BANKRUPTCY and the SUPREME COURT

Bankruptcy
and the
Supreme Court

KENNETH N. KLEE

Professor of Law
UNIVERSITY OF CALIFORNIA, LOS ANGELES
Partner
KLEE, TUCHIN, BOGDANOFF & STERN LLP

Library of Congress Cataloging-in-Publication Data

Klee, Kenneth N.

Bankruptcy and the Supreme Court / by Kenneth N. Klee.

p. cm.

Includes index.

ISBN 978-1-4224-2751-4 (hardcover)

1. Bankruptcy--United States--Cases. 2. United States. Supreme Court. I. Title.

KF1524.K54 2009

346.7307'8--dc22

2008040158

LEXISNEXIS EDITORIAL OFFICES
744 Broad Street, Newark, New Jersey 07102   973-820-2000
201 Mission Street, San Francisco, California 94105   415-908-3200
Customer Services Department: 800-833-9844

DEDICATION

This book is dedicated to my mentor and teacher
Professor Vern Countryman

Preface

This book is a beginning and not an end. The universe of 570 Supreme Court bankruptcy and insolvency cases from 1898-2008 embodies a comprehensive database from which additional research may be done.[*] Moreover, this book only scratches the surface of the rich material contained in the Justices' private papers that were gathered as part of the research for this book. Most of these papers are available at the National Bankruptcy Archives for use by judges, lawyers, and scholars.[**] Indeed the collection of the bankruptcy Supreme Court case database and assembly of the Justices' papers should be of lasting significance to the development of bankruptcy scholarship and law.

Writing this book was facilitated by financial assistance from the American College of Bankruptcy; American College of Bankruptcy Foundation; Klee, Tuchin, Bogdanoff & Stern LLP; the UCLA School of Law; and the UCLA Academic Senate, and by the able research assistance of the UCLA Law Library staff and many fine research assistants provided through the Law Library at the UCLA School of Law. I acknowledge and appreciate the efforts of research assistants Arthur Wille of the UCLA Law Class of 2003, Ryan Bunker and Roshan Sonthalia of the UCLA Law Class of 2004, Lesley Wasser and Robert J. Wood of the UCLA Law Class of 2005, Michael Akiva, Arthur Kim, and Tiffany Parcher of the UCLA Law Class of 2006, George Azadian and William Holzer of the UCLA Law Class of 2007, Shaun Hoting of the UCLA Law Class of 2008, Edwin Hermawan of the UCLA Law Class of 2009, and Gary K. Li of the UCLA Law Class of 2010. I am likewise grateful to Courtney Pozmantier, my colleague at Klee, Tuchin, Bogdanoff & Stern LLP, for research assistance. In addition, I offer thanks to United States Bankruptcy Judges Charles Case, Randolph J. Haines, Christopher Klein, and Geraldine Mund for providing useful research materials, to Prof.

---

[*]   *See* http://www.law.ucla.edu/home/apps/supremecourtcases/

[**]   *See* http://www.law.upenn.edu/bll/archives/bankruptcy/scjpapers.html

Douglas Baird for suggesting I read BANKRUPTCY LAW STORIES, to Scott Clarkson for suggesting I look at papers of the Justices in the National Archives, to Mitchell A. Harwood for editorial suggestions, and to Thomas Mayer for suggesting I look at the Cravath lectures on corporate reorganization. I am grateful to Myra Saunders, Laura Cadra, Amy Atchison, Nancy Berkowitz, Scott Dewey, Kevin Gerson, Cheryl Kelly Fischer, Jenny Lentz, Linda O'Connor, Tammy Pettinato, John Wilson and others on the fabulous UCLA School of Law library staff for research assistance and coordination of my quest to obtain the Justices' bankruptcy papers. I also offer thanks and appreciation to my talented UCLA assistant Tal Grietzer for his skill in assembling this book for publication, to Mary Scott for her patience in editing the book, to Joseph Doherty for assistance on the statistical tests in Chapter 1, and to my colleagues Prof. Daniel Bussel, Prof. William Klein, and Prof. William Warren for their substantive suggestions. I am grateful to colleagues at my law firm, Klee, Tuchin, Bogdanoff & Stern LLP, for enthusiastically supporting the invest-ment of my time to write this book. I also express deep–heartfelt thanks to my wife Doreen for her steadfast support and encourage-ment and the sacrifices she made during this seven-year project.

K.N.K.

Los Angeles, California
October 2008

Summary of Contents

Table of Contents

CHAPTER 3—BANKRUPTCY AND CONSTITUTIONAL LAW: SOVEREIGN IMMUNITY, FEDERAL PREEMPTION, FEDERALISM, AND THE USE OF STATE LAW IN BANKRUPTCY   121

CHAPTER 6—LANDMARK CASES AND OLD FAVORITES 439

Table of Cases

Tables of Authorities

U.S. Constitution:

Statutes: The Bankruptcy Act of 1898 (as amended)

STATUTES: BANKRUPTCY CODE

OTHER BANKRUPTCY ACTS

STATUTES: OTHER

BANKRUPTCY RULES AND GENERAL ORDERS

Books, Law Reviews, and Journals:

Introduction

The United States Supreme Court is a complex institution. Discussing its bankruptcy jurisprudence of the past 111 years could easily yield a multivolume treatise. This book is far more modest and circumscribed. Instead of a treatise, this book is a comprehensive desk reference for lawyers, judges, and scholars examining the Supreme Court's bankruptcy decisions from 1898 through 2008 from six different perspectives.

Chapter 1 examines the Court as a governmental and political institution devoting attention to the Court's business and habits, i.e., the processes by which the Court receives bankruptcy cases and decides them and the rules it promulgates to regulate bankruptcy courts and practice. This chapter examines issues that might confront the Court in several areas of law, yet present themselves in this book in a bankruptcy context. In particular, Chapter 1 looks at the process by which the Court grants, denies, and dismisses certiorari and opinions in which it has a change of heart by ducking the issue on which it voted to grant review. This chapter also looks at articulated methods by which the Court makes decisions including legal maxims and canons of statutory construction. Chapter 1 continues with analysis of the role of politics in bankruptcy decisions and looks behind the scenes at internal communications among the Justices as reflected in their private papers. Finally, this chapter concludes with a discussion of the Supreme Court's rule making and supervisory authority.

Chapter 2 examines how the Court tends to resolve conflicts between bankruptcy law and other areas of state and federal law, such as administrative law, family law, labor law, pension law, probate law, real estate law, and tax law. This discussion is linked closely to Chapter 3 which discusses the constitutional breadth of the bankruptcy power and analyzes how the Court reconciles bankruptcy law with constitutional law, sovereign immunity, federal preemption, and federalism, as well as the use of state law in bankruptcy.

Chapter 4 discusses the Court's treatment of the bankruptcy court as a judicial institution. In particular, it examines how the Court has sculpted and restricted the bankruptcy court's subject matter jurisdiction, powers of the bankruptcy court, and res judicata and collateral estoppel effects of bankruptcy court and non-bankruptcy court judgments. Not surprisingly, these issues have plagued the Court for years.

Chapter 5 analyzes, in considerable detail, bankruptcy law, doctrine, and policies that arise primarily or exclusively of the context of the Bankruptcy Code, such as avoiding powers, dischargeability, claims priority and distribution, and plan confirmation. Although it is the longest chapter in the book, Chapter 5 is not exhaustive and does not review the cases from every possible perspective. For example, the partnership cases are included under the topics in which they arise rather than in a separate section on partnerships in bankruptcy. Nevertheless, this chapter might be of most interest to bankruptcy judges and practicing bankruptcy lawyers.

Chapter 6 discusses some of the bankruptcy cases over the past 111 years in which the Court sharply changed the course of bankruptcy law. It also includes my favorite cases, regardless of their impact on bankruptcy law or doctrine.

CHAPTER 1

THE BUSINESS AND HABITS OF THE SUPREME COURT

INTRODUCTION

Before embarking on a substantive discussion of the 570 Supreme Court bankruptcy cases from 1898-2008, an evaluation of the business and habits of the Court that decided these cases proved instructive. The Court is a continuous body that changes over time as its composition is altered due to shifting societal norms as well as the views of particular Justices.[1] It is nevertheless possible to identify some aspects of the Court as an institution that have shaped its bankruptcy decisions.

When first approached to write about this subject, I thought there would be a couple hundred cases to review. Astoundingly, the Court has decided 570 bankruptcy and insolvency cases over the past 111 years.

THE COURT'S CASELOAD

Although during some terms the Court has decided a large number of bankruptcy decisions, such as the 2004 term which yielded six, in more recent years the Court decided only a few cases with bankruptcy issues. It could be expected that the decisions would be bunched in the years following major changes in the bankruptcy statute, but the data

---

1.   The dynamics of the Court may shift dramatically over a short period of time. Within four months, from September 4, 2005 to January 31, 2006, Chief Justice Rehnquist died and was replaced by Chief Justice Roberts and Justice O'Connor retired and was replaced by Justice Alito. *See:* http://www.supremecourtus.gov/about/biographiescurrent.pdf
(last visited June 25, 2008).

show that in the 10 years following the effective date of the Bank-ruptcy Code, the Supreme Court decided only 17 bankruptcy cases. By comparison, in the 10 years following the effective date of the Bankruptcy Act of 1898, the Court decided 77 bankruptcy cases. What could account for this disparity? Was the drafting of the 1978 Bankruptcy Code so much clearer than that of the Bankruptcy Act of 1898 that the Court had fewer occasions to intervene? Could the answer lie elsewhere than in the drafting of the two laws?

In 1898 the Supreme Court heard bankruptcy cases on appeal, writ of error, certification, or writ of certiorari. In 1979 the Supreme Court essentially[2] heard bankruptcy cases only on writ of certiorari. Over the years, Congress has limited the appellate jurisdiction of the Supreme Court and increased its discretionary jurisdiction.[3] "Perhaps the decisive factor in the history of the Supreme Court is its progressive contraction of jurisdiction. This tendency has been particularly significant since the Civil War."[4] Indeed, in 1915 Congress "shut off reviews as of right by the Supreme Court in bankruptcy litigation."[5] In 1925 Congress expressly repealed "so much of sections 24 and 25 of the Bankruptcy Act . . . as regulates the mode of review by the Supreme Court in the proceedings, controversies, and cases therein named."[6] One year later, however, for reasons that remain unclear, Congress created some confusion by re-enacting section 24 of the

---

2.   Some cases involve the Court's appellate jurisdiction, such as where the United States appeals from a decision holding a statute of the United States unconstitutional. *See* United States v. Sec. Indus. Bank, 459 U.S. 70, 74 (1982).

3.   The topic of the Supreme Court's jurisdiction is discussed at length in a thorough book by FELIX FRANKFURTER & JAMES M. LANDIS, THE BUSINESS OF THE SUPREME COURT: A STUDY IN THE FEDERAL JUDICIAL SYSTEM (The MacMillan Company 1927) ("*Business*").

4.   *See id.* at 187.

5.   *See* Act of Jan. 28, 1915, 38 Stat. 803.

6.   *See* Act of Feb. 13, 1925, ch. 229, § 13, 43 Stat. 936, 942 discussed in *Business* at 282 & n.95.

Bankruptcy Act.[7] Ultimately, in 1988, Congress withdrew the right of appeal to the Supreme Court in most cases,[8] including bankruptcy cases and proceedings. Thereafter, review was almost exclusively by writ of certiorari.[9]

Thus, today the Court has discretion to review bankruptcy proceedings and almost never exercises this discretion except to resolve a Circuit split or some pressing issue of national importance. The vast majority of bankruptcy cases and proceedings stand little to no chance of being heard by the United States Supreme Court. Yet, theoretically the cases the Court does decide should clarify the law, provide some finality and predictability, and offer insights about how the Court resolves issues of bankruptcy law. On the other hand, because Justices at a particular time may be unfamiliar with bankruptcy law, the Court may render a decision that causes more problems than it resolves. The chapters below analyze the extent to which the Court has done the former rather than the latter.

CERTIORARI GRANTED OR DENIED

Because the Supreme Court has discretion to grant or deny certiorari,[10] it is useful to analyze the bases on which the Court

---

7. *See* Act of May 27, 1926, § 9, 44 Stat. 662 discussed in *Business* at 282 & n.95. *See also* James A. McLaughlin, *Amendment of the Bankruptcy Act*, 40 HARV. L. REV. 341, 344 (1927).

8. For example, in 1988, Congress repealed § 1252 of the Judicial Code which provided for direct appeals to the Supreme Court in cases invalidating an Act of Congress. *See* Pub. L. No. 100-352, § 1, 102 Stat. 662 (1988). Direct appeal still lies from 3-judge district court cases, but it is improbable this kind of suit would arise in a bankruptcy context.

9. It is conceivable for the appellate jurisdiction of the Court to be implicated in bankruptcy cases or proceedings, but this is a remote possibility. *See* 28 U.S.C. § 1251(b) (2000) (allowing appeal in civil actions involving ambassadors, suits by the United States against a state, and suits by a state against citizens of another state).

10. The procedure by which the Court considers writs for certiorari has changed over the years. For example, in the mid-1920's the procedure

exercises its discretion.[11] Of course it is well known, even apart from the Court's review of bankruptcy cases, that one reason the Court grants certiorari is to resolve a Circuit split.[12] Under the Rule of Four,[13]

---

included the staff distributing copies of the briefs and record to all Justices, each Justice examining the papers and preparing a memorandum or note indicating an appropriate disposition, the discussing of each petition at a conference of the Justices, and finally, the taking a recorded vote on each petition. *See* Justice John Paul Stevens, *The Life Span of a Judge-Made Rule*, 58 N.Y.U. L. REV. 1, 12 (1983) (citing 1924 testimony of Chief Justice Taft and Justice Van Devanter). By 1947 not every petition was discussed; the Chief Justice instead circulated a "dead list" identifying cases deemed unworthy of conference unless a Justice requested its discussion at conference. *See id.* at 13. By 1975, the "dead list" had been replaced by a "discuss list" which limits the petitions to be discussed in conference unless a Justice adds a petition to the list. *See id.* Today the record is not routinely filed with the petition for certiorari, and not every Justice examines the original papers in the case; instead, law clerks prepare "pool memos" analyzing the petitions. *See id.*

11.   David O'Brien has conducted an interesting statistical analysis of the Court's propensity to grant or deny petitions for certiorari. *See* D. O'Brien, *Join-3 Votes, The Rule of Four, The Cert. Pool, and the Supreme Court's Shrinking Plenary Docket*, 13 J.L. & POL. 779 (1997).

12.   *See, e.g.,* Howard Delivery Serv., Inc. v. Zurich Am. Ins. Co., 547 U.S. 651, 657 (2006) ("We granted certiorari . . . to resolve a split among the Circuits . . . .") (citation omitted); Rousey v. Jacoway, 544 U.S. 320, 325 (2005) ("We granted certiorari to resolve this division among the Courts of Appeals . . . .); Bank of Am. Nat'l Trust & Sav. Ass'n v. 203 N. LaSalle St. P'ship, 526 U.S. 434, 443 (1999) ("We granted certiorari, 523 U.S. 1106 (1998), to resolve a Circuit split on the issue."); Patterson v. Shumate, 504 U.S. 753, 757 (1992) ("We granted certiorari . . . to resolve the conflict among the Courts of Appeals . . . ."); Farrey v. Sanderfoot, 500 U.S. 291, 295 (1991) ("We granted certiorari to resolve the conflict of authority."). *See generally*, Lawrence Baum, *The Supreme Court* 92 (CQ Press 2007) ("Justice Ginsberg said that 'the overwhelming factor' in the granting of certiorari 'is the division of opinions in the circuits.'").

13.   For more than 80 years, the Supreme Court has operated under an internal Rule of Four that requires the Court to grant review when at least four Justices vote to grant a writ of certiorari. *See* Testimony of Justice Van Devanter, *Hearings on H.R. 8206 Before the House Comm. on the Judiciary*, 68th Cong., 2d Sess. 8 (1924) ("We always grant the petition when as many as four think that it should be granted, and sometimes when as many as three think that way."). *Accord Hearings on*

however, sometimes a Justice must lobby other Justices to persuade them that a Circuit split exists and the Court should grant certiorari. One such example arose in *Case v. Los Angeles Lumber Products Co.*,[14] in which Justice Douglas wrote an extensive memorandum and addendum that persuaded Justice Reed to vote to grant certiorari.[15]

CERTIORARI GRANTED AND ISSUE DUCKED

On occasion, the Court exercises its discretion to grant certiorari to resolve an issue but then changes its mind. For the most part, we are left to speculate what caused the Court's about face.

For example, the Court has been careful to avoid resolving whether the Constitution permits a bankruptcy judge to conduct a jury trial

---

S. 1932 Before the Senate Comm. on the Judiciary, 75th Cong., 1st Sess., Pt. 3, 490 (1937) (Letter of Chief Justice Charles Hughes, "the petition is always granted if four so vote."). *See generally, e.g.*, Lawrence Baum, *The Supreme Court* 89 (CQ Press 2007); Justice John Paul Stevens, *The Life Span of a Judge-Made Rule*, 58 N.Y.U. L. REV. 1, 10 (1983) ("Whenever four justices of the United States Supreme Court vote to grant a petition for a writ of certiorari, the petition is granted even though a majority of the Court votes to deny."); R. Revez & P. Karlan, *Nonmajority Rules and the Supreme Court*, 136 U. PA. L. REV. 1067, 1068-70 (1988) (opining that since 1937 the rule has become a hard and fast Rule of Four because the Court denies certiorari even over the strong dissent of three Justices); Leiman, *The Rule of Four*, 57 COLUM. L. REV. 975, 976 (1957) (discussing the process of the Court's exercise of discretionary review before 1925).

14. 308 U.S. 106 (1939).

15. *See* May 10, 1939 Memorandum from Justice Douglas to Justice Reed and May 15, 1939 Addendum to Memorandum of 5-10-39. In his private papers (23-124), Justice Reed writes a Memo on *Case v. Los Angeles Lumber Products Co.* as follows: "Mr, [sic] Justice Douglas this morning convinced me that his position on this is correct and that my trouble of yesterday evening was born of misconception." He then sets forth at length his reasons for being convinced. On May 22, 1939, the Court voted 5-4 to grant certiorari in the case. *See* 307 U.S. 619 (1939) and private papers of Justice Douglas (23-124) October Term 1939 noting that Justices Douglas, Frankfurter, Reed, Black, and Roberts voted to grant certiorari whereas Justices Stone, Butler, McReynolds, and Hughes voted to deny the petition.

in a core proceeding. In 1989, the Court decided *Granfinanciera, S.A. v. Nordberg*,[16] in which a chapter 11 trustee filed a suit in the bankruptcy court to recover fraudulent transfers. Section 157(b)(2)(H) of the Judicial Code[17] explicitly provides that actions to recover fraudulent conveyances are core proceedings. The bankruptcy court held that it could hear the action without a jury, despite the petitioners' demand for a jury trial, and both the district court and the Eleventh Circuit affirmed. The Supreme Court, however, reversed, holding that when a party makes a jury demand for a claim that is inherently legal, "Congress cannot eliminate [that] party's Seventh Amendment right to a jury trial merely by relabeling the cause of action to which it attaches and placing exclusive jurisdiction in an administrative agency or a specialized court of equity."[18]

In 1990, the Second Circuit had to decide whether a bankruptcy judge could hold jury trials in proceedings that are both legal and, at the same time, core pursuant to section 157(b) of the Judicial Code.[19] The Court had left that question open in *Granfinanciera*.[20] After careful consideration, the Second Circuit held "that *Granfinanciera* does not foreclose the possibility of jury trials in the bankruptcy court."[21]

The Court granted certiorari in *Ben Cooper*[22] to consider the legality of non-tenured bankruptcy judges conducting jury trials in

---

16.   492 U.S. 33 (1989).

17.   28 U.S.C. § 157(b)(2)(H) (2000).

18.   *See Granfinanciera*, 492 U.S. at 61.

19.   *See* Ben Cooper, Inc. v. Ins. Co. of Pa. (*In re* Ben Cooper, Inc.), 896 F.2d 1394 (2d Cir. 1990).

20.   *See Granfinanciera*, 492 U.S. at 64.

21.   *See Ben Cooper, Inc. v. Ins. Co. of Pa.*, 896 F.2d at 1401.

22.   *See* Ins. Co. of Pa. v. Ben Cooper, Inc., 497 U.S. 1023 (1990) (granting certiorari from the Second Circuit's decision 896 F.2d 1394 (2d Cir. 1990)). As noted previously, under the Supreme Court's Rule of Four, at least four Justices had to vote to grant certiorari in order for the Court to take this action. *See supra* n.13.

core bankruptcy proceedings. After the United States intervened and asked the Court to affirm the decision of the Second Circuit, the Court, on its own motion, vacated the grant of certiorari and remanded the case to the Second Circuit as follows:[23]

> The United States, whose motion to intervene filed in this Court on September 28, 1990 was granted, has raised a question concerning the Court of Appeals' jurisdiction over this case and hence a question about our own jurisdiction. Motion of the United States to Intervene and Brief of the United States, pages 9 through 17. Because the Court of Appeals should address the jurisdictional issue in the first instance, we vacate the judgment of the United States Court of Appeals for the Second Circuit and remand the case for consideration of the jurisdictional issue raised by the United States.

On remand, the Second Circuit held that it had jurisdiction and reinstated its prior opinion.[24] Again the Court considered a petition for writ of certiorari. This time, however, without explanation, the Court voted to deny certiorari with only Justice White voting to grant certiorari.[25] At least three Justices who originally voted to grant certiorari had changed their minds, and the public is left to wonder why.

There are also cases in which the Court might prefer to duck an issue but must resolve it on the merits. For example, in *Maggio v. Zeitz (In re Luma Camera Service, Inc.)*,[26] Justice Jackson decided that a turnover order was res judicata even though his memorandum to the Justices noted that "whichever way [the res judicata issue] is decided, would make matters worse."[27]

---

23. *See* Ins. Co. of Pa. v. Ben Cooper, Inc., 498 U.S. 964 (1990).

24. *See* Ben Cooper, Inc. v. Ins. Co. of Pa. (*In re* Ben Cooper, Inc.), 924 F.2d 36 (2d Cir. 1991).

25. *See* Ins. Co. of Pa. v. Ben Cooper, Inc., 500 U.S. 928 (1991).

26. 333 U.S. 56 (1948).

27. *See* January 21, 1948, Memorandum for the Court from Justice Jackson (contained in Justice Black's papers).

The Supreme Court is a political institution. Because its judgments cannot be reversed,[28] the Court has the freedom to make legal determinations that arguably are laced with policy considerations. It is plausible that the Court recognized the systemic importance of not deciding *Ben Cooper*. If the Court had granted certiorari and rendered a decision on the merits, the Court would have had to determine whether the judicial power of the United States, which must be vested in life-tenured judges under Article III of the Constitution,[29] permits or precludes non-tenured bankruptcy judges from holding jury trials. In the latter case, the result would have been to impose all bankruptcy jury trials on the already overburdened federal district courts. By ducking the issue, the Court avoided making this Hobson's choice.

Ben Cooper is not the only instance in which the Court has changed its mind about resolving an issue. There are other examples in the bankruptcy context when the Court has granted certiorari to resolve a question but then issues an opinion that does not answer the question on which certiorari was granted. These instances arise not only when technical defects in the record properly preclude the Court from reaching the merits, but when reaching the merits would require the Court to decide a sensitive issue on which it prefers to postpone consideration. In *Tennessee Student Assistance Corp. v. Hood*,[30] the Court granted certiorari to review the Sixth Circuit's holding that "the States ceded their immunity from private suits in bankruptcy in the Constitutional Convention, and therefore, the Bankruptcy Clause,

---

28.   Of course when the Court's judgment is based on statutory construction rather than the Constitution, Congress may amend the statute to overturn the Court's construction and has done so on many occasions. *See, e.g.,* Daniel J. Bussel, *Textualism's Failures: A Study of Overruled Bankruptcy Decisions*, 53 VAND. L. REV. 889 (2000) (discussing legislatively overruled Supreme Court and lower court decisions).

29.   *See* U.S. CONST. art. III, § 1 ("The judicial Power of the United States, shall be vested in one supreme Court, and in such inferior Courts as the Congress may from time to time ordain and establish. The Judges, both of the supreme and inferior Courts, shall hold their Offices during good Behaviour . . . .").

30.   541 U.S. 440 (2004).

U.S. Const., Art. I, § 8, cl. 4, provided Congress with the necessary authority to abrogate state sovereign immunity in 11 U.S.C. § 106(a)."[31] The Court held that even though the state is served with a summons, the bankruptcy court's discharge of a student loan is *in rem* and does not implicate a state's Eleventh Amendment immunity, so the Court is not required to reach the broader question.[32] Thus, the Court avoided deciding the difficult and important question on which it granted certiorari.

As a result, lower courts were left to grapple with the scope of *in rem* jurisdiction in bankruptcy cases and proceedings. But they didn't have to wait long, because one year later, the Court granted certiorari in *Central Virginia Community College v. Katz*,[33] "to consider the question left open by our opinion in *Hood*: whether Congress' attempt to abrogate state sovereign immunity in 11 U.S.C. § 106(a) is valid."[34] Although the Court again failed to answer the question on which it granted certiorari, it held that Congress had the power to "treat States in the same way as other creditors insofar as concerns 'Laws on the subject of Bankruptcies . . . .'"[35]

A more striking example involves the Court's refusal to decide whether the new value principle of the absolute priority rule[36] survived enactment of the 1978 Bankruptcy Code. After raising and

---

31.   *See id.* at 445.

32.   *See id.* at 443. ("Because we conclude that a proceeding initiated by a debtor to determine the dischargeability of a student loan debt is not a suit against the State for purposes of the Eleventh Amendment, . . . we do not reach the question on which certiorari was granted."). The substance of *Hood* is discussed more fully *infra* in Ch. 3 in the broader discussion of sovereign immunity and bankruptcy. *See infra* pp. 161-164.

33.   544 U.S. 960 (2005).

34.   *See* Cent. Va. Cmty. Coll. v. Katz, 546 U.S. 356, 361 (2006).

35.   *See id.* at 379. *See* additional discussion *infra* in Ch. 3, pp. 161-164.

36.   *See* Case v. Los Angeles Lumber Prods. Co., 308 U.S. 106, 121-22 (1939) (discussing the elements of the new value principle or exception to the absolute priority rule) and additional discussion *infra* in Ch. 5, pp. 377–381.

not deciding the issue in 1988,[37] the Court again had an opportunity to resolve the question in 1999 in *Bank of America National Trust & Savings Ass'n v. 203 North LaSalle Street Partnership*.[38] The Court stated that it granted certiorari to resolve a Circuit split on the issue.[39] Instead of addressing whether the new value principle survived enactment of the 1978 Bankruptcy Code, and, if so, whether it was applied properly based on the facts in the *203 N. LaSalle* case, the Court framed the issue as "whether a debtor's prebankruptcy equity holders may, over the objection of a senior class of impaired creditors, contribute new capital and receive ownership interests in the reorganized entity, when that opportunity is given exclusively to the old equity holders under a plan adopted without consideration of alternatives."[40] Holding that the exclusive opportunity to contribute new capital and receive ownership interests violates the new value principle, the Court found it unnecessary to decide whether the new value principle survived enactment of the 1978 Bankruptcy Code.[41] This backward decision-making enabled the Court to avoid resolving an important question that could have provided much-needed guidance to the lower courts and resolved the Circuit split on which the Court granted certiorari. Instead, the Court left the question to fester for another day.

A few years after the effective date of the 1978 Bankruptcy Code,[42] the Court was asked to decide whether application of Bankruptcy

---

37.   *See* Norwest Bank Worthington v. Ahlers, 485 U.S. 197, 203 n.3 (1988).

38.   526 U.S. 434 (1999).

39.   *See id.* at 443 ("We granted certiorari, 523 U.S. 1106 (1998), to resolve a Circuit split on the issue.").

40.   *See id.* at 437.

41.   *See id.* at 443. ("We do not decide whether the statute includes a new value corollary or exception, but hold that on any reading respondent's proposed plan fails to satisfy the statute . . . .").

42.   The 1978 Bankruptcy Code became effective for cases filed on or after October 1, 1979. *See* Pub. L. No. 95-598, § 402(a), 92 Stat. 2549, 2682 (1978).

Code § 522(f) to permit a debtor to avoid liens acquired before the date of enactment violates the Fifth Amendment.[43] After writing several pages of dictum about the questionable constitutionality of a retroactive application of the statute, Justice Rehnquist ducked ruling on the constitutional question by invoking a rule of statutory construction concluding that Congress intended the statute to apply prospectively with respect to the avoidance of property rights.[44]

HOW THE COURT APPEARS TO DECIDE CASES

The Court goes out of its way to avoid deciding constitutional issues. Therefore, before addressing a constitutional issue, the Court will look for a jurisdictional or statutory basis to resolve the case before it. A good example is the Court's decision in *United States v. Security Industrial Bank*[45] which held that the avoiding powers of the Bankruptcy Code did not apply retroactively rather than addressing whether the retroactive application of the statute would offend the Fifth Amendment of the Constitution.[46]

In order to give the appearance that it decides cases according to a rational rule of law, the Court often articulates rules of statutory construction or legal maxims that inform its decisions. Although these rules and maxims simply might be a veneer for the bald political forces that many suspect underlie case outcomes, they must be briefed and argued as part of the formalism of the Court. Admittedly, there

---

43. *See* United States v. Sec. Indus. Bank, 459 U.S. 70, 73-74 (1982) ("*Security Industrial Bank*"). Strictly speaking, because a lower court held a statute of the United States unconstitutional and the United States appealed, *Security Industrial Bank* involved the Supreme Court's appellate jurisdiction rather than its certiorari jurisdiction.

44. *See id.* at 78-79. ("We consider the statutory question because of the 'cardinal principle that this Court will first ascertain whether a construction of the statute is fairly possible by which the constitutional question may be avoided.'") (citations omitted).

45. 459 U.S. 70 (1982).

46. *See id.* at 82 (holding that Bankruptcy Code § 522(f)(2) does not apply retroactively, thereby avoiding a difficult constitutional question).

are some Justices who are new textualists[47] whose vote might be tied inextricably to these rules and maxims, unless an issue of great policy would be contravened by blindly adhering to them. A brief examination of the rules of statutory construction and legal maxims helps to understand the complexity woven into the Court's rhetorical bases for making legal decisions.

STATUTORY CONSTRUCTION

"The bankruptcy law has now been so thoroughly construed that there is not much doubt about any of its provisions . . . ."[48]

Numerous articles and books discuss statutory construction, and some analyze the Supreme Court's use of statutory construction to decide cases.[49] A few do so specifically with respect to the Court's use of statutory construction in bankruptcy cases.[50] Although this book does not have the depth or breadth of analysis contained in articles

---

47.   Justices Alito, Roberts, Scalia, and Thomas are new textualists whose first approach to resolving a dispute over the Bankruptcy Code is to begin with the plain language of the statute. Other Justices, such as Justice Breyer, are purposivists who will look to the purpose the statute addresses as a point of first inquiry. Other Justices, such as Justice Stevens, might take a mixed approach, first addressing what is fair as a matter of policy or equity.

48.   *See* H.R. REP. NO. 1182, 63d Cong., 2d Sess. 1 (1914), reprinted in 52 CONG. REC. 435.

49.   *See, e.g.,* Antonin Scalia, *Common-Law Courts in a Civil-Law System: The Role of United States Federal Courts in Interpreting the Constitution and Laws,* in A MATTER OF INTERPRETATION 3 (Amy Gutmann ed., 1997); Michael H. Koby, *The Supreme Court's Declining Reliance on Legislative History: The Impact of Justice Scalia's Critique,* 36 HARV. J. LEGIS. 368-95 (1999). *See generally,* H.L.A. HART, THE CONCEPT OF LAW 121-44 (Oxford: Clarendon Press, 1961) (arguing for "open texture" position on judicial interpretation between formalism and rule-skepticism).

50.   *See, e.g.,* Daniel J. Bussel, *Textualism's Failures: A Study of Overruled Bankruptcy Decisions,* 53 VAND. L. REV. 889 (2000) (discussing legislatively overruled Supreme Court and lower court decisions); Karen M. Gebbia-Pinetti, *Interpreting the Bankruptcy Code: An Empirical Study of the Supreme Court's Bankruptcy Decisions,* 3 CHAPMAN L. REV. 173 (Spring 2000) (discussing the interpretive conflict and the Bankruptcy Code and reviewing bankruptcy cases from the Court's 1981 through 1998 terms).

and books dedicated solely to this topic, it might provide the reader with interesting insights about the Supreme Court's use of statutory construction in bankruptcy decisions.

The analysis begins by identifying and then examining the Court's use of maxims of statutory construction in bankruptcy cases. An illustration of their uses with specific examples, noting the use of conflicting maxims, and concluding with a discussion whether the Court uses the maxims as a basis for decision or to rationalize a decision *ex post*, follows.

During the twentieth century, the Court used several maxims of statutory construction in bankruptcy decisions generally reflective of the guiding principle that the Court is to interpret statutes, not make them.[51] Among the more important and frequently used are the following:

1. When the language of the statute is unambiguous, courts must interpret the language in accordance with its plain meaning[52]

---

51.   *See* N.Y. County Nat'l Bank v. Massey, 192 U.S. 138, 146 (1904) ("We are to interpret statutes, not to make them."). *See generally* ABNER J. MIKVA & ERIC LANE, AN INTRODUCTION TO STATUTORY INTERPRETATION AND THE LEGISLATIVE PROCESS 24-27 (Aspen Law & Business 1997) (explaining and criticizing the use of canons because "canons are not a coherent, shared body of law from which correct answers can be drawn, and . . . viewed individually, many canons are wrong." *Id.* at 25); Karl N. Llewellyn, *Remarks on the Theory of Appellate Decision and the Rules or Canons About How Statutes Are To Be Construed*, 3 VAND. L. REV. 395-406 (1950) (describing 28 pairs of canons of statutory construction and their opposites and how the current temper of the Court and needs to be addressed affects their use).

52.   *See, e.g.,* Patterson v. Shumate, 504 U.S. 753, 760 (1992) (party seeking to defeat plain meaning of the Bankruptcy Code bears an "exceptionally heavy burden") (internal quotation marks omitted); Conn. Nat'l Bank v. Germain, 503 U.S. 249, 254 (1992) ("When the words of a statute are unambiguous, then . . . 'judicial inquiry is complete.'") (citation omitted); Gleason v. Thaw, 236 U.S. 558, 560 (1915) ("[T]he Bankrupt Law is a prosy thing intended for ready application to the everyday affairs of practical business, and when construing its terms we are constrained by their usual acceptation in that field of endeavor."); Citizens Banking Co. v. Ravenna Nat'l Bank, 234 U.S. 360, 368 (1914) ("The advantages and disadvantages have been balanced by Congress,

without regard to legislative history,[53] except in the rare case in which the literal application of the "statute will produce a result demonstrably at odds with the intentions of its drafters."[54]

2. When the language of the statute is clear, the court must enforce it in accordance with its terms notwithstanding prior practice.[55]

---

and its will has been expressed in terms which are plain and therefore controlling."); Crawford v. Burke, 195 U.S. 176, 189 (1904) ("The language of this section is so clear as to require no construction.").

53. *See, e.g.,* Barnhill v. Johnson, 503 U.S. 393, 401 (1992) ("[W]e note that appeals to statutory history are well taken only to resolve 'statutory ambiguity.'") (citation omitted); Toibb v. Radloff, 501 U.S. 157, 162 (1991) ("[T]his Court has repeated with some frequency: 'Where, as here, the resolution of a question of federal law turns on a statute and the intention of Congress, we look first to the statutory language and then to the legislative history if the statutory language is unclear.'"); United States v. Ron Pair Enters., Inc., 489 U.S. 235, 240-41 (1989) ("[A]s long as the statutory scheme is coherent and consistent, there is generally no need for a court to inquire beyond the plain language of the statute. The task of resolving the dispute over the meaning of [the statute] begins where all such inquiries must begin: with the language of the statute itself.") (*"Ron Pair"*); Kuehner v. Irving Trust Co., 299 U.S. 445, 449 (1937) ("The legislative history of this provision . . . cannot affect its interpretation, since the language of the act as adopted is clear.").

54. *See Ron Pair*, 489 U.S. at 242 (quoting Griffin v. Oceanic Contractors, Inc., 458 U.S. 564, 571 (1982)); United States v. Am. Trucking Ass'ns, 310 U.S. 534, 543 (1940) ("There is, of course, no more persuasive evidence of the purpose of a statute than the words by which the legislature undertook to give expression to its wishes. Often these words are sufficient in and of themselves to determine the purpose of the legislation. In such cases we have followed their plain meaning. When that meaning has led to absurd or futile results, however, this Court has looked beyond the words to the purpose of the act. Frequently, however, even when the plain meaning did not produce absurd results but merely an unreasonable one 'plainly at variance with the policy of the legislation as a whole' this Court has followed that purpose, rather than the literal words." (citation omitted; quoted with approval in Perry v. Commerce Loan Co., 383 U.S. 392, 400 (1966)). *Cf.* Sturges v. Crowninshield, 17 U.S. (4 Wheat.) 122, 202-03 (1819) (adopting a rule of contract construction that overrides plain meaning to avoid "absurdity and injustice").

55. *See, e.g.,* Hartford Underwriters Ins. Co. v. Union Planters Bank, N.A., 530 U.S. 1, 10 (2000) ("[W]hile pre-Code practice 'informs our understanding of the language of the Code,' it cannot overcome that

3. Even when the language of the statute is clear, courts must consider the legislative history and issues of policy and previous practice to determine congressional intent.[56]

---

language. It is a tool of construction, not an extratextual supplement.") (citation omitted); BFP v. Resolution Trust Corp., 511 U.S. 531, 546 (1994) ("Where the 'meaning of the Bankruptcy Code's text is itself clear,' . . . its operation is unimpeded by contrary state law or prior practice."); Pa. Dep't of Pub. Welfare v. Davenport, 495 U.S. 552, 563 (1990); United States v. Ron Pair Enters., Inc., 489 U.S. 235, 245-46 (1989).

56. *See, e.g.,* Kelly v. Robinson, 479 U.S. 36, 43 (1986) ("[T]he text is only the starting point . . . . In expounding a statute, we must not be guided by a single sentence or member of a sentence, but look to the provisions of the whole law, and to its object and policy.") (internal quotation marks and citations omitted); Bank of Marin v. England, 385 U.S. 99, 103 (1966) ("[We] do not read these statutory words with the ease of a computer. There is an overriding consideration that equitable principles govern the exercise of bankruptcy jurisdiction."); Wright v. Union Cent. Life Ins. Co., 311 U.S. 273, 279 (1940) ("And so long as that right is protected the creditor certainly is in no position to insist that doubts or ambiguities in the Act be resolved in its favor and against the debtor. Rather, the Act must be liberally construed to give the debtor the full measure of the relief afforded by Congress, lest its benefits be frittered away by narrow formalistic interpretations which disregard the spirit and the letter of the Act.") (internal citations omitted); Wright v. Vinton Branch of Mountain Trust Bank, 300 U.S. 440, 459 (1937); ("The new Act does not in terms provide for 'The right to protect its [the mortgagee's] interest in the property by bidding at such sale whenever held.' But the committee reports and the explanations given in Congress make it plain that the mortgagee was intended to have this right. We accept this view of the statute.") (footnote omitted; parenthetical in original); City of Lincoln v. Ricketts, 297 U.S. 373, 376 (1936) ("In construing the words of an act of Congress, we seek the legislative intent. We give to the words their natural significance unless that leads to an unreasonable result plainly at variance with the evident purpose of the legislation.") (citations omitted); Wis. Pub. Intervenor v. Mortier, 501 U.S. 597, 611 n.4 (1991) ("[C]ommon sense suggests that inquiry benefits from reviewing additional information rather than ignoring it."); United States v. Am. Trucking Ass'ns, 310 U.S. 534, 543-44 (1940) ("When aid to construction of the meaning of words, as used in the statute, is available, there certainly can be no 'rule of law' which forbids its use, however clear the words may appear on 'superficial examination.'") (footnotes omitted); Williams v. U.S. Fid. & Guar. Co., 236 U.S. 549, 555 (1915)

4. The Court must not erode a past bankruptcy practice absent a clear indication in the legislative history that Congress intended such a departure.[57]

5. When Congress uses different language in a successor statute, the Court presumes that Congress has changed its intent.[58]

("And nothing is better settled than that statutes should be sensibly construed, with a view to effectuating the legislative intent.") (citations omitted). *Cf.* Corn Exch. Nat'l Bank & Trust Co. v. Klauder, 318 U.S. 434, 438 (1943) ("[W]e find nothing in Congressional policy which warrants taking this case out of the letter of the Act."); United States v. Emory, 314 U.S. 423, 430 (1941) ("We are aware of no canon of statutory construction compelling us to hold that the word 'first' in a 150 year old statute means 'second' or 'third', unless Congress later has said so or implied it unmistakably.").

57.   *See, e.g.,* Cohen v. de la Cruz, 523 U.S. 213, 221 (1998) ("We . . . will not read the Bankruptcy Code to erode past bankruptcy practice absent a clear indication that Congress intended such a departure.") (internal quotation marks and citation omitted); Dewsnup v. Timm, 502 U.S. 410, 419 (1992) ("[T]his Court has been reluctant to accept arguments that would interpret the Code, however vague the particular language under consideration might be, to effect a major change in pre-Code practice that is not the subject of at least some discussion in the legislative history."); Midlantic Nat'l Bank v. New Jersey Dep't of Envtl. Protection, 474 U.S. 494, 501 (1986) ("The normal rule of construction is that if Congress intends for legislation to change the interpretation of a judicially created concept, it makes that intent specific. . . . The Court has followed this rule with particular care in construing the scope of bankruptcy codifications.") (citation omitted) (cited with approval in United States v. Noland, 517 U.S. 535, 539 (1996)).

58.   *See* Crawford v. Burke, 195 U.S. 176, 190 (1904) ("Our own view, however, is that a change in phraseology creates a presumption of a change in intent, and that Congress would not have used such different language . . . without thereby intending a change in meaning."). *Cf.* Williams v. Austrian, 331 U.S. 642, 661-62 (1947) ("This negation of long-standing policy should be given effect . . . and should not be hedged by judge-made principles not in accord with those aims. Congress need not document its specific actions in elaborate fashion in order to direct this Court's attention to statutory policy and purpose. The failure to provide appropriate fanfare for . . . the consequent expansion of federal jurisdiction, hardly invites our opinion as to the advisability of the action which Congress has taken."). *But see* Maynard v. Elliott, 283 U.S. 273, 277 (1931) ("Only compelling language in the statute itself would warrant the rejection of a construction so long and so generally accepted,

6. A later statute that does not apply retroactively cannot be invoked to influence construction of an earlier statute.[59]

7. Under the rule of *stare decisis*, once the Supreme Court has decided an issue of statutory construction, the decision is final and binding in future cases, even if the plain meaning of the text is to the contrary.[60]

8. If possible, every word of a statute must be given meaning.[61]

---

especially where overturning the established practice would have such far reaching consequences as in the present case."); Van Huffel v. Harkelrode, 284 U.S. 225, 227 (1931) (finding the right to sell free and clear of encumbrances by implication under the Bankruptcy Act of 1898 even though the Bankruptcy Act of 1867 contained an express provision allowing the power to sell free and clear).

59.   *See* Levy v. Indus. Fin. Corp., 276 U.S. 281, 284 (1928) ("But that statute did not govern this case and cannot be invoked for the construction of the earlier law."). *But cf.* United States v. Emory, 314 U.S. 423, 430 (1941) ("We are aware of no canon of statutory construction compelling us to hold that the word 'first' in a 150 year old statute means 'second' or 'third,' unless Congress later has said so or implied it unmistakably.").

60.   Technically speaking, the doctrine of *stare decisis* is not a rule of statutory construction but is a court-created doctrine that applies to preclude the Court from reconsidering its previous interpretation of statutory language. As with rules of statutory construction, however, the Court appears to invoke *stare decisis* only when its application suits the outcome that a majority of the Court want's to reach. For example, in Tenn. Student Assistance Corp. v. Hood, 541 U.S. 440, 446 (2004), the Court construed the Eleventh Amendment of the United States Constitution to apply to suits against a state by citizens of its own state even though the text of the Eleventh Amendment "refers only to suits against a State by citizens of another State." *But see, e.g.,* Perez v. Campbell, 402 U.S. 637 (1971) (overruling *Kesler* and *Reitz* as misinterpreting the Supremacy Clause of the Constitution). *Accord* Washington v. W. C. Dawson & Co., 264 U.S. 219, 238 (1924) (Frankfurter, J., dissenting) ("Stare decisis is ordinarily a wise rule of action. But it is not a universal, inexorable command. The instances in which the Court has disregarded its admonition are many.") (footnote omitted).

61.   *See, e.g.,* Rake v. Wade, 508 U.S. 464, 471 (1993) ("To avoid deny[ing] effect to a part of a statute we accord significance and effect ... to every word.") (citations and internal quotation marks omitted); Hoffman v. Conn. Dep't of Income Maintenance, 492 U.S. 96, 103 (1989) ("It is our duty to give effect, if possible, to every clause and word of a statute . . . .")

9. Redundancy is not the same as surplusage.[62]
10. That a statute is awkward and ungrammatical does not make it ambiguous.[63]
11. A court must not interpret a statute to produce an absurd result.[64]
12. If literal interpretation of the statute produces an unfair result, it is up to Congress to amend the statute to remedy the problem.[65]
13. Congress "says in a statute what it means and means in a statute what it says there."[66]

(citations and internal quotation marks omitted); D. Ginsburg & Sons, Inc. v. Popkin, 285 U.S. 204, 208 (1932) ("[I]f possible, effect shall be given to every clause and part of a statute.") (citations omitted). *But see* Chickasaw Nation v. United States, 534 U.S. 84, 94 (2001) ([T]he Court's preference for avoiding surplusage "is sometimes offset by the canon that permits a court to reject words 'as surplusage' if 'inadvertently inserted or if repugnant to the rest of the statute.'") (citation omitted).

62.   *See, e.g.,* Conn. Nat'l Bank v. Germain, 503 U.S. 249, 253 (1992) ("Redundancies across statutes are not unusual events in drafting, and so long as there is no positive repugnancy between two laws . . . a court must give effect to both.") (internal citation and quotation marks omitted).

63.   *See* Laime v. United States Trustee, 540 U.S. 526, 534 (2004) ("The statute is awkward, and even ungrammatical; but that does not make it ambiguous . . . .").

64.   *See, e.g.,* Hartford Underwriters Ins. Co. v. Union Planters Bank, N.A., 530 U.S. 1, 6 (2000) (It is well established that "when the statute's language is plain, the sole function of the courts—at least where the disposition required by the text is not absurd—is to enforce it according to its terms.") (internal quotation marks omitted); INS v. Cardoza-Fonseca, 480 U.S. 421, 452 (1987) (Scalia, J., concurring) (nonbankruptcy case).

65.   *See* Cent. Trust Co. v. Official Creditors' Comm. of Geiger Enters., Inc., 454 U.S. 354, 360 (1982) (*per curiam*) ("While the Court of Appeals may have reached a practical result, it was a result inconsistent with the unambiguous language used by Congress."). *But see* Tinker v. Colwell, 193 U.S. 473, 490 (1904) ("[W]e think Congress did not intend to permit such an injury [criminal conversation] to be released by a discharge in bankruptcy. An action to redress a wrong of this character should not be taken out of the exception [to discharge] on any narrow and technical construction of the language of such exception.").

66.   *See* Conn. Nat'l Bank v. Germain, 503 U.S. 249, 253-54 (1992) ("In any event, canons of construction are no more than rules of thumb that help courts determine the meaning of legislation, and in interpreting a

14. Different parts of a statute must be interpreted together (*in pari materia*).[67]

15. A word is presumed to have the same meaning in all parts of the same statute.[68]

16. As a general proposition, the Court will construe a statute to affect only property rights created after the date of enactment.[69]

---

statute a court should always turn first to one, cardinal canon before all others. We have stated time and again that courts must presume that a legislature says in a statute what it means and means in a statute what it says there."). *Accord Ron Pair*, 489 U.S. at 241-42.

67. *See, e.g.*, Duparquet Huot & Moneuse Co. v. Evans, 297 U.S. 216, 218 (1936) ("There is need to keep in view also the structure of the statute, and the relation, physical and logical, between its several parts."); Lockwood v. Exch. Bank, 190 U.S. 294, 300 (1903) ("The two provisions of the statute must be construed together, and both be given effect."); Pirie v. Chicago Title & Trust Co., 182 U.S. 438, 449 (1901) ("Undoubtedly all the sections of the act must be construed together . . . ."). The same rule does not hold for words in other statutes. Although "[h]ere and there in the Bankruptcy Code Congress has included specific directions that establish the significance for bankruptcy law of a term used elsewhere in the federal statutes," in the absence of such specific directions the Court will not look to other statutes to define bankruptcy law terms. *See* Howard Delivery Serv., Inc. v. Zurich Am. Ins. Co., 547 U.S. 651, 662 (2006) (citing United States v. Reorganized CF&I Fabricators of Utah, Inc., 518 U.S. 213, 219-20 (1996)).

68. *See* Cohen v. de la Cruz, 523 U.S. 213, 220 (1998) (there is a presumption in the Bankruptcy Code that "equivalent words have equivalent meaning when repeated in the same statute . . . .") (citation omitted); Patterson v. Shumate, 504 U.S. 753, 758 n.2 (1992) (citing Morrison-Knudsen Constr. Co. v. Director, Office of Workers' Comp. Programs, 461 U.S. 624, 633 (1983) ("[A] word is presumed to have the same meaning in all subsections of the same statute."). *But see* Dewsnup v. Timm, 502 U.S. 410, 417 n.3 (1992) ("[W]e express no opinion as to whether the words 'allowed secured claim' have different meaning in other provisions of the Bankruptcy Code.").

69. *See* United States v. Sec. Indus. Bank, 459 U.S. 70, 79-81 (1982) ("The principle that statutes operate only prospectively . . . is familiar to every law student. . . . This principle has been repeatedly applied to bankruptcy statutes affecting property rights. . . . *Holt v. Henley*, 232 U.S. 637 (1914) . . . . No bankruptcy law shall be construed to eliminate property rights which existed before the law was enacted in the absence of an explicit command from Congress."); Holt v. Henley, 232 U.S. 637,

17. In a statute, "includes" is illustrative, not limiting or exclusive.[70]

The Court has used conflicting maxims of statutory construction in numerous bankruptcy cases and sometimes within the same case.[71] For example, in *Keppel v. Tiffin Savings Bank*[72] the Court was required to interpret the meaning of "surrender" in section 57g of the Bankruptcy Act of 1898.[73] Under that statute, "the claims of creditors who have received preferences shall not be allowed unless such creditors shall surrender their preferences." The Sixth Circuit certified to the Supreme Court three questions, the first of which was "[c]an a creditor of a bankrupt, who has received a merely voidable preference, and who has in good faith retained such preference until deprived thereof by the judgment of a court upon a suit of the trustee, thereafter prove the debt so voidably preferred?"[74] In a 5-4 opinion, the Court held that even creditors who involuntarily "surrender" their preferences may prove claims in bankruptcy.[75] Both the majority[76] and

---

639 (1914) ("[T]he reasonable and usual interpretation of statutes is to confine their effect, so far as may be, to property rights established after they were passed."). The same principle does not apply to contract rights where the bankruptcy statutes usually are construed to apply to pre-existing rights. *See, e.g.,* Hanover Nat'l Bank v. Moyses, 186 U.S. 181, 188 (1902) (cited with approval in *Sec. Indus. Bank*, 459 U.S. at 80).

70.   *See* Am. Sur. Co. v. Marotta, 287 U.S. 513, 517 (1933).

71.   One commentator has concluded that "the Court does not apply a single interpretive method in its Bankruptcy Code cases." *See* Karen M. Gebbia-Pinetti, *Interpreting the Bankruptcy Code: An Empirical Study of the Supreme Court's Bankruptcy Decisions*, 3 CHAPMAN L. REV. 173, 298 (Spring 2000).

72.   197 U.S. 356 (1905) ("*Keppel*").

73.   11 U.S.C. § 93g (1976) (repealed 1979). Section 57g of the Bankruptcy Act is the predecessor of Bankruptcy Code § 502(d). *See* STAFF OF SUBCOMM. ON CIVIL AND CONSTITUTIONAL RIGHTS OF THE HOUSE COMM. ON THE JUDICIARY, 95th CONG., TABLE OF DERIVATION OF H.R. 8200, 7 (Comm. Print 1977).

74.   *See Keppel*, 197 U.S. at 359.

75.   *See id.* at 374.

76.   *See id.* at 361. ("Let us first consider the meaning of this provision, guided by the cardinal rule which requires that it should, if possible, be

dissent[77] focused on the plain meaning of the statute and the policy it was intended to accomplish. The majority looked to the dictionary definition of "surrender" and determined that it applied to both voluntary and involuntary actions.[78] The majority buttressed its statutory construction by noting that the fundamental purpose of the provision was to secure an equality of distribution among creditors, and that denying a creditor who disgorges a preference the opportunity to prove a claim would create an inequality.[79] The dissent countered that a creditor who resists the trustee and disgorges a preference after judgment has nothing left to surrender; to hold otherwise would defeat the statute's policy of a prompt, equal, and inexpensive distribution of the estate.[80] The majority believed that to deprive the preferred creditor of a claim after disgorgement of the preference would be punitive and would "disregard the elementary rule that a penalty is not to be readily implied . . . unless the words of the statute plainly impose it."[81] Thus, each side passionately used maxims of statutory construction to support different interpretations and meanings of the same word.[82]

More recently, in *United States v. Ron Pair Enterprises, Inc.*,[83] the Court decided whether Bankruptcy Code § 506(b)[84] entitles a creditor

---

given a meaning in accord with the general purpose which the statute was intended to accomplish.").

77. *See id.* at 380 (Day, J., with whom Harlan, Brewer, and Brown, JJ., joined, dissenting). ("Therefore the sole question here is: What is meant by the term 'surrender' as used in the act of 1898?").

78. *See id.* at 362. ("The word 'surrender,' however, does not exclude compelled action, but, to the contrary, generally implies such action.").

79. *See id.* at 361.

80. *See id.* at 378, 384.

81. *See id.* at 362.

82. For a more recent example of a 5-4 decision that follows a similar pattern of disagreement over statutory interpretation, *see* United States v. Sotelo, 436 U.S. 268 (1978) discussed *infra* in Ch. 2., p. 116.

83. 489 U.S. 235 (1989).

04. 11 U.S.C. § 506(b) (2000).

to receive postpetition interest on an allowed, nonconsensual, oversecured claim. To resolve this issue, both the majority and dissent invoked different maxims of statutory construction. The war of the maxims resulted in a 5-4 decision in favor of granting postpetition interest to the oversecured-nonconsensual lien creditor. The majority invoked the maxim that a statute must be construed in accordance with its plain meaning.[85] In this case, the placement of the second of four commas in section 506(b) meant that interest was available to any oversecured creditor and did not have to be provided in an agreement. "The language and punctuation Congress used cannot be read in any other way."[86] The dissent noted that based on the position of a comma in the statute, the majority had adopted a statutory construction that reversed a clear past practice and Supreme Court ruling without any clear evidence that Congress intended a different result when it adopted Bankruptcy Code § 506(b).[87] The dissent contended that the majority's approach violated the maxims that "[p]unctuation is not decisive of the construction of a statute" and "if Congress intends for legislation to change the interpretation of a judicially created concept, it makes that intent specific."[88]

Indeed, several Supreme Court cases have held that as a matter of statutory construction, courts should "not read the Bankruptcy Code to erode past bankruptcy practice absent a clear indication that Congress intended such a departure."[89] Sometimes the Court will go to

---

85.   *See Ron Pair*, 489 U.S. at 241 ("[W]here, as here, the statute's language is plain, 'the sole function of the courts is to enforce it according to its terms.'") (quoting Caminetti v. United States, 242 U.S. 470, 485 (1917)).

86.   *See Ron Pair*, 489 U.S. at 242.

87.   *See id.* at 252-53 (O' Connor, J., with whom Brennan, Marshall, and Stevens, JJ., joined, dissenting).

88.   *See id.* at 250, 252 (citations omitted).

89.   Pa. Dep't of Pub. Welfare v. Davenport, 495 U.S. 552, 563 (1990). *Accord, e.g.*, Cohen v. de la Cruz, 523 U.S. 213 (1998); United States v. Reorganized CF&I Fabricators of Utah, Inc., 518 U.S. 213, 221 (1996); United States v. Ron Pair Enters., Inc., 489 U.S. 235, 244-45 (1989);

an extreme to find such a past practice. For example, in *Midlantic National Bank v. New Jersey Department of Environmental Protection*,[90] despite "unequivocal language"[91] in the statute authorizing a trustee to abandon "any property of the estate that is burdensome," the Court held that Bankruptcy Code § 554(a)[92] does not authorize a trustee to abandon hazardous property in contravention of a state statute or regulation reasonably designed to protect the public health or safety. Relying on only three pre-Code cases (including one that did not deal with state laws and another in which the relevant language was arguably dicta), the Court concluded that under pre-Code bankruptcy law there were restrictions on a trustee's power to abandon property."[93] On the other hand, the Court has limited the maxim of reliance on prior practice by noting that "where the meaning of the Bankruptcy Code's text is itself clear . . . its operation is unimpeded by contrary . . . prior practice."[94]

The Court also has adhered to the maxim that in the absence of express language, courts will not construe statutes to affect property rights established before they were passed. For example, in *Holt v. Henley*,[95] Justice Holmes wrote for a unanimous Court in refusing to

---

United Sav. Ass'n v. Timbers of Inwood Forest Assocs., Ltd., 484 U.S. 365, 380 (1988); Kelly v. Robinson, 479 U.S. 36, 53 (1986).

90.   474 U.S. 494 (1986).

91.   *See* United States v. Ron Pair Enters., Inc., 489 U.S. 235, 251 (1989) (O'Connor, J., dissenting).

92.   11 U.S.C. § 554(a) (1988).

93.   *See* United States v. Ron Pair Enters., Inc., 489 U.S. 235, 251-52 (1989) (O'Connor, J., dissenting). In *Midlantic*, Justice Rehnquist's dissent, in which Justice O'Connor joined, made plain that a close reading of the three cases relied on by the majority "reveals that none supports the rule" of *Midlantic*. *See Midlantic*, 474 U.S. at 510 (Rehnquist, J., dissenting).

94.   *See* Hartford Underwriters Ins. Co. v. Union Planters Bank, N.A., 530 U.S. 1, 10 (2000) (quoting BFP v. Resolution Trust Corp., 511 U.S. 531, 546 (1994)).

95.   *232 U.S. 637 (1914) ("Holt")*.

apply the trustee's newly enacted lien rights[96] to defeat the pre-existing rights of a vendor who installed a sprinkler system for the debtor. "[T]he reasonable and usual interpretation of such statutes is to confine their effect, so far as may be, to property rights established after they were passed."[97] The Court relied on this precedent 62 years later in *Security Industrial Bank*[98] when it refused to retroactively apply the Bankruptcy Code's newly-created section 522(f)[99] power to avoid liens in household goods and furnishings:[100] "No bankruptcy law shall be construed to eliminate property rights which existed before the law was enacted in the absence of an explicit command from Congress."

The rule of *stare decisis* plays a large role in Supreme Court decisions. Even if a statute has a plain meaning, if the Court previously has ruled against the plain meaning, a later court generally will not overturn the result.[101] The Court's recent Eleventh Amendment jurisprudence illustrates this point nicely. For example, the Eleventh Amendment, by its terms, plainly applies only to suits against a state by a citizen of another state.[102] But long ago, in *Hans v. Louisiana*[103] the Court construed the amendment to cover suits against a state by

---

96.   The Act of June 25, 1910, ch. 412, § 8, 36 Stat. 838, 840 amended section 47a(2) of the Bankruptcy Act to give the trustee the rights of a lien creditor.

97.   *See Holt*, 232 U.S. at 639.

98.   *See* United States v. Sec. Indus. Bank, 459 U.S. 70, 80 (1982).

99.   *See* 11 U.S.C. § 522(f)(2) (Supp. 1980).

100.   *Sec. Indus. Bank*, 459 U.S. at 81.

101.   Of course, *stare decisis* does not preclude the Supreme Court from overturning previous holdings, but this is seldom done on the basis of textualism as opposed to policy concerns. *See* United States v. Ron Pair Enters., Inc., 489 U.S. 235, 241-43 (1989).

102.   *See* U.S. CONST. amend. XI ("The Judicial power of the United States shall not be construed to extend to any suit in law or equity, commenced or prosecuted against one of the United States by Citizens of another State, or by Citizens or Subjects of any Foreign State.").

103.   134 U.S. 1 (1890).

its own citizens.[104] This expansive construction served the policy that it would be unseemly for a state to be sued by its own citizens even more than foreign citizens.[105] It also violated the maxim of statutory construction that every word must be given meaning or significance.[106] In *Hans* the Supreme Court effectively read "other" out of the Eleventh Amendment. Despite this plain departure from textualist principles, after *Hans*, Justices who adhere to textualism have followed *stare decisis* and refused to use textualism to overrule *Hans*.[107] Yet on other occasions, the Court has changed its position despite *stare decisis*. For example, in *Perez v. Campbell*,[108] the Court

---

104. *See id.* at 20 ("[T]he obligations of a State rest for their performance upon its honor and good faith, and cannot be made the subjects of judicial cognizance unless the State consents to be sued, or comes itself into court . . . .").

105. *See* Alden v. Maine, 527 U.S. 706, 749 (1999) ("In some ways, of course, a congressional power to authorize private suits against nonconsenting States in their own courts would be even more offensive to state sovereignty than a power to authorize the suits in a federal forum.").

106. *See, e.g.,* Rake v. Wade, 508 U.S. 464, 471 (1993) ("To avoid deny[ing] effect to a part of a statute we accord significance and effect . . . to every word.") (citations and internal footnotes omitted); Hoffman v. Conn. Dep't of Income Maintenance, 492 U.S. 96, 103 (1989) ("It is our duty to give effect, if possible, to every clause and word of a statute . . . .") (citations and internal footnotes omitted); D. Ginsburg & Sons, Inc. v. Popkin, 285 U.S. 204, 208 (1932) ("[I]f possible, effect shall be given to every clause and part of a statute.") (citations omitted). *But see* Chickasaw Nation v. United States, 534 U.S. 84, 94 (2001) ([T]he Court's preference for avoiding surplusage "is sometimes offset by the canon that permits a court to reject words 'as surplusage' if 'inadvertently inserted or if repugnant to the rest of the statute.'") (citation omitted).

107. "Regardless of what one may think of Hans, it has been assumed to be the law for nearly a century. During that time, Congress has enacted many statutes—including the Jones Act and the provisions of the Federal Employers' Liability Act (FELA) which it incorporates—on the assumption that States were immune from suits by individuals." Welch v. Tex. Dep't of Highways & Pub. Transp., 483 U.S. 468, 496 (1987) (Scalia, J., concurring).

108. 402 U.S. 637 (1971).

overruled its earlier decisions in *Kesler v. Department of Public Safety*[109] and *Reitz v. Mealey*[110] as misinterpreting the Supremacy Clause of the Constitution. In his April 9, 1971 letter to Justice Blackmun regarding *Perez*, Justice Harlan urges Justice Blackmun to turn his draft opinion into a dissent upholding *Kesler* with greater emphasis on *stare decisis*.[111]

Some commentators hold the view that the Supreme Court's bankruptcy jurisprudence adopts "a 'plain meaning' posture where the language of the statute meets with judicial approval, and use[s] legislative intent to contradict the language of the statute where a literal reading is not kind to the desired result."[112] This pragmatic, perhaps somewhat cynical, view of the Court is borne out by the research of the decisions by most, but not all, Justices.[113] Over the years, a significant number of Justices appear to care deeply about the legislative history[114] and view their role as interpreting statutes to

---

109.   369 U.S. 153 (1962).

110.   314 U.S. 33 (1941).

111.   *See* April 9, 1971 letter from Justice Harlan to Justice Blackmun (contained in Blackmun papers) ("From my standpoint <u>Kesler</u> was correctly decided, and, further, I think that <u>stare decisis</u> should stand in the way of overruling.").

112.   *See* Kenneth N. Klee & Frank A. Merola, *Ignoring Congressional Intent: Eight Years of Judicial Legislation*, 62 AM. BANKR. L.J. 1, 2 (1988). *See also* Justice Powell's notes on a clerk's memorandum dated September 19, 1986 regarding congressional intent and Kelly v. Robinson, 479 U.S. 36 (1986) ("Congress could not have intended that restitution orders, analogous to criminal fines, are dischargeable.").

113.   The tendency of courts to sometimes depart from "plain meaning" has caused one Supreme Court Justice to "question whether our legal culture has so far departed from attention to text, or is so lacking in agreed-upon methodology for creating and interpreting text, that it any longer makes sense to talk of 'a government of laws, not of men.'" *See* Patterson v. Shumate, 504 U.S. 753, 766 (1992) (Scalia, J., concurring).

114.   In the context of the Bankruptcy Code, the Court has recognized that "[b]ecause of the absence of a conference and the key roles played by Representative [Don] Edwards and his counterpart floor manager Senator DeConcini, we have treated their floor statements on the Bankruptcy Reform Act of 1978 as persuasive evidence of congressional intent." *See* Begier v. I.R.S., 496 U.S. 53, 64 n.5 (1990). *See also*

achieve congressional intent even when the statutory language is inconsistent with the desired outcome. For example, Bankruptcy Act § 75(s)(3)[115] permitted the debtor to redeem an encumbered farm by paying its appraised value. But the remedy was subject to two provisos, the second of which authorized the secured creditor to demand a public sale of the property.[116] In *Wright v. Union Central*

Commodity Futures Trading Comm'n v. Weintraub, 471 U.S. 343, 350 (1985) (quoting statements made by members of Congress). *But see* Fid. Fin. Servs. v. Fink, 522 U.S. 211, 220 (1998) ("Whatever weight some Members of this Court might accord to floor statements about proposals actually under consideration, remarks that purport to clarify 'related' areas of the law can have little persuasive force, and in this case none at all."); Hoffman v. Connecticut, 492 U.S. 96, 103-04 (1989) (in refusing to rely on floor statements, the Court noted that "'legislative history generally will be irrelevant to a judicial inquiry into whether Congress intended to abrogate the Eleventh Amendment.'") (citation omitted). The Court also has relied on House and Senate Reports in construing bankruptcy statutes. *See, e.g.,* Commodity Futures Trading Comm'n v. Weintraub, 471 U.S. 343, 351 (1985) (("Both the House and the Senate Reports state that § 542(e) 'is a new provision . . . .'"). *But see Begier*, 496 U.S. at 69 (Scalia, J., concurring) ("I think it both demeaning and unproductive for us to ponder whether to adopt literal or not-so-literal readings of Committee Reports, as though they were controlling statutory text."). When congressional reports are silent, the Court has even looked at hearing testimony to determine legislative history. *See* United States v. Whiting Pools, Inc., 462 U.S. 198, 207 (1983) ("Although the legislative reports are silent on the precise issue before us, the House and Senate hearings . . . provide guidance."). In some instances, even when the congressional reports address the issue, the Court will refer to hearing testimony. *See, e.g.,* Norwest Bank Worthington v. Ahlers, 485 U.S. 197, 205 n.5 (1988). *But see* Kelly v. Robinson, 479 U.S. 36, 51 n.13 (1986) ("We acknowledge that a few comments in the hearings . . . may suggest that the language bears the interpretation adopted [below] . . . . But none of those statements was made by a Member of Congress, nor were they included in the official Senate and House Reports. We decline to accord any significance to these statements.").

115. The Frazier-Lemke Act, ch. 869, 48 Stat. 1289 (1934) (formerly codified at 11 U.S.C. § 203(s)) (repealed 1949) (adding subsection (s) to Bankruptcy Act § 75).

116. *See id.* ("[U]pon request in writing by any secured creditor or creditors, the court shall order the property upon which such secured creditors have a lien to be sold at public auction.").

Life Insurance Co.[117] the Court was asked to decide whether a debtor could redeem farmland at a value fixed by the court before the secured creditor could cause the farm to be sold in a public sale.[118] In deliberating about the Court's decision in *Wright*, Justice Roberts wrote Justice Douglas a letter specifically referencing congressional debates to influence the Court's interpretation of the statute. Justice Roberts writes to Justice Douglas as follows:[119]

> This was the congressional view: "Under existing language of the bill, whether or not there may be foreclosure in a case where the award is less than the debt secured is left to the discretion of the judge. Now, that is not a clear explanation, but it will suffice for the present purpose. I would make it clearer if it were important. However, the amendment proposed removes the judge's discretion, if the original debt has not been fully paid, and gives the creditor the right, as a matter of right, to have a foreclosure of the property in the event his debt has not been in full." (79 Cong. Rec. 14333)

This concern is evidenced in the unanimous reported opinion which states that "the [Bankruptcy] Act must be liberally construed to give the debtor the full measure of the relief afforded by Congress, lest its benefits be frittered away by narrow formalistic interpretations which disregard the spirit and the letter of the Act."[120]

Similar themes pervade other Supreme Court bankruptcy decisions. For example, "[i]n expounding a statute, we must not be guided by a single sentence or member of a sentence, but look to the

---

117.   311 U.S. 273 (1940).

118.   *See id.* at 275-76 ("The narrow issue presented . . . is whether under § 75(s)(3) the debtor must be accorded an opportunity . . . to redeem the property at the reappraised value or at a value fixed by the court before the court may order a public sale.").

119.   *See* December 2, 1940 letter from Justice Roberts to Justice Douglas regarding Wright v. Union Cent. Life Ins. Co., 311 U.S. 273 (1940).

120.   *See* Wright v. Union Cent. Life Ins. Co., 311 U.S. 273, 279 (1940) (citations omitted). *Accord* Wright v. Logan, 315 U.S. 139 (1942).

provisions of the whole law, and to its object and policy."[121] Justice Douglas made this point quite clearly in *Bank of Marin v. England*[122] when he wrote, "[y]et we do not read these statutory words with the ease of a computer."[123]

Certain Justices are devoted textualists even when their politics would appear to favor a different outcome. For example, in *Dewsnup v. Timm*,[124] Justice Scalia, an avowed textualist, wrote a scathing dissent to a majority opinion that forbade lien-stripping of liens securing claims of undersecured creditors.[125] The substance of the dissent was that Congress could not have intended to use "secured claim" one way in Bankruptcy Code § 506(a) and another way in § 506(d). In *Bank of Marin*, Justice Harlan chided the Court for disregarding "both the proper principles of statutory construction and the most permanent interests of bankruptcy administration" in fashioning a pragmatic result "in its haste to alleviate an indisputable inequity to the bank."[126]

Yet, if the policy at stake is overwhelmingly important, even the most ardent textualist might compromise his principles of statutory interpretation.[127] For example, in *BFP v. Resolution Trust Corp.*,[128] Justice Scalia wrote for the Court interpreting "reasonably equivalent value" in Bankruptcy Code § 548.[129] In order to protect 400 years of real estate mortgage foreclosure practices from fraudulent transfer

---

121.   Kelly v. Robinson, 479 U.S. 36, 43 (1986) (quoting United States v. Heirs of Boisdoré, 49 U.S. [8 How.] 113, 122 (1850)).

122.   385 U.S. 99 (1966) (*"Bank of Marin"*).

123.   *See id.* at 103.

124.   502 U.S. 410 (1992).

125.   *See id.* at 420-36 (1992) (Scalia, J., dissenting).

126.   *See Bank of Marin*, 385 U.S. at 103 (Harlan, J., dissenting).

127.   *See, e.g.,* Young v. United States, 535 U.S. 43 (2002) (Scalia, J., writing for a unanimous Court). *Young* is discussed more fully *infra* in Ch. 2, pp. 116-118.

128.   511 U.S. 531 (1994) (*"BFP"*).

129.   11 U.S.C. § 548 (2000).

attack, Justice Scalia wrote that the value received at a regularly conducted real property foreclosure sale is per se reasonably equivalent to the value of the property sold.[130] Outside the real property foreclosure context, however, "the 'reasonably equivalent value' criterion will continue to have independent meaning (ordinarily a meaning similar to fair market value)."[131]

The dissent made two textualist arguments, both of which had been used by Justice Scalia in other cases, to refute the soundness of the majority opinion. First, the dissent noted that engrafting a "foreclosure-sale exception" onto Bankruptcy Code § 548 was "in derogation of the straightforward language used by Congress,"[132] noting that neither congressional intent nor the plain meaning of the statute support the conclusion that the distressed prices normally fetched at foreclosure sales qualify for "reasonably equivalent value" in section 548. In fact, "rejecting such a reading of the statute is as easy as statutory interpretation is likely to get."[133] Second, the dissent noted that the Court's construction of the statute to only permit avoidance of collusive or procedurally deficient foreclosure sales rendered several congressional amendments to the Bankruptcy Code superfluous.[134] This interpretation transgresses a well-known rule of statutory construction that every part of a statute must be given some meaning.[135] Moreover, the Court eviscerates another canon of statutory construction by interpreting the same words in section 548 to have one meaning for real property foreclosures and another meaning for all other transfers.[136] As Justice Scalia wrote in his dissent in *Dewsnup v. Timm*, "'Normal rule[s] of statutory construction'" require

---

130. *See BFP*, 511 U.S. at 542-43.

131. *See id.* at 545.

132. *See id.* at 549 (Souter, J., with whom Blackmun, Stevens, and Ginsburg, JJ., joined, dissenting).

133. *See id.* at 550-51.

134. *See id.* at 555.

135. *See supra* n.61 and accompanying text.

136. *See BFP*, 511 U.S. at 556-57.

that "identical words [used] *in the same section of the same enact-ment*" must be given the same effect.[137]

Instead of simply resting the *BFP* decision on policy grounds, however, Justice Scalia went to great efforts to answer the dissent's textualist attack on his opinion.[138] He countered that the meaning of the statute is not plain because it creates an ambiguity by failing to define what a foreclosed property is worth.[139] He wrote that the Court's opinion does not render congressional amendments super-fluous because "[p]rior to 1984, it was at least open to question wheth-er § 548 could be used to invalidate even a *collusive* foreclosure sale . . . . It is no superfluity for Congress to clarify what had at best been unclear, which is what it did here by making the provision apply to involuntary as well as voluntary transfers and by including foreclosures within the definition of 'transfer.'"[140] Finally, he noted that his opinion did not give two inconsistent meanings to "reasonably equivalent value."[141] The inquiry whether the debtor received reasonably equivalent value is "the same for all transfers"; but the fact that "a piece of property is legally subject to a forced sale . . . necessarily affects its worth [and] completely redefin[es] the market in which the property is offered for sale . . . ."[142]

The exchange among the Justices in *BFP* is not an isolated example of sharp differences over statutory construction. For example, in *FCC v. NextWave Personal Communications, Inc.,*[143]

---

137. *See* Dewsnup v. Timm, 502 U.S. at 422 (Scalia, J., dissenting) (emphasis in original).

138. *See BFP*, 511 U.S. at 546. ("The dissent's insistence here that no doubt exists—that our reading of the statute is 'in derogation of the *straight-forward language* used by Congress,' . . . does not withstand scrutiny.") (emphasis in original).

139. *See id.* at 547. ("But what *is* the 'value'? The dissent has no re-sponse . . . .") (emphasis in original).

140. *See id.* at 543 n.7 (emphasis in original).

141. *See id.* at 548.

142. *See id.*

143. 537 U.S. 293 (2003).

Justice Scalia, writing for the Court, takes sharp issue with Justice Breyer's dissent,[144] at one point writing that "[i]n addition to distorting the text of the provision, the dissent's interpretation renders the provision superfluous."[145] Justice Breyer's dissent attacks the majority opinion in kind, largely based on issues of statutory construction,[146] at one point writing that the majority's reasoning "rests too heavily upon linguistic deduction and too little upon human purpose."[147]

In fact, Justice Breyer's observation is characteristic of some of the Court's bankruptcy decisions. On occasion, the Court will adhere to plain meaning and overturn a pragmatic result that departs from the language of the statute. For example, the Court's *per curiam* opinion in *Central Trust Co. v. Official Creditors' Committee*[148] interpreted section 403(a) of the Bankruptcy Reform Act of 1978 to prohibit dismissal of a chapter XI case filed under the Bankruptcy Act and refiling it as a chapter 11 case under the Bankruptcy Code.[149] Even if the dismissal was in the best interests of the estate and would conserve judicial resources, the bankruptcy court was not free to disregard a clear congressional directive.[150] "While the Court of Appeals may have reached a practical result, it was a result inconsistent with the unambiguous language used by Congress."[151]

In other instances, however, the Court will doggedly adhere to a plain meaning rule of statutory interpretation even when the result is harsh. For example, in *Laime v. United States Trustee*,[152] in a straight forward manner, the Court dealt with Congress' 1994 deletion of an

---

144. *See id.* at 305-07.

145. *See id.* at 307.

146. *See id.* at 313-21.

147. *See id.* at 321.

148. 454 U.S. 354 (1982).

149. *See id.* at 359-60.

150. *See id.* at 359.

151. *See id.* at 360.

152. 540 U.S. 526 (2004).

award of compensation from the bankruptcy estate "to the debtor's attorney" under section 330 of the Bankruptcy Code.[153] Even though the 1994 deletion left the statute "awkward, and even ungrammatical," the Court found it unambiguous.[154] The Court relied on its previous statement in *Hartford Underwriters Insurance Co. v. Union Planters Bank, N.A.* and previous opinions that "when the statute's language is plain, the sole function of the courts—at least where the disposition required by the text is not absurd—is to enforce it according to its terms."[155] The plain meaning of the statute did not lead to absurd results because the statute does not prevent debtors from engaging counsel before filing for chapter 7, even though those same attorneys could not be compensated out of the estate after the filing.[156] The Court recognized that deference to the supremacy of the Legislature caused its "unwillingness to soften the import of Congress' chosen words even if . . . the words lead to a harsh outcome . . . ."[157]

Sometimes the Court will adopt a sensible rule of construction that Congress later codifies. For example, in *American Surety Co. v. Marotta,*[158] the Court interpreted the meaning of the word "includes" in the definition of "creditor" in section 1(9) of the Bankruptcy Act of

153. *See* Bankruptcy Reform Act of 1994, Pub. L. No. 103-394, 108 Stat. 4106, 4130-31 (§ 224(b) of the Act amending 11 U.S.C. § 330(a) (1994)).

154. *See Laime*, 540 U.S. at 534.

155. *See* Hartford Underwriters Ins. Co. v. Union Planters Bank, N.A., 530 U.S. 1, 6 (2000) (internal quotation marks omitted).

156. *See Laime*, 540 U.S. at 535-36.

157. *See id.* at 538; Corn Exch. Nat'l Bank & Trust Co. v. Klauder, 318 U.S. 434, 437-38 (1943) ("Such a construction is capable of harsh results . . . but we find nothing in Congressional policy which warrants taking this case out of the letter of the Act."). *But see* Duparquet Huot & Moneuse Co. v. Evans, 297 U.S. 216, 223 (1936) ("Such a reading of the act will help at the same time in the avoidance of other consequences too harsh or incongruous to have been intended by the Congress.").

158. *See* Am. Sur. Co. v. Marotta, 287 U.S. 513 (1933).

1898.[159] The Court rejected the interpretation of the lower court which had interpreted "the word 'include' to be one of limitation, the equivalent of 'include only,' and to exclude every person not having a demand presently provable."[160] Rather, the Court noted that "[i]n definitive provisions of statutes and other writings, 'include' is frequently, if not generally, used as a word of extension or enlargement rather than as one of limitation or enumeration."[161] In the context of the Bankruptcy Act, the Court contrasted "shall include" with "shall mean" and concluded that in the context of section 1(9), "it is plain that 'shall include' . . . cannot reasonably be read to be the equivalent of 'shall mean' or 'shall include only.'"[162] Congress later adopted this reasonable rule of construction for the entire 1978 Bankruptcy Code.[163]

LEGAL MAXIMS

The Court uses numerous legal maxims that have nothing to do with statutory construction per se. As noted previously,[164] the doctrine of *stare decisis* appears to require the Court to follow its previous decisions. Even then, the command is not inexorable; the Court has

---

159.   *See id.* at 516 ("(9) 'creditor' shall include anyone who owns a demand or claim provable in bankruptcy, and may include his duly authorized agent, attorney, or proxy.").

160.   *See id.* at 516-17.

161.   *See id.* at 517.

162.   *See id.*

163.   *See* 11 U.S.C. § 102(3) (1978) ("In this title, 'includes' and 'including' are not limiting."). *See also* H.R. REP. NO. 595, 95th Cong., 1st Sess. 315 (1977) ("Paragraph (3) is a codification of *American Surety Co. v. Marotta*, 287 U.S. 513 (1933)."). The Table of Derivation of the Bankruptcy Code also indicates this rule of construction was taken from *American Surety Co. v. Marotta. See* TABLE OF DERIVATION OF H.R. 8200, SUBCOMM. ON CIVIL AND CONSTITUTIONAL RIGHTS OF THE HOUSE COMM. ON THE JUDICIARY, 95th Cong., 1st Sess. 2 (Comm. Print No. 6 1977).

164.   *See* n.60 *supra* and accompanying text.

overruled previous decisions that were directly on point to the issue before it.[165] When the Court invokes *stare decisis*, however, it applies only to holdings of a decision or those legal principles necessary to the conclusions reached.

The principle of *stare decisis* does not hold with respect to obiter dicta or statements contained in an opinion that are not necessary to its conclusion. Early in the history of our Republic, Chief Justice Marshall established the principle that the Court was "not bound to follow our dicta in a prior case in which the point now at issue was not fully debated."[166] This principle remains vital today. The majority opinion in *Central Virginia Community College v. Katz*[167] relied on it verbatim: "It is a maxim not to be disregarded, that general expressions, in every opinion, are to be taken in connection with the case in which those expressions are used. If they go beyond the case, they may be respected, but ought not to control the judgment in a subsequent suit when the very point is presented for decision."[168]

ORAL ARGUMENT

As an empirical matter, it is difficult to determine the impact of oral argument on the Court's bankruptcy decisions. The Court's bankruptcy cases at times involve inexperienced advocates arguing about issues with which the Court is unfamiliar.[169] In many cases it

---

165. *See, e.g.,* Perez v. Campbell, 402 U.S. 637 (1971) (overruling *Kesler* and *Reitz* as misinterpreting the Supremacy Clause of the Constitution). *Accord* Washington v. W. C. Dawson & Co., 264 U.S. 219, 238 (1924) (Frankfurter, J., dissenting) ("Stare decisis is ordinarily a wise rule of action. But it is not a universal, inexorable command. The instances in which the Court has disregarded its admonition are many.") (footnote omitted).

166. *See* Cohens v. Virginia, 19 U.S. (6 Wheat.) 264 (1821).

167. 546 U.S. 356, 363 (2006).

168. *See id.* citing *Cohens v. Virginia* at 399-400.

169. *See, e.g.,* Justice Douglas' Memorandum to the Conference dated January 23, 1946, in Meyer v. Fleming (*In re* Chicago, R.I. & Pac. Ry. Co.), 327 U.S. 161 (1946) ("The problem presented by this case was

appears that the bankruptcy lawyer who argued the case below is reluctant to relinquish the opportunity to make a Supreme Court argument. In commenting on a bankruptcy case argued during the October 1999 term, Justice O'Connor remarked that the two bankruptcy "lawyers were experienced in the field and explained a good deal about the case since [we—Supreme Court Justices] do not hear too many bankruptcy cases. They will probably never come back to argue before the Supreme Court."[170] Although it is understandable that an attorney would not want to give up the highlight of a career to argue before the United States Supreme Court, a decision to forego bringing in a Supreme Court specialist who is known to the Justices might not be in the client's best interest.

It may also be true that at least some of the Justices appear to be unfamiliar with and devote less attention to bankruptcy cases.[171] Anecdotally, according to a former Supreme Court law clerk and corroborated by a Justice's former student, in the past few years one of the Justices has confessed that the Justices do not lose a lot of sleep over bankruptcy cases, because, unlike constitutional cases or capital cases, if the Court makes a mistake, Congress can fix it prospectively by amending the statute. At the 1999 Ninth Circuit Judicial Conference, another Justice acknowledged that bankruptcy issues are complicated, and the Justices do not understand them very well; they

---

inadequately argued. It is a question of first impression in this Court.") (contained in Burton papers).

170. *See* 2000 Ninth Circuit Judicial Conference, Conversation with Justice O' Connor (on file with Assistant Circuit Executive for Judicial Conference and Education, Office of the Circuit Executive for the Ninth Circuit).

171. Authors and scholars also appear to largely ignore the Court's bankruptcy cases. *See* Richard E. Ellis, *Ogden v. Saunders*, in THE OXFORD GUIDE TO UNITED STATES SUPREME COURT DECISIONS 224-25 (Kermit L. Hall ed., 1999); Peter J. Coleman, *Sturges v. Crowninshield*, in THE OXFORD GUIDE TO UNITED STATES SUPREME COURT DECISIONS 297 (Kermit L. Hall ed., 1999) (guide reviews important Supreme Court cases but discusses only two bankruptcy decisions, both from the early 19th century).

answer these questions narrowly by taking small steps to avoid doing too much damage.[172]

These Justices' views are not isolated examples of the Justices' perception of bankruptcy law. The Justices' public opinions and private papers reinforce these perceptions.[173] For example, Justice Douglas' dissent in *St. Joe Paper Co. v. Atlantic Coast Line Railroad Co.*,[174] states directly that Justice Frankfurter's majority decision "reveals a basic misunderstanding of the system of bankruptcy reorganization."[175] Moreover, the private exchange between Justices Powell and Douglas in *Otte v. United States*,[176] shows a similar lack of concern or familiarity on the part of those Justices with bankruptcy cases. *Otte* required the Court to decide whether a trustee had to withhold taxes from payments of priority wage claims for prepetition wages. Justice Powell wrote a note to himself on January 18, 1974, referring to the case as a "Pee-Wee conflict, but it does exist. (& I don't think it makes any difference how it is resolved)."[177] Justice Douglas sent Justice Powell a note dated November 9, 1974, disagreeing with the treatment of wages as well as priority but said he would acquiesce because "I think it is more important that the rule of bankruptcy

---

172. This account is verified by a bankruptcy judge and attorney who attended the Conference. The Circuit Executive's office could not locate the official tape of the conference.

173. The Justices' private papers also reveal that lower court judges share these perceptions. For example, in a letter dated February 8, 1961 addressed to Justice Harlan about Lewis v. Mfrs. Nat'l Bank, 364 U.S. 603 (1961), Judge Brown of the Fifth Circuit writes, "[w]ith the Court so occupied with provocative and highly controversial questions of great public importance, I am sure that you welcome the occasional cases such as *Lewis* presenting just nice, little neat legal questions." (contained in Harlan papers).

174. 347 U.S. 298 (1954).

175. *See id.* at 329 (Douglas, J., dissenting).

176. 419 U.S. 43 (1974).

177. *See* Jan. 18, 1974 note from Justice Powell to self re: *Otte v. United States* (contained in Powell papers).

administration be settled than that it be settled right."[178] This sentiment is echoed in a letter from Justice Whittaker to Justices Black and Clark in which Justice Whittaker writes that "it seems to me more important that the rule be clearly declared than which way it is declared."[179] Furthermore, with respect to the opinion of the Court in *National Labor Relations Board v. Bildisco & Bildisco*,[180] Justice Rehnquist states in a note to Justice Stevens dated November 17, 1983, that "I do not feel that I am qualified to make any sort of exegesis on the meaning of the Bankruptcy Code . . . ." Likewise, in a March 4, 1985 memorandum to file, Justice Powell writes about the Court's decision in *Commodity Futures Trading Commission v. Weintraub*,[181] "[t]his is not an area of the law in which I have any expertise or any great interest; . . . [t]he issue is hardly one of national importance." In light of these exchanges, perhaps the expertise of a seasoned bankruptcy lawyer appearing at oral argument and articulating bankruptcy law, policy, and practice could, arguably, make the difference in a close case.

POLITICS AND THE COURT

As useful as rules of statutory construction and legal maxims might be to lead the Court to reasoned decisions, in many cases the Court resolves the policies at stake based on other principles such as legal ethics, societal norms, the national interest, or other political considerations.[182] From its inception, the United States Supreme Court

---

178. *See* Nov. 9, 1974 note from Justice Douglas to Justice Powell re: *Otte v. United States* (contained in Powell papers).

179. *See* February 13, 1959, letter from Justice Whittaker to Justices Black and Clark commenting on the Court's decision in United States v. Embassy Rest., Inc., 359 U.S. 29 (1959) (contained in Clark papers).

180. 465 U.S. 513 (1984).

181. 471 U.S. 343 (1985).

182. *See, e.g.,* Grable & Sons Metal Prods., Inc. v. Darue Eng'g & Mfg., 545 U.S. 308, 312-20 (2005) (holding the national interest in providing a federal forum for federal tax litigation is sufficiently substantial to support the exercise of federal-question jurisdiction over the disputed

has functioned as a political institution with its members serving as statesmen as well as jurists.[183] Although some Justices publicly proclaim that the Court decides cases basically based on legal principles,[184] it is apparent that politics and policy drive outcomes at the Court in many important areas.[185] Moreover, on rare occasions,

---

issue on removal); Burnham v. Superior Court of Cal., County of Marin, 495 U.S. 604, 630 n.2 (1990) ("We recognized that contemporary societal norms must play a role in our analysis.") (citation omitted); Flournoy v. Wiener, 321 U.S. 253, 264 (1944) ("This far-reaching political consideration was decisive even after the Civil War in settling the rule that not only do we not review a case from a state court that can rest on a purely state ground. . . .") (citation omitted).

183. *See* FELIX FRANKFURTER & JAMES M. LANDIS, THE BUSINESS OF THE SUPREME COURT: A STUDY IN THE FEDERAL JUDICIAL SYSTEM (The MacMillan Company 1927) at 317-18 (*"Business"*) ("Throughout its history, the Supreme Court has called for statesmanship—the gifts of mind and character fit to rule nations. . . . The accents of statesmen are the recurring motif of Supreme Court opinions. From the beginning, the Court had to resolve what were essentially political issues . . . .").

184. *See, e.g.*, EARL WARREN, THE MEMOIRS OF CHIEF JUSTICE EARL WARREN (Madision Books 2001) (*"Warren"*) at 6 ("Through politics . . . progress could be made . . . by compromising and taking half a loaf. . . . The opposite is true so far as the judicial process was concerned. [P]articularly in the Supreme Court, the basic ingredient of the decision is principle, and it should not be compromised . . . ."). *See also id.* at 282-84 describing in detail the Court's "usual manner of proceeding" to decide cases.

185. *See Business* at 310, 318 ("[T]he process of constitutional interpretation compels the translation of policy into judgment, and the controlling conceptions of the Justices are their 'idealized political picture' of the existing social order. . . . That its business is of a different order from the common run of litigation has been recognized by the Court. . . . * * * From the beginning, the Court had to resolve what were essentially political issues—the proper accommodation between the states and the central government. These political problems will persist as long as our federalism endures; and the Supreme Court will remain the ultimate arbitrator between Nation and States."). *See also* THE FEDERAL COURTS: YESTERDAY, TODAY, AND TOMORROW at 62-68 (United States District Court for the N.D. Cal. Historical Society 1990) (panel discussion between Judge A. Leon Higginbotham, Jr. and Prof. Gerald Gunther describing the political and philosophical basis of the Court's decision in

sitting Justices engage in politics outside the confines of Supreme Court decisions.[186] It would not be surprising, then, that partisan politics could play a significant role in the Court's resolution of bankruptcy cases.

It is possible that researching the party of the President who appointed the 63 Supreme Court Justices serving during 1898-2008 might inform the discussion.[187] Of the Justices serving on the Court during that period, 22 presidents appointed 63 justices, of whom 39 were appointed by Republicans and 24 by Democrats,[188] and, of the Justices appointed by Democratic presidents, Franklin Roosevelt

---

Brown v. Board of Education). But see Warren at 285-86 (describing the Court's deliberations in *Brown v. Board of Education* without mention of politics or philosophy).

186. For example, Chief Justice Warren Burger actively lobbied to prevent enactment of the 1978 Bankruptcy Code. He lobbied congressional staff. *See* Kenneth N. Klee, Assoc. Counsel, House Comm. on the Judiciary, 95th Cong., 1st Sess., May 13, 1977 Memorandum to Files. And he lobbied President Carter directly. *See* October 27, 1978 letter from Chief Justice Warren E. Burger to President Carter. President Carter's Chief Counsel prepared a Memorandum to the President dated October 31, 1978, which stated in part as follows:

> It is rare that I express myself as being indignant about something, but I must do so to you after reading the October 27 letter to you from the Chief Justice. It is appalling to note that the Chief Justice, the highest official in the Judicial Branch of our government, has grossly distorted the facts to you, in an attempt to persuade you to make a political judgment in this matter about which he has some very strong feelings.

See October 31, 1978 Memorandum to The President from Bob Lipschutz re: Bankruptcy Law Revision Bill—H.R. 8200. Notwithstanding the views of the Chief Justice, President Carter signed the 1978 Bankruptcy Code into law on November 6, 1978.

187. This study looked at 570 Court bankruptcy and insolvency cases from 1898 to 2008.

188. *See generally* Lee Epstein, Jeffrey A. Segal, Harold J. Spaeth & Thomas G. Walker, *Supreme Court Compendium*, (2d Edition Congressional Quarterly, Inc. 1994).

See also: http://www.supremecourtus.gov/about/members.pdf.

appointed nine. On the Republican side, William Howard Taft appointed six. The tenure of the Justices varied dramatically. For example, William O. Douglas, a Democrat appointed by Franklin Roosevelt, served over 36 years on the Court,[189] whereas James Byrnes, another Democrat appointed by Franklin Roosevelt, served a little more than one year.[190] The disparity in the number of Republican appointments compared to Democratic appointments mirrors the actual difference in years of service by Supreme Court Justices from the two parties. The data on time served show that Republican Justices served in the aggregate more than 603 years from January 1, 1898, through October 1, 2008, whereas Democratic Justices served in the aggregate more than 377 years during that period.[191] Thus, the number of appointments shows a 62.5% disparity (39 Republicans vs. 24 Democrats), and similarly the years served reveals an excess of 59.9% (603 years for Republicans vs. 377 years for Democrats).

Interestingly, although the data suggest a strong partisanship in government cases,[192] the differences between the parties of the presidents appointing the Justices were not statistically significant or correlated in fresh-start or dischargeability cases.[193] So, although the

---

189. Franklin Roosevelt appointed William O. Douglas to the Court, and Justice Douglas served from April 17, 1939 until November 12, 1975.

190. Franklin Roosevelt appointed James F. Byrnes to the Court, and Justice Byrnes served from July 8, 1941 until October 3, 1942.

191. *See* http://www.supremecourtus.gov/about/members.pdf.

192. *See infra* Appendix A. Justices appointed by Republican presidents are significantly more likely to favor the debtor against the government than are Justices appointed by Democratic presidents.

193. For purposes of analysis, the bankruptcy cases are grouped by topic, such as cases involving dischargeability, the government, the debtor's fresh start, or pro-creditor cases. There is also an assumption that the partisan politics of a particular Justice would correlate with the politics of the party by whom the Justice was appointed. (There is no doubt that there are sharp exceptions to this assumption. The most often cited example: the politics of the Republican Party did not correlate highly with Chief Justice Earl Warren's politics on the Court.) Then the data were sifted to determine if politics was correlated with the outcome in

Court might be a political institution, it does not appear, for the most part, that the partisanship of its Justices is predictive of their voting patterns in bankruptcy cases, with the exception of cases in which the debtor is adverse to the government.

THE JUSTICES' PRIVATE PAPERS

Partisanship aside, there is a different kind of politics that might operate in the Court: the politics of coalition building and vote trading. In order to gain insight into the internal politics of the Court, archives around the country were scoured and over nine linear feet of the Justices' private papers were collected and reviewed.[194] The papers reveal interesting if not conclusive insights into the internal operation of the Court.[195] For example, the papers show that sometimes Justices will defer to those Justices whom they hold in high regard or who are perceived to have expertise in an area.[196] On other occasions, Justices

---

various categories of bankruptcy cases. The methodology used in this analysis is more particularly described *infra* in Appendix A.

194. Not all of the Justice's papers are available for research. For example, according to Daun van Ee, Historical Specialist, Manuscript Division, The Library of Congress, Justice Byron White's papers are inaccessible until 2012. The papers of Justices Brewer, Fortas, and Stewart are archived at Yale University, which apparently only makes them available for research to Yale affiliates or those who apply to do research at Yale; moreover, the Stewart papers are closed to researchers until Justice Stevens retires from the Court.

195. On the other hand, some of the Justices' papers, including those of Justices Goldberg, Moody, Peckham, and Sutherland, contained little or nothing of value from a bankruptcy law perspective.

196. *See, e.g.,* Justice Marshall's March 18, 1970, Memorandum for the Conference in United States v. Key, 397 U.S. 322 (1970) explaining the basis for revision of his opinion: "It is difficult to gainsay Brother Douglas on the subject of corporate reorganization . . . ." (contained in Marshall papers). *But see* Justice Powell's handwritten notes on Justice Douglas' second draft opinion in Baker v. Gold Seal Liquors, Inc., 417 U.S. 467 (1974) in which Powell writes in the margin, "This is a juvenile opinion, long on meaningless generalities (some inaccurately expressed), & short on comprehension of a 77 Reorg. & on analysis." (contained in Powell papers).

evidence testiness in their correspondence. For example, in his December 20, 1940, letter to Justice Douglas concerning *Palmer v. Connecticut Railway & Lighting Co.*,[197] Justice Frankfurter writes, "I am really troubled by your opinion. . . . What does trouble me is that you are not disclosing what you are really doing. As you know, I am no poker player and naturally, therefore, I do not believe in poker playing in the disposition of cases."[198] Of similar tenor, in his February 16, 1966, letter joining Justice Clark's opinion in *Perry v. Commerce Loan Co.*,[199] Justice Fortas attaches a letter he sent to Justices Harlan and Stewart dripping with sarcasm: "I am totally overcome by the matchless eloquence and irresistible logic of Brother Clark's opinion in this case . . . . it is not my weakness or vacillation, but Brother Clark's mighty strength that has caused this catastrophy [sic]."[200]

There are occasions when the author of the opinion by the Court changes. Sometimes Justices who author dissenting opinions do so because they thought they were drafting the majority opinion and then lost support for their views.[201] Alternatively, sometimes Justices who thought they were writing a dissent persuade enough other Justices to switch votes that the opinion becomes the majority, even if

---

197.   311 U.S. 544 (1941).

198.   *See* December 20, 1940, letter from Justice Frankfurter to Justice Douglas (contained in Douglas papers).

199.   383 U.S. 392 (1966).

200.   *See* February 16, 1966, letter from Justice Fortas to Justice Clark attaching February 16, 1966, letter from Justice Fortas to Justices Harlan and Stewart (contained in Clark papers).

201.   *See, e.g.,* Perez v. Campbell, 402 U.S. 637 (1971) in which the Court used the Supremacy Clause to preclude a state from refusing to renew a debtor's driver's license based on the failure to pay an automobile related tort judgment. On April 5, 1971, Justice Blackmun proposed an opinion purporting to represent the majority with Justices Black and Douglas dissenting. Following shifting alliances on whether *Kesler* should be overruled, Justice Blackmun decided not to rewrite his opinion but instead recommended the case be reassigned so he could write a dissent. Justice White then wrote the majority opinion. For a more complete discussion of *Perez* and *Kesler, see infra* Ch. 2, pp. 175-177.

it is written by another Justice.[202] In certain cases, Justices assigned to write a 5-4 majority opinion may change their views and nevertheless write the majority opinion coming out the other way. For example, Justice Black wrote the opinion of the Court in *Pearlman v. Reliance Insurance Co.*,[203] even though he switched his vote from the position he took in conference, because a majority of the Justices had shifted from reversing the court of appeals to affirmance.[204]

Sometimes dissenting Justices keep their dissents within the Court in recognition of the importance of the appearance of unanimity in Court decisions.[205] In the early 1900's, very few bankruptcy cases had published dissents[206] whereas published dissents became more common in later years.[207] Justice Stevens noted that "[p]ublished

---

202. For example, in United States v. Durham Lumber Co., 363 U.S. 522 (1960), Justice Brennan drafted a dissent in December 1959 followed up by correspondence to other Justices in December 1959 and January 1960 that became the basis for Chief Justice Warren's majority opinion. (*See* Brennan Papers, correspondence dated December 10, 1959, December 11, 1959, January 21, 1960, & June 16, 1960).

203. 371 U.S. 132 (1962).

204. *See* Justice Black's November 6, 1962, Memorandum for the Conference (contained in Black papers).

205. For example, in his November 18, 1982, letter to Justice Blackmun commenting on *United States v. Security Industrial Bank*, Justice Stevens writes that "there is some virtue in trying to have Court opinions as unanimous as possible." Even though Justice Stevens shared Justice Blackmun's analysis in the dissent, he decided to join Justice Rehnquist's majority opinion. *See id.* (contained in Blackmun papers).

206. From 1900–1910, five percent of the bankruptcy cases had dissenting opinions, and there were none in the next two decades. Dissents also appear to have been rare in cases before 1900 based on Justices electing "to suppress fundamental differences of view" in the interest of the appearance of harmony. *See* David P. Currie, "The Constitution in the Supreme Court: The First Hundred Years 1789-1888" at 150 & nn.201-04 (Univ. of Chicago Press 1990).

207. The data show that dissenting opinions became a regular part of the Court's bankruptcy decisions following significant statutory amendments in the 1930's. From 1930-1940, 25 percent of the Court's

dissents from denials of certiorari were unknown in 1925 but are now [in 1983] a regular occurrence."[208] The raw data substantiate Justice Stevens' view.[209]

The Justices' papers reveal that there were sharp disagreements within the internal deliberations of the Court even when there was no published dissent.[210] As the Justices' regard for the unanimity of Court decisions diminished, published dissents increased dramatically in bankruptcy decisions.

On some occasions Justices who disagreed about a decision follow up with an exchange of correspondence after the case is decided. For example, in *United States v. Kras*,[211] an indigent debtor filed a motion asserting his Fifth Amendment Due Process rights to be able to file a voluntary bankruptcy petition without paying the required $50 filing fee. Justice Blackmun's clerk suspected the case was a sham suit and the Justice appeared to agree, writing a decision distinguishing *Boddie v. Connecticut*[212] on the basis that there was no constitutional right to bankruptcy and that the bankruptcy discharge was not the only way for a debtor to receive a fresh start. Several Justices, including Justices Douglas and Stewart filed dissenting opinions lamenting that indigents would be unable to avail themselves of this important right.

---

bankruptcy decisions had dissents, a trend that grew to 57 percent and, ultimately, 100 percent during the next three decades.

208. *See* Justice John Paul Stevens, *The Life Span of a Judge-Made Rule*, 58 N.Y.U. L. Rev. 1, 13 & n.63 (1983).

209. *See infra* Appendix B.

210. In a letter sent on November 4, 1939, from Chief Justice Hughes to Justice Douglas regarding Case v. Los Angeles Lumber Prods. Co., 308 U.S. 106 (1939), Chief Justice Hughes writes that he does not agree with Justice Douglas' reasoning but will not dissent because the holding is narrow and the effect of the decision is salutary. In a handwritten note to Justice Brandeis regarding Security Mortgage Co. v. Powers, 278 U.S. 149 (1928), Justice McReynolds writes, "I voted the other way, but if you get a majority I shall not say anything." (contained in Brandeis papers).

211. *See* United States v. Kras, 409 U.S. 434 (1973).

212. 401 U.S. 371 (1971).

Within a year after the *Kras* decision was rendered, the Solicitor General wrote to Justice Blackmun and advised him that Kras paid the filing fee shortly after the Court's decision was rendered.[213] Two days later Justice Blackmun advised the Solicitor General that he "had a feeling there was something wrong with this case"[214] and the next day he sent a note to Justices Stewart and Douglas advising them that Kras paid the filing fee.[215]

THE COURT'S REGULATION OF BANKRUPTCY PROCEDURE[216]

Aside from its legal decision making, the Supreme Court from time to time has adopted rules of court to address abuses in bankruptcy administration. In 1925, the Court promulgated rules[217] recommended by a joint committee of The Conference of Senior Circuit Judges (which Congress authorized by the Act of 1922), the American Bar Association, the National Association of Credit Men, and the Commercial Law League of America.[218] For many years, the Supreme Court promulgated General Orders which governed the procedure of bankruptcy courts.[219] The Court amended or abrogated the General

---

213. *See* June 17, 1974 letter from Solicitor General Korman to Justice Blackmun (contained in Blackmun papers).

214. *See* June 19, 1974 letter from Justice Blackmun to Solicitor General Korman (contained in Blackmun papers).

215. *See* June 20, 1974 note from Justice Blackmun to Justices Stewart and Douglas (contained in Blackmun papers).

216. "After all, procedure is instrumental; it is the means of effectuating policy." *See* FELIX FRANKFURTER & JAMES M. LANDIS, THE BUSINESS OF THE SUPREME COURT: A STUDY IN THE FEDERAL JUDICIAL SYSTEM (The MacMillan Company 1927) at 2 ("*Business*").

217. *See* 267 U.S. 613 (1925).

218. *See Business* at 246-47. The Conference was held in Philadelphia in January, 1924. The report was published at 49 Am. Bar Assn. Rep. 461, 3 Docket, 2795.

219. On May 16, 1867, the Supreme Court promulgated "General Orders and Forms in Bankruptcy." *See* Compilation of Federal Court Rules published by Anne Ashmore (on file with author appended to transmittal

Orders or rules from time to time[220] and had occasion to render opinions on their validity.[221] To replace the General Orders in liquidating bankruptcy and Chapter XIII wage earner cases and following passage of the Rules Enabling Act,[222] the Supreme Court in 1973 promulgated Federal Rules of Bankruptcy Procedure.[223]

Promulgation of the Bankruptcy Rules fostered some dissent. Although the Supreme Court promulgates the Bankruptcy Rules, as has been the case since at least 1924, the Court takes little role in actually drafting the Rules. Justice Douglas' disagreement with the Court's delegation of rule drafting to the Judicial Conference and Rule 920, giving bankruptcy referees the power to punish for contempt, led him to dissent from the Court's promulgation of the 1973 Bankruptcy Rules[224] in pertinent part as follows:

---

cover sheet from Linda Corbelli, Library, Supreme Court of the United States, January 24, 2005).

220. *See, e.g.*, 93 U.S. vii; 172 U.S. 653; 199 U.S. 618; 210 U.S. 567; 239 U.S. 623; 244 U.S. 641; 267 U.S. 613; 268 U.S. 712; 280 U.S. 617; 283 U.S. 870; 286 U.S. 573; 288 U.S. 619; 288 U.S. 655; 295 U.S. 771; 297 U.S. 735; 298 U.S. 695; 300 U.S. 689; 302 U.S. 787; 303 U.S. 671; 305 U.S. 681; 310 U.S. 661; 331 U.S. 871; 355 U.S. 969; & 368 U.S. 1043.[288 US 653]

221. *See, e.g.,* Meek v. Ctr. County Banking Co., 268 U.S. 426, 434 (1925) ("The authority conferred upon this court by § 30 of the Bankruptcy Act to prescribe all necessary rules, forms and orders as to procedure and for carrying the Act into effect, is plainly limited to provisions for the execution of the Act itself, and does not authorize additions to its substantive provisions. . . . General Order No. 8 and Form No. 2, in purporting to authorize one or less than all of the partners to file a petition against the partnership without the consent of the others, do not relate to the execution of any of the provisions of the Act itself; and therefore are without statutory warrant and of no effect.") (citations omitted).

222. *See* 28 U.S.C. § 2075 (1970) which led to the Court's promulgation of Bankruptcy Rules commencing in 1973.

223. *See* 411 U.S. 991 (1973).

224. *See* 411 U.S. 991, 992-94 (1973) (Douglas, J., dissenting). The quoted matter omits an extensive diatribe by Justice Douglas on giving the contempt power to bankruptcy referees.

I cannot agree to the Court's submission of the proposed Bankruptcy Rules to the Congress.

Once I was knowledgeable in the bankruptcy field, having taught the course for some years, made my own field studies of it, and written extensively about various bankruptcy problems. . . .

* * *

I would not extend the contempt power to bankruptcy referees. Perhaps I am wrong. But that issue has never been considered, debated, or voted upon by this Court. The Court is merely the conduit for the Rules. It does not purport to approve or disapprove. As I have said on other occasions, it has merely placed its imprimatur on the Rules without reading, let alone discussing, these Rules.

* * *

[F]or most of these Rules I do not have sufficient insight and experience to know whether they are desirable or undesirable. I must, therefore, disassociate myself from them.

If these Rules go to the Congress they should be sent by the Judicial Conference, not by this Court.

Justice Douglas' passionate dissent was not an isolated incident. In 1975 when the Court promulgated the Chapter X Rules for reorganization cases, Justice Douglas supplied a more abbreviated but quite spirited dissent, noting in part that "[b]ecause this Court is no more than a 'rubber stamp' I think it should not participate in the rule-making process."[225]

Despite Justice Douglas' strong feelings, the Court has continued to promulgate federal rules of bankruptcy procedure that have a far-reaching impact on bankruptcy cases and proceedings. Enactment of the 1978 Bankruptcy Code led the Court in 1983 to abrogate the Rules pertaining to the Bankruptcy Act and to promulgate new rules

---

225.   *See* 421 U.S. 1021, 1022 (1975) (Douglas, J., dissenting).

applicable to the Bankruptcy Code.[226] Since then the Court has amended the Bankruptcy Rules on several occasions based on recommendations of the Judicial Conference.[227]

The Court's dual role as adjudicator and rule maker has influenced the outcome of some of the Court's bankruptcy decisions.[228] For example, in *Maggio v. Zeitz (In re Luma Camera Service, Inc.)*,[229] the Court considered the plight of Maggio, the president and manager of debtor Luma Camera Service, Inc., who was jailed for contempt of court in failing to turn over .property he possessed that he had knowingly and fraudulently concealed from the bankruptcy trustee.[230] In affirming the contempt order, the Second Circuit stated: "Although we know that Maggio cannot comply with the order, we must keep a straight face and pretend that he can, and must thus affirm orders which first direct Maggio 'to do an impossibility, and then punish him for refusal to perform it.'" This put the Court in the position of both doing justice in the case before it and acting in its supervisory capacity over courts of bankruptcy. The Court's published opinion frames the issue candidly:[231]

> Whether this [statement of the court of appeals] is to be read
> literally as its deliberate judgment of the law of the case or is

---

226. *See* 461 U.S. 973 (1983) (promulgating Rules for bankruptcy cases and proceedings and abrogating Rules for cases and proceedings under the Bankruptcy Act of 1898).

227. *See* 471 U.S. 1147 (1985); 480 U.S. 1077 (1987); 490 U.S. 1119 (1989); 500 U.S. 1017 (1991); 507 U.S. 1077 (1993); 511 U.S. 1171 (1994); 514 U.S. 1145 (1995); 517 U.S. 1263 (1996); 520 U.S. 1285 (1997); 526 U.S. 1169 (1999); 529 U.S. 1147 (2000); 532 U.S. 1077 (2001); 535 U.S. 1139 (2002); 155 L. Ed. 2d lxv (2003). The Judicial Conference in turn receives recommendations from its Standing Committee on Practice and Procedure and the Advisory Committee on Bankruptcy Rules.

228. Thus, one strategy for counsel to examine in Supreme Court advocacy is to urge the Court to use its supervisory power as a basis for disposition of the case.

229. 333 U.S. 56 (1948).

230. *See id.* at 58-59.

231. *See id.* at 59.

something of a decoy intended to attract our attention to the problem, the declaration is one which this Court, in view of its supervisory power over courts of bankruptcy, cannot ignore.

In his Memorandum for the Court, Justice Jackson, who authored the opinion of the Court, states his position even more bluntly suggesting that the Court "look upon this decision more in the light of an exercise of our rule-making power to straighten out the tangle in these proceedings than as the mere decision of this case."[232]

CONCLUSION

The Supreme Court is a complex institution with its own special rules, customs, and procedures. Parties who study the Court's habits and tendencies might improve their chances of persuading the Court to grant certiorari and ultimately rule in their favor. These tendencies appear to be influenced by general principles involving conflicts in the Circuits and legal maxims, but they also might vary depending on the specific context in which the cases arise.

The balance of this book examines and discusses how the Court decides bankruptcy and insolvency cases involving substantive bankruptcy law as well as when bankruptcy law conflicts with constitutional law, jurisdictional limitations, and federalism principles. Chapter 2 examines the Court's decisions in which bankruptcy law conflicts with other federal and state and local laws.

---

232. *See* Justice Jackson's January 21, 1948, Memorandum for the Court (contained in Justice Black's papers).

APPENDIX A: EMPIRICAL CASE STUDY

SUPREME COURT BANKRUPTCY CASE STUDY METHODOLOGY

The data were coded using a two-pass system. After grouping the bankruptcy cases by topic, each topic was placed in a spreadsheet. When a Justice voted with the majority, the vote was recorded as a "1." When a Justice dissented, the vote was recorded as a "2." If a Justice took no part in the opinion, the vote was recorded as "5." Using a statistical analysis program (SPSS v.14), the second pass of the process was implemented. In this second pass, the outcome of the case was incorporated into the data so that the data were modified according to whether the case resulted in a pro-debtor or pro-creditor outcome. After incorporating the outcome of the case, the result was that the data were coded for each Justice with a "1" or "0" or "-1" depending on the topic at issue and the way the Justice voted. For example, in a dischargeability case when the outcome was pro-debtor or anti-debtor, the vote of each Justice was coded "1." In other words, if the majority opinion was pro-debtor and a Justice voted with the majority, or if the decision was anti-debtor and a Justice voted with the minority they were coded "1." A Justice was coded "-1" if the opinion was anti-debtor, and the Justice voted with the majority, or if the opinion was pro-debtor, and the Justice voted with the minority. All other outcomes were given a code of "0" and were not included in the calculations.

RESULTS OF STUDY ON SUPREME COURT DISCHARGEABILITY CASES AND GOVERNMENT CASES

The data were studied to determine whether the Justices were motivated by political partisanship in the following kinds of bankruptcy cases: government; pro-creditor; pro-debtor; dischargeability; and fresh start cases. Precisely 46 cases were categorized under the topic "Dischargeability." In these cases, a total of 412 votes were cast by 51 separate Justices, 17 of whom were appointed by Democratic presidents and 34 of whom were appointed by Republican presidents. Democratic-appointed Justices cast 103 votes, and Republican-appointed Justices cast 309 votes. The mean value of the votes was calculated for each political party. On balance, the Court sided against the debtor 15.52% of the time more than it sided with the debtor (57.76% anti-debtor vs. 42.24% pro-debtor). The on-balance difference between the parties indicates that Justices appointed by a Republican president were more anti-debtor (16.56% anti-debtor) than Justices appointed by a Democratic president (12.73% anti-debtor). This difference is not statistically significant by conventional statistical standards (F=0.927, p=.336), and suggests no meaningful difference between the political parties on dischargeability cases.

On the other hand, the data suggest a significant difference in the Justices' votes in government cases. In 100 cases, the Court sided against the debtor and for the government 21.46% of the time more than it sided with the debtor (60.73% anti-debtor vs. 39.27% pro-debtor). The on-balance difference between the parties, however, indicates that Justices appointed by a Democratic president were more anti-debtor and pro-government (29.77% anti-debtor) than Justices appointed by a Republican president (14.70% anti-debtor). This difference of more than 15% is statistically significant (F=72.835; p <.000).

Note that there was a slight issue with Justices White and Stone. Both of these Justices were appointed by presidents of one party, but then elevated to Chief Justice by a president of the opposite party. For the calculations these Justices were coded by the political party of the president that *originally* appointed them. However, it might be argued that the elevation could be attributable to a change in perception that would more closely align the Justices' beliefs with that of the president that elevated them. Accordingly, the Justices' votes might be properly attributable to the party that they represented at a particular time. The data were recoded and analyzed to reflect this possibility. As can be seen from the following tables, the differences were not statistically significant.

Statistical Analysis of Political Party and Voting in Supreme Court Bankruptcy Cases [single political party]								
	N		On-balance votes (Positive values are pro-debtor)				Statistical significance	
	Cases	Votes	Total	Republican	Democrat	Diff.	F	p-value
Dischargeability	46	412	-15.53%	-16.56%	-12.73%	3.83%	.927	.336
Government	100	876	-21.46%	-14.70%	-29.77%	-15.07%	72.835	.000
Pro-Creditor	82	717	-5.44%	-4.85%	-6.46%	-1.61%	.399	.528
Fresh Start	7	61	96.72%	95.35%	100%	-4.65%	.204	.816

	N		On-balance votes (Positive values are pro-debtor)				Statistical significance	
Statistical Analysis of Political Party and Voting in Supreme Court Bankruptcy Cases [dual political party]								
	Cases	Votes	Total	Republican	Democrat	Diff.	F	p-value
Dischargeability	46	412	-15.53%	-15.86%	-14.56%	1.30%	.099	.753
Government	100	876	-21.46%	-12.97%	-31.66%	-18.69%	108.45	.000
Pro-Creditor	82	717	-5.44%	-3.96%	-7.98%	-4.02%	2.296	.130
Fresh Start	7	61	96.72%	95.45%	100%	-4.55%	.188	.829

APPENDIX B: DATA ON DISSENTING OPINIONS

Years	Percentage of Decisions with Dissenting Opinions	Years	Percentage of Decisions with Dissenting Opinions
1900-1910	5	1961-1970	100
1911-1920	0	1971-1980	67
1921-1930	0	1981-1990	71
1931-1940	25	1991-2000	20
1941-1950	57	2001-2005	33
1951-1960	75		

A polynomial equation describes these data well.[233]

Term	Coefficient	SE	P	95% CI of Coefficient
Intercept	-0.5278	0.2434	0.0619	-1.0890 to 0.0333
Decade	0.3435	0.0932	0.0062	0.1286 to 0.5584
Decade^2	-0.0244	0.0076	0.0122	-0.0418 to -0.0069

In order to test the hypothesis that Justices published dissents more in recent years than in the early 1900's, a statistical analysis compared the Court's discharge decisions from 1900-1940 period with the 1971-2004 period.[234] The differences are statistically significant.[235]

Period	Discharge			Cases with Dissents	
	No	Yes	Total	Number	Percentage
1900-1940	19	11	30	1	3.3%
1971-2004	7	7	14	7	50%
Total	26	18	44	8	18.2%

Other tests on the data did not show statistical significance.

---

233. The dependent variable is the percentage of cases with dissents in each decade. The independent variable, Decade, is coded "1" in 1900-1910, "2" in 1911-1920, etc. The over-time change in the percentage of dissents is well-described (adjusted r-square = .59) by the following polynomial equation:

%Dissent = -0.5278 + Decade*0.3435 + Decade^2*-0.0244.

234. Note that the total number of cases involving discharge for use in this table (44) is different than the earlier mention of discharge cases (46) *supra* in Appendix A, because two of the cases fell outside the date range (1962 & 1964).

235. p=.001, two-tailed Fisher Exact.

CHAPTER 2

THE COURT RESOLVES CONFLICTS BETWEEN BANKRUPTCY LAW AND OTHER AREAS OF STATE AND FEDERAL LAW

INTRODUCTION

Occasionally the Court chooses to decide a bankruptcy case when bankruptcy policy directly conflicts with competing policies of other federal or state laws. Over the past 111 years, the Court has resolved conflicts between bankruptcy law and federal administrative law, environmental law, labor law, pension law, and tax law.[236] This chapter also discusses how the Court has resolved conflicts between bankruptcy law and state family law, probate law, and real estate law. Chapter 3 discusses more broadly how the Court reconciles bankruptcy law with constitutional law, sovereign immunity, federal preemption, federalism, and the use of state law in bankruptcy.

At the outset, it is important to note that the Court sometimes side-steps policy conflicts by purporting to "harmonize" conflicting laws. "[W]hen two statutes are capable of co-existence, it is the duty of the courts, absent a clearly expressed congressional intention to the contrary, to regard each as effective."[237]

Occasionally, however, the Court recognizes a direct conflict between the statutory directives or policy objectives of competing federal laws. The resolution of this conflict usually depends on wheth-

---

236. *See generally* EDMUND H. DRYER, SUPREME COURT BANKRUPTCY LAW (The W.H. Anderson Co. 1937 & Supp. 1938) (internal quotation marks omitted) (digesting all Supreme Court bankruptcy decisions through volume 301 U.S.) ("*Dryer*").

237. *See* G.E.M. Ag Supply, Inc. v. Pioneer Hi-Bred Int'l, Inc., 534 U.S. 124, 143-44 (2001) (quoting Morton v. Mancari, 417 U.S. 535, 551 (1974)).

er the majority of Justices view the question presented primarily from the perspective of bankruptcy law or nonbankruptcy law.[238] For example, in *Midlantic National Bank v. New Jersey Department of Environmental Protection*,[239] the Court resolved the irreconcilable conflict between federal bankruptcy law, which permits the trustee to abandon any kind of property, and the federal environmental law which prohibits the abandonment of property contaminated with toxic waste. In *National Labor Relations Board v. Bildisco & Bildisco*,[240] the Court resolved the conflict between federal bankruptcy law, which permits rejection of any executory contract, including a collective-bargaining agreement, and federal labor law, which prohibits unilateral abrogation of a collective-bargaining agreement before the parties bargain to an impasse.

There is no way to predict with certainty how the Court will resolve a conflict between competing federal laws or between bankruptcy law and state laws. Of course the Court may adopt a policy that it considers to be more important to protecting the public interest. On the other hand, however, if legal issues overwhelm the importance of the policy conflict, the Court may resolve the case in a manner that protects the integrity of its legal decision-making. Finally, the Court's decision may be guided by the importance of the decision to a particular body of law separate and apart from a public policy analysis or principles of statutory construction.

ADMINISTRATIVE LAW

On occasion, the Court has examined the interface between the bankruptcy laws and administrative laws. Some cases involve conflicts between the Bankruptcy Act or Bankruptcy Code and a regulatory statute. Other cases involve the bankruptcy estate or

---

238. *See* Karen M. Gebbia-Pinetti, *Interpreting the Bankruptcy Code: An Empirical Study of the Supreme Court's Bankruptcy Decisions*, 3 CHAPMAN L. REV. 173, 256 (Spring 2000).

239.   474 U.S. 494 (1986).

240.   465 U.S. 513 (1984).

trustee as successor to the debtor's rights or obligations under a regulatory statute. In the former cases the Court does not permit a regulatory agency to undercut a supervening bankruptcy law or policy.[241] The Court grants deference to the agency acting within the scope of its expertise but not when it violates regulatory statutes or bankruptcy laws.

In *Pension Benefit Guarantee Corp. v. LTV Corp.*[242] the PBGC sued to require LTV to reinstate and pay for its previously terminated ERISA pension plans. During its chapter 11 case, LTV Steel Co., Inc., a subsidiary of LTV, consented to the PBGC's termination of its three ERISA defined benefit pension plans, thereby transferring liability for the shortfall to the PBGC.[243] Later, however, as part of settling an adversary proceeding with the Steelworkers, LTV Steel adopted follow-on plans to pay the retirees the difference between the amounts they would receive from the PBGC and what they would have received had the former never been terminated. The PBGC determined that LTV Steel's action was in violation of the PBGC's policies under ERISA. It restored the terminated plans thereby making the LTV corporate group liable for all amounts owing as if the plans had never been terminated.[244]

The Court held that the PBGC's decision to restore LTV's plans under ERISA was not arbitrary or capricious or contrary to law within section 5 of the Administrative Procedures Act. Although the PBGC did not apprise LTV of the material on which it was to base its

---

241. There are occasions where bankruptcy law and policy is not supervening, such as when the bankruptcy trustee asserts a claim against the receiver of an insolvent bank or the receiver brings a fraudulent transfer suit against the bankruptcy estate. *See, e.g.,* 12 U.S.C. § 1821(d)(13)(C)-(D) & (17)(D) (2000) ("RIGHTS UNDER THIS PARAGRAPH. —The rights under this paragraph of the Corporation and any conservator described in subparagraph (A) shall be superior to any rights of a trustee or any other party (other than any party which is a Federal agency) under title 11, United States Code.").

242. 496 U.S. 633 (1990).

243. *See id.* at 640-41.

244. *See id.* at 642-43.

decision or give LTV a statement applying its reasoning in light of articulated standards, neither the APA nor ERISA gave LTV the procedural rights that it sought to invoke.[245] Because the administrative record gave the lower courts a sufficient basis to review the PBGC's rationale at the time of its decision, the APA was satisfied and the courts were not authorized to impose additional procedural burdens on the agency.[246]

Although the Court often will grant deference to an administrative agency with respect to statutes over which it has expertise, the Court will grant no deference to an agency outside the area of its expertise.[247] For example in *Federal Communications Commission v. NextWave Personal Communications, Inc.,*[248] the Court considered whether the FCC's revocation of NextWave's spectrum licenses, based on its failure to make timely payments on its purchase obligation, violated the non-discrimination provisions in Bankruptcy Code § 525.[249] The FCC contended, inter alia, that it had a valid regulatory motive for terminating the licenses in addition to nonpayment and that failure to permit it to do so would create a conflict between the Bankruptcy Code and the Communications Act.[250] The Court had no trouble rejecting the FCC's arguments based on the plain language of the statute and the lack of conflict between the two laws.[251] The Court noted that "[t]he Administrative Procedure Act requires federal courts

---

245. *See id.* at 655.

246. *See id.* at 654-55.

247. *See, e.g.,* N.L.R.B. v. Bildisco & Bildisco, 465 U.S. 513, 529 n.9 (1984) ("While the [National Labor Relations] Board's interpretation of the NLRA should be given some deference, the proposition that the Board's interpretation of statutes outside its expertise is likewise to be deferred to is novel. We see no need to defer to the Board's interpretation of Congress' intent in passing the Bankruptcy Code.").

248. 537 U.S. 293 (2003).

249. *See id.* at 295.

250. *See id.* at 301, 304.

251. *See id.* at 301. ("We find none of these contentions persuasive . . . .").

to set aside federal agency action that is 'not in accordance with law,' . . . which means, of course, *any* law, and not merely those laws that the agency itself is charged with administering."[252] Significantly, none of the opinions in *NextWave* considers whether the FCC's position should be given special deference. Presumably the Justices recognized implicitly that the administrative agency was entitled to no deference in its interpretation of a statute beyond its regulatory authority.

The Court also has not deferred to the actions of an administrative agency when the Court viewed the agency's actions as conflicting with the Bankruptcy Act or a regulatory act, such as the Interstate Commerce Act ("ICA").[253] In *St. Joe Paper Co. v. Atlantic Coast Line Railroad Co.*,[254] the Supreme Court reversed the Court of Appeals' holding that the ICC's proposed reorganization plan, which called for a forced merger between the debtor and a third party, was fair and equitable.[255] In reaching its decision, the Court turned to Bankruptcy Act § 77(b)(3)[256] which, as enacted in 1933, provided:

> (b) A plan of reorganization within the meaning of this section . . . (3) shall provide adequate means for the execution of the plan, which may, so far as may be consistent with the provisions of sections 1 and 5 of the Interstate Commerce Act (ICA) as amended, include . . . the merger of the Debtor with any other railroad corporation . . . .

The Court concluded, after reviewing the legislative history of this provision, that § 77(b)(3) was designed to ensure that the Bankruptcy Act did not permit reorganizations that were inconsistent with the provisions of the ICA, particularly the provisions related to the merger of railroads.[257] By reviewing the relevant provisions of the ICA

---

252. *See id.* at 300 (emphasis original; citations omitted).

253. 49 U.S.C. §§ 10101 *et seq.* (1982).

254. 347 U.S. 298 (1954).

255. *See id.* at 302, 315.

256. Act of Mar. 3, 1933, chs. 203-204, 47 Stat. 1467, 1475.

257. *See St. Joe Paper*, 347 U.S. at 305.

and their legislative history, the Court determined that "only mergers voluntarily initiated by the participating carriers" were permitted by the ICA.[258] Therefore, because the merger here was initiated by the Interstate Commerce Commission ("ICC") alone and not by the participating carriers, the plan violated both Bankruptcy Act § 77 and section 5 of the ICA and could not stand.[259]

Justices Douglas, Burton, and Minton dissented. The dissent argued that the majority misstated the issue in the case because the ICC did not attempt to force a merger but merely included a merger provision in its proposed plan.[260] The dissenters thought the issue was whether the ICC may include, in a plan of reorganization, a provision that the debtor should be merged with another railroad and submit the plan for the approval or disapproval to the security holders who were entitled to vote on the plan.[261] The dissenters argued that the ICC could include such a provision, and because the merger would not follow automatically from such inclusion in the plan, but would require a vote of security holders for approval, the instant case did not involve an attempted forced merger.[262]

Moreover, the Court has gone further and, even in the absence of a conflict with bankruptcy-law policy, not granted deference to an administrative agency's interpretation of its own statute when its interpretation is at odds with the plain meaning of the statute. For example in *Maislin Industries, U.S., Inc. v. Primary Steel, Inc.*,[263] the Court did not grant deference to the ICC's interpretation of the ICA.

---

258. *See id.* at 305.

259. *See id.* at 307.

260. *See id.* at 321.

261. *See id.* at 322.

262. *See id.* 24 years later with the adoption of the Bankruptcy Code, the dissent would be vindicated by Congress. Bankruptcy Code § 1123(a)(5)(C), 11 U.S.C. § 1123(a)(5) (2000), was designed to legislatively overrule *St. Joe Paper* to permit a plan to provide for a forced merger. *See* H.R. REP. NO. 95-595, 407(1977).

263. 497 U.S. 116 (1990).

The ICA provided that "except as provided in this subtitle," both shippers and carriers must adhere to those rates.[264] The Act also provided that the ICC ensure that a rate or a practice is reasonable.[265] The ICC began interpreting these statutes to mean that shippers and carriers did not have to adhere to their filed rates if they privately negotiated a lower rate.[266] In *Maislin Industries*, the Maislin Corporation reached a private agreement with Primary Steel for shipping at a rate lower than the rate on file with the ICC.[267] As a result, Maislin underbilled Primary Steel nearly $200,000.[268] When Maislin filed for chapter 11 relief in 1983, the agents of its bankruptcy estate sought to collect from Primary Steel the amount of the undercharges.[269] Primary Steel argued that because the companies had agreed on a lower rate, collecting the higher rate would be unreasonable and in violation of the Act.[270] The ICC agreed with Primary Steel and found, based on the parties' agreement to the lower rate, that it would be unreasonable to permit Maislin's bankruptcy estate to collect the higher rate.[271] The district court and the Eighth Circuit agreed with the ICC.[272]

The Supreme Court reversed, holding that the plain language of the ICA required that shippers and carriers adhere to the filed rates and did not provide equitable defenses to parties who violated that order through a voluntary arrangement.[273] The Court refused to concede that the ICC was entitled to deference to decide which prac-

---

264. *See* 49 U.S.C. § 10761(a) (1982).

265. *See* 49 U.S.C. § 10701(e) (1982).

266. *See Maislin Indus.*, 497 U.S. at 121-22.

267. *See id.* at 122-23.

268. *See id.* at 123.

269. *See id.* The suit alleged a violation of the ICA's filed rate doctrine and did not implicate bankruptcy law or policy.

270. *See id.*

271. *See id.* at 123-25.

272. *See id.* at 125.

273. *See id.* at 130-33.

tices were unreasonable under the ICA.[274] To the contrary, the Court held that the ICC was not permitted to find that collecting the filed rate was unreasonable when such a construction would be flatly inconsistent with the plain mandate of the statute that shippers and carriers adhere to the filed rates.[275]

Justice Stevens, joined by Chief Justice Rehnquist, dissented. The dissent argued that the ICC rationally interpreted its statute and that in light of the proposition in *Chevron U.S.A. Inc. v. Natural Resources Defense Council, Inc.*,[276] that deference should be paid to an agency's interpretation of its statute, the Court should affirm the ICC's decision.[277]

Five years after its decision in *Maislin Industries*, the Court decided *Interstate Commerce Commission v. Transcon Lines*,[278] this time supporting the ICC's interpretation of its regulations.[279] Transcon Lines was a regulated interstate motor carrier that was placed in involuntary bankruptcy before enactment of the Negotiated Rates Act of 1993[280] and the Trucking Industry Regulatory Reform Act of 1994,[281]

---

274.   *See id.* at 130-31.

275.   *See id.* at 134-35. Although the ICC was not permitted to contradict the filed-rate doctrine, Congress was not so restricted. In response to an outcry from customers who were being sued by bankruptcy trustees of insolvent motor carriers to pay freight undercharges, Congress enacted corrective legislation. *See infra* nn.280-281.

276.   467 U.S. 837, 843 (1984).

277.   *See Maislin Indus.*, 497 U.S. at 151-53.

278.   513 U.S. 138 (1995).

279.   *See id.* at 145 ("Although the ICC's authority to determine proper remedies for violations under the Act is not without limits, its judgment that a particular remedy is an appropriate exercise of its enforcement authority under 49 U.S.C. § 11702(a)(4) is entitled to some deference. Two substantial reasons support our conclusion that the remedy chosen by the agency is an appropriate one.").

280.   Pub. L. No. 103-180, 107 Stat. 2044 (1993).

281.   Pub. L. No. 103-311, 108 Stat. 1683 (1994).

which changed a trustee's ability to sue for freight undercharges.[282] Transcon's bankruptcy trustee sued to collect undercharges, including unpaid freight charges and liquidated damages, from Transcon's former customers.[283] The Court found that the ICC was authorized to file a civil action to enforce its regulations, and its exercise of this remedy is entitled to some deference[284] as is its promulgation of a regulation in accordance with the ICA.[285] Accordingly, the Court sustained the ICC's suit to enjoin the trustee from collecting loss-of-discount liquidated damages in violation of ICC regulations.[286]

ENVIRONMENTAL LAW

For the most part, since the 1970's, federal and state governments have enacted environmental laws designed to prohibit or remediate environmental hazards by requiring violators to clean up or pay to clean up the hazards.[287] This policy directly conflicts with congressional bankruptcy policy to give the debtor an opportunity to reorganize, preserve jobs, discharge debts, and avoid liquidation.[288] It is not surprising, therefore, that on two occasions during the mid-1980's, the Court addressed some of the conflicts between bankruptcy law and

---

282. *See Transcon Lines*, 513 U.S. at 139-40.

283. *See id.* at 140.

284. *See id.* at 145.

285. *See id.* at 148.

286. *See id.* at 148-49.

287. For example, in 1970, Congress enacted the Clean Air Act, 42 U.S.C. §§ 7401-7642; in 1972, Congress enacted the Federal Water Pollution Control Act, 33 U.S.C. §§ 1251-1387 ("Clean Water Act"); in 1976, Congress enacted the Resource, Conservation, and Recovery Act, 42 U.S.C. §§ 6902-6992 ("RCRA"); and, in 1980, Congress enacted the Comprehensive Environmental Response, Compensation, and Liability Act ("CERCLA").

288. *See, e.g.,* N.L.R.B. v. Bildisco & Bildisco, 465 U.S. 513, 528 (1984) ("The fundamental purpose of reorganization is to prevent a debtor from going into liquidation, with an attendant loss of jobs and possible misuse of economic resources.").

environmental laws.[289] The Court has resolved these conflicts to protect the public health and safety, but not the public fisc.

In *Ohio v. Kovacs*,[290] Ohio obtained a stipulated judgment and injunction against the debtor chief executive officer of a polluting corporation requiring him and the corporation to desist from further pollution and to clean up a hazardous waste disposal site.[291] The debtor refused to perform and Ohio sought and obtained the appointment of a receiver to take possession of the debtor's property to satisfy the judgment by cleaning up the property.[292] While the receiver was cleaning up the property, the debtor filed for bankruptcy and argued that his obligation under the injunction to clean-up the property was dischargeable because it was not one of the nondischargeable debts described in Bankruptcy Code § 523(a).[293] Ohio argued that the clean-up order was not a debt, both because it occurred as a breach of a statute and not a contract and because the debtor's breach did not give rise to a right to payment.[294] The Court disagreed with both of Ohio's arguments, holding that the breach of a statute can give rise to a claim and to a right to payment as evidenced by Ohio's seizure of the debtor's assets in partial satisfaction of its claim.[295] Because Ohio had cleaned up the property, there was nothing left for the debtor to do other than the payment of money.[296] Thus, by its own actions, Ohio reduced the clean-up order to a monetary obligation that was dischargeable as a prepetition debt.

---

289. *See* Midlantic Nat'l Bank v. New Jersey Dep't of Envtl. Protection, 474 U.S. 494 (1986); Ohio v. Kovacs, 469 U.S. 274 (1985).

290. *Id.*

291. *See id.* at 275-76.

292. *See id.* at 276.

293. *See id.* at 276-77; 11 U.S.C. § 523(a) (Supp. 1984).

294. *See Ohio v. Kovacs*, 469 U.S. at 279.

295. *See id.* at 279-81.

296. *See id.* at 283.

The next year, in *Midlantic National Bank v. New Jersey Department of Environmental Protection*,[297] the Court held that the chapter 7 trustee of a bankrupt corporation could not use Bankruptcy Code § 554 to abandon contaminated properties in violation of environmental statutes and regulations designed to protect the public unless the court approved procedures to adequately protect the public.[298] The Court limited its holding, however, by stating that "[t]he abandonment power is not to be fettered by laws or regulations not reasonably calculated to protect the public health or safety from imminent and identifiable harm."[299]

The Court's *Midlantic* holding was based on four questionable propositions. First, the Court noted that under the former Bankruptcy Act, the power of abandonment was judge-made and was circumscribed by an established line of cases to condition any abandonment on compliance with state and federal laws.[300] The Court inferred that Congress intended to include this established corollary when it codified the abandonment power in Bankruptcy Code § 554; if Congress intends to change the interpretation of a judicially-created concept, it makes that intent explicit.[301] Second, the Court noted that ensuring compliance with state safety laws was important to Congress because Congress made it an express exception to the automatic stay.[302] Thus, it was not unlikely that Congress' concern was incorporated into the abandonment provision. Third, the Court noted that section 959(b) of

---

297.   474 U.S. 494 (1986).

298.   *See id.* at 507. Justifying its holding, the Court noted that "Congress has repeatedly expressed its legislative determination that the trustee is not to have *carte blanche* to ignore nonbankruptcy law [, and that] . . . the efforts of the trustee to marshal and distribute the assets of the estate must yield to governmental interest in public health and safety." *Id.* at 502.

299.   *See id.* at 507 n.9.

300.   *See id.* at 500-01.

301.   *See id.* at 501.

302.   *See id.* at 503-04.

the Judicial Code,[303] while not directly applicable to the abandonment provision, requires a trustee who operates the debtor's business to manage property of the estate in compliance with state laws.[304] Thus, it was clear that Congress did not intend for the Bankruptcy Code to pre-empt all state laws that otherwise constrain the exercise of the trustee's powers. Fourth, the Court noted the congressional enactment of federal legislation designed to protect the environment against toxic pollution as evidence of Congress' intent that a bankruptcy trustee not abandon property in derogation of a state environmental law.[305]

The problem with *Midlantic* is not so much its result as its methodology. Instead of deciding the case on policy grounds, the Court went to great lengths to do so through legal reasoning. The dissent, authored by Justice Rehnquist, joined by Chief Justice Burger, Justice White, and Justice O'Connor, shredded the integrity of the majority opinion. The dissent attacked each of the grounds used by the majority to support its holding. First, the dissent noted that the language of Bankruptcy Code § 554 is clear and limits the trustee's power only insofar as the property must burden the estate.[306] Second, Congress explicitly exempted state environmental protection violations from the automatic stay.[307] Thus, if it had that same concern under abandonment, it would have expressly put an environmental limitation in the abandonment statute. Third, the dissent distin-guished the cases the majority used to argue that under the Act there was a judicially created doctrine limiting the trustee's abandonment power to compliance with state law.[308] Although the dissent attacked the majority's holding, it would have left open a narrow exception. When abandonment by the trustee itself might create a genuine

---

303. 28 U.S.C. § 959(b) (1982).

304. *See Midlantic*, 474 U.S. at 505.

305. *See id.* at 505-06.

306. *See id.* at 509.

307. *See id.*

308. *See id.* at 510.

emergency that the trustee uniquely would be able to guard against, abandonment would be inappropriate.[309] Absent that situation, notice of abandonment of the polluted property would adequately protect the public's health and safety.

Thus, the Court has set the outside limits to resolve conflicts between bankruptcy law and environmental law. When all that is involved is an issue of money, bankruptcy law and policy will prevail. When there is a danger to the public health and safety, environmental law and policy will prevail.

In fact, lower courts appear to follow the *Midlantic* majority's dictum[310] to limit *Midlantic* to preclude abandonment only when there is an emergency or imminent danger to public health and safety.[311] In balancing these competing policies, there are many issues left for the Court to clarify, including, among others, (1) what happens when there are insufficient funds in the bankruptcy estate to clean up the contaminated property; (2) what is the personal liability of the trustee for failing to clean up contaminated property; (3) what is the priority of the clean up cost relative to administrative expenses and prepetition claims; and (4) what is the dischargeability of clean-up injunctions and judgments and their status as claims when the state has not cleaned up the property?

---

309. *See id.* at 515.

310. *See id.* at 507 n.9 ("This exception to the abandonment power vested in the trustee by § 554 is a narrow one. . . . The abandonment power is not to be fettered by laws or regulations not reasonably calculated to protect the public health and safety from imminent and identifiable harm.").

311. *See, e.g.,* New Mexico Envt'l Dep't v. Foulston (*In re* L.F. Jennings Oil Co.), 4 F.3d 887, 890 (10th Cir. 1993) (abandonment permitted when the trustee's only violation was a failure to file reports and the state's own expert could not state that an immediate threat existed); Lancaster v. Tennessee (*In re* Wall Tube & Metal Prods. Co.), 831 F.2d 118, 121 (6th Cir. 1987) (abandonment denied when hazardous substances on property could cause injury or death); *In re* Brio Ref., Inc., 86 B.R. 487 (N.D. Tex. 1988) (because the hazardous nature of the property was unknown, abandonment was permitted).

Although the Court has not considered the direct interaction of environmental law and bankruptcy law after *Midlantic*, the Court has decided environmental law cases that will have a significant impact on bankruptcy cases. In *Cooper Industries v. Aviall Services, Inc.*,[312] based on the plain meaning of the CERCLA statute,[313] the Court held that a purchaser, who voluntarily pays to clean up four environmentally contaminated properties, cannot assert a contribution claim against the seller or other potentially responsible parties ("PRP's") under section 113(f)(1) of CERCLA;[314] because the purchaser was never sued by an environmental authority in a civil action under sections 106 or 107(a) of CERCLA[315] to clean up the properties, therefore, the PRP's did not fall within the express language of CERCLA § 113(f)(1).[316] The Court remanded to let the lower courts determine whether the purchaser could pursue a cost recovery action or had an implied right of contribution under section 107 of CERCLA against the seller.[317]

Although *Cooper Industries* does not address bankruptcy law, it has important implications for debtors who are PRP's or might be PRP's. Debtors with contaminated sites sometimes base their reorganization plans on the ability to discharge fixed or contingent contribution claims under chapter 11 plans. Because a PRP cannot sue until an environmental authority files a clean-up suit, *Cooper Industries* may make these contribution claims so attenuated that they will not be discharged unless a clean up suit has been filed.[318] On

---

312.   543 U.S. 157 (2004).

313.   *See id.* at 167. ("Given the clear meaning of the text, there is no need . . . to consult the purpose of CERCLA at all.").

314.   *See* 42 U.S.C. § 9613(f)(1) (2000).

315.   *See* 42 U.S.C. §§ 9606, 9607(a) (2000).

316.   *See Cooper Indus.*, 543 U.S. at 160-61.

317.   *See id.* at 170-71.

318.   *See In re* Hillsborough Holdings Corp., 325 B.R. 334 (Bankr. M.D. Fla. 2005) (holding that there is no contingent claim for CERCLA

the other hand, if all of the environmental contamination occurred before the debtor filed for bankruptcy, courts might conclude that the PRP contribution claims are still contingent claims subject to discharge in chapter 11 even if a suit cannot be filed outside of bankruptcy.

Cooper Industries is but one example of how the Court's nonbankruptcy decisions can affect bankruptcy law dramatically in cases when, in all likelihood, the Justices are oblivious to bankruptcy law and policy implications. In such cases the Court unwittingly might create or increase the conflict between bankruptcy law and other areas rather than providing a basis for conflict resolution.

FAMILY LAW

The Court's decisions resolving conflicts between bankruptcy law and family law frequently concern alimony, maintenance, and child or spousal support.[319] In his digest of the Court's bankruptcy decisions through 1938, Edmund Dryer summarizes four decisions between 1901 and 1931 all concluding in part that obligations for alimony are nondischargeable.[320] Indeed, on February 5, 1903, Congress amended Bankruptcy Act § 17 to make debts for "alimony due or to become due, or for maintenance or support of wife or child," nondischargeable.[321]

---

reimbursement until the government files an enforcement action against the claimant).

319. *See* Owen v. Owen, 500 U.S. 305 (1991); Farrey v. Sanderfoot, 500 U.S. 291 (1991); Taylor v. Voss, 271 U.S. 176 (1926); Cohn v. Malone, 248 U.S. 450 (1919); Robert Moody & Son v. Century Sav. Bank, 239 U.S. 374 (1915); Hull v. Dicks, 235 U.S. 584 (1915); Wetmore v. Markoe, 196 U.S. 68 (1904); Tinker v. Colwell, 193 U.S. 473 (1904); Dunbar v. Dunbar, 190 U.S. 340 (1903); Audubon v. Shufeldt, 181 U.S. 575 (1901).

320. *See Dryer*, at 31, citing *Maynard v. Elliott, Wetmore v. Markoe, Dunbar v. Dunbar*, and *Audubon v. Shufeldt. Maynard v. Elliott* actually involves a debtor's liability as an endorser on a promissory note and does not concern alimony except to the extent the Court cites *Dunbar v. Dunbar* with approval. *See* Maynard v. Elliott, 283 U.S. 273, 278 (1931).

321. *See* Pub. L. No. 62, 57th Cong., 1st Sess., 32 Stat. 797 (Feb. 5, 1903).

Before enactment of the 1903 amendment, the Court thrice held[322] that alimony or support claims were not provable debts and therefore nondischargeable under Bankruptcy Act § 63. Most interestingly, before the 1903 amendment, based on the plain language of the statute, prepetition liquidated debts, including those for alimony, were provable and dischargeable under the Bankruptcy Act.[323] Nevertheless, the Court held on policy grounds that the amount owing for liquidated prepetition alimony was not a debt and, therefore, was not discharged.[324] First, the Court held that "[t]he mere fact that a judgment has been rendered does not prevent the Court from looking into the proceedings with a view of determining the nature of the liability which has been reduced to judgment."[325] The Court then quoted from its 1901 decision in *Audubon v. Shufeldt* that "[p]ermanent alimony is regarded rather as a portion of the husband's estate to which the wife is equitably entitled, than as strictly a debt . . . ."[326] In *Audubon v. Shufeldt* the Court set out a history of the treatment of alimony under English and United States law[327] before holding that "neither the alimony in arrear at the time of the adjudication in bankruptcy, nor

---

322. *See* Wetmore v. Markoe, 196 U.S. 68 (1904); Dunbar v. Dunbar, 190 U.S. 340 (1903); and Audubon v. Shufeldt, 181 U.S. 575 (1901).

323. *See Wetmore v. Markoe*, 196 U.S. at 72:

> "Sec. 63. Debts which may be proved:—
>
> "Debts of the bankrupt may be proved and allowed against his estate which are (1) a fixed liability, as evidenced by a judgment or an instrument in writing, absolutely owing at the time of the filing of the petition against him, whether then payable or not, with any interest thereon which would have been recoverable at that date or with a rebate of interest upon such as were not then payable and did not bear interest."

324. *See id.* at 73-74.

325. *See id.* at 72.

326. *See id.* at 73 (quoting *Audubon v. Shufeldt*, 181 U.S. at 577-78).

327. *See Audubon v. Shufeldt*, 181 U.S. at 578-80.

alimony accruing since that adjudication, was provable in bankruptcy, or barred by the discharge."[328]

The Court's decision in *Dunbar v. Dunbar* went one step further by holding that a husband's contractual obligation to support his wife and minor children was not provable or dischargeable.[329] After the Court reviewed United States and English precedents, it based its decision on policy grounds: "We think it was not the intention of Congress, in passing a bankruptcy act, to provide for the release of the father from his obligation to support his children by his discharge in bankruptcy, and if not, then we see no reason why his contract to do that which the law obliged him to do should be discharged in that way."[330] The Court also noted the nondischargeability of alimony and support obligations under the 1903 amendment and stated that even though the amendment was prospective and could not be relied on in *Dunbar v. Dunbar*, it could be "referred to here for the purpose of showing the legislative trend in the direction of not discharging an obligation of the bankrupt for the support and maintenance of wife or children."[331]

The Court's decision in *Dunbar v. Dunbar* paved the way for it to hold in *Wetmore v. Markoe* that a fixed and unalterable judgment or decree providing for the support of minor children "is not a debt in any just sense."[332] Having been convinced by the logic of its own decisions, the Court concluded that the 1903 amendment was not a change in the law, but based on the Court's decision in *Audubon v. Shufeldt* was "merely declaratory of the true meaning and sense of the statute."[333] The Court concluded this trilogy of alimony cases with the sweeping pronouncement that "[t]he bankruptcy law should received (sic) such an interpretation as will effectuate its beneficent purposes

---

328. *See id.* at 580.

329. *See* Dunbar v. Dunbar, 190 U.S. 340, 345, 350-51 (1903).

330. *See id.* at 351-52.

331. *See id.* at 353.

332. *See Wetmore v. Markoe*, 196 U.S. at 76.

333. *See id.* at 77.

and not make it an instrument to deprive dependent wife and children of the support and maintenance due them from the husband and father, which it has ever been the purpose of the law to enforce."[334]

The lesson to be learned from these early cases is that even when the bankruptcy statute appears on its face to override family law, the Court has not hesitated to reach a contrary conclusion, unless its hands are tied. The Court in *Wetmore v. Markoe* said as much: "Unless positively required by direct enactment the courts should not presume a design upon the part of Congress in relieving the unfortunate debtor to make the law a means of avoiding enforcement of the obligation, moral and legal, devolved upon the husband to support his wife and to maintain and educate his children."[335] Thus, it should come as no surprise that 11 years later in *Hull v. Dicks*,[336] the Court held that when a debtor dies after filing for bankruptcy, a bankruptcy trustee's title to the debtor's property is subject to a widow's state law right of support.[337]

More than 80 years later, the Court revisited analogous issues involving the intersection of bankruptcy law and family law. Would the Court's trend toward "plain meaning" lead to a different outcome or would the Court continue to craft its opinions to protect family law even at the price of straining its interpretation of the Bankruptcy Code? *Farrey v. Sanderfoot* and *Owen v. Owen* provide the substance for an analysis of this question.

In *Farrey v. Sanderfoot*,[338] the Court considered whether a debtor could use Bankruptcy Code § 522(f)(1)[339] to avoid a judicial lien that the divorce court had created on his exempt residence to secure his obligations to his spouse as part of a property division in a divorce

---

334. *See id.*

335. *See id.*

336. 235 U.S. 584 (1915).

337. *See id.* at 587.

338. Farrey v. Sanderfoot, 500 U.S. 291 (1991).

339. 11 U.S.C. § 522(f)(1) (Supp. 1990).

proceeding.[340] The plain language of the statute permits a debtor to "avoid the fixing of a lien on an interest of the debtor in property to the extent that such lien impairs an exemption to which the debtor would have been entitled . . . if such lien is . . . a judicial lien . . . ." Without dissent the Court decided that the debtor could not use this section of the Bankruptcy Code to avoid a former spouse's judicial lien, because, as a matter of plain meaning,[341] it only applies when the lien attaches after the debtor obtains an interest in property; in this case the divorce court awarded the judicial lien simultaneously with granting Sanderfoot a fee simple interest in the house.[342] In this case Sanderfoot did own an undivided one-half interest in the house before the divorce court entered its decree. But under state law, the divorce court extinguished the old property interests of both spouses in the house and gave Sanderfoot a new property interest at the same time the judicial lien attached.[343] Moreover, the new lien did not secure a

---

340. *See Farrey v. Sanderfoot*, 500 U.S. at 293.

341. "We agree with Judge Posner that to permit a debtor in these circumstances to use the Code to deprive a spouse of this protection would neither follow the language of the statute nor serve the main goal it was designed to address." *See id.* at 301.

342. *See id.* at 296. "Therefore, unless the debtor had the property interest to which the lien attached at some point *before* the lien attached to that interest, he or she cannot avoid the fixing of the lien under the terms of § 522(f)(1)." (emphasis original). This quotation begs the question whether a lien that attaches simultaneously with the creation of a property interest should be treated as having "fixed" to the debtor's interest in property. The Court is correct that the debtor did not own the property in fee simple without a lien; but it is also true that there was no property to which the judicial lien had attached before the debtor acquired it. The term "fixing" does have a temporal component, but no rule of construction limits it to property acquired "before" the creation of the lien as opposed to "before or concurrently with" the lien's creation. At the very least, the language of the statute is not "plain" regarding its application to the simultaneous creation of property and the fixing of a lien. That is why the lower courts were split and the Court granted certiorari. *See id.* at 295. ("We granted certiorari to resolve the conflict of authority.").

343. *See id.* at 299.

value more than the value of the former spouse's interest in the house.[344]

The Court's opinion notes that its conclusion is consistent with congressional purpose and the legislative history.[345] The concurrence understandably notes that the "result the Court reaches consists with fairness and common sense."[346] Even if the debtor owned the house as sole and separate property during the marriage, however, based on the Court's history of preventing bankruptcy law from unduly interfering with state family law, it is likely that the Court would have strained to reach the same result regardless of the statute's plain meaning. The concurrence, however, posits a different outcome and believes that "the Bankruptcy Code may be used in some later case to allow a spouse to avoid otherwise valid obligations under a divorce court decree."[347] Based on the Court's uniform deference to state family law, it is doubtful that the Court would countenance such a result.

There is some merit to the Court's simply deciding a matter according to common sense instead of stretching the doctrine of plain meaning to warp the interpretation of the Bankruptcy Code. Common sense is a flexible concept making it entirely possible that using common sense in resolving the intersection of bankruptcy law and family law might not comport with common sense in other cases. Moreover, when the Circuit courts are split on the meaning of a statute, it is problematic for the Court to say that "plain meaning" can

---

344. *See id.* at 292. ("[T]he lien is granted to the debtor's former spouse under a divorce decree that extinguishes all previous interests the parties had in the property, and in no event secured more than the value of the nondebtor spouse's former interest.").

345. *See id.* at 297-99. "As noted, the legislative history suggests that Congress primarily intended § 522(f)(1) as a device to thwart creditors who, sensing an impending bankruptcy, rush to court to obtain a judgment to defeat the debtor's exemptions. That is not what occurs in a divorce proceeding such as this." *Id.* at 300.

346. *See id.* at 303 (Kennedy, J., with whom Souter, J., joins, concurring).

347. *See id.*

be used to resolve the matter. The Court's use of plain meaning in *Farrey v. Sanderfoot* founders on the Court's requirement that the debtor must own the property *before* the lien fixes to the debtor's interest in property. This requirement is made up out of whole cloth;[348] the Court just as easily could have found that the lien affixes to an interest in property that the debtor acquires before or simultaneously with the creation of the lien.

The Court's strained interpretation of the meaning of "fixing" could have disturbing implications when applied to other Code sections. For example, based on the Court's construction, the estate will never be able to avoid the fixing of a statutory lien on the debtor's after-acquired property because the lien attaches simultaneously with the debtor's acquisition of the property.[349] And in the preference context, it is possible that under the Court's rule in *Farrey v. Sanderfoot*, a debtor with floating inventory or receivables financing would acquire future inventory or receivables "subject to" the lien, meaning there is no transfer of property of the debtor for the estate to avoid.[350]

---

348. After citing the Black's Law Dictionary definition of "fix" the Court correctly concludes that "fixing" refers to a temporal event. Then the Court leaps to the conclusion that the object to which the lien affixes must be "pre-existing" and never explains why a lien cannot affix to an interest that the debtor acquires concurrently with the fixing of the lien. *See id.* at 296.

349. The Court was aware that the Bankruptcy Code refers to "fixing" of a lien in § 545 respecting the avoidance of statutory liens. *See id.* at 296 n.3. And the reasoning of *Farrey v. Sanderfoot* can extend to all judicial liens outside the bounds of a lien created in a divorce proceeding. Justice Scalia dodged this very issue in *Owen v. Owen* when he crafted the opinion of the Court by assuming "without deciding that [the judicial lien] fixed 'on an interest of the debtor in property.'" *See* Owen v. Owen, 500 U.S. 305, 309 (1991). In fact, since the former wife recorded her judicial lien before the former husband purchased property, the lien attached simultaneously, and under *Farrey v. Sanderfoot,* Justice Scalia would have been forced to decide *Owen v. Owen* the other way. Justice Stevens' dissent in *Owen v. Owen* makes this point precisely. *See id.* at 315.

350. Courts should reject such a construction because it would make Bankruptcy Code § 547(c)(5) surplusage.

Some courts have used the reasoning of *Farrey v. Sanderfoot* to disturb the traditional working of other avoiding powers.[351]

On the same day it decided *Farrey v. Sanderfoot*, the Court decided *Owen v. Owen*[352] in which the Court confronted an effort by a state to opt out of the debtor's ability under Bankruptcy Code § 522(f)(1) to avoid a judicial lien that impairs an exemption. In *Owen v. Owen*, a former wife obtained and recorded a judgment against her former husband before he acquired any property in the county in which the judgment was recorded.[353] Several years later, he purchased property in that county and the judgment lien attached.[354] One year later, the state passed an exemption law allowing the property to be claimed exempt, and the former husband filed bankruptcy under chapter 7 one year after that.[355]

During the chapter 7 bankruptcy case, the debtor sought to use § 522(f)(1) to avoid the judicial lien to the extent it impaired his homestead. Under Florida law, the debtor could not avoid the encumbrance because the state defined exempt property in such a way that it excluded property encumbered by judicial liens.[356] The Court determined, however, that the debtor's entitlement to an exemption, and accordingly his ability to avoid a lien which impairs it, in a state that has opted out of the federal exemptions is determined under federal law and not the law of the individual state.[357] Thus, the Court

---

351. *See* Owen v. Owen, 961 F.2d 170, 172 (11th Cir.), *cert. denied*, 506 U.S. 1022 (1992) (applying *Farrey v. Sanderfoot* to prevent the avoidance of a judicial lien on after-acquired exempt property).

352. *See* Owen v. Owen, 500 U.S. 305 (1991). The Court decided both *Owen v. Owen* and *Farrey v. Sanderfoot* on May 23, 1991.

353. *See Owen v. Owen*, 500 U.S. at 306.

354. *See id.* at 307.

355. *See id.*

356. *See id.*

357. *See id.* at 312-14.

permitted the debtor to avoid the judicial lien to the extent it impaired the exemption he could have taken had there been no lien.[358]

Because the Court assumed, without deciding, that the lien attached to an interest of the debtor in property, the Court reversed and remanded.[359] On remand, the Eleventh Circuit held, based on *Farrey v. Sanderfoot*, that indeed there was no interest of the debtor to which the lien attached because it attached simultaneously with the debtor's acquisition of the property.[360] Thus, the Court's well-intentioned decision in *Farrey v. Sanderfoot* to uphold judicial liens created in divorce proceedings was questionably expanded to uphold judgment liens created outside the context of the actual divorce proceeding.

Occasionally, the Court's family law cases also extend outside the divorce setting. For example, in *Cunningham v. Brown*,[361] the Court held that a preference defendant's status as a minor did not justify the retention of an avoidable preference.[362] Also, in *Tinker v. Colwell*,[363] the Court held that the crime of criminal conversation, or the seduction of another's spouse, was nondischargeable as a willful and malicious injury to the property of the husband because the husband "has certain personal and exclusive rights with regard to the person of his

---

358. *See id.* at 312-13 ("ask first whether avoiding the lien would entitle the debtor to an exemption, and if it would, then avoid and recover the lien"). At least some courts believe that the rule in *Owen v. Owen* has been overruled with respect to exempt tools of the trade by legislative enactment Bankruptcy Code § 522(f)(3), 11 U.S.C. § 522(f)(3) (2000). *See In re* Parrish, 186 B.R. 246, 247 n.1 (Bankr. W.D. Wis. 1995) ("[W[ith the passage of § 522(f)(3), the state has been given the ability to prohibit the avoiding of a lien to the extent it exceeds $ 5,000.").

359. *See Owen v. Owen*, 500 U.S. at 314.

360. *See* Owen v. Owen, 961 F.2d 170, 172 (11th Cir.), *cert. denied*, 506 U.S. 1022 (1992).

361. 265 U.S. 1 (1924).

362. *See id.* at 13-14. Cunningham was the trustee of Charles Ponzi whose criminal exploits are discussed in the opinion. *See id.* at 7-9.

363. 193 U.S. 473 (1904).

wife . . . and that an assault of this nature may properly be described as an injury to the personal rights and property of the husband, which is both malicious and willful."[364] As a result of this decision, Congress codified the nondischargeability of debts for criminal conversation,[365] but this exception to discharge was repealed on enactment of the 1978 Bankruptcy Code.[366]

By way of further example, in *Taylor v. Voss*,[367] the Court considered the competing claims to real property between a debtor's bankruptcy trustee and his deceased spouse's testamentary trustee. The bankruptcy trustee wanted to sell the property free and clear of the spouse's interest whereas the testamentary trustee alleged that the spouse became absolutely vested in her dower interest in the property on the adjudication of the bankruptcy.[368] The Court held, in reliance on *Stellwagen v. Clum*,[369] that "[i]n the absence of any conflicting provision in the Bankruptcy Act the question of a wife's interest in the bankrupt's property is governed by the local law."[370] Under state law the adjudication of the husband "as a bankrupt, when followed by the appointment of the trustee in bankruptcy, operated as a 'judicial sale' of his real estate within the meaning of the statute, and made absolute his wife's interest therein."[371] It is doubtful whether the result in *Taylor v. Voss* would apply under the 1978 Bankruptcy Code, because Bankruptcy Code § 541(c) should be held to operate to override the

---

364.   *See id.* at 481.

365.   Bankruptcy Act § 17a(2), 11 U.S.C. § 35a(2), Act of Feb. 5, 1903, ch. 487, 30 Stat. 550, made debts "for seduction of an unmarried female, or for criminal conversation" nondischargeable.

366.   *See* Pub. L. No. 95-598, § 401(a), 92 Stat. 2549, 2682 (Nov. 6, 1978); H.R. REP. NO. 95-595 at 365 (1977).

367.   271 U.S. 176 (1926).

368.   *See id.* at 178.

369.   245 U.S. 605 (1918).

370.   *See* Taylor v. Voss, 271 U.S. 176, 190 (1926).

371.   *See id.*

ipso facto aspect of state law that vests the wife's interest on the entry of the order for relief.

Not all of the Court's family law decisions rule in favor of the debtor's spouse, particularly when the interests of the spouse conflict with creditors rather than the debtor. For example, in *Cohn v. Malone*,[372] before filing for bankruptcy, the debtor assigned two life insurance policies to his wife, but, as the insured, he retained the right to change beneficiaries. The bankruptcy trustee demanded the policies to get the cash surrender value. The Court held for the trustee against the wife finding that the insured's contractual right to change beneficiaries passed to the trustee and that a state statute dealing with the policies gave the wife no "vested and indefeasible interest in [the] policies . . . ."[373]

LABOR LAW

The Court has encountered the interface between bankruptcy and labor law infrequently, but its decisions in this area are of tremendous importance as matters of social policy. The Court appears to construe the specific provisions and policies of the Bankruptcy Code to prevail over more general provisions and policies of the labor laws.

Although the Court has authored several opinions concerning the wage priority in bankruptcy, two are probably its most significant.[374] In 1952, the Court held in *Nathanson v. National Labor Relations Board* that the N.L.R.B.'s back pay award entered against the debtor prepetition was not entitled to priority under the Bankruptcy Act.[375]

---

372.   248 U.S. 450 (1919).

373.   *See id.* at 453.

374.   *See* United States v. Embassy Rest., Inc., 359 U.S. 29 (1959); Nathanson v. Nat'l Labor Relations Bd., 344 U.S. 25 (1952).

375.   *See Nathanson*, 344 U.S. at 28-29. 53 years later, Congress amended the Bankruptcy Code to accord administrative expense priority to the postpetition portion of the back pay award if payment of the award will not substantially increase the probability of layoff or termination of current employees or of nonpayment of domestic support obligations

Harmonizing the policies of labor law and bankruptcy law, the Court noted that:[376]

> The policy of the National Labor Relations Act is fully served by recognizing the [N.L.R.B.'s] claim for back pay as one to be paid from the estate. The question whether it should be paid in preference to other creditors is a question to be answered from the Bankruptcy Act. When Congress came to claims for unpaid wages, it did not grant all of them priority. . . . We would depart from that policy if we granted priority to one class of wage claimants irrespective of the amount of the claim or the time of its accrual.

Thus, the Court interpreted the specific priority provisions of the Bankruptcy Act restrictively. "The theme of the Bankruptcy Act is 'equality of distribution'; and if one claimant is to be preferred over others, the purpose should be clear from the statute."[377]

The Court's decision in *Nathanson* blazed the trail for its reasoning seven years later in *United States v. Embassy Restaurant, Inc.* when it narrowly construed the wage priority to exclude contributions to union welfare funds required under a collective bargaining agreement.[378] The Court declined to let business practicalities, in which unions bargain for these benefits as though they were wages and business regards them as part of the wage package, override the language of the statute.[379] Even though fringe benefits qualified as wages under the National Labor Relations Act and the Social Security Act, the Court viewed its responsibility to "construe

---

during the bankruptcy case. *See* 11 U.S.C. § 503(b)(1)(A)(ii) (Supp. 2005), as added by Pub. L. No. 109-8, § 329, 119 Stat. 23, 101 (2005).

376. *See Nathanson*, 344 U.S. at 28-29.

377. *See id.* at 29 (citing Sampsell v. Imperial Paper Corp., 313 U.S. 215, 219 (1941)). *Accord* Howard Delivery Serv., Inc. v. Zurich Am. Ins. Co., 547 U.S. 651, 667 (2006) (narrowly construing § 507(a)(5) employee benefit plan priority to exclude claims for unpaid workers' compensation premiums); Kuehner v. Irving Trust Co., 299 U.S. 445, 451 (1937); Kothe v. R.C. Taylor Trust, 280 U.S. 224, 227 (1930).

378. *See Embassy Restaurant*, 359 U.S. at 31.

379. *See id.* at 33. ("This approach overlooks the fact that we deal with a statute, not business practice.").

the priority section of the Bankruptcy Act, not those statutes."[380] The Court left it to Congress to enlarge the priority class to include these claims,[381] and Congress did so almost 20 years later when it enacted the Bankruptcy Code.[382]

Without doubt, the Court's most significant decision involving bankruptcy and labor law is *National Labor Relations Board v. Bildisco & Bildisco*,[383] in which the Court held that a chapter 11 debtor in possession, upon an appropriate showing, could reject a collective bargaining agreement under Bankruptcy Code § 365,[384] and could, without committing an unfair labor practice, unilaterally modify or terminate one or more provisions of the agreement before court approval of rejection of the agreement.[385] The Court's opinion is noteworthy in several respects. First, in harmonizing bankruptcy law and labor law policies, the Court requires the debtor in possession to make "reasonable efforts to negotiate a voluntary modification" and that negotiations "are not likely to produce a prompt and satisfactory solution."[386] The Court determined that "[t]he NLRA requires no less" and found that the debtor in possession was under a duty to bargain based on labor law and "the national labor policies of avoiding labor strife and encouraging collective bargaining."[387] It refused to find that a debtor in possession is a new entity (with no duty to bargain under the unassumed collective bargaining agreement), stating that "it is sensible to view the debtor in possession as the same 'entity' which existed before the filing of the bankruptcy petition."[388] Nevertheless,

---

380. *See id.*

381. *See id.* at 35. ("If this class is to be so enlarged, it must be done by the Congress.").

382. *See* 11 U.S.C. § 507(a)(4) (1979).

383. 465 U.S. 513 (1984).

384. *See id.* at 516.

385. *See id.* at 516-17.

386. *See id.* at 526.

387. *See id.*

388. *See id.* at 528.

before bargaining to impasse or obtaining a court-ordered rejection of the agreement, the debtor in possession did not commit an unfair labor practice by unilaterally modifying or terminating provisions under the collective bargaining agreement, because it is "empowered by virtue of the Bankruptcy Code to deal with its contracts and property in a manner it could not have employed absent the bankruptcy filing."[389] As a matter of bankruptcy law and policy,[390]

> the filing of a petition in bankruptcy means that the collective-bargaining agreement is no longer immediately enforceable, and may never be enforceable again. Consequently, Board enforcement of a claimed violation of § 8(d) [of the NLRA] under these circumstances would run directly counter to the express provisions of the Bankruptcy Code and to the Code's overall effort to give the debtor-in-possession some flexibility and breathing space.

Second, *Bildisco* contains powerful dicta about the purposes of bankruptcy and the rights of debtors in possession. For example, regarding the purpose of chapter 11, the Court notes that "[t]he fundamental purpose of reorganization is to prevent a debtor from going into liquidation, with an attendant loss of jobs and possible misuse of economic resources."[391] Regarding the power of the bankruptcy court as a court of equity,[392] the Court states that "[t]he Bankruptcy Code does not authorize freewheeling consideration of every conceivable

---

389. *See id.*

390. *See id.* at 532.

391. *See id.* at 528.

392. The 1978 Bankruptcy Code specified that the Bankruptcy Court was a court of law, equity, and admiralty. *See* 28 U.S.C. § 1481 (1982) (repealed 1984). As more fully discussed *infra* in Ch. 4, pp. 223-229, in its post-1984 cases, notwithstanding the 1984 repeal of Judicial Code § 1481, the Court continues to describe the bankruptcy court as a court of equity. Some commentators who have taken a closer look have questioned whether the bankruptcy court is a statutory court rather than a court of equity. *See, e.g.,* Alan Ahart, *The Limited Scope of Implied Powers of a Bankruptcy Judge: A Statutory Court of Bankruptcy, Not a Court of Equity*, 79 AM. BANKR. L.J. 1 (2005).

equity, but rather only how the equities relate to the success of the reorganization."[393] Regarding the rights of a debtor in possession under an executory contract before assumption or rejection, the Court reaffirmed its holding in *Philadelphia Co. v. Dipple*[394] that "[i]f the debtor-in-possession elects to continue to receive benefits from the other party to an executory contract pending a decision to assume or reject the contract, the debtor-in-possession is obligated to pay the reasonable value of those services . . . ."[395] These quotes are of lasting duration and apply equally as well today as when they were written.

The same cannot be said for *Bildisco*'s standard for rejecting a collective bargaining agreement. Perhaps the most important consequence of *Bildisco* is that its holding prompted Congress to almost immediately enact the Bankruptcy and Federal Judgeship Amendments Act of 1984.[396] Even though the Court had declared the Bankruptcy Code to be unconstitutional in 1982,[397] by the time *Bildisco* was decided Congress had failed to enact amendatory legislation. *Bildisco*'s holding so infuriated organized labor that it quickly provided the political impetus for legislation to overrule *Bildisco* through the enactment of Bankruptcy Code § 1113.[398] As a byproduct, Congress enacted legislation to deal with the constitutional defects in the bankruptcy courts' jurisdiction raised in *Northern Pipeline*. This topic is discussed more fully in Chapter 3.

PENSION LAW

During the past 30 years, the Court has decided a few cases resolving the conflict between bankruptcy law and pension law. The

---

393.　*See Bildisco*, 465 U.S. at 527.

394.　312 U.S. 168, 174 (1941).

395.　*See Bildisco*, 465 U.S. at 531.

396.　Bankruptcy Amendments and Federal Judgeship Act of 1984, Pub. L. No. 353, 98 Stat. 333 (1984).

397.　*See* N. Pipeline Constr. Co. v. Marathon Pipe Line Co., 458 U.S. 50 (1982).

398.　*See* 11 U.S.C. § 1113 (Supp. 1984).

Bankruptcy Code seeks to assemble the debtor's property into an estate for distribution to creditors in liquidation or under a plan. On the other hand, pension laws seek to preserve a fund of money, securities, or other property to pay for the debtor's retirement.[399] The Court, through its interpretation of the relevant statutes,[400] has uniformly resolved these conflicting policies in favor of the pension law and its policy to protect the debtor's retirement.

For example, in *Patterson v. Shumate*,[401] the Court held that a qualified retirement plan covered by ERISA[402] was excluded from property of the estate under Bankruptcy Code § 541(c)(2).[403] Basing its holding on the statutory interpretation that § 541(c)(2)'s reference to "nonbankruptcy law" covered anti-alienation provisions in federal law, such as those required by section 206(d)(1) of ERISA,[404] as well as spendthrift trusts under state law,[405] the Court noted that its holding was consistent with both bankruptcy and ERISA policies.[406] The

---

399. *See, e.g.*, Guidry v. Sheet Metal Workers Nat'l Pension Fund, 493 U.S. 365, 376 (1990) ("Section 206(d) [of ERISA] reflects a considered congressional policy choice, a decision to safeguard a stream of income for pensioners . . . even if that decision prevents others from securing relief for the wrongs done to them.").

400. Although the Court considered policy issues, its analysis started with the plain language of the statute. *See* Patterson v. Shumate, 504 U.S. 753, 757 (1992) ("In our view, the plain language of the Bankruptcy Code and ERISA is our determinant.").

401. 504 U.S. 753 (1992).

402. ERISA is an acronym that refers to the Employee Retirement Income Security Act of 1974, 88 Stat. 832, as amended, (2000). *See* Patterson v. Shumate, 504 U.S. 753, 755 (1992).

403. *See id.* at 760.

404. *See* 29 U.S.C. § 1056(d)(1) (1988).

405. *See Patterson v. Shumate*, 504 U.S. at 758 ("Nothing in § 541 suggests that the phrase 'applicable nonbankruptcy law' refers . . . exclusively to *state* law. The text contains no limitation on 'applicable nonbankruptcy law' relating to the source of the law.").

406. *See id.* at 763-65. *See also* Mechele Dickerson, "The Story of *Patterson*: Plainly Protecting Pensions," BANKRUPTCY LAW STORIES 118,

Court first noted that the policy of broad inclusion of property of the estate is not a policy that underlies "the Code as a whole."[407] The Court also noted that its decision "ensures that the treatment of pension benefits will not vary based on the beneficiary's bankruptcy status."[408] Thus, there is no asymmetry between pension rights in and outside bankruptcy.[409] The Court continued by pointing out that its opinion gives appropriate effect to three ERISA policies: no exceptions to ERISA's anti-alienation provisions; ERISA's goal of protecting pension benefits; and uniform national treatment of pension benefits.[410] Having held that the pension plan is excluded from the estate under Bankruptcy Code § 541(c)(2), the Court concluded its opinion by leaving open whether a debtor's interest in an ERISA-qualified pension plan qualifies for exemption under Bankruptcy Code § 522(b)(2)(A).[411]

In 2004 the Court considered, in *Yates v. Hendon*,[412] whether a debtor who is a sole shareholder and owner of a professional corporation may qualify as a "participant" in an ERISA pension plan sponsored by the debtor's corporation.[413] The Court held that as long as the pension "plan covers one or more employees other than the business owner and his or her spouse, the working owner may participate on equal terms with other plan participants."[414] The Court left open, to be decided on remand, whether Yates qualifies as a

---

141-44 (Robert K. Rasmussen, ed., Foundation Press 2007) (explaining the retirement landscape in America and justifying the result in *Patterson* on policy grounds).

407. *See id.* at 763-64.

408. *See id.* at 764.

409. *See id.* (citing Butner v. United States, 440 U.S. 48, 55 (1979)).

410. *See* Patterson v. Shumate, 504 U.S. 753, 764-65 (1992).

411. *See id.* at 765-66.

412. 541 U.S. 1 (2004).

413. *See id.* at 6.

414. *See id.*

beneficiary under the pension plan[415] and whether Yates' trustee has the power to recover loan repayments to the plan as a preference.[416]

In *Rousey v. Jacoway*,[417] the Court answered a variant of the question left open in *Patterson v. Shumate*, holding that a debtor's interest in an IRA[418] may be exempted from the bankruptcy estate under Bankruptcy Code § 522(d)(10)(E), presumably to the extent reasonably necessary for the support of the debtor or a dependent of the debtor.[419] In *Rousey*, an Arkansas couple, following termination of their employment, rolled over the lump sum distributions from their employer-sponsored pension plan into two IRA accounts.[420] Several years later, they filed a joint bankruptcy petition under chapter 7 and claimed a portion of their IRA's as exempt property under Bankruptcy Code § 522(d)(10)(E).[421] Unlike the defined benefit pension plan in *Patterson v. Shumate*, which was subject to ERISA, the IRA accounts in *Rousey* were not subject to ERISA and had no anti-alienation provision. In fact, the debtors could withdraw money from the accounts at anytime, as long as they paid the applicable 10% penalty for early withdrawals.[422] Accordingly, these accounts became

---

415.   *See id.* at 11 n.2.

416.   *See id.* at 23-24.

417.   544 U.S. 320 (2005).

418.   IRA is an acronym for Individual Retirement Account.

419.   *See Rousey*, 544 U.S. at 322, 334-35. The Court in *Patterson v. Shumate* did note that "[a]lthough a debtor's interest [in an IRA] could not be excluded [from property of the estate] under § 541(c)(2) . . ., that interest nevertheless could be exempted under § 522(d)(10)(E)." *See Patterson*, 504 U.S. at 762-63 (footnote omitted).

420.   *See Rousey*, 544 U.S. at 322.

421.   *See id.* at 323-25.

422.   *See id.* at 327-28. An IRA beneficiary may withdraw from an IRA account at any time, but withdrawals before age 59½ are subject to a 10% surtax. *See* 26 U.S.C. § 72(t) (2000). Unlike the defined benefit pension plan in *Patterson v. Shumate* which was subject to ERISA, the IRA accounts in *Rousey* were not subject to ERISA. Thus, these accounts became property of the bankruptcy estates because the

property of the bankruptcy estates because the exclusion in Bankruptcy Code § 541(c)(2) does not apply. By its terms, however, Bankruptcy Code § 522(d)(10)(E) preserves the debtors' right to receive
retirement payments "on account of illness, disability, death, age or
length of service."[423]

The dispute in *Rousey* is whether the debtors' right to receive IRA
payments is (1) from "a stock bonus, pension, profitsharing, annuity,
or similar plan or contract," and (2) "on account of illness, disability,
death, age, or length of service."[424] Resolving a three-way Circuit split,
the Court held that IRAs are age-based, because the IRA 10% penalty
for withdrawals under age 59 1/2 "erects a substantial barrier to early
withdrawal."[425] Moreover, the Court held that the IRAs met
§ 522(d)(10)(E)'s requirement of being similar to a "stock bonus,
pension, profit sharing, or annuity plan," because "[t]he common
feature of all of these plans is that they provide income that substi-
tutes for wages earned as salary or hourly compensation."[426]
Accordingly, the IRAs were exempt, presumably to the extent
reasonably necessary for the support of the debtors or a dependent of
the debtors.[427]

---

exclusion in Bankruptcy Code § 541(c)(2) did not apply. *See Patterson*,
504 U.S. at 762-63 (footnote omitted).

423. *See* 11 U.S.C. § 522(d)(10)(E). This federal exemption is available to
the debtor only if the state in which the debtor may claim exemptions has
not opted out of the federal exemptions. *See* 11 U.S.C. § 522(b)(1).
Currently, 15 states, the District of Columbia, Puerto Rico, and the
Virgin Islands allow access to the federal exemptions, and other states,
such as California, Iowa, and New York, have incorporated them as part
of their exemption laws.

424. *See Rousey*, 544 U.S. at 325.

425. *See id.* at 332-34.

426. *See id.* at 330-32.

427. After the Court decided *Rousey*, Congress passed the 2005
Amendments expanding the statutory protection of most kinds of
retirement accounts under federal and state exemptions, subject to a $1
million cap on IRAs that may be increased by the bankruptcy judge if the
interests of justice so require or with respect to certain rollover contribu-

The Court also has addressed a debtor's rights and obligations with respect to its pension plan. For example, as noted previously in the discussion of administrative law, the Court held in *PBGC v. LTV Corp.*[428] that the PBGC could use its anti-follow-on policy under the Administrative Procedure Act[429] to force the debtors to reinstate terminated ERISA defined benefit pension plans.[430] Also, in *Joint Industry Board of Electrical Industry v. United States*,[431] the Court held that an employer's liability for contributions to a multi-employer annuity plan established under a collective bargaining agreement was not entitled to priority under Bankruptcy Act § 64a(2).[432] Following its holding in *United States v. Embassy Restaurant, Inc.*,[433] the Court held that the annuity fund was not intended to relieve the distress of temporary unemployment which was the fundamental purpose of the priority for wages due to workmen under Bankruptcy Act § 64a(2).[434] The Court concluded that it was not inclined to overrule *Embassy Restaurant* and that the matter was more appropriately left to Congress.[435]

PROBATE LAW

It is a universal principle of United States bankruptcy law that the filing of a bankruptcy petition creates a bankruptcy estate comprised

---

tions. *See* 11 U.S.C. § 522(b)(3)(C), 522(d)(12), & 522(n) (Supp. 2005), as added by Pub. L. No. 109-8, § 224(a), (e), 119 Stat. 23, 62-65 (2005).

428.   496 U.S. 633 (1990).

429.   5 U.S.C. § 706 (1988).

430.   *See PBGC v. LTV, Corp.*, 496 U.S. at 656.

431.   391 U.S. 224 (1968).

432.   *See id.* at 226-28.

433.   359 U.S. 29 (1959).

434.   *See Joint Indus. Bd.*, 391 U.S. at 227-28.

435.   Congress embraced the Court's invitation and overruled *Embassy Restaurant* when it enacted § 507(a)(4) of the 1978 Bankruptcy Code, 11 U.S.C. § 507(a)(4). *See* H.R. REP. NO. 95-595, at 357 (1977).

of the debtor's property wherever located and by whomever held. This estate forms a legal *res* over which the bankruptcy court has exclusive jurisdiction.

But when an individual debtor dies, all of his or her property comprises a legal *res* known as a decedent's estate that is probated or processed under nonbankruptcy law, creating a potential conflict between the bankruptcy court and the probate court or the bankruptcy trustee and the executor over the decedent's property. The conflict can arise not only when a debtor dies, but when a debtor asserts a claim against property in a decedent's estate.

The Court has considered this potential conflict on three occasions over the past 111 years. In 1917 the Court considered a case in which the decedent left a trust to his son subject to the condition that the trust principal could be drawn only if the son became solvent and able to pay his debts from resources other than the trust fund.[436] The prodigal son filed a bankruptcy petition and received a discharge, after which the trust company instituted judicial proceedings resulting in an order giving the son the trust principal. The son's bankruptcy trustee, not a party to the distribution action, filed suit against the son and the trust company to recover the principal as an asset of the bankruptcy estate. Affirming the lower courts, the Court held that son could retain the principal. "Here the testator has merely prescribed the condition on which he will make a gift of the principal. . . . The Bankruptcy Act presents no obstacle to carrying out the testator's intention."[437]

In 1943 the Court considered whether a decedent-debtor's administrator had a right to file a bankruptcy petition or revive one that had been abated on the debtor's death.[438] The administrator wanted to reopen the bankruptcy to set aside a foreclosure on the debtor's real estate. Seeking to harmonize state and federal law, the Court held the administrator could file the petition only if state law

---

436. *See* Hull v. Farmers' Loan & Trust Co., 245 U.S. 312 (1917).

437. *Id.* at 314-15.

438. *See* Harris v. Zion Sav. Bank & Trust Co., 317 U.S. 447 (1943).

permitted him to do so. The Court based its decision on the principle that "[t]he probate court, not the bankruptcy court, is the appropriate forum for weighing the respective benefits or detriments to those who share in the equity of the decedent's estate."[439] This holding is part of a larger principle known as the probate exception to federal jurisdiction which holds that "matters of strict probate are not within the jurisdiction of courts of the United States" but within the realm of state courts.[440] The dissent interpreted the Bankruptcy Act to be preemptive, empowering a personal representative of the bankrupt to intervene without regard to state law. Nevertheless, the majority rule subordinates bankruptcy policies to more vital state law concerns.

Despite the Court's tendency to elevate pure probate law concerns over bankruptcy law and policy, in its 1946 non-bankruptcy decision *Markham v. Allen*,[441] the Court established an exception to this general rule, thereby permitting bankruptcy courts and other federal courts to resolve disputes among the parties that do not directly implicate property in probate. In *Markham*, the Court reaffirmed its previous holdings that although Congress never conferred *in rem* jurisdiction on the federal courts to probate wills or administer decedents' estates, when there is a statutory basis for exercising federal jurisdiction over disputes between parties, federal courts may adjudicate those disputes even if they concern probate assets or could be resolved in state probate courts.[442] Thus, after *Markham* one could surmise that if it

---

439.   *Id.* at 450.

440.   *See* Sutton v. English, 246 U.S. 199, 205 (1918).

441.   326 U.S. 490 (1946).

442.   *See id.* at 494 ("[I]t has been established by a long series of decisions of this Court that federal courts of equity have jurisdiction to entertain suits 'in favor of creditors, legatees and heirs' and other claimants against a decedent's estate 'to establish their claims' so long as the federal court does not interfere with the probate proceedings or assume general jurisdiction of the probate or control of the property in the custody of the state court. *Waterman v. Canal-Louisiana Bank Co.*, 215 U.S. 33, 43, and cases cited. *See* Sutton v. English, [246 U.S. 199], 205; United States v. Bank of New York Co., 296 U.S. 463, 477; Common-

were presented with the right set of facts, the Court might permit a bankruptcy court to adjudicate the rights of parties before the bankruptcy court when the bankruptcy court's judgment could have an indirect impact on the probate estate.[443] Sixty years would pass before the Court answered the question in the bankruptcy context.

In 2006 the Court considered in *Marshall v. Marshall*[444] whether a debtor could, in the bankruptcy court, bring a counterclaim against a decedent's son in tort for interfering with her prospects of receiving an intervivos gift.[445] The decedent's son filed a post-trial motion in the bankruptcy court to dismiss the counterclaim to his proof of claim for lack of jurisdiction, arguing that based on the probate exception to federal jurisdiction, the matter could only be tried in the probate court. Although the lower federal courts ruled in favor of the debtor, the Ninth Circuit reversed; the Ninth Circuit chose to adopt a broad expansion of the probate exception to strip the federal courts of jurisdiction over matters that ordinarily would be decided by the probate court, such as tortuous interference with the testator's intent. Without dissent, the Supreme Court reversed the Ninth Circuit and remanded the case, relying on the Court's *Markham* decision which circumscribes the exercise of federal jurisdiction from disturbing or affecting property in custody of the probate court.[446] The Court held that the probate exception did not implicate the suit in *Marshall* because the suit sought to establish *in personam* liability against the decedent's son rather than to assert any claim against the *res* in

---

wealth Trust Co. v. Bradford, 297 U.S. 613, 619; United States v. Klein, 303 U.S. 276; Princess Lida v. Thompson, 305 U.S. 456, 466.").

443. For example, based on *Markham v. Allen*, it is possible that the bankruptcy court could properly determine whether the debtor's estate or one of its creditor's holds title to a claim against the decedent's probate estate.

444. 547 U.S. 293 (2006).

445. *See id.* at 300-01.

446. In other words, the Court interpreted *Markham* as precluding a federal court from exercising jurisdiction over a *res* that is within the jurisdiction of the probate court.

probate. Thus, as it did in *Ankenbrandt v. Richards*,[447] when it narrowly construed the domestic relations law exception to federal jurisdiction, the Court in *Marshall* chose to limit the probate exception to preclude the exercise of federal jurisdiction only on matters directly within the jurisdiction of the specialized state forum.

REAL ESTATE LAW

The Court appears to resolve conflicts between bankruptcy law and real estate law by deferring to real estate law and policy unless clear and explicit statutory language or congressional intent requires a different result. In *Taylor v. Voss*,[448] the Court considered a deceased wife's entitlement to share in proceeds from the sale of real estate of her bankrupt husband, holding that "[i]n the absence of any conflicting provision in the Bankruptcy Act the question of a wife's interest in the bankrupt's property is governed by the local law."[449] Moreover, in *Security Mortgage Co. v. Powers*,[450] the Court followed the principle that when there is no overriding federal law, the construction of a mortgagee's entitlement to attorney's fees under a real property note and mortgage will be determined under nonbankruptcy law.[451] Fur-

---

447.   504 U.S. 689, 701-03 (1992) (non-bankruptcy case relying, inter alia, on dictum in Barber v. Barber, 62 U.S. (21 How.) 582, 584 (1859), to limit domestic relations law exception to exercise of federal jurisdiction to preclude federal courts only from granting or modifying a divorce, alimony, or child custody decree).

448.   271 U.S. 176 (1926).

449.   *See id.* at 190 (citing Stellwagen v. Clum, 245 U.S. 605 (1918) (dispute over white pine timber)).

450.   278 U.S. 149 (1928).

451.   *See id.* at 153-54 ("The validity of the lien claimed by the Mortgage Company for attorney's fees must be determined by the law of Georgia; for the contract was there made and was secured by real estate there situate. The construction of the contract for attorney's fees presents no obstacle to enforcing it in bankruptcy, either as a provable claim or by way of a lien upon specific property.") (citations omitted). Presumably, under the Bankruptcy Code, the Court would find that the clear and

thermore, in *Butner v. United States*,[452] the Court reaffirmed the well-known rule that bankruptcy courts will look to nonbankruptcy law to establish property entitlements[453] unless an overriding federal purpose provides a reason to change those entitlements.[454] In essence, the Court is loath to create an asymmetry between bankruptcy and nonbankruptcy property rights unless Congress has clearly forced the difference.

Evidently the Court has adopted a stringent test for finding clear language to the contrary. For example, in *BFP v. Resolution Trust Corp.*,[455] the Court refused to permit the trustee to use the constructive fraudulent conveyance avoiding powers of Bankruptcy Code § 548 to unwind a real property foreclosure sale, despite statutory language that had been applied by several lower courts to do so.[456] A majority of the Court refused to believe that Congress could have intended to upset over 400 years of mortgage foreclosure law by allowing bank-

---

explicit language of Bankruptcy Code § 506(b) requires the fees to be reasonable as a matter of federal law. *See In re* A.J. Lane & Co., 113 B.R. 821, 823-24 (Bankr. D. Mass. 1990). *Cf.* United States v. Ron Pair Enters., Inc., 489 U.S. 235 (1989) (interpreting Bankruptcy Code § 506(b)).

452.   440 U.S. 48 (1979).

453.   *See id.* at 54. ("Congress has generally left the determination of property rights in the assets of a bankrupt's estate to state law." (footnote omitted)).

454.   *See id.* at 55. ("Property interests are created and defined by state law. Unless some federal interest requires a different result, there is no reason why such interests should be analyzed differently simply because an interested party is involved in a bankruptcy proceeding."). *Cf.* Barry E. Adler, "The Questionable Axiom of *Butner v. United States*," BANKRUPTCY LAW STORIES 11, 18-20 (Robert K. Rasmussen, ed., Foundation Press 2007) (arguing that *Butner*'s rationale leaves nonconsensual creditors, such as tort claimants, in a subordinate position without their consent).

455.   511 U.S. 531 (1994). For a more complete discussion of *BFP*, *see supra* Ch. 1, pp. 31-33 and *infra* Chs. 3, 5 & 6, pp. 182, 191, 244, 354, 450.

456.   *See id.* at 536.

ruptcy judges to determine whether the value received at the sale constituted a reasonably equivalent value.[457]

In *Rake v. Wade*,[458] however, the Court implicitly found clear statutory language that would override state law to benefit the secured creditor. *Rake* considered whether the language of Bankruptcy Code §§ 506(b) and 1325(a)(5) entitled an oversecured mortgagee to receive payment of postpetition interest on arrearages cured under a plan even though neither state law nor the mortgage documents provided for it.[459] Following its decision in *United States v. Ron Pair Enterprises, Inc.*,[460] the Court held that the oversecured creditor would be entitled to accrue postpetition interest between the filing of the petition and confirmation of a plan, regardless of the provision in Bankruptcy Code § 1322(b)(2) that a plan may not modify a claim secured by a lien on only the debtor's principal residence.[461] The Court reached a similar conclusion with respect to the oversecured creditor's right to receive postconfirmation interest.[462] The opinion in *Rake* fails to mention *Butner* but instead focuses on statutory interpretation rather than analysis of the creditor's rights under non-bankruptcy law or the asymmetry between bankruptcy and non-bankruptcy law created by the Court's holding. Not surprisingly, in 1994 Congress amended the Bankruptcy Code to legislatively overrule the result in *Rake* by requiring the amount to cure a default to "be determined in accordance with the underlying agreement and applicable nonbankruptcy law."[463]

---

457. *See id.* at 542-43.

458. 508 U.S. 464 (1993).

459. *See id.* at 465.

460. 489 U.S. 235, 241 (1989).

461. *See Rake*, 508 U.S. at 471-72.

462. *See id.* at 474-75.

463. *See* § 305 of the Bankruptcy Reform Act of 1994, Pub. L. No. 103-394, 108 Stat. 4106, 4134 (Oct. 22, 1994) (adding Bankruptcy Code §§ 1123(d), 1222(d) & 1322(e), 11 U.S.C. §§ 1123(d), 1222(d) & 1322(e)

Some of the most significant cases involving bankruptcy law and real estate law concern the bankruptcy court's power or jurisdiction,[464] raise takings issues under the Fifth Amendment,[465] or involve application of adequate protection, lien stripping,[466] or cram down[467] of a lender's lien against real estate.[468] These cases are examined in

---

(2000); § 1123(d) failed to override § 1124(2), 11 U.S.C. § 1124(2) (2000), discussed *infra* n.2158).

464. *See, e.g.,* Emil v. Hanley, 318 U.S. 515 (1943) (no power to require non-bankruptcy receiver to account to bankruptcy court unless receivership is superseded); Van Huffel v. Harkelrode, 284 U.S. 225 (1931) (power to sell real estate free and clear of liens); Straton v. New, 283 U.S. 318 (1931) (lack of power to enjoin state court creditors' suit to marshal and enforce liens and sell real estate).

465. *See, e.g.,* Wright v. Vinton Branch of the Mountain Trust Bank, 300 U.S. 440 (1937); Louisville Joint Stock Land Bank v. Radford, 295 U.S. 555 (1935).

466. "Lien stripping" refers to a two step practice. First, the court bifurcates a partially secured creditor's claim into an allowed secured claim equal to the value of the creditor's interest in the collateral and an unsecured claim for the deficiency. Second, in an adversary proceeding or under a plan, the court strips the lien to secure only the allowed secured claim but not the deficiency.

467. "Cram down" involves confirming a plan over the dissent of a class of claims. This concept was first considered by the Supreme Court in Reconstruction Fin. Corp. v. Denver & R.G.W.R. Co., 328 U.S. 495, 531 (1946). It applies in modified form under the Bankruptcy Code. *See generally,* K. Klee, *All You Ever Wanted to Know About Cram Down Under the New Bankruptcy Code,* 53 AM. BANKR. L.J. 133-71 (1979). This topic is discussed more fully *infra* in Ch. 5, pp. 370-384, 392-396.

468. *See, e.g.,* Nobelman v. Am. Sav. Bank, 508 U.S. 324 (1993) (chapter 13 case prohibiting lien stripping of claim partially secured by lien on debtor's principal residence); Dewsnup v. Timm, 502 U.S. 410 (1992) (chapter 7 case holding that Bankruptcy Code § 506(d) could not be used to lien strip an undersecured creditor's lien for deficiency); Bank of Am. Nat'l Trust & Sav. Ass'n v. 203 N. LaSalle St. P'ship, 526 U.S. 434 (1999) (denying confirmation of a chapter 11 cramdown plan that exclusively gives former owners equity in reorganized company in exchange for new value); United Sav. Ass'n v. Timbers of Inwood Forest Assocs., 484 U.S. 365 (1988) (secured party's state law right to take possession of property on foreclosure is not entitled to adequate protection).

Chapters 3, 4, and 5 as part of a general analysis of constitutional, jurisdictional, and substantive law that applies beyond the limited context of real estate cases.

The Court has decided some cases, however, in which the real estate issues provide an interesting interface with bankruptcy law. For example, *Johnson v. Collier*[469] determined that until a trustee is elected, a bankrupt holds defeasible title to causes of action and may institute and maintain a lawsuit for the unlawful sale of his real property.[470] Moreover, *Johnson v. Home State Bank*[471] held that the functional equivalent of a nonrecourse mortgage[472] qualifies as a claim subject to treatment in a bankruptcy case because of the breadth of the definition of claim in Bankruptcy Code § 101 and the rule of construction in Bankruptcy Code § 102(2) that a "'claim against the debtor' includes [a] claim against property of the debtor."[473] The Court noted that the definition of "claim" under the 1978 Bankruptcy Code was derived from the definition under Chapter X of the Bankruptcy Act in which the nonrecourse mortgage was included as a claim.[474]

---

469.   222 U.S. 538 (1912).

470.   *See id.* at 539. Under Bankruptcy Code § 541(a)(1), 11 U.S.C. § 541(a)(1) (2000), the result would be different because the filing of a petition immediately vests title to all of the debtor's causes of action in the bankruptcy estate. *See* Bailey v. Household Fin. Corp. III (*In re Bailey*), 306 B.R. 391, 394 (Bankr. D.D.C. 2004). Unless the trustee (or debtor in possession) abandons the cause of action, the debtor cannot bring it during the pendency of the bankruptcy case.

471.   501 U.S. 78 (1991). *Johnson* is perhaps better known for its additional holding that a debtor who receives a chapter 7 discharge is not categorically prohibited from filing a sequential case under chapter 13. *See id.* at 87.

472.   A nonrecourse mortgage is one where the lender agrees to look only to the collateral for repayment of the debt; the debtor has no personal liability. In *Johnson*, the mortgage was recourse but the debtor had received a chapter 7 discharge before filing a new case under chapter 13. In the chapter 13 case, the mortgage functionally was nonrecourse, having been reduced to an *in rem* judgment lien against the property. *See id.* at 80, 86-87.

473.   *See id.* at 84-85.

474.   *See id.* at 85-86.

TAX LAW

Over the past 111 years, the Supreme Court has had ample opportunity to encounter the interface of bankruptcy law and federal, state, and local tax law in numerous contexts. About 10 percent of the Supreme Court cases involving bankruptcy or insolvency law involve a tax lien, claim, or priority in some respect.[475] Although it is difficult to generalize principles from a data set this large, one is able to conclude that the Court resolves most of these issues on the basis of statutory construction rather than tax or bankruptcy policy. For purposes of discussion, the cases are grouped into six categories: (1) tax refunds or withholdings as property of the estate; (2) adjudication of the trustee's duty to file tax returns or pay taxes; (3) determination of tax claims; (4) determination of tax priorities; (5) dischargeability of tax claims; and (6) disposition of tax liens.

TAX REFUNDS OR WITHHOLDINGS AS PROPERTY OF THE ESTATE

On at least two occasions during the past 111 years, the Court has examined whether a debtor's tax refunds or withheld taxes constitute property of the estate. In *Segal v. Rochelle*,[476] the Court held that federal income tax refunds received by the debtors' postpetition are sufficiently rooted in the prebankruptcy past and so little entangled with the debtors' ability to make a fresh start that they should be regarded as property of the estate.[477] Because the Bankruptcy Act vested title to all of a debtor's transferable property in the trustee, the Court interpreted the term "property" broadly to include contingent property interests such as tax loss-carrybacks.[478] Thus, the refund

---

475. Of 570 cases in the Supreme Court database, 58 mention taxes in some manner.

476. 382 U.S. 375 (1966).

477. *See id.* at 380.

478. *See id.* at 379.

deriving from application of the tax loss-carryback represents proceeds of property of the estate and is not property of the debtor.

In *Begier v. I.R.S,*[479] the debtor paid federal income tax and FICA tax withholding installments and excise tax payments to the Internal Revenue Service out of a special tax account and also out of its general operating account.[480] The debtor's bankruptcy trustee sued the IRS to avoid the payments as preferential transfers.[481] The Court held that trust-fund taxes the debtor is required to withhold are not property of the debtor when paid to the Internal Revenue Service.[482] The holding applies to payments out of the debtor's special tax account as well as to payments out of the general operating account. Essentially, the trustee could not avoid these payments as preferential transfers because the money paid was not a transfer of property of the debtor. The bankruptcy court had reasoned that funds paid out of the debtor's special tax account are held in trust for the taxing authorities, because the tax trust is established and the funds are traceable.[483] As such, the bankruptcy court held that these monies are property in which the debtor had no equitable interest and, had they not been remitted to the IRS, would have been excluded from property of the estate under Bankruptcy Code § 541(d).[484] The Court held, however, that whether the funds were segregated in a separate account is irrelevant; instead, funds paid out of the debtor's general operating account are implicitly held in trust for the IRS the moment the debtor collects the excise taxes from its customers or withholds payroll taxes,

---

479. 496 U.S. 53 (1990).

480. *See id.* at 56.

481. *See id.* at 57.

482. *See id.* at 55, 61-62, 67.

483. *See id.* at 57.

484. *See id.* at 58. ("[P]roperty of the debtor subject to the preferential transfer provision is best understood as that property that would have been part of the estate had it not been transferred before the commencement of bankruptcy proceedings.") (internal quotation marks omitted).

which occurs simultaneously with the debtor's payment of wages to its employees.[485]

The Court's holdings in *Segal* and *Begier* can be reconciled based on principles of statutory interpretation. In *Segal*, the Court broadly interpreted the Bankruptcy Act to resolve a dispute between a debtor and the trustee. Similarly, in ruling for the government and against the trustee in *Begier*, the Court broadly interpreted both the trust fund provisions of the Internal Revenue Code and the Bankruptcy Code's no-equitable-interest exclusion from property of the estate.[486]

ADJUDICATION OF THE TRUSTEE'S DUTY TO FILE TAX RETURNS AND PAY TAXES

Periodically the Court has resolved disputes about the bankruptcy trustee's duty to file tax returns and pay taxes. In 1904 the Court decided in *Swarts v. Hammer*[487] that the trustee is obligated to pay state, school, and city taxes on the debtor's property. Although the filing of a petition under the Bankruptcy Act vests title to non-exempt property in the trustee, there is nothing that withdraws the property "from the necessity of protection by the State and municipality, or which should exempt it from its obligations to either [to pay taxes]."[488] The Court affirmed the Eighth Circuit's holding that, although the trustee is required to pay taxes, the trustee is not obligated to pay accrued penalties or fees provided by nonbankruptcy law.[489] Thus, the Court maintained the symmetry between bankruptcy and nonbankruptcy law on the amount of the tax, but recognized implicitly that the

---

485. *See id.* at 61-62, 67.

486. Based on this limited universe of cases, one might tentatively conclude that in resolving bankruptcy tax matters, the Court will set a hierarchy, preferring the taxing authority over the trustee and the trustee over the debtor.

487. 194 U.S. 441 (1904).

488. *See id.* at 444.

489. *See id.*

government would have to bear the cost of delay in bankruptcy administration the same as any other unsecured creditor.[490]

In a highly specialized opinion, *Reinecke v. Gardner*,[491] the Court performed a statutory interpretation of the War Revenue Act of 1917 and held that a trustee carrying on the business of a bankrupt corporation was not subject to the excess profits tax to which the debtor would have been subjected had it continued to operate the business. The statute only imposed the tax on corporations, not on trustees or other fiduciaries. As a matter of tax policy, the Court disfavors extension of a tax by implication to persons not mentioned in the statute.[492]

Not surprisingly, Congress responded legislatively to impose the postpetition tax obligations of a business debtor on an operating bankruptcy trustee. As a general proposition, section 960 of the Judicial Code[493] imposes on a trustee or other court officer who conducts any business all of the federal, state, and local taxes applicable to that business as if the business were conducted by an individual or corporation. Regarding federal income taxes, section 6012(b)(3) of the Internal Revenue Code requires the trustee of a corporation in a bankruptcy case to file a corporate income tax return in the same manner and form as the corporation.[494] The Internal Revenue Code imposes a

---

490.   The Court echoed this theme years later with respect to suspension of the accrual of interest on taxes incurred during a Chapter XI case following its supersession by a liquidating bankruptcy case. *See* Nicholas v. United States, 384 U.S. 678, 689 (1966) ("creditors of a bankruptcy estate should not be disadvantaged solely by means of the law's delay [; therefore, we confine] the accrual of interest on Chapter XI obligations to the arrangement proceeding itself . . . .").

491.   277 U.S. 239 (1928).

492.   *But see* Nicholas v. United States, 384 U.S. 678, 693 (1966) ("[T]here can be no question that . . . the trustee [in a liquidating bankruptcy case] was under an obligation to file returns for these taxes, even though the taxes themselves were incurred by the debtor in possession during the pendency of the [chapter XI] arrangement proceeding.").

493.   28 U.S.C. § 960 (2000).

494.   26 U.S.C. § 6012(b)(3) (2000).

similar obligation on the chapter 7 or chapter 11 estate of an individual debtor.[495]

Nothing in the Internal Revenue Code,[496] however, explicitly addresses the trustee's obligation to file tax returns or pay taxes for a liquidating trust set up under a confirmed chapter 11 plan. In *Holywell Corp. v. Smith*,[497] the Court held that since the liquidating trustee is an assignee of the corporate debtors, the trustee has the duties to pay taxes and file a corporate income tax return in the same manner and form as the corporations are required to file. Moreover, since the trustee is also the fiduciary of a trust of an individual debtor, the Internal Revenue Code expressly requires the trustee to file an income tax return on behalf of one of the individual debtors.[498]

DETERMINATION OF TAX CLAIMS

On several occasions, the Court has addressed the power of a bankruptcy judge to determine tax claims.[499] These cases frequently implicate doctrines of jurisdiction,[500] and res judicata, and federalism,

---

495. 26 U.S.C. § 6012(a)(9) (2000).

496. It is possible that § 6012(a)(4) of the Internal Revenue Code applies since the statute covers "any trust." *See* 26 U.S.C. § 6012(a)(4) (2000).

497. 503 U.S. 47 (1992).

498. *See* Internal Revenue Code § 1398(c)(1), 26 U.S.C. § 1398(c)(1) (2000).

499. *See, e.g.,* Gardner v. New Jersey, 329 U.S. 565, 572, 580 (1947) (reorganization court may exercise jurisdiction over and constitutionally determine proof and allowance of state tax claims); Arkansas Corp. Comm'n v. Thompson, 313 U.S. 132, 138-39 (1941) (Bankruptcy Act § 64a does not give the bankruptcy court the power to redetermine the value of property that was subject to a previous quasi-judicial property tax assessment); New Jersey v. Anderson, 203 U.S. 483, 491-92 (1906) (bankruptcy court had the power to determine the amount or legality of tax claims).

500. *See, e.g.,* Phelps v. United States, 421 U.S. 330 (1975) (when IRS has levied on assets before bankruptcy, bankruptcy court lacks summary jurisdiction to adjudicate controversy over proceeds of the assets without the IRS' consent); Gardner v. New Jersey, 329 U.S. 565, 572-73 (1947) (reorganization court has jurisdiction to determine proof and allowance

but also deal with substantive issues such as interest,[501] penalties,[502] and the like.

As a general proposition, the bankruptcy judge has the power to determine all claims against the *res* that comprises the bankruptcy estate. This includes the power to set a bar date applicable to federal, state, and local tax claims.[503] "The federal government possesses supreme power in respect of bankruptcies. . . . If a state desires to participate in the assets of a bankrupt, she must submit to appropriate requirements by the controlling power; otherwise, orderly and expeditious proceedings would be impossible and a fundamental

---

of state tax claims and jurisdiction over property subject to state tax liens).

501. *See, e.g.,* Nicholas v. United States, 384 U.S. 678, 689-90 (1966) (liquidating trustee not liable for interest on taxes accrued during superseded Ch. XI arrangement); Bruning v. United States, 376 U.S. 358, 360 (1964) (debtor remains liable for postpetition interest on nondischargeable tax debt); City of New York v. Saper, 336 U.S. 328, 341 (1949) (unsecured tax claims subject to the general rule that interest stops accruing at the date of bankruptcy); United States v. Childs, 266 U.S. 304, 307-08 (1924) (discussing the difference in treatment of interest and penalties on tax claims under Bankruptcy Act § 57j: "a penalty is a means of punishment; interest is a means of compensation.").

502. *See, e.g.,* Nicholas v. United States, 384 U.S. 678 (1966) (holding a liquidating trustee liable for tax penalties); Simonson v. Granquist, 369 U.S. 38, 40 (1962) (holding that Bankruptcy Act § 57j requires the disallowance of all non-pecuniary loss penalties, even those that are secured by a valid tax lien); Meilink v. Unemployment Comm'n, 314 U.S. 564, 568-69 (1942) (holding that tax interest is not a penalty); Boteler v. Ingels, 308 U.S. 57, 60 (1939) (holding that Bankruptcy Act § 57j only disallows tax penalties incurred by the debtor, not those tax penalties incurred by a trustee or receiver); United States v. Childs, 266 U.S. 304, 309-10 (1924) (Court distinguishes tax interest from tax penalty).

503. *See* New York v. Irving Trust Co., 288 U.S. 329, 331-32 (1933). Bankruptcy Code § 502(b)(9) provides statutory minimum time periods for a governmental unit to file a proof of claim for a prepetition tax and § 503(b)(1)(D) eliminates the requirement to file a request for payment of tax entitled to priority as an administrative expense. *See* 11 U.S.C. §§ 502(b)(9), 503(b)(1)(D) (2000).

purpose of the Bankruptcy Act would be frustrated."[504] The bankruptcy court also has the power to determine whether a bankruptcy sale of assets is subject to state stamp taxes when the sale is made before confirmation of a reorganization plan.[505]

In litigating the merits of the tax claim, the risk of non-persuasion is part of the substance of the claim.[506] Normally, in a bankruptcy case, although the filing of a proof of claim is *prima facie* evidence of its validity and amount,[507] the risk of non-persuasion is on the claimant. In resolving a dispute over a state tax claim, however, the Court has held that absent some modification expressed in the Bankruptcy Code, the state's allocation of the burden of proof on the taxpayer will control in bankruptcy to place the risk of non-persuasion on the trustee or other party opposing the tax claim.[508]

DETERMINATION OF TAX PRIORITIES

Several of the Court's bankruptcy tax cases determine the priority of the taxing authority's claim. Of course, to be entitled to priority as a tax claim, the debt must be for taxes rather than a non-tax debt. Thus, in *New Jersey v. Anderson*,[509] the Court found that the exaction in question was a tax because it matched the following tax characteristic: "a tax is a pecuniary burden laid upon individuals or property for the purpose of supporting the Government."[510] Over the decades, in

---

504. *See* New York v. Irving Trust Co., 288 U.S. 329, 333 (1933) (citation omitted).

505. *See* Fla. Dep't of Revenue v. Piccadilly Cafeterias, Inc., 553 U.S. ___, 128 S. Ct. 2326, 2336-37 (2008), discussed more fully *infra* at p. 190, n.963.

506. *See* Raleigh v. Ill. Dep't of Revenue, 530 U.S. 15, 20-21 (2000) ("Given its importance to the outcome of cases, we have long held the burden of proof to be a 'substantive' aspect of a claim.").

507. *See* Fed. R. Bankr. P. 3002(f).

508. *See Raleigh*, 530 U.S. at 26.

509. 203 U.S. 483 (1906).

510. *See id.* at 492.

deciding whether exactions were entitled to priority as tax claims under Bankruptcy Act § 64a, the Court used the *Anderson* definition to characterize debts under federal or state statutes.[511] In *City of New York v. Feiring*,[512] the Court applied the *Anderson* test and held that a city duty on sales that could be collected from either the buyer or the seller of personal property is a tax entitled to priority in the bankruptcy case of a seller who failed to collect the tax.[513] Analyzing Bankruptcy Act § 64a irrespective of any label adopted by state law or statutes,[514] the Court concluded that the duty in question was "laid upon the bankrupt seller for the support of government, and without his consent . . . ."[515] The Court refined its definition of what constitutes a "tax" in cases under the Bankruptcy Code when it decided *United States v. Reorganized CF&I Fabricators of Utah, Inc.*,[516] in which it characterized the exaction of 10% on certain pension funding deficiencies as a penalty rather than a tax. The Court reasoned that "a tax was an enforced contribution to provide for the support of government; a penalty, as the word was here used, was an exaction imposed by statute as punishment for an unlawful act."[517]

Not every claim for a tax debt is entitled to priority. Specifically, among other things, in order to be eligible for priority treatment, the tax must be owed by the debtor or the estate and not only by some third party to whom the debtor is contractually liable. Section 960(a)

---

511. *See* United States v. New York, 315 U.S. 510, 512 n.2 (1942) (considering whether exactions under two federal statutes were taxes entitled to priority under Bankruptcy Act § 64a); City of New York v. Feiring, 313 U.S. 283, 285 (1941) (considering whether a New York sales tax was a "tax" entitled to priority under Bankruptcy Act § 64a); New York v. Jersawit, 263 U.S. 493, 495-96 (1924) (considering whether New York franchise tax due in advance was subject to proration and whether penalty interest was a tax).

512. 313 U.S. 283 (1941).

513. *See id.* at 287-88.

514. *See id.* at 285.

515. *See id.* at 287.

516. 518 U.S. 213 (1996).

517. *See id.* at 224 (citation omitted).

of the Judicial Code[518] and its predecessor statutes[519] obligate trustees and debtors in possession conducting a business to pay applicable federal, state, and local taxes. The obligation to pay taxes arises, however, only with respect to taxes imposed on conducting businesses of the debtor as opposed to taxes imposed on businesses of third parties. For example, in *Palmer v. Webster & Atlas National Bank*,[520] the Court held that when the obligation to pay taxes is not imposed directly on the debtor, but on a company whose property is leased or operated by the debtor, the trustee should not use the estate's assets to make priority payments on the tax obligations of another company.[521] The Court reached a similar conclusion in *Philadelphia Co. v. Dipple*,[522] when it considered whether taxes incurred by non-debtor property owners would be entitled to priority as taxes against a debtor operating company that leased and operated street railway companies;[523] the Court held that the obligations to pay taxes were contractual only and not entitled to be paid in priority to other unsecured claims.[524] When an innocent third party has paid tax obligations, before enactment of the 1978 Bankruptcy Code the bank-

---

518.   28 U.S.C. § 960(a) (Supp. 2005) (as amended by Pub. L. No. 109-8, § 712(a), 119 Stat. 23, 127 (2005)) ("Any officers and agents conducting any business under authority of a United States court shall be subject to all Federal, State and local taxes applicable to such business to the same extent as if it were conducted by an individual or corporation.").

519.   *See, e.g.*, Act of Mar. 3, 1887, ch. 373, § 2, 24 Stat. 552, 554; Act of Mar. 3, 1911, ch. 231, § 65, 36 Stat. 1104; 28 U.S.C. § 124 (1940) (forerunners of 28 U.S.C. § 960(a) (Supp. 2005)) (as amended by Pub. L. No. 109-8, § 712(a), 119 Stat. 23, 127 (2005)) that the Court analyzed with respect to tax obligations in *Palmer* and *Dipple*.

520.   312 U.S. 156 (1941).

521.   *See id.* at 167. Of course, the trustee could use estate assets to pay such tax obligations as general unsecured claims.

522.   312 U.S. 168, 174 (1941).

523.   *See id.* at 169-70.

524.   *See id.* at 174-75. The Court noted that the predecessor statute to 28 U.S.C. § 960 that requires an operating trustee to pay taxes was not applicable because the trustees were "not operating the business of the various underlying companies."

ruptcy court could use its equitable powers to subrogate the third party to the tax priority.[525] Bankruptcy Code § 507(d), however, prohibits a person subrogated to the rights of a tax creditor from being subrogated to the tax priority.[526] Nevertheless, a party taking an assignment of the claim may gain priority that way.[527] Thus, courts will recognize priority status for priority tax claims assigned by contract or statute but not by subrogation.

Once the taxing authority establishes that it holds a tax claim against the debtor or estate entitled to priority under Bankruptcy Act § 64a or Bankruptcy Code § 507(a), the bankruptcy court must determine the extent of the tax priority. Early on, the Court held that tax claims entitled to priority in bankruptcy had priority over unsecured claims but not over valid liens unless non-bankruptcy law so provides.[528] Sometimes the Court is required to resolve where tax claims rank within the range of all priority claims. In *Otte v. United*

---

525. *See* Dayton v. Stanard, 241 U.S. 588, 590 (1916).

526. *See* 11 U.S.C. § 507(d) (2000). *See also, e.g., In re* Beverages Int'l, Ltd., 96 B.R. 407 (Bankr. D. Mass.), *aff'd*, 105 B.R. 145 (D. Mass. 1989) (a surety which paid to the state the state's excise tax was subrogated to the claim with respect to the amount paid, but not to the state's tax priority status); *In re* Henzler Mfg. Corp., 89 B.R. 655 (Bankr. N.D. Ohio 1988) (individual officers not subrogated to tax priority based on § 507(d); IRS contended that § 6672 liability is a separate tax liability, so no subrogation); *In re* Tentex Marine, Inc., 83 B.R. 530 (Bankr. W.D. Tenn. 1988) (officers were allowed subrogation to amount of trust fund taxes paid by them, but § 507(d) precluded subrogation to priority).

527. *See* Wilson v. Brooks (*In re* Missionary Baptist Found. of Am., Inc.), 661 F.2d 1244, 1244-46 (5th Cir. 1982). *Cf.* Shropshire, Woodliff & Co. v. Bush, 204 U.S. 186, 189 (1907) (allowing assignee of priority wage claim to assert wage priority).

528. *See* City of Richmond v. Bird, 249 U.S. 174, 177 (1919) (holding that Bankruptcy Act § 64a does not give taxing authority priority over property encumbered by bona fide liens to which the tax would be inferior under nonbankruptcy law). Before 1926, tax claims also had priority over administrative expenses. *See* United States v. Randall, 401 U.S. 513, 516 nn.2-3 (1971); Dayton v. Stanard, 241 U.S. 588, 590 (1916).

States,[529] for example, the Court determined that withholding taxes due on the trustee's postpetition payment of prepetition priority wage claims were entitled to be treated ratably with the wage priority of which they were a part rather than granted first priority as an administrative expense or fourth priority as a prepetition tax claim.[530]

The Court confronted a more difficult question in *United States v. New York*,[531] when it not only had to decide the priority of federal social security and excise tax claims and penalties but also had to resolve a distributive issue when the estate lacked sufficient funds to pay interdependent state unemployment taxes; the Court opted for an algebraic solution that had the "incongruous" result of paying the United States more on its excise tax claim than it would have received in the event the funds were sufficient to pay all priority claims in full.[532]

The Court also has confronted the extent of the tax priority in partner and partnership bankruptcy cases. For example, in *United States v. Kaufman*,[533] the Court held that the jingle rule[534] applied to

---

529.   419 U.S. 43 (1974).

530.   *See id.* at 56-58.

531.   315 U.S. 510 (1942).

532.   *See id.* at 518-20.

533.   267 U.S. 408 (1925).

534.   "The rule of distribution . . . may be made to run like some jingle, 'firm estate to firm creditors, separate estate to separate creditors, anything left over from either goes to the other.'" *See* Note, *The Separate Estates of Non-Bankrupt Partners in the Bankruptcy of a Partnership under the Bankruptcy Act of 1898*, 20 HARV. L. REV. 589, 591-92 (1907). Thus, under the jingle rule, claims of partnership creditors are satisfied first from partnership assets and secondly from partners assets and claims of partner creditors are satisfied first from partner's assets and secondly from partnership assets. The "jingle rule" was set forth in Bankruptcy Act § 5g and was included in Uniform Partnership Act § 40 so that state partnership law would correspond to the Bankruptcy Act. *See In re* Safren, 65 B.R. 566, 573 (Bankr. C.D. Cal. 1986). By contrast, Bankruptcy Code § 723(c) entitles the trustee of a bankrupt partnership to share in the estate of a bankrupt partner on the same general basis as any other creditor of the partner. *See In re* El Paso Ref., Inc., 192 B.R.

priority tax claims; i.e., because the United States only had a priority tax claim against the partners, the priority only extended to the partners' share in any surplus of partnership property after partnership creditors were paid.[535]

Finally, the Court has considered the relative priority of multiple tax claims within the context of a chapter 11 reorganization plan. In *United States v. Energy Resources Co.*,[536] the Court held "that a bankruptcy court has the authority to order the Internal Revenue Service" to allocate payments made under a confirmed chapter 11 plan of reorganization first to trust fund taxes and second to other tax claims "where the bankruptcy court determines that this designation is necessary for the success of a reorganization plan."[537] Thus, when necessary for the success of the plan under which tax liabilities of equal priority are paid over time, the plan proponent may draft a plan that directs the taxing authority to apply the payments to specific tax liabilities in a particular order.

The Court has defended the bankruptcy priority structure against efforts by bankruptcy courts' efforts to use equitable power to alter the structure. In *United States v. Noland*,[538] the Court held that bankruptcy judges could not use the power of equitable subordination under Bankruptcy Code § 510(c) to categorically subordinate a tax penalty claim in direct contradiction to the priority ordering estab-

---

144, 147 (Bankr. W.D. Tex. 1996) ("[s]ection 723(c) was drafted in order to overrule the inequities of the 'jingle rule.' . . . Congress drafted § 723 to provide that when a partner enters bankruptcy the unsatisfied partnership's creditors share in the partner's estate at the same level as the partner's own creditor's [sic]").

535. *See Kaufman*, 267 U.S. at 412-13.

536. 495 U.S. 545 (1990).

537. *See id.* at 546, 549.

538. 517 U.S. 535 (1996).

lished by Congress.[539] Thus, the Court accorded the postpetition, non-compensatory tax penalty first priority as an administrative expense.[540] The Court reached a similar conclusion in *United States v. Reorganized CF&I Fabricators of Utah, Inc.*,[541] when it refused to allow the bankruptcy court to use Bankruptcy Code § 510(c) to categorically subordinate a non-priority tax penalty to other general unsecured claims.[542] Therefore, the principle in *Noland* applies not only to preclude categorical reordering of priority tax claims but also to prevent reordering of claims within a class.[543]

Occasionally, the Court has resolved the issue of tax priority in a bankruptcy case by referring to a non-bankruptcy statute. In *United States v. Key*,[544] the Court held that Revised Statute § 3466's requirement that, when the debtor is insolvent, the debts owing to the United States must be first paid,[545] was not inconsistent with the provisions of section 199 of Chapter X of the Bankruptcy Act requiring a tax claim to be paid in full under a reorganization plan.[546] The Court harmonized the statutes by requiring the insolvent Chapter X debtor to pay

---

539. *See id.* at 536 ("We hold that the bankruptcy court may not equitably subordinate claims on a categorical basis in derogation of Congress's scheme of priorities.").

540. *See id.* at 543.

541. 518 U.S. 213 (1996).

542. *See id.* at 229 ("[T]he categorical reordering of priorities that takes place at the legislative level of consideration is beyond the scope of judicial authority to order equitable subordination under § 510(c).").

543. *See id.* at 229 ("[T]he principle of *Noland* has nothing to do with transfers between classes, as distinct from ranking within one of them.").

544. 397 U.S. 322 (1970).

545. Since 1797, until its Amendment by the Bankruptcy Reform Act in 1978, Rev. Stat. § 3466 provided in pertinent part that "whenever any person indebted to the United States is insolvent . . . the debts due to the United States shall be first satisfied." *See* Act of March 3, 1797, § 5, 1 Stat. 515, as amended by Act of Mar. 2, 1799, § 65, 1 Stat. 676; 31 U.S.C. § 191 (1968). Currently, Rev. Stat. § 3466 is codified at 31 U.S.C. § 3713 (2000) and does not apply in cases under title 11.

546. *See Key*, 397 U.S. at 328-29, 332-33.

the debts owing to the United States before any other debts but permitting the solvent Chapter X debtor to confirm a plan that pays the debts in full under the plan.[547]

The Internal Revenue Service has used provisions of the Internal Revenue Code to assert priority in bankruptcy cases with mixed results. In *United States v. Randall*,[548] the debtor in possession was supposed to maintain a separate tax account for withholding taxes but failed to do so. Following the debtor's adjudication as a bankrupt, the IRS argued that the withholding taxes that the debtor was supposed to hold in trust under section 7501(a) of the Internal Revenue Code[549] were held in trust for the IRS and were not part of the bankruptcy estate.[550] The Court, in a 5-4 opinion, did not resolve the trust issue but held that Bankruptcy Act § 64a is "an overriding statement of federal policy on this question of priorities" and that obligations for with-holding taxes are subordinate to the payment of administrative expenses.

The Internal Revenue Service turned the *Randall* result around in *Begier v. I.R.S.*,[551] when it successfully used Bankruptcy Code § 541(d) to resist a preference attack by persuading the Court that general funds paid by the debtor to the IRS are not property of the debtor but are held in trust under section 7501 of the Internal Revenue Code.[552] By excluding property from property of the estate, the Internal Revenue Service asserts a form of priority, but it must be able to trace the payments to section 7501 trust property in order to do so.[553] The *Begier*

---

547.   *See id.* at 328-29 (defining solvency in the bankruptcy or balance sheet sense as opposed to the equity sense and citing United States v. Oklahoma, 261 U.S. 253, 260-61 (1923)).

548.   401 U.S. 513 (1971).

549.   26 U.S.C. § 7501(a) (2000).

550.   *See Randall*, 401 U.S. at 515.

551.   496 U.S. 53 (1990).

552.   *See id.* at 55, 67.

553.   *See* United States v. Whiting Pools, Inc., 462 U.S. 198, 205 n.10 (1983).

holding, that any voluntary prepetition payment of trust-fund taxes satisfies the tracing rules, is very generous to the IRS.[554]

DETERMINATION OF DISCHARGEABILITY OF TAX CLAIMS

Tax claimants have aggressively litigated to make nondischargeable all tax obligations owed to them including interest and penalties. In deciding these cases, the Court has retreated from its general rule that exceptions to discharge are to be narrowly construed[555] and instead ruled broadly to prevent the discharge of tax debts and accompanying interest and penalties. In *Bruning v. United States*,[556] the Court permitted the IRS to apply tax credits to postpetition interest on FICA and withholding taxes; although the estate did not owe postpetition interest on these taxes,[557] the debtor remained liable for the tax debt and the Court decided that interest was an integral part of the nondischargeable tax debt.[558] The Court reasoned that Congress intended that personal liability for interest on the tax also be nondischargeable.[559]

---

554. *See Begier*, 496 U.S. at 67.

555. *Compare, e.g.*, Gleason v. Thaw, 236 U.S. 558, 562 (1915) ("In view of the well-known purposes of the Bankrupt Law exceptions to the operation of a discharge thereunder should be confined to those plainly expressed . . . .") *with, e.g.*, Bruning v. United States, 376 U.S. 358, 361 (1964) (Bankruptcy Act "§ 17 is not a compassionate section for debtors. Rather it demonstrates congressional judgment that certain problems— *e.g.*, those of financing government—override the value of giving the debtor a wholly fresh start.") (footnote omitted).

556. 376 U.S. 358 (1964).

557. *See* New York v. Saper, 336 U.S. 328, 330-32 (1949) (applying rule of Sexton v. Dreyfus, 219 U.S. 339, 344 (1911) to stop interest on unsecured tax claims as of the date of the filing of the bankruptcy petition).

558. *See Bruning*, 376 U.S. at 360.

559. *See id.* at 361 ("Congress clearly intended that personal liability for unpaid tax debts survive bankruptcy. The general humanitarian purpose of the Bankruptcy Act provides no reason to believe that Congress has a different intention with regard to the personal liability for interest on such debts.").

Similarly, in *United States v. Sotelo*,[560] the Court held in a 5-4 opinion that a responsible party's 100% penalty for the corporation's failure to pay withholding taxes is a nondischargeable tax debt rather than a dischargeable penalty.[561] The Court based its holding on "the most natural reading of statutory language" as well as the legislative history.[562] That the Internal Revenue Code labeled the amount owing a "penalty" was not dispositive because the funds due were "unquestionably 'taxes'" at the time they were "collected or withheld from others" and the responsible officer failed to pay them over.[563] In dissent, Justice Rehnquist noted that the normal reading of the statute would only apply to preclude discharge of taxes owed by the bankrupt within the three years preceding bankruptcy and he would "want far clearer language than can be found in this statute to reach the conclusion that this liability is not dischargeable" in the bankruptcy case of a third party.[564] Moreover, Justice Rehnquist would have narrowly construed any exception to the general discharge provisions of the Bankruptcy Act in order to preserve the Court's longstanding tradition of reading the Bankruptcy Act to rehabilitate bankrupts.[565] Nevertheless, Justice Marshall, writing for the majority, found that the Court could not rely on policy factors or sympathy to override the specific policy judgments made by Congress in enacting the Bankruptcy legislation.[566]

The Court had another occasion to consider the nondischargeability of tax claims in *Young v. United States*,[567] when it decided that

---

560. 436 U.S. 268 (1978).

561. *See id.* at 274.

562. *See id.* at 275-77.

563. *See id.* at 275.

564. *See id.* at 283-84 (Rehnquist, J., dissenting).

565. *See id.* at 285-86 (Rehnquist, J., dissenting) (citing Gleason v. Thaw, 236 U.S. 558, 562 (1915)).

566. *See Sotelo*, 436 U.S. at 279-80.

567. 535 U.S. 43 (2002).

the three-year lookback period[568] for priority income tax claims was tolled during the pendency of the debtors' previous joint chapter 13 case.[569] Writing for the Court, Justice Scalia never referred to maxims requiring the Court to adhere to the plain language of the statute, which instead he characterized as a "loophole" that the debtors tried to use to their advantage.[570] Instead of ruling for the debtors and requiring Congress to amend the Bankruptcy Code to close the loophole, the Court characterized the lookback period for priority and nondischargeable income taxes as a limitations period rather than a substantive component of the Bankruptcy Code.[571] This characterization enabled the Court to invoke the "hornbook law" that limitations periods, such as the lookback period, are subject to traditional principles of equitable tolling unless tolling would be inconsistent with the text of the statute.[572] Despite the fact that the Bankruptcy Code specifically references tolling in other sections, the Court concluded that these references supplement rather than displace principles of equitable tolling of which Congress could be presumed to be aware in writing the Bankruptcy Code.[573] Reaching a result that is sound as a matter of policy and questionable as a matter of statutory interpreta-

---

568. Under Bankruptcy Code § 523(a)(1)(A) certain tax debts of individual debtors are nondischargeable if they are entitled to priority under § 507(a)(8), a provision that applies to claims for income taxes for a taxable year for which the return was required to be filed "after three years before the date of the filing of the petition . . . ." *See* 11 U.S.C. §§ 523(a)(1)(A) & 507(a)(8)(A)(i) (2000).

569. *See Young*, 535 U.S. at 53.

570. *See id.* at 46-47.

571. *See id.* at 47-48.

572. *See id.* at 47, 49. Without analyzing the 1984 amendment that repealed the statutory designation of bankruptcy courts as courts of equity, Bankruptcy Amendments and Federal Judgeship Act of 1984, Pub. L. No. 353, 98 Stat. 333 (1984), the Court notes in passing that bankruptcy courts are courts of equity. *See id.* at 50. The Court also fails to analyze whether "equitable tolling" remains within the equity power of the bankruptcy court. *See infra* Ch. 4 pp. 223-229.

573. *See id.* at 53.

tion, the Court refused to permit the debtors to file sequential bankruptcies[574] in a way that would prevent the IRS from protecting the nondischargeability of its tax claim.

DISPOSITION OF TAX LIENS

Sometimes the government's prepetition tax claim is secured by a tax lien.[575] If the lien encumbers property of the estate, then the taxing authority holds a secured claim in the bankruptcy case unless the lien is avoided[576] or junior to a prior choate[577] lien that subsumes the value of the property. The lien attaches only to the debtor's interest in property as determined by applicable nonbankruptcy law, not to property

---

574. In Johnson v. Home State Bank, 501 U.S. 78 (1991), the Court found that the Bankruptcy Code specifically permitted serial bankruptcy filings that were filed in good faith. In *Young* the Court noted in dictum that whether the serial filing was done in good faith or to "run down the lookback period" would not alter the result in *Young*. See *Young*, 535 U.S. at 50.

575. *See, e.g.,* 26 U.S.C. §§ 6321 et seq. (2000) (federal tax lien).

576. United States v. Speers, 382 U.S. 266, 275 (1965) (holding that the trustee's strong arm power under Bankruptcy Act § 70c, read together with Internal Revenue Code § 6323, would defeat a federal tax lien that was unrecorded at the time of bankruptcy). The same result would pertain under Bankruptcy Code § 545(2), 11 U.S.C. § 545(2) (2000).

577. In order for a lien to prevail against a federal tax lien or the general priority of the United States under Rev. Stat. § 3466, 31 U.S.C. § 3713 (2000), the lien must be "choate," i.e. a perfected lien in specific property. *See, e.g.,* United States v. Texas, 314 U.S. 480, 488 (1941) (holding that a Texas gasoline tax lien was too general and inchoate to prevail over a claim of the United States under Rev. Stat. § 3466; the Court left open whether a perfected lien on property in possession of debtor would prevail over the government's claim under Rev. Stat. § 3466). The Court has not extended the requirement of choateness when the government is a voluntary creditor such as in a Small Business Administration or Federal Housing Administration loan. *See* United States v. Kimbell Foods, Inc., 440 U.S. 715, 740 (1979) (holding that "absent a congressional directive, the relative priority of private liens and consensual liens arising from these Government lending programs is to be determined under nondiscriminatory state laws").

that the debtor holds in trust or as agent for a third party. Thus, in *United States v. Durham Lumber Co.*,[578] the Court refused to permit the federal government's tax lien to attach to contract payments received by the debtor general contractor in which nondebtor subcontractors had superior rights under applicable state law.[579] Refusing to adopt a rule of federal property law in determining the scope of the debtor's interest in the contract payment,[580] the Court endorsed a rule of deference that adopts the decision of the Fourth Circuit construing state law "unless their conclusions are shown to be unreasonable."[581]

If the bankruptcy estate is in possession of property subject to the tax lien, the bankruptcy court has power to sell the property free and clear of encumbrances, including the tax lien, and the lien will attach to proceeds of sale.[582] Under the Bankruptcy Code, the bankruptcy court may exercise its power to authorize a sale of property free and clear of tax liens either during case administration[583] or under a chapter 11 plan.[584]

The Court also has considered cases in which the taxing authority is in possession of the debtor's property as of the time of the filing of the bankruptcy petition but has not yet conducted a tax sale. Under the Bankruptcy Act, if a tax lien claimant was in possession of personal property at the time of the filing of the petition, the tax claimant did not lose rights by turning the property over to a receiver or bankruptcy trustee; as noted by the Court in *Goggin v. Division of Labor Law Enforcement*,[585] the validity of the lien is determined as of

---

578. 363 U.S. 522 (1960).

579. *See id.* at 526.

580. *See id.* at 526 n.4.

581. *See id.* at 526-27 (citation omitted).

582. *See* Van Huffel v. Harkelrode, 284 U.S. 225, 227-28 (1931).

583. *See* 11 U.S.C. § 363(f) (2000).

584. *See* 11 U.S.C. § 1123(a)(5)(D) (2000).

585. 336 U.S. 118 (1949).

the time of bankruptcy and to rule otherwise would put the taxing authority in conflict with the trustee over turnover of property in which the bankruptcy estate might have equity.[586] Under the Bankruptcy Code, the result is similar; the Court held in *United States v. Whiting Pools, Inc.*,[587] that, until title to property passes out of the estate, as long as the taxing authority demands adequate protection of its interest in property as a condition of turnover, the taxing authority's rights are preserved.[588]

CONCLUSION

The Court does its best to avoid conflicts by harmonizing bankruptcy laws and other laws. When the Court cannot resolve a conflict, it generally appears to decide the conflict by ruling in favor of the more important policy. Thus, almost without regard to the language of the bankruptcy laws, the Court has protected family law claimants and laws protecting the public health and safety. In other areas, the Court appears to avoid any policy hierarchy, and instead resolves disputes based on the language of the statutes and legislative intent. Chapter 3 analyzes, inter alia, how the Court resolves conflicts between bankruptcy law and the Constitution.

---

586. *See id.* at 130-31.

587. 462 U.S. 198 (1983).

588. *See id.* at 211-12.

BANKRUPTCY AND CONSTITUTIONAL LAW: SOVEREIGN IMMUNITY, FEDERAL PREEMPTION, FEDERALISM, AND THE USE OF STATE LAW IN BANKRUPTCY

INTRODUCTION

Even before the Court confronts the problems of reconciling conflicting federal and state laws of the kind discussed in Chapter 2, it considers over-arching legal principles imbedded in the fabric of our Republic. The very nature of our constitutional system sometimes restricts the Court's ability to evaluate laws on the merits without first deciding a meta issue. Our Constitution gives Congress the power to write uniform laws on the subject of bankruptcies throughout the United States, but states have long promulgated their own insolvency statutes. The prospect for conflict between federal and state laws implicates principles of federalism as well as federal preemption. Moreover, the doctrine of sovereign immunity might limit the manner and extent to which Congress may validly authorize a bankruptcy trustee[589] to sue a federal or state government. Furthermore, the absence of a general federal property or secured transactions law sometimes requires the Court to address whether state law or federal

---

589. To the extent a federal bankruptcy trustee is held to act in the capacity of the United States in representing a federally-created bankruptcy estate, sovereign immunity would not limit this authority. "[N]othing in [the Eleventh Amendment] or any other provision of the Constitution prevents or has ever been seriously supposed to prevent a State's being sued by the United States." *See* United States v. Mississippi, 380 U.S. 128, 140 (1965).

law[590] provides the basis for the rule of decision in bankruptcy cases. The resolution of these issues has led to strong differences of opinion among the Justices both in a particular case and over time. The resulting case law, therefore, may be susceptible to change as the composition of the Court changes.

CONSTITUTIONAL LAW

The United States Constitution affects bankruptcy law[591] in at least three different ways. First, the Bankruptcy Clause and its uniformity requirement provide the source of power for Congress to legislate bankruptcy laws.[592] Second, the Court considers the extent to which

---

590. In 1938 *Erie v. Tompkins* overruled *Swift v. Tyson* and held that "[t]here is no federal general common law." *See* Erie R. Co. v. Tompkins, 304 U.S. 64, 78 (1938) (overruling Swift v. Tyson, 41 U.S. (16 Pet.) 1 (1842)). More recently, the Court has stated that "cases in which judicial creation of a special federal rule would be justified . . . are 'few and restricted,' limited to situations where there is a 'significant conflict between some federal policy or interest and the use of state law.'" *See* O'Melveny & Myers v. FDIC, 512 U.S. 79, 87 (1994) (citations omitted). Thus, if a bankruptcy court applies federal law, it must be within a properly enacted federal statute or within the court's inherent equity powers. *See infra* Ch. 4, pp. 221-229.

591. The Constitution also affects state insolvency laws. *See, e.g.,* Blake v. McClung, 176 U.S. 59, 63-65, 67 (1900) and Blake v. McClung, 172 U.S. 239, 253-55 (1898) (holding that a state priority statute giving priorities to state residents violates the Privileges and Immunities Clause, U.S. CONST. art. IV, § 2, which protects non-corporate citizens of other states).

592. The Court has considered and rejected whether Congress' bankruptcy legislation may be authorized by the Commerce Clause. *See* Ry. Labor Executives' Ass'n v. Gibbons, 455 U.S. 457, 468 (1982) ("Unlike the Commerce Clause, the Bankruptcy Clause itself contains an affirmative limitation or restriction upon Congress' power: bankruptcy laws must be uniform throughout the United States. Such uniformity in the applicability of legislation is not required by the Commerce Clause. Thus, if we were to hold that Congress had the power to enact nonuniform bankruptcy laws pursuant to the Commerce Clause, we would eradicate from the Constitution a limitation on the power of Congress to enact bankruptcy laws.") (citations omitted).

other provisions of the Constitution[593] limit, restrict, or are overridden by the Bankruptcy Clause. Third, the Court considers the manner and extent to which sovereign immunity circumscribes Congress' power to exercise its bankruptcy power. In part, these decisions turn on the Court's interpretation of the Eleventh Amendment, but they also address the independent doctrine of constitutional sovereign immunity and the waiver of sovereign immunity in the plan of the Convention.

SCOPE AND CONSTITUTIONALITY OF THE BANKRUPTCY POWER

Article one, section eight, clause four of the United States Constitution grants Congress the power to enact uniform Laws on the subject of Bankruptcies throughout the United States.[594] In its first interpretation of the Bankruptcy Clause, the Court noted that "[t]he peculiar terms of the grant [of bankruptcy power] certainly deserve notice [because] Congress is not authorized merely to pass laws, the operation of which shall be uniform, but to establish uniform laws on

---

593. Specifically, the Court has considered conflicts between the Bankruptcy Clause and the Commerce Clause, the Takings Clause, the Due Process Clause, the Seventh Amendment right to jury trial, and Eleventh Amendment sovereign immunity, among others. *See, e.g.,* Ry. Labor Executives' Ass'n v. Gibbons, 455 U.S. 457, 468-69 (1982) (Commerce Clause conflict); United States v. Sec. Indus. Bank, 459 U.S. 70, 75 (1982) and Louisville Joint Stock Land Bank v. Radford, 295 U.S. 555 (1935) (Takings Clause conflicts); Mullane v. Cent. Hanover Bank & Trust Co., 339 U.S. 306, 314-19 (1950) and Wright v. Union Cent. Life Ins. Co., 304 U.S. 502, 518 (1938) (due process limits); Granfinanciera, S.A. v. Nordberg, 492 U.S. 33, 59-61 (1989) (conflict with the Seventh Amendment right to jury trial); and Tenn. Student Assistance Corp. v. Hood, 540 U.S. 440 (2004) (conflict with Eleventh Amendment sovereign immunity). *See infra* pp. 154-155 & Ch. 4, pp. 201, 213-214, which discusses constitutional limitations on the bankruptcy courts' jurisdiction imposed by Article III of the Constitution. *See, e.g.,* N. Pipeline Constr. Co. v. Marathon Pipe Line Co., 458 U.S. 50, 87 (1982).

594. *See* U.S. CONST. art. I, § 8, cl. 4.

the subject throughout the United States."[595] More recently the Court has stated, somewhat broadly, that "[t]he power of Congress to establish uniform laws on the subject of bankruptcies throughout the United States is unrestricted and paramount."[596] Nevertheless, litigants have challenged the scope of the bankruptcy power, and the Court has held that "a debtor has no constitutional or 'fundamental' right to a discharge in bankruptcy."[597] One might have expected that most constitutional challenges to the bankruptcy laws would have been resolved during the early years of the Republic. Surprisingly, however, the Supreme Court considered many fresh constitutional issues during the past 111 years.

Perhaps the most puzzling part of the Bankruptcy Clause is its requirement that the enacted laws be "uniform."[598] Just past the turn of the 20th century, the Court decided *Hanover National Bank v. Moyses*[599] in which it held that "[t]he laws passed on the subject must, however, be uniform throughout the United States, but that uniformity is geographical, and not personal, and we do not think that the provision of the act of 1898 as to exemptions is incompatible with the

---

595. *See* Sturges v. Crowninshield, 17 U.S. (4 Wheat.) 122, 193-94 (1819) (Marshall, C.J.).

596. *See* Int'l Shoe v. Pinkus, 278 U.S. 261, 265 (1929).

597. *See* Grogan v. Garner, 498 U.S. 279, 286 (1991) (characterizing and citing the Court's holding in United States v. Kras, 409 U.S. 434, 445-46 (1973)).

598. The Bankruptcy Clause is not the only part of the Constitution that requires uniformity. Within Article I, the Constitution requires all duties, imposts and excises to be uniform throughout the United States and also specifies that rules of naturalization must be uniform. *See* U.S. CONST. art. I, § 8, cls. 1 & 4. The Court has looked to its interpretation of each uniformity clause in determining the meaning of the others. *See* United States v. Ptasynski, 462 U.S. 74, 84 n.13 (1983) (relying on interpretation of Bankruptcy Clause uniformity to aid interpretation of indirect Tax Clause uniformity); Reg'l Rail Reorganization Act Cases, 419 U.S. 102, 161 (1974) (relying on interpretation of indirect Tax Clause uniformity in Head Money Cases, 112 U.S. 580, 594 (1884), to aid interpretation of Bankruptcy Clause uniformity).

599. 186 U.S. 181 (1902).

rule."[600] Through a turn of phrase, the Court deftly upheld congressional enactment of a national bankruptcy law that permitted each state to adopt specific exemptions for its residents which would differ from state to state but nevertheless be enforced in federal bankruptcy cases. Thus, "[t]he uniformity requirement of the Bankruptcy Clause is not an Equal Protection Clause for bankrupts."[601]

Nor is the Uniformity Clause an Equal Protection Clause for creditors. In *Stellwagen v. Clum*,[602] the Court commented favorably on the Bankruptcy Act's empowerment of the trustee to avoid transfers using state fraudulent transfer laws,[603] even though creditors might be subject to different laws depending on where the debtor filed its bankruptcy petition.[604] The Court noted that the rationale of the Uniformity Clause protects the bankruptcy policy of ratable distribution, not the ability of a particular creditor to resist fraudulent transfer attack:[605]

> This state [fraudulent transfer] statute is not opposed to the policy of the bankruptcy law or in contravention of the rules and principles established by it with a view to the fair distribution of the assets of the insolvent. It is only state laws which conflict with the bankruptcy laws of Congress that are suspended; those which are in aid of the Bankruptcy Act can stand.

---

600. *See id.* at 188.

601. *See* Ry. Labor Executives' Ass'n v. Gibbons, 455 U.S. 457, 471 n.11 (1982).

602. 245 U.S. 605 (1918).

603. *See* Bankruptcy Act § 70e, 11 U.S.C. § 110e (1976) (repealed 1979).

604. *See Stellwagen*, 245 U.S. at 613 ("Notwithstanding this requirement as to uniformity the bankruptcy acts of Congress may recognize the laws of the State in certain particulars, although such recognition may lead to different results in different States.").

605. *See id.* at 615 (citation omitted).

The Court's charitable interpretation of "uniformity" encouraged Congress to pass laws that were uniform in name only.[606] In 1974 the Supreme Court upheld the Regional Rail Reorganization Act against constitutional challenge even though the statute applied in practice only to railroads in reorganization in the northeastern states.[607] But even the United States Supreme Court has its limits. In 1982 the Court decided *Railway Labor Executives' Ass'n v. Gibbons*[608] and, on Uniformity Clause grounds, struck down bankruptcy legislation drafted so specifically on its face that it would apply in practice to only one large railroad debtor.[609] In *Gibbons*, the Court hedged its opinion by noting that "the uniformity requirement is not a straightjacket that forbids Congress to distinguish among classes of debtors."[610]

---

606. Although the Court has not defined "uniformity" with precision, it has held a tax to be uniform "when it operates with the same force and effect in every place where the subject of it is found." *See Head Money Cases*, 112 U.S. at 594.

607. *See* Reg'l Rail Reorganization Act Cases, 419 U.S. 102, 158-60 (1974). The Court justified its outcome in large part on the basis of the *Head Money Cases*, where the effect of the tax statute distinguished between geographic regions, and rejected the "argument that the Rail Act differs from the head tax statute because by its own terms the Rail Act applies only to one designated region . . . . The definition of the region does not obscure the reality that the legislation applies to all railroads under reorganization . . . during the time the Act applies." *See id.* at 161. *But see* Sturges v. Crowninshield, 17 U.S. (4 Wheat.) 122, 193-94 (1819) ("The peculiar terms of the grant [of the bankruptcy power] certainly deserve notice. Congress is not authorized merely to pass laws, the operation of which shall be uniform, but to establish uniform laws on the subject throughout the United States.").

608. 455 U.S. 457 (1982).

609. *See id.* at 469-73. ("A law can hardly be said to be uniform throughout the country if it applies only to one debtor and can be enforced only by the one bankruptcy court having jurisdiction over that debtor.") *Id.* at 470.

610. *See id.* at 469.

Nevertheless, the opinion in *Gibbons* was not unanimous, with Justices Marshall and Brennan concurring in the judgment. Note 2 of the concurrence expresses a concern that, under the Court's approach, bankruptcy legislation respecting Conrail might be invalid.[611] Indeed this concern caused Justice Brennan to write a two page letter to Justice Rehnquist withdrawing from his majority opinion: "I joined your opinion and I dislike being an 'Indian giver'. But I think I'll feel more comfortable if I withdraw my join and either write on my own or work out with Thurgood whether I can join him."[612] Justice Brennan's concern raises the intriguing question whether regional legislation that may apply constitutionally to eight railroads might apply unconstitutionally once the railroads are rolled up into one large operation.

The past 111 years also witnessed several constitutional challenges to bankruptcy laws that had nothing to do with the Uniformity Clause. "From the beginning, the tendency of legislation and of judicial interpretation has been uniformly in the direction of progressive liberalization in respect of the operation of the bankruptcy power."[613] Indeed, the Court has recognized as "broad" the scope of Congress' power under the Bankruptcy Clause.[614] The Court also has noted that the specific grant of power under the Bankruptcy Clause is augmented by the Necessary and Proper Clause[615] which gives Congress the power "[t]o make all laws which shall be necessary and proper for carrying into Execution the" bankruptcy power.[616] Never-

---

611.   *See id.* at 477 n.2 (Marshall and Brennan, JJ., concurring).

612.   *See* February 17, 1982, letter from Justice Brennan to Justice Rehnquist regarding *Gibbons* (included in Marshall papers).

613.   *See* Cont'l Ill. Nat'l Bank & Trust Co. v. Chicago, R.I. & Pac. Ry. Co., 294 U.S. 648, 668 (1935).

614.   *See* Reg'l Rail Reorganization Act Cases, 419 U.S. 102, 154 (1974).

615.   U.S. CONST. art. I, § 8, cl.18.

616.   *See* Wright v. Union Cent. Life Ins. Co., 304 U.S. 502, 513 (1938). Despite this reference, it does not appear that the Court has ever used the Necessary and Proper Clause to justify the constitutionality of a bankruptcy statute.

theless, "[t]he subject of bankruptcies is incapable of final definition."[617]

The year 1935 was a watershed in which the Court decided two
key cases concerning the scope of the bankruptcy power. In *Continental Illinois National Bank & Trust Co. of Chicago v. Chicago, Rock
Island & Pacific Railway Co.*,[618] the Court held that the railroad
reorganization provisions in Bankruptcy Act § 77 did not exceed the
scope of the bankruptcy power. Some might have thought that
congressional power to enact bankruptcy laws would be limited to
bankruptcy laws in England at the time of the founding of our
nation.[619] The Court had rejected this view in *Hanover National Bank
v. Moyses*, however, holding that "[t]he framers of the Constitution
were familiar with Blackstone's Commentaries, and with the bankrupt laws of England, yet they granted plenary power to Congress
over the whole subject of 'bankruptcies,' and did not limit it by the
language [that they] used."[620] Indeed *Moyses* noted that Congress
constitutionally expanded United States bankruptcy laws beyond
those in England to permit individuals who were not traders to
become debtors and file voluntary bankruptcy petitions.[621]

In *Chicago Rock Island*, the Court also used broad language to
reject the argument that bankruptcy laws were confined to liquidation
cases, noting that, taken as a group, the bankruptcy laws passed by

---

617. *See id.*

618. 294 U.S. 648 (1935) ("*Chicago Rock Island*").

619. *Cf.* Grupo Mexicano de Desarrollo, S.A. v. Alliance Bond Fund,
Inc., 527 U.S. 308 (1999) (a nonbankruptcy case in which the Court
sharply restricted the general equity power of the United States district
court to what it was in English courts of Chancery in 1789).

620. *See Moyses*, 186 U.S. at 187. *See also, e.g., Chicago Rock Island*,
294 U.S. at 669 ("[T]he power of Congress under the bankruptcy clause is
not to be limited by the English or Colonial law in force when the
Constitution was adopted . . . .").

621. *See Moyses*, 186 U.S. at 186. Accord, *e.g.*, Wright v. Union Cent.
Life Ins. Co., 304 U.S. 502, 513 (1938); *Chicago Rock Island*, 294 U.S. at
668.

Congress before enactment of Bankruptcy Act § 77, "far-reaching though they be, have not gone beyond the limit of congressional power; but rather have constituted extensions into a field whose boundaries may not yet be fully revealed."[622] The Court approved Congress' power to provide for railroad reorganizations by noting that § 77 "does no more than follow the line of historical and progressive development projected by previous acts."[623] In *Gibbons* the Court stated, "although we have noted that '[t]he subject of bankruptcies is incapable of final definition,' we have previously defined 'bankruptcy' as the 'subject of relations between an insolvent or nonpaying or fraudulent debtor and his creditors, extending to his and their relief.' * * * Congress' power under the Bankruptcy Clause 'contemplate[s] an adjustment of a failing debtor's obligations.'"[624]

Yet the Court went further in *Wright v. Union Central Life Insurance Co.* holding that the bankruptcy power is not limited to adjustment of the debtor-creditor relationship but can extend to a purchaser at a judicial sale who takes subject to the debtor's right of redemption.[625] Specifically, Congress acted within the scope of the bankruptcy power in extending a state equity of redemption period.[626]

Nevertheless, the Court has recognized that although "the power of Congress under the bankruptcy clause is not to be limited by the English or Colonial law in force when the Constitution was adopted, it does not follow that the power has no limitations."[627] Yet the Court

---

622. *See Chicago Rock Island*, 294 U.S. at 671.

623. *See id.* at 672.

624. *See Gibbons*, 455 U.S. at 466 (citations omitted). *Accord* N. Pipeline Constr. Co. v. Marathon Pipe Line Co., 458 U.S. 50, 71 (1982) (Congress has the power to enact legislation permitting the restructuring of relations between debtors and creditors.). The adjustment also can take the form of a composition agreement when the debtors debts are reduced under a plan. *See, e.g.,* United States v. Bekins, 304 U.S. 27, 47 (1938).

625. *See* Wright v. Union Cent. Life Ins. Co., 304 U.S. 502, 514-15 (1938).

626. *See id.* at 515.

627. *See Chicago Rock Island*, 294 U.S. at 669.

has refused to define the outer limits of the "subject of Bankruptcies." It is fair to ask whether these limits are exceeded when bankruptcy legislation applies to "both solvent and liquid" debtors.[628] Stated differently, the subject of Bankruptcies could well apply to a company that is insolvent in the balance sheet sense, when its liabilities exceed the fair saleable value of its assets, or in the equity sense, when it is generally unable to pay its debts as they mature.[629] But as a matter of constitutional law does the subject of bankruptcies extend to a company that is neither insolvent in the bankruptcy sense nor the equity sense?[630]

From a constitutional perspective, during the past century the Court has equated bankruptcy and insolvency.[631] "While attempts have been made to formulate a distinction between bankruptcy and insolvency, it has long been settled that, within the meaning of the

---

628. *See* First Nat'l Bank v. Flershem, 290 U.S. 504, 517 (1934) (overturning federal equity receivership in which the debtor was both solvent and liquid).

629. *See, e.g.,* Ashton v. Cameron County Water Improvement Dist., 298 U.S. 513, 536-37 (1936) (Cardozo, J., dissenting) (reading the Bankruptcy Clause to apply when a person is unable to pay his debts).

630. At least one commentator has argued that the Bankruptcy Power cannot extend to a solvent debtor because a solvent debtor is in no sense "bankrupt" within the meaning of the constitutional requirement. *See* G. Eric Brunstad, Jr., "Good Faith, Solvent Debtors, and the Subject of Bankruptcies," (manuscript on file with author). *But see In re* Marshall, 300 B.R. 507, 509, 526 (Bankr. C.D. Cal. 2003) (holding "that the Bankruptcy Clause of the United States Constitution does not require that a debtor in bankruptcy be insolvent under any test").

631. *But see* Sturges v. Crowninshield, 17 U.S. (4 Wheat.) 122, 194-95 (1819) ("[T]he subject [of bankruptcy law] is divisible in its nature into bankrupt and insolvent laws; though the line of partition between them is not so distinctly marked as to enable any person to say, with positive precision, what belongs exclusively to the one, and not the other . . . . Although the two systems have existed apart from each other, there is such a connection between them, as to render it difficult to say how far they may be blended together.").

[Bankruptcy Clause], the terms are convertible."[632] Thus, unless the subject of bankruptcies is limited by the requirement that the debtor be insolvent in the balance sheet or equity sense, it is difficult to surmise the contours of the outer limit of the bankruptcy power. To be sure, it might suffice that the debtor's insolvency be imminent if not already in existence.[633] Public policy supports permitting a company to file for bankruptcy reorganization or liquidation before it is on death's door. But this leeway should not extend to a debtor that is both solvent and liquid with full ability to pay its debts as they become due.

The issue is not purely theoretical. Although Congress limited access to Chapters X, XI, XII, and XIII of the Bankruptcy Act to debtors who stated that they were insolvent,[634] Congress dropped the

---

632. *See Chicago Rock Island*, 294 U.S. at 667-68. *See also* Thomas E. Plank, *Bankruptcy and Federalism*, 71 FORD. L. REV. 1063, 1076-77 (2002).

633. Courts, without deciding the constitutional issue, have allowed companies to file bankruptcy petitions when facing a serious threat to the companies' long term viability. *See, e.g.,* Baker v. Latham Sparrowbush Assocs. (*In re* Cohoes Indus. Terminal, Inc.), 931 F.2d 222, 228 (2d Cir. 1991) ("Although a debtor need not be in extremis in order to file [a Chapter 11] petition, it must, at least, face such financial difficulty that, if it did not file at that time, it could anticipate the need to file in the future.").

634. *See* Bankruptcy Act §§ 130(1), 323, 423 & 623, 11 U.S.C. §§ 530(1), 723, 823 & 1023 (1976) (repealed 1979) (requiring a petitioning debtor to state that the debtor "is insolvent or unable to pay its debts as they mature"). Even if the debtor was balance sheet solvent, it was eligible to be a debtor as long as it was unable to pay its debts. *See* United States v. Key, 397 U.S. 322, 329 (1970) ("Chapter X proceedings are not open merely to corporations that are insolvent, in that their liabilities exceed their assets, but also to those that are solvent in the bankruptcy or asset-liability sense and yet are unable to meet their obligations as they mature."). Before the Bankruptcy Act of 1898, no United States bank-ruptcy law incorporated a balance sheet insolvency test. *Compare* § 1(19) of the Bankruptcy Act of 1898, ch. 541, 30 Stat. 544, 11 U.S.C. § 1(19) (1976) (repealed 1979) *with* Bankruptcy Act of 1867, ch. 176, 14 Stat. 517 (1867) (repealed 1878); Bankruptcy Act of 1841, ch. 9, 5 Stat. 440 (1841) (repealed 1843); and Bankruptcy Act of 1800, ch. 19, 2 Stat. 19 (1800) (repealed 1803). The Acts of 1867 and 1841 required the voluntary debtor to allege equity insolvency. *See* Act of 1867 § 11 ("inability to pay all his debts in full"); Act of 1841 § 1 ("unable to meet their debts and engage-ments").

allegation of insolvency when it enacted the 1978 Bankruptcy Code.[635] Thus, the prospect remains for the Court to determine whether the Bankruptcy Code is unconstitutional as applied to a debtor that is both solvent and liquid.[636]

Congress has only permitted courts to function as tribunals for the adjudication of matters within the bankruptcy jurisdiction,[637] but the Constitution does not appear to so limit the bankruptcy power. One Justice was of the view that Congress could entrust administration of the bankruptcy laws to nonbankruptcy tribunals because "the scope of the bankruptcy power is not restricted to that which has been exercised."[638] No other Justice concurred with this view. Nevertheless, the Court's recent arbitration decisions[639] have led some lower courts to conclude that core bankruptcy matters, such as damages for

635.   *See* 11 U.S.C. § 301 (2000) (containing no insolvency requirement).

636.   Lower courts considering the issue have held that the Bankruptcy Clause of the Constitution does not preclude solvent debtors from seeking bankruptcy relief. *See, e.g., In re* Marshall, 300 B.R. 507, 510 (Bankr. C.D. Cal. 2003) (finding that the Bankruptcy Clause requires neither balance sheet nor liquidity insolvency to invoke federal bankruptcy jurisdiction) (dictum as to equity insolvency). *See also In re* Integrated Telecom Express, 384 F.3d 108, 121-23 (3d Cir. 2004) (citing *In re Marshall* with approval); *In re* Rose, 318 B.R. 771 (Bankr. S.D.N.Y. 2004). Most courts avert the constitutional issue by deciding the case on a motion to dismiss the bankruptcy petition for bad faith filing. *See In re* SGL Carbon Corp., 200 F.3d 154 (3d Cir. 1999); *In re* RBGSC Inv. Corp., 253 B.R. 352 (E.D. Pa. 2000) (citing *SGL* with approval); *In re* Liptak, 304 B.R. 820 (Bankr. N.D. Ill. 2004).

637.   *See, e.g.,* 28 U.S.C. § 1334(a), (e) (2000) (granting the United States district courts original and exclusive jurisdiction over bankruptcy cases and property of the debtor, as of the commencement of the case, and of the estate). *But see* 28 U.S.C. § 1334(b) (2000) (granting the United States district courts non-exclusive jurisdiction over bankruptcy proceedings).

638.   *See* RFC v. Bankers Trust Co., 318 U.S. 163, 175 (1943) (Douglas, J., concurring).

639.   *See, e.g.,* Buckeye Check Cashing, Inc. v. Cardegna, 546 U.S. 440, 447-48 (2006) (A challenge to the validity of the contract as a whole, and not specifically to the arbitration clause within it, must go to the arbitrator for decision, not to the court.).

violation of the automatic stay, are subject to mandatory arbitration and the bankruptcy judge has no discretion to hear them in the bankruptcy court unless the arbitration conflicts with, or jeopardizes the goals of, the Bankruptcy Code.[640]

CONFLICTS WITH OTHER CONSTITUTIONAL PROVISIONS

The Court has considered conflicts between the Bankruptcy Clause and several other constitutional provisions, including the Fourth, Fifth, Tenth, and Eleventh Amendments of the Constitution.[641]

The Fifth Amendment Privilege Against Self Incrimination

In *McCarthy v. Arndstein*,[642] the Court held that a debtor's Fifth Amendment privilege against self incrimination applies in bankruptcy cases and other civil proceedings as well as in criminal proceedings.[643] Nevertheless, on several occasions the Court has considered whether the debtor's Fifth Amendment privilege conflicts with the right of the bankruptcy estate to acquire property from the debtor or creditors.

---

640. *See* MBNA Am. Bank, N.A. v. Hill, 436 F.3d 104, 109-10 (2d Cir. 2006) (when arbitration would not seriously jeopardize the objectives of the Bankruptcy Code, a core proceeding, such as an individual debtor's action for damages for a bank's violation of the automatic stay under Bankruptcy Code § 362(k), must be sent to arbitration). *See also* Hays & Co. v. Merrill Lynch, Pierce, Fenner & Smith, Inc., 885 F.2d 1149, 1156-57 (3d Cir. 1989); *In re* U.S. Lines, Inc., 197 F.3d 631 (2d Cir. 1999); *In re* Brown, 354 B.R. 591 (D.R.I. 2006). *But see,* Allegaert v. Perot, 548 F.2d 432, 436-37 (2d Cir. 1977); *In re* Merrill, 343 B.R. 1 (Bankr. D. Me. 2006).

641. The Court also has noted, in passing, congressional concern that subjecting a debtor to a chapter 13 repayment plan involuntarily would violate the Thirteenth Amendment's prohibition against involuntary servitude. *See* Toibb v. Radloff, 501 U.S. 157, 165-66 (1991).

642. 266 U.S. 34 (1924).

643. *See id.* at 39-40 ("The privilege is not ordinarily dependent upon the nature of the proceeding in which the testimony is sought or is to be used. It applies alike to civil and criminal proceedings, wherever the answer might tend to subject to criminal responsibility him who gives it.").

Early on, in *In re Harris*,[644] the Court held that the Self Incrimination Clause of the Fifth Amendment did not apply to permit a debtor to refuse to turn over to a bankruptcy receiver books and records containing incriminating statements, as long as the books could not be used against the debtor in a criminal trial.[645] A few years later, the Court went further, holding that once the trustee or receiver has the books and records, even if a protective arrangement is not in place, the bankruptcy court has discretion to order the books and records turned over by the trustee or receiver to the prosecutor or Grand Jury.[646]

Moreover, in *Watkins v. Sedberry*,[647] the Court held that neither the Fourth nor Fifth Amendments applied to permit individual debtors to delay transfer of their property to their bankruptcy trustee, even if the property contained incriminating information. The Court offered a compelling rationale in *Ex parte Fuller*[648] as follows:[649]

> A man who becomes a bankrupt or who is brought into a bankruptcy court has no right to delay the legal transfer of the possession and title of any of his property to the officers ap-

---

644.   221 U.S. 274 (1911).

645.   *See id.* at 279-80 (1911) ("The question is not of testimony but of surrender—not of compelling the bankrupt to be a witness against himself in a criminal case, present or future, but of compelling him to yield possession of property that he no longer is entitled to keep."). *See also* 11 U.S.C. §§ 344 & 542(e) (2000) (requiring turn over of books and records in Bankruptcy Code cases).

646.   *See* Dier v. Banton, 262 U.S. 147, 150 (1923) (holding that neither the Fourth Amendment nor the Fifth Amendment protected the bankrupt against the receiver's turnover of lawfully delivered books and records to the prosecutor and Grand Jury); Johnson v. United States, 228 U.S. 457, 458-59 (1913) (holding that books turned over to the bankruptcy trustee could be used against the bankrupt in a criminal prosecution without violating the bankrupt's Fifth Amendment privilege against self incrimination).

647.   261 U.S. 571 (1923).

648.   262 U.S. 91 (1923).

649.   *See id.* at 93-94.

pointed by law for its custody or for its disposition, on the ground that the transfer of such property will carry with it incriminating evidence against him. His property and its possession pass from him by operation and due proceedings of law, and when control and possession have passed from him, he has no constitutional right to prevent its use for any legitimate purpose. His privilege secured to him by the Fourth and Fifth Amendments to the Constitution is that of refusing himself to produce, as incriminating evidence against him, anything which he owns or has in his possession and control, but his privilege in respect to what was his and in his custody ceases on a transfer of the control and possession which takes place by legal proceedings and in pursuance of the rights of others, even though such transfer may bring the property into the ownership or control of one properly subject to subpoena duces tecum.

The Takings Clause

The Court also has construed the intersection of the Bankruptcy Clause with both the Takings Clause and Due Process Clause of the Fifth Amendment. The Takings Clause of the Fifth Amendment prohibits the federal government from taking private property for public use without just compensation.[650] It "does not prohibit the taking of private property, but instead places a condition on the exercise of that power."[651] This proscription applies both to appropriations of and physical ouster from property as well as to regulatory takings.[652] Therefore economic regulatory statutes, such as bankruptcy

---

650. *See* U.S. CONST. amend. V ("[N]or shall private property be taken for public use, without just compensation.").

651. *See* First English Evangelical Lutheran Church v. County of Los Angeles, 482 U.S. 304, 314 (1987).

652. *See, e.g.,* Kelo v. City of New London, 545 U.S. 469, 488 (2005); Lingle v. Chevron U.S.A., Inc., 544 U.S. 528, 537-39 (2005); E. Enters. v. Apfel, 524 U.S. 498, 522-23 (1998); Lucas v. S.C. Coastal Council, 505 U.S. 1003, 1014-15 (1992); Hodel v. Irving, 481 U.S. 704, 714 (1987); Penn Cent. Transp. Co. v. New York City, 438 U.S. 104, 124 (1978).

legislation, could effect a taking within the scope of the Takings Clause.[653]

The inevitable conflict between the Bankruptcy Clause and the Takings Clause squarely presents the question which clause prevails.[654] Each time it has considered the issue, however, the Court has stated that Congress' power under the Bankruptcy Clause is limited by the Takings Clause.[655] For example, in *United States v. Security Industrial Bank*,[656] the Court considered a Takings Clause challenge to a Bankruptcy Code provision permitting debtors to avoid certain liens, possibly including those predating the statute's enactment. The Court expressed "substantial doubt whether the retroactive destruction of the appellees' liens . . . comport[ed] with the Fifth Amend- Amendment," and therefore construed the statute as applying only to lien interests vesting after the legislation took effect.[657] In dictum, the Court noted that the Bankruptcy Code's complete destruction of state law property rights, even of insubstantial value, would merit protection under the Fifth Amendment's Takings Clause.[658]

---

653. *See, e.g.,* United States v. Sec. Indus. Bank, 459 U.S. 70, 75 (1982) (dictum). *Cf.* Leider v. United States, 301 F.3d 1290, 1296 (Fed. Cir. 2002) ("[U]nlocated creditor has a property right in his or her distributive share of the funds of a bankruptcy estate.").

654. Commentators have speculated about the answer to this question. *See, e.g.,* Julia Patterson Forrester, *Bankruptcy Takings*, 51 FLA. L. REV. 851, 866-70 (1999); James Steven Rogers, *The Impairment of Secured Creditors' Rights in Reorganization: A Study of the Relationship Between the Fifth Amendment and the Bankruptcy Clause*, 96 HARV. L. REV. 973 (1983).

655. *See* United States v. Sec. Indus. Bank, 459 U.S. 70, 75, 78 (1982) (dictum); Wright v. Vinton Branch of Mountain Trust Bank, 300 U.S. 440, 456-58 (1937) ("*Vinton Branch*"); Louisville Joint Stock Land Bank v. Radford, 295 U.S. 555, 589 (1935).

656. 459 U.S. 70 (1982).

657. *See id.* at 78-79.

658. *See id.* at 77-78. *See also* Kener v. La Grange Mills, 231 U.S. 215, 217-18 (1913) (holding that neither the Georgia constitution nor the Bankruptcy Act of 1867 could exempt property from existing liens).

Nearly 80 years earlier, in *Louisville Joint Stock Land Bank v. Radford*,[659] the Court unanimously struck down the first Frazier-Lemke Act[660] for unconstitutionally taking a mortgagee's property rights without just compensation.[661] Specifically, the Court held that the Act unconstitutionally deprived the mortgagee of the following specific state property rights:[662]

- The right to retain the lien until the indebtedness thereby secured is paid.

- The right to realize upon the security by a judicial public sale.

- The right to determine when such sale shall be held, subject only to the discretion of the court.

- The right to protect its interest in the property by bidding at such sale whenever held, and thus to assure having the mortgaged property devoted primarily to the satisfaction of the debt, either through receipt of the proceeds of a fair competitive sale or by taking the property itself.

- The right to control meanwhile the property during the period of default, subject only to the discretion of the court, and to have the rents and profits collected by a receiver for the satisfaction of the debt.

The taking of these rights occurred because the Act deprived the mortgagee of possession for five years while the debtor was permitted to retain possession by paying a fair annual rent or purchasing the property at its appraised value with deferred payments bearing annual interest at 1% and paid under an amortization that has 85% of the principal paid after six years.[663]

---

659.   295 U.S. 555 (1935).

660.   Pub. L. No. 73-486, 48 Stat. 1289 (1934).

661.   *See Radford*, 295 U.S. at 588-90.

662.   *See id.* at 594-95.

663.   *See id.* at 591-92, 601-02 & n.21.

Although the Court's opinion in *Radford* was unanimous, at least one Justice was troubled by its import. In his May 24, 1935 letter to Justice Brandeis about *Radford*, Justice Stone wrote as follows:[664]

> This is a very good opinion, but I am a little troubled about one feature of it . . . . Can you say that the Fifth Amendment protects rights of the mortgagee without saying likewise that congressional action destroying or cutting down those rights in a bankruptcy proceeding is not an exercise of the bankruptcy power? In other words, whatever impairment of the rights of creditors is within the scope of the bankruptcy power is withdrawn from the protection of the Fifth Amendment . . . .

The import of *Radford* is precisely the opposite: whatever rights of secured creditors are protected by the Fifth Amendment are withdrawn from Congress' power to legislate under the Bankruptcy Clause. Indeed, in different contexts the Court has held that other constitutional amendments limit Congress' Article I powers.[665]

Almost immediately after the Court declared the first Frazier-Lemke Act unconstitutional, Congress enacted the second Frazier-Lemke Act.[666] The Act contained amendments that were largely cosmetic. For example, the five year stay of the first Act was reduced to a three year stay that could be terminated by the court.[667] The Supreme Court quickly, and again unanimously, reversed course, upholding the constitutionality of the second Frazier-Lemke Act,[668] because, among other things, it "adequately preserves three of the five above enumerated rights of a mortgagee."[669] The three preserved rights

---

664. *See* May 24, 1935 letter from Justice Stone to Justice Brandeis regarding *Radford* (contained in Brandeis papers).

665. *See, e.g.,* Seminole Tribe of Fla. v. Florida, 517 U.S. 44, 71-72 (1996) (holding that the Eleventh Amendment limits Congress' power under the Indian Commerce Clause, U.S. CONST. art. I, § 8, cl. 3).

666. Act of Aug. 28, 1935, Pub. L. No. 74-384, 49 Stat. 941 (1935).

667. *See id.*, § 75(s)(2), 49 Stat. 944.

668. *See* Wright v. Vinton Branch of the Mountain Trust Bank, 300 U.S. 440, 458-61 (1937).

669. *See id.* at 458.

were the right to retain the lien until the secured indebtedness is paid; the right to realize on the security by a judicial public sale; and the right to bid in the secured debt at a foreclosure sale.[670]

It is no coincidence, at least to some extent, that the Bankruptcy Code preserves the essence of these very rights. For example, if the estate has no equity in the collateral and it is not necessary to an effective reorganization, Bankruptcy Code § 362(d)(2) gives the secured creditor a basis to seek relief from the automatic stay to foreclose its lien under nonbankruptcy law.[671] Moreover, if the trustee proposes to sell the lender's collateral, Bankruptcy Code § 363(k) generally preserves the lender's right to credit bid up to the amount of the indebtedness secured at a foreclosure sale.[672] Also, if the secured creditor does not vote in favor of a chapter 11 plan, and the plan proponent seeks to cram down the plan under § 1129(b)(2)(A)(i), the Bankruptcy Code preserves that creditor's right to retain its lien until the indebtedness secured is paid.[673] If the plan proponent chooses to cram down the plan under § 1129(b)(2)(A)(ii) or (iii), however, apparently this protection is lost.[674] Thus, we can infer that the Bank-

---

670. *See id.* at 458-59 (noting that the last of these rights was not provided for in the Act but in the legislative history).

671. *See* 11 U.S.C. § 362(d)(2) (2000) cited with approval in United Sav. Ass'n v. Timbers of Inwood Forest Assocs., Ltd., 484 U.S. 365, 374-76 (1988) (dictum).

672. *See* 11 U.S.C. §§ 363(k) & 1129(b)(2)(A)(ii) (2000). If the court, for cause, orders otherwise, the secured creditor will lose its right to credit bid at a sale under § 363(k). *See* 11 U.S.C. § 363(k) (2000). But if the creditor retains its right to credit bid, it may do so up to the amount of the allowed claim. *See id.*

673. *See* 11 U.S.C. § 1129(b)(2)(A)(i) (2000). Under Bankruptcy Code § 506(a), however, in a chapter 11 case the secured indebtedness that is protected might be less than the debt when the value of the collateral is less than the allowed claim. The secured creditor can remedy this problem by causing the class containing its allowed secured claim to elect to be treated as fully secured under § 1111(b)(2). This election is not available if the property is sold under a process that allows the creditor to credit bid its claim. *See* 11 U.S.C. § 1111(b)(1)(A)(ii) & (B)(ii) (2000).

674. *See* 11 U.S.C. § 1129(b)(2)(A)(ii)-(iii) (2000).

ruptcy Code only protects the value of a secured creditor's interest in collateral rather than the lien or any property interest in the collateral.[675] This certainly was the Court's view under the Bankruptcy Act when it held that the Fifth Amendment only protects the value of the creditors' collateral.[676] Significantly, at least in the context of a railroad reorganization when the public interest is at stake, the Court has held that creditors have no Fifth Amendment taking claim for operating losses that diminish the value of their collateral during the reorganization case.[677]

Reading *Vinton Branch* and *Radford* together, it is fair to ask whether *Radford* retains any vitality after *Vinton Branch*. Courts and commentators do not agree. The Supreme Court has noted that *Vinton Branch* corrected the Court's error in *Radford*.[678] Thus, some lower courts have paid *Radford* short shrift.[679] Other courts rely on

675. *But cf.* Dewsnup v. Timm, 502 U.S. 410, 417 (1992) (contorting statutory interpretation of § 506(d) to avoid a potential Fifth Amendment problem if lien stripping applies to pre-existing liens).

676. *See, e.g.,* New Haven Inclusion Cases, 399 U.S. 392, 489-90 (1970) ("We thereby accord the bondholders the right to a liquidation and a per-parcel sale that is theirs by virtue of their mortgage liens. The Bankruptcy Act does not require that they be given more."); Wright v. Union Cent. Life Ins. Co., 311 U.S. 273, 278 (1940) (The Fifth Amendment requires the Bankruptcy Act "to protect the rights of secured creditors, throughout the proceedings, to the extent of the value of the property. There is no constitutional claim of the creditor to more than that.")

677. *See* New Haven Inclusion Cases, 399 U.S. 392, 491 (1970) ("We do not doubt that the time consumed in the course of the proceedings in the reorganization court has imposed a substantial loss upon the bondholders. But in the circumstances presented by this litigation we see no constitutional bar to that result. The rights of the bondholders are not absolute.").

678. *See* Helvering v. Griffiths, 318 U.S. 371, 401 n.52 (1943) (dictum in tax case noting instances in which the Court has overruled its previous opinions and reversed course). Nevertheless the Court cited *Radford* with approval in *Dewsnup v. Timm* as properly invoking the Takings Clause. *See* Dewsnup v. Timm, 502 U.S. 410, 419 (1992).

679. *See, e.g.,* Yi v. Citibank (Md.) N.A. (*In re* Yi), 219 B.R. 394, 401 (E.D. Va. 1998) ("*Radford* . . . has been all but overruled by *Wright v.*

Radford as good law,[680] at least for the proposition that the bankruptcy power is subject to the Fifth Amendment.[681] According to one commentator, the holding in *Radford* that the bankruptcy power is subject to the Fifth Amendment "must be taken to mean nothing more than the fifth amendment, through either the due process clause or the takings clause, is the constitutional foundation for the proposition that states that retroactively disrupt settled expectations may be subject to particularly attentive judicial scrutiny."[682] Several courts have adopted this interpretation in holding that the Bankruptcy Code's authorization of lien avoidance does not implicate takings under the Fifth Amendment.[683] Moreover, the Court itself has held that statutory limitations on allowance of a secured indenture trustee's claims for compensation for services and attorneys fees and for reimbursement of expenses do not violate the Fifth Amendment.[684] If *Radford* is not a dead letter, it is of limited vitality. Thus, secured creditors cannot rely

---

Vinton Branch of Mountain Trust Bank . . . ."); In re Gulf States Steel, Inc., 285 B.R. 497, 511 (Bankr. N.D. Ala. 2002) ("*Radford* has been seriously eroded if not overruled by *Wright v. Vinton Branch of Mountain Trust Bank . . . ."*).

680. *See, e.g.,* Woods v. Mich. Nat'l Bank-Valley (*In re* Woods), 9 B.R. 325, 328 (Bankr. E.D. Mich. 1981) ("Wright did not overrule *Radford* but rather limited and clarified its holding. . . . that the bankruptcy power is subject to the constraints of the Fifth Amendment.").

681. *See Radford*, 295 U.S. at 589 ("The bankruptcy power . . . is subject to the Fifth Amendment . . . .").

682. *See* James Steven Rogers, *The Impairment of Secured Creditors' Rights in Reorganization: A Study of the Relationship Between the Fifth Amendment and the Bankruptcy Clause*, 96 HARV. L. REV. 973, 985 (1983).

683. *See, e.g.,* Travelers Ins. Co. v. Bullington, 878 F.2d 354, 359 n.6 (11th Cir. 1989); Yi v. Citibank (Md.) N.A. (*In re* Yi), 219 B.R. 394, 401 (E.D. Va. 1998).

684. *See* Reconstruction Fin. Corp. v. Bankers Trust Co., 318 U.S. 163, 168-70 (1943) (§ 77 railroad reorganization case in which claims for compensation for services, attorneys fees, and expenses of indenture trustee of secured mortgage bonds was referred to interstate commerce commission for determination).

on the Takings Clause to limit the modification of their property rights in bankruptcy cases.

In the final analysis, however, the Due Process Clause, not the Takings Clause, provides secured creditors with the baseline protection of property rights in bankruptcy. "Property rights do not gain any absolute inviolability in the bankruptcy court because created and protected by state law. Most property rights are so created and protected. But if Congress is acting within its bankruptcy power, it may authorize the bankruptcy court to affect these property rights, provided the limitations of the due process clause are observed."[685]

The Due Process Clause

In the Nineteenth Century, the Court decided *Canada Southern Railway v. Gebhard*[686] interpreting the Due Process Clause to accord substantive due process to United States holders of bonds in a Canadian out of court scheme of arrangement.[687] The Court analyzed the bondholders' rights in comparison to their rights in bankruptcy:[688]

> The confirmation and legalization of "a scheme of arrange-ment" under such circumstances is no more than is done in bankruptcy when a "composition" agreement with the bank-rupt debtor, if assented to by the required majority of credi-tors, is made binding on the non-assenting minority. In no just sense do such governmental regulations deprive a person of his property without due process of law. They simply require each individual to so conduct himself for the general good as not unnecessarily to injure another.

The Court went on to note that even secured creditors must yield some rights in bankruptcy:[689]

> Every member of a political community must necessarily part with some of the rights which, as an individual, not affected by his relation to others, he might have retained. Such concessions

---

685. *See* Wright v. Union Cent. Life Ins. Co., 304 U.S. 502, 518 (1938).

686. 109 U.S. 527 (1883).

687. *See id.* at 537-39.

688. *See id.* at 536.

689. *See id.*

make up the consideration he gives for the obligation of the body politic to protect him in life, liberty, and property. Bankrupt laws, whatever may be the form they assume, are of that character.

Even though economic substantive due process fell into disfavor after the Court overturned *Lochner v. New York*[690] and its progeny[691] in 1937,[692] the Court's analysis in *Gebhard* continues to inform its decisions on procedural due process.

Early on, the Court held that the Due Process Clause[693] trumps the Bankruptcy Clause.[694] For example, in *Moyses*[695] the Court considered a due process challenge to a debtor receiving a discharge in bankruptcy without service of process or personal notice to creditors of the

---

690. *See* Lochner v. New York, 198 U.S. 45, 52 (1905) (striking down as violative of substantive due process and freedom of contract a law prohibiting employers from allowing employees to work more than ten hours in one day).

691. *See, e.g.,* Adkins v. Children's Hosp., 261 U.S. 525, 539 (1923) (overturning minimum wage statute for women as violative of freedom of contract); Coppage v. Kansas, 236 U.S. 1 (1915) (overturning as violative of freedom of contract a statute prohibiting employers from requiring employees to agree not to join unions).

692. *See* W. Coast Hotel Co. v. Parrish, 300 U.S. 379, 400 (1937) (overturning *Adkins* and the *Lochner* line of substantive due process cases).

693. The Due Process Clause of the Fifth Amendment applies to limit the federal government's exercise of its bankruptcy power. With respect to state insolvency statutes, a similar analysis would apply under the Fourteenth Amendment. *See, e.g.,* Neblett v. Carpenter, 305 U.S. 297 (1939) (holding that a state statute for the rehabilitation of insurance companies authorizing the insurance commissioner, subject to the approval of the court, to mutualize or reinsure the business of the company or to enter into rehabilitation agreements, is not so vague that a decision by the state court construing the statute to authorize a certain plan and procedure would deprive policyholders of their property without due process of law).

694. Of course the Due Process Clause of the Fourteenth Amendment also trumps state insolvency statutes, but a state statute subordinating claims of a foreign corporation to claims of state residents does not violate due process of law. *See* Blake v. McClung, 172 U.S. 239, 259-60 (1898) (holding that foreign corporation was not denied due process of law simply because its claim was subordinated to state creditors).

695. *See* Hanover Nat'l Bank v. Moyses, 186 U.S. 181, 187 (1902) (notice requirements of Fifth Amendment apply and are satisfied).

discharge adjudication in the bankruptcy case.[696] The Court noted that the Due Process Clause applied and proceeded to define the scope of procedural process that has influenced notice in bankruptcy cases to the present:[697]

> Creditors are bound by the proceedings in distribution on notice by publication and mail, and when jurisdiction has attached and been exercised to that extent, the court has jurisdiction to decree discharge, if sufficient opportunity to show cause to the contrary is afforded, on notice given in the same way. . . . Service of process or personal notice is not essential to the binding force of the decree.

Thus, the Court set the predicate for notice by mail and publication in bankruptcy cases and proceedings and further established that the Constitution only requires creditors to have the opportunity to request a hearing.[698]

Nearly 50 years after *Moyses*, the Court decided *Mullane v. Central Hanover Bank & Trust Co.*,[699] refining its definition of notice that comports with procedural due process in the context of a state trust distribution dispute.[700] The trustee gave notice of settlement of its first accounting only by publication, and certain beneficiaries challenged the notice as violative of their due process rights.[701] The Court resolved the matter by setting forth a rule that has survived the ages: when the claimant's interest and whereabouts is known or reasonably ascertainable, actual notice, rather than notice by publication is required; when the claimant's interest and whereabouts is unknown and not reasonably ascertainable, proper notice by publication will

---

696. *See id.* at 191-92.

697. *See id.* at 192.

698. *See* 11 U.S.C. § 102(1) (2000) (construing "after notice and a hearing") and Fed. R. Bankr. P. 2002(a), (f), & (*l*) (providing for notice by first class mail or by publication when first class mail is impracticable).

699. 339 U.S. 306 (1950).

700. *See id.* at 307 (considering due process under the Fourteenth Amendment).

701. *See id.* at 309-11.

satisfy the constitutional requirement of due process of law.[702] With respect to the scope and form of notice, it must be "reasonably calculated to reach those who could easily be informed" because "notice reasonably certain to reach most of those interested in objecting is likely to safeguard the interests of all."[703]

Aside from considering the Due Process Clause in the context of appropriate bankruptcy notices, the Court has also addressed due process issues in bankruptcy as applied to the rights of secured creditors. The Bankruptcy Clause gives Congress broad powers to modify the rights of secured creditors subject to the constraints of the Due Process Clause of the Fifth Amendment.[704] For example, in *Continental Illinois National Bank & Trust Co. of Chicago v. Chicago, Rock Island & Pacific Railway Co.*,[705] the Court held that the bankruptcy court's injunction enjoining secured bondholders from selling their collateral did not destroy contract rights without due process of law, but simply delayed the enforcement of a contractual remedy.[706]

In *Wright v. Vinton Branch of the Mountain Trust Bank*,[707] Justice Brandeis, writing for a unanimous Court, summarized the Court's jurisprudence affecting the interests of secured creditors:[708]

> A court of bankruptcy may affect the interests of lienholders in many ways. To carry out the purposes of the Bankruptcy Act, it may direct that all liens upon property forming part of

---

702. *See id.* at 317-18.

703. *See id.* at 319.

704. *See, e.g.*, Wright v. Union Cent. Life Ins. Co., 304 U.S. 502, 518 (1938) ("Property rights do not gain any absolute inviolability in the bankruptcy court because created and protected by state law. Most property rights are so created and protected. But if Congress is acting within its bankruptcy power, it may authorize the bankruptcy court to affect these property rights, provided the limitations of the due process clause are observed.").

705. 294 U.S. 648 (1935).

706. *See id.* at 680-81.

707. 300 U.S. 440 (1937).

708. *See id.* at 470.

a bankrupt's estate be marshaled; or that the property be sold free of encumbrances and the rights of all lien holders be transferred to the proceeds of the sale. *Van Huffel v. Harke-lrode*, 284 U.S. 225, 227. Despite the peremptory terms of a pledge, it may enjoin the sale of the collateral, if it finds that the sale would hinder or delay preparation or consummation of a plan of reorganization. *Continental Illinois National Bank & Trust Co. v. Chicago, R.I. & P. Ry. Co.*, 294 U.S. 648, 680-681. It may enjoin like action by a mortgagee which would defeat the purpose of subsection (s) [of the Frazier-Lemke Act] to effect rehabilitation of the farmer mortgagor.

Thus, the Court evaluates whether bankruptcy legislation modifies a secured creditor's substantive or remedial rights "to such an extent as to deny the due process of law guaranteed by the Fifth Amendment."[709]

Not every procedural delay imposed on a secured creditor constitutes a violation of the Due Process Clause. For example, in the Court's first decision in *Wright v. Union Central Life Insurance Co.*,[710] the Court upheld as constitutional a statute extending for up to three years a statutory period for the debtor to redeem an equity of redemption.[711] Every contract is "made subject to constitutional power in the Congress to legislate on the subject of bankruptcies. . . . The rights of the purchaser are preserved, the possibility of enjoyment is merely delayed."[712]

The Court elaborated this principle in its second decision in *Wright v. Union Central Life Insurance Co.*,[713] when it held that the debtor had a statutory right to have the property appraised for pur-

---

709. *See id.*

710. 304 U.S. 502 (1938).

711. *See id.* at 515-16 (citing Home Bldg. & Loan Ass'n v. Blaisdell, 290 U.S. 398, 448 (1934) (neither Contracts Clause nor Due Process Clause of Fourteenth Amendment violated by two year extension of redemption period)).

712. *See Wright*, 304 U.S. at 516.

713. 311 U.S. 273 (1940).

poses of redemption before the creditor has a right to public sale.[714] Writing for the Court, Justice Douglas rebuffed the secured creditor's objection, noting that the statute provided safeguards "to protect the rights of secured creditors, throughout the proceedings, to the extent of the value of the property. There is no constitutional claim of the creditor to more than that."[715] The Court expanded this rationale in *Reconstruction Finance Corp. v. Denver & Rio Grande Western Railroad Co.,*[716] when it held, in the context of a § 77 railroad reorganization case, that there was no constitutional impediment to the Interstate Commerce Commission's elimination of valueless secured claims from participating under the reorganization plan.[717]

Earlier, in *Kuehner v. Irving Trust Co.,*[718] the Court had held that a "reasonable limitation" on the amount of an allowed claim, even though it results in the destruction of the creditor's contractual remedies, does not violate the Due Process Clause.[719] *Kuehner* involved a § 77B reorganization case in which the debtor invoked § 77B(b)(10) of the bankruptcy law to limit to three-year's rent a lessor's indemnity claim for damages under a rejected lease.[720] The lessor, whose state law damages exceeded the three-year cap, asserted a Fifth Amend-

---

714. *See id.* at 277 ("We think that the denial of an opportunity for the debtor to redeem at the value fixed by the court before ordering a public sale was error.").

715. *See id.* at 278 (citations omitted). *Accord* Borchard v. Cal. Bank, 310 U.S. 311, 317 (1940) ("[T]he secured creditors' rights are protected to the extent of the value of the property.").

716. 328 U.S. 495 (1946).

717. *See id.* at 509 ("[T]he congressional authority to the Commission to eliminate valueless claims from participation in reorganization is a valid exercise of the federal bankruptcy power. . . . We see no more constitutional impediment to the elimination of claims against railroad debtors by the Interstate Commerce Commission's determination of values . . . than we do to their elimination by an accepted bid in a depression market.").

718. 299 U.S. 445 (1937).

719. *See id.* at 452, 455.

720. *See id.* at 447.

ment challenge under the Due Process Clause which the Court rejected.[721] The Court held that:[722]

> [w]hile, therefore, the Fifth Amendment forbids the destruction of a contract it does not prohibit bankruptcy legislation affecting the creditor's remedy for its enforcement against the debtor's assets, or the measure of the creditor's participation therein, if the statutory provisions are consonant with a fair, reasonable, and equitable distribution of those assets.

The Seventh Amendment

In *Granfinanciera, S.A. v. Nordberg,*[723] the Court held that Congress' exercise of power under the Bankruptcy Clause was subject to preservation of the right to jury trial under the Seventh Amendment.[724] "Congress cannot eliminate a party's Seventh Amendment right to a jury trial merely by relabeling the cause of action to which it attaches and placing exclusive jurisdiction in an administrative agency or a specialized court of equity."[725]

The *Granfinanciera* Court noted the ambiguity of the current statutory provisions for jury trials in bankruptcy cases.[726] Section 1411(a) of the Judicial Code[727] provides that the Bankruptcy Code and the Judicial Code "do not affect any right to trial by jury that an individual has under applicable nonbankruptcy law with regard to a personal injury or wrongful death tort claim."[728] This might lead one to conclude that the Bankruptcy Code only protects the right to jury

---

721. *See id.* at 448-49.

722. *See id.* at 452.

723. 492 U.S. 33 (1989).

724. *See id.* at 59-61.

725. *See id.* at 61.

726. *See id.* at 42 (citing S. Elizabeth Gibson, *Jury Trials in Bankruptcy: Obeying the Commands of Article III and the Seventh Amendment,* 72 Minn. L. Rev. 967, 989-96 (1988)).

727. *See* 28 U.S.C. § 1411(a) (2000).

728. *See id.*

trial in personal injury tort and wrongful death cases. But a contrary inference can be drawn from section 1411(b) which provides that "[t]he district court may order the issues arising [in connection with involuntary bankruptcy petitions] to be tried without a jury."[729] This implies that litigants have rights to jury trials in proceedings other than personal injury tort and wrongful death claims.

Finding the statute and legislative history to be unclear, the *Granfinanciera* Court held that "[t]he Seventh Amendment protects a litigant's right to a jury trial only if a cause of action is legal in nature and it involves a matter of 'private right.'"[730] After observing that restructuring of debtor-creditor relationships is not itself a public right,[731] the Court focused on whether the bankruptcy trustee's pursuit of a fraudulent conveyance action was a public right.[732] More than 50 years earlier, the Court held in *Schoenthal v. Irving Trust Co.*[733] that preference avoiding powers "constitute no part of the proceedings in bankruptcy but concern controversies arising out of it."[734] As a result, the *Granfinanciera* Court held that fraudulent conveyance causes of action are matters of private right rather than public right because they more nearly represent a contract claim brought by a debtor to enhance the size of the estate than they do disputes among creditors to divide the *res*.[735] The Court's holding should apply to preference and

---

729. *See* 28 U.S.C. § 1411(b) (2000).

730. *See Granfinanciera*, 492 U.S. at 42 n.4. Even then, if the defendant has filed a proof of claim with the bankruptcy court, it will waive its right to jury trial with respect to any objection to claim or an avoiding power counterclaim. *See* Langenkamp v. Culp, 498 U.S. 42 (1990) (Bankruptcy Code case); Katchen v. Landy, 382 U.S. 323 (1966) (Bankruptcy Act case).

731. *See Granfinanciera*, 492 U.S. at 56 n.11.

732. *See id.* at 56.

733. 287 U.S. 92 (1932).

734. *See id.* at 94-95.

735. *See Granfinanciera*, 492 U.S. at 56.

other avoiding power causes of action[736] as well, unless they request equitable relief.[737] The Court clarified that "[i]f a claim that is legal in nature asserts a 'public right,' . . . then the Seventh Amendment does not entitle the parties to a jury trial if Congress assigns its adjudication to an administrative agency or specialized court of equity."[738] The Court held that if a legal right is not closely intertwined with a federal regulatory program and the right neither belongs to nor is asserted against the federal government, then the right "carries with it the Seventh Amendment's guarantee of a jury trial."[739] The Court left for another day, which has not yet come, the question whether the Constitution permits non-Article III judges to conduct jury trials, either outright or subject to the supervision of an Article III United States district court.[740]

The Tenth Amendment

The Tenth Amendment reserves to the states those powers not delegated to the United States by the Constitution.[741] The Court has rejected as "futile" arguments by secured creditors or purchasers at

---

736. *See id.* at 58 n.13 (citing, inter alia, *Katchen v. Landy* for the proposition that if the creditor had not filed a proof of claim, it could have demanded a jury trial on the trustee's preference suit that solely sought legal damages).

737. *See In re* Wood & Henderson, 210 U.S. 246, 258 (1908) (holding no Seventh Amendment right to jury trial in an action under Bankruptcy Code § 60d (the forbear of Bankruptcy Code § 329) to recover excessive fees paid prepetition to the debtor's attorney in contemplation of the bankruptcy filing).

738. *See Granfinanciera*, 492 U.S. at 42 n.4.

739. *See id.* at 54-55 (characterizing a bankruptcy trustee's right to bring a fraudulent transfer cause of action as a private right rather than a public right for purposes of the Court's Seventh Amendment analysis).

740. *See Granfinanciera*, 492 U.S. at 64.

741. Specifically, the Tenth Amendment provides that "[t]he powers not delegated to the United States by the Constitution, nor prohibited by it to the States, are reserved to the States respectively, or to the people." U.S. CONST. amend. X.

judicial sales that, because the regulation of property rights is left to the states under the Tenth Amendment, Congress has no power under the Bankruptcy Clause to alter their property rights.[742] "Bankruptcy proceedings constantly modify and affect property rights established by state law."[743]

An entirely separate matter, however, is the extent to which the Tenth Amendment precludes Congress from exercising the bankruptcy power to provide for the adjustment of debts of municipalities or other arms of the state. The Court addressed the issue for the first time in *Ashton v. Cameron County Water Improvement District*,[744] holding that Congress lacked the power to require creditors to accept a composition plan offered by a public corporation.[745] The Court never mentioned the Tenth Amendment directly but based its conclusion on principles of state sovereignty protected by the Tenth Amendment. First, the Court noted that since Congress cannot exercise the taxing power to tax municipal bonds without infringing state sovereignty, it likewise cannot exercise its bankruptcy power to infringe municipal bonds because the bankruptcy power cannot have any higher "rank or importance in our scheme of government" than the taxing power.[746] Second, because the Contracts Clause[747] forbids the states from impairing the obligations of their municipal bonds, the states cannot consent to federal legislation under the Bankruptcy Clause that accomplishes an end run around this restriction.[748] Moreover, for Congress to do so directly without the consent of the states would

---

742. *See, e.g.,* Wright v. Union Cent. Life Ins. Co., 304 U.S. 502, 517 (1938).

743. *See id.*

744. 298 U.S. 513 (1936).

745. *See id.* at 530-31.

746. *See id.* at 530.

747. U.S. CONST. art. I, § 10.

748. *See Ashton*, 298 U.S. at 531.

impermissibly violate state sovereignty.[749] Thus, the Court struck down Chapter IX of the Bankruptcy Act[750] as unconstitutional.[751]

Two years later in *United States v. Bekins*,[752] however, the Court examined the constitutionality of Chapter X of the Bankruptcy Act,[753] a municipal debt adjustment statute, which Congress enacted after the Court's decision in *Ashton* struck down Chapter IX. The Court held that Congress could constitutionally provide a composition chapter applicable to arms of the state, without violating state sovereignty reserved under the Tenth Amendment, as long as the state retains both ultimate approval of the composition plan under state law and the ability to limit access of its instrumentalities to bankruptcy relief.[754] The Court distinguished its decision in *Ashton* by noting that Chapter X was carefully crafted to avoid federal interference with the power of the state or its subdivisions to manage their own affairs.[755] "The statute is carefully drawn so as not to impinge on the sovereignty of the State. The State retains control of its fiscal affairs."[756]

A comparison of Chapters IX and X, however, leads one to wonder what statutory differences were constitutionally significant. Perhaps there were none. In fact, Chapter IX had a requirement that the state or its subdivision approve the petition when required by local law, but this was deleted in Chapter X.[757]

---

749. *See id.*

750. Act of May 24, 1934, Pub. L. No. 73-251, 73d Cong., 2d Sess., ch. 345, §§ 78-80, 48 Stat. 798.

751. *See Ashton*, 298 U.S. at 532.

752. 304 U.S. 27 (1938).

753. Act of Aug. 16, 1937, Pub. L. No. 75-302, 75th Cong., 1st Sess., ch. 657, 50 Stat. 653.

754. *See Bekins*, 304 U.S. at 54.

755. *See id.* at 49-50.

756. *See id.* at 51.

757. *See id.* at 49. ("We attach no importance to this omission.").

A change in the composition of the Court also cannot explain the about face. In *Ashton*, Justice McReynolds wrote for a Court in which only Justice Cardozo dissented. In *Bekins*, after Justice Van Devanter left the Court and Justice Reed joined, Chief Justice Hughes wrote for a Court in which Justices McReynolds and Butler dissented and in which Justice Cardozo took no part. Was it possibly that Franklin Roosevelt's threat to pack the Court had an impact on the "Nine Old Men" and led the Court to a change of heart to sustain legislation that was of critical importance in combating the depression?[758] The *Bekins* opinion recites the conditions[759] in which the states alone were unable to provide relief based on the restrictions of the Contracts Clause.[760] Without federal and state cooperation under a municipal debt restructuring act, there would be no hope to solve this serious financial crisis.[761]

Article III

Article III of the Constitution requires the judicial power of the United States to be vested in the Supreme Court "and in such inferior Courts as the Congress may from time to time ordain and establish."[762]

---

758. In A.L.A. Schechter Poultry Corp. v. United States, 295 U.S. 495 (1935), notwithstanding the crisis of the great depression, a Supreme Court that was conservative, both economically and philosophically, unanimously struck down as unconstitutional the National Recovery Administration, the heart of President Franklin Roosevelt's New Deal. In response, President Roosevelt threatened to pack the Court with younger, more progressive Justices. *See*, Laura Kalman, *Law, Politics, and the New Deal(s)*, 108 YALE L.J. 2165 (1999); Barry Cushman, *Rethinking the New Deal Court*, 80 VA. L. REV. 201 (1994). *See generally*, Steven G. Calabresi & James Lindgren, *Term Limits for the Supreme Court: Life Tenure Reconsidered*, 29 HARV. J.L. & PUB. POL'Y 769 (2006).

759. *See Bekins*, 304 U.S. at 48 (describing the onerous burden of tax assessments, the high level of delinquencies, and the devastating impact on taxing districts to perform governmental functions).

760. *See* U.S. CONST. art. I, § 10 (precluding states from impairing obligations of contract).

761. *See Bekins*, 304 U.S. at 53-54.

762. U.S. CONST. art. III, § 1.

The Constitution further requires that the "Judges, both of the supreme and inferior Courts, shall hold their Offices during good Behavior" and receive compensation that may not be diminished during their tenure.[763] Nevertheless, despite warnings from the House Judiciary Committee,[764] Congress enacted the 1978 Bankruptcy Code which vested pervasive jurisdiction in non-Article III courts.[765]

Four years later, in *Northern Pipeline Construction Co. v. Marathon Pipe Line Co.*,[766] the Court[767] declared the Bankruptcy Code's pervasive grant of jurisdiction to non-Article III judges to be unconstitutional.[768] Although the controversy arose in an adversary proceeding in which the debtor in possession, as plaintiff, asserted a state law breach of contract and warranty cause of action,[769] the Court held the jurisdictional infirmity to be non-severable and struck the constitutionality of the entire bankruptcy court system.[770] In no sense

---

763. *Id.*

764. The 1977 report of the House Committee on the Judiciary to accompany H.R. 8200 contained a lengthy analysis concluding that a pervasive grant of jurisdiction to a non-Article III judge would be unconstitutional. *See* H.R. REP. NO. 95-595, 95th Cong., 1st Sess., 21-39 (1977).

765. *See* Pub. L. No. 95-598, §§ 201(a), 241(a), 92 Stat. 2549, 2657-60, 2668-69, enacting 28 U.S.C. §§ 151 et seq. & 1471 et seq.

766. 458 U.S. 50 (1982).

767. The *Northern Pipeline* decision must be analyzed with great care because the judgment of the Court was accompanied by a four-Justice plurality opinion authored by Justice Brennan, a two-Justice opinion authored by Justice Rehnquist concurring in the judgment, and a three-Justice dissent authored by Justice White. Chief Justice Burger joined in Justice White's dissent and wrote his own dissenting opinion. *See id.*

768. *See id.* at 87.

769. *See id.* at 56, 89.

770. *See id.* at 87-88, 91-92. Justice Rehnquist's concurrence, joined in by Justice O'Connor, was more measured: "I would, therefore, hold so much of the Bankruptcy Act of 1978 as enables a Bankruptcy Court to entertain and decide Northern's lawsuit over Marathon's objection to be violative of Art. III of the United States Constitution." *See id.* at 91. Ultimately, however, the concurrence opted to strike the entire grant of

could the estate's pursuit of the debtor's action for breach of contract be said to involve a "public right" that might warrant an exception to the strictures of Article III.[771] Rather, the estate's right to recover contract damages implicated state-created private rights that required adjudication by an Article III judge if it was to be pursued in a federal forum as opposed to trial by a state court judge and jury.[772] The plurality opinion implied, however, that the restructuring of debtor-creditor relations, which is at the heart of the federal bankruptcy power, might well constitute a public right subject to adjudication by a non-Article III tribunal.[773] The resolution of that issue is for another day. The scope of bankruptcy court jurisdiction, including the congressional and judicial response to *Northern Pipeline*, is discussed more fully in Chapter 4.[774]

SOVEREIGN IMMUNITY

The application of Sovereign Immunity in bankruptcy cases has been the focus of many law review articles, and an in-depth analysis of the subject could well fill a short book.[775] During the past 111 years,

---

jurisdiction as unconstitutional based on non-severability: "Because I agree with the plurality that this grant of authority is not readily severable from the remaining grant of authority to bankruptcy courts under § 1471, *see ante*, at 87-88, n.40, I concur in the judgment." *See id.* at 91-92.

771. *See id.* at 71, 91.

772. *See id.* at 71-72, 90.

773. *See id.* at 71.

774. *See infra* Ch. 4, pp. 214-215 & nn.1057-1061 (discussing the Bankruptcy Amendments and Federal Judgeship Act of 1984, Pub. L. No. 353, 98th Cong., 2d Sess., 98 Stat. 333 (1984)).

775. *See, e.g.,* Randolph J. Haines, *The Uniformity Power: Why Bankruptcy Is Different*, 77 AM. BANKR. L.J. 129 (2003); Ralph Brubaker, *Of State Sovereign Immunity and Prospective Remedies: The Bankruptcy Discharge as a Statutory* Ex parte Young Relief, 76 AM. BANKR. L.J. 461 (2002); Shauna Fuller Veach, *Dissension Among the Ranks—The Courts are at Odds Over 11 U.S.C. § 106 and its Purported Abrogation of Sovereign Immunity In the Bankruptcy Code*, 32 U. MEM. L. REV. 475, 475-519 (2002); Randolph J. Haines, *Getting to Abrogation*, 75 AM. BANKR.

the Court has considered when, and under what conditions, federal and state sovereigns may be sued in bankruptcy courts and other forums. In part, the Court's jurisprudence turns on whether sovereigns have consented to jurisdiction by an affirmative act or waiver. The Court has also examined when Congress may abrogate sovereign immunity. Although the United States and each particular state may assert sovereign immunity, different legal considerations apply to the waiver or abrogation of federal and state sovereign immunity.

Federal Sovereign Immunity

Sovereign immunity protects a non-consenting sovereign against suits to establish *in personam* liability. On the other hand, when the federal government has possession of an intangible asset over which the debtor asserts ownership, sovereign immunity will not preclude a federal court from proceeding *in rem* to order turnover of the asset.[776]

There are several forms of sovereign immunity depending on the form of the sovereign.[777] The doctrine of Federal sovereign immunity is a court-made doctrine that preserves the integrity of the federal sovereign against suits by its citizens without its consent. The doctrine derives from English law when the King reigned supreme and could do no wrong.[778]

Without question, Congress has the power to waive or abrogate federal sovereign immunity and has attempted to do so in several

---

L.J. 447 (2001); Chad J. Kutmas, *Piercing Sovereign Immunity in Bankruptcy: Myth or Reality?*, 37 TUL. L. REV. 457, 457-79 (2001); Kenneth N. Klee, James O. Johnston & Eric Winston, *State Defiance of Bankruptcy Law*, 52 VAND. L. REV. 1527, 1527-1606 (1999).

776. *See* United States v. Whiting Pools, Inc., 462 U.S. 198, 211 (1983).

777. Courts have recognized sovereign immunity to prevent suits against federal, state, foreign, and domestic sovereign entities without their consent. *See, e.g.,* Alden v. Maine, 527 U.S. 706, 714-16 (1999) (state government); United States v. Nordic Vill., Inc., 503 U.S. 30, 37-39 (1992) (federal government).

778. *See, e.g.,* Alden v. Maine, 527 U.S. 706, 715-16 (1999).

instances.[779] The Court, however, has imposed strict rules that define when it will honor a congressional waiver. In *United States v. Nordic Village, Inc.*,[780] the Court held that Bankruptcy Code § 106(c),[781] which generally waived sovereign immunity whenever the Bankruptcy Code used the term "governmental unit," did not waive federal sovereign immunity against money claims asserted against the United States.[782] The Court reasoned that waivers of the government's sovereign immunity must be expressed unequivocally to be effective, and they are not to be construed liberally to give effect to general waivers.[783]

Evidently Congress was not pleased with the Court's *Nordic Village* decision and, in 1994 amended Bankruptcy Code § 106 to expressly abrogate sovereign immunity in 60 separate sections of the Bankruptcy Code.[784] After enactment of the 1994 amendment, the Court has uniformly concluded that Congress' intent to abrogate sovereign immunity under the Bankruptcy Code is unmistakably clear.[785] The debate has therefore turned to its power to do so. Although congressional power to abrogate federal sovereign immunity, foreign sovereign immunity, and Indian tribe sovereign immunity is

779. *See, e.g.,* Federal Tort Claims Act, Pub. L. No. 79-601, §§ 401-22, 60 Stat. 842 (1946) (codified as amended at 28 U.S.C. §§ 2671-80 (2000)); 11 U.S.C. § 106(a) (2000).

780. 503 U.S. 30 (1992).

781. 11 U.S.C. § 106(c) (1990). *See infra* n.784 regarding the 1994 amendment rewriting the substance of § 106(c).

782. *See Nordic Village,* 503 U.S. at 34.

783. *See id.*

784. *See* Pub. L. No. 103-394 § 113, 108 Stat. 4106, 4117 (Oct. 22, 1994) (rewriting section 106(c) of the original 1978 Bankruptcy Code as section 106(a)).

785. *See, e.g.,* Tenn. Student Assistance Corp. v. Hood, 541 U.S. 440, 463 (2004); Vt. Agency of Natural Res. v. United States *ex rel.* Stevens, 529 U.S. 765, 790-91 (2000).

unquestionable, its power to abrogate state sovereign immunity has been much less clear.[786]

Eleventh Amendment Immunity

For many years, the Court considered congressional efforts to abrogate state sovereign immunity in light of the protection afforded the states by the Eleventh Amendment.[787] Under Eleventh Amendment law, as is true with respect to abrogation or waiver of federal sovereign immunity, the Court will not find abrogation of state sover-

---

786. With respect to suits against foreign sovereigns, Congress has passed legislation that preempts the field; the Foreign Sovereign Immunities Act of 1976, 28 U.S.C. § 1602 *et seq.*, "establishes a comprehensive framework for determining whether a court in this country, state or federal, may exercise jurisdiction over a foreign state." *See* Argentina v. Weltover, Inc., 504 U.S. 607, 610 (1992) (allowing Argentina to be sued in the United States district court for a default on Argentine government bonds). With respect to suits against domestic sovereign nations, i.e., Indian tribes, Congress likewise has complete power to abrogate their immunity and has done so in limited circumstances. *See, e.g.,* Kiowa Tribe v. Mfg. Techs., Inc., 523 U.S. 751, 754, 758 (1998) ("As a matter of federal law, an Indian tribe is subject to suit only where Congress has authorized the suit or the tribe has waived its immunity."). With respect to abrogation of the sovereign immunity of states of the United States, however, the issue is more nuanced as discussed below.

787. The Eleventh Amendment provides that "the judicial power of the United States shall not be construed to extend to any suit in law or equity, commenced or prosecuted against one of the United States by Citizens of another State, or by Citizens or Subjects of any Foreign State." U.S. CONST. amend. XI. The Court has expanded application of the Eleventh Amendment well beyond its text to shield states against suits by their own citizens, Indian tribes, and foreign sovereigns. *See* Hans v. Louisiana, 134 U.S. 1, 10 (1890) (state may not be sued without its consent by its own citizens); Blatchford v. Native Vill. of Noatak, 501 U.S. 775, 786 (1991) (state may not be sued without its consent by Indian tribe); Principality of Monaco v. Mississippi, 292 U.S. 313, 330 (1934) (state may not be sued without its consent by foreign sovereign). *Cf.* Krystal Energy Co. v. Navajo Nation, 357 F.3d 1055, 1058 (9th Cir. 2004) (because Indian tribes are domestic governments, their sovereign immunity is congressionally abrogated by Bankruptcy Code §§ 106(a) & 101(27)).

eign immunity unless the language of the statute is unmistakably clear.[788] Moreover, abrogation is only effective if Congress has the power to do so. Although the Court has recognized congressional power to abrogate the states' Eleventh Amendment and sovereign immunity under section 5 of the Fourteenth Amendment,[789] the Court has stated broadly, outside of the bankruptcy context, that Congress may not use its Article I powers to abrogate state sovereign immunity.[790] In fact, in *Seminole Tribe of Florida v. Florida*,[791] both the majority and dissenting opinions contain dicta that reflect an assumption that Congress may not use its Article I powers to abrogate state sovereign immunity in the bankruptcy context.[792] These dicta came after the Court's analysis in *Hoffman v. Connecticut Department of Income Maintenance*,[793] holding that Bankruptcy Code § 106(c)[794] did not abrogate sovereign immunity because Congress did not make

---

788. *See, e.g.,* Hoffman v. Conn. Dep't of Income Maint., 492 U.S. 96, 102-03 (1989) (restricting then § 106(c)'s waiver of sovereign immunity to injunctive and declaratory relief because Congress' intentions to abrogate the states' sovereign immunity was not unmistakably clear).

789. *See* Coll. Sav. Bank v. Fla. Prepaid Postsecondary Educ. Expense Bd., 527 U.S. 666, 672 (1999); City of Boerne v. Flores, 521 U.S. 507, 519 (1997); Seminole Tribe of Fla. v. Florida, 517 U.S. 44, 65-66 (1996); Fitzpatrick v. Bitzer, 427 U.S. 445, 456 (1976).

790. *See* Fla. Prepaid Postsecondary Educ. Expense Bd. v. Coll. Sav. Bank, 527 U.S. 627, 635-36 (1999) (invalidating legislation promulgated under the Patent Clause, U.S. CONST. art. I, § 8, cl. 8, and the Interstate Commerce Clause, U.S. CONST. art. I, § 8, cl. 3); Seminole Tribe of Fla. v. Florida, 517 U.S. 44, 71-72 (1996) (invalidating legislation promulgated under the Indian Commerce Clause, U.S. CONST. art. I, § 8, cl. 3).

791. 517 U.S. 44 (1996).

792. *See id.* at 73 n.16, 77, 77 n.1.

793. 492 U.S. 96 (1989).

794. 11 U.S.C. § 106(c) (1978). As enacted in 1978, § 106(c), the forerunner of current Bankruptcy Code § 106(a), used general references to "creditor," "entity," or "governmental" unit as a device to bind governmental units and thereby waive or abrogate sovereign immunity. *See* 92 Stat. 2556.

sufficiently explicit its intention to withdraw the state sovereign immunity defense in certain bankruptcy actions.[795]

Even if Congress does not abrogate the states' sovereign immunity, however, a state may, by consent or conduct, waive its immunity under certain circumstances. For example, a state may consent to suit in federal court by a clear waiver in a contract or state statute. Alternatively, a state may surrender its immunity by engaging in conduct that manifests clearly its intention to waive its immunity.[796] For example, in the bankruptcy context, the Court has long held that a state waives its sovereign immunity by conduct when it files a proof of claim in a bankruptcy case.[797]

In circumstances when the bankruptcy court proceeds *in rem*, the doctrine of sovereign immunity will have limited application to fetter the bankruptcy court's power to administer the bankruptcy estate and enforce the bankruptcy discharge.[798] For example, in *New York v. Irving Trust Co.*,[799] the Court held that a state must comply with applicable bankruptcy procedures in order to participate in the division of the bankruptcy estate. In *Van Huffel v. Harkelrode*,[800] the Court held that the bankruptcy court has the power to sell the estate's property free and clear of a state's tax lien: "Realization upon the lien created by state law must yield to the requirements of bankruptcy administration."[801]

---

795. *See id.* at 104.

796. *See, e.g.,* Lapides v. Bd. of Regents, 535 U.S. 613, 618 (2002); Coll. Sav. Bank v. Fla. Prepaid Postsecondary Educ. Expense Bd., 527 U.S. 666, 675-76 (1999).

797. *See* Gardner v. New Jersey, 329 U.S. 565, 574 (1947). *See also* Lapides v. Bd. of Regents, 535 U.S. 613 (2002) and Cent. Va. Cmty. Coll. v. Katz, 546 U.S. 356 (2006) (both citing *Gardner* with approval).

798. *See* Cent. Va. Cmty. Coll. v. Katz, 546 U.S. 356, 362-63 (2006).

799. 288 U.S. 329, 332 (1933).

800. 284 U.S. 225 (1931).

801. *See id.* at 228.

The so-called *in rem* exception to the assertion of state sovereign immunity has its roots in admiralty cases when a federal court administering a *res* has power to require a state to turnover personal property in its possession, at least when the state has no colorable claim to title.[802] Moreover, when property, such as a shipwreck, is already in custody of a federal court, the court may quiet title to the property notwithstanding an assertion of sovereign immunity.[803] There is an exception to this doctrine, however, that permits the state to assert sovereign immunity in an *in rem* proceeding when the state's sovereignty interest is uniquely implicated or otherwise involves an "essential attribute of sovereignty," such as title to submerged lands in its possession.[804]

Recently, the Court extended the logic of its admiralty *in rem* decisions to bankruptcy cases,[805] noting that "[b]ankruptcy courts have exclusive jurisdiction over a debtor's property, wherever located, and over the estate[,] . . . [and a] bankruptcy court's *in rem* jurisdiction permits it 'to determin[e] all claims that anyone . . . has to the property or thing in question.'"[806] Thus, the bankruptcy court has *in rem* jurisdiction to enforce the debtor's discharge even when the bankruptcy rules require the debtor to file a complaint and serve a summons against the state.[807]

---

802. *See* Florida v. Treasure Salvors, Inc., 485 U.S. 670, 687 (1982).

803. *See* California v. Deep Sea Research, Inc., 523 U.S. 491, 507-08 (1998).

804. *See* Idaho v. Coeur D'Alene Tribe of Idaho, 521 U.S. 261, 283-88 (1997).

805. *See* Tenn. Student Assistance Corp. v. Hood, 541 U.S. 440, 451 (2004) ("Although both bankruptcy and admiralty are specialized areas of the law, we see no reason why the exercise of the federal courts' in rem bankruptcy jurisdiction is more threatening to state sovereignty than the exercise of their in rem admiralty jurisdiction.").

806. *See id.* at 447-48.

807. *See id.* at 453-54.

Nevertheless, even the bankruptcy court's *in rem* jurisdiction is not without limits. In *United States v. Nordic Village, Inc.*,[808] the Court held that a bankruptcy court's *in rem* jurisdiction could not overcome the federal government's sovereign immunity assertion against a bankruptcy trustee's suit for money damages.[809] One might assume that the same result would hold when a trustee asserts a bankruptcy avoiding power to recover money in the hands of a state. As noted in Chapter 1, the Court granted certiorari in *Central Virginia Community College v. Katz*,[810] "to consider the question left open . . . in *Hood*: whether Congress' attempt to abrogate state sovereign immunity in 11 U.S.C. § 106(a) is valid."[811] Although the Court again failed to answer the question on which it granted certiorari, it held, in a 5-4 decision, that the trustee could recover a preferential transfer from an agency that was the arm of a state because Congress had the power to "treat States in the same way as other creditors insofar as concerns 'Laws on the subject of Bankruptcies.'"[812] This holding was not based on congressional abrogation of state sovereign immunity but on considerations of constitutional sovereign immunity.[813]

Constitutional Sovereign Immunity

Separate and apart from the Eleventh Amendment, the Court has held that the doctrine of state sovereign immunity must be analyzed on a constitutional basis as evidenced in the plan of the Convention.[814]

---

808.   503 U.S. 30 (1992).

809.   *See id.* at 38 (holding that when the statute did not clearly waive federal sovereign immunity, a bankruptcy court's *in rem* jurisdiction could not sustain a bankruptcy trustee's suit to recover property wrongfully transferred to the IRS).

810.   544 U.S. 960 (2005).

811.   *See* Cent. Va. Cmty. Coll. v. Katz, 546 U.S. 356, 361 (2006).

812.   *See id.* at 1005.

813.   *See id.* at 1004.

814.   *See id.* at 1004-05 (citing Alden v. Maine, 527 U.S. 706, 713 (1999) (non-bankruptcy case holding that state sovereign immunity is constitutional in scope without regard to the Eleventh Amendment) and

In other words, there is a presumption under our constitutional system that the states have retained their sovereign immunity against suit without their consent in the federal courts unless a plaintiff shows by conclusive evidence that the states surrendered their immunity as part of the plan of the Convention.[815]

Although some lower courts held that the uniformity aspect of the Bankruptcy Clause constitutes such evidence, until its holding in *Central Virginia Community College v. Katz*, the Court refused to resolve this issue. For example, in *Hood*, the precise question presented was whether the plan of Convention abrogated the states' sovereign immunity with respect to bankruptcy cases. As noted previously, the Court decided *Hood* on the basis of *in rem* jurisdiction instead of deciding the question presented.[816]

In *Central Virginia Community College v. Katz*, however, the Court reached "[t]he ineluctable conclusion . . . that States agreed in the plan of the Convention not to assert any sovereign immunity defense they might have had in [bankruptcy] proceedings . . . ."[817] The Court's holding was contrary to statements made in both the majority and dissenting opinions in *Seminole Tribe* that Congress had no power under the Bankruptcy Clause to abrogate state sovereign

---

Blatchford v. Native Vill. of Noatak, 501 U.S. 775, 779 (1991) (non-bankruptcy case observing that a state is not subject to suit in federal court unless it has consented either expressly or in the plan of the Convention)).

815. *See* Hans v. Louisiana, 134 U.S. 1, 12-13 (1890) (quoting The Federalist No. 81) and Welch v. United States, 409 F.3d 646 (4th Cir. 2005) (holding in a nonbankruptcy case that plaintiff has the burden to prove a waiver of sovereign immunity). *See generally*, Kenneth N. Klee, James O. Johnston & Eric Winston, *State Defiance of Bankruptcy Law*, 52 VAND. L. REV. 1527 (1999). *See also* Amicus Brief of Professors William Cohen & Kenneth N. Klee in Support of Debtor/Appellee Kathryn Bliemeister, Arizona v. Bliemeister (*In re* Bliemeister), 296 F.3d 858 (9th Cir. 2002) (No. 01-16058) (on file with author).

816. *See Hood*, 541 U.S. at 454-55 (refusing to decide constitutionality of Bankruptcy Code § 106).

817. 546 U.S. 356, 377 (2006).

immunity.[818] But, based largely on the efforts of Justice O'Connor,[819] the Court carefully considered the history of the plan of the Convention and rejected this erroneous dictum.[820] At least with respect to "orders ancillary to the bankruptcy courts' *in rem* jurisdiction, like orders directing turnover of preferential transfers, . . . the States agreed in the plan of the Convention not to assert that immunity."[821]

Thus, the Court has drawn an *in rem* line that recognizes the Bankruptcy Clause as the source of congressional power to intrude on state sovereign immunity. Time will tell whether the Court will reach a different conclusion when a trustee sues a state not to collect the *res* but to impose *in personam* liability.

Ex parte Young Relief

Whether a state asserts constitutional sovereign immunity or Eleventh Amendment immunity, the Court has held that federal courts may fashion prospective injunctive relief to prevent state officials from ongoing violations federal law.[822] The genesis for this remedy is *Ex parte Young*[823] in which the Court reasoned that if[824]

> [t]he act to be enforced is alleged to be unconstitutional, and if it be so, the use of the name of the State to enforce an unconstitutional act to the injury of complainants is a proceeding without the authority of and one which does not affect the State in its sovereign or governmental capacity. It is simply an illegal act upon the part of a State official in attempting by the

---

818. *See id.* at 363 (acknowledging this point).

819. In one of her last acts on the Court before retiring, Justice O'Connor apparently persuaded four of her colleagues to uphold the integrity of the bankruptcy system against the assertion of state sovereign immunity.

820. *See* Cent. Va. Cmty. Coll. v. Katz, 546 U.S. at 363.

821. *See id.* at 373.

822. *See Seminole Tribe*, 517 U.S. at 73.

823. 209 U.S. 123, 149 (1908).

824. *See id.* at 159.

use of the name of the State to enforce a legislative enactment which is void because unconstitutional.

Therefore, if a debtor has advance notice that a state official is about to continue an ongoing violation of binding federal law, the debtor may petition the bankruptcy court to issue an *Ex parte Young* injunction against the state official. The relief should be available unless "Congress has prescribed [a statute that contains] a *detailed remedial scheme* for the enforcement against a State of a statutorily created right."[825] Presumably, the Bankruptcy Code is not such a statute. In fact, to the contrary, one commentator argues that the bankruptcy discharge itself is a self-executing *Ex parte Young* injunction that statutorily enjoins state officers from collecting a discharged debt.[826]

FEDERAL PREEMPTION AND FEDERALISM

When bankruptcy law conflicts with state law, considerations of federalism compound the Court's difficulty in resolving the conflict. At the outset, it is important to note that the Court sometimes sidesteps policy conflicts by purporting to "harmonize" conflicts between federal bankruptcy law and inconsistent state laws.[827] For example, in *Harris v. Zion Savings Bank & Trust Co.*,[828] the Court, seeking to harmonize state and federal law, held that a deceased farmer's administrator was authorized to file a federal bankruptcy petition only if

---

825. *See Seminole Tribe*, 517 U.S. at 74. As noted previously, the injunctive relief is not permissible if it implicates a state's "special sovereignty interests." *See also Coeur D'Alene Tribe*, 521 U.S. at 281.

826. *See* Ralph Brubaker, *Of State Sovereign Immunity and Prospective Remedies: The Bankruptcy Discharge as a Statutory* Ex parte Young *Relief*, 76 AM. BANKR. L.J. 461, 470, 505, 511-33 (2002).

827. The Court also endeavors to harmonize conflicting federal laws as well. *See, e.g.,* Morton v. Mancari, 471 U.S. 535, 551 (1971) ("[W]hen two statutes are capable of co-existence, it is the duty of the courts, absent a clearly expressed congressional intention to the contrary, to regard each as effective.").

828. 317 U.S. 447 (1943).

state law permitted him to do so. The Court based its decision on a belief that the probate court was the proper forum for weighing the respective benefits or detriments to those who shared in the equity of the decedent's estate. There was no conflict with federal bankruptcy law because it only permitted filings by persons authorized under state law to file bankruptcy petitions.[829] Likewise, in *Johnson v. Star*,[830] the Court, following its recent decision in *Pobreslo v. Joseph M. Boyd Co.*,[831] held that a state statute which barred non-consenting creditors from seizing property covered by a general assignment for the benefit of creditors was not in conflict with the Bankruptcy Act because it was not an insolvency statute. Under the state statute, the assignment conveyed all of the debtor's property for the equal benefit of all of his creditors who accepted under the assignment and, thus, was in harmony with the Bankruptcy Act, as it sought to ensure better protection of creditors.[832] Moreover, in *Faitoute Iron & Steel Co. v. City of Asbury Park*,[833] the Court harmonized federal and state interests by holding that congressional passage of a municipal bankruptcy law did not operate retroactively to preempt state legislation providing for the restructuring of defaulted municipal bonds.[834] The Court doubted that a federal statute "carefully drawn so as not to impinge upon the sovereignty of the State" could have been intended by Congress to preempt a state from regulating the fiscal management

---

829.   *See id.* at 451-53. *See also* Price v. Gurney, 324 U.S. 100 (1945) (shareholder was not authorized to file a bankruptcy petition for debtor corporation because a corporation may file a voluntary petition only if its representative is authorized to do so under state law).

830.   287 U.S. 527 (1933).

831.   287 U.S. 518 (1933).

832.   The Court also noted that general assignments for the benefit of creditors were valid, even under common law, except with respect to nondischargeability proceedings instituted under the Bankruptcy Act, which would then supersede the assignment statute. *See id.* at 526.

833.   316 U.S. 502 (1942).

834.   *See id.* at 507-09.

of its instrumentalities.[835] Furthermore, in *Marine Harbor Properties, Inc. v. Manufacturers Trust Co.*,[836] the Court held that the enactment of Bankruptcy Act Chapter X did not preempt conflicting proceedings pending in state or federal courts, even though Congress could have done so.[837]

When the Court cannot harmonize federal bankruptcy and state law, it decides which law will prevail based on the Federal Rules of Decision Act: "The laws of the several states, except where the Constitution or treaties of the United States or Acts of Congress otherwise require or provide, shall be regarded as rules of decision in civil actions in the courts of the United States, in all cases where they apply."[838] In some cases the Court holds that federal bankruptcy principles preempt inconsistent state laws.[839] In other cases, however, the Court holds that federal bankruptcy law must yield to inconsistent state law.

On occasion, the Court frames the issue as a jurisdictional matter. In a non-bankruptcy case, *Sutton v. English*,[840] the Court held that state courts have exclusive jurisdiction to decide probate matters. The Court reasoned that once a probate estate is opened, the state court has exclusive *in rem* jurisdiction over all of the decedent's property.

---

835. *See id.* at 508 (citing United States v. Bekins, 304 U.S. 27, 50-51 (1938)).

836. 317 U.S. 78 (1942).

837. *See id.* at 83.

838. *See* 28 U.S.C. § 1652 (2000) originally enacted as the Act of Sept. 24, 1789, ch. 20, § 35, 1 Stat. 92. The only significant change was made in 1948 when the original reference to "trials at common law" was replaced by "civil actions." *See* Act of June 25, 1948, ch. 646 § 1652, 62 Stat. 944. Bankruptcy cases probably qualify as civil actions within the scope of the statute even to the extent they are *in rem*.

839. *See, e.g.,* Local Loan Co. v. Hunt, 292 U.S. 234, 244 (1934) (holding that the Rules of Decision Act docs not require the bankruptcy court to follow a state rule allowing a lien on future wages because the state rule conflicts with "the clear and unmistakable policy of the bankruptcy act").

840. 246 U.S. 199, 205 (1918).

Therefore, it would be inappropriate for a federal court to exercise competing jurisdiction over the *res*.[841] Likewise, through an extension of the *Younger*[842] doctrine, the Court has not permitted bankruptcy judges to issue injunctions interfering with state criminal proceedings.[843] Nor, under the Rooker-Feldman doctrine,[844] may lower federal courts exercise subject matter jurisdiction in an action that seeks to review or collaterally attack a final state court judgment.

PREEMPTION

Once a federal court determines that it has jurisdiction, it performs a federal preemption analysis. Early on, in *Gibbons v. Ogden*,[845] the Court interpreted the Supremecy Clause of the Constitution[846] to

---

841. As noted *supra* in Ch. 2, however, in Marshall v. Marshall, 547 U.S. 293, 311-12 (2006), the Court sharply restricted the probate exception to limit bankruptcy jurisdiction only with respect to matters purely within the *in rem* jurisdiction of the probate court. *See supra* pp. 95-96.

842. Younger v. Harris, 401 U.S. 37, 46 (1971).

843. *See* Kelly v. Robinson, 479 U.S. 36, 47 (1986) ("Our interpretation of the Code also must reflect . . . a deep conviction that federal bankruptcy courts should not invalidate the results of state criminal proceedings. . . . This Court has emphasized repeatedly the fundamental policy against federal interference with state criminal prosecutions.").

844. The so-called Rooker-Feldman doctrine is based on two non-bankruptcy Supreme Court decisions, Rooker v. Fid. Trust Co., 263 U.S. 413 (1923) and D.C. Court of Appeals v. Feldman, 460 U.S. 462 (1983), discussed more fully *infra* in Ch. 4, p. 236. In Exxon Mobil Corp. v. Saudi Basic Indus. Corp., 544 U.S. 280 (2005), the Court limited the Rooker-Feldman doctrine and emphasized its statutory, rather than constitutional, underpinnings. *See id.* at 284 (noting that the Rooker-Feldman doctrine is confined to deny federal court subject matter jurisdiction to "cases brought by state-court losers complaining of injuries caused by state-court judgments rendered before the district court proceedings commenced and inviting district court review and rejection of those judgments").

845. 22 U.S. (9 Wheat.) 1 (1824).

846. U.S. CONST. art. VI, § 2.

override state laws that "interfere with, or are contrary to," federal laws.[847] Preemption may be express, when federal law specifically overrides state law, or implied, if the Court infers a congressional intent to completely displace and preempt state law.[848] Preemption may also occur, if Congress has not completely displaced state law, when a state law actually conflicts with the accomplishment of the full federal purposes envisioned by Congress in enacting the federal law.[849]

When bankruptcy law preempts the field,[850] the Court uses the Supremacy Clause to strike down inconsistent state laws.[851] Curiously,

---

847.   *See Gibbons v. Ogden*, 22 U.S. at 211.

848.   *See, e.g.,* Cal. Fed. S&L Ass'n v. Guerra, 479 U.S. 272, 280-81 (1987). *See generally,* Josef S. Athanas & Peter P. Knight, *Resolving Conflicts Between The Bankruptcy Code and Other Federal and State Laws*, 11 J. BANKR. L. & PRAC. 237 (2002).

849.   *See, e.g.,* Cal. Fed. S&L Ass'n v. Guerra, 479 U.S. 272, 281 (1987) ("[I]n those areas where Congress has not completely displaced state regulation, federal law may nonetheless pre-empt state law to the extent it actually conflicts with federal law.").

850.   The Court will preempt a state statute if the statute stands as an obstacle to achieving the objectives of Congress in enacting the federal law. *See, e.g., id.* at 284 (the "'purpose of Congress is the ultimate touchstone' of the pre-emption inquiry") (citations omitted); Hines v. Davidowitz, 312 U.S. 52, 67 (1941) ("There is not—and from the very nature of the problem there cannot be—any rigid formula or rule which can be used as a universal pattern to determine the meaning and purpose of every act of Congress. This Court, in considering the validity of state laws in the light of treaties or federal laws touching the same subject, has made use of the following expressions: conflicting; contrary to; occupying the field; repugnance; difference; irreconcilability; inconsistency; violation; curtailment; and interference. But none of these expressions provides an infallible constitutional test or an exclusive constitutional yardstick. In the final analysis, there can be no one crystal clear distinctly marked formula. Our primary function is to determine whether, under the circumstances of [a] particular case, [state] law stands as an obstacle to the accomplishment and execution of the full purposes and objectives of Congress.") (citations and footnotes omitted).

851.   *See, e.g.,* Vanston Bondholders Protective Comm. v. Green, 329 U.S. 156, 162-63 (1947) (holding that federal bankruptcy law, rather than state law, determines the allowance of postpetition interest in bankruptcy cases); Am. Sur. Co. v. Sampsell, 327 U.S. 269, 272 (1946) (using federal

however, the Court has held that when no federal bankruptcy law is in effect, the Bankruptcy Clause of the Constitution,[852] standing alone, does not preempt the field.[853] If Congress chooses not to pass a bankruptcy law, the Court will, however, strike down state insolvency statutes to the extent they discharge debts retroactively[854] or extraterritorially, but not to the extent that the discharge is prospective and confined to the boundaries of the state.[855]

When a federal bankruptcy law is effective, as has been the case continuously since 1898,[856] consideration of the relationship between federal and state laws inevitably implicates the doctrine of federal preemption. Preemption presents at least three questions. First, in the absence of a federal bankruptcy statute, does the Uniformity Clause in

---

bankruptcy principles of equitable distribution to equitably subordinate a surety's claim to claims that it was not obligated to pay under state law); Kalb v. Feuerstein, 308 U.S. 433, 438-40 (1940) (holding that the broad policy of the Frazier-Lemke Act to exert peremptory federal power over bankrupt farmers and their property preempted state courts from conducting foreclosure proceedings against a bankrupt farmer's property); Int'l Shoe Co. v. Pinkus, 278 U.S. 261, 265, 268 (1929) (holding that federal bankruptcy law preempted an inconsistent state insolvency statute "at least in so far as it relates to the distribution of property and releases to be given").

852.   U.S. CONST. art. I, § 8, cl. 4.

853.   *See* Sturges v. Crowninshield, 17 U.S. (4 Wheat.) 122, 196 (1819) (states may enact bankruptcy laws, as long as Congress has not done so).

854.   *See id.* at 196-97 (state bankruptcy statute may not violate the Contracts Clause, Article I, § 10, by discharging a debt entered into before enactment of the law because to do so would impair an obligation of contract unconstitutionally). *Cf.* Kener v. La Grange Mills, 231 U.S. 215, 217-18 (1913) (holding, in the alternative, that a state constitution may not exempt property from existing liens without violating the Contracts Clause of the United States Constitution).

855.   *See* Ogden v. Saunders, 25 U.S. (12 Wheat.) 213, 267-68 (1827).

856.   The Bankruptcy Act of 1898 was enacted on July 1, 1898, and operated without interruption until it was repealed on October 1, 1979, when the 1978 Bankruptcy Code became effective. *See* Pub. L. No. 95-598, § 401(a), 92 Stat. 2549, 2682 (1978).

Article I, section 8, clause 4 of the Constitution preempt state insolvency statutes? Second, when Congress passes a pervasive uniform law on the subject of bankruptcies, does that bankruptcy law preempt state insolvency statutes or other state laws? Third, if the federal bankruptcy law conflicts with state laws, does the doctrine of preemption apply?[857]

States are not barred from passing insolvency laws, as long as those laws are not "in competition" with federal statutes. The relevant question in a preemption analysis is, therefore, whether the state law "trespasses" on federal turf. In turn, this analysis depends primarily on whether state law offers the debtor a discharge:[858]

> It is settled that [when a federal bankruptcy law is effective,] a state may not pass an insolvency law which provides for a discharge of the debtor from his obligations, ... [A]ll the cases lay stress upon the fact that one of the principal requisites of a true bankruptcy law is for the benefit of the debtor in that it discharges his future acquired property from the obligation of existing debts.

Stellwagen v. Clum made clear that state laws are suspended "only to the extent of actual conflict with the system provided" by federal bankruptcy legislation,[859] while state laws "which are in aid of the Bankruptcy Act can stand."[860]

The Court decided *Stellwagen* in 1918, upholding section 6343 of Ohio's Revised Statutes against a claim that the law was "suspended" by the Bankruptcy Act of 1898. At the time, section 6343 provided for avoidance, by any creditor, of any "sale, conveyance, transfer, mortgage or assignment" made by a debtor "in contemplation of insolvency, and with a design to prefer one or more creditors to the

---

857. *See* Gade v. Nat'l Solid Wastes Mgmt. Ass'n, 505 U.S. 88, 98 (1992) (under the doctrine of conflict preemption, preemption is implied when "compliance with both federal and state regulation is a physical impossibility") (internal quotation marks omitted).

858. *See* Stellwagen v. Clum, 245 U.S. 605, 615-16 (1918).

859. *See id.* at 613.

860. *See id.* at 615-16.

exclusion in whole or in part of others . . . ."[861] The statute, the Court explained, would be upheld because it did not "provide for the discharge of the debtor from his existing debts,"[862] and, thus, was "not opposed to the policy of the bankruptcy law or in contravention of the rules and principles established by it with a view to the fair distribution of the assets of the insolvent."[863]

By contrast, in *International Shoe Co. v. Pinkus*,[864] the Arkansas insolvency act in question provided for full discharge of the debtor. The Court had no problem holding that the federal bankruptcy law preempted the state insolvency statute:[865]

> Congress did not intend to give insolvent debtors seeking discharge, or their creditors seeking to collect claims, choice between the relief provided by the Bankruptcy Act and that specified in state insolvency laws. States may not pass or enforce laws to interfere with or complement the Bankruptcy Act or to provide additional or auxiliary regulations. . . . It is clear that the provisions of the Arkansas law governing the distribution of property of insolvents for the payment of their debts and providing for their discharge, or that otherwise relate to the subject of bankruptcies are within the field entered by Congress when it passed the Bankruptcy Act, and therefore such provisions must be held to have been superseded.

In *Pobreslo v. Joseph M. Boyd Co.*,[866] the Court was asked to decide whether "the provisions of [chapter 128 of the Wisconsin Statutes] which relate to voluntary assignments for the benefit of creditors . . . conflict with the National Bankruptcy Act."[867] The statutes at issue provided, among other things, that if an insolvent

---

861. *See id.* at 609 n.1.

862. *See id.* at 617.

863. *See id.* at 615.

864. 278 U.S. 261 (1929).

865. *See id.* at 265-66 (citations omitted).

866. 287 U.S. 518 (1933).

867. *See id.* at 521.

debtor made a preferential transfer to a creditor, an assignee could file suit to avoid and recover the conveyance.[868] The Court upheld the Wisconsin statutes, observing that an improper discharge provision in the state statute had been severed by the state courts, and that the remainder of the statute was "quite in harmony with the purposes of the federal act, the provisions of [the state statute] that are regulatory of . . . voluntary assignments serve to protect creditors against each other and . . . to assure equality of distribution unaffected by any requirement or condition in respect of discharge."[869]

Preemption applies, however, only when federal bankruptcy legislation embraces a federal policy or states a federal rule that occupies the field. Thus, when federal law provides for the avoidance of certain judicial liens that impair exemptions, the Court will not uphold state laws opting out of the lien avoidance provisions.[870] Generally speaking, however, when federal law does not preempt the field, the Court appears to apply a comity principle to resolve conflicts between federal bankruptcy law and competing state laws. For example, in *Butner v. United States*,[871] the Court held that ordinarily a bankruptcy court must apply state law unless a competing bankruptcy principle indicates that state law must be overridden.[872] Moreover, in

---

868. *See* Moskowitz v. Prentice (*In re* Wis. Builders Supply Co.), 239 F.2d 649, 654-55 (7th Cir. 1956) (describing Wisconsin assignment statutes in effect at time of *Pobreslo*).

869. *See Pobreslo*, 287 U.S. at 525-26. *See also* Johnson v. Star, 287 U.S. 527 (1933) (upholding, against preemption challenge, Texas voluntary assignment statutes which, inter alia, allowed assignees to recover pre-assignment preferences).

870. *See, e.g.,* Owen v. Owen, 500 U.S. 305, 313-14 (1991) ("On the basis of the analysis we have set forth above with respect to federal exemptions, and in light of the equivalency of treatment accorded to federal and state exemptions by § 522(f), we conclude that Florida's exclusion of certain liens from the scope of its homestead protection does not achieve a similar exclusion from the Bankruptcy Code's lien avoidance provision.").

871. 440 U.S. 48 (1979).

872. *See id.* at 55.

Midlantic National Bank v. New Jersey Department of Environmen-tal Protection,[873] the Court found that Congress did not intend for the Bankruptcy Code to pre-empt state environmental disposal laws and other laws that govern the operation of a debtor's business.[874]

Almost from the inception, states enacted legislation to avoid the impact of federal bankruptcy laws. For many years, commencing in the early 1900's,[875] states successfully dodged Supremacy Clause attacks by passing laws with a valid state law purpose that only had an incidental impact on the payment of discharged debts. For example, in *Reitz v. Mealey*,[876] the Court upheld the constitutionality of a New York statute that permitted a county clerk to suspend a driver's motor vehicle license for failure to pay a dischargeable judg-ment rendered for injury caused by operation of the motor vehicle.[877] The Court reasoned that the statute was a valid exercise of the state's police power,[878] and even if part of the statute unconstitutionally interfered with the driver's discharge under the Bankruptcy Act, that part was severable from the rest of the statute which was clearly valid.[879] The Court left open whether creditor control over the suspension of driving privileges was constitutionally preempted as contrary to the Bankruptcy Act.[880]

---

873.   474 U.S. 494 (1986).

874.   *See id.* at 505.

875.   For an extensive history of highway safety financial responsibility laws, *see* Justice Frankfurter's opinion in Kesler v. Dep't of Pub. Safety, 369 U.S. 153, 158-69 (1962).

876.   314 U.S. 33 (1941).

877.   *See id.* at 36-37. Justice Douglas dissented.

878.   *See id.* at 37 (Before its amendment, the statute constituted "a valid exercise of the State's police power not inconsistent with § 17 of the Bankruptcy Act.").

879.   *See id.* at 38-40.

880.   *See id.* at 38, 40.

A little more than 20 years later, the Court answered this open question in the negative in *Kesler v. Department of Public Safety.*[881] In *Kesler* the Court upheld the constitutionality of a Utah statute that required a debtor to satisfy an automobile accident judgment as a condition to reinstatement of his driver's license, notwithstanding the discharge of the judgment in bankruptcy.[882] The debtor had operated his vehicle negligently and the judgment creditor caused the state to suspend his registration and operator's license.[883] After suspension of the license, the debtor filed for bankruptcy and obtained a discharge of the judgment.[884] When the debtor sought reinstatement of his license and vehicle registration, the state refused because the state statute required payment of the judgment as a condition of reinstatement and specifically provided that a discharge in bankruptcy does not relieve the judgment debtor from this requirement.[885] The Supreme Court voted 5 to 3 to affirm the judgment of a three-judge district court[886] upholding the constitutionality of the Utah statute on the basis that it served a valid police power purpose that was wholly unrelated to the bankruptcy discharge.[887]

Nine years later in *Perez v. Campbell,*[888] however, with Justices Black and Douglas in the majority, the Court voted 5 to 4 to overturn *Kesler* and *Reitz* and strike down an Arizona motor vehicle safety responsibility statute as unconstitutional under the Supremacy

881. 369 U.S. 153 (1962).

882. *See id.* at 174.

883. *See id.* at 155.

884. *See id.*

885. *See id.*

886. The Court heard this case on direct appeal from a three-judge district court rather than on certiorari from a Court of Appeals. *See id.*

887. *See id.* at 174 ("Utah is not using its police power as a devious collecting agency under the pressure of organized creditors. . . . [T]he bearing of the statute on the purposes served by bankruptcy legislation is essentially tangential."). Warren, Black, and Douglas, JJ., dissenting.

888. 402 U.S. 637 (1971).

Clause.[889] In *Perez*, the Court considered whether Arizona's Motor
Vehicle Safety Responsibility Act was invalid under the Supremacy
Clause as inconsistent with the dischargeability provisions of the
Bankruptcy Act.[890] Adolfo Perez and his wife confessed judgment in a
suit arising from personal injuries and property damage he caused
while operating his uninsured motor vehicle. Shortly after the confession of judgment, Mr. and Mrs. Perez each filed voluntary bankruptcy
petitions and received a discharge of the judgment. Because the
Perez's did not pay the judgment, the Superintendent of the Arizona
Motor Vehicle Division suspended their drivers' licenses as required
by the Arizona statute, notwithstanding discharge of the judgment.[891]
The Court engaged in "a two-step process of first ascertaining the
construction of the two statutes and then determining the constitutional question whether they are in conflict."[892] After ascertaining that
the Arizona statute was designed to protect judgment creditors from
"financially irresponsible persons" and the Bankruptcy Act was
designed to give the financially-troubled debtor a fresh start, the
Court determined that the Arizona statute unconstitutionally interfered with and frustrated the discharge provisions of the Bankruptcy
Act because it stood "as an obstacle to the accomplishment and execution of the full purposes and objectives of Congress."[893] The Court
noted that both *Kesler* and *Reitz* "ignored this controlling principle"

---

889. *See id.* at 651-52. ("Thus, we conclude that *Kesler* and *Reitz* have
no authoritative effect to the extent they are inconsistent with the
controlling principle that any state legislation which frustrates the full
effectiveness of federal law is rendered invalid by the Supremacy
Clause."). For a discussion of the internal Court coalition building in
Perez, see supra Ch. 1, p. 27-28.

890. *See id.* at 638 (The Arizona statute was based on the Uniform
Motor Vehicle Safety Responsibility Act.).

891. *See id.* at 641-42.

892. *See id.* at 644.

893. *See id.* at 644-49 (citation omitted).

by looking to the purpose for which the state statute was enacted rather than to its effect.[894] As a result, the Court concluded:[895]

> We can no longer adhere to the aberrational doctrine of *Kesler* and *Reitz* that state law may frustrate the operation of federal law as long as the state legislature in passing its law had some purpose in mind other than one of frustration. Apart from the fact that it is at odds with the approach taken in nearly all our Supremacy Clause cases, such a doctrine would enable state legislatures to nullify nearly all unwanted federal legislation by simply publishing a legislative committee report articulating some state interest or policy—other than frustration of the federal objective—that would be tangentially furthered by the proposed state law.

Congress codified and expanded the principle of *Perez* in Bankruptcy Code § 525(a).[896] As enacted, with certain exceptions not relevant here, section 525(a) provides that:

> [A] governmental unit may not deny, revoke, suspend, or refuse to renew a license, permit, charter, franchise, or other similar grant to, condition such a grant to, discriminate with respect to such grant against, deny employment to, terminate the employment of, or discriminate with respect to employment against, a person that is or has been a debtor . . . solely because such bankrupt or debtor is or has been a debtor . . . or a bankrupt or . . . has been insolvent . . . or has not paid a debt that is dischargeable . . . .

This language expands *Perez* in at least three significant respects. First, the section applies to foreign and federal as well as state govern-

---

894. *See id.* at 650-51.

895. *See id.* at 651-52. The dissent lamented that the very Supremacy Clause argument in *Perez* had been considered and rejected in *Kesler* and *Reitz. See id.* at 657. So much for *stare decisis*. This point was not overlooked by the Justices. In fact, on April 9, 1971, Justice Harlan wrote a letter to Justice Blackmun stating in part as follows: "From my standpoint <u>Kesler</u> was correctly decided, and, further, I think that <u>stare decisis</u> should stand in the way of overruling." (contained in papers of Justice Blackmun).

896. *See* 11 U.S.C. § 525(a) (2000).

mental units.[897] Second, section 525(a) expands the categories of prohibited governmental actions well beyond the revocation of a driver's license. Third, the section protects all debtors that are "persons" including partnership and corporate debtors.[898]

The breadth of this new provision could be used by debtors to overturn several governmental regulatory actions. For example, in *FCC v. NextWave Personal Communications, Inc.,*[899] the Court considered whether the FCC's postpetition revocation of the debtor NextWave's broadband spectrum licenses violated Bankruptcy Code § 525.[900] Nextwave had agreed to make installment payments to the FCC to purchase the licenses and the licenses provided that failure to make timely payment "will result in the automatic cancellation" of the licenses.[901] Although NextWave made a timely down payment to the FCC, it ran into financing difficulties and the FCC suspended the requirement of installment payments through October 29, 1998 and set June 8, 1998 as a deadline for Nextwave to elect a restructuring option.[902] Instead, on June 8, 1998, NextWave filed a chapter 11 petition and, in accordance with bankruptcy law, suspended payments on prepetition debts to all creditors including the FCC pending the confirmation of a chapter 11 plan.[903] Following the conclusion of some litigation over the value of the licenses, the FCC took the position that NextWave's licenses had been automatically

---

897. *See* 11 U.S.C. § 101(27) (2000) (broadly defining the term "governmental unit").

898. *See* 11 U.S.C. § 101(41) (2000) (defining the term "person" to include an individual, partnership, or corporation, but not most governmental units).

899. 537 U.S. 293 (2003).

900. *See id.* at 295. The facts of *NextWave* are quite complex and the reader is encouraged to review the opinion to appreciate the extent of the conflict between the debtor and the FCC.

901. *See id.* at 297.

902. *See id.*

903. *See id.*

cancelled when it missed the first payment deadline in October 1998.[904] Ultimately the FCC argued that Bankruptcy Code § 525(a) did not preclude it from cancelling NextWave's licenses solely due to NextWave's failure to make installment payments, because, the FCC argued, it had a "valid regulatory motive" for the cancellation.[905] The Court held "that factor . . . irrelevant."[906] Otherwise a governmental unit could avoid the policy of § 525 simply by pointing to some "further motive behind the cancellation. . . . Section 525 means nothing more or less than that the failure to pay a dischargeable debt must alone be the proximate cause of the cancellation—the act or event that triggers the agency's decision to cancel, whatever the agency's ultimate motive in pulling the trigger may be."[907] The Court also noted that § 525's express exception for certain regulatory purposes precludes a general exception for cancellations that have a valid regulatory purpose.[908] As a result, the Court overturned the cancellation and sent a clear message that Bankruptcy Code § 525 will seriously restrict governmental regulators from confiscating property of the estate based on non-payment of debt. The Court's decision is correct because it enhances equality of distribution among creditors and the debtor's prospects for reorganization by preserving property of the estate and treating the government the same as any other creditor who voluntarily extends credit to the debtor.

---

904. *See id.* at 298.

905. *See id.* at 301.

906. *See id.*

907. *See id.* at 301-02.

908. *See id.* at 302.

FEDERALISM[909]

> [I]n construing legislation this court has disfavored in-roads by implication on state authority and resolutely confined restrictions upon the traditional power of states to regulate their local transportation to the plain mandate of Congress.[910]

Some of the most important issues of federalism concern whether a dispute involving local law will be resolved in federal court or state court. Congress often resolves this issue by interpreting statutes defining the scope of federal bankruptcy jurisdiction. This topic is discussed more fully in Chapter 4. Beyond legislative decisions to allocate jurisdiction, the judiciary has adopted principles of federalism to permit or limit federal jurisdiction. Historically the Court has interpreted federal legislation and the power of federal courts narrowly to avoid interference with state criminal proceedings;[911] the Court's interpretation of the federal Bankruptcy Code is no exception.[912] "The right to formulate and enforce penal sanctions is an important aspect of the sovereignty retained by states."[913] This reflection on federalism led the majority in *Kelly v. Robinson* to conclude that a debtor's restitution obligation, imposed as a condition of probation in state

---

909.   "From the beginning, the Court had to resolve what were essentially political issues—the proper accommodation between the states and the central government. These political problems will persist as long as our federalism endures; and the Supreme Court will remain the ultimate arbitrator between Nation and States." *See* FELIX FRANKFURTER & JAMES M. LANDIS, THE BUSINESS OF THE SUPREME COURT: A STUDY IN THE FEDERAL JUDICIAL SYSTEM (The MacMillan Company 1927) at 318.

910.   *See* Palmer v. Massachusetts, 308 U.S. 79, 84 (1939) (§ 77 railroad reorganization case concerning the power of railroad reorganization trustees to discontinue local transportation service).

911.   *See, e.g.,* Younger v. Harris, 401 U.S. 37, 46 (1971).

912.   Kelly v. Robinson, 479 U.S. 36, 47 (1986) ("Our interpretation of the Code also must reflect . . . a deep conviction that federal bankruptcy courts should not invalidate the results of state criminal proceedings. . . . This Court has emphasized repeatedly 'the fundamental policy against federal interference with state criminal prosecutions.'").

913.   *See id.*

criminal proceedings, was nondischargeable under Bankruptcy Code
§ 523(a)(7), because the restitution obligation was *not* compensation
for actual pecuniary loss.[914] The Court did so to uphold principles of
federalism "[d]espite the clear statutory language" to the contrary.[915]
On the other hand, when the statute is plain, the Court has construed
chapter 13 of the Bankruptcy Code to discharge state court restitution
orders imposed as a condition of probation,[916] notwithstanding
federalism concerns.[917] Congress promptly overruled the Court's result
in *Davenport* thereby reinstituting the nondischargeability of criminal
restitution claims across the board.[918]

THE USE OF STATE LAW IN BANKRUPTCY[919]

Although Congress and the federal courts might have the power to
override state law in bankruptcy cases, that does not mean they will
choose to exercise their power to do so. The Court's cases are replete
with examples of the use of state law in bankruptcy.

As already noted, "[b]ankruptcy proceedings constantly modify
and affect the property rights established by state law."[920] Thus, it is
within the province of federal bankruptcy law to determine claims

---

914. *See id.* at 52-53.

915. *See id.* at 45.

916. *See* Pa. Dep't of Pub. Welfare v. Davenport, 495 U.S. 552, 558-60
(1990) ("The language employed to define 'claim' in § 101(4)(A) makes no
reference to purpose. The plain meaning of a 'right to payment' is
nothing more nor less than an enforceable obligation, regardless of the
objectives the State seeks to serve in imposing the obligation.").

917. *See id.* at 564. ("[T]he concerns animating *Younger* cannot justify
rewriting the Code to avoid federal intrusion. Where, as here, congressional intent is clear, our sole function is to enforce the statute according
to its terms.").

918. *See* Criminal Victims Protection Act of 1990, Pub. L. No. 101-581,
§ 3, 104 Stat. 2865.

919. Vern Countryman, *The Use of State Law in Bankruptcy Cases
(Part I)*, 47 N.Y.U. L. REV. 407 (1972); Vern Countryman, *The Use of
State Law in Bankruptcy Cases (Part II)*, 47 N.Y.U. L. REV. 631 (1972).

920. *See* Wright v. Union Cent. Life Ins. Co., 304 U.S. 502, 517(1938).

priorities in bankruptcy.[921] Likewise, federal bankruptcy law determines a creditor's entitlement to postpetition interest.[922] And federal bankruptcy law determines the period within which a creditor may act to perfect its lien for purposes of the enabling loan exception to the preference statute.[923] The lack of federal corporate, commercial, and property law, however, has influenced the Court to use state corporate, commercial, and property laws as norms in bankruptcy cases unless the Bankruptcy Code overrides the entitlement or a conflicting federal interest requires another result.[924] The Court has also enforced

---

921. *See, e.g.,* Prudence Realization Corp. v. Geist, 316 U.S. 89 (1942) (federal bankruptcy law, rather than state liquidation law, determines whether a guarantor of mortgage certificates shares ratably with certificate participants whom it has guaranteed). *See infra* Ch. 5, p. 290.

922. *See* Rake v. Wade, 508 U.S. 464, 455-56 (1993) (holding that Bankruptcy Code § 506(b) requires accrual of postpetition interest on the claim of an oversecured creditor whether or not the creditor would be entitled to interest on such claim under state law).

923. *See* First Fid. Fin. Servs., Inc. v. Fink, 522 U.S. 211, 212-13 (1998).

924. *See, e.g.,* Raleigh v. Ill. Dep't of Revenue, 530 U.S. 15, 20 (2000); BFP v. Resolution Trust Corp., 511 U.S. 531, 544-45 (1994); Nobelman v. Am. Sav. Bank, 508 U.S. 324, 329-30 (1993); Barnhill v. Johnson, 503 U.S. 393, 398 (1992); Butner v. United States, 440 U.S. 48, 54-55 (1979) ("Congress has generally left the determination of property rights in the assets of a bankrupt's estate to state law. . . . Property interests are created and defined by state law. Unless some federal interest requires a different result, there is no reason why such interests should be analyzed differently simply because an interested party is involved in a bankruptcy proceeding.") (footnote omitted)); McKenzie v. Irving Trust Co., 323 U.S. 365, 370 (1945) ("In the absence of any controlling federal statute, a creditor or bona fide purchaser could acquire rights in the property transferred by the debtor, only by virtue of a state law."); Corn Exch. Nat'l Bank & Trust Co. v. Klauder, 318 U.S. 434, 436-37 (1943) ("This is undoubtedly the effect of a literal reading of [§ 60(b) of] the [Bankruptcy] Act. Its apparent command is to test the effectiveness of a transfer, as against the trustee, by the standards which applicable state law would enforce against a good-faith purchaser.") (footnote omitted); Sec. Mortgage Co. v. Powers, 278 U.S. 149, 153-54 (1928) ("The validity of the lien claimed by the Mortgage Company for attorney's fees must be determined by the law of Georgia; for the contract was there made and was secured by real estate there situate.") (citations omitted); Taylor v.

state tax laws in bankruptcy cases absent a conflicting federal statute.[925]

Although the bankruptcy law establishes the conditions determining who may be a debtor,[926] legal capacity or existence to file for bankruptcy relief is determined by nonbankruptcy law.[927] For example, a corporation that has been dissolved under state law has no capacity to file for bankruptcy relief because it has ceased to exist according to the

---

Voss, 271 U.S. 176, 190 (1926) ("In the absence of any conflicting provision in the Bankruptcy Act the question of a wife's interest in the bankrupt's property is governed by the local law."). *See also* Stellwagen v. Clum, 245 U.S. 605, 613 (1918) ("[I]t has been settled from an early date that state laws to the extent that they conflict with the laws of Congress, enacted under its constitutional authority, on the subject of bankruptcies are suspended. While this is true, state laws are thus suspended only to the extent of actual conflict with the system provided by the Bankruptcy Act of Congress.") (footnotes omitted); Hiscock v. Varick Bank of N.Y., 206 U.S. 28 (1907); *Ex parte* Christy, 44 U.S. (3 How.) 292, 316 (1845) ("There is no doubt that the liens, mortgages, and other securities within the purview of this proviso, so far as they are valid by the state laws, are not to be annulled, destroyed, or impaired under the proceedings in bankruptcy; but they are to be held of equal obligation and validity in the courts of the United States as they would be in the state courts."); Nugent v. Boyd, 44 U.S. (3 How.) 426 (1845). *See generally*, Ogden v. Saunders, 25 U.S. (12 Wheat.) 213 (1827); Sturges v. Crowninshield, 17 U.S. (4 Wheat.) 122 (1819).

925. *See* Cal. State Bd. of Equalization v. Sierra Summit, Inc., 490 U.S. 844, 851-52 (1989) (allowing state sales and use taxes to be imposed on bankruptcy liquidation sales).

926. *See* Bankruptcy Code § 109(a), 11 U.S.C. § 109(a) (2000), and Bankruptcy Act § 4, 11 U.S.C. § 22 (1976) (repealed 1979).

927. *Compare* Wragg v. Fed. Land Bank of New Orleans, 317 U.S. 325 (1943) (debtor whose property was sold could commence serial bankruptcy case on the day before her state law redemption period expired); *with* State Bank of Hardinsburg v. Brown, 317 U.S. 135 (1942) (when sale of property cuts off redemption rights under state law, the debtor's ownership interest in the property is extinguished and there is no basis to file a bankruptcy petition to protect the property). *See also* Harris v. Zion Sav. Bank & Trust Co., discussed *supra* nn.438-439 and accompanying text.

law under which it was formed.[928] Similarly, when state law authorizes the corporation's directors to act on its behalf, a shareholder of the corporation has no right directly or derivatively to file a bankruptcy petition on behalf of the corporation.[929]

Although Bankruptcy Code § 541[930] creates a bankruptcy estate as a matter of federal law, a large part[931] of that estate is comprised of the debtor's non-bankruptcy property interests owned, for the most part, as of the date of the filing of the bankruptcy petition.[932] The determi-

928. *See* Chicago Title & Trust Co. v. Forty-One Thirty-Six Wilcox Bldg. Corp., 302 U.S. 120 (1937).

929. *See* Price v. Gurney, 324 U.S. 100 (1945).

930. *See* 11 U.S.C. § 541 (2000).

931. Although in most cases the bulk of the property of the estate will be property of the debtor under § 541(a)(1), in some cases recoveries through use of federal avoiding powers causes of actions will comprise the bulk of the estate under § 541(a)(3). *See, e.g.,* Cunningham v. Brown, 265 U.S. 1 (1924) (the "original" Ponzi Scheme case); *In re* M&L Bus. Mach. Co., 84 F.3d 1330 (10th Cir. 1996); *In re* Hedged-Invs. Assocs., Inc., 48 F.3d 470 (10th Cir. 1995); First Fed. of Mich. v. Barrow, 878 F.2d 912 (6th Cir. 1989); *In re* The Fla. Fund of Coral Gables, Ltd., 144 Fed. Appx. 72 (11th Cir. 2005). *See also In re* French, 440 F.3d 145 (4th Cir. 2006) (holding that federal avoidance powers may be used to reach extraterritorial real properties). The prominent role of state law on avoiding powers is discussed more fully *infra* in Ch. 5, pp. 329-331, 337-340, 346-366. The Bankruptcy Code also brings into the bankruptcy estate certain property that an individual debtor acquires after bankruptcy. *See* 11 U.S.C. §§ 541(a)(5), 1115(a), 1207(a), & 1306(a) (2000).

932. *See* 11 U.S.C. § 541(a)(1) (2000) which brings the debtor's interests in property, as of the date of the filing of the bankruptcy petition, into the federal bankruptcy estate. Bankruptcy Code § 541(a) is the successor to Bankruptcy Act § 70a, 11 U.S.C. § 110a (1976) (repealed 1979), which initially gave the bankruptcy trustee the title of the bankrupt "as of the date he was adjudged a bankrupt" and later "as of the date of the filing of the petition." *Compare* The Bankruptcy Act, Act of July 1, 1898, ch. 541, § 70a, 30 Stat. 565 *with* The Chandler Act, Act of June 22, 1938, ch. 575, § 70a, 52 Stat. 879. The 1938 amendment was consistent with the Court's interpretation of the former standard in Everett v. Judson, 228 U.S. 474, 479 (1913).

nation whether an item constitutes "property" is a federal question,[933] but the scope, character, and other attributes of the debtor's property interests depends on nonbankruptcy (usually state) law.[934] In determining the nature of property rights created by state statutes, the Court is "hesitant to overrule decisions by [lower] federal courts skilled in the law of particular states unless their conclusions are shown to be unreasonable."[935] But when a federal treaty or Act of Congress is involved, the Court has consistently construed "property" broadly to include expectancies and other inchoate prospects that do not become tangible until after the date of the filing of the petition.[936]

---

933. *See, e.g.,* Chicago Bd. of Trade v. Johnson, 264 U.S. 1, 10 (1924) (refusing to accept the state court's characterization of a seat of the Chicago Board of Trade as "not property").

934. *See, e.g.,* Butner v. United States, 440 U.S. 48, 53-55 (1979) (state law, rather than federal equity principles, determines debtor's dispute with mortgagee over entitlement to rents and profits collected after bankruptcy and before foreclosure); Thompson v. Magnolia Petroleum Co., 309 U.S. 478, 481 (1940) (looking to state law to determine ownership of oil and land); Taylor v. Voss, 271 U.S. 176, 190 (1926) (construing the debtor's adjudication as a bankrupt to be a "judicial sale" under state law giving the debtor's wife an absolute interest in the bankrupt's real estate as of the date of the filing of the petition; "[i]n the absence of any conflicting provision in the Bankruptcy Act the question of a wife's interest in the bankrupt's property is governed by the local law."); Harrigan v. Bergdoll, 270 U.S. 560, 564 (1926) (looking to state law to determine when statute of limitations began to run on debtor's cause of action to call unpaid stock subscriptions).

935. *See* United States v. Durham Lumber Co., 363 U.S. 522, 525-27 (1960) (citing Propper v. Clark, 337 U.S. 472, 486-87 (1949) to justify the Court's deference to the court of appeals' interpretation that under state law, the general contractor did not have a property interest in the face amount of the construction contract, but only in the residual fund after subcontractors were paid). Interestingly in this case, the Court's deference to the lower federal court was crucial to forming a majority opinion of Justices who agreed that state law should apply but could not agree among themselves what the state law was. *See* January 21, 1960, Letter of Justice Brennan to Douglas, Whittaker, and Stewart, JJ. (contained in Brennan papers).

936. *See, e.g.,* Williams v. Heard, 140 U.S. 529, 540-41 (1891) (case under Bankruptcy Act of 1867 involving war risk insurance premium claim);

The Court reached a similar result under the Bankruptcy Act of 1898 in construing rights under the Internal Revenue Code, holding that the bankruptcy trustee has a right to a refund for federal taxes paid by the bankrupt in prepetition years based on losses generated during the year of the filing of the petition.[937]

But when the issue directly implicates the debtor's fresh start, the Court has drawn a different line. In *Lines v. Frederick*,[938] the Court retreated from its decision in *Segal v. Rochelle*, holding that accrued but unused vacation pay based on prepetition services was not property.[939] Whether the item in question was property had to be resolved in light of the purposes of the Bankruptcy Act and not simply based on the time when the benefits vested or state law definitions of property.[940]

The Court's conclusion in *Lines v. Frederick* is difficult to reconcile with the Court's holding in *Milnor v. Metz*.[941] Milnor was a federal government employee who was ordered to perform, and did perform, increased duties without increased pay.[942] He petitioned Congress for compensation. Before Congress acted, Milnor filed a petition under a state insolvency statute to make an assignment of property to a creditors' representative and received a discharge of his

---

Phelps v. McDonald, 99 U.S. 298, 304-05 (1878) (case under Bankruptcy Act of 1867 involving indemnity claim for cotton destroyed during the Civil War); Comegys v. Vasse, 26 U.S. (1 Pet.) 193, 213-14 (1828) (case under Bankruptcy Act of 1800 involving compensation for vessel illegally captured). *See* generally, Vern Countryman, *The Use of State Law in Bankruptcy Cases (Part I)*, 47 N.Y.U. L. REV. 407, 438-47 (1972).

937.   *See* Segal v. Rochelle, 382 U.S. 375, 384-85 (1966).

938.   400 U.S. 18 (1970).

939.   *See id.* at 19-20.

940.   *See id. Cf.* Local Loan v. Hunt, 292 U.S. 234, 243 (1934) (invoking debtor's fresh start as a basis to override a state statute providing for a present lien to secure the enforcement of the assignment of a debtor's future wages).

941.   41 U.S. (16 Pet.) 221 (1842).

942.   *See id.* at 224.

debts. Then Congress passed a bill that paid Milnor for the duties he performed before the filing of the insolvency proceeding. The Court, following its earlier decision in *Comegys v. Vasse*,[943] held that the payment was tied to Milnor's equitable claim to compensation for prepetition services and that it was property assigned in the insolvency proceeding; as such, the creditors' representative was entitled to the payment rather than the debtor.[944]

If anything, the definition of property of the estate in Bankruptcy Code § 541 is broader that the definition in Bankruptcy Act § 70a or any of its predecessors. Nevertheless, it is apparent that the Court has switched its approach to this topic over time, ranging from the broad construction of property of the estate in some eras and placing more emphasis on the debtor's fresh start in others. Based on its policy of strict statutory construction (which would support broad interpretation of property of the estate under Bankruptcy Code § 541), today's Court probably would limit *Lines v. Frederick* to its facts, follow the Court's older precedents, and include all of the debtor's prepetition expectancies as property of the estate as long as the loss giving rise to the debtor's equitable claim arose prepetition.[945]

Defining the debtor's property interest also might have important distributive implications. For example, in *United States v. Durham Lumber Co.*,[946] the Court looked to a contractor's state property rights

---

943. 26 U.S. (1 Pet.) 193 (1828).

944. *See Milnor*, 41 U.S. at 227.

945. For an interesting lower court decision arising in the context of a statute enacted post-discharge that provided the debtor with retroactive crop-disaster relief, *see* Burgess v. Sikes (*In re* Burgess), 438 F.3d 493, 499, 503 (5th Cir. en banc 2006) (holding 8 to 7 that because the compensatory statute was enacted postpetition, the debtor had no interest in property at the time of the filing of the petition). *Accord* Bracewell v. Kelley (*In re* Bracewell), 454 F.3d 1234, 1237 (11th Cir. 2006); Drewes v. Vote (*In re* Vote), 276 F.3d 1024, 1026-27 (8th Cir. 2002). According to these cases, it is not enough that the loss occurs prepetition; in order for the crop relief payment to be property of the estate, the debtor must have a prepetition right to compensation.

946. 363 U.S. 522 (1960).

in funds owed to it under a construction contract to resolve competing claims of a federal tax lien claimant and subcontractors: if the entire fund were property of the contractor's bankruptcy estate, the federal tax lien claimant would prevail whereas the subcontractors would prevail if, under state law, they had a prior right to payment so that only the residual in the fund would become property of the estate.[947] Similarly, in *Farrey v. Sanderfoot*,[948] the debtor's ability to avoid a judicial lien turned on whether, under state law, the divorce court's judicial lien on a home attached to the debtor's joint property interest or a new property interest in the home.[949] And in *Security Warehousing Co. v. Hand*,[950] the Court sustained the trustee's ability to avoid pledges of warehouse receipts when there was no change of possession of the underlying goods as required under state law for a valid pledge.[951]

Likewise, as a general proposition,[952] under the Bankruptcy Act and the Bankruptcy Code, Congress has adopted state law as a rule of decision to determine which property an individual debtor may

---

947.   *See id.* at 525-26.

948.   500 U.S. 291 (1991).

949.   *See id.* at 299. The Court held that the debtor must hold an interest in property prior to the time the judicial lien attaches, not simultaneously; since state law determined that the debtor's spouse's interest in the house was a new interest created at the time the judicial lien attached, the debtor lost and could not avoid the lien under Bankruptcy Code § 522(f). *See id.* at 301.

950.   206 U.S. 415 (1907).

951.   *See id.* at 425-27.

952.   The Bankruptcy Act and Bankruptcy Code have recognized certain specific federal exemptions, such as federal pensions paid to winners of a congressional Medal of Honor. *See* Bankruptcy Act § 6, 11 U.S.C. § 24 (1976) (repealed 1979); 11 U.S.C. § 522(b)(3) & 38 U.S.C. § 1562 (formerly § 3101) (2000). *See also* H.R. REP. NO. 595, 95th Cong., 1st Sess. 360 (1977). Moreover, the 1978 Bankruptcy Code allows an individual debtor to choose federal Bankruptcy Code exemptions established in § 522(d) unless the pertinent state opted out of the election. *See* 11 U.S.C. § 522(b)(2) & (d) (2000) and *infra* Ch. 5, pp. 272-273 & n.1390.

exempt from the bankruptcy estate.[953] Thus, the Court has held that a debtor could claim insurance policies as exempt based on state law, even though Bankruptcy Act § 70a(5) had an express proviso governing when insurance policies become property of the estate.[954] In addition, the Court has held that a debtor may not exempt disability payments issued under a contract that supplemented a life insurance contract when the supplementary contract is not insurance within the meaning of state laws defining the exemption.[955] Furthermore, the Court has held that Congress may not use the federal bankruptcy law to exempt property from a lien which attached before enactment of the bankruptcy law.[956]

Although one might think that abandonment of property from the estate under Bankruptcy Code § 554 is purely a matter of federal law, in the context of polluted property the Court has held otherwise. In *Midlantic National Bank v. New Jersey Department of Environmental Protection*,[957] the Court held that the bankruptcy trustee's abandonment power is limited by a judicially-developed doctrine that required the abandonment to comply with state and federal law.[958] This holding is not surprising as a matter of sound public policy, but it

---

953. *See, e.g.,* White v. Stump, 266 U.S. 310, 312-13 (1924) (holding that the date of the filing of the bankruptcy petition is the appropriate time to determine exemptions under state law); Lockwood v. Exch. Bank, 190 U.S. 294, 299-300 (1903) (holding that Bankruptcy court had jurisdiction to enforce a state law claim of exemption).

954. *See* Holden v. Stratton, 198 U.S. 202, 212-13 (1905) (analyzing former § 70a(5) of the Bankruptcy Act, 11 U.S.C. § 110a(5) (1898) (repealed 1979) and resolving the conflict in favor of the bankrupt's right to claim exemptions under Bankruptcy Act § 6, 11 U.S.C. § 24 (1898) (repealed 1979)).

955. *See* Legg v. St. John, 296 U.S. 489, 493 (1936).

956. *See* Kener v. La Grange Mills, 231 U.S. 215, 217-18 (1913) (holding, in the alternative, that the Bankruptcy Act of 1867 could not exempt property from a lien that had attached before bankruptcy, notwithstanding exemption of the property under the Georgia Constitution).

957. 474 U.S. 494 (1986).

958. *See id.* at 506-07.

is surprising as a matter of statutory construction, particularly since Congress enacted a statute expressly requiring bankruptcy trustees to comply with state law when they are operating a debtor's business.[959]

Likewise, because property of the estate is within the exclusive jurisdiction of the bankruptcy court,[960] one might think that a use, sale, or lease of property under Bankruptcy Code § 363 would be controlled exclusively by federal law. Although the express provisions of the Bankruptcy Code do control certain aspects of the estate's use, sale, and lease of property, the Court has held that state law governs interpretation of the use, sale, or lease contract, whether it arises prepetition or under a plan.[961] Similarly, state law may condition transferability of the property on the payment of debts connected with it, such as was the case with a trustee's ability to sell the debtor's seat on the Chicago Board of Trade.[962] And bankruptcy law does not preclude a state from charging a sales or use tax on the liquidation of estate assets.[963]

---

959.   *See* 28 U.S.C. § 959(b) (2000) ("[A] trustee, . . . including a debtor in possession, shall manage and operate the property in his possession as trustee[ ] . . . according to the requirements of the valid laws of the State in which such property is situated, in the same manner that the owner or possessor thereof would be bound to do if in possession thereof.") (and by implication not otherwise).

960.   *See* 28 U.S.C. § 1334(e) (2000).

961.   *See* Callaway v. Benton, 336 U.S. 132, 137-38 (1949) (holding that ordinary rules of offer and acceptance govern third party's option to sell leased property to the debtor or to have its lease rejected and purchase the estate's interest in the leased property).

962.   *See* Bd. of Trade v. Johnson, 264 U.S. 1, 8-9 (1924).

963.   *See* Cal. State Bd. of Equalization v. Sierra Summit, Inc., 490 U.S. 844, 850-53 (1989) (allowing state sales and use taxes to be imposed on bankruptcy liquidation sales). *But see* Bankruptcy Code § 1146(a), 11 U.S.C. § 1146(a) (2000), preempting state stamp taxes and similar transfer taxes under chapter 11 plans (and by implication not otherwise). *Accord* Fla. Dep't of Revenue v. Piccadilly Cafeterias, Inc., 553 U.S. ___, 128 S. Ct. 2326, 2339 (2008) (permitting state to assess stamp tax on bankruptcy sale made before a plan is confirmed).

Even in the realm of federal avoiding powers causes of action, the Court has looked to state law on occasion. To be sure, "[w]hat constitutes a transfer and when it is complete . . . is necessarily a federal question, since it arises under a federal statute . . . ."[964] And, as noted previously, the time within which a transfer may be perfected for purposes of the avoiding powers is determined by federal bankruptcy law.[965] In some cases, however, the Court has examined state law to flesh out a term left undefined in the Bankruptcy Code. For example, state law determines the validity of a mortgage against the debtor's property.[966] Moreover, in *BFP v. Resolution Trust Corp.*,[967] in evaluating the merits of a federal fraudulent conveyance action under Bankruptcy Code § 548, the Court held that whether a real property foreclosure was made for a reasonably equivalent value turned on whether the foreclosure was conducted in accordance with applicable nonbankruptcy law.[968] In other instances, the Court has looked to state law to provide an independent source of avoiding powers.[969] For example, in *Miller v. New Orleans Acid & Fertilizer Co.*,[970] the Court held that the trustee in bankruptcy could avoid a preference under state law[971] even though it was not avoidable under Bankruptcy Act

---

964. *See* McKenzie v. Irving Trust Co., 323 U.S. 365, 369-70 (1945). For a more complete discussion of the trustee's avoiding powers, *see infra* Ch. 5, pp. 323-366.

965. *See* First Fid. Fin. Servs. v. Fink, 522 U.S. 211, 220 (1998) (holding that federal bankruptcy law controls period within which an enabling loan may be perfected for purposes of establishing a preference defense under Bankruptcy Code § 547(c)(3)).

966. *See* Humphrey v. Tatman, 198 U.S. 91, 93-94 (1905).

967. 511 U.S. 531 (1994).

968. *See id.* at 545.

969. The Court has held that the Bankruptcy Act did not prevent a state from properly enacting legislation avoiding fraudulent transfers. *See* Stellwagen v. Clum, 245 U.S. 605, 614 (1918).

970. 211 U.S. 496 (1909).

971. Louisiana state law considered creditors of a partnership to be creditors of the individual debtor general partner whereas Bankruptcy Act

§ 60.[972] In *Benedict v. Ratner*,[973] the Court upheld the bankruptcy trustee's use of state fraudulent transfer law to avoid a creditor's lien on the assignment of the debtor's future accounts.[974] Of course the Bankruptcy Code itself incorporates state law by reference in several federal avoiding powers.[975] Moreover, the Bankruptcy Code gives the trustee the rights of actual unsecured creditors to avoid transfers (usually based on state law rights).[976] Thus, state law plays a prominent role with respect to federal avoiding powers.

For the most part bankruptcy law does not create claims;[977] rather, claims against the estate are established under nonbankruptcy law (usually state law).[978] Under Bankruptcy Code § 558,[979] the bankruptcy

---

§§ 5 & 60, 11 U.S.C. §§ 23 & 96 (1900) (repealed 1979), did not. *See* Miller v. New Orleans Acid & Fertilizer Co., 211 U.S. 496, 497, 503-05 (1909).

972.   *See id.* at 505-06.

973.   268 U.S. 353 (1925).

974.   *See id.* at 359, 364-65; the Court also allowed the trustee to assert a federal preference action against the creditor to recover amounts paid to the creditor on the accounts within four months of bankruptcy. *See id.* at 365.

975.   *See, e.g.,* 11 U.S.C. §§ 547(e) & 548(d)(1) (2000).

976.   *See* 11 U.S.C. § 544(b) (2000) which is based on Bankruptcy Act § 70e, 11 U.S.C. § 110e (1928) (repealed 1979), as interpreted by the Court in Moore v. Bay, 284 U.S. 1 (1931). *See infra* Ch. 5, pp. 353-356.

977.   *But see* Bankruptcy Code § 1111(b)(1)(A), 11 U.S.C. § 1111(b)(1)(A) (2000) (establishing chapter 11 non-recourse deficiency claim where none would exist under state law; and former § 77(b) which gave landlords claims in railroad reorganization cases that did not exist under common law or state law). *See* City Bank Farmers Trust Co. v. Irving Trust Co., 299 U.S. 433 (1937).

978.   *See, e.g.,* Raleigh v. Ill. Dep't of Revenue, 530 U.S. 15, 20 (2000); Sec. Mortgage Co. v. Powers, 278 U.S. 149, 153-54 (1928); Bryant v. Swofford Bros. Dry Goods Co., 214 U.S. 279, 290-91 (1909) (finding conditional sales contract under state law).

979.   11 U.S.C. § 558. *See also* Bankruptcy Act § 70c, 11 U.S.C. § 110c (1976) (repealed 1979).

estate may assert any defenses of the debtor to defeat the claim.[980] Also, Bankruptcy Code § 502(b)(1) generally permits the court to sustain an objection to claim based on nonbankruptcy law.[981] As a general rule, federal bankruptcy law does not change the burden of proving a claim; rather, the burden of proof is part of the substance of the claim that is allocated by state law.[982]

Under the Bankruptcy Act of 1898, however, only provable claims[983] could be allowed.[984] Thus, it was possible that a claim that might be asserted against the debtor under state law would not be provable in bankruptcy. Early on, the Court held that a landlord's claim for loss of future rents, based on the trustee's rejection of the lease, was not provable under the Bankruptcy Act.[985] The Court

---

980. The estate also may disallow the claim to the extent it is unenforceable under any agreement or applicable law, other than because the claim is contingent or unliquidated. *See* 11 U.S.C. § 502(b)(1) (2000).

981. *See* 11 U.S.C. § 502(b)(1) (2000) and *infra* Ch. 5, pp. 274-277. Note, however, that under Bankruptcy Code § 502(b)(1) & (c), claims that would be disallowed under state law because they are unmatured or contingent may be allowed in bankruptcy. Moreover, there are federal bases to disallow claims set forth in Bankruptcy Code §§ 502(b)(2)-(9), (d), (e), (j), & 724. In particular, the Court has upheld federal disallowance of state tax penalties. *See* New York v. Jersawit, 263 U.S. 493 (1924).

982. *See* Raleigh v. Ill. Dep't of Revenue, 530 U.S. 15, 20-21 (2000) (in the context of a state tax statute that put the burden of proof on the taxpayer, absent some federal interest that would require a different result, the state's allocation of the burden of proof is controlling in bankruptcy).

983. The concept of "provability" was defined in Bankruptcy Act § 63, 11 U.S.C. § 103 (1976) (repealed 1979). As such, the Court has ruled that whether a claim is provable is a federal question. *See, e.g.,* Tindle v. Birkett, 205 U.S. 183, 185-86 (1907).

984. *See* Bankruptcy Act § 57d, 11 U.S.C. § 93d (Supp. 1942) (repealed 1979). The allowance of a claim is a federal question. *See, e.g.,* Heiser v. Woodruff, 327 U.S. 726, 732 (1946).

985. *See* Manhattan Props., Inc. v. Irving Trust Co., 291 U.S. 320, 338-39 (1934). In 1938, Congress enacted Bankruptcy Act § 63a(9), 11 U.S.C. § 103a(9) (1940) (repealed 1979), to make a landlord's claim for future rent provable, but Congress capped the claim in dollar amount at one

reached its holding based on statutory interpretation that Congress did not intend the provability in Bankruptcy Act § 63a(4)[986] of contingent claims based on contracts to extend to real property leases.[987] The Court acknowledged that "[t]he issue is not one of power, for plainly Congress may permit such claims or exclude them."[988] In passing, however, the Court noted that in four of its previous cases[989] it had not "expressed disapproval" and in fact had cited several lower court decisions based on the state law notion that "[r]ent issues from the land, is not due until the rent day, and is due in respect of the enjoyment of the premises let."[990] This citation led one commentator to speculate that the Court's decision in *Manhattan Properties, Inc. v. Irving Trust Co.* "was largely influenced by the fact that the common law did not recognize a claim for future rent . . . ."[991]

When the lease termination occurred based on the filing of the bankruptcy case, however, the Bankruptcy Act reached a different result.[992] For many years, the Bankruptcy Act enforced an ipso facto clause if the parties contracted in advance that the lease would

---

year's rent for purposes of allowance. *See* Act of June 22, 1938 ("Chandler Act"), Pub. L. No. 696, 52 Stat. 840, 873. The concept of provability was eliminated when Congress enacted the 1978 Bankruptcy Code, but the cap on a landlord's claim of damages for rejection damages was retained in a modified form in Bankruptcy Code § 502(b)(6), 11 U.S.C. § 502(b)(6) (2000).

986.   *See* 11 U.S.C. 103a(4) (1940) (repealed 1979).

987.   *See Manhattan Props.*, 291 U.S. 320 at 332 ("The sole inquiry is the intent of the Act." (setting forth a detailed history of the proof and allowance of contingent claims in bankruptcy)).

988.   *See id.*

989.   *See id.* at 336 (citing Maynard v. Elliott, 283 U.S. 273, 278 (1931); William Filene's Sons Co. v. Weed, 245 U.S. 597 (1918); Gardinier v. Butler & Co., 245 U.S. 603, 605 (1918) (receivership case); Cent. Trust Co. v. Chicago Auditorium Ass'n, 240 U.S. 581, 589-90 (1916).

990.   *See* William Filene's Sons Co. v. Weed, 245 U.S. 597, 601 (1918).

991.   *See* Vern Countryman, *The Use of State Law in Bankruptcy Cases (Part I)*, 47 N.Y.U. L. REV. 407, 424 (1972).

992.   The Bankruptcy Code largely overrides ipso facto clauses. *See* 11 U.S.C. §§ 541(c)(1)(B), 363(*l*), & 365(e) (2000).

terminate automatically on the filing of a bankruptcy case.[993] The Court held that damages resulting from ipso facto termination of the lease gave rise to a provable claim,[994] except when the measure of damages was so unreasonable to constitute a penalty.[995]

Both the Bankruptcy Act and the Bankruptcy Code contain provisions limiting or disallowing claims or liens that are valid and enforceable under nonbankruptcy law. The Court has noted that the *Erie* doctrine[996] does not require "a court of bankruptcy . . . to adopt local rules of law in determining what claims are provable, or to be allowed, or how the bankrupt's estate is to be distributed . . . ."[997] As mentioned previously, the Court has upheld a reasonable limitation on the allowance of a landlord's claim for lease rejection damages.[998] Moreover, the Court has upheld federal bankruptcy law that generally

---

993. *See* Finn v. Meighan, 325 U.S. 300, 301-02 (1945) (Chapter X reorganization case interpreting Bankruptcy Act § 70b, 11 U.S.C. § 110b (1942) (repealed 1979) ("an express covenant that an assignment by operation of law or the bankruptcy of a specified party thereto or of either party shall terminate the lease . . . is enforceable")). *Accord* Smith v. Hoboken R.R., 328 U.S. 123, 126-28 (1946) (applying Bankruptcy Act § 70b in a § 77 railroad reorganization case subject to other statutory requirements).

994. *See* Irving Trust Co. v. A.W. Perry, Inc., 293 U.S. 307, 310-11 (1934).

995. *See* Kothe v. R.C. Taylor Trust, 280 U.S. 224, 226 (1930).

996. In Erie R. Co. v. Tompkins, 304 U.S. 64 (1938), the Court held that in those federal cases when jurisdiction is based on diversity of citizenship and not governed by the federal Constitution or acts of Congress, the federal court is bound to apply state substantive law, whether statutory or common law. *See id.* at 78.

997. *See* Heiser v. Woodruff, 327 U.S. 726, 731 (1946) (dictum). *See also* Vanston Bondholders Protective Comm. v. Green, 329 U.S. 156, 162 (1947) ("In determining what claims are allowable and how a debtor's assets shall be distributed, a bankruptcy court does not apply the law of the state where it sits. *Erie R. Co. v. Tompkins* . . . has no such implication.").

998. *See supra* n.985 and accompanying text.

disallows postpetition interest on unsecured[999] or undersecured[1000] claims and interest on unpaid interest.[1001] Before the codification of equitable subordination in Bankruptcy Code § 510(c),[1002] the Court upheld the inherent equitable power of the bankruptcy court to equitably subordinate[1003] or disallow claims.[1004] At the same time, it refused to compel the bankruptcy court to follow a state rule of subordination.[1005] It is for the federal bankruptcy "court—not without appropriate regard for rights acquired under rules of state law—to define and apply federal law in determining the extent to which the inequitable conduct of a claimant in acquiring or asserting his claim in bankruptcy requires its subordination to other claims . . . ."[1006]

---

999. *See* City of New York v. Saper, 336 U.S. 328, 330-32 (1949) (unsecured tax claims).

1000. *See* Sexton v. Dreyfus, 219 U.S. 339, 343-44 (1911).

1001. *See* Vanston Bondholders Protective Comm. v. Green, 329 U.S. 156, 163-64 (1947) (using equitable powers to disallow interest on unpaid interest).

1002. *See* 11 U.S.C. § 510(c) (2000), discussed more fully *infra* in Chs. 4 & 5, pp. 226 & 299-302. Bankruptcy Code § 510(c) provides a statutory basis for courts to equitably subordinate claims to claims and interests. Bankruptcy Code § 502(j), 11 U.S.C. § 502(j) (2000), is the successor to Bankruptcy Act § 57k and arguably supports equitable disallowance of claims. *See infra* n.1004 describing *Pepper v. Litton*.

1003. *See* Taylor v. Standard Gas & Elec. Co., 306 U.S. 307, 323-24 (1939) (subordinating parent corporation's claim against subsidiary to preferred stock interests in subsidiary).

1004. *See* Pepper v. Litton, 308 U.S. 295, 303-04 (1939) (equitably disallowing owner's claim based on court's equitable powers derived from Bankruptcy Act § 57k, 11 U.S.C. § 93k (1934) (repealed 1979)).

1005. *See* Prudence Realization Corp. v. Geist, 316 U.S. 89, 95 (1942) (the *Erie* doctrine does not require the bankruptcy court to apply a local rule of subordination).

1006. *See id. See generally*, Vern Countryman, *The Use of State Law in Bankruptcy Cases (Part I)*, 47 N.Y.U. L. REV. 407, 429 (1972).

CONCLUSION

In the United States, state and federal legal systems co-exist providing great variety and richness in American civil law. Our federal bankruptcy laws incorporate some state laws by reference, adopt others as a base line, harmonize with many, and conflict with a few. This chapter reveals that resolving conflicts among conflicting federal and state laws is no simple task; rather considerations of supremacy, preemption, federalism, states' rights, and sovereign immunity may be implicated. Chapter 4 examines the extent to which bankruptcy courts may exercise jurisdiction to resolve these disputes, among others.

JUDICIAL POWER: JURISDICTION, POWERS OF THE BANKRUPTCY COURT, RES JUDICATA AND COLLATERAL ESTOPPEL

INTRODUCTION

Although Congress may constitutionally enact uniform laws on the subject of bankruptcies throughout the United States, Congress is not required to do so. During the early years of the Republic, bankruptcy laws were few and far between. Since 1898, however, the United States has always had a bankruptcy law in force.

Once Congress decides to legislate a federal bankruptcy law, it must decide the manner of bankruptcy case adjudication. To date, Congress has decided to vest jurisdiction over bankruptcy cases exclusively in federal courts, but has been less uniform in vesting jurisdiction over controversies arising in such cases. Although Congress has permitted the day to day work of the bankruptcy courts to be done by non-tenured judges, it has not been consistent with regard to the scope and magnitude of the power that may be exercised by those judges. An examination of Supreme Court decisions regarding federal court jurisdiction over bankruptcy cases and controversies and the power wielded by bankruptcy referees and judges to resolve disputes,[1007] as well as an analysis of the Court's cases

---

1007. Extended discussion of Supreme Court cases involving appellate jurisdiction in bankruptcy cases and proceedings is beyond the scope of this Chapter. Most of those cases arose between enactment of the Bankruptcy Act in 1898, when parties could appeal as of right to the Supreme Court in bankruptcy cases and proceedings, and January 28, 1915, when Congress repealed that direct right of appeal; moreover, for the most part, those cases involve straight-forward dismissal for lack of appellate jurisdiction or perfunctory or technical discussions of statutes that no longer apply. *See, e.g.,* Taylor v. Voss, 271 U.S. 176 (1926); William R.

dealing with res judicata and collateral estoppel, helps to determine the contours of the exercise of judicial power in the bankruptcy arena.

JURISDICTION

Within the framework of bankruptcy law, no other topic demanded as much attention of the Supreme Court over the last 111 years as did bankruptcy court jurisdiction. Although state courts are courts of general jurisdiction, federal courts may only exercise jurisdiction conferred on them by Congress. If Congress adopts a federal statute but fails to vest jurisdiction in a federal court, then the

---

Staats Co. v. Sec. Trust & Sav. Bank, 243 U.S. 121 (1917); Swift & Co. v. Hoover, 242 U.S. 107 (1916); Cent. Trust Co. v. Lueders, 239 U.S. 11 (1915); Scotten v. Littlefield, 235 U.S. 407 (1914); Lazarus, Michel & Lazarus v. Prentice, 234 U.S. 263 (1914); Yazoo & Miss. Valley R.R. v. Brewer, 231 U.S. 245 (1913); Lovell v. Newman & Son, 227 U.S. 412 (1913); James v. Stone & Co., 227 U.S. 410 (1913); Wynkoop, Hallenbeck, Crawford Co. v. Gaines, 227 U.S. 4 (1913); *In re* Loving, 224 U.S. 183 (1912); J.W. Calnan Co. v. Doherty, 224 U.S. 145 (1912); Munsuri v. Fricker, 222 U.S. 121 (1911); Tefft, Weller & Co. v. Munsuri, 222 U.S. 114 (1911); Duryea Power Co. v. Sternbergh, 218 U.S. 299 (1910); Blake v. Openhym, 216 U.S. 322 (1910); Kenney v. Craven, 215 U.S. 125 (1909); Miller v. New Orleans Acid & Fertilizer Co., 211 U.S. 496 (1909); Chapman v. Bowen, 207 U.S. 89 (1907); *Ex parte* First Nat'l Bank of Chicago, 207 U.S. 61 (1907); Frederic L. Grant Shoe Co. v. W.M. Laird Co., 203 U.S. 502 (1906); First Nat'l Bank of Chicago v. Chicago Title & Trust Co., 198 U.S. 280 (1905); Plymouth Cordage Co. v. Smith, 194 U.S. 311 (1904); Schweer v. Brown, 195 U.S. 171 (1904); Spencer v. Duplan Silk Co., 191 U.S. 526 (1903); Holden v. Stratton, 191 U.S. 115 (1903); Elliott v. Toeppner, 187 U.S. 327 (1902); First Nat'l Bank of Denver v. Klug, 186 U.S. 202 (1902); Bardes v. Hawarden First Nat'l Bank, 175 U.S. 526 (1899). A few modern cases deal with general removal statutes that are not limited specifically to removal of bankruptcy cases or proceedings. *See* Rivet v. Regions Bank of La., 522 U.S. 470 (1998); Things Remembered v. Petrarca, 516 U.S. 124 (1995). One modern case addresses appellate jurisdiction in bankruptcy cases and proceedings. *See* Conn. Nat'l Bank v. Germain, 503 U.S. 249 (1992).

state courts are bound to hear cases and controversies regarding the federal statute.[1008]

Since the founding of the Republic, however, whenever Congress has enacted comprehensive bankruptcy legislation, it has vested bankruptcy jurisdiction in federal courts. After 1867[1009] these have been called courts of bankruptcy or bankruptcy courts.[1010] Bankruptcy

---

1008. *See, e.g.,* Testa v. Katt, 330 U.S. 386, 391 (1947) ("If an act of Congress gives a penalty to a party aggrieved, without specifying a remedy for its enforcement, there is no reason why it should not be enforced, if not provided otherwise by some act of Congress, by a proper action in a State court.") (citations omitted). *Cf.* United States v. Bank of New York & Trust Co., 296 U.S. 463, 479 (1936) ("Upon the state courts, equally with the courts of the Union, rests the obligation to guard and enforce every right secured by the Constitution and laws of the United States whenever those rights are involved in any suit or proceedings before them.").

1009. *See* Bankruptcy Act of 1867, § 1, Act of March 2, 1867, 39th Cong., 2d Sess., ch. 176 at 517.

1010. *See* Bankruptcy Act of 1800, § 2, Act of April 4, 1800, 6th Cong., 1st Sess., 2 Stat. 19, 21 (1845) (repealed 1803 by the Act of Dec. 19, 1803, 8th Cong., 1st Sess., 2 Stat. 248 (1845)); Bankruptcy Act of 1841, § 8, Act of Aug. 19, 1841, 27th Cong., 1st Sess., 5 Stat. 440, 446-47 (1846) (repealed Mar. 3, 1843, 9th Cong., 1st Sess., 5 Stat. 614 (1846)); Bankruptcy Act of 1867, § 1, Act of March 2, 1867, 39th Cong., 2d Sess., 14 Stat. 517 (1868) (repealed June 7, 1878, 45th Cong., 2d Sess., 20 Stat. 99 (1879)). Under the Bankruptcy Act of 1898, Congress vested bankruptcy jurisdiction in "courts of bankruptcy" which included all United States district courts, not only the court in which the case is filed. *See* § 1(10) of the Bankruptcy Act of 1898, 11 U.S.C. § 1(10) (1976) (repealed 1979); Williams v. Austrian, 331 U.S. 642, 644 (1947) (holding that bankruptcy jurisdiction is conferred on all United States district courts, not only the court in which the case is filed). Under the 1978 Bankruptcy Code, Congress first vested bankruptcy jurisdiction in the United States district courts and specified that the jurisdiction would be exercised by independent bankruptcy courts. *See* 28 U.S.C. § 1471 (1978) (repealed 1984). In 1982 the Court decided *Northern Pipeline* finding the 1978 jurisdictional scheme to be unconstitutional. *See* N. Pipeline Constr. Co. v. Marathon Pipe Line Co., 458 U.S. 50, 87 (1982). Congress responded in 1984 by once again vesting bankruptcy jurisdiction in the United States district courts but allowed the district courts to refer bankruptcy cases to bankruptcy

courts have always had power to decide whether they have jurisdiction over a particular case or controversy.[1011] This power can extend beyond the conclusion of the case or proceeding.[1012] For instance, it is well-settled that unless the bankruptcy court's order is on appeal, it has jurisdiction to determine the scope of its previous order.[1013]

It is useful to separately consider jurisdiction under the Bankruptcy Act of 1898 (the "Bankruptcy Act" or "Act") and the 1978 Bankruptcy Code (the "Bankruptcy Code" or "Code"). Although jurisdiction under the Bankruptcy Act is largely of historical interest, important insights may be gained by examining the Court's approach to bankruptcy jurisdiction over a period of years. As time passes and the Court renders more decisions interpreting the jurisdictional provisions of the Bankruptcy Act, the bankruptcy system adapts and Congress sometimes responds by expanding and fine-tuning the scope of bankruptcy court jurisdiction. Once this process is examined under the Bankruptcy Act, it can be compared to the Court's approach to jurisdiction under the Bankruptcy Code.

---

judges who functioned as "units" of the district courts known as "bankruptcy courts." *See* 28 U.S.C. §§ 151, 1334 (Supp. 1984).

1011. *See, e.g.,* Chicot County Drainage Dist. v. Baxter State Bank, 308 U.S. 371, 377 (1940); Stoll v. Gottlieb, 305 U.S. 165, 171 (1938); First Nat'l Bank v. Klug, 186 U.S. 202, 204 (1902) (dictum). As noted below, a bankruptcy court's determination of jurisdiction is res judicata and cannot be collaterally attacked even if the jurisdiction was asserted erroneously. *See, e.g.,* Chicot County Drainage Dist. v. Baxter State Bank, 308 U.S. 371, 378 (1940); Stoll v. Gottlieb, 305 U.S. 165, 171-72 (1938).

1012. For instance, under Bankruptcy Code § 550, 11 U.S.C. § 550 (2000), bankruptcy courts have the power to reopen closed cases. *See, e.g., In re Slali,* 282 B.R. 225, 229 (C.D. Cal. 2002) (affirming bankruptcy court's decision to reopen case to modify discharge injunction). A bankruptcy court also might reopen an adversary proceeding to reform a judgment under Fed. R. Bankr. P. 9024, or reopen a case when the court has retained jurisdiction under a confirmed plan.

1013. *See* Local Loan Co. v. Hunt, 292 U.S. 234, 239 (1934) (holding that courts have jurisdiction to interpret and enforce their own orders).

From 1898 to 1979, bankruptcy jurisdiction was set forth in sections 2 and 23 of the Bankruptcy Act of 1898.[1014] Section 2a of the Bankruptcy Act of 1898,[1015] provided that:

> The courts of the United States hereinbefore defined as courts of bankruptcy [i.e., the judge or referee of the United States district courts or territorial courts] are hereby created courts of bankruptcy and are hereby invested, within their respective territorial limits . . ., with such jurisdiction at law and in equity as will enable them to exercise original jurisdiction in proceedings under this Act . . . to [administer bankruptcy cases, e.g., adjudicating persons bankrupt, allowing and disallowing claims, and the like].

Moreover, section 23 of the Bankruptcy Act of 1898,[1016] provided that:[1017]

1014. *See* 11 U.S.C. §§ 11, 46 (1976) (repealed 1979).

1015. 11 U.S.C. § 11 (1976) (repealed 1979). The Bankruptcy Act also contained a territorial restriction on bankruptcy court jurisdiction limiting the power of the court to adjudge persons bankrupt to those who had their principal place of business, residence, or domicile within the district for the greater portion of the six months preceding the date of the filing. *See* Bankruptcy Act, § 2a(1), 11 U.S.C. § 11a(1) (1976) (repealed 1979). This constraint led to litigation in which the Court held that the commencement of an equity receivership in one district did not change the location of the debtor's principal place of business for purposes of determining bankruptcy court jurisdiction. *See* Royal Indem. Co. v. Am. Bond & Mortgage Co., 289 U.S. 165, 168-70 (1933).

1016. 11 U.S.C. § 46 (1976) (repealed 1979). The Bankruptcy Act's reference to a debtor as a "bankrupt" is archaic. For ease of reference and to reduce stigma, the Bankruptcy Code calls a person seeking relief a "debtor" rather than a "bankrupt." *See* H.R. REP. NO. 595, 95th Cong., 1st Sess. 310 (1977).

1017. As originally enacted, Bankruptcy Act § 23b contained no exception for §§ 60, 67 & 70. *See* Bankruptcy Act of 1898 § 23b, Pub. L. No. 171 (July 1, 1898), 30 Stat. 544, 552 (1898). In 1903, however, Congress amended § 23b to provide an exception for cases under §§ 60b & 67e. *See* Pub. L. No. 62, 57th Cong., 2d Sess. § 8 (Feb. 5, 1903), 32 Stat. 797, 798 (1903). With the law so written, the Court dismissed for lack of jurisdiction suits to avoid liens brought by the trustee under § 67f. *See, e.g.,* Taubel-Scott-Kitzmiller Co. v. Fox, 264 U.S. 426, 433-38 (1924). In 1926, Congress added § 70e to the exclusion. *See* Pub. L. No. 301, 69th

a. The United States district courts shall have jurisdiction of all cases at law and in equity, as distinguished from proceedings under this Act, between receivers and trustees as such and adverse claimants, concerning the property acquired or claimed by the receivers or trustees, in the same manner and to the same extent as though such proceedings had not been instituted and such controversies had been between the bankrupt and such adverse claimants.

b. Suits by the receiver and trustee shall be brought or prosecuted only in the courts when the bankrupt might have brought or prosecuted them if proceedings under this Act had not been instituted, unless by consent of the defendant, except as provided in sections 60, 67, and 70 of this Act.

The Court made clear that the Bankruptcy Act's conferral of jurisdiction "at law" did not turn bankruptcy court adjudication into a common law action.[1018] Rather, as discussed below, the Court has long-recognized that bankruptcy cases and proceedings are equitable in nature.[1019]

For the most part,[1020] these jurisdictional provisions gave the bankruptcy courts summary jurisdiction over bankruptcy cases[1021] and over

---

Cong., 1st Sess., ch. 406, § 8 (May 27, 1926), 44 Stat. 662, 664 (1927). Ultimately, in 1938 when it enacted the Chandler Act, Congress amended the Bankruptcy Act to broaden the exception as it reads above. *See* Pub. L. No. 696, 75th Cong., 3d Sess., ch. 575 (June 22, 1938), 52 Stat. 840, 854 (1938).

1018. *See* Meek v. Ctr. County Banking Co., 268 U.S. 426, 429 (1925) (holding that the bankruptcy proceeding was not in the nature of a common law action nor "abated by any rule of the common law").

1019. *See, e.g.,* Pepper v. Litton, 308 U.S. 295, 304 (1939).

1020. The Court's decision in *Texas v. Donoghue* appears to be an aberration that undermines this principle. *See* Texas v. Donoghue, 302 U.S. 284, 289 (1937) (holding that even though oil was in possession of the debtor's trustee, it was an abuse of discretion for the bankruptcy court to deny Texas' application for permission to decide a dispute over title to the oil in state court).

1021. The bankruptcy court's jurisdiction over the case is summary and exclusive. The Court has held that a bankruptcy court is "not at liberty to

property in which the debtor had actual or constructive possession.[1022] This principle held true even though the property was in the custody of a state court at the time of the bankruptcy filing, as long as the state court had not entered a final judgment.[1023] Unless the parties con-

---

surrender its exclusive control over matters of administration" such as determining priorities in distribution. *See* U.S. Fid. & Guar. Co. v. Bray, 225 U.S. 205, 218 (1912). But as a general proposition, the bankruptcy court may exercise its discretion to allow general litigation to proceed in a nonbankruptcy forum. *See, e.g., Ex Parte* Baldwin, 291 U.S. 610, 619 (1934) (§ 77 railroad reorganization case in which the Court states that "the bankruptcy court might, in the exercise of its discretion, conclude that it is desirable to have the litigation proceed in the state court."). If, however, a state court asserts jurisdiction over property of the bankruptcy estate, it is clear that the bankruptcy court exercises paramount jurisdiction. *See* Taylor v. Sternberg, 293 U.S. 470, 472 (1935) ("Upon the filing of a petition in bankruptcy the jurisdiction of the bankruptcy court becomes paramount and exclusive, and thereafter that court's possession and control of the estate cannot be affected by proceedings in other courts, whether state or federal; and this applies while the possession is constructive as well as when it becomes actual."); *In re* Watts & Sachs, 190 U.S. 1, 27 (1903) ("The bankruptcy law is paramount, and the jurisdiction of the Federal courts in bankruptcy, when properly invoked, in the administration of the affairs of insolvent persons and corporations, is essentially exclusive."). Apparently, paramount federal jurisdiction can be retained even after the property is sold, as long as the sale order expressly retains jurisdiction. *Cf.* Wabash R.R. Co. v. Adelbert Coll., 208 U.S. 38, 47 (1908) (non-bankruptcy federal district court railroad reorganization proceeding).

1022. *See, e.g.,* Page v. Ark. Natural Gas Corp., 286 U.S. 269, 271 (1932) (because the bankruptcy trustee had possession of the leasehold, the bankruptcy referee had jurisdiction to adjudicate all questions respecting its title, possession, or control). Evidently title to the property was sufficient to constitute constructive possession. *See infra* n.1046 and accompanying text.

1023. *Compare, e.g.,* Kalb v. Feuerstein, 308 U.S. 433, 443 (1940) (§ 75 case filed by farmer ousts state court of jurisdiction to foreclose on farm); Gross v. Irving Trust Co., 289 U.S. 342, 344 (1933) (bankruptcy filing ousts state court of jurisdiction to award compensation to receivers); *and* Isaacs v. Hobbs Tie & Timber Co., 282 U.S. 734, 737 (1931) (bankruptcy court has exclusive jurisdiction over property in which the debtor had title and right to possession as of the filing of the bankruptcy petition even if creditor has commenced a foreclosure action in a nonbankruptcy

sented to adjudication before the bankruptcy court,[1024] however, in lieu of summary jurisdiction, the Bankruptcy Act required plenary jurisdiction to be exercised by United States district courts[1025] over certain avoiding power actions[1026] or controversies arising in bank-

---

forum) *with, e.g.,* Straton v. New, 283 U.S. 318, 326 (1931) (when creditor obtained and docketed a court judgment against the debtor's real estate prepetition, the debtor's bankruptcy would not oust the state court of jurisdiction or permit the bankruptcy court to enjoin the foreclosure sale).

1024. *See, e.g.,* Schumacher v. Beeler, 293 U.S. 367, 377 (1934) (explaining that consent of parties can confer jurisdiction); MacDonald v. Plymouth County Trust Co., 286 U.S. 263, 267 (1932) (holding that parties could consent to have matters ordinarily subject to trial under plenary jurisdiction before the district court instead tried in summary proceedings before the bankruptcy referee); Bryan v. Bernheimer, 181 U.S. 188, 197 (1901) (creditor consented to summary jurisdiction by filing a proof of claim).

1025. The district court exercising plenary jurisdiction did not necessarily have to be the court in which the bankruptcy petition was filed. Moreover, if the parties consented, an action normally triable as a plenary suit could be adjudicated by the bankruptcy referee in a summary proceeding. *See* MacDonald v. Plymouth County Trust Co., 286 U.S. 263, 265, 277 (1932).

1026. Without regard to the debtor's possession or title to property, Bankruptcy Act § 23b granted the district courts plenary jurisdiction over preference, certain fraudulent transfer, and strong arm clause causes of action under Bankruptcy Act §§ 60, 67 & 70. *See supra* n.1017 *and e.g.,* Flanders v. Coleman, 250 U.S. 223, 227 (1919) (fraudulent transfer cause of action); Collett v. Adams, 249 U.S. 545, 549 (1919) (preference action). This special jurisdictional grant also covered actions to recover the payment of excessive attorneys fees under § 60d of the Bankruptcy Act. *See In re* Wood, 210 U.S. 246, 253 (1908). The jurisdictional grant did not cover, however, an action to recover property of the debtor obtained by false pretenses when there was no transfer by the debtor. *See* Park v. Cameron, 237 U.S. 616, 618 (1915) ("Those [allegations] that we have recited seem to us in their conclusion to import not that the corporation had done anything, but that certain of its officers by false pretenses have withdrawn its funds. If so the suit is not to avoid a transfer by the bankrupt of its property, but a suit against wrongdoers who have appropriated it without the bankrupt's assent, and therefore not within §§ 23b and 70e of the [Bankruptcy] Act.").

ruptcy cases over which they would have had jurisdiction had the bankruptcy case not been filed.[1027] If the debtor had neither actual nor constructive possession of the property[1028] and there was no basis for federal court jurisdiction in the absence of a bankruptcy case,[1029] then the federal district court lacked jurisdiction over the controversy,

---

1027. *See, e.g.,* Bush v. Elliott, 202 U.S. 477, 482 (1906) (holding that federal circuit court had plenary jurisdiction in case where diversity jurisdiction tests met). The limitations of § 23 on the jurisdiction conferred by Bankruptcy Act § 2a did not apply in corporate reorganization cases under Chapter X of the Bankruptcy Act. *See* Williams v. Austrian, 331 U.S. 642, 644 (1947).

1028. Of course if the debtor had actual or constructive possession of the property at the time of the bankruptcy petition, a wrongful replevin of the property postpetition would not oust the district court of summary jurisdiction over the property even though the replevin took the property out of the possession of the bankruptcy trustee. *See* White v. Schloerb, 178 U.S. 542, 548 (1900). *Cf.* Murphy v. John Hofman Co., 211 U.S. 562, 569-70 (1909) (jurisdiction remains in bankruptcy court despite postpetition replevin by sheriff who nevertheless left property in possession of the bankruptcy receiver). Nor would turnover to the secured party by a temporary bankruptcy receiver acting without an order of the bankruptcy court oust the bankruptcy court of jurisdiction. *See* Whitney v. Wenman, 198 U.S. 539, 553 (1905) ("We do not think this jurisdiction can be ousted by a surrender of the property by the receiver, without authority of the court . . . . What we hold is that under the allegations of this bill the District Court had the right in a proceeding in the nature of a plenary action . . . to determine their rights, and to grant full relief . . . .").

1029. For example, federal diversity jurisdiction would be a basis for the district court to exercise jurisdiction in the absence of bankruptcy. *See, e.g.,* Bush v. Elliott, 202 U.S. 477, 484 (1906). Even so, courts exercising plenary jurisdiction have no power to interfere with claims administration or other matters exclusively within the jurisdiction of the bankruptcy court. *See* Knauth, Nachod & Kuhne v. Latham & Co., 242 U.S. 426, 428 (1917) (holding that federal Circuit court hearing action by receivers (and later bankruptcy trustee) to recover fraudulently transferred property had no jurisdiction to hear a cross bill of the transferee seeking to impress a trust on the property based on alleged fraud of the debtor in obtaining money from the transferee; the transferee's effort was little more than an effort to gain priority against property of the estate on account of money that the debtors fraudulently obtained).

unless Bankruptcy Act § 23b provided otherwise.[1030] For instance, in *Harris v. First National Bank of Mt. Pleasant*,[1031] the Court affirmed the district court's dismissal for lack of jurisdiction of a suit by a bankruptcy trustee against a bank for wrongfully withholding collateral. The bank had not consented to jurisdiction and there was no provision of the Bankruptcy Act that applied to confer federal jurisdiction.[1032] If the property at issue was not in the debtor's actual or constructive possession and a third party asserted a bona fide claim adverse to the bankruptcy trustee, the dispute was beyond the summary jurisdiction of the bankruptcy court.[1033] The mere assertion of an adverse claim, however, did not oust the bankruptcy court of jurisdiction; if the claim was colorable or unwarranted, the bankruptcy court retained jurisdiction; but if it was real and substantial, the bankruptcy court was required to relinquish jurisdiction.[1034] Moreover, district courts outside the district in which the bankruptcy case was commenced could exercise summary ancillary jurisdiction with respect to such property[1035] including "ancillary jurisdiction to make

---

1030. *See, e.g.,* Daniel v. Guar. Trust Co., 285 U.S. 154, 163-64 (1932); Kelley v. Gill, 245 U.S. 116, 121 (1917); Wall v. Cox, 181 U.S. 244, 247 (1901); Hicks v. Knost, 178 U.S. 541, 542 (1900); Mitchell v. McClure, 178 U.S. 539, 540 (1900); Bardes v. Hawarden First Nat'l Bank, 178 U.S. 524, 536 (1900) (holding that without consent of the defendant, district court lacked jurisdiction over turnover action or fraudulent transfer action to recover money or property in possession of a third party).

1031. 216 U.S. 382 (1910).

1032. *See id.* at 383-84.

1033. *See, e.g.,* Galbraith v. Vallely, 256 U.S. 46, 50 (1921).

1034. *See, e.g.,* Harrison v. Chamberlin, 271 U.S. 191, 194 (1926).

1035. *See, e.g.,* Babbitt v. Dutcher, 216 U.S. 102, 113 (1910) (A United States district court had ancillary jurisdiction in cases in which there is "no claim of adverse title based on any transfer prior to the bankruptcy, but when the property is in the physical possession of a third party or of an agent of the bankrupt, or of an officer of a bankrupt corporation, who refuses to deliver it to the trustee in bankruptcy."). *Cf.* Fulton Nat'l Bank v. Hozier, 267 U.S. 276, 280 (1925) (although not the facts in this case, the Court noted the existence of ancillary jurisdiction was appropriate where the subsidiary controversy had a direct relation to property or assets

orders and issue process in aid of proceedings pending and being administered in the District Court of another district."[1036]

In many cases under the Bankruptcy Act, the bankruptcy court's jurisdiction to resolve a controversy turned on whether the non-debtor party had consented to jurisdiction.[1037] Unless the non-debtor party objected to the bankruptcy court's exercise of summary jurisdiction before entry of a final order, the Court fashioned a rule that by not challenging jurisdiction the non-debtor party waived the right to do so.[1038] But if the party objected to the bankruptcy court's exercise of summary jurisdiction before the entry of a final order, its appearance in the bankruptcy court alone did not constitute consent to summary jurisdiction.[1039] The Court determined that "consent" could be inferred by the filing of a proof of claim with the bankruptcy court[1040] or simply

---

actually or constructively drawn into the court's possession or control by the principal suit).

1036. *See In re* Elkus, 216 U.S. 115, 117 (1910).

1037. As referenced *supra* in n.1017, after the 1903 amendments and before the 1926 amendments, the bankruptcy court had summary jurisdiction over preference and certain federal fraudulent transfer suits for the recovery of property under Bankruptcy Act §§ 60b & 67e, but unless the defendant consented, no summary jurisdiction for fraudulent transfer suits under Bankruptcy Act § 70e. *See, e.g.,* Wood v. A. Wilbert's Sons Shingle & Lumber Co., 226 U.S. 384, 388-89 (1912).

1038. *See, e.g.,* Harris v. Avery Brundage Co., 305 U.S. 160, 164 (1938).

1039. *See, e.g.,* Galbraith v. Vallely, 256 U.S. 46, 49-50 (1921) (even though the assignee for the benefit of creditors appeared in bankruptcy court and filed an accounting and paid over assigned assets net of fees, the bankruptcy court lacked summary jurisdiction to require the assignee to turnover fees and expenses retained and subject to his adverse claim); Louisville Trust Co. v. Comingor, 184 U.S. 18, 26 (1902) (sustaining challenge to exercise of summary jurisdiction when assignee for the benefit of creditors appeared in the district court but objected to summary jurisdiction before the entry of a final order).

1040. *See, e.g.,* Katchen v. Landy, 382 U.S. 323, 334 (1966) (holding that a creditor's filing a proof of claim confers summary jurisdiction on the bankruptcy court to decide preference actions and orders to surrender property filed by the bankruptcy trustee in a responsive action to disallow the claim); Bryan v. Bernheimer, 181 U.S. 188, 197 (1901) (credi-

the failure of a non-debtor party to timely object to the bankruptcy court's exercise of jurisdiction.[1041] Among those in the bankruptcy bar, this process came to be known affectionately as "jurisdiction by ambush."

Although there was no simple test to determine whether a matter fell within the summary or plenary jurisdiction of the bankruptcy court, possession of the property was the most important factor that influenced the decision. If the debtor had actual or constructive possession of an asset that was property of the bankruptcy estate, the bankruptcy court could exercise summary jurisdiction because the *res* was *in custodia legis*; that is, based on the court's custody over the asset in the possession of the estate, the court could exercise pervasive *in rem* jurisdiction.[1042]

But if the debtor's possession was solely as a custodian for the benefit of a third party, the bankruptcy court lacked summary jurisdiction. In *Phelps v. United States*[1043] the Court applied this reasoning to hold that the bankruptcy court lacked summary

---

tor consented to summary jurisdiction by filing a proof of claim). *Cf.* Alexander v. Hillman, 296 U.S. 222, 238-39, 242-43 (1935) (claim filed in federal equity receivership submits claimant to court's jurisdiction in respect of all defenses, objections, and counterclaims that might be interposed to the validity, priority, or amount of claims).

1041. *See* Cline v. Kaplan (*In re* Gold Medal Laundries, Inc.), 323 U.S. 97, 99 (1944) (dictum because timely objection to jurisdiction made on facts of this case). *Cf.* Bankruptcy Act § 2a(7), 11 U.S.C. § 11a(7) (1976) (repealed 1979) ("[W]here in a controversy arising in a proceeding under this Act an adverse party does not interpose objection to the summary jurisdiction of the court of bankruptcy, by answer or motion filed before the expiration of the time prescribed by law or rule of court[,] . . . he shall be deemed to have consented to such jurisdiction[.]").

1042. *See, e.g.,* Isaacs v. Hobbs Tie & Timber Co., 282 U.S. 734, 738 (1931) (holding that once the debtor filed for bankruptcy, title to the property vested in the trustee and the bankruptcy court acquired exclusive jurisdiction over the property, thereby precluding a state court from continuing with foreclosure proceedings or determining the scope of a secured creditor's lien).

1043. 421 U.S. 330 (1975).

jurisdiction to hear the trustee's request that an assignee for the benefit of creditors turnover property subject to a valid prepetition tax lien in favor of the Internal Revenue Service.[1044] The tax levy created a custodial relationship between the assignee and the IRS thereby placing the property in the constructive possession of the IRS and beyond the summary jurisdiction of the bankruptcy court.[1045]

On the other hand, if the debtor had a colorable claim to title of an asset in the debtor's actual or constructive possession that would be vested in the bankruptcy trustee as property of the bankruptcy estate, then the bankruptcy court had summary jurisdiction over the asset and could resolve disputes of ownership.[1046] Nevertheless, in certain exceptional circumstances, the bankruptcy court retained the discretion to allow a matter to be litigated in a nonbankruptcy forum. For instance, when the trustee and a third person dispute title to property in possession of the bankruptcy estate and interpretation of unsettled questions of state property law is central to the suit, the bankruptcy court might allow the state court to resolve the controversy.[1047]

By comparison, when the debtor lacks actual or constructive possession of the property, absent the consent of the parties, the bankruptcy court lacks jurisdiction to decide controversies regarding the

---

1044. *See id.* at 335-37.

1045. *See id.* at 336-37 ("[W]here possession is assertedly held not for the bankrupt, but for others prior to the bankruptcy . . . the holder is not subject to summary jurisdiction.") (citation omitted).

1046. *See, e.g.,* Thompson v. Magnolia Petroleum Co., 309 U.S. 478, 481(1940) (bankruptcy court has jurisdiction to adjudicate controversies relating to property over which the debtor has actual or constructive possession as of the date of the filing of the bankruptcy petition).

1047. *See* Mangus v. Miller, 317 U.S. 178, 185 (1942) (suggesting that bankruptcy court should afford debtor joint tenant of a land purchase contract and his wife opportunity to litigate with assignor of land vendor in state court to determine parties' rights to land); Thompson v. Magnolia Petroleum Co., 309 U.S. 478, 483-84 (1940) (allowing Illinois state court to determine disputed fee ownership to the right of way lands in an oil field).

property. For example, when the debtor is not in possession of an asset to which it asserts an interest, and a third person asserts a bona fide claim adverse to the bankruptcy estate, the bankruptcy court lacks summary jurisdiction over the dispute.[1048] Moreover, suits regarding property to which the debtor does not have title or an equity of redemption are outside the court's summary jurisdiction.[1049]

Finally, if the matter is central to the administration of the bankruptcy case, the bankruptcy court would exercise exclusive jurisdiction over the matter. For instance, in *Brown v. Gerdes*,[1050] the issue was whether the bankruptcy court had jurisdiction to award professional fees for counsel who represented the bankruptcy trustee in filing a suit in state court. The Court held that the bankruptcy court had exclusive jurisdiction to award fees because the Bankruptcy Act established a comprehensive system of supervision over compensation and allowance of administrative expenses.[1051] Indeed, the Court has denounced efforts by bankruptcy courts to delegate the resolution of

---

1048. *See, e.g.,* Cline v. Kaplan (*In re* Gold Medal Laundries, Inc.), 323 U.S. 97, 98-100 (1944) (absent consent, no summary jurisdiction to turnover property in which both the debtor and a third person assert an interest); Taubel-Scott-Kitzmiller Co. v. Fox, 264 U.S. 426, 438 (1924) (no summary jurisdiction over action to avoid a prepetition execution lien and levy because trustee does not have possession of property and is confronted with substantial adverse claim); Galbraith v. Vallely, 256 U.S. 46, 50 (1921) (denying summary jurisdiction over action to turnover fees held by assignee for the benefit of creditors who asserted an adverse claim) Louisville Trust Co. v. Comingor, 184 U.S. 18, 26 (1902) (same).

1049. *See, e.g.,* State Bank of Hardinsburg v. Brown, 317 U.S. 135, 137 (1942) (when sheriff holds foreclosure sale of debtor's real estate before bankruptcy and cuts off equity of redemption under state law, the bankruptcy court lacks jurisdiction over the property even if the deed is not delivered until after the filing of the petition).

1050. 321 U.S. 178 (1944).

1051. *See id.* at 182. *Cf.* Barton v. Barbour, 104 U.S. 126, 128 (1881) (previously evidencing the comprehensive system of supervision of court-appointed officials and establishing the *Barton Doctrine* that an estate administrator cannot be sued without leave of the court appointing the official).

bankruptcy compensation disputes to state courts, even when the compensation is not payable out of the estate.[1052]

Nor did the jurisdictional uncertainties cease with the establishment of the 1978 Bankruptcy Code. To be sure, the Byzantine jurisdictional scheme of the Bankruptcy Act led Congress to grant bankruptcy courts pervasive jurisdiction under the Bankruptcy Code.[1053] But the Code's broad grant of jurisdiction to non-tenured bankruptcy judges left the Code ripe for constitutional challenge. As noted in Chapter 3, in 1982 the Court's *Northern Pipeline* decision struck down the entire jurisdiction of the bankruptcy courts as unconstitutional.[1054] Congress refused to respond, and the Administrative Office of United States Courts, somewhat questionably, disseminated an Emergency Rule, to be adopted in each judicial district, purporting to maintain bankruptcy jurisdiction in the federal courts.[1055] Instead of leaving bankruptcy cases to be adjudicated in state courts of general jurisdiction, the Emergency Rule provided that United States district judges could assert jurisdiction and could refer cases to non-tenured bankruptcy judges. Although five Circuit courts upheld the constitutionality of the Emergency Rule, the Supreme

---

1052. *See* Leiman v. Guttman, 336 U.S. 1, 5, 9 (1949) (requiring bankruptcy court to assert jurisdiction over the allowance of fees incident to the reorganization but not payable out of the estate).

1053. *See* Pub. L. No. 598, 95th Cong., 2d Sess., 92 Stat. 2549, 2668 § 241(a) (1978) (enacting 28 U.S.C. § 1471) (repealed 1984); H.R. REP. NO. 595, 95th Cong., 1st Sess. 445 (1977) ("Actions that formerly had to be tried in State court or in Federal district court, at great cost and delay to the estate, may now be tried in the bankruptcy courts. The idea of possession or consent as the sole bases for jurisdiction is eliminated. The bankruptcy court is given in personam as well as *in rem* jurisdiction to handle everything that arises in a bankruptcy case.").

1054. *See* N. Pipeline Constr. Co. v. Marathon Pipe Line Co., 458 U.S. 50 (1982), discussed more fully *supra* in Ch. 3, pp. 123, 129, & 154-155.

1055. *See* H.R. REP. NO. 807, 97th Cong., 2d Sess. at 30 (1982). Some courts appended the text of the Emergency Rule to their reported decisions. *See, e.g.,* White Motor Corp. v. Citibank, N.A., 704 F.2d 254, 265-67 (6th Cir. 1983).

Court denied certiorari on two occasions and never did rule on the unconstitutionality of this judicial legislation.[1056]

In 1984, Congress responded to the Court's 1982 *Northern Pipeline* decision.[1057] Instead of vesting bankruptcy jurisdiction in tenured Article III bankruptcy judges, Congress amended the Bankruptcy Code to nominally vest comprehensive jurisdiction in Article III United States district courts.[1058] Recognizing that district courts would have neither the time nor interest to administer most bankruptcy cases, the amendment permitted district courts to make a more circumscribed jurisdictional reference to non-tenured bankruptcy judges.[1059] Not surprisingly, each district court quickly adopted a local rule referring bankruptcy cases to non-tenured bankruptcy judges for disposition unless the district court withdrew the reference. Non-tenured bankruptcy judges have the ability to enter final judgments in core matters or, when the parties consent to jurisdiction, in non-core matters related to bankruptcy cases or proceedings.[1060] Otherwise,

---

1056. Five Circuit courts upheld the constitutionality of the Emergency Rule and interpreted *Northern Pipeline* to invalidate the grant of jurisdiction to bankruptcy judges only, thereby permitting the district courts to retain original jurisdiction over bankruptcy cases. *See* Coastal Steel Corp. v. Tilghman Wheelabrator Ltd., 709 F.2d 190, 200 (3d Cir.), *cert. denied*, 464 U.S. 938 (1983); *In re* Braniff Airways, Inc., 700 F.2d 214, 214 (5th Cir.), *cert. denied sub nom.* Am. Airlines, Inc. v. Braniff Airways, Inc., 461 U.S. 944 (1983); Salomon v. Kaiser (*In re* Kaiser), 722 F.2d 1574, 1582 (2d Cir. 1983); White Motor Corp. v. Citibank, N.A., 704 F.2d 254, 260 (6th Cir. 1983); *In re* Hansen, 702 F.2d 728, 729 (8th Cir. 1983).

1057. *See* Bankruptcy Amendments and Federal Judgeship Act of 1984, Pub. L. No. 353, 98th Cong., 2d Sess., 98 Stat. 333 (1984) ("BAFJA").

1058. *See id.*, § 101, enacting 28 U.S.C. § 1334 (Supp. 1984).

1059. *See id.*, § 104(a), 98 Stat. 336, 340-41, enacting, inter alia, 28 U.S.C. §§ 152(a)(1) & 157 (Supp. 1984).

1060. *See* 28 U.S.C. §§ 152(a)(1) & 157(b)-(c) (2000). In Celotex Corp. v. Edwards, 514 U.S. 300, 308 (1995), the Court adopted the definition of "related to" jurisdiction set forth by the Third Circuit in Pacor, Inc. v. Higgins, 743 F.2d 984, 994 (1984): "[T]he 'related to' language of [28 U.S.C.] § 1334(b) must be read to give district courts (and bankruptcy

bankruptcy judges may only make reports and recommendations to United States district court judges, who alone have the power to enter final orders in non-core proceedings when at least one party has not consented to bankruptcy court jurisdiction.[1061] Remarkably, the Court has not had occasion to review the constitutionality of this patch-work system in which the judicial power of the United States is routinely exercised by non-tenured judges under the theoretical supervision of the United States district courts.

Although the core/non-core distinction is not identical with the jurisdictional scheme under the Bankruptcy Act of 1898, the older jurisdictional decisions retain some vitality in shaping the contours of jurisdiction under the 1978 Bankruptcy Code. To be sure, the list of core proceedings in section 157(b)(2) of the Judicial Code is broader than summary jurisdiction conferred under the Act. It is doubtful, however, that the Court would find a matter that it formerly included within summary jurisdiction to be outside the scope of core proceedings. Thus, knowledge of the Act precedents may prove persuasive in resolving future jurisdictional disputes, even though not binding under the jurisdictional scheme of the Bankruptcy Code.

Of course, because the Bankruptcy Code abolished the distinction between summary and plenary jurisdiction, the facts of some cases have been decided differently under the Bankruptcy Code than under the Act. In *United States v. Whiting Pools, Inc.*,[1062] the Court permit-

---

courts under § 157(a)) jurisdiction over more than simply proceedings involving the property of the debtor or the estate . . . . The usual articulation of the test for determining whether a civil proceeding is related to bankruptcy is whether *the outcome of that proceeding could conceivably have any effect on the estate being administered in bankruptcy.* . . . Thus, the proceeding need not necessarily be against the debtor or against the debtor's property. An action is related to bankruptcy if the outcome could alter the debtor's rights, liabilities, options, or freedom of action (either positively or negatively) and which in any way impacts upon the handling and administration of the bankrupt estate." (emphasis in original; citations omitted).

1061. *See* 28 U.S.C. § 157(c)(1) (2000).

1062. 462 U.S. 198 (1983).

ted a chapter 11 debtor in possession to obtain turnover of property in the hands of the Internal Revenue Service, which had pursued creditor remedies to gain possession of the property as a secured creditor with a perfected tax lien.[1063] Thus, the Court reached a different result in *Whiting Pools* than it reached in *Phelps v. United States*, which the Court distinguished as a liquidation case.[1064]

The Court has also rendered a few decisions interpreting jurisdiction under the 1978 Bankruptcy Code, some of which raise issues that did not arise under the Bankruptcy Act.[1065] For instance, the Court has hinted that the bankruptcy court's jurisdiction in a chapter 11 reorganization case may be broader than in a chapter 7 liquidation case.[1066] Moreover, in *Kontrick v. Ryan*,[1067] the Court held that time constraints in the bankruptcy rules are claims-processing rules that do not affect federal subject matter jurisdiction.[1068] Furthermore,

---

1063. *See id.* at 206-07. The Court was careful to leave open the question whether turnover under Bankruptcy Code § 542 would apply to a pledge of collateral or other situation when the creditor had possession of the property outside the context of pursuing default remedies. *See id.* at 207 n.14.

1064. *See id.* at 206 n.13. *See also supra* nn.1043-1045 and accompanying text.

1065. As mentioned *supra* in n.1007, the Court's decision in Conn. Nat'l Bank v. Germain, 503 U.S. 249 (1992) discusses appellate jurisdiction from interlocutory orders and reconciles §§ 158 & 1292 of the Judicial Code. Moreover, as discussed in Ch. 3, the Court rendered several sovereign immunity decisions interpreting the scope of bankruptcy court jurisdiction under the Bankruptcy Code against governmental units.

1066. *See* Celotex Corp. v. Edwards, 514 U.S. 300, 310 (1995) ("[I]t is relevant to note that we are dealing here with a reorganization under Chapter 11, rather than a liquidation under Chapter 7. The jurisdiction of bankruptcy courts may extend more broadly in the former case than in the latter.").

1067. 540 U.S. 443 (2004).

1068. *See id.* at 456 ("Characteristically, a court's subject-matter jurisdiction cannot be expanded to account for the parties' litigation conduct; a claim-processing rule, on the other hand, even if unalterable on a party's application, can nonetheless be forfeited if the party

although the Court has refused to decide whether a bankruptcy judge may conduct a jury trial without the consent of the parties,[1069] the Court nevertheless has reaffirmed precedents allowing a bankruptcy judge to resolve a controversy without a jury trial when the creditor has filed a proof of claim. In *Granfinanciera, S.A. v. Nordberg*, the Court cited with approval its decision in *Katchen v. Landy* in which the Court held that the creditor's filing of a proof of claim triggers the process of the allowance and disallowance of claims and waives any jury trial right of a creditor on avoiding power actions filed against the creditor.[1070] The Court reaffirmed this reasoning in *Langenkamp v. Culp*,[1071] holding that a creditor's filing of a proof of claim waives its right to jury trial in a later-filed preference action.[1072]

---

asserting the rule waits too long to raise the point."). *See also* Fed. R. Bankr. P. 9030, recognizing that the Bankruptcy Rules cannot expand or limit a court's jurisdiction.

1069. *See* Ins. Co. of Pa. v. Ben Cooper, Inc., 497 U.S. 1023 (1990) (granting certiorari to decide whether bankruptcy judges may conduct jury trials without the consent of the parties), 498 U.S. 964 (1990) (vacating the grant of certiorari and remanding), and 500 U.S. 928 (1991) (denying certiorari after the Second Circuit reinstated its opinion on remand), discussed more fully *supra* in Ch. 1, pp.8-10.

1070. *See* Granfinanciera, S.A. v. Nordberg, 492 U.S. 33, 58 n.13 (1989) (citing with approval Katchen v. Landy, 382 U.S. 323, 336 (1966) ("although petitioner might be entitled to a jury trial on the issue of preference if he presented no claim in the bankruptcy proceeding and awaited a federal plenary action by the trustee, Schoenthal v. Irving Trust Co., 287 U.S. 92, when the same issue arises as part of the process of allowance and disallowance of claims, it is triable in equity")). *Katchen*, in turn, rooted its holding in *Alexander v. Hillman*, a federal equity receivership case in which the Court allowed the federal district court to adjudicate legal counterclaims filed by receivers against claimants. *See* Alexander v. Hillman, 296 U.S. 222, 238-39, 242-43 (1935) (claim filed in federal equity receivership submits claimant to court's jurisdiction in respect of all defenses, objections, and counterclaims that might be interposed to the validity, priority, or amount of claims). For a more thorough discussion of *Granfinanciera, see supra* Chs. 1 & 3, pp.8, 123, & 148.

1071. 498 U.S. 42 (1990) (*per curiam*).

1072. *See id.* at 44-45.

LIMITATIONS ON BANKRUPTCY COURT JURISDICTION

For the most part, a bankruptcy court has exclusive jurisdiction over a bankruptcy case and is "not at liberty to surrender its exclusive control over matters of administration, or to confide them to another tribunal."[1073] A bankruptcy court may defer the exercise of its jurisdiction when Congress has entrusted the matter in controversy to an administrative agency[1074] or when compelling issues of state law should be determined by state courts.[1075] Moreover, a bankruptcy court may act in such a manner that it relinquishes all or part of its jurisdiction.[1076] Sometimes the act is inadvertent. In *Acme Harvester Co. v. Beekman Lumber Co.*,[1077] the Court held that the district court lost jurisdiction to issue an *ex parte* injunction enjoining a creditor

---

1073. *See* U.S. Fid. & Guar. Co. v. Bray, 225 U.S. 205, 218 (1912) (district court improperly allowed a creditor who had filed a claim in bankruptcy to bring a bill in equity in a non-bankruptcy forum).

1074. Indeed, deference of jurisdiction may be required. *See, e.g.,* Nathanson v. N.L.R.B., 344 U.S. 25, 30 (1952) (suggesting that wise administration demands the bankruptcy court to refer liquidation of a back pay claim against the debtor to the N.L.R.B.); Thompson v. Tex. Mexican Ry. Co., 328 U.S. 134, 142 (1946) (requiring bankruptcy court to permit the Interstate Commerce Commission to determine railroad reorganization debtor's request to abandon operations under a trackage agreement); Smith v. Hoboken R., Warehouse & S.S. Connecting Co., 328 U.S. 123, 129-30 (1946) (requiring the bankruptcy court to permit the Interstate Commerce Commission to determine whether lessor to a railroad reorganization debtor-lessee could cause forfeiture and termination of a lease of terminal switching line).

1075. *See, e.g., supra* n.1047 and accompanying text.

1076. Sometimes the relinquishment of jurisdiction is intentional. Bankruptcy Code § 305, 11 U.S.C. § 305 (2000), authorizes the court to dismiss or suspend all proceedings in a bankruptcy case. The Judicial Code specifies when a district court exercising bankruptcy jurisdiction may or must abstain from deciding a proceeding. *See* 28 U.S.C. § 1334(c) (2000). Likewise, the court to which a claim or cause of action is removed has the power to relinquish jurisdiction by remanding the removed claim or cause of action. *See* 28 U.S.C. § 1452(b) (2000).

1077. 222 U.S. 300 (1911).

from pursuing a state court action against the debtor.[1078] In that case, creditors of Acme Harvester filed an involuntary petition. Instead of adjudicating the debtor as bankrupt, however, the district judge allowed a committee of creditors to continue to resolve the debtor's financial affairs extra-judicially, without the appointment of a trustee or receiver.[1079] As a result of this abstention-like approach, the Court held that the district court lost jurisdiction to issue an injunction protecting property of the estate which became "subject to the ordinary methods of procedure in courts of competent jurisdiction."[1080]

Furthermore, occasionally limitations in the bankruptcy court's jurisdiction may preclude the court from granting relief necessary to resolve problems, thereby causing messy conflicts with state courts over title and possession to property and equitable relief. In *Hebert v. Crawford*,[1081] such a situation arose. Creditors brought a summary proceeding in the bankruptcy court and obtained judgment against LeBlanc for converting the debtor's rice crop.[1082] LeBlanc claimed he had the right to pay the judgment with money of Beaumont Mills, a partnership in which he was a partner. Beaumont disagreed and brought a state court action obtaining an injunction against LeBlanc to prevent withdrawal of funds from the partnership. Nevertheless, LeBlanc withdrew the partnership funds and paid them into the bankruptcy court in violation of the state court's injunction. Le-Blanc's successor brought an action in bankruptcy court to enjoin Beaumont from proceeding in state court on the basis that the bankruptcy court had exclusive jurisdiction to determine possession of the rice and entitlement to the conversion payment. The Court held that although the bankruptcy court had jurisdiction to determine possession of the rice in summary proceedings, it did not choose to

---

1078. *See id.* at 306-07.

1079. *See id.* at 302-03.

1080. *See id.* at 310.

1081. 228 U.S. 204 (1913).

1082. *See id.* at 210.

determine title to the rice.[1083] Therefore, the bankruptcy court lacked jurisdiction to enjoin LeBlanc's partners from proceeding in state court for equitable relief to enjoin LeBlanc from using partnership money to satisfy his personal judgment. Incident to that jurisdiction, the state court could determine whether the bankruptcy trustee received the money, with notice that it was partnership assets, in violation of the state court's injunction.[1084] But the state court had no jurisdiction to determine possession of the rice or who was entitled to its proceeds. Thus, without the consent of all parties, each court lacked jurisdiction to resolve the entire controversy.[1085]

Finally, on the rare occasion when bankruptcy court jurisdiction arguably conflicts with important state jurisdictional interests, the Court has required Congress to clearly and explicitly confer federal bankruptcy jurisdiction before the state courts will be ousted of jurisdiction. In *Palmer v. Massachusetts*,[1086] the Court held that since the history of railroads has great importance to local areas, a general grant of bankruptcy court jurisdiction was insufficient to oust a state commission of jurisdiction to decide whether to stop railroad service.[1087]

1083. *See id.* at 208-09.

1084. *See id.* at 210 in which the Court resolves the conflict of jurisdiction between the bankruptcy court and state court on several issues.

1085. A similar jurisdictional conflict arose between two federal courts conducting the reorganization and merger of the Penn Central and New Haven Railroads. One court had jurisdiction over the railroad reorganization whereas the other had jurisdiction over the merger. *See* New Haven Inclusion Cases, 399 U.S. 392, 425-28 (1970) (noting that the reorganization court should exercise paramount jurisdiction and that it also was the first court with jurisdiction over the *res*).

1086. 308 U.S. 79 (1939).

1087. *See id.* at 87-88. *But see* 11 U.S.C. § 1170 (2000) granting federal bankruptcy jurisdiction over the abandonment of railroad lines.

POWERS OF THE BANKRUPTCY COURT

INHERENT POWERS OF BANKRUPTCY COURT

The Court has recognized that the bankruptcy court, like any court, has certain inherent powers. For instance, in *Marrama v. Citizens Bank of Massachusetts*,[1088] the Court held, despite apparently clear language in the statute to the contrary,[1089] that Bankruptcy Code § 105(a) gave the bankruptcy court power to deny a debtor's right, under Bankruptcy Code § 706(a), to convert a chapter 7 case to a chapter 13 case.[1090] The Court also intimated that such a power was inherent and not dependent on congressional enactment of § 105(a): "[E]ven if § 105(a) had not been enacted, the inherent power of any court to sanction 'abusive litigation practices,' . . . might well provide an adequate justification for a prompt, rather than a delayed, ruling on an unmeritorious attempt to qualify as a debtor under Chapter 13."[1091]

In another context, the Court has recognized that in addition to statutory authority to impose punishment for contempt,[1092] the bank-

---

1088. 549 U.S. 365, 127 S. Ct. 1105 (2007).

1089. *See id.*, 127 S. Ct. at 1112 (Alito, J., with whom Roberts, C.J., Scalia and Thomas, JJ., joined, dissenting) ("The Bankruptcy Code unambiguously provides that a debtor who has filed a bankruptcy petition under Chapter 7 has a broad right to convert the case to another chapter.").

1090. *See id.*

1091. *See id.*

1092. *See* Bankruptcy Act § 2a(13), (15), & (16), 11 U.S.C. § 11a(13), (15), & (16) (1976) (repealed 1979). The Court has upheld orders imposing punishment for contempt in bankruptcy cases. *See* Oriel v. Russel; Prela v. Hubshman, 278 U.S. 358, 365-66 (1929) (upholding the punishment of bankrupts for failure to turn over property of the estate). The Bankruptcy Code has no statutory provision authorizing the court to punish for contempt. In 1978, Congress enacted § 1481 of the Judicial Code, 28 U.S.C. § 1481, which, effective April 1, 1984, provided a source for such power by limiting the contexts in which it could be used. *See* Pub. L. No. 598, 95th Cong., 2d Sess., § 241(a), 92 Stat. 2671 (1978). On July 12, 1984,

ruptcy court has the inherent power to punish for contempt. In *Mueller v. Nugent*,[1093] the Court sustained a contempt order against the bankrupt's son who, acting as the debtor's agent with no adverse claim, refused to turn over money that was property of the estate.[1094] The Court held that under the circumstances, the bankruptcy referee lawfully issued an order to show cause why the son should not be held in contempt.[1095]

The Court also has had occasion to limit the exercise of the bankruptcy court's contempt power.[1096] In *Maggio v. Zeitz (In re Luma Camera Service, Inc.)*, the Court held that the bankruptcy court has no power to impose a purely punitive contempt order.[1097] Both the

---

the President signed the Bankruptcy Amendments and Federal Judgeship Act of 1984 into law, apparently repealing this statutory grant. *See* Pub. L. No. 353, 98th Cong. 2d Sess., § 113, 98 Stat. 343 (1984) ("BAFJA"). *But see* Adam J. Levitan, *Toward a Federal Common Law of Bankruptcy: Judicial Lawmaking in a Statutory Regime*, 80 AM. BANKR. L.J. 1, 29 (2006) (arguing that the conflict between §§ 113 & 121 of BAFJA means that § 1481 was never repealed). Nevertheless, the bankruptcy court has inherent power to impose sanctions even beyond the strictures of contempt. *Cf.* Chambers v. NASCO, Inc., 501 U.S. 32, 46 (1991) (non-bankruptcy case involving federal district court sitting in diversity).

1093. 184 U.S. 1 (1902).

1094. *See id.* at 13.

1095. *See id.* ("We think the referee has the power to act in the first instance in matters such as this, when the case has been referred, and in aid of the court of bankruptcy, and exercises in such cases 'much of the judicial authority of that court.'") (citation omitted).

1096. *See* Maggio v. Zeitz (*In re* Luma Camera Serv., Inc.), 333 U.S. 56, 62 (1948); McCarthy v. Arndstein, 262 U.S. 355, 360-61 (1923); Arndstein v. McCarthy, 254 U.S. 71, 73 (1920) (debtor who properly asserts Fifth Amendment privilege against self incrimination may not be held in contempt); *In re* Watts & Sachs, 190 U.S. 1, 29 (1903) (holding that counsel could not be held in contempt for rendering advice to clients in good faith).

1097. *See Maggio v. Zeitz*, 333 U.S. at 72. As discussed *infra* in n.1100, the Court also limited the power of the bankruptcy court to order turn over

bankruptcy referee and the district court had held an alleged recipient of a fraudulent transfer in contempt for failing to turnover property.[1098] The Court believed that the lower courts wrongly ignored credible evidence that the transferee no longer had possession of the property when the turnover action was brought.[1099] When the trustee sued the transferee for turnover, if the transferee was not in possession of the property or its proceeds, the turnover action was inappropriate.[1100] Moreover, the lower courts should not be able to punish the transferee for failing to turnover property outside the transferee's control.[1101] Therefore, the Court vacated the contempt order.[1102]

EQUITY POWERS OF BANKRUPTCY COURT

> [W]hatever equitable powers remain in the bankruptcy courts must and can only be exercised within the confines of the Bankruptcy Code.[1103]

The Supreme Court has recognized for many years that bankruptcy courts "are essentially courts of equity, and their proceedings [are] inherently proceedings in equity."[1104] Under the Bankruptcy Act of 1898, the Court interpreted broadly the scope of the bankruptcy

---

of property to situations when the defendant has possession of the property or its proceeds.

1098. *See id.* at 77.

1099. *See id.* at 76-77.

1100. *See id.* at 63-64 ("The nature and derivation of the [turnover] remedy make clear that it is appropriate only when the evidence satisfactorily establishes the existence of the property or its proceeds, and possession thereof by the defendant at the time of the proceeding. While some courts have taken the date of bankruptcy as the time to which the inquiry is directed, we do not consider resort to this particular proceeding appropriate if, at the time it is instituted, the property and its proceeds have already been dissipated, no matter when that dissipation occurred.").

1101. *See id.* at 75-77.

1102. *See id.* at 77-78.

1103. Norwest Bank Worthington v. Ahlers, 485 U.S. 197, 206 (1988).

1104. *See* Local Loan Co. v. Hunt, 292 U.S. 234, 240 (1934).

courts' equity power.[1105] In *Pepper v. Litton*,[1106] the Court held that a bankruptcy court, as a court of equity, may look through form to substance when determining the true nature of a transaction as it relates to the rights of parties against a bankrupt's estate.[1107] This pronouncement followed earlier Court decisions collapsing circuitous arrangements into a single transaction for purposes of preference avoidance[1108] and recharacterizing a trust receipt as a secured loan for nondischargeability purposes.[1109] Moreover, in *Steelman v. All Continent Corp.*,[1110] the Court held that a bankruptcy court could use its powers as a court of equity to preserve the status quo by enjoining nonbankruptcy litigation that, if prosecuted to judgment, might cause

---

1105. *See, e.g.,* Robertson v. Howard, 229 U.S. 254, 263 (1913) ("[B]ankruptcy courts are given full and complete equitable power in matters of the administration and sale of the bankrupt estate.").

1106. 308 U.S. 295 (1939).

1107. *See id.* at 305 (The bankruptcy court's equitable powers "have been invoked to the end that fraud will not prevail, that substance will not give way to form, that technical considerations will not prevent substantial justice from being done."). This sweeping language broadened the approach taken by the Court in Bailey v. Baker Ice Mach. Co., 239 U.S. 268, 272 (1915), in which Justice Van Devanter, writing for a unanimous Court, stated that whether a contract was to be treated as a conditional sale, or an absolute sale with a mortgage back, turned on the intent of the parties: "[T]he question whether a particular contract shows one or the other turns upon the ruling intention of the parties as disclosed by the entire contract, and not upon any single provision separately considered."

1108. *See* Nat'l Bank of Newport v. Nat'l Herkimer County Bank, 225 U.S. 178, 184 (1912) ("If the bankrupt has made a transfer of his property, the effect of which is to enable one of his creditors to obtain a greater percentage of his debt than another creditor of the same class, circuity of arrangement will not avail to save it.").

1109. *See* Davis v. Aetna Acceptance Co., 293 U.S. 328, 334 (1934) ("The trust receipt may state that the debtor holds the car as the property of the creditor; in truth it is his own property, subject to a lien. The substance of the transaction is this, and nothing more . . . . The resulting obligation is not turned into one arising from a trust because the parties to one of the documents have chosen to speak of it as a trust.") (citations omitted).

1110. Steelman v. All Continent Corp., 301 U.S. 278 (1937).

a fraud to come to fruition and defeat or impair bankruptcy court jurisdiction.[1111] And in *Local Loan Co. v. Hunt*,[1112] the Court upheld the equity power of the bankruptcy court, in what was essentially a supplemental and ancillary bill in equity, to enjoin a lender's state court suit to enforce a wage assignment that threatened to interfere with the bankruptcy court's discharge order.[1113] Moreover, the Court concluded that the bankruptcy court could exercise ancillary injunctive jurisdiction even if the court would have lacked jurisdiction over an original proceeding:[1114]

> That a federal court of equity has jurisdiction of a bill ancillary to an original case or proceeding in the same court, whether at law or in equity, to secure or preserve the fruits and advantages of a judgment or decree rendered therein, is well settled. And this, irrespective of whether the court would have jurisdiction if the proceeding were an original one. The proceeding being ancillary and dependent, the jurisdiction of the court follows that of the original cause . . . .

Furthermore, even in the absence of explicit statutory language in the Bankruptcy Act delineating equitable powers, the Court has upheld the equitable powers of the bankruptcy court to resolve liens or claims against, or distributions from, a bankruptcy estate. Thus, in *Van Huffel v. Harkelrode*,[1115] the Court held that a bankruptcy court may direct that all liens upon property forming a part of the bankrupt's estate be marshaled[1116] and that the bankruptcy court's power to sell property free and clear of encumbrances "must be implied from the general equity powers of the court . . . ."[1117] Previously the Court had held that bankruptcy courts, as courts of equity, could sell proper-

---

1111. *See id.* at 288-89.

1112. 292 U.S. 234 (1934).

1113. *See id.* at 241.

1114. *See id.* at 239 (citations omitted).

1115. 284 U.S. 225 (1931).

1116. *See id.* at 227-28.

1117. *See id.* at 228.

ty of the estate wherever located and by whomever held without the commencement of an ancillary proceeding.[1118] And the Court has allowed the bankruptcy court to equitably disallow or subordinate an insider's claim when it would be inequitable to allow the claim to share ratably with creditors.[1119] In other words, "[t]he power of the bankruptcy court to subordinate claims or adjudicate equities arising out of the relationship between the several creditors is complete."[1120] In this regard, the Court has sustained the bankruptcy court's power to subordinate the entire claim of a claimant when it is difficult to quantify the extent of the damage caused by the claimant's inequitable conduct.[1121] Moreover, the Court has sustained the bankruptcy court's equity power to disallow a claim for interest on interest even when the claimant could assert such a claim against the debtor under nonbankruptcy law.[1122] Many years earlier, the Court interpreted the Bankruptcy Act to apply English precedents requiring an undersecured creditor to apply to principal, rather than to postpetition interest, the proceeds of securities collateral sold postpetition, except

---

1118. *See* Robertson v. Howard, 229 U.S. 254, 261 (1913).

1119. *See* Pepper v. Litton, 308 U.S. 295, 304, 308 (1939).

1120. *See* Sampsell v. Imperial Paper & Color Corp., 313 U.S. 215, 219 (1941) (citing, inter alia, Taylor v. Standard Gas & Elec. Co., 306 U.S. 307 (1939) & Pepper v. Litton, 308 U.S. 295 (1939)).

1121. *See* Taylor v. Standard Gas & Elec. Co., 306 U.S. 307, 323-24 (1939) (because it was impossible to recast the debtor's financial condition to determine damages, the Court affirmed the subordination of the claim to stock awarded to public preferred shareholders). Although this result was permissible under the Bankruptcy Act, it is impermissible to equitably subordinate a claim to an ownership interest under Bankruptcy Code § 510(c), 11 U.S.C. § 510(c) (2000).

1122. *See* Vanston Bondholders Protective Comm. v. Green, 329 U.S. 156, 163 (1947) ("[W]e think that allowance of interest on interest ... would not be in accord with the equitable principles governing bankruptcy distributions.").

for any postpetition interest or dividends issued on the securities which the Court permitted to be applied to postpetition interest.[1123]

The Court also has upheld the equity powers of bankruptcy courts in other contexts. For example, the court has recognized the equitable power of a bankruptcy court to enjoin a secured creditor from selling collateral when the sale would hinder or prevent preparation and consummation of a plan of reorganization.[1124] "The power to issue an injunction when necessary to prevent the defeat or impairment of its jurisdiction is, therefore, inherent in a court of bankruptcy, as it is in a duly established court of equity."[1125] On the other hand, the Court has recognized the equitable power of the bankruptcy court to curtail a stay when necessary to protect the property interests of a secured creditor.[1126] Also, the Court has upheld the equitable power of the bankruptcy court to penalize a creditor acting in bad faith or with improper motives in a bankruptcy case.[1127] Thus, from the time of the enactment of the Bankruptcy Act of 1898, the Court recognized the

---

1123. *See* Sexton v. Dreyfus, 219 U.S. 339, 345-46 (1911) (holding that delay in sale of the collateral should not benefit secured creditors). Although the Court's decision in *Sexton* appears to be based on following English precedents, in *Vanston* the Court characterized its *Sexton* opinion as having been based on "equitable considerations." *See Vanston*, 329 U.S. at 164.

1124. *See* Cont'l Ill. Nat'l Bank & Trust Co. v. Chicago, R.I. & Pac. Ry. Co., 294 U.S. 648, 675 (1935) (affirming the equity power of the bankruptcy court to enjoin a sale of collateral in a § 77 railroad reorganization case).

1125. *Id.*

1126. *See* Wright v. Vinton Branch of the Mountain Trust Bank of Roanoke, Va., 300 U.S. 440, 464 (1937) (construing second Frazier-Lemke Act to give courts discretion to terminate the stay where necessary to protect a mortgagee).

1127. *See* Woods v. City Nat'l Bank & Trust Co. of Chicago, 312 U.S. 262, 265 (1941) (denial of compensation to mortgage bondholders' protective committee under Ch. X of Bankruptcy Act where, inter alia, committee member "was heavily invested in the equity . . . and that fact was not disclosed").

bankruptcy court as a court of equity with the capacity to exercise equitable powers in many different contexts.

Moreover, the character of bankruptcy courts as courts of equity has survived enactment of the 1978 Bankruptcy Code.[1128] In *United States v. Energy Resources Co.*,[1129] the Court held that, in exercising its powers as a court of equity, "a bankruptcy court has the authority to order the IRS to apply [plan] payments to trust fund liabilities if the bankruptcy court determines that this designation is necessary to the success of a reorganization plan."[1130] The Court reached its holding even though "[t]he Bankruptcy Code does not explicitly authorize the bankruptcy courts to approve reorganization plans designating tax payments as either trust fund or nontrust fund."[1131] The Court relied on the residual power given to bankruptcy courts as courts of equity in Bankruptcy Code §§ 105(a) and 1123(b)(5) as "consistent with the traditional understanding that bankruptcy courts, as courts of equity, have broad authority to modify creditor-debtor relationships."[1132] Section 105(a) also served as a basis of power in *Celotex Corp. v. Edwards*[1133] to support a bankruptcy court's injunction against a judgment creditor's proceeding against a surety on a supersedeas bond posted by the debtor prepetition.[1134] Because the outcome of proceeding on the bond could conceivably affect the bankruptcy estate and

---

1128. *See* Young v. United States, 535 U.S. 43, 50 (2002) ("[B]ankruptcy courts [ ] are courts of equity and 'apply the principles and rules of equity jurisprudence.'" (quoting Pepper v. Litton, 308 U.S. 295, 304 (1939)); United States v. Energy Res. Co., 495 U.S. 545, 549 (1990) ("[B]ankruptcy courts, as courts of equity, have broad authority to modify debtor-creditor relationships."); N.L.R.B. v. Bildisco & Bildisco, 465 U.S. 513, 527 (1984) ("The Bankruptcy Court is a court of equity, and in making this determination it is in a very real sense balancing the equities . . . .").

1129. 495 U.S. 545 (1990).

1130. *See id.* at 549.

1131. *Id.*

1132. *Id.* (citations omitted).

1133. 514 U.S. 300 (1995).

1134. *See id.* at 302.

the debtor's ability to reorganize, the Court found that the proceeding on the bond was related to the bankruptcy case and the bankruptcy court could exercise jurisdiction.[1135] The Court noted in dictum that the result might be otherwise if the bankruptcy court's exercise of jurisdiction led to an order that was "only a frivolous pretense to validity."[1136] Even if the injunction were invalid, however, if the creditor disagreed with it, the proper recourse was to object to the injunction and not to collaterally attack it or ask the district court to ignore it.[1137]

LIMITATIONS ON THE BANKRUPTCY COURT'S EQUITY POWERS

Although the bankruptcy court has broad equitable power to issue orders in aid of its jurisdiction, the Court has limited this power when the relief granted is inconsistent with provisions of the Bankruptcy Act or Bankruptcy Code.[1138] For instance, the Court has held that the bankruptcy court lacks the power to issue an injunction involving litigation over property that is not property of the estate.[1139] Specifically, in *Callaway v. Benton*, the Court held that the district judge,

---

1135. *See id.* at 308 n.6, 309.

1136. *See id.* at 312 n.9 (quoting dissenting opinion).

1137. *See id.* at 313. Analysis of collateral attack is developed more fully, nn.1159-1197 *infra*, in the discussion of res judicata.

1138. *See, e.g.,* Norwest Bank Worthington v. Ahlers, 485 U.S. 197, 206 (1988) (Bankruptcy Code case in which the Court holds that the bankruptcy court has no power to permit cramdown of a sweat equity plan where the statute precludes the residual equity holder's retention of any property on account of its interest); D. Ginsberg & Sons, Inc. v. Popkin, 285 U.S. 204, 206-08 (1932) (Bankruptcy Act case in which the Court holds that the bankruptcy court has no equitable power under Bankruptcy Act § 2a(15) or otherwise to make an order to arrest or issue a writ *ne exeat* against the debtor's officers to compel testimony on a more stringent basis than that set forth in Bankruptcy Act § 9).

1139. *See, e.g.,* Callaway v. Benton, 336 U.S. 132, 147, 150 (1949); Lockwood v. Exch. Bank of Fort Valley, 190 U.S. 294, 299 (1903) (holding that the bankruptcy court had no power to administer and distribute exempt property).

acting as a bankruptcy court, should not have issued an injunction preventing continuation of a state court suit to determine whether a unanimous vote of a lessor's shareholders was necessary to sell property to the debtor.[1140] Moreover, in *Emil v. Hanley*, the Court held that as long as a non-bankruptcy receivership remained in effect, the bankruptcy court lacked power to order an accounting from the receiver.[1141] Furthermore, the Court has held that when a state court has acquired jurisdiction over the debtor's property in an action to enforce a judicial lien, unless the lien is avoidable in bankruptcy, the bankruptcy court lacks power to interfere with the state court action.[1142]

And, with the notable exception of *Marrama v. Citizens Bank of Massachusetts*,[1143] many recent decisions of the Court have made clear that whatever equitable powers bankruptcy courts have, they "must and can only be exercised within the confines of the Bankruptcy Code."[1144] As Justice Rehnquist noted in *Bildisco*, "the Bankruptcy Court must focus on the ultimate goal of Chapter 11 when considering these equities. The Bankruptcy Code does not authorize freewheeling consideration of every conceivable equity, but rather only how the equities relate to the success of the reorganization."[1145]

The Court also has imposed limits on the scope of the bankruptcy courts' equitable powers. Specifically, "[b]ankruptcy courts are not authorized in the name of equity to make wholesale substitution of underlying law controlling the validity of creditors' entitlements, but

---

1140. *See* Callaway v. Benton, 336 U.S. 132, 147, 150 (1949).

1141. *See* Emil v. Hanley, 318 U.S. 515, 520 (1943) (no power to require non-bankruptcy receiver to account to bankruptcy court unless receivership is superseded).

1142. *See* Straton v. New, 283 U.S. 318, 326 (1931) (lack of power to enjoin state court creditors' suit to marshal and enforce liens and sell real estate).

1143. 549 U.S. 365 (2007). *See supra* nn.1088-1091 and accompanying text.

1144. Norwest Bank Worthington v. Ahlers, 485 U.S. 197, 206 (1988).

1145. N.L.R.B. v. Bildisco & Bildisco, 465 U.S. 513, 527 (1984).

are limited to what the Bankruptcy Code itself provides."[1146] Nor can the bankruptcy court rely on legislative history to support the use of equitable powers to override the statute. In *United States v. Noland*,[1147] the Court warned that "statements in legislative history cannot be read to convert statutory leeway for judicial development of a rule on particularized exceptions into delegated authority to revise statutory categorization, untethered to any obligation to preserve the coherence of substantive congressional judgments."[1148]

In a nonbankruptcy context, the Court has held that the equity powers of a United States district court are limited to those that existed in 1789.[1149] It remains to be seen whether the Court will impose this restriction on the bankruptcy courts, which are units of the district courts[1150] and depend on them for the source of bankruptcy court jurisdiction.[1151]

POWER OF BANKRUPTCY COURT TO SUBSTANTIVELY CONSOLIDATE

Substantive consolidation is one of the key equitable powers that bankruptcy judges exercise to consolidate the estate of a debtor with one or more other entities. The Court has addressed the doctrine of substantive consolidation only once in *Sampsell v. Imperial Paper & Color Corp.*[1152] *Sampsell* involved the recovery of assets fraudulently

---

1146. Raleigh v. Ill. Dep't of Revenue, 530 U.S. 15, 24-25 (2000) (citing United States v. Reorganized CF&I Fabricators of Utah, Inc., 518 U.S. 213, 228-29 (1996); United States v. Noland, 517 U.S. 535, 543 (1996)).

1147. United States v. Noland, 517 U.S. 535 (1996).

1148. *See id.* at 542.

1149. *See* Grupo Mexicano de Desarrollo, S.A. v. Alliance Bond Fund, Inc., 527 U.S. 308 (1999) (nonbankruptcy case in which the Court sharply restricted the equity power of the United States district court to what it was in English courts of Chancery in 1789.)

1150. *See* 28 U.S.C. § 151 (2000).

1151. *See* 28 U.S.C. §§ 157, 1334 (2000).

1152. 313 U.S. 215, 219-20 (1941).

transferred from a debtor sole proprietor to his newly formed family-owned corporation.[1153] The bankruptcy court, noting that the corporation was "nothing but a sham and a cloak" that was devised for the purpose of hindering, delaying, and defrauding the debtor's creditors, substantively consolidated the assets of the non-filed corporation into the shareholder's estate.[1154] After consolidation, a corporate creditor that was not a party to the consolidation motion sought priority against distribution of the corporate assets.[1155] On the facts of the case, the Court held that the corporate creditor, who had knowledge of the fraudulent transfer,[1156] was not entitled to priority but was entitled only to be treated equally with the debtor's unsecured creditors.[1157] With respect to the bankruptcy court's power, the Court stated that "[t]he power of the bankruptcy court to subordinate claims or to adjudicate equities arising out of the relationship between the several creditors is complete."[1158] Thus, at least in the context of a fraudulent transfer made with actual intent to hinder, delay, or defraud creditors, the Court viewed the bankruptcy court's power to substantively consolidate to be derivative of its general equity powers to subordinate claims or to adjudicate equities among creditors.

RES JUDICATA AND COLLATERAL ESTOPPEL

As a general proposition, the Court has applied the doctrines of res judicata (or claim preclusion) and collateral estoppel (or issue preclusion) as rules of finality of judgments in bankruptcy cases and

---

1153. *See id.* at 215-16.

1154. *See id.* at 217-19.

1155. *See id.* at 217.

1156. *See id.*

1157. *See id.* at 219-21.

1158. *Id.* at 219, citing, inter alia, Taylor v. Standard Gas & Elec. Co., 306 U.S. 307 (1939) & Pepper v. Litton, 308 U.S. 295 (1939).

proceedings.[1159] As in other civil litigation, issue preclusion in bank-ruptcy ordinarily prevents a party from relitigating an issue that was fully and fairly litigated in a previous action.[1160] By comparison, claim preclusion ordinarily prevents a party from asserting any claim (even a different claim) that could have been litigated in previous litigation involving a transaction.[1161] The principle underlying claim preclusion is that once a party has a chance to fairly and finally litigate a claim before a fair tribunal of competent jurisdiction, ordinarily it will be inappropriate to relitigate the claim or related claims that arise out of the same transaction or series of transactions. The principle underlying issue preclusion is more narrow: One who has actually finally litigated an issue in a fair forum ordinarily will not be permitted to relitigate it. Because issues of notice and fairness of the forum are imbedded in these rules, courts apply them only when it is equitable to do so based on the intuition and discretion of the judge in the subsequent litigation.[1162]

If a court renders a final judgment in a contested action, res judicata "precludes the parties from litigating the question of the court's subject matter jurisdiction in a subsequent litigation" unless "[t]he subject matter of the action was so plainly beyond the court's jurisdiction that its entertaining the action was a manifest abuse of

---

1159. *See generally* The American Law Institute, *Restatement of the Law, Second, Judgments* (1982) ("Restatement") which sets forth in some detail the law of res judicata.

1160. *See id.* §§ 27-28 ("When an issue of fact is actually litigated and determined by a valid and final judgment, and the determination is essential to the judgment, the determination is conclusive in a subsequent action between the parties, whether on the same or a different claim[, except as provided in § 28]."). *See id.* § 27. Restatement § 29 also provides guidelines when issue preclusion applies in subsequent litigation with other persons, such as parties in privity with an original litigant.

1161. *See id.* §§ 18-26 (Ordinarily, when a valid final judgment is rendered, there may be no further action on the original claim or any part thereof including all remedies "with respect to all or any part of the transaction, or series of connected transactions, out of which the action arose." *Id.* at § 24(1)). *See id.* Ch. 1, Introduction, Scope Note & § 24.

1162. *See id.* Scope Note at 13.

authority . . . ."[1163] For example, in *Oriel v. Russell*,[1164] the Court held that a turnover order issued under the Bankruptcy Act could not be collaterally attacked in a later contempt proceeding.[1165] Moreover, as noted previously,[1166] in *Celotex Corp. v. Edwards*,[1167] the Court upheld as within the bankruptcy court's "related to" jurisdiction, the bankruptcy court's issuance of an injunction in a Bankruptcy Code case against a judgment creditor proceeding to execute on a surety bond posted by the debtor.[1168] In so holding, however, the Court noted in dictum that if the creditor contended the power to issue the injunction was beyond the jurisdiction of the court, its recourse was to object to the injunction in the court that issued it and challenge it on direct appeal rather than through a collateral attack.[1169] Earlier, in *Chicot County Drainage District v. Baxter State Bank*,[1170] the Court held that a bondholder could not collaterally attack an order confirming a municipal readjustment plan even when the statute on which the plan was based was later declared unconstitutional.[1171] The Court reasoned that the district court that confirmed the plan had jurisdiction to determine its own jurisdiction, and if the bondholder wanted to challenge the jurisdiction, it was required to do so in the bankruptcy case or in a direct appeal, not in a collateral attack.[1172] This holding is

---

1163. *See id.* § 12. Res judicata may be raised as a defense in the subsequent litigation. *See* Rivet v. Regions Bank of La., 522 U.S. 470, 476 (1998) (res judicata could be asserted as a federal law affirmative defense, but did not transmute the plaintiff's state law claim into a federal question for purposes of removal jurisdiction).

1164. 278 U.S. 358 (1929).

1165. *See id.* at 363.

1166. *See supra* nn.1133-1137 and accompanying text.

1167. 514 U.S. 300 (1995).

1168. *See id.* at 307-10.

1169. *See id.* at 306-07, 313.

1170. 308 U.S. 371 (1940).

1171. *See id.* at 375.

1172. *See id.* at 376.

strikingly similar to the Court's prior holding in *Stoll v. Gottlieb*[1173] in which a reorganization plan eliminated a creditor's right to proceed against a third party guarantor; even if the bankruptcy court lacked jurisdiction to issue such an order, the creditor's sole remedy was to object to plan confirmation and take a direct appeal rather than engage in a collateral attack.[1174] Likewise, when creditors fail to appeal a sale order, they may not later ask for return of property transferred under the order.[1175]

Of course, the Court has rendered several more bankruptcy decisions in which the application of res judicata is straight forward. Sometimes, claims and issues litigated before the commencement of bankruptcy will be binding in litigation before the bankruptcy court. In *Heiser v. Woodruff*,[1176] the Court held that because the issue of fraud in obtaining a state court default judgment had been previously litigated and not appealed, res judicata precluded a bankruptcy trustee from prosecuting an objection to claim which sought to set aside the default judgment on the basis that it had been procured by fraud.[1177] Similarly, if the debtor's fraud is established in state court

---

1173. 305 U.S. 165 (1938).

1174. *See id.* at 171-72.

1175. *See* New Haven Inclusion Cases, 399 U.S. 392, 481 (1970) ("[W]e agree with Penn Central that the Committee's request for the return of the stock is foreclosed by *res judicata*. For the Committee—as well as all the other bondholders—took no appeal from the order of the reorganization court directing the transfer of the New Haven assets subject to a later determination of value.") (footnote omitted).

1176. 327 U.S. 726 (1946).

1177. *See id.* at 735-36. *See also* Myers v. Int'l Trust Co., 263 U.S. 64, 77 (1923) (holding that where a creditor appeared before the bankruptcy court and objected to confirmation of a composition plan on the basis that the debtors had induced it to extend credit based on false statements, it was precluded from relitigating that issue in later litigation asserting deceit against the debtors). But when the bankruptcy court does not determine the issue of deceit, a state court is free to decide the issue in nondischargeability litigation (which before 1970 was not within the exclusive jurisdiction of the bankruptcy court). *See* Friend v. Talcott, 228 U.S. 27, 40-43 (1913). Likewise, when the state court does not determine

litigation prepetition, that issue will be binding on the debtor in bankruptcy nondischargeability litigation under principles of collateral
estoppel.[1178]

Moreover, under the Rooker-Feldman doctrine, lower federal
courts may not exercise subject matter jurisdiction in an action that
seeks to review or collaterally attack a final state court judgment. The
so-called Rooker-Feldman doctrine is based on two non-bankruptcy
Supreme Court decisions, *Rooker v. Fidelity Trust Co.*[1179] and *District
of Columbia Court of Appeals v. Feldman.*[1180] *Rooker* held that only a
state appellate court or the United States Supreme Court have the
power to modify or reverse a state court judgment because lower
federal courts have no appellate jurisdiction but only exercise original
jurisdiction. *Feldman* followed *Rooker* and held that a United States
district court has no subject matter jurisdiction to review a final judgment of a state court. Thus, a final state court judgment, and matters
inextricably intertwined with it, cannot be challenged in a lower
federal court but must be challenged by appeal up to the highest court
of the state and then to the United States Supreme Court.

When a state court decides an issue within the exclusive or
primary jurisdiction of a federal court, however, the Rooker-Feldman
doctrine will not apply to deprive a federal court of subject matter
jurisdiction.[1181] Thus, lower courts have held that federal bankruptcy

---

whether a judgment has been obtained by fraud, the bankruptcy court
can look behind the judgment in deciding whether to disallow or
subordinate the claim. *See* Pepper v. Litton, 308 U.S. 295, 302-03 (1939)
(res judicata is not a bar where the state court decides whether to enforce
a judgment but does not determine its validity).

1178. *See* Grogan v. Garner, 498 U.S. 279, 291 (1991) (Court applies
collateral estoppel because the burden of proof in bankruptcy nondischargeability litigation is preponderance of the evidence and is not more
stringent than the standard applied in nonbankruptcy litigation).

1179. 263 U.S. 413 (1923).

1180. 460 U.S. 462 (1983).

1181. Thus, the Rooker-Feldman doctrine does not apply to deprive
federal courts of habeas corpus jurisdiction. *See, e.g.,* Plyler v. Moore,

court jurisdiction to avoid preferences and fraudulent transfers is an exception to the general Rooker-Feldman doctrine.[1182] Federal bankruptcy courts also will have final authority to determine the scope and applicability of the automatic stay.[1183]

Issues litigated in the bankruptcy court will sometimes be binding in later non-bankruptcy litigation. For instance, if a bankruptcy court determines title to a lease, that determination will be res judicata in later litigation among successors in interest to the litigants.[1184] Moreover, if a bankruptcy court determines that a debtor's property is exempt, that determination is res judicata in subsequent state court litigation involving the property.[1185] Furthermore, in *Prudence Realization Corp. v. Ferris*[1186] the Court upheld on principles of res judicata a provision of a reorganization plan in which the bankruptcy court refused to retain jurisdiction to determine priorities in distribution of the estate, instead leaving the matter to be determined by another court of competent jurisdiction.[1187]

---

129 F.3d 728, 732 (4th Cir. 1997); Ritter v. Ross, 992 F.2d 750, 753 (7th Cir. 1993); Blake v. Papadakos, 953 F.2d 68, 71 n.2 (3d Cir. 1992).

1182. *See* Noel v. Hall, 341 F.3d 1148 (9th Cir. 2003).

1183. *See* Gruntz v. County of Los Angeles (*In re* Gruntz), 202 F.3d 1074, 1079-83 (9th Cir. en banc 2000) (citing Kalb v. Feuerstein, 308 U.S. 433, 438-39 (1940) ("It is generally true that a judgment by a court of competent jurisdiction bears a presumption of regularity and is not thereafter subject to collateral attack. But Congress, because its power over the subject of bankruptcy is plenary, may by specific bankruptcy legislation create an exception to that principle and render judicial acts taken with respect to the person or property of a debtor whom the bankruptcy law protects nullities and vulnerable collaterally.")).

1184. *See* Page v. Ark. Natural Gas Corp., 286 U.S. 269, 272 (1932).

1185. *See* Smalley v. Laugenour, 196 U.S. 93, 97 (1905) (dictum).

1186. 323 U.S. 650 (1945).

1187. *See id.* at 654-55.

238   Chapter 4—Judicial Power
Res Judicata and Collateral Estoppel

Limitations on Res Judicata

In some instances, the Court will not apply principles of res judicata. For example, when bankruptcy law preempts the field, res judicata will not prevent a debtor from attacking a state court foreclosure judgment entered after the debtor's bankruptcy filing when the state court lost jurisdiction.[1188] Moreover, because a bankruptcy case is an *in rem* proceeding, facts determined in a bankruptcy adjudication will not be res judicata in later litigation with creditors who were not before the bankruptcy court.[1189] In addition, the Court has held that when a respondent fails to assert res judicata below, the Court will not consider it for the first time at the Supreme Court.[1190] Furthermore, when a creditor, debtor, and guarantor agree to entry of a stipulated judgment without indicating a basis for the debtor's liability, the Court will not allow res judicata to bar evidence in a later nondischargeability proceeding that the debtor's fraudulent misrepresentations induced a guarantor to guarantee the debt.[1191] The Court reasoned that "neither the interest served by res judicata, the process of orderly adjudication in state courts, nor the policies of the Bankruptcy Act would be well served by foreclosing [the guarantor] from submitting additional evidence to prove his case."[1192]

1188. *See* Kalb v. Feuerstein, 308 U.S. 433, 439, 440 n.12 (1940) (permitting collateral attack of state court's foreclosure proceedings conducted postpetition, without the farmer's consent, against a bankrupt farmer's property).

1189. *See* Gratiot Co. State Bank v. Johnson, 249 U.S. 246, 249 (1919) (bankruptcy adjudication and finding of debtor's insolvency is only a judgment *in rem* and is not res judicata in trustee's preference suit against creditor who has not appeared before the bankruptcy court).

1190. *See* Cal. State Bd. of Equalization v. Sierra Summit, Inc., 490 U.S. 844, 846 n.3 (1989). *But see id.* at 854-55 (Blackmun, J., dissenting).

1191. *See* Brown v. Felsen, 442 U.S. 127, 138-39 (1979). But, as noted previously, if the debtor's fraud is established in state court litigation prepetition, that issue will be binding on the debtor in bankruptcy nondischargeability litigation under principles of collateral estoppel. *See* Grogan v. Garner, 498 U.S. 279, 284-85 (1991).

1192. *See* Brown v. Felsen, 442 U.S. 127, 132 (1979).

Competing policy considerations have led the Court to occasionally prescribe narrow restrictions on general principles of res judicata and collateral estoppel. In *United States v. United States Fidelity & Guaranty Co.*,[1193] the United States represented the sovereign interests of Indian nations as the lessee of Indian lands to a lessee that became bankrupt.[1194] The United States sued the lessee for royalties and the lessee cross-claimed in state court and won a judgment.[1195] The United States then sued the surety of the lease payments in federal court and argued that the state court judgment was a nullity because the court lacked jurisdiction.[1196] The Court held that since Indian sovereignty cannot be waived, the United States, acting on behalf of sovereign Indian nations, could object to state court jurisdiction at any time, even if the state trial court entered a judgment from which the United States did not appeal.[1197] In this narrow context, the normal rules of res judicata do not apply.

CONCLUSION

It is difficult not to get lost in the thicket of case law interpreting and defining the jurisdiction and power of the bankruptcy courts. From a broad perspective, however, the Court appears to balance competing policies with the language of the bankruptcy statutes and limitations of the constitution. The Court has been reluctant to allow non-tenured bankruptcy judges to exercise comprehensive jurisdiction outside the context of administering the bankruptcy estate unless the parties consent. Almost certainly, the Court will not find a non-tenured bankruptcy judge to have jurisdiction or power that a United States district judge lacks. By the same token, the Court does not want to restrict the function of bankruptcy judges so far as to impose

---

1193. 309 U.S. 506 (1940).

1194. *See id.* at 512.

1195. *See id.* at 510.

1196. *See id.* at 511.

1197. *See id.* at 514.

on either the federal district courts or state courts the burden of adjudicating day to day aspects of most bankruptcy cases and proceedings.

These unarticulated underlying constraints help explain the Court's refusal to review the Emergency Rule or to decide the constitutionality of bankruptcy judges presiding over jury trials. They also provide one explanation for the modern Court's reluctance to recognize broad equitable powers in the bankruptcy courts outside the context of case administration.

There is no set of constraints, however, that neatly explains the Court's jurisdiction and power jurisprudence over the last 111 years. Notably, the general trend of the modern Court against judicial activism provides a sharp contrast to the Court's opinions from the 1930's to 1970's that broadly empowered the bankruptcy courts, as courts of equity, to do justice beyond the confines of the Bankruptcy Act. Chapter 5 explores substantive bankruptcy law and determines whether there is a similar shift in the Court's decisions on matters of substantive bankruptcy law.

CHAPTER 5

FEDERAL BANKRUPTCY LAWS AND POLICIES

INTRODUCTION

This Chapter analyzes the Court's treatment of bankruptcy doctrines and policies that arise primarily or exclusively in the context of the Bankruptcy Code. These doctrines and policies include avoiding powers, dischargeability, claims priority and distribution, and plan confirmation. At times, as discussed more fully in Chapter 2, matters involve the intersection or conflict between bankruptcy and non-bankruptcy laws and policies. In other cases, the Court determines matters purely as a matter of bankruptcy law and policy, subject to the political realities that influence any legislation. For example, federal bankruptcy law exclusively governs the priorities and distributions from a bankruptcy estate. Likewise, federal bankruptcy law determines the extent to which a general unsecured creditor may assert a claim for postpetition interest against the bankruptcy estate.[1198] Similarly, the Court has held that federal bankruptcy law determines whether an oversecured creditor is entitled to accrue postpetition interest on its claim.[1199]

1198. *See* Bankruptcy Code §§ 502(b)(2), 506(b), & 726(a)(5), 11 U.S.C. §§ 502(b)(2), 506(b), & 726(a)(5) (2000). *See, e.g.,* Vanston Bondholders Protective Comm. v. Green, 329 U.S. 156, 163 (1947) (refusing to apply state law to determine postpetition interest on interest and holding that "an allowance of interest on interest under the circumstances shown by this case would not be in accord with the equitable principles governing bankruptcy distributions").

1199. *See* Rake v. Wade, 508 U.S. 464, 471 (1993) (holding that Bankruptcy Code § 506(b), 11 U.S.C. § 506(b) (2000), requires accrual of postpetition interest on the claim of an oversecured creditor whether or not the creditor would be entitled to interest on such claim under state law).

In most of these cases, the Court does its best to interpret the Bankruptcy Code in a manner consistent with fundamental bankruptcy policies: 1) Equality of distribution among creditors similarly situated;[1200] 2) discouraging a race of diligence among creditors;[1201] 3) discouraging secret liens;[1202] 4) favoring the debtor's fresh start;[1203]

1200. *See, e.g.,* Howard Delivery Serv. v. Zurich Am. Ins. Co., 547 U.S. 651, 667, 669 (2006) (holding that workers' compensation premium claims do not qualify as a priority claim based on the Bankruptcy Code's equal distribution norm); Young v. Higbee, 324 U.S. 204, 210 (1945) ("one of the prime purposes of the bankruptcy law has been to bring about a ratable distribution among creditors of a bankrupt's assets"); Clarke v. Rogers, 228 U.S. 534, 548 (1913) ("Equality between creditors is necessarily the ultimate aim of the Bankrupt[cy] Law . . . ."); Pirie v. Chicago Title & Trust Co., 182 U.S. 438, 449 (1901) ("It is hardly necessary to assert that the object of a bankrupt[cy] act, so far as creditors are concerned, is to secure equality of distribution among them of the property of the bankrupt—not among some of the creditors, but among all of them.").

1201. *See, e.g.,* Union Bank v. Wolas, 502 U.S. 151, 162 (1991) (construing payments on long term debts to come within the ordinary course of business preference defense to deter a race of diligence).

1202. *See, e.g.,* United States v. Speers, 382 U.S. 266, 276 (1965) (noting that an unrecorded federal tax lien lacks priority based on the Bankruptcy Act's policy of discouraging secret liens).

1203. *See, e.g.,* FCC v. NextWave Pers. Communs., Inc., 537 U.S. 293, 306 n.4 (2003) (holding that Bankruptcy Code § 525(b) sought to prohibit government action that would undercut the fresh start that was bankruptcy's promise); Williams v. U.S. Fid. & Guar. Co., 236 U.S. 549, 554-55 (1915) ("It is the purpose of the Bankrupt[cy] Act to convert the assets of the bankrupt into cash for distribution among creditors and then to relieve the honest debtor from the weight of oppressive indebtedness and permit him to start afresh free from the obligations and responsibilities consequent upon business misfortunes.").

5) maximizing the value of the bankruptcy estate;[1204] 6) favoring business, farmer, railroad, or municipal reorganizations;[1205] and 7) generally precluding the allowance of postpetition interest on prepetition unsecured claims.[1206] Thus, the Court narrowly interprets

---

1204. *See, e.g.,* Toibb v. Radloff, 501 U.S. 157, 163 (1991) ("Chapter 11 also embodies the general Code policy of maximizing the value of the bankruptcy estate.").

1205. *See, e.g.,* N.L.R.B. v. Bildisco & Bildisco, 465 U.S. 513, 527-28 (1984) (noting that "the policy of Chapter 11 is to permit successful rehabilitation of debtors" and that "[t]he fundamental purpose of reorganization is to prevent a debtor from going into liquidation"); United States v. Whiting Pools, Inc., 462 U.S. 198, 203 (1983) ("Thus, to facilitate the rehabilitation of the debtor's business, all the debtor's property must be included in the reorganization estate."); Conn. Ry. & Lighting Co. v. Palmer, 305 U.S. 493, 501 (1939) ("It is first to be noted that the successive acts of the Congress, on extension of individual debts and corporate and railroad reorganization, are directed generally at the rehabilitation of debtors."); Adair v. Bank of Am. Nat'l Trust & Sav. Ass'n, 303 U.S. 350, 354 (1938) ("Progressive liberalization of bankruptcy and insolvency laws, in an effort to avert the evils of liquidation, has furnished opportunity for composition in bankruptcy proceedings and later for composition and extension of debts in relief proceedings for individual debtors, for reorganization of railroads and other corporations, and for public debtor proceedings."); Wright v. Vinton Branch of Mountain Trust Bank, 300 U.S. 440, 470 (1937) (holding that the court may enjoin the sale of collateral if the effect is to hinder the rehabilitation of the farmer mortgagor); Reconstruction Fin. Corp. v. Denver & R.G.W.R. Co., 328 U.S. 495, 505-06 (1946) ("By provisions for adjustment of creditors' claims [in § 77 railroad reorganization cases], Congress intended to avoid the delays, costs and sacrifices of liquidation."); United States v. Bekins, 304 U.S. 37, 54 (1938) ("[The State] invites the intervention of the bankruptcy power to save its agency which the State itself is powerless to rescue. Through its cooperation with the national government the needed relief is given.").

1206. *See, e.g.,* Nicholas v. United States, 384 U.S. 678, 683 (1966) (disallowing postpetition interest on administrative tax claims following a conversion to liquidation because "creditors should not be disadvantaged *vis-a-vis* one another by legal delays attributable solely to the time-consuming procedures inherent in the administration of the bankruptcy laws"); New York v. Saper, 336 U.S. 328, 337-38 (1949) (disallowing the

statutory priorities in order to promote the policy of equality of distribution among creditors of equal rank.[1207] Similarly, to prevent a race of diligence among creditors or to facilitate the debtor's fresh start, the Court, for the most part, has broadly interpreted avoiding powers.[1208] On occasion, however, when strict interpretation of bankruptcy policy would have a disruptive effect outside of bankruptcy, the Court has coupled the plain language of the Bankruptcy Code with a competing policy justification to reach a different result.[1209]

---

accrual of postpetition interest on unsecured priority tax claims); Vanston Bondholders Protective Comm. v. Green, 329 U.S. 156, 163 (1947) (holding that "an allowance of interest on interest under the circumstances shown by this case would not be in accord with the equitable principles governing bankruptcy distributions"); Sexton v. Dreyfus, 219 U.S. 339, 344-45 (1911) (based on equitable principles, the accumulation of interest on unsecured claims is suspended as of the date of the bankruptcy petition).

1207. *See, e.g.,* Howard Delivery Serv. v. Zurich Am. Ins. Co., 547 U.S. 651, 667, 669 (2006) (holding that workers' compensation premium claims do not qualify as a priority claim based on the Bankruptcy Code's policy that priorities must be strictly construed).

1208. *See, e.g.,* Owen v. Owen, 500 U.S. 305, 313 (1991) (broadly defining the debtor's avoiding powers to avoid a judicial lien placed on the debtor's residence before the debtor filed for bankruptcy under chapter 7: "Just as it is not inconsistent with the policy of permitting state-defined exemptions to have another policy disfavoring waiver of exemptions, whether federal- or state-created; so also it is not inconsistent to have a policy disfavoring the impingement of certain types of liens upon exemptions, whether federal- or state-created."). *But see* Union Bank v. Wolas, 502 U.S. 151, 158, 162 (1991) (broadly interpreting ordinary course of business preference defense in order to prevent a race of diligence).

1209. These conflicts are discussed in Chapter 2 and are not repeated here. *See, e.g.,* BFP v. Resolution Trust Corp., 511 U.S. 531, 545 (1994) (protecting regularly conducted, non-collusive real property foreclosure sales from fraudulent transfer attack); Union Bank v. Wolas, 502 U.S. 151, 162 (1991) (protecting ordinary commercial transactions and holding that payments to a bank on long term debt are within the ordinary course of business defense to preference recovery).

Substantive Bankruptcy Law

Commencement of the Case: Capacity to File, Who May Be a Debtor, Involuntary Petitions

In order to commence a bankruptcy case, the debtor must have capacity to file the bankruptcy petition. When the debtor is a corporation or other non-human being, the Court has held that state law determines whether the entity exists, and, if so, who has the power to act on its behalf. In *Chicago Title & Trust Co. v. Forty-One Thirty-Six Wilcox Bldg. Corp.*,[1210] the Court held that a corporation had been dissolved under Illinois law and, therefore, no longer had the legal capacity to transact business or to file a bankruptcy petition;[1211] nothing in the federal bankruptcy law conflicted with the exclusive power of the state to determine how long its corporations continued to exist.[1212] Moreover, in *Price v. Gurney*,[1213] the Court held that a dissident shareholder could not file a bankruptcy petition under Chapter X of the Bankruptcy Act on behalf of the corporation because state corporate law dictated that only the directors had the power to authorize the filing of a petition.[1214] Nor could the petition be commenced by way of a shareholder derivative action, because a derivative action is a suit by a shareholder to enforce a cause of action

---

1210. 302 U.S. 120 (1937).

1211. *See id.* at 126.

1212. *See id.* at 127-28. ("[T]he Federal Government is powerless to resurrect a corporation which the state has put out of existence for all purposes . . . ."). *Id.* at 128.

1213. 324 U.S. 100 (1945).

1214. *See id.* at 104 ("[T]he initiation of the proceedings, like the run of corporate activities, is left to the corporation itself, i.e. to those who have the power of management."); and at 106 ("If the District Court finds that those who purport to act on behalf of the corporation have not been granted authority by local law to institute the proceedings, it has no alternative but to dismiss the petition.").

by the corporation against a third party, not a bankruptcy petition for its own reorganization.[1215]

In addition to having the capacity to file, the debtor also must be eligible to file. Sections 109 and 303 of the Bankruptcy Code,[1216] like sections 4 and 5 of the Bankruptcy Act,[1217] specify who may be a debtor in voluntary and involuntary bankruptcy cases. Certain categories of debtors, such as most insurance companies and banks, are excluded because there are other statutory procedures that provide for their insolvency.[1218] In *Vallely v. Northern Fire & Marine Ins. Co.*,[1219] the Court held that the bankruptcy court lacked jurisdiction to adjudicate the bankruptcy of an insurance company, even though the debtor's time to appeal the order of adjudication had expired and the bankruptcy court had appointed a trustee who had incurred expenses and paid out money.[1220]

In addition to rules of exclusion, the bankruptcy statutes also have rules of inclusion because only certain categories of debtors are eligible to file. In order to be eligible to file a petition under chapter 12 of the Bankruptcy Code or section 75 of the Bankruptcy Act, the debtor had

---

1215. *See id.* at 105 ("It is a misnomer to speak of the filing of the petition on behalf of the corporation as a derivative action.").

1216. 11 U.S.C. §§ 109, 303 (2000).

1217. 11 U.S.C. §§ 22-23 (1976) (repealed 1979).

1218. *See* Bankruptcy Act § 4a, 11 U.S.C. § 22a (1976) (repealed 1979), and Bankruptcy Code § 109(b), 11 U.S.C. § 109(b) (2000). Currently, insurance insolvency proceedings are administered under state law and most bank insolvencies are subject to federal proceedings under title 12 of the United States Code. *See* McCarran-Ferguson Act, 15 U.S.C. § 1012(a) (1945) (leaving the business of insurance to be regulated by state laws); 12 U.S.C. § 91 (Supp. 2007) (precluding federal bank insolvencies from being handled under state law).

1219. 254 U.S. 348 (1920).

1220. *See id.* at 351-56.

to be a family farmer or farmer respectively.[1221] In *First Nat'l Bank & Trust Co. v. Beach*,[1222] the Court interpreted section 75, based on the totality of the facts and circumstances in the case before it, to permit a debtor to file for relief as a farmer because he spent the majority of the time working the land, even though the majority of his income was not derived from his labor.[1223] In reaching its conclusion, the Court went out of its way not to be constrained by a rigid interpretation of the statute[1224] because the debtor was within the class of protected farmers contemplated by Congress.[1225] On the other hand, the Court has not permitted a farmer to collaterally attack an eligibility decision of a lower court that dismissed the farmer's bankruptcy case. Thus, in

---

1221. When Bankruptcy Act § 75 was amended on May 15, 1935, subsection (r) defined "farmer" as follows: "For the purposes of this section, section 4(b), and section 74, the term 'farmer' includes not only an individual who is primarily bona fide personally engaged in producing products of the soil, but also any individual who is primarily bona fide personally engaged in dairy farming, the production of poultry or livestock, or the production of poultry products or livestock products in their unmanufactured state, or the principal part of whose income is derived from any one or more of the foregoing operations, and includes the personal representative of a deceased farmer; and a farmer shall be deemed a resident of any county in which such operations occur." Act of May 15, 1935, ch. 114, § 3, 49 Stat. 246; 11 U.S.C. § 203r (1936) (expired March 1, 1949; repealed 1979). Currently, Bankruptcy Code § 109(f) provides that only a family farmer or family fisherman with regular family income may be a debtor under chapter 12. *See* 11 U.S.C. §§ 101(18)-(19) & 109(f) (Supp. 2005).

1222. 301 U.S. 435 (1937).

1223. *See id.* at 439-41.

1224. *See id.* at 440-41. ("We emphasize the fact afresh that the words of the statute to which meaning is to be given are not phrases of art with a changeless connotation. They have a color and a content that may vary with the setting.").

1225. *Accord* Wright v. Logan, 315 U.S. 139 (1942) (reversing dismissal of a § 75 case and holding that the Bankruptcy Act must be construed liberally to give the debtor the full measure of relief).

Bernards v. Johnson,[1226] the Court held that state foreclosures could proceed because the farmers failed to directly appeal the orders dismissing their bankruptcy cases.[1227]

By the same token, the Court has broadly construed the bankruptcy laws to provide access to broad categories of debtors. In *Toibb v. Radloff*,[1228] the Court interpreted the plain language of the Bankruptcy Code to allow an individual debtor (human being) to convert a voluntary chapter 7 case to a case under chapter 11 even though the individual had no business to reorganize.[1229] The Court rested its reasoning on the broad policy in favor of maximizing the value of the bankruptcy estate.[1230] On the other hand, gaining access to the bankruptcy court does not insure that the debtor will get relief. In *United States v. Kras*,[1231] the Court held that an indigent individual debtor had to pay the fee to file the bankruptcy petition as a condition to getting a discharge; there is no constitutional right to a discharge in bankruptcy.[1232]

Another issue of eligibility arises in the context of sequential filings. The Court has held that the Bankruptcy Act should be interpreted liberally to grant the debtor the full measure of relief intended by Congress.[1233] In this regard, the Court has held uniformly that dismissal or failure of a previous case does not constitute a basis

---

1226. 314 U.S. 19 (1941).

1227. *See id.* at 29-31.

1228. 501 U.S. 157 (1991).

1229. *See id.* at 160-61 ("The Code contains no ongoing business requirement for reorganization under Chapter 11, and we are loath to infer the exclusion of certain classes of debtors from the protections of Chapter 11, because Congress took care in § 109 to specify who qualifies . . . ."). *Id.* at 161.

1230. *See id.* at 164-66.

1231. 409 U.S. 434 (1973).

1232. *See id.* at 446-49.

1233. *See* Wright v. Logan, 315 U.S. 139, 141-42 (1942).

to deny relief to a debtor in a subsequent case. In *Wragg v. Federal Land Bank of New Orleans*,[1234] the Court held that the debtor's equity of redemption was sufficient to warrant a sequential filing under section 75 of the Bankruptcy Act even though the debtor's first section 75 case was dismissed.[1235] A few years earlier in *John Hancock Mutual Life Insurance Co. v. Bartels*,[1236] the Court permitted a farmer to seek adjudication (liquidation) under section 75(s) of the Bankruptcy Act following a failed attempt at restructuring under section 75(a)-(r).[1237] Three years later, the Court reaffirmed this decision in *Wright v. Logan*.[1238] Citing its decisions in *John Hancock Mutual Life Insurance Co. v. Bartels* and *Wright v. Union Central Life Insurance Co.*,[1239] the Court based its holding on the proposition that "the Act must be liberally construed to give the debtor the full measure of the relief afforded by Congress . . . lest its benefits be frittered away by narrow formalistic interpretations which disregard the spirit and the letter of the Act."[1240] Moreover, in *Johnson v. Home State Bank*,[1241] the Court permitted a chapter 7 debtor, immediately after receiving a chapter 7 discharge, to file a sequential chapter 13 case to restructure debts that

---

1234. 317 U.S. 325 (1943).

1235. *See id.* at 328. ("[T]he dismissal of the original proceeding and denial of the application to reopen it were not bars to a new proceeding under § 75 to secure whatever relief the Act would afford with respect to petitioner's remaining interest in the mortgaged property. We find no intimation in the language and purposes of the Act that an unsuccessful earlier proceeding would preclude a new petition so long as the farmer retains an interest which could be administered in a proceeding under § 75.").

1236. 308 U.S. 180 (1939).

1237. *See id.* at 183-85 (finding no basis to dismiss the petition based on the farmer's plight; taking advantage of the statute is not bad faith).

1238. 315 U.S. 139, 141-42 (1942).

1239. Wright v. Union Cent. Life Ins. Co., 311 U.S. 273, 279 (1940).

1240. *See* Wright v. Logan, 315 U.S. at 141-42.

1241. 501 U.S. 78 (1991).

were not discharged under chapter 7.[1242] Although creditor Home State Bank argued that Congress had a policy against serial filings, the Court rejected this argument, noting that the Bankruptcy Code dealt extensively with serial filings.[1243] Because the Code did not specifically prohibit a debtor from filing for chapter 13 after filing for chapter 7, Congress must not have considered that an abuse of the system or it would have included that in the extensive provisions dealing with serial filings.[1244]

A different result follows when the debtor files a bankruptcy petition in bad faith, and the statute explicitly requires dismissal for bad faith filing. Sections 141 and 146 of Chapter X of the Bankruptcy Act required dismissal of a petition if not approved as filed in good faith.[1245] In *Marine Harbor Properties, Inc. v. Manufacturers Trust Co.*,[1246] the Court affirmed the dismissal of a Chapter X petition as not being filed in good faith because the debtor failed to show that Chapter X would produce a superior result to state foreclosure proceedings.[1247] A year later, the Court followed suit in *Fidelity Assurance Ass'n v. Sims*,[1248] dismissing as a bad faith filing the Chapter X petition of a company that primarily sold investment contracts.[1249] The

---

1242. *See id.* at 87.

1243. *See id.*

1244. *See id.*

1245. *See* 11 U.S.C. §§ 541, 546 (1976) (repealed 1979). A filing is not in good faith as defined in §146 if, inter alia, "(4) a prior proceeding is pending in any court and it appears that the interests of creditors and stockholders would be best subserved in such prior proceeding." *See* 11 U.S.C. § 546(4) (1976) (repealed 1979).

1246. 317 U.S. 78 (1942).

1247. *See id.* at 85-86. The debtor had no equity in the property and there was no showing that shareholders would make a new value contribution under a Chapter X plan.

1248. 318 U.S. 608 (1943).

1249. *See id.* at 616.

Court found that the debtor could not comply with regulatory requirements to sell investment contracts and insurance, and, therefore,
creditors would be better served by allowing state court litigation to
continue.[1250]

A separate issue concerns which petitioning creditors have the
legal capacity to file an involuntary bankruptcy petition. Both the
Bankruptcy Act[1251] and the Bankruptcy Code[1252] authorize qualifying
creditors to file involuntary petitions.[1253] Moreover, section 303(b)(3) of
the Bankruptcy Code authorizes fewer than all of the general partners
of a partnership to file an involuntary bankruptcy petition[1254] against
an insolvent partnership. The Bankruptcy Act, however, as originally
enacted had no such provision.[1255] This deficiency led the Court, in
Meek v. Centre County Banking Co.,[1256] to reverse the denial of a
motion to dismiss an involuntary petition because it was filed by
partners and not by creditors.[1257]

1250. *See id.* at 620.

1251. Bankruptcy Act § 59, 11 U.S.C. § 95 (1976) (repealed 1979).

1252. Bankruptcy Code § 303(b), 11 U.S.C. § 303(b) (2000).

1253. Under the Bankruptcy Act, a creditor holding an unliquidated
claim for damages qualified as a petitioning creditor with standing to file
an involuntary petition. *See* Frederic L. Grant Shoe Co. v. W.M. Laird
Co., 212 U.S. 445, 448 (1909) (unliquidated claim for breach of express
warranty). The result should be the same under the Bankruptcy Code
unless the claim is subject to a bona fide dispute as to liability or amount.
See 11 U.S.C. § 303(b)(1) (Supp. 2005).

1254. *See* 11 U.S.C. § 303(b)(3) (2000).

1255. *See* § 5 of Bankruptcy Act of 1898, 30 Stat. 544, 547-48 (1899).

1256. 268 U.S. 426 (1925).

1257. *See id.* at 434-35. In response to the Court's decision in *Meek*,
Congress amended section 5b of the Bankruptcy Act, 11 U.S.C. § 23b, to
provide for fewer than all of the general partners to be able to file a
voluntary petition on behalf of the partnership if they averred that the
partnership was insolvent. *See* Pub. L. No. 75-696, ch. 575, § 5b, 52 Stat.
840, 845-46 (1938). In 1973, Bankruptcy Rule 105 permitted non-
petitioning general partners to contest the petition, but did not clearly

The Court's decision in *Meek* led to an interesting chain of events affecting the character of the petition filed by fewer than all of the general partners of a general partnership debtor. Different laws and procedures apply depending on whether the petition is voluntary or involuntary. In 1938, in response to *Meek*, Congress amended section 5b of the Bankruptcy Act[1258] to provide for fewer than all of the general partners to be able to file a voluntary petition on behalf of the partnership if they averred that the partnership was insolvent.[1259] In 1973, Bankruptcy Rule 105 permitted non-petitioning general partners to contest the petition, but did not clearly denominate the filing as an involuntary petition.[1260] Although Bankruptcy Code section 303(b) clearly specifies that fewer than all of the general partners of an insolvent general partnership may file an involuntary petition against it, the Code does not expressly preclude fewer than all of the general partners from filing a voluntary petition on behalf of the general partnership when the partnership agreement so provides.[1261] The first Bankruptcy Rules promulgated in response to the 1978 Bankruptcy Code assumed that such a petition would be an involuntary petition.[1262] Years later, however, the Court amended the Rules to allow for the possibility that, as a matter of substantive law, fewer than all

---

denominate the filing as an involuntary petition. *See* Bankruptcy Rule 105 (1973).

1258. 11 U.S.C. § 23b (1976) (repealed 1979).

1259. *See* Pub. L. No. 75-696, ch. 575, § 5b, 52 Stat. 840, 845-46 (1938).

1260. *See* Bankruptcy Rule 105 (1973).

1261. *See* 11 U.S.C. § 303 (2000).

1262. *See* Fed. R. Bankr. P. 1004(a) (1983) (requiring all general partners to consent to the bankruptcy filing of a voluntary petition: "1004(a): Voluntary Petition: A voluntary petition may be filed on behalf of the partnership by one or more general partners if all general partners consent to the petition.").

of the general partners might be able to file a voluntary petition on behalf of the partnership.[1263]

The filing of an involuntary petition also raises an issue whether the debtor is eligible to be placed into bankruptcy involuntarily. Both the Bankruptcy Act[1264] and the Bankruptcy Code[1265] contain provisions limiting the categories of debtors against whom involuntary petitions may be commenced. Although the Court has protected excluded classes from being placed into bankruptcy involuntarily, the Court also has not hesitated to sustain filings against debtors outside the excluded classes. For example, in *Armstrong v. Fernandez*,[1266] the Court sustained the filing of the petition against a debtor who claimed to be a wage earner or person chiefly engaged in the tillage of the soil, because the record sustained the court's finding that the debtor was in fact a merchant.[1267] On the other hand, in *Toxaway Hotel Co. v. J.L. Smathers & Co.*,[1268] the Court required the dismissal of an involuntary petition against a hotel, holding that "a corporation engaged primarily in running hotels is not a corporation engaged principally in 'trading' or 'mercantile pursuits.'" The Court reasoned that the corporation was not engaged in trading or mercantile pursuits because its principal profit was not from commerce but from rent.[1269] Writing *per*

1263. *See* Fed. R. Bankr. P. 1004 (Dec. 1, 2002) (deleting Rule 1004(a)).

1264. *See* Bankruptcy Act § 4b, 11 U.S.C. § 22b (1976) (repealed 1979) (excluding, inter alia, wage earners, farmers, and corporations that are not moneyed, business, or commercial corporations from involuntary relief).

1265. *See* Bankruptcy Code § 303(a) (2000) (excluding farmers, family farmers, and corporations that are not moneyed, business, or commercial corporations from involuntary relief).

1266. 208 U.S. 324 (1908).

1267. *See id.* at 332.

1268. 216 U.S. 439 (1910).

1269. *See id.* at 447-49 (interpreting the hotel as not within the class of corporations specified in the Bankruptcy Act of 1898, § 4b, as amended, namely corporations engaged in manufacturing, printing, publishing,

curiam in *Nollman & Co. v. Wentworth Lunch Co.*,[1270] the Court extended this holding to exclude from involuntary bankruptcy relief a corporation engaged in carrying on a general restaurant business.[1271] The Court reasoned that, like a hotel, a restaurant is not engaged in manufacturing, printing, publishing, trading, and mercantile pursuits: "[A]n occupation that is not trading is not a mercantile pursuit."[1272]

When the debtor does not contest the involuntary petition, however, the Court has interpreted the exclusion more narrowly and allowed the debtor to be adjudicated a bankrupt. In *Friday v. Hall & Kaul Co.*,[1273] the Court overturned the holding of the Circuit Court of Appeals that the debtor construction company was not a corporation principally engaged in manufacturing.[1274] The Court noted that whether the company was engaged in manufacturing depended upon what it was actually doing and not on what it was authorized to do.[1275] Moving on to the meaning of "manufacturing" within Bankruptcy Act § 4, the Court determined that the intention of Congress was to subject all businesses engaged in any type of manufacturing as their principal, not merely incidental, business to the law; thus, the word should be given a "liberal rather than a narrow meaning."[1276] Therefore, the Court held that the company was engaged in manufacturing because its "production of concrete arches, or piers, or abutments, is the result

---

trading or mercantile pursuits). *See* Bankruptcy Act § 4b, 30 Stat. 544, 547 (1899).

1270. 217 U.S. 591 (1910).

1271. *See id.* at 592 n.1.

1272. *See id.*

1273. 216 U.S. 449 (1910).

1274. *See id.* at 455-56.

1275. *See id.* at 454.

1276. *See id.*

of successive steps [and] the combination of raw material . . . produced a product, which undoubtedly was 'manufactured.'"[1277]

In 1923, the Court clarified that the filing of an involuntary petition by three creditors of the debtor is sufficient on its face to give the bankruptcy court jurisdiction.[1278] The Court noted that the bankruptcy court has jurisdiction even if one of the petitioning creditors is later disqualified, as long as other creditors join in the petition.[1279] This result was codified over 50 years later in section 303(c) of the Bankruptcy Code,[1280] following its inclusion in 1973 in Bankruptcy Rule 104(e).[1281]

When the requisite number of creditors file an involuntary petition against an eligible debtor, the debtor can either consent to entry of the order for relief or controvert the filing. If the debtor challenges the petition, the court will enter relief if the requisite financial tests are met. Under section 303(h) of the Bankruptcy Code,[1282] the court will order relief only if the debtor is generally not paying debts as they become due, other than debts that are subject to a bona fide dispute as to liability or amount, or within 120 days before the date of the filing of the petition a receiver was appointed or took possession of substantially all of the debtor's property.[1283] The Bankruptcy Code's exclusion of a trustee, receiver, or custodian appointed to take charge of less than substantially all of the debtor's property to enforce a lien

---

1277. *See id.* at 455.

1278. *See* Canute S.S. Co. v. Pittsburgh & W. Va. Coal Co., 263 U.S. 244, 248-49 (1923).

1279. *See id.* at 249.

1280. 11 U.S.C. § 303(c)(2000).

1281. Bankruptcy Rule 104(e) (1973). Bankruptcy Rule 104(e) was more expansive than Bankruptcy Act § 59f, 11 U.S.C. § 95f (1976) (repealed 1979), which simply provided for creditors to join in the involuntary petition without specifying the legal effect.

1282. 11 U.S.C. § 303(h) (2000).

1283. *See id.*

derives from the Court's decision under the Bankruptcy Act of *Duparquet Huot & Moneuse Co. v. Evans*.[1284] Under Bankruptcy Act § 3, the debtor could be adjudicated a bankrupt involuntarily for committing one or more acts of bankruptcy.[1285] The fifth act of bankruptcy occurred when a debtor who was insolvent had a receiver or trustee take charge of his property,[1286] and under § 77B of the Bankruptcy Act, a debtor could be placed into reorganization involuntarily if it was the subject of an "equity receivership."[1287] In *Duparquet*, the Court held that the Bankruptcy Act's reference to "equity receivership" excluded a limited and special receivership incident to foreclosure.[1288] Moreover, the Court held that the fifth act of bankruptcy was not present because, on the facts of the case before it, the debtor was solvent.[1289] As such, the Court left open whether a limited receivership would qualify for the fifth act of bankruptcy, but implied that it would not.[1290] In 1978, some 42 years later, Bankruptcy Code § 303(h)(2) resolved the ambiguity as a matter of statute.

1284. 297 U.S. 216 (1936).

1285. *See* 11 U.S.C. § 21 (1976) (repealed 1979).

1286. *See id.* § 21a(5).

1287. *See* Act of June 7, 1934, 73d Cong., 2d Sess., ch. 424, § 77B(a), 48 Stat. 911-22, enacting Bankruptcy Act § 77B, 11 U.S.C. § 207 (1934) (superseded in 1938 by Chapter X, 52 Stat. 883, 11 U.S.C. §§ 501 et seq.).

1288. *See Duparquet*, 297 U.S. at 218 ("History and structure will be found to teach together that a receivership in a foreclosure suit is not an equity receivership within the meaning of the law."). In Tuttle v. Harris, 297 U.S. 225, 226 (1936), the Court likewise sustained the dismissal of an involuntary § 77B petition, holding that a mortgagee in possession was a property owner, not a receiver, for purposes of § 77B.

1289. *See Duparquet*, 297 U.S. at 224.

1290. *See id.* ("There is support for the view that to satisfy this provision the receivership must be general, as contrasted with a receivership incidental to the enforcement of a lien.... We need not go into that question now.").

PROPERTY OF THE ESTATE, EXEMPTIONS, AND EXCLUSIONS FROM THE ESTATE

Both the Bankruptcy Act[1291] and the Bankruptcy Code[1292] create a federal bankruptcy estate in which the assets of the debtor are administered during the bankruptcy case. Generally, unless the statute provides otherwise,[1293] the date of filing of the bankruptcy petition operates as a date of cleavage when property of the debtor[1294] owned on that date passes into the estate and after-acquired property remains

---

1291. *See* Bankruptcy Act § 70a, 11 U.S.C. § 110a (1976) (repealed 1979).

1292. *See* Bankruptcy Code § 541(a), 11 U.S.C. § 541(a) (2000).

1293. Both the Bankruptcy Act and the Bankruptcy Code include an individual debtor's postpetition earnings in property of the estate in chapters that call for payments out of future earnings. *See, e.g.,* § 611 of Chapter XIII of the Bankruptcy Act, 11 U.S.C. § 1011 (1976) (repealed 1979), and Bankruptcy Code §§ 1115(a)(2), 1207(a)(2) & 1306(a)(2), 11 U.S.C. §§ 1115(a)(2), 1207(a)(2) & 1306(a)(2) (Supp. 2005). Moreover, both the Bankruptcy Act and the Bankruptcy Code include as property of the estate limited categories of property that the debtor acquires within six months or 180 days after the date of the filing of the petition, respectively. *See* Bankruptcy Act § 70a(7), 11 U.S.C. § 110a(7) (1976) (repealed 1979) & Bankruptcy Code § 541(a)(5), 11 U.S.C. § 541(a)(5) (2000).

1294. *See, e.g.,* White v. Stump, 266 U.S. 310, 313 (1924) ("[P]rovisions of the bankruptcy law show that the point of time which is to separate the old situation from the new in the bankrupt's affairs is the date when the petition is filed."); Everett v. Judson, 228 U.S. 474, 479 (1913) ("We think that the purpose of the law was to fix the line of cleavage with reference to the condition of the bankrupt estate as of the time at which the petition was filed . . . .") In addition to traditional property interests in assets of value, the bankruptcy estate also includes the debtor's books and records which the debtor or a third party must turn over, even if they contain incriminating statements. *See, e.g., Ex parte* Fuller, 262 U.S. 91, 93-94 (1923) (partners required to turn over books and records to trustee of bankrupt partnership even if the books and records contain incriminating information); *In re* Harris, 221 U.S. 274, 279 (1911) ("If a trustee had been appointed, the title to the books would have vested in him by the express terms of § 70, and the bankrupt could not have withheld possession of what he no longer owned, on the ground that otherwise he might be punished."); 11 U.S.C. § 542(e) (2000).

with the debtor.[1295] Under the Bankruptcy Act, the bankruptcy trustee was vested with title by operation of law[1296] to most[1297] of the non-exempt property of the debtor[1298] that became property of the estate,[1299]

1295. *See, e.g.,* Segal v. Rochelle, 382 U.S. 375, 377 (1966) (holding that "the trustee must acquire the bankrupt's 'property' as of the date the petition is filed and property subsequently acquired belongs to the bankrupt."); Cameron v. United States, 231 U.S. 710, 717 (1914) (noting that "the filing of the petition in bankruptcy operates to place the property of the alleged bankrupt in *custodia legis* and prevents any creditor from attaching it"); Cramer v. Wilson, 195 U.S. 408, 416-17 (1904) (case under Bankruptcy Act of 1867 holding that debtor had no title on the date of the filing and taking title postpetition was irrelevant).

1296. *See, e.g.,* Thomas v. Sugarman, 218 U.S. 129, 134 (1910) (holding that legal title to the bankrupt's assets had transferred to the trustee by operation of law under the Bankruptcy Act); Gazlay v. Williams, 210 U.S. 41, 47 (1908) ("The passage of the lessee's estate from Brown, the bankrupt, to Williams, the trustee, as of the date of the adjudication, was by operation of law and not by the act of the bankrupt, nor was it by sale."). *See also* Cent. Trust Co. v. Chicago Auditorium Ass'n, 240 U.S. 581, 590 (1916) (dictum that a clause in an executory contract permitting assignment only with the consent of the non-debtor party did not prevent the option to perform and assume the contract from passing to the bankruptcy trustee by operation of law).

1297. *See, e.g.,* Swarts v. Hammer, 194 U.S. 441, 444 (1904) (noting that "the title to all of the property of the bankrupt not declared to be exempt is vested in the trustee"). Moreover, the Bankruptcy Act included, as property of the estate, property that was transferable by the debtor or on which creditors could have levied. *See* Bankruptcy Act § 70a(5), 11 U.S.C. § 110a(5) (1976) (repealed 1979). Therefore, as discussed more fully below, property upon which creditors could not levy or that was non-transferable was excluded from the estate under the Bankruptcy Act.

1298. Property of the debtor does not include services rendered to the debtor or ownership of goods consigned to the debtor. *Cf.* Gleason v. Thaw, 236 U.S. 558, 561 (1915) (holding that attorney's services rendered to debtor did not constitute property for nondischargeability purposes); Ludvigh v. Am. Woolen Co., 231 U.S. 522, 528 (1913) (holding no transfer of property of the debtor when the debtor returns goods held in bailment to consignor).

1299. *See* Bankruptcy Act § 70a, 11 U.S.C. § 110a (1976) (repealed 1979); Thomas v. Sugarman, 218 U.S. 129, 134 (1910) ("The legal title to the

subject to any conditions on the property in the hands of the debtor.[1300] During the early 1900's, the Court probably went astray in augmenting property of the estate by holding that the bankruptcy trustee could use Bankruptcy Act § 70a(5)[1301] to avoid prepetition transfers.[1302] On the other hand, the Court has restricted the scope of property of the estate by noting that property subject to a resulting trust or constructive trust is not property of the estate, even if it is in the debtor's

---

money had been in the bankrupt, and was transferred by the statute to the trustee, § 70. He was entitled to have that money in his hands as against the bankrupt in any event . . . . The law had put him in the bankrupt's shoes with additional powers.").

1300. *See, e.g.,* Bd. of Trade v. Johnson, 264 U.S. 1, 11 (1924) (holding that proceeds of the debtor's seat on the Chicago Board of Trade could not be distributed without first satisfying the claims of members of the board of trade); Hull v. Dicks, 235 U.S. 584, 587 (1915) (holding that the debtor's spouse was entitled to the support payments out of property of the estate because the trustee's title was subject to the condition that if the debtor died during the pendency of the bankruptcy case, the widow and children were entitled to receive the allowance given them by state law); Zartman v. First Nat'l Bank, 216 U.S. 134, 138 (1910) ("[T]he trustee takes the property of the bankrupt, not as an innocent purchaser, but as the debtor had it at the time of the petition, subject to all valid claims, liens and equities."); York Mfg. Co. v. Cassell, 201 U.S. 344, 352 (1906) (reasoning that "[u]nder the provisions of the bankrupt[cy] act the trustee in bankruptcy is vested with no better right or title to the bankrupt's property than belonged to the bankrupt at the time when the trustee's title accrued").

1301. 11 U.S.C. § 110a(5) (1976) (repealed 1979).

1302. *See* Knapp v. Milwaukee Trust Co., 216 U.S. 545, 556 (1910) (trustee may use Bankruptcy Act § 70a(5) to avoid unfiled shifting stock mortgage on inventory); Sec. Warehousing Co. v. Hand, 206 U.S. 415, 427 (1907) (trustee permitted to avoid field warehousing arrangement); Vern Countryman, *The Use of State Law in Bankruptcy Cases (Part I),* 47 N.Y.U. L. REV. 407, 434-38 (1972) (Bankruptcy Act § 70a only vested the trustee with title to property, not title to any property interest that a levying creditor could reach). Under the Bankruptcy Code, avoiding power recoveries are explicitly property of the estate. *See* 11 U.S.C. § 541(a)(3) (2000).

possession.[1303] Likewise, the Court held that under the Bankruptcy Act, shares of stock owned by a customer in possession of a broker are not property of an insolvent stockbroker's general bankruptcy estate, even though the shares are not specifically identifiable as customer-name securities.[1304]

Under the Bankruptcy Code, on the other hand, almost[1305] all legal and equitable interests of the debtor in property become property of the estate initially,[1306] and the bankruptcy trustee simply serves as a legal representative of the estate.[1307] Avoiding power recoveries are included as property of the estate, even though the powers themselves are not.[1308]

Over the past 111 years, the Court has rendered several important decisions interpreting the contours of property of the estate. Generally,

---

1303. Cunningham v. Brown, 265 U.S. 1, 11 (1924) (dictum noting that property subject to a resulting or constructive trust would not be property of the estate).

1304. *See* Gorman v. Littlefield, 229 U.S. 19, 23-25 (1913) ("It is therefore unnecessary for a customer, where shares of stock of the same kind are in the hands of a broker, being held to satisfy his claims, to be able to put his finger upon the identical certificates of stock purchased for him. It is enough that the broker has shares of the same kind which are legally subject to the demand of the customer."). *Id.* at 24.

1305. As discussed more fully below, certain property of the estate is excluded under Bankruptcy Code § 541(b) & (c)(2), 11 U.S.C. § 541(b) & (c)(2) (2000).

1306. *See* Bankruptcy Code § 541(a), 11 U.S.C. § 541(a) (2000). As noted *supra* in Ch. 4, pp. 215-216, 223, if the estate does not have possession of property of the estate, the estate representative may sue to obtain turn over from a party in possession of the property or its proceeds. *See, e.g,* United States v. Whiting Pools, Inc., 462 U.S. 198 (1983) (interpreting turnover under Bankruptcy Code § 542, 11 U.S.C. § 542 (1982)); Maggio v. Zeitz (*In re* Luma Camera Serv., Inc.), 333 U.S. 56, 62-64 (1948) (interpreting turnover under the Bankruptcy Act to require the defendant to be in possession of the property or its proceeds at the time turnover is sought).

1307. *See* Bankruptcy Code § 323(a), 11 U.S.C. § 323(a) (2000).

1308. *See* Bankruptcy Code § 541(a)(3), 11 U.S.C. § 541(a)(3) (2000).

non-bankruptcy law (usually state law) determines whether the debtor or a creditor *has* an interest in property.[1309] On the other hand, federal bankruptcy law determines whether the debtor's interest in property *becomes* property of the bankruptcy estate.[1310]

In this respect, the Court rendered decisions under the Bankruptcy Act narrowly interpreting forfeiture clauses that, if enforced under nonbankruptcy law, would remove property from the estate. For example, in *Gazlay v. Williams*,[1311] the Court refused to apply a lessor's forfeiture clause to the transfer from a real property lessee to his bank-

---

1309. *See, e.g.*, Butner v. United States, 440 U.S. 48, 55 (1979) ("Property interests are created and defined by state law. Unless some federal interest requires a different result, there is no reason why such interests should be analyzed differently simply because an interested party is involved in a bankruptcy proceeding."); Sec. Mortgage Co. v. Powers, 278 U.S. 149, 157 (1928) (holding that property rights existing before bankruptcy in persons other than the debtor had to be recognized and respected in bankruptcy); Taylor v. Voss, 271 U.S. 176, 190 (1926) ("In the absence of any conflicting provision in the Bankruptcy Act the question of a wife's interest in the bankrupt's property is governed by the local law."); Bd. of Trade v. Johnson, 264 U.S. 1, 10 (1924) ("[W]here the bankrupt[cy] law deals with property rights which are regulated by the state law, the federal courts in bankruptcy will follow the state courts; but when the language of Congress indicates a policy requiring a broader construction of the statute than the state decisions would give it, federal courts can not be concluded by them."). *But see* Page v. Edmunds, 187 U.S. 596, 602 (1903) (holding that if the decisions of a State Supreme Court "are declarations of general law—mere definitions of property—we may dispute their conclusions if their reasoning does not persuade.").

1310. *See, e.g.*, Segal v. Rochelle, 382 U.S. 375, 381 n.6 (1966) ("The 'choice of law' rules relevant to this question [whether property is transferable and therefore property of the estate] are not in dispute. What would constitute a 'transfer' is a matter of federal law. Whether an item could have been so transferred is determined generally by state law, save that on rare occasions overriding federal law may control this determination or bear upon it.") (citations omitted).

1311. 210 U.S. 41 (1908).

ruptcy trustee because the transfer occurred by operation of law.[1312] As such, the forfeiture clause was not implicated because it applied only to voluntary assignments by the lessee or sales of the lessee's interest under execution or other legal process.[1313] Moreover, the forfeiture clause did not apply when the trustee sold the lease out of the estate because "[i]t would not be a voluntary assignment by the lessee, nor a sale of the lessee's interest, but of the trustee's interest held under the bankruptcy proceedings for the benefit of creditors."[1314]

The Court also has provided insights into how a bankruptcy court should characterize property. In *Hewit v. Berlin Machine Works*,[1315] the Court upheld a conditional sale contract, holding that title did not pass to the bankrupt until payments under the purchase notes were completed, and the bankruptcy trustee had no greater rights in the property than the bankrupt had.[1316] In *Bailey v. Baker Ice Machine Co.*,[1317] the Court provided further guidance for determining whether property subject to a conditional sale contract under which the debtor was the vendee was property of the bankruptcy estate. If the contract was held to be a conditional sale contract, title would not pass until the debtor made all of the required payments. Before that time, there would only be a possessory interest held by the estate. On the other hand, if the contract was in substance an absolute sale with a mortgage back as security, title to the property would be in the bankruptcy trustee subject to the secured party's lien. The Court held that the distinction between a contract for a conditional sale and an absolute sale with a mortgage back depended on the intention of the

---

1312. *See id.* at 47-48.

1313. *See id.*

1314. *See id.* at 47.

1315. 194 U.S. 296 (1904).

1316. *See id.* at 301-02.

1317. 239 U.S. 268 (1915).

parties as shown by the entire contract and not on any single provision considered on its own.[1318]

Moreover, characterization of property ownership can turn on facts from which courts infer the fair the intention of the parties. In *Manson v. Williams*,[1319] the Court upheld as not clearly erroneous the findings of the lower courts that proceeds of the sale of goods were owned by a de facto partnership rather than by either of two brothers individually.[1320] The parties commingled monies in a business account and the capital of one was used to pay the liabilities of the other.[1321] Even though the brothers did not formally establish a partnership or use the business name among themselves, courts will imply the partnership "if that is the fair result of what they did understand and intend."[1322] Moreover, in *Equitable Trust Co. v. First National Bank*,[1323] the Court relied on the intent of the parties and the operative documentation to distinguish a promise from a property right, holding that "what the parties meant to establish and what [First National Bank] got was the assurance of a credit abroad to the extent of its check as in the case of a letter of credit, not an attenuated property right in an account to which no special funds were attached and the

---

1318. *See id.* at 272 ("[T]he question whether a particular contract shows one or the other turns upon the ruling intention of the parties as disclosed by the entire contract, and not upon any single provision separately considered."). Although the Court held the contract to be a conditional sale contract and denied the trustee's efforts at recharacterization, the Court's early recognition of a bankruptcy court's need to consider the totality of the contract in determining the intention of the parties foreshadowed the Court's more expansive equity jurisprudence in years to come. *See supra* Ch. 4, pp. 223-229.

1319. 213 U.S. 453 (1909).

1320. *See id.* at 457.

1321. *See id.*

1322. *See id.*

1323. 275 U.S. 359 (1928).

particulars of which neither the respondent nor the purchaser of the check could know."[1324]

Segal v. Rochelle[1325] required the Court to consider the boundary of the Bankruptcy Act's reference to property, when both the trustee and individual debtors claimed the proceeds of refunds arising from application of a postpetition net operating loss to recoup income taxes paid prepetition.[1326] Specifically, the Court reasoned that in light of the policies of the Act, the term "property" should be interpreted broadly and that an interest was not outside its reach because it was novel or contingent or because enjoyment must be postponed.[1327] The Court found that the refunds were sufficiently rooted in the prebankruptcy past and so little entangled with the bankrupt's ability to make a fresh start that they should be regarded as property under Bankruptcy Act § 70a(5).[1328]

Four years later in *Lines v. Frederick*,[1329] the Court refused to extend its holding in *Segal v. Rochelle* to apply to a debtor's prepetition accrued but unpaid vacation pay.[1330] In a *per curiam* opinion, the Court reaffirmed that property of the estate should be construed broadly, but not so far as to prohibit the debtor from enjoying a fresh start.[1331] Incorporating the debtor's vacation pay into the bankruptcy estate is inimical to the debtor's fresh start because it would force the debtor either to forego a vacation or take it without pay.[1332] Therefore, in order to be included as property of the estate, not only must the

---

1324. *See id.* at 369.

1325. 382 U.S. 375 (1966).

1326. *See id.* at 380.

1327. *See id.* at 379.

1328. *See id.* at 380.

1329. 400 U.S. 18 (1970).

1330. *See id.* at 19-20.

1331. *See id.* at 20.

1332. *See id.*

funds be "sufficiently rooted in the pre-bankruptcy past" but *also* "so little entangled with the bankrupt's ability to make an unencumbered fresh start."[1333]

Four years later in *Kokoszka v. Belford*,[1334] the Court resolved the tension between *Segal v. Rochelle* and *Lines v. Frederick*[1335] in deciding that a postpetition income tax refund for income earned prepetition was property of the estate and that federal wage garnishment limitations did not limit the amount of the refund available to the trustee.[1336] Chief Justice Burger, writing for a unanimous Court, noted that the "crucial analytical key" lay "in an analysis of the nature of the asset involved" in light of the twin bankruptcy principles of broadly defining property of the estate and not fettering the debtor's fresh start.[1337] Because "[t]he income tax refund at issue in the present case does not relate conceptually to future wages and it is not the equivalent of future wages for the purpose of giving the bankrupt a 'fresh start[,]'" the Court included the refund as property of the estate.[1338]

Under the Bankruptcy Act, property of the debtor was included in the bankruptcy estate only if it was transferable by the debtor and could be levied on by creditors.[1339] Thus, in *Eaton v. Boston Safe*

1333. *See id.*

1334. 417 U.S. 642 (1974).

1335. *See id.* at 646 ("*Segal* and *Lines*, while construing § 70a(5) in almost identical language, reached contrary results.").

1336. *See id.* at 648, 651-52.

1337. *See id.* at 646.

1338. *See id.* at 647-48.

1339. *See* § 70a(5) of the Bankruptcy Act, 11 U.S.C. § 110a(5) (1976) (repealed 1979) ("The trustee of the estate . . . shall . . . be vested . . . with the title of the bankrupt . . . to . . . (5) property, including rights of action, which prior to the filing of the petition he could by any means have transferred or which might have been levied upon . . . .").

Deposit & Trust Co.,[1340] the Court affirmed a decision of the Massachusetts Supreme Judicial Court that a spendthrift trust under which the debtor was the beneficiary was not property of the bankruptcy estate. The law of Massachusetts treated state trust restrictions on transferability to creditors and the bankruptcy trustee as limiting the character of the equitable property and inherent in it.[1341] In *Page v. Edmunds,*[1342] however, the Court interpreted the Bankruptcy Act's transferability language to include the debtor's seat on the Philadelphia Stock Exchange in the bankruptcy estate because the debtor could transfer it, even if creditors could not levy on the seat under state law.[1343] The Court followed its earlier precedent in *Hyde v. Woods*[1344] and held that the seat had value and was property, even though the transferee of the seat might take it subject to restrictions and conditions, such as election to membership by the exchange.[1345] Because stock exchanges impose restrictions on seats and memberships from their inception, the debtor's property interest is never absolute and unconditional, but is limited by the restrictions *ab initio.*[1346] In *Board of Trade v. Johnson,*[1347] the Court held that the

1340. 240 U.S. 427 (1916).

1341. *See id.* at 429.

1342. 187 U.S. 596 (1903).

1343. *See id.* at 601-02.

1344. 94 U.S. 523, 524-25 (1877) (holding, under the Bankruptcy Act of 1867, that the debtor's seat on the San Francisco Stock and Exchange Board is property that, had he not transferred it prepetition, would have become property of his bankruptcy estate subject to the rules of the stock board (e.g., providing for the application of the proceeds of sale of the membership to debts due to the members of the exchange)).

1345. *See Page v. Edmunds,* 187 U.S. at 601, 604-05.

1346. *See Hyde v. Woods,* 94 U.S. at 525. ("A seat in this board is not a matter of absolute purchase. Though we have said it is property, it is incumbered with conditions when purchased, without which it could not be obtained.").

1347. 264 U.S. 1 (1924).

district court erred in ordering the transfer and sale of the debtor's seat on the Chicago Board of Trade free and clear of the objections of other members of the Board.[1348] Although the Board's rules provided for sale of the seat only in the absence of objection by the other members, the Court held that the debtor's bankruptcy trustee could sell the seat without the members' vote if the claims of the other members were satisfied before the trustee realized any proceeds for the bankruptcy estate.[1349] In *West v. Oklahoma Tax Commission*,[1350] however, the court noted that Indian Headrights (interests held by tribe members in tribal mineral estates) are not transferable and therefore not property of the bankruptcy estate.[1351]

Unless the debtor holds property as an agent or in trust, the property will become property of the estate and subject to bankruptcy administration. Thus, in *Mahon v. Stowers*,[1352] the Court refused to impose a trust on cattle held by the debtor because the seller remained unpaid in what the parties intended to be a cash transaction; there was only a debtor-creditor relationship and no indication of an express trust.[1353] Likewise, in *Equitable Trust Co. v. Rochling*,[1354] the debtor had ownership, dominion, and control over the proceeds of two cashier's checks but there was no indication that the debtor acted as an agent for a third party in cashing the checks; the Court held that

---

1348. *See id.* at 15. The Court analogizes the members' right to prevent the transfer of a seat to a common law lien. *See id.* at 11. If so, the trustee should have been able to sell free and clear under the principles of Van Huffel v. Harkelrode, 284 U.S. 225, 228 (1931), which the Court would decide seven years later. *See also* Thomas H. Jackson & Douglas G. Baird, *Kovacs and Toxic Wastes in Bankruptcy*, 36 STAN. L. REV. 1199, 1207 (1984).

1349. *See* Bd. of Trade v. Johnson, 264 U.S. 1, 6, 11-12 (1924).

1350. West v. Okla. Tax Comm'n, 334 U.S. 717 (1948).

1351. *See id.* at 719 n.2.

1352. 416 U.S. 100 (1974).

1353. *See id.* at 107.

1354. 275 U.S. 248 (1927).

the third party had no right of reclamation in the proceeds and was an ordinary creditor.[1355]

Both the Bankruptcy Act[1356] and the Bankruptcy Code[1357] include, as property of the estate, property of the debtor wherever located and by whomever held, including a third party. Several Court decisions have illuminated when property remains property of the estate and when it becomes third party property outside of the estate.[1358] In *Bryan v. Bernheimer*,[1359] the Court held that the bankruptcy estate included property of the debtor in the hands of a third party who, with full knowledge of the bankruptcy petition, purchased property of the debtor from an assignee for the benefit of the debtor's creditors.[1360] Moreover, in *Clarke v. Larremore*,[1361] the Court held that the bankruptcy estate included proceeds of a prepetition execution sale in the hands of

1355. *See id.* at 253-54. *Accord* Latzko v. Equitable Trust Co., 275 U.S. 254, 257 (1927).

1356. *See* Bankruptcy Act § 70a, 11 U.S.C. § 110a (1976) (repealed 1979).

1357. *See* the preamble to Bankruptcy Code § 541(a), 11 U.S.C. § 541(a) (preamble) (2000), and § 1334(e) of the Judicial Code, 28 U.S.C. § 1334(e) (2000).

1358. As discussed below, transfers of the debtor's property sometimes may be avoidable even if the property transferred is no longer property of the estate.

1359. 181 U.S. 188 (1901).

1360. *See id.* at 193, 197. This holding apparently led Congress in 1938 to add § 70a(8) to the Bankruptcy Act to specifically confer summary jurisdiction in cases similar to *Bryan v. Bernheimer*. *See* The Chandler Act, Act of June 22, 1938, 75th Cong., 3d Sess., ch. 575, §1, 52 Stat. 840, 880, amending Bankruptcy Act § 70a(8) (giving the trustee title to all "(8) property held by an assignee for the benefit of creditors appointed under an assignment which constituted an act of bankruptcy, which property shall . . . be deemed to be held by the assignee as the agent of the bankrupt and shall be subject to the summary jurisdiction of the court. . . .").

1361. 188 U.S. 486 (1903).

the levying sheriff because they had not been paid to the levying creditor in satisfaction of the judgment.[1362]

Under the Bankruptcy Act, an individual debtor's exempt property did not become property of the estate.[1363] Although the Bankruptcy Act did not itself create new categories of exempt property, it did recognize state and non-bankruptcy federal exemptions.[1364] As noted in Chapter 3, the Court upheld the constitutionality of this exemption formula.[1365] In order to claim property as exempt, the debtor's strict compliance with state law is essential. For example, in *White v. Stump*,[1366] the Court held that the date of the filing of the bankruptcy petition marked a point of cleavage whereupon property passed out of the control of the debtor into the bankruptcy estate.[1367] Unless the

---

1362. *See id.* at 488-90.

1363. *See* Bankruptcy Act § 70a (preamble), 11 U.S.C. § 110a (preamble) (1976) (repealed 1979) ("The trustee of the estate of a bankrupt . . . shall . . . be vested by operation of law with the title of the bankrupt . . . except insofar as it is to property which is held to be exempt . . . ."). Under the Bankruptcy Code, certain property (other than exempt property) is excluded from the estate. *See* nn.1394-1398 *infra* and accompanying text.

1364. Section 6 of the Bankruptcy Act, 11 U.S.C. § 24 (1976) (repealed 1979), provided that the Bankruptcy Act would "not affect the allowance to bankrupts of the exemptions which are prescribed by the laws of the United States or by the State laws . . . [excluding certain fraudulently transferred property]." *See* Holden v. Stratton, 198 U.S. 202, 213-14 (1905) ("It has always been the policy of Congress, both in general legislation and in bankrupt acts, to recognize and give effect to the state exemption laws.").

1365. *See* Hanover Nat'l Bank v. Moyses, 186 U.S. 181 (1902) (discussed more fully *supra* in Ch. 3, pp. 124-125). In *Kener v. La Grange Mills*, however, the Court held that neither the Georgia constitution nor the Bankruptcy Act of 1867 could exempt property from existing liens. *See* Kener v. La Grange Mills, 231 U.S. 215, 217-18 (1913) (citing Gunn v. Barry, 82 U.S. (15 Wall.) 610, 622-23 (1873)).

1366. 266 U.S. 310 (1924).

1367. *See id.* at 313.

debtor claimed a homestead in accordance with state law before the filing of the bankruptcy petition, the property would become general property of the estate subject to liquidation for the benefit of creditors.[1368] On the other hand, in *Holden v. Stratton*,[1369] the Court sustained the ability of the debtors to exempt insurance policies from the bankruptcy estate as long as the policies were also exempt under state law (notwithstanding the Bankruptcy Act's conflicting reference in a proviso to section 70a(5) when insurance policies with cash surrender values become property of the estate).[1370] The Court stated that "the purpose of the proviso was to confer a benefit upon the insured bankrupt by limiting the character of the interest in a non-exempt life insurance policy which should pass to the trustee . . . ."[1371]

In *Legg v. St. John*,[1372] the Court again considered the Bankruptcy Act's insurance policy proviso and held that a disabled debtor's future disability benefits payable under a life insurance policy were not themselves insurance policies, because the benefits payable were not insurance within the meaning of Bankruptcy Act § 70a; as such they

---

1368. *See id.* at 311. Thus, the debtor's spouse was not able to claim the homestead after the bankruptcy filing. Section 522(*l*) of the Bankruptcy Code specifically permits a dependent of the debtor to file a list of exemptions if the debtor fails to do so. The right to file a list generally only applies, however, to property that is exempt as of the date of the filing of the petition. Therefore the result in *White v. Stump* would not differ under the Bankruptcy Code.

1369. 198 U.S. 202 (1905).

1370. *See id.* at 212 ("Considering the matter originally, it is we think apparent that section 6 is couched in unlimited terms, and is accompanied with no qualification whatever. Even a superficial analysis of section 70*a* demonstrates that that section deals not with exemptions, but solely with the nature and character of property, title to which passes to the trustee in bankruptcy.").

1371. *See id.* at 213.

1372. 296 U.S. 489 (1936).

became property of the estate, except to the extent exempt as disability benefits under state law.[1373]

Under the Bankruptcy Code, almost all property of the debtor becomes property of the estate,[1374] including property of the debtor in the possession of a secured creditor.[1375] As discussed in Chapter 4, generally, under the Bankruptcy Act, a bankruptcy court's summary jurisdiction was limited to property in the debtor's possession as of the filing of the petition.[1376] Under Bankruptcy Code § 542(a),[1377] however, the trustee may invoke the bankruptcy court's jurisdiction to compel turnover of property of the estate in the hands of a third party by adequately protecting the third party's property interest.[1378]

1373. *See id.* at 492-93.

1374. As explained below, § 541(b) & (c)(2) excludes certain property from becoming property of the estate. *See* 11 U.S.C. § 541(b) & (c)(2) (2000).

1375. *See* United States v. Whiting Pools, Inc., 462 U.S. 198, 209 (1983) (holding that "the reorganization estate includes property of the debtor that has been seized by a creditor prior to the filing of a petition . . . .").

1376. *See, e.g.,* Phelps v. United States, 421 U.S. 330, 335-36 (1975) (liquidation case in which the IRS levy transferred constructive possession of the property, thereby ousting the bankruptcy court of summary jurisdiction); Taubel-Scott-Kitzmiller Co. v. Fox, 264 U.S. 426, 432-34 (1924) ("But in no case where it lacked possession, could the bankruptcy court, under the law as originally enacted, nor can it now (without consent) adjudicate in a summary proceeding the validity of a substantial adverse claim.").

1377. 11 U.S.C. § 542(a) (2000).

1378. *See* United States v. Whiting Pools, Inc., 462 U.S. 198, 211-12 (1983) (holding that Internal Revenue Service was required to turn over debtor's property seized to secure a tax lien: "When the property seized prior to the filing of a petition is drawn into the Chapter 11 reorganization estate, the Service's tax lien is not dissolved; nor is its status as a secured creditor destroyed. The IRS, under § 363(e), remains entitled to adequate protection for its interests, to other rights enjoyed by secured creditors, and to the specific privileges accorded tax collectors.").

The Bankruptcy Code also permits an individual debtor to exempt property out of the estate.[1379] The Court has decided a few cases under the Bankruptcy Code answering questions about bankruptcy exemptions that were not resolved under the Bankruptcy Act. In *Taylor v. Freeland & Kronz*,[1380] the Court resolved whether a bankruptcy trustee could file a late objection to exemptions that the debtor improperly claimed.[1381] Specifically, the Court strictly enforced both Bankruptcy Code § 522(*l*), that "unless a party in interest objects, the property claimed as exempt on such list is exempt,"[1382] and Federal Rule of Bankruptcy Procedure 4003(b), which requires a party to object to exemptions within 30 days after the conclusion of the section 341(a)[1383] meeting of creditors.[1384] Even though the debtor claimed an exemption in an asset to which she had no colorable right to exempt, because no party timely objected, the Court affirmed the Circuit court's denial of the objection.[1385] The Court noted, however, that it was not deciding whether the equitable power of the bankruptcy court could be used to reach a different result.[1386]

In *Rousey v. Jacoway*,[1387] the Court reaffirmed its suggestion in *Patterson v. Shumate*[1388] and held that a debtor could use the Bank-

---

1379. *See* 11 U.S.C. § 522(b) (Supp. 2005).

1380. 503 U.S. 638 (1992).

1381. *See id.* at 642.

1382. 11 U.S.C. § 522(*l*) (2000).

1383. *See* 11 U.S.C. § 341(a) (2000).

1384. *See* Taylor v. Freeland & Kronz, 503 U.S. 638, 644 (1992) ("Deadlines may lead to unwelcome results, but they prompt parties to act and they produce finality.").

1385. *See id.* at 641-42.

1386. *See id.* at 645-46 (declining to consider for the first time on appeal the equitable power of the bankruptcy court under Bankruptcy Code § 105(a)).

1387. 544 U.S. 320 (2005).

1388. 504 U.S. 753, 762-63 (1992), discussed more fully below.

ruptcy Code to exempt an Individual Retirement Account ("IRA") from property of the estate.[1389] Specifically, debtors selecting the federal exemptions under section 522(b)[1390] could use section 522(d)(10)(E)[1391] to exempt their IRAs both because the IRAs provide a right to payment "on account of . . . age"[1392] and are "similar plan[s] or contract[s]" to the "stock bonus, pension, profitsharing, [or] annuity . . . plan[s]."[1393]

Not all of the debtor's property becomes property of the bankruptcy estate. As noted previously, under the Bankruptcy Act, an individual debtor's exempt property does not become property of the estate. Nor does the bankruptcy estate include title to property in which a third party has title good against the debtor and the trustee.[1394]

1389. *See* Rousey v. Jacoway, 544 U.S. 320, 326 (2005).

1390. Generally, unless the debtor's state has opted out, Bankruptcy Code § 522(b), in addition to non-bankruptcy federal exemptions, gives individual debtors the right to elect federal bankruptcy exemptions under § 522(d) or, in the alternative, state exemptions. *See* 11 U.S.C. § 522 (Supp. 2005).

1391. Under Bankruptcy Code § 522(d)(10)(E), a debtor who elects the federal exemptions set forth in § 522(d) may exempt from the bankruptcy estate his right to receive "a payment under a stock bonus, pension, profitsharing, annuity, or similar plan or contract . . ., to the extent reasonably necessary for the support of the debtor and any dependent of the debtor." *See* 11 U.S.C. § 522(d)(10)(E) (2000).

1392. *See Rousey v. Jacoway*, 544 U.S. at 326-29.

1393. *See id.* at 329-35.

1394. *See* Thomas v. Taggart, 209 U.S. 385, 389 (1908) (holding that "if the title to property claimed is good as against the bankrupt and his creditors at the time the trustee's title accrued, the title does not pass [to the bankruptcy estate] and the property should be restored to its true owner."). But in the absence of a statute, agreement, or court order establishing a trust, property of the estate will include goods supplied to the debtor even though the debtor has not paid the purchase price. *See* Mahon v. Stowers, 416 U.S. 100, 111 (1974) (holding that lender with security interest in debtor's property prevailed against creditor who had supplied goods to debtor on a cash basis but had not been paid).

Under the Bankruptcy Code, section 541(b) and (c)(2)[1395] sets forth exclusions from property of the estate. In particular, section 541(c)(2) enforces in a bankruptcy case "[a] restriction on transfer of a beneficial interest of the debtor in a trust that is enforceable under applicable nonbankruptcy law . . . ."[1396] In *Patterson v. Shumate*,[1397] the Court held that the statutory reference to "nonbankruptcy law" was broad enough to include state or federal nonbankruptcy law; thus, the Court excluded from the estate the debtor's interest in a corporate pension plan that was subject to the anti-alienation provisions of ERISA.[1398]

CLAIMS: ALLOWANCE, DISALLOWANCE, PRIORITY, SUBORDINATION

Allowance and Disallowance of Claims

Once the bankruptcy estate is formed, in order to participate in a distribution from the estate or under a plan, creditors must file proofs of claims or have them deemed filed on their behalf.[1399] In general,[1400] a

---

1395. 11 U.S.C. § 541(b) & (c)(2) (2000).

1396. 11 U.S.C. § 541(c)(2) (2000).

1397. 504 U.S. 753 (1992).

1398. *See id.* at 759-60. The anti-alienation provisions of ERISA, the Employee Retirement Income Security Act of 1974, prevents a debtor from assigning or alienating the debtor's interest in a corporate pension that is qualified under ERISA. *See* 29 U.S.C. § 1056(d)(1) (2000) (commonly known as section 206(d)(1) of ERISA) ("each pension plan shall provide that benefits provided under the plan may not be assigned or alienated").

1399. *See generally* Bankruptcy Code §§ 501, 726(a) & 1111, 11 U.S.C. §§ 501, 726(a) & 1111 (2000); Fed. R. Bankr. P. 3001, 3002 & 3003; Bankruptcy Act §§ 57, 106(1), 307(2), 336(2), 406(2), 436(2), 451, 606(1), & 633(1), 11 U.S.C. §§ 93, 506(1), 707(2), 736(2), 806(2), 836(2), 851, 1006(1) & 1033(1) (1976) (repealed 1979); and Bankruptcy Rules 302, 10-401(e), 11-33, 12-24(a)(2), 12-30 & 13-302 (repealed 1979).

1400. Under the Bankruptcy Code, the term "claim" also includes rights to certain equitable remedies for breach of performance if such breach of

claim is a right to payment[1401] or property[1402] as opposed to an ownership interest in the debtor. Moreover, a debt[1403] is a debtor's liability on a claim,[1404] and only debts are dischargeable in bankruptcy.[1405] Thus, if a party does not hold a debt or claim, in general[1406] there is no basis to participate in the bankruptcy distribution or to be subject to the bankruptcy discharge.[1407]

Once a proof of claim is timely filed, it is deemed *prima facie* valid[1408] and allowed unless a party in interest timely objects.[1409] Under

---

performance gives rise to a right to payment. *See* 11 U.S.C. § 101(5)(B) (2000). Thus, in Ohio v. Kovacs, 469 U.S. 274, 283 (1985), the Court held that a court order requiring the debtor to repay Ohio for environmental cleanup damages was a claim, even though the order was entered originally as a cleanup remedy for a statutory violation.

1401. *See* 11 U.S.C. § 101(5)(A) (2000).

1402. *See* 11 U.S.C. § 102(2) (2000). In Johnson v. Home State Bank, 501 U.S. 78, 84 (1991), the Court held that the nonrecourse right of a mortgagee to proceeds of the debtor's property was a claim for purposes of the Bankruptcy Code.

1403. Section 1(14) of the Bankruptcy Act defined debt to "include and debt, demand, or claim provable in bankruptcy." *See* 11 U.S.C. § 1(14) (1976) (repealed 1979).

1404. *See* 11 U.S.C. § 101(5), (12) (2000) for a complete definition of "debt" and "claim" under the Bankruptcy Code.

1405. *See* 11 U.S.C. §§ 524, 727, 944, 1141, 1228 & 1328 (2000); 11 U.S.C. § 35a (1976) (repealed 1979).

1406. Even though they are not claims, certain "demands" are subject to a discharge-like injunction in asbestos bankruptcies. *See* 11 U.S.C. § 524(g)(4)(B)-(5) (2000).

1407. *See, e.g.,* Wetmore v. Markoe, 196 U.S. 68, 77 (1904) (holding that a husband's accrued obligations for alimony and support under a divorce decree were not debts under the Bankruptcy Act).

1408. *See* Fed. R. Bankr. P. 3001(f) (2007); Bankruptcy Act § 57a, 11 U.S.C. § 93a (1976) (repealed 1979); Bankruptcy Rule 301(b) (1973) (repealed 1979); & Whitney v. Dresser, 200 U.S. 532, 535 (1906).

1409. *See* Bankruptcy Code § 502, 11 U.S.C. § 502 (2000); Bankruptcy Act § 57d, 11 U.S.C. § 93d (1976) (repealed 1979).

the Bankruptcy Act, in a straight bankruptcy liquidation case, a claim had to be provable[1410] in order to be allowable.[1411] The Bankruptcy Code dropped the requirement of provability,[1412] but delineates nine

---

1410. For the most part, a claim was provable if it was fixed, reduced to judgment, based on a contract (express or implied), or contingent, but not unliquidated, unless it was a pending negligence action or for anticipatory breach of contract. *See* Bankruptcy Act § 63, 11 U.S.C. § 103 (1976) (repealed 1979). *See also, e.g.,* Nathanson v. N.L.R.B., 344 U.S. 25, 27 (1952) (N.L.R.B. back pay award was a provable claim based on an implied contract); Miller v. Irving Trust Co., 296 U.S. 256, 259 (1935) (holding that lessor's rejection damages claim was not provable because it was, at the time the petition in bankruptcy was filed, uncertain and a mere matter of speculation whether any liability would ever arise); Maynard v. Elliott, 283 U.S. 273, 275-76 (1931) (holding that claims on unmatured notes were provable as claims based upon a contract express or implied); Lewis v. Roberts, 267 U.S. 467, 468 (1925) (holding that a tort claim for negligence was provable under Bankruptcy Act § 63a(1)). If the contingent claim was not liquidated or estimated during the case, under Bankruptcy Act § 57d it would be disallowed and deemed not provable under Bankruptcy Act § 63d. *See* 11 U.S.C. §§ 93d & 103d (1976) (repealed 1979). In straight bankruptcy cases, only provable debts were dischargeable under Bankruptcy Act § 17a. *See* 11 U.S.C. § 35a (1976) (repealed 1979).

1411. *See* Bankruptcy Act §§ 57d & 63, 11 U.S.C. §§ 93d & 103 (1976) (repealed 1979), requiring claims to be provable in order to be allowable. On the other hand, in all other kinds of bankruptcy cases under the Bankruptcy Act, claims were defined to include claims that were not provable. *See, e.g.,* § 77(b)(2), 11 U.S.C. § 205(b)(2) (1976) (repealed 1979), dealing with railroad reorganizations, § 81(1) of Chapter IX, 11 U.S.C. § 401(1) (1976) (repealed 1979), dealing with adjustments of debts of political subdivisions and public agencies and instrumentalities, §§ 106(1) & 201 of Chapter X, 11 U.S.C. §§ 506(1) & 601 (1976) (repealed 1979), dealing with corporate reorganizations, § 307(2) of Chapter XI, 11 U.S.C. § 707(2) (1976) (repealed 1979), dealing with arrangements, § 406(2) of Chapter XII, 11 U.S.C. § 806(2) (1976) (repealed 1979), dealing with real property arrangements, and § 606(1) of Chapter XIII, 11 U.S.C. § 1006(1) (1976) (repealed 1979), dealing with individual debt adjustment plans.

1412. Therefore, the concept of provability is of historical interest only and, for the most part, is not discussed in this book.

separate bases on which claims may be disallowed[1413] as well as a few bases to disallow specialized claims.[1414] Moreover, like the Bankruptcy Act before it,[1415] the Bankruptcy Code authorizes the disallowance of claims based on the equities of the case.[1416]

Soon after Congress passed the Bankruptcy Act of 1898, the Court established several fundamental principles regarding allowance and disallowance of claims. In *Hutchinson v. Otis, Wilcox & Co.*,[1417] a creditor attached debts during the preference period, was paid, and recorded a satisfaction of judgment.[1418] Later, after the bankruptcy trustee sued the creditor and avoided the payments, the creditor sought to prove a claim in the bankruptcy for the amounts disgorged.[1419] The trustee objected to allowance on the basis of satisfaction.[1420] The Court held that the creditor's claim was allowed and the recorded satisfaction of judgment was not a bar to recovery because

---

1413. *See* 11 U.S.C. § 502(b) (2000).

1414. *See, e.g.,* Bankruptcy Code § 502(e), 11 U.S.C. § 502(e) (2000), dealing with disallowance of certain claims for contribution or reimbursement.

1415. *See* Bankruptcy Act § 57k, 11 U.S.C. § 93k (1976) (repealed 1979) ("Claims which have been allowed may be reconsidered and rejected, in whole or in part according to the equities of the case . . . ."); Pepper v. Litton, 308 U.S. 295, 305 (1939) (citing Bankruptcy Act § 57k to support equitable disallowance of a claim, because "a claim which has been allowed may be later 'rejected in whole or in part, according to the equities of the case,' disallowance or subordination in light of equitable considerations may originally be made.").

1416. *See* Bankruptcy Code § 502(j), 11 U.S.C. § 502(j) (2000), containing the language of Bankruptcy Act § 57k on which the Court relied in *Pepper v. Litton* to equitably disallow a claim. *See supra* n.1415 and Ch. 4, p. 223-229.

1417. 190 U.S. 552 (1903).

1418. *See id.* at 553.

1419. *See id.*

1420. *See id.*

the creditor had disgorged the payments.[1421] In *Keppel v. Tiffin Savings Bank*,[1422] the Court extended this reasoning in reliance on the equality principle to hold that "whenever the preference has been abandoned or yielded up, and thereby the danger of inequality has been prevented, such creditor is entitled to stand on an equal footing with other creditors and prove his claims."[1423] In answering the certified question before it, however, the Court also addressed a good faith requirement: "a creditor of a bankrupt, who has received a merely voidable preference, and who has in good faith retained such preference until deprived thereof by the judgment of a court upon a suit of the trustee, [may] thereafter prove the debt so voidably preferred."[1424] Congress later codified this principle, without regard to the creditor's good faith, in both the Bankruptcy Act[1425] and Bankruptcy Code.[1426] By the same token, if the creditor refuses to return an avoidable transfer, both the Bankruptcy Act[1427] and the Bankruptcy Code[1428] include a so-

---

1421. *See id.*

1422. 197 U.S. 356 (1905).

1423. *See id.* at 363-64.

1424. *See id.* at 359, 374.

1425. *See* The Chandler Act, Act of June 22, 1938, 75th Cong., 3d Sess., ch. 575, §1, 52 Stat. 840, 867, amending Bankruptcy Act § 57n, 11 U.S.C. § 93n (Supp. 1938) (repealed 1979), to read in pertinent part: "*And provided further*, That a claim arising in favor of a person by reason of the recovery by the trustee from such person of money or property, or the avoidance by the trustee of a lien held by such person, may be filed within thirty days from the date of such recovery is by way of a proceeding in which a final judgment has been entered against such person, the claim shall not be allowed if the money is not paid or the property is not delivered to the trustee within thirty days from the date of the rendering of such final judgment, or within such further time as the court may allow."

1426. *See* Bankruptcy Code § 502(h), 11 U.S.C. § 502(h) (2000).

1427. *See* Bankruptcy Act § 57g, 11 U.S.C. § 93g (1976) (repealed 1979).

1428. *See* Bankruptcy Code § 502(d), 11 U.S.C. § 502(d) (2000).

called "surrender clause"[1429] providing for disallowance of the claim unless and until the creditor disgorges the avoidable transfer.[1430] Thus, in *Gardner v. Chicago Title & Trust Co.*,[1431] the Court precluded a bank from receiving dividends on its unsecured claim against the debtor's estate until the bank paid postpetition debts it owed on deposits made by the bankruptcy trustees.[1432]

The Court also loosely construed provisions that proofs of claim, in order to be allowed, had to be timely filed with the bankruptcy court. In *J.B. Orcutt Co. v. Green*,[1433] the Court held that proofs of claim delivered to the bankruptcy trustee before the bar date would be allowed, even though the trustee's attorney negligently failed to file the proofs with the bankruptcy court.[1434] In essence, the Court charitably construed delivery to the trustee to be delivery to the bankruptcy court because the trustee was an officer of the court.[1435] "If the trustee inadvertently neglects to perform that duty it is the neglect of an officer of the court, and the creditors are in no way responsible therefor."[1436] The Court extended this charitable policy 86 years later when it decided *Pioneer Investment Services Co. v. Brunswick*

1429. *See, e.g., Keppel* at 363-64 (interpreting the "surrender clause" of Bankruptcy Act § 57g).

1430. As noted in more detail *infra* in nn.1440-1442 and accompanying text, the creditor may be able to net the amount of the bankruptcy dividend against the amount of the transfer required to be disgorged. *See* Page v. Rogers, 211 U.S. 575, 581 (1908).

1431. 261 U.S. 453 (1923).

1432. *See id.* at 456. Technically, the Court allowed the bank's unsecured claim in the amount above security, but precluded the trustee from paying dividends on the claim until the bank disgorged postpetition deposits owed to the trustee.

1433. 204 U.S. 96 (1907).

1434. *See id.* at 102.

1435. *See id.*

1436. *See id.*

Associates Ltd. Partnership.[1437] In *Pioneer*, a creditor received a timely notice of the claims bar date and gave its file, including the notice, to its attorney who failed to timely file a proof of claim on the creditor's behalf. Relying on Bankruptcy Rule 9006(b)(1),[1438] the Court decided 5-4 that the claim could be late filed. The Court reached its conclusion by balancing the equities based on "excusable neglect," holding that neglect was not limited to filings missed due to intervening circumstances beyond the party's control but included mistake, inadvertence, and carelessness.[1439] Thus, the Court has shown long-term lenience in allowing late-filed proofs of claim.

Another realm in which the Court charitably treated creditors arose in *Page v. Rogers*,[1440] when the Court permitted a preference defendant to net the amount of his anticipated bankruptcy distribution dividend against the amount required to be disgorged as a preference.[1441] The Court premised its decision on the basis of efficiency: "[I]t is entirely practicable to avoid the circuitous proceeding of compelling the defendant to pay into the bankruptcy court the full amount of the preference which he has received, and then to resort to the same court to obtain part of it back by way of dividend."[1442]

1437. 507 U.S. 380 (1993).

1438. Fed. R. Bankr. P. 9006(b)(1) (1993) permits the bankruptcy court to exercise its discretion to enlarge the time within which an act may be done; if the motion to enlarge time is made after the time has expired, the court may "permit the act to be done where the failure to act was the result of excusable neglect."

1439. *See Pioneer*, 507 U.S. at 392.

1440. 211 U.S. 575 (1909).

1441. *See id.* at 581.

1442. *See id.* Presumably the Court was influenced by the advanced stage of the distribution because the bankruptcy court already had entered the final decree in the bankruptcy case. *See id.*

Finally, in *Ivanhoe Building & Loan Ass'n v. Orr*,[1443] the Court clarified that the presence of and realization on third party collateral securing an unsecured claim against the debtor does not diminish a creditor's allowed unsecured claim against the bankruptcy estate.[1444] Of course the creditor is entitled only to a single satisfaction and is not permitted recovery in excess of principal and interest owed.[1445]

Although the Court is inclined to allow creditors holding bona fide claims to participate in a bankruptcy distribution, the Court has not enlarged the universe of claims that is allowable. Even though parties have the freedom of contract to negotiate liquidated damages clauses, in order to be allowed, the amount of the claim must be reasonable and not a penalty. In *Kothe v. R.C. Taylor Trust*,[1446] the Court disallowed a landlord's unreasonably large liquidated damages claim as a penalty on the following rationale:[1447]

> The broad purpose of the Bankruptcy Act is to bring about an equitable distribution of the bankrupt's estate among creditors holding just demands based upon adequate consideration. Any agreement which tends to defeat that beneficent design must be regarded with disfavor.

The parties' freedom to contract did not include a provision designed to give the landlord preferential treatment ahead of the other

---

1443. 295 U.S. 243 (1935), discussed more fully *infra* in Ch. 6, pp. 455-457.

1444. *See Ivanhoe*, 295 U.S. at 245-46. Eleven years later, the Court reaffirmed the vitality of the *Ivanhoe* principle in a § 77 railroad reorganization case. Reconstruction Fin. Corp. v. Denver & R.G.W.R. Co., 328 U.S. 495, 529 (1946). Some lower courts have applied this principle under the Bankruptcy Code where a third party pays the guarantor on an unsecured guarantee. *See, e.g.,* Nat'l Energy & Gas Transmission, Inc. v. Liberty Elec. Power, LLC (*In re* Nat'l Energy & Gas Transmission, Inc.), 492 F.3d 297, 301 (4th Cir. 2007).

1445. *See Ivanhoe*, 295 U.S. at 246.

1446. 280 U.S. 224 (1930).

1447. *See id.* at 227.

unsecured creditors based on the large amount of its liquidated damages claim.[1448]

The Bankruptcy Act and Bankruptcy Code have specialized provisions limiting the allowance of certain claims.[1449] For instance, as a general proposition, both the Bankruptcy Act[1450] and the Bankruptcy Code[1451] disallow claims for postpetition interest on unsecured claims. The Court clarified its position on allowance of claims for postpetition interest in *Nicholas v. United States*[1452] when it held that interest accrues on claims during the period in which the claims are incurred,

---

1448. *See id.* at 226-27.

1449. *See, e.g.,* Bankruptcy Code § 502(b)(6)-(7), 11 U.S.C. § 502(b)(6)-(7) (2000) (limiting certain landlord and employment contract damage claims); Bankruptcy Act §§ 63a(9) *proviso* & 202, 11 U.S.C. §§ 103a(9) *proviso* & 602 (1976) (repealed 1979). *But see* Conn. Ry. & Lighting Co. v. Palmer, 305 U.S. 493, 502 (1939) (rejecting any limitation on landlords' rejection damage claims in railroad reorganization cases under the Act).

1450. Under the Bankruptcy Act, the Court affirmed case law disallowing postpetition interest on unsecured and undersecured claims based on equitable principles. *See, e.g.,* Nicholas v. United States, 384 U.S. 678, 683 (1966) (disallowing postpetition interest on administrative tax claims following a conversion to liquidation because "creditors should not be disadvantaged *vis-a-vis* one another by legal delays attributable solely to the time-consuming procedures inherent in the administration of the bankruptcy laws."); New York v. Saper, 336 U.S. 328, 337-38 (1949) (disallowing the accrual of postpetition interest on unsecured priority tax claims); Vanston Bondholders Protective Comm. v. Green, 329 U.S. 156, 163 (1947) (holding that "an allowance of interest on interest under the circumstances shown by this case would not be in accord with the equitable principles governing bankruptcy distributions"); Sexton v. Dreyfus, 219 U.S. 339, 344-45 (1911) (based on equitable principles, the accumulation of interest on unsecured claims is suspended as of the date of the bankruptcy petition).

1451. *See* 11 U.S.C. § 502(b)(2) (2000) (generally disallowing claims for postpetition interest). *But see* 11 U.S.C. § 726(a)(5) (2000) (allowing postpetition interest on all unsecured claims against a solvent estate).

1452. 384 U.S. 678 (1966).

but not beyond.[1453] Thus, a prepetition unsecured claim accrues post-petition interest until the date of the filing of the petition, a postpetition reorganization or arrangement administrative expense claim accrues interest from the time it is incurred until it is paid or the case is converted, and a postpetition liquidation administrative expense claim accrues interest from the time it is incurred (or allowed) until it is paid.[1454]

Moreover, under both the Bankruptcy Code and Bankruptcy Act, a landlord's claim for damages arising from the rejection of a prepetition unexpired real property lease is limited.[1455] The limits came about as a result of Congressional action[1456] responding to two Supreme Court cases with opposite financial outcomes. In the first, *Manhattan Properties, Inc. v. Irving Trust Co.*,[1457] the Court disallowed a landlord's rejection damage claim based on Congress' "failure to include [within the section] a provision for claims for loss of rent, or for damages consequent on the abrogation of leases."[1458] In the second, *Irving Trust Co. v. A.W. Perry, Inc.*,[1459] the Court upheld the allowance of a landlord's liquidated damage claim measured in the amount of the rent reserved by the lease, even though the lessee's bankruptcy

1453. *See id.* at 686.

1454. *See id.* ("A tax incurred within any one of these three periods would, we think, be entitled to bear interest against the bankrupt estate until, but not beyond, the close of the period in which it was incurred.").

1455. *See* 11 U.S.C. § 502(b)(6) (2000), Bankruptcy Act §§ 63a(9) *proviso* & 202, 11 U.S.C. §§ 103a(9) *proviso* & 602 (1976) (repealed 1979). *But see* Conn. Ry. & Lighting Co. v. Palmer, 305 U.S. 493, 502 (1939) (rejecting any limitation on landlords' rejection damage claims in railroad reorganization cases under the Act).

1456. Congress enacted the *proviso* to Bankruptcy Act § 63a(9) in the Chandler Act, Act of June 22, 1938, Pub. L. No. 696, 75th Cong., 3d Sess., ch. 575, 52 Stat. 840, 873 (repealed 1979).

1457. 291 U.S. 320 (1934).

1458. *See id.* at 335.

1459. 293 U.S. 307 (1934).

was, ipso facto, the default that terminated the lease and triggered the liquidated damages clause.[1460] The Court reasoned that the claim in *Perry* was not for the rent reserved by the lease, but based on a separate express contract for liquidated damages.[1461]

Neither the Bankruptcy Act nor the Bankruptcy Code contains a bright-line rule requiring the disallowance or subordination of claims held by insiders of a debtor such as officers and directors. To be sure, corporate fiduciaries might be held to a higher standard to demonstrate good faith and fair dealing in the acquisition of their claims, and the court should disallow insider claims that are not fair and equitable to other creditors.[1462] But the Court has refused to hold insiders to the standard of a trustee of a true trust whereby the trustee can make no profit from his trust.[1463] The Court has held that when insiders purchase claims at a discount either prepetition or postpetition, the claims will be allowed in full in the absence of unfair dealing, bad faith, misrepresentation, deception, the use of inside information, or unjust enrichment,[1464] at least if the debtor is a going concern, though technically insolvent, at the time of purchase.[1465]

The Court has decided several cases regarding the allowance of creditors' claims for attorneys' fees. If the creditor incurs attorneys' fees prepetition with respect to the debt, they are included as part of

---

1460. *See id.* at 310-11.

1461. *See id.* at 311.

1462. *See* Pepper v. Litton, 308 U.S. 295, 304-07 (1939).

1463. *See* Mfrs. Trust Co. v. Becker, 338 U.S. 304, 311-12 (1949) (refusing to apply the true trust standard of Magruder v. Drury, 235 U.S. 106 (1914), to insiders in a reorganization case).

1464. *See Mfrs. Trust Co. v. Becker* at 310-11 (Chapter XI Arrangement case in which the Court discusses the acquisition of claims by relatives and an office associate of a director of the debtor).

1465. *See id.* at 313-14 (leaving unanswered whether insiders claims will be disallowed if acquired after judicial insolvency proceedings for the debtor are expected or have begun).

the creditor's allowed claim to the extent allowable under applicable nonbankruptcy law.[1466] With respect to claims for postpetition attorneys' fees, however, a different rule may apply. Early on, in *Randolph v. Scruggs*,[1467] the Court held that an assignee for the benefit of creditors could not recover attorneys fees against the estate for services rendered postpetition.[1468] When the creditor is oversecured, however, the Court has reached a different result. In *Security Mortgage Co. v. Powers*,[1469] the Court held that under the terms of a note secured by a lien on property of the debtor, an oversecured creditor could credit bid at a sale of the property to recover attorneys fees for services rendered postpetition in collection of the debt.[1470] Section 506(b) of the Bankruptcy Code limits this holding by statute to require the fees to be reasonable. If the creditor is unsecured, however, it is unclear whether the Court will allow an unsecured claim for attorneys fees that is contingent as of the time of the filing of the petition when services are rendered postpetition. In *Travelers Casualty & Surety Co. of America v. Pacific Gas & Electric Co.*,[1471] the Court overturned the *Fobian* rule[1472] that generally disallowed an

---

1466. *See, e.g.,* Cohen v. de la Cruz, 523 U.S. 213, 223 (1998) (holding that prepetition attorneys fees associated with a nondischargeable debt are also nondischargeable); Sec. Mortgage Co. v. Powers, 278 U.S. 149, 154 (1928) (holding that property of the estate was encumbered by a creditor's lien for prepetition attorneys' fees valid under state law).

1467. Randolph v. Scruggs, 190 U.S. 533 (1903).

1468. *See id.* at 539.

1469. 278 U.S. 149 (1928).

1470. *See id.* at 156-57.

1471. 549 U.S. 443 (2007).

1472. In Fobian v. Western Farm Credit Bank (*In re* Fobian), 951 F.2d 1149, 1153 (9th Cir. 1991), the Ninth Circuit held that when an unsecured creditor incurs postpetition attorneys fees and the litigated issues involve not basic contract enforcement questions, but issues peculiar to federal bankruptcy law, attorney's fees generally will not be awarded.

unsecured creditor's claim for attorneys fees from bankruptcy related litigation.[1473] By the same token, the Court left open whether section 506(b) or some other section of the Bankruptcy Code could be used to disallow the claim for fees.[1474] Moreover, the Court failed to discuss its previous holding in *Randolph v. Scruggs* disallowing such a claim. Presumably courts deciding this issue on the merits will follow *Randolph v. Scruggs* and disallow claims of unsecured creditors for postpetition attorneys fees.[1475]

Secured Claims

The allowance of secured claims presents special issues in bankruptcy. Under both the Bankruptcy Act[1476] and the Bankruptcy Code,[1477] a claim is treated as a secured claim if it is secured by a lien[1478] encumbering property of the estate.[1479] If the claim is secured only by collateral owned by a third party, it is not a secured claim against the estate.[1480]

1473. *See* Travelers Cas. & Sur. Co. of Am. v. Pac. Gas & Elect. Co., 549 U.S. 443, 127 S. Ct. 1199, 1206 (2007).

1474. *See id.* at 1207-08.

1475. *See, e.g., In re* WCS Enters., Inc., 381 B.R. 206, 209-10 (Bankr. E.D. Va. 2007).

1476. *See* Bankruptcy Act §§ 1(28) & 57h, 11 U.S.C. §§ 1(28), 93h (1976) (repealed 1979).

1477. *See* Bankruptcy Code § 506(a), 11 U.S.C. § 506(a) (2000).

1478. A "lien" is a charge against or an interest in property to secure the payment of a debt or the performance of an obligation. *See* Bankruptcy Code § 101(37), 11 U.S.C. § 101(37) (2000).

1479. Under the Bankruptcy Act, the claim was also treated as secured if it was backed by a surety of the bankrupt whose reimbursement claim was secured by a lien on property of the estate. *See* Bankruptcy Act § 1(28), 11 U.S.C. § 1(28) (1976) (repealed 1979).

1480. *See* Ivanhoe Bldg. & Loan Ass'n v. Orr, 295 U.S. 243, 245-46 (1935) (holding that a creditor with a claim secured by a lien only encumbering third party property is an unsecured creditor holding no allowed secured

A creditor's valid, perfected, and unavoidable lien[1481] interest is a property right that is respected under both the Bankruptcy Act and the Bankruptcy Code.[1482] This property right may give the creditor the ability to recover kinds of liabilities that ordinarily are not recoverable by unsecured creditors.[1483] For instance, in *United States v. Ron Pair Enterprises, Inc.*,[1484] the Court held that under Bankruptcy Code § 506(b), an oversecured creditor holding a statutory lien could recover postpetition interest out of its collateral.[1485] A few years later, the Court clarified that federal bankruptcy law may permit an oversecured creditor to accrue postpetition interest on its claim whether or not the creditor would be entitled to interest on such claim under

---

claim against the bankruptcy estate), discussed more fully in Ch. 6, pp. 455-457.

1481. If the lien is avoided, the creditor's claim will no longer be treated as secured and the trustee may be able to recover amounts paid to the creditor prepetition. *See, e.g.,* Benedict v. Ratner, 268 U.S. 353, 364-65 (1925).

1482. In Butner v. United States, 440 U.S. 48, 55 (1979), the Court held that unless some federal interest requires a different result, the bankruptcy court must respect property interests established under state law. Likewise, in Sec. Mortgage Co. v. Powers, 278 U.S. 149, 156-57 (1928), the Court held that the property rights existing before bankruptcy in persons other than the debtor had to be recognized and respected in bankruptcy.

1483. For example, creditors holding allowed secured claims may recover reasonable fees, costs, or charges provided under an agreement, typically a security agreement, and postpetition interest whether or not there is a security agreement. *See* 11 U.S.C. § 506(b) (2000). It is unclear whether creditors holding unsecured claims also have allowed claims for postpetition attorneys fees. *Compare* Travelers Cas. & Sur. Co. of Am. v. Pac. Gas & Elect. Co., 549 U.S. 443, 127 S. Ct. 1199, 1206 (2007) (reversing disallowance of claim for postpetition fees under *Fobian* rule) with Randolph v. Scruggs, 190 U.S. 533, 539 (1903) (no allowed claim for postpetition fees not beneficial to the estate).

1484. 489 U.S. 235 (1989).

1485. *See id.* at 241.

state law.[1486] This holding followed case law under the Bankruptcy Act which held that the allowance of interest in a federal bankruptcy case is a matter of federal law, not state law.[1487] But unlike Bankruptcy Act cases such as *Vanston Bondholders Protective Committee v. Green*,[1488] which determined the allowance of interest in bankruptcy cases based on general equitable principles,[1489] Bankruptcy Code § 506(b) makes the issue one of statutory interpretation in Bankruptcy Code cases.[1490]

In some cases, the trustee will incur costs to preserve the secured party's collateral. If so, Bankruptcy Code § 506(c)[1491] allows the trustee to surcharge the secured party's collateral to recoup administrative expenses of preservation.[1492] In *Hartford Underwriters Insurance Co. v. Union Planters Bank, N.A.*,[1493] the Court held that the Bankruptcy Code limited to the trustee the right to assert the surcharge power and

---

1486. *See* Rake v. Wade, 508 U.S. 464, 471-72 (1993) (holding that Bankruptcy Code § 506(b) requires accrual of postpetition interest on the claim of an oversecured creditor notwithstanding contrary state law).

1487. *See* Vanston Bondholders Protective Comm. v. Green, 329 U.S. 156, 163 (1947) ("When and under what circumstances federal courts will allow interest on claims against debtors' estates being administered by them has long been decided by federal law.").

1488. *Id.*

1489. *See id.* at 162-63 (applying equitable principles disallowing postpetition interest on interest to holders of mortgage bonds).

1490. *See* United States v. Ron Pair Enters., Inc., 489 U.S. 235, 241 (1989).

1491. 11 U.S.C. § 506(c) (2000).

1492. The same principle applied in cases under the Bankruptcy Act. *See, e.g.,* Adair v. Bank of Am. Nat'l Trust & Sav. Ass'n, 303 U.S. 350, 360-61 (1938).

1493. Hartford Underwriters Ins. Co. v. Union Planters Bank, N.A., 530 U.S. 1 (2000).

forbade a third party administrative claimant from moving to surcharge the collateral.[1494]

Bankruptcy Code § 506(d)[1495] ostensibly permits the trustee to avoid a secured creditor's lien to the extent the lien does not secure an allowed claim. Thus, if the claim is disallowed under section 502(b), the lien can be avoided in most circumstances. In *Dewsnup v. Timm*,[1496] however, the Court considered whether a chapter 7 individual debtor could use Bankruptcy Code § 506(d) to strip an undersecured real property lien down to the judicially-determined value of the collateral.[1497] Bankruptcy Code § 506(a)[1498] bifurcates an undersecured recourse claim into an allowed claim equal to the value of the collateral and an unsecured claim for the deficiency. Thus, a claim is an allowed secured claim only to the extent of the value of the collateral. Despite the plain language of Bankruptcy Code § 506(a) and (d), however, the Court forbade a chapter 7 individual debtor from using Bankruptcy Code § 506(d) to strip liens securing claims of undersecured creditors.[1499] In doing so, the Court found the statutory

---

1494. *See id.* at 14. The Court noted that § 506(c) was based on Bankruptcy Act "cases establishing an equitable principle that where a court has custody of property, costs of administering and preserving the property are a dominant charge . . . ." *Id.* at 9 (citations omitted). In this case, however, pre-Code practice did not serve as a basis to clarify the plain language of the Bankruptcy Code limiting to the trustee the power to surcharge. *See id.* at 11.

1495. 11 U.S.C. § 506(d) (Supp. 1992) ("(d) To the extent that a lien secures a claim against the debtor that is not an allowed secured claim, such lien is void . . . .") (exceptions omitted)).

1496. 502 U.S. 410 (1992).

1497. *id.* at 411.

1498. 11 U.S.C. § 506(a) (Supp. 1992) ("(a) An allowed claim of a creditor secured by a lien on property in which the estate has an interest . . . is a secured claim to the extent of the value of [the collateral], and is an unsecured claim to the extent that the value of [the collateral] is less than the amount of such allowed claim. . . .").

1499. *See id.* at 417.

language to be ambiguous.[1500] Instead of reading § 506 (a) and (d) together, the Court instead embraced the secured creditor's position that subsection (d) could be construed without regard to subsection (a):[1501]

> [T]he words "allowed secured claim" in § 506(d) need not be read as an indivisible term of art defined by reference to § 506(a), which by its terms is not a definitional provision. Rather, the words should be read term-by-term to refer to any claim that is, first, allowed, and, second, secured. Because there is no question that the claim at issue here has been "allowed" pursuant to § 502 of the Code and is secured by a lien with recourse to the underlying collateral, it does not come within the scope of § 506(d), which voids only liens corresponding to claims that have *not* been allowed and secured.

Priorities and Distributions in Bankruptcy[1502]

"[F]ederal bankruptcy law, not state law, governs the distribution of a bankrupt's assets to his creditors."[1503] As a matter of federal bankruptcy law, the Court has long recognized that bankruptcy claim priorities must be "tightly construed."[1504] Thus, for the most part, the

---

1500. *See id.*

1501. *See id.* at 415. As noted in Ch. 1, nn.118-119 and accompanying text, Justice Scalia authored a scathing dissent attacking the Court's statutory interpretation. *See* Dewsnup v. Timm, 502 U.S. 410, 420-36 (1992) (Scalia, J., dissenting).

1502. The Court has noted that bankruptcy priorities do not apply outside of bankruptcy in state court or non-bankruptcy proceedings. *See* United States v. Emory, 314 U.S. 423, 426 (1941).

1503. *See* Am. Sur. Co. v. Sampsell, 327 U.S. 269, 272 (1946); Prudence Realization Corp. v. Geist, 316 U.S. 89, 95 (1942).

1504. *See, e.g.,* Howard Delivery Serv., Inc. v. Zurich Am. Ins. Co., 547 U.S. 651, 667, 669 (2006). *See also id.* at 655 (2006) ("[W]e are mindful that the Bankruptcy Code aims, in the main, to secure equal distribution among creditors." (citations omitted); United States v. Embassy Rest., Inc., 359 U.S. 29, 31 (1959); Nathanson v. N.L.R.B., 344 U.S. 25, 29 (1952); Sampsell v. Imperial Paper & Color Corp., 313 U.S. 215, 219 (1941); Kothe v. R.C. Taylor Trust, 280 U.S. 224, 227 (1930).

Court has rejected creditors' attempts to assert priority status outside the express terms of the statute. As originally enacted, Bankruptcy Act § 64 contained a general catchall granting priority to "debts owing to any person who by the laws of the States or the United States is entitled to priority."[1505] Nevertheless, in *Davis v. Pringle*,[1506] the Court refused to interpret the term "person" in § 64 to include the United States.[1507] Therefore the Court held that the general priority of the United States under Revised Statute § 3466[1508] would not be recognized in bankruptcy cases.[1509] It took Congress only one year to overturn the Court's decision by amending the Bankruptcy Act to define the term "person" to include the United States.[1510] Not surprisingly, the

---

1505. Bankruptcy Act § 64b(5), 11 U.S.C. § 104b(5) (1898) (repealed 1979).

1506. 268 U.S. 315 (1925).

1507. *See id.* at 317-18. ("It is incredible that after the conspicuous mention of the United States in the first place at the beginning of the section and the grant of a limited priority, Congress should have intended to smuggle in a general preference by muffled words at the end.").

1508. In one form or other, Rev. Stat. § 3466 has existed almost from the founding of the Republic. The Act of July 31, 1789, § 21, ch. 5, 1 Stat. 29, 42, first gave the United States priority but was limited to debts due on bonds for duties. The Act of May 2, 1792, § 18, ch. 27, 1 Stat. 259, 263, allowed sureties who paid their debts to the United States to exercise the priority. The Act of March 3, 1797, § 5, ch. 20, 1 Stat. 512, 515, extended the priority to all debts due to the United States from any person. The Act of March 2, 1799, § 65, ch. 22, 1 Stat. 627, 676, applied to bonds for duties. Rev. Stat. § 3466 is derived from the Acts of 1797 and 1799. Before it was amended in 1978, § 191 of title 31, the successor to Rev. Stat. § 3466, provided that when a debtor was insolvent, the debts owing to the United States must be paid first. *See* 31 U.S.C. § 191 (1927) & Rev. Stat. § 3466 (1878). A 1982 amendment relocated the provision to § 3713 of title 31 where it remains today. *See* Pub. L. No. 97-258, 96 Stat. 877 (Sept. 13, 1982), enacting 31 U.S.C. § 3713; 31 U.S.C. § 3713 (2000).

1509. *See Davis v. Pringle*, 268 U.S. at 318.

1510. *See* Pub. L. No. 69-301, chs. 405-406, § 15, 44 Stat. 662, 667 (May 27, 1926). Over 50 years later, the 1978 Bankruptcy Code amended the successor to Rev. Stat. § 3466 to make it inapplicable in bankruptcy cases. *See* Pub. L. No. 95-595, § 322(a), 92 Stat. 2549, 2678 (Nov. 6, 1978).

next time the Court considered the term in *Lincoln v. Ricketts*,[1511] it noted the amendment to the Bankruptcy Act[1512] and adopted a more expansive interpretation, holding the term "person" to include a municipal corporation for purposes of bankruptcy priority.[1513] In *Nathanson v. National Labor Relations Board*,[1514] however, the Court once again narrowly construed the amended Bankruptcy Act and Revised Statute § 3466 to deny priority to a back-pay award claim asserted by the N.L.R.B. against the debtor.[1515] The Court reasoned that even though the debt was owed to an agency of the United States, the debt was not entitled to priority status because it was incurred for the benefit of private laborers rather than to secure adequate revenue to sustain public burdens.[1516]

Section 64 of the Bankruptcy Act also contains a priority for "wages and commissions . . . due to workmen . . . ."[1517] In *United States v. Embassy Restaurant, Inc.*,[1518] the Court pointed out that "The broad purpose of the Bankruptcy Act is to bring about an equitable

---

The priority remains applicable when the debtor is insolvent outside of a bankruptcy case, such as when the debtor makes a general assignment for the benefit of creditors. *See* United States v. Moore, 423 U.S. 77, 85-86 (1975) (granting priority to claim of the United States that was unliquidated at the time of the general assignment for the benefit of creditors).

1511. 297 U.S. 373 (1936).

1512. *See id.* at 376-77 (distinguishing Davis v. Pringle based on the 1926 Amendment to Bankruptcy Act § 64).

1513. *See id.* at 374-75. Moreover, in Small Bus. Admin. v. McClellan, 364 U.S. 446, 451-52 (1960), the Court held that the Small Business Administration was an agency of the United States entitled to the priority both for debts it originated and for those it acquired by assignment.

1514. 344 U.S. 25 (1952).

1515. *See id.* at 27-29.

1516. *See id.*

1517. *See* Bankruptcy Act § 64a(2), 11 U.S.C. § 104a(2) (1976) (repealed 1979).

1518. 359 U.S. 29 (1959).

distribution of the bankrupt's estate. . . ." and that "if one claimant is to be preferred over others, the purpose should be clear from the statute."[1519] These principles led the Court to narrowly construe the Bankruptcy Act to deny priority status to plan trustees' collectively bargained claims for contributions to employee benefit plans because the claims were not due to workmen or in the nature of wages.[1520] The Court rejected the union's policy arguments, noting that the Court deals with interpretation of a statute, not a business practice.[1521] In 1968, the Court decided *Joint Industry Board of Electrical Industry v. United States*[1522] reaffirming its *Embassy Restaurant* position by denying priority status to claims for unpaid contributions to an employees' annuity plan.[1523] In 1978, however, Congress changed the result in *Embassy Restaurant* and *Joint Industry Board* by enacting as part of the Bankruptcy Code, a limited priority for contributions to employee benefit plans.[1524]

As noted in Chapter 2,[1525] some of the Court's priority decisions resolve claims for priority asserted by taxing authorities. In *Otte v. United States*,[1526] the Court decided that under the Bankruptcy Act, when a bankruptcy trustee pays priority wage claims, the withholding

---

1519. *See id.* at 31 (citations omitted).

1520. *See id.* at 33.

1521. *See id.*

1522. 391 U.S. 224 (1968).

1523. *See id.* at 226-28.

1524. *See* Pub. L. No. 95-598, enacting 11 U.S.C. § 507(a)(4), 92 Stat. 2549, 2584 (Nov. 6, 1978); H.R. REP. NO. 595, 95th Cong., 1st Sess., 357 (1977) (noting that the enactment of Bankruptcy Code § 507(a)(4) overrules *Embassy Restaurant*). Currently the limited priority for employee benefit plans is found in Bankruptcy Code § 507(a)(5), 11 U.S.C. § 507(a)(5) (Supp. 2005).

1525. For a more thorough discussion of the Court's tax priority decisions, *see supra* Ch. 2, pp. 107-115.

1526. 419 U.S. 43 (1974).

taxes due on those wages are entitled to second priority, the same as the wages.[1527] Writing for the Court, Justice Douglas reasoned that the withholding taxes were not fourth-priority tax claims because they were not incurred by the bankrupt prepetition.[1528] The Court also refused to grant the withholding tax claims a first priority as an administrative expense, because "more than a general observation that the taxes arose during bankruptcy is required to dignify withholding taxes with the prime status of first priority."[1529] Surprisingly, the Court stated that withholding taxes "do not strike us as costs or expenses of doing business."[1530] Moreover, the Court found it anomalous that the withholding taxes could be accorded a higher priority than the wage claims that gave rise to the taxes.[1531] Thus, the Court reasoned that second priority was the appropriate priority for the taxes, because the payment of the second-priority wage claims gave rise to the tax obligation.[1532]

In *United States v. Kaufman*,[1533] the Internal Revenue Service asserted a priority claim for taxes owed by individual partners in the bankruptcy of their partnership.[1534] The Court narrowly construed the tax priority in Bankruptcy Act § 64a to only grant priority to taxes owed by the partnership rather than its partners.[1535] In deciding

---

1527. *See id.* at 57-58.

1528. *See id.* at 56.

1529. *See id.* at 56-57.

1530. *See id.* at 57.

1531. *See id.*

1532. *See id.* at 57-58.

1533. 267 U.S. 408 (1925).

1534. *See id.* at 409-10.

1535. *See id.* at 411. The result might be different under Bankruptcy Code § 507(a)(8) (2000) based on different statutory language and the repeal of the so-called jingle rule in Bankruptcy Act § 5f. *See* 11 U.S.C. § 23f (1976) (repealed 1979). For a more thorough discussion of the jingle rule, *see supra* Ch. 2, pp. 111-112 & n.534.

whether the tax priority applies, the Court must first answer the federal question whether the claim is for a tax.[1536] Thus, in *City of New York v. Feiring*,[1537] the Court held that a New York City sales tax was a tax because the debtor-seller was not simply a tax collector from the buyer, but a party from whom the City could collect the tax involuntarily.[1538] As such, the City held a tax claim for which it could assert priority.[1539] The Court applied similar reasoning, in *United States v. New York*,[1540] to confer tax status to a claim of the United States for unpaid social security and excise taxes, because the debtor-employer was liable for amounts that it was required to collect from its employees.[1541]

Under the Bankruptcy Code, the Court has continued to wrestle with priority tax claims. In *Young v. United States*,[1542] the Court held that the three-year lookback period for unsecured priority tax claims in Bankruptcy Code § 507(a)(8)(A)(i)[1543] is a limitation period that required the Court to equitably toll the lookback period during the pendency of a previous bankruptcy case.[1544] Accordingly when the debtor filed a chapter 7 bankruptcy case after dismissal of a chapter 13 case, the Court added the duration of the previous chapter 13 case

---

1536. *See* City of New York v. Feiring, 313 U.S. 283, 285 (1941).

1537. 313 U.S. 283 (1941).

1538. *See id.* at 285-88.

1539. *See id.* at 288.

1540. 315 U.S. 510 (1942).

1541. *See id.* at 515.

1542. 535 U.S. 43 (2002).

1543. 11 U.S.C. § 507(a)(8)(A)(i) (2000).

1544. *See Young*, 535 U.S. at 54.

to the three-year reachback period for the purpose of determining priority tax claim and nondischargeability status.[1545]

More recently, the Court denied priority status to claims for unpaid workers compensation premiums as falling outside the Bankruptcy Code's priority for claims for contributions to employee benefit plans.[1546] The Court reasoned that since the statute was unclear whether workers compensation premiums fell within the priority for claims for contributions to employee benefit plans, the policy of narrowly construing priorities[1547] and furthering the equality of distribution among creditors would prevail and priority was denied.[1548] This was particularly true because, unlike the wage and benefit priority which provided exclusive benefit to employees, the workers compensation premiums provided benefit to *employers* by limiting their tort liability and was entitled to general unsecured claim treatment similar to other liability insurance premiums.[1549]

Nevertheless, once the Court decides that a claim is entitled to priority, it is the character of the claim and not the status of the claim holder that determines priority status. In *Shropshire, Woodliff & Co.*

1545. *See id.* at 47 ("The three-year lookback period is a limitations period subject to traditional principles of equitable tolling. Since nothing in the Bankruptcy Code precludes equitable tolling of the lookback period, we believe the courts below properly excluded from the three-year limitation the period during which the Youngs' Chapter 13 petition was pending.").

1546. *See* Howard Delivery Serv., Inc. v. Zurich Am. Ins. Co., 547 U.S. 651, 669 (2006) ("Unless and until Congress otherwise directs, we hold that [insurance] carriers' claims for unpaid workers' compensation premiums remain outside the priority allowed by § 507(a)(5).").

1547. This policy is reinforced in the context of a tax priority claim based on the Court's parallel policy that "[w]here there is a reasonable doubt as to the meaning of a taxing Act, it should be construed most favorably to the taxpayer." *See, e.g.,* White v. Aronson, 302 U.S. 16, 20 (1937) (citation omitted).

1548. *See Howard Delivery*, 547 U.S. at 655, 667-69.

1549. *See id.* at 662-63.

v. Bush,[1550] the Court held, based on the plain language of the statute, that an assignee of a wage claim was entitled to assert priority status even though the assignee was not a laborer.[1551] Likewise, in *Bramwell v. United States Fidelity & Guaranty Co.*,[1552] the Court applied the law of assignment and granted priority under Revised Statute § 3466 to a surety who had guaranteed a debt owed to the United States.[1553]

Bankruptcy law fixes the right to priority status as of the date of the filing of the bankruptcy petition.[1554] In *United States v. Marxen*,[1555] the Court held that the general priority of the United States under

---

1550. 204 U.S. 186 (1907).

1551. *See id.* at 188-89 (holding that under Bankruptcy Act § 64, the right of prior payment is attached to the claim of the wage earner rather than the person).

1552. 269 U.S. 483 (1926).

1553. *See id.* at 490 (applying priority for the benefit of the surety in the insolvency of a bank not subject to the Bankruptcy Act: "There is nothing in the language of [Rev. Stat. § 3466], and no reason has been suggested, to indicate a purpose to give priority in the case of a debt due the United States from a debtor subject to the Bankruptcy Act and to deny priority, under like circumstances, when the debt is due from an insolvent bank or other debtor to whom the Act does not apply.").

1554. The status of a lien against property is also fixed as of the date of the filing of the bankruptcy petition. *See, e.g.,* Goggin v. Div. of Labor Law Enforcement of Cal., 336 U.S. 118, 130 (1949) (holding that priority of claimant's tax lien determined at the time of the filing of the petition); Sec. Mortgage Co. v. Powers, 278 U.S. 149, 156 (1928) (holding that property of the estate was encumbered at the time of the filing of the bankruptcy petition by a creditor's lien for prepetition attorneys' fees valid under state law); Lazarus, Michel & Lazarus v. Prentice, 234 U.S. 263, 269 (1914) (dismissing appeal on the basis that rights in property fixed as of the time of filing and attorneys could not obtain lien for prepetition attorneys' fees by proceeding outside of bankruptcy court postpetition).

1555. 307 U.S. 200 (1939).

Revised Statute § 3466[1556] and Bankruptcy Act § 64 does not apply when the United States acquires a claim postpetition, because the rights of creditors are fixed as of the date of the filing of the bankruptcy petition.[1557]

Subordination[1558]

The Bankruptcy Code contains several provisions subordinating claims. Some provisions subordinate claims to specific other claims. For instance, Bankruptcy Code § 509(c) subordinates the claim of a surety to the claim of the principal creditor until the principal's claim is paid in full.[1559] Section 510(b) subordinates a securities rescission claim to all claims that are senior or equal to the claim represented by the security.[1560] And patterned on the provisions in Bankruptcy Act

---

1556. Before it was amended in 1978, § 191 of title 31, the successor to Rev. Stat. § 3466, provided that when a debtor was insolvent, the debts owing to the United States must be paid first. *See* 31 U.S.C. § 191 (1927) & Rev. Stat. § 3466 (1878) as amended by Pub. L. No. 95-598, § 322(a), 92 Stat. 2549, 2678 (Nov. 6, 1978). A 1982 amendment relocated the provision to § 3713 of title 31 where it remains today but is not applicable in bankruptcy cases. *See* Pub. L. No. 97-258, 96 Stat. 877 (Sept. 13, 1982), enacting 31 U.S.C. § 3713; 31 U.S.C. § 3713 (2000).

1557. *See Marxen*, 307 U.S. at 207 ("We are of the view that § 3466 is inapplicable to general claims in bankruptcy transferred to the United States, or to which it has become subrogated on payment, after the filing of the petition, for the reason that the rights of creditors are fixed by the Bankruptcy Act as of the filing of the petition in bankruptcy. This is true both as to the bankrupt and among themselves.").

1558. *See also* the discussion of the bankruptcy court's power to subordinate *supra* in Ch. 4, pp. 226 & 232.

1559. *See* 11 U.S.C. § 509(c) (2000) (subordinating claims for subrogation, reimbursement, or contribution). Under the Bankruptcy Act, the Court reached the same result as a matter of general equitable principles. *See* Am. Sur. Co. v. Sampsell, 327 U.S. 269, 272-73 (1946); Am. Sur. Co. v. Westinghouse Elec. Mfg. Co., 296 U.S. 133, 137-38 (1935).

1560. *See* 11 U.S.C. § 510(b) (2000) (subordinating claims arising from the purchase, sale, or rescission of a security).

§ 67c(3),[1561] Bankruptcy Code § 724(b) subordinates certain claims secured by tax liens[1562] to many kinds of priority claims.[1563]

Other Bankruptcy Code provisions subordinate claims to all general unsecured claims. In a chapter 7 liquidation case, tardily filed claims are subordinated to timely filed claims. Moreover, unlike the Bankruptcy Act, which disallowed penalties or forfeitures owing to any state or the United States,[1564] chapter 7 of the Bankruptcy Code subordinates non-pecuniary loss penalties owing to all kinds of claimants.[1565]

Finally, as discussed more thoroughly in Chapter 4, in cases under the Bankruptcy Act or the Bankruptcy Code, the bankruptcy court has the power to equitably subordinate or equitably disallow claims.

1561. Bankruptcy Act § 67c(3), 11 U.S.C. § 107c(3) (1976) (repealed 1979), provided for the subordination of tax liens on personal property, not accompanied by possession of the taxing agency, to certain priority claims. *Cf.* Goggin v. Div. of Labor Law Enforcement of Cal., 336 U.S. 118, 127 (1949) (upholding priority of claimant's tax lien because it had possession of debtor's personal property at the time of the filing of the petition).

1562. Based on the 2005 amendment to § 724(b), there is no subordination of tax liens securing ad valorem taxes on real or personal property. *See* 11 U.S.C. § 724(b) (Supp. 2005).

1563. *See id.* (excluding from the benefit of subordination administrative expenses, other than wages, salaries, and commissions, incurred in a chapter 11 case before conversion to chapter 7).

1564. *See* Bankruptcy Act § 57j, 11 U.S.C. § 93j (1976) (repealed 1979) & Simonson v. Granquist, 369 U.S. 38, 40 (1962) (disallowing secured governmental penalty claim). Bankruptcy Code § 724(a) modifies the result in *Simonson* by permitting the chapter 7 trustee to avoid a lien that secures a subordinated penalty claim. *See* 11 U.S.C. § 724(a) (2000).

1565. *See* Bankruptcy Code § 726(a)(4), 11 U.S.C. § 726(a)(4) (2000). Neither equitable subordination under Bankruptcy Code § 510(c) nor this provision supports the categorical subordination of penalty claims in chapter 11 reorganization cases. *See* United States v. Reorganized CF&I Fabricators of Utah, Inc., 518 U.S. 213, 228-29 (1996); United States v. Noland, 517 U.S. 535, 543 (1996).

Under the Bankruptcy Act, the bankruptcy court's power to equitably subordinate claims was based on general equitable principles.[1566] In two cases involving the American Surety Company, the Court set forth one principle of equitable subordination derived from the law of suretyship: the claim of a surety will be subordinated to that of its principal until the claim of the principal is paid in full.[1567] In *Taylor v. Standard Gas & Electric Co.*,[1568] the Court established a second principle of equitable subordination derived from breach of fiduciary duty or trust: a parent company's claim against its affiliate will be subordinated when the parent mismanaged the affiliate and harmed its creditors or shareholders.[1569] But, as the Court held in *Comstock v. Group of Institutional Investors*,[1570] if the parent company did not mismanage the affiliate, act in bad faith, or harm the affiliate's creditors, its claim would not be subordinated in the affiliate's bankruptcy case.[1571] Building on its decision in *Comstock*, the Court, in *Manufacturers Trust Co. v. Becker*,[1572] clearly defined a third principle of equitable subordination: insider's claims, including those of corporate fiduciaries, will not be equitably subordinated in the absence of unfair dealing, bad faith, misrepresentation, deception, use of inside

---

1566. *See, e.g.,* Am. Sur. Co. v. Sampsell, 327 U.S. 269, 272-73 (1946); Pepper v. Litton, 308 U.S. 295, 310-11 (1939); Taylor v. Standard Gas & Elec. Co., 306 U.S. 307, 324 (1939); Am. Sur. Co. v. Westinghouse Elec. Mfg. Co., 296 U.S. 133, 137-38 (1935).

1567. *See, e.g.,* Am. Sur. Co. v. Sampsell, 327 U.S. 269, 272-73 (1946); Am. Sur. Co. v. Westinghouse Elec. Mfg. Co., 296 U.S. 133, 137-38 (1935).

1568. 306 U.S. 307 (1939).

1569. *See, e.g., id.* at 324.

1570. 335 U.S. 211 (1948).

1571. *See, e.g., id.* at 228-30 (5-4 decision in § 77 railroad reorganization case holding that parent company's receipt of dividends and borrowings from its affiliate was in good faith and beneficial to affiliate, and, even though parent dominated affiliate, there was no basis to subordinate its claim).

1572. 338 U.S. 304 (1949).

information, or unjust enrichment.[1573] Likewise, in *Pepper v. Litton*,[1574] the Court set forth a basic principle of equitable disallowance: the bankruptcy court may equitably disallow claims under Bankruptcy Act § 57k when allowance of the claims would not be fair and equitable to other creditors.[1575]

Under the Bankruptcy Code, § 502(j) incorporates the substance of Bankruptcy Act § 57k.[1576] But unlike the Bankruptcy Act, Bankruptcy Code § 510(c) codifies the bankruptcy court's power of equitable subordination in a limited manner.[1577] The Court has had occasion to determine circumstances under which a bankruptcy court may equitably subordinate priority claims. In *United States v. Noland*,[1578] the Court held that the bankruptcy court could not categorically subordinate all administrative tax penalty claims.[1579] The Court extended this principle in *United States v. Reorganized CF&I Fabricators of Utah, Inc.*[1580] when it held that the bankruptcy courts also lacked power to categorically subordinate general unsecured

---

1573. *See id.* at 310-11.

1574. 308 U.S. 295 (1939).

1575. *See id.* at 305-06.

1576. *See* 11 U.S.C. § 502(j) (2000).

1577. *See* 11 U.S.C. § 510(c) (2000). Bankruptcy Code § 510(c) only allows subordination of claims to claims and ownership interests to interests, thereby appearing to preclude the result reached in *Taylor v. Standard Gas* where the Court required a reorganization plan to subordinate a claim to preferred stock. *See* Taylor v. Standard Gas & Elec. Co., 306 U.S. 307, 324 (1939).

1578. 517 U.S. 535 (1996).

1579. *See id.* at 543 ("Congress could have, but did not, deny noncompensatory, postpetition tax penalties the first priority given to other administrative expenses, and bankruptcy courts may not take it upon themselves to make that categorical determination under the guise of equitable subordination.").

1580. 518 U.S. 213 (1996).

penalty claims based on the character of the claims alone.[1581] Thus, equitable subordination must be based on the facts and circumstances of each claim rather than the general character or category of the claim. In *Noland*, however, the Court expressly left open "whether a bankruptcy court must always find creditor misconduct before a claim may be equitably subordinated."[1582]

ESTATE ADMINISTRATION: TRUSTEES, RECEIVERS, ADMINISTRATIVE EXPENSES AND COMPENSATION

Trustees and Receivers[1583]

The Court has held bankruptcy estate representatives, such as trustees and receivers, to a negligence standard that requires them to exercise ordinary care in the performance of fiduciary functions. In *United States ex rel. Willoughby v. Howard*,[1584] the Court confronted a fact pattern in which one individual served as trustee or receiver of

---

1581. *See id.* at 229 ("[C]ategorical reordering of priorities that takes place at the legislative level of consideration is beyond the scope of judicial authority to order equitable subordination.").

1582. *See* United States v. Noland, 517 U.S. 535, 543 (1996).

1583. Under the Bankruptcy Code, the bankruptcy court lacks authority to appoint a receiver. *See* 11 U.S.C. § 105(b) (2000). Under Bankruptcy Act § 2a(3), 11 U.S.C. 11a(3) (1976) (repealed 1979), however, the bankruptcy court could appoint a receiver to take possession of the debtor's property pending dismissal of the case or the appointment of a trustee; but the receiver had no authority to transfer the estate's property without a court order. *See* Whitney v. Wenman, 198 U.S. 539, 553 (1905) ("But the receiver had no power or authority under the allegations of this bill to turn over the property. He was appointed a temporary custodian, and it was his duty to hold possession of the property until the termination of the proceedings or the appointment of a trustee for the bankrupt."). The bankruptcy court also could authorize a receiver to operate the debtor's business in straight bankruptcy or a Chapter XI reorganization case. *See* Bankruptcy Act §§ 2a(5) & 343, 11 U.S.C. §§ 11a(5) & 743 (1976) (repealed 1979).

1584. 302 U.S. 445 (1938).

123 bankruptcy estates and deposited estate funds into commercial accounts at a court-qualified depository bank that later became insolvent.[1585] Writing for the Court, Justice Brandeis wrote that "every trustee or receiver of an estate has the duty of exercising reasonable care in the custody of the fiduciary estate."[1586] Although the bankruptcy court circumscribed the exercise of trustee's discretion by designating qualified depository banks into which estate funds could be deposited, it did not relieve the trustee of the duty of ordinary care to make and maintain deposits prudently.[1587] Thus, both the trustee/receiver and the surety that issued the trustee's fidelity bond could be held liable under a simple negligence standard when the bank into which the trustee deposited estate funds became insolvent.[1588] Moreover, as discussed more fully below, the negligence of a trustee or receiver in administering an estate can give rise to an administrative expense claim against the estate.[1589]

Bankruptcy trustees and receivers have specific custodial obligations and duties. Under the Bankruptcy Act, the Court held that a receiver was a temporary custodian who had no power to turn over property to third parties; "it was his duty to hold possession of the property until the termination of the proceedings or the appointment of a trustee for the bankrupt."[1590] In another case under the Act, the

---

1585. *See id.* at 447.

1586. *See id.* at 450.

1587. *See id.* at 451-52.

1588. *See id.* at 454 and Reading Co. v. Brown, 391 U.S. 471 (1968), in which the Court left open and refused to reaffirm dictum in McNulta v. Lochridge, 141 U.S. 327, 332 (1891) that a judgment against a receiver was not personal but could only be collected out of the funds in his hands. *See also Reading Co.*, 391 U.S. at 478 n.7.

1589. *See* Reading Co. v. Brown, 391 U.S. 471, 476, 485 (1968) (holding that damages resulting from the negligence of a Chapter XI receiver acting within the scope of his authority as receiver give rise to an administrative expense claim).

1590. *See* Whitney v. Wenman, 198 U.S. 539, 553 (1905).

Court held that bankruptcy trustees are obligated to file tax returns for taxes incurred by the estate and may be penalized by taxing authorities for failing to do so.[1591] The same result applies in Bankruptcy Code cases.[1592] Moreover, under the Bankruptcy Code, if the debtor confirms a reorganization plan and transfers its assets by assignment into a liquidating trust, the Court has held that the liquidating trustee has an obligation to file tax returns in the same manner and form as the debtor, whether a corporation or individual.[1593] Powers of trustees and receivers, including the avoiding powers, are discussed in other parts of this chapter.

Administrative Expense Claims

Both the Bankruptcy Act and the Bankruptcy Code grant priority for expenses of administration.[1594] Although most of these expenses involve actual benefit to the estate, in order to avoid a moral hazard, the category also includes postpetition tort claims against the representative of the estate. In *Reading Co. v. Brown*,[1595] a court-appointed receiver negligently failed to insure the Chapter XI debtor's leased industrial premises.[1596] When a fire destroyed the premises

---

1591. *See* Nicholas v. United States, 384 U.S. 678, 693-94 (1966) (citing Internal Revenue Code § 6011(a), 26 U.S.C. § 6011(a) (1954) & 28 U.S.C. § 960 (1964) (requiring a trustee who operates a business to pay state taxes)). In 2005, Congress amended § 960 of the Judicial Code to require a trustee conducting business under authority of any United States Court to be subject to all federal, state and local taxes. *See* Act of April 20, 2005, Pub. L. No. 109-8, § 712(a), 119 Stat. 127.

1592. *See id.* and Bankruptcy Code §§ 346(b), (h), & 503(b)(1)(B), 11 U.S.C. §§ 346(b), (h), & 503(b)(1)(B) (Supp. 2005).

1593. *See* Holywell Corp. v. Smith, 503 U.S. 47, 52-53 (1992) (relying on Internal Revenue Code § 6012(b)(3)-(4), 26 U.S.C. § 6012(b)(3)-(4) (1988)).

1594. *See* Bankruptcy Code §§ 503(b) & 507(a)(2), 11 U.S.C. §§ 503(b) & 507(a)(2) (Supp. 2005); Bankruptcy Act § 64a(1), 11 U.S.C. § 104a(1) (1976) (repealed 1979).

1595. 391 U.S. 471 (1968).

1596. *See id.* at 473.

and spread to adjoining property, the owner of the neighboring premises filed an administrative expense claim for damages.[1597] Overruling the bankruptcy trustee's objection to priority status for the claim, the Court held that negligence of a receiver administering an estate under a Chapter XI arrangement gave rise to an actual and necessary cost of operating Debtor's business.[1598] As such, the claim was entitled to priority as an administrative expense under Bankruptcy Act § 64a(1).[1599] Postpetition penalties incurred by the estate provide another category of administrative expense claim that provides no benefit to the estate. In *Boteler v. Ingels*,[1600] the Court held that the state could collect, as an administrative expense, postpetition penalties on vehicle licenses and registrations that were not timely paid by the trustee.[1601]

Compensation in Bankruptcy Cases[1602]

The Court has long recognized that the bankruptcy court has the power to review all professional fees and expenses incurred during the course of bankruptcy administration and exclusive jurisdiction to

---

1597. *See id.* at 474.

1598. *See id.* at 485.

1599. *See id.*

1600. 308 U.S. 57 (1939).

1601. *See id.* at 60-61 (relying on the substance of 28 U.S.C. § 959(b) (1934) as promulgated in the Act of June 18, 1934, ch. 576, 48 Stat. 987. In Palmer v. Webster & Atlas Nat'l Bank of Boston, 312 U.S. 156 (1941), the Court limited the scope of 28 U.S.C. § 959(b) so that where the debtor operates the business of a third party, neither the debtor's receiver nor trustee would be obligated to pay taxes incurred by operation of the underlying business. *See id.* at 163.

1602. Bankruptcy Act § 60d, 11 U.S.C. § 96d (1976) (repealed 1979), and Bankruptcy Code § 329, 11 U.S.C. § 329 (2000) also give the bankruptcy court power to review the reasonableness of debtors' attorneys fees paid by debtors before the filing of the petition in relation to the filing and to disgorge any excessive payments. *See In re* Wood, 210 U.S. 246, 250 (1908).

allow reasonable compensation for services rendered in the bankruptcy case or on behalf of the estate.[1603] Thus, in *Watkins v. Sedberry*,[1604] the Court held that without court approval, the bankruptcy court could not enforce a postpetition contract between a trustee and the trustee's attorney that obligates the estate to pay attorneys' fees.[1605] Moreover, "[t]he amount of attorney's fees to be charged against the estate as an expense of administration is subject to the examination and approval of the court,"[1606] and entering into an invalid attorneys' fee contract does not deprive the trustee's attorney of the right to fair and reasonable compensation allowed by the bankruptcy court.[1607]

A generation later, in *Brown v. Gerdes*,[1608] the Court held that persons seeking compensation for services or reimbursement for expenses are held to a fiduciary standard.[1609] This includes not only counsel for the debtor in possession or trustee, but members of

---

1603. *See, e.g.,* Leiman v. Guttman, 336 U.S. 1, 9 (1949) (bankruptcy court has exclusive jurisdiction to determine stockholders' committee's attorneys' entitlement to fees out of escrow established under contract between the parties, even though property in escrow was not property of the estate); Brown v. Gerdes, 321 U.S. 178, 187-88 (1944) (bankruptcy court has exclusive jurisdiction to allow attorneys' fees as administrative expenses and when attorney for estate sues in state court, the bankruptcy law supersedes conflicting state fee procedures); Woods v. City Nat'l Bank & Trust Co., 312 U.S. 262, 268-69 (1941). *But see* Reconstruction Fin. Corp. v. Bankers Trust Co., 318 U.S. 163, 173-74 (1943) (holding that ICC had exclusive authority to fix maximum fee allowances in § 77 railroad reorganization cases, subject to limited judicial review).

1604. 261 U.S. 571 (1923).

1605. *See id.* at 574-75 (holding postpetition contract for attorneys fees invalid as having been obtained without court approval and without notice to creditors).

1606. *See id.* at 575.

1607. *See id.* at 577.

1608. Brown v. Gerdes, 321 U.S. 178 (1944).

1609. *See id.* at 182.

creditors' committees, protective committees, and indenture trustees as well:[1610]

> A fiduciary who represents security holders in a reorganization may not perfect his claim to compensation by insisting that, although he had conflicting interests, he served his several masters equally well or that his primary loyalty was not weakened by the pull of his secondary one. Only strict adherence to these equitable principles can keep the standard of conduct for fiduciaries "at a level higher than that trodden by the crowd."

Thus, if fiduciary insiders of the debtor trade in the debtor's stock postpetition based on insider information, they can be denied all postpetition compensation and required to disgorge any amounts paid.[1611]

Nevertheless, the Court has distinguished between standards for allowing or disallowing claims for compensation and reimbursement of expenses. With respect to compensation, the Court has stated that:[1612]

> "[R]easonable compensation for services rendered" necessarily implies loyal and disinterested service in the interest of those for whom the claimant purported to act. Where a claimant, who represented members of the investing public, was serving more than one master or was subject to conflicting interests, he should be denied compensation. It is no answer to say that fraud or unfairness were not shown to have resulted.

On the other hand, even Justice Douglas recognized that ordinarily claims for reimbursement of expenses that have clearly benefited the

---

1610. *See* Woods v. City Nat'l Bank & Trust Co., 312 U.S. 262, 268-69 (1941) (Chapter X business reorganization case) (citation omitted).

1611. *See* Wolf v. Weinstein, 372 U.S. 633, 643 (1963) (Ch. X business reorganization case denying all postpetition compensation to debtor's president and general manager for trading in debtor's stock postpetition while acting as fiduciaries in possession of inside information).

1612. *See Woods*, 312 U.S. at 268 (citations omitted).

estate should be allowed. Speaking for the Court in *Woods v. City National Bank & Trust Co.*, he wrote:[1613]

> Some discrimination, however, is necessary in applying the foregoing rule to claims for expenses. Reimbursement for "proper costs and expenses incurred in connection with the administration" of the estate may be allowed. The rule disallowing compensation because of conflicting interests may be equally effective to bar recovery of the expenditures made by a claimant subject to conflicting interests. Plainly expenditures are not "proper" within the meaning of the Act where the claimant cannot show that they were made in furtherance of a project exclusively devoted to the interests of those whom the claimant purported to represent. On the other hand, those expenditures normally should be allowed which have clearly benefited the estate. Thus, where taxes have been paid, needful repairs or additions to the property have been made, or the like, equity does not permit the estate to retain those benefits without paying for them.

Section 504 of the Bankruptcy Code[1614] sets forth a bright line provision prohibiting splitting of attorneys' fees awarded in bankruptcy cases in most situations. The Court held that this was the policy under the Bankruptcy Act as well, at least when counsel for several creditors signed a contract to take a portion of the fees awarded to the trustee's counsel.[1615]

Section 330 of the Bankruptcy Code authorizes compensation for services rendered by estate representatives be paid as administrative expenses.[1616] This category includes the attorney for the debtor in possession in a chapter 11 case.[1617] Moreover, an attorney for an individual chapter 12 or 13 debtor may be compensated for reasonable

---

1613. *See id.* at 269-70 (citations omitted).

1614. 11 U.S.C. § 504 (2000).

1615. *See* Weil v. Neary, 278 U.S. 160, 173-74 (1929).

1616. *See* 11 U.S.C. § 330(a) (2000).

1617. *See id.* & §§ 327(a) & 1107(b).

attorneys fees under the Bankruptcy Code.[1618] Since 1994, however, based on the Court's strict construction of an amendment to the statute deleting the reference to the debtor's attorney,[1619] counsel for an individual debtor, in a chapter 7 case or in a chapter 11 case when a trustee is serving, is ineligible to receive compensation allowable as an administrative expense under Bankruptcy Code § 330.[1620] Of course, under Bankruptcy Code § 329, such counsel might be able to keep a reasonable prepetition fee or retainer.[1621] Once the bankruptcy petition is filed, however, the bankruptcy court has exclusive jurisdiction to award compensation out of the property of the estate.[1622]

ADMINISTRATIVE POWERS: AUTOMATIC STAY, USE OF COLLATERAL AND OTHER PROPERTY, ABANDONMENT, SALES, FINANCING, EXECUTORY CONTRACTS

Automatic Stay

The Court has decided some important cases concerning the scope of the automatic stay. Although Bankruptcy Act § 11a[1623] provided

---

1618. *See* 11 U.S.C. § 330(a)(4)(B) (2000).

1619. *See* The Bankruptcy Reform Act of 1994, Pub. L. No. 103-394, § 224(b), 108 Stat. 4106, 4130 (Oct. 22, 1994) (amending 11 U.S.C. § 330(a) to delete reference to debtor's attorney).

1620. *See* Lamie v. United States, 540 U.S. 526, 538-39 (2000).

1621. *See* 11 U.S.C. § 329 (2000). Courts will be called on to determine whether, as a matter of state law, the retainer is property of the attorney or property of the bankruptcy estate. Moreover, courts might be required to decide whether a prepetition security retainer may secure an individual chapter 7 debtor's attorney's claim for postpetition services as part of an allowed secured claim even though compensation may not be awarded as an administrative expense.

1622. *See, e.g.,* Gross v. Irving Trust Co., 289 U.S. 342, 344 (1933) (holding that once bankruptcy commenced, a state court lacked jurisdiction to award compensation to receivers it appointed out of the bankrupt's assets in possession of the receivers).

1623. 11 U.S.C. § 29a (1976) (repealed 1979).

that suits founded on dischargeable claims "shall be stayed," in *Connell v. Walker*[1624] the Court interpreted this language not to grant an automatic stay in ordinary bankruptcy cases.[1625] Nevertheless, in *Continental Illinois National Bank & Trust Co. of Chicago v. Chicago, Rock Island & Pacific Railway Co.*,[1626] the Court affirmed the power of a railroad reorganization court to affirmatively enjoin collateral foreclosure.[1627] Likewise, in *Thompson v. Texas Mexican Railway Co.*,[1628] the Court noted that Bankruptcy Act § 77(j)[1629] did not provide an automatic stay in railroad reorganization cases, but the reorganization court could issue stay orders consistent with the statute.[1630] In *Kalb v. Fuerstein*,[1631] however, the Court held that the filing of a Bankruptcy Act § 75[1632] petition by a farmer under the Frazier-Lemke

---

1624. 291 U.S. 1 (1934).

1625. *See id.* at 6 ("[T]he authority given by that section [11a] to stay pending suits after adjudication, which has taken place here, is not mandatory, but permissive, to be exercised in the sound discretion of the court."). From 1973 through 1976, the Supreme Court promulgated Federal Rules of Bankruptcy Procedure providing for an automatic stay in most kinds of bankruptcy cases under the Bankruptcy Act. *See* Bankruptcy Rules 401, 601, & 13-401, 411 U.S. 989 (1973) (effective Oct. 1, 1973) (repealed 1979); Bankruptcy Rule 11-44, 415 U.S. 1003 (1974) (effective July 1, 1974) (repealed 1979); Bankruptcy Rules 10-601 & 12-43, 421 U.S. 1019 (1975) (effective Aug. 1, 1975) (repealed 1979); & Bankruptcy Rules 8-501 & 9-4, 425 U.S. 1004 (1976) (effective Aug. 1, 1976) (repealed 1979).

1626. 294 U.S. 648 (1935).

1627. *See id.* at 666.

1628. 328 U.S. 134 (1946).

1629. 11 U.S.C. § 205(j) (1976) (repealed 1979).

1630. *See Thompson,* 328 U.S. at 138 & n.5.

1631. 308 U.S. 433 (1940).

1632. *See* 11 U.S.C. § 203 (1940) (repealed 1949).

Act automatically stayed all state court actions without any need on the part of the debtor to obtain a federal court order.[1633]

The 1978 Bankruptcy Code codified the automatic stay in § 362,[1634] and applied it in almost all bankruptcy cases.[1635] The automatic stay generally protects the estate and the debtor from the commencement or continuation of suits on prepetition claims and from lien enforcement and setoff.[1636] In *Citizens Bank of Maryland v. Strumpf*,[1637] the Court interpreted the automatic stay in Bankruptcy Code § 362(a)(7)[1638] to apply to the exercise of a right of setoff, but held that a bank's placement of a temporary administrative freeze on a deposit account was not a setoff.[1639] The bank could maintain the temporary administrative freeze and dishonor checks only to the extent it was entitled to seek relief from the automatic stay and to condition the estate's use of cash collateral by the provision of adequate protection.[1640]

1633. *See Kalb* at 441-42. *See also* Bernards v. Johnson, 314 U.S. 19, 32 (1941) (discussing the automatic stay but refusing to analyze it in the § 75 case based on mootness).

1634. 11 U.S.C. § 362 (2000).

1635. From its inception, the automatic stay applied to voluntary petitions, joint petitions, and involuntary petitions filed under Bankruptcy Code §§ 301, 302, and 303 respectively. *See* 11 U.S.C. § 362(a) (2000). The automatic stay also applies in chapter 9 municipality reorganizations. *See* 11 U.S.C. § 901(a) (2000). The automatic stay never applied, however, to § 304 cases ancillary to foreign proceedings or to foreign proceedings under chapter 15 of the Bankruptcy Code. *See* 11 U.S.C. § 362(a) (2000 & Supp. 2005).

1636. *See* 11 U.S.C. § 362(a) (2000).

1637. 516 U.S. 16 (1995).

1638. 11 U.S.C. § 362(a)(7) (2000).

1639. *See Strumpf*, 516 U.S. at 19. The Court also rejected debtor in possession's arguments that the freeze violated the automatic stay under § 362(a)(3) and (a)(6). *See id.* at 21.

1640. *See id.* at 21. The Court raised but did not consider whether the bank would be entitled to freeze the deposit account and dishonor the

The Court also has had occasion to interpret the scope of exceptions to the automatic stay in Bankruptcy Code § 362(b).[1641] In *Midlantic National Bank v. New Jersey Department of Environmental Protection,*[1642] the Court noted in dictum that the automatic stay is "one of the fundamental debtor protections provided by the bankruptcy laws,"[1643] and that the stay is subject to a police or regulatory power exception to protect the public health and safety.[1644] Moreover, in *Board of Governors of the Federal Reserve System v. MCorp Financial, Inc.,*[1645] the Court interpreted the police and regulatory power exception to permit the Board of Governors of the Federal Reserve System to continue administrative proceedings against the debtor charging violations of the Board's Source of Strength regulation and § 23A of the Federal Reserve Act.[1646]

Even when the automatic stay does not apply, the debtor or estate representative may seek an affirmative injunction to protect the estate or the debtor. In *Celotex Corp. v. Edwards,*[1647] the Court held that parties were bound to respect a bankruptcy court injunction pre-

---

trustee's checks if it were oversecured so that honoring the checks would not affect the amount of its allowed secured claim. *See id.* at 19 ("Whether that temporary refusal [freeze] was otherwise wrongful is a separate matter—we do not consider, for example, respondent's contention that the portion of the account subjected to the 'administrative hold' exceeded the amount properly subject to setoff.").

1641. 11 U.S.C. § 362(b) (2000).

1642. 474 U.S. 494 (1986).

1643. *See id.* at 503 (internal quotation marks omitted) citing S. REP. NO. 95-989, 54 (1978); H.R. REP. NO. 95-595, 340 (1977).

1644. *See Midlantic,* 474 U.S. at 503-04. The exception is currently codified in § 362(b)(4), 11 U.S.C. § 362(b)(4) (2000).

1645. 502 U.S. 32 (1991).

1646. *See id.* at 41.

1647. 514 U.S. 300 (1995).

cluding them from proceeding against a supersedeas bond unless and until the injunction was modified or reversed.[1648]

Parties subject to an affirmative injunction or the automatic stay may seek relief. Under Bankruptcy Code § 362(d),[1649] a party with an interest in property of the estate may be entitled to obtain relief from the automatic stay if (1) the party's interest is not adequately protected; or (2) the debtor has no equity in the property and it is not necessary to an effective reorganization. In *United Savings Ass'n v. Timbers of Inwood Forest Associates, Ltd.*,[1650] Justice Scalia, writing for a unanimous Court, interpreted the adequate protection standard not to entitle undersecured creditors to compensation for the delay imposed by the automatic stay. The Court held that the lien of the undersecured creditors was adequately protected, because the creditor's protected interest in property does not include the secured party's right to take immediate possession of the collateral and apply it in payment of the debt.[1651] As a result, as long as the creditor's collateral is not declining in value and is otherwise protected,[1652] the undersecured creditor is not entitled to condition maintenance of the automatic stay on the receipt of postpetition interest or other adequate protection payments.[1653]

1648. *See id.* at 309-10 (holding that the bankruptcy court had jurisdiction to issue the injunction and its order was not a frivolous pretense to validity, because parties proceeding against the surety bond would cripple the debtor's efforts to reorganize and therefore could conceivably have an effect on the estate).

1649. 11 U.S.C. § 362(d) (2000).

1650. 484 U.S. 365 (1988).

1651. *See id.* at 371 ("[T]he 'interest in property' protected by § 362(d)(1) does not include a secured party's right to immediate foreclosure.").

1652. Other forms of protection might include insurance and maintenance of collateral and collateral documentation.

1653. Secured creditors reacted to *Timbers* by bargaining for more security, taking security interests in rents, and requiring subordination agreements from junior creditors, among other responses. *See generally* Edward R. Morrison, "*Timbers of Inwood Forest*, the Economics of Rent,

In influential dictum, the *Timbers* Court also interpreted what Bankruptcy Code § 362(d)(2) means by "not necessary to an effective reorganization":[1654]

> What this requires is not merely a showing that if there is conceivably to be an effective reorganization, this property will be needed for it; but that the property is essential for an effective reorganization *that is in prospect*. This means . . . that there must be "a reasonable possibility of a successful reorganization within a reasonable time."

Use of Collateral and Other Property

The Bankruptcy Code codifies the trustee's right to use collateral in § 363.[1655] The Bankruptcy Act, however, contained no formal statutory provision for the use of collateral,[1656] although it gave the court jurisdiction to control the debtor's property in the best interests of the debtor and its creditors[1657] and authorized the court to permit the trustee or debtor in possession to operate the debtor's business.[1658] Nevertheless, in *Adair v. Bank of America National Trust & Savings*

---

and the Evolving Dynamics of Chapter 11," BANKRUPTCY LAW STORIES 21, 47-49 (Robert K. Rasmussen, ed., Foundation Press 2007) (contending that the *Timbers* holding on adequate protection is unimportant for many lenders who can avoid its impact in many ways).

1654. *See Timbers*, 484 U.S. at 375-76.

1655. *See* 11 U.S.C. § 363 (2000).

1656. The Bankruptcy Act contained provisions authorizing the sale of property, as discussed more fully *infra*, pp. 317-318.

1657. *See, e.g.,* Bankruptcy Act § 75(e) ("[T]he court shall exercise such control over the property of the farmer as the court deems in the best interests of the farmer and his creditors.") & (n) ("The filing of a petition . . . shall subject the farmer and his property, wherever located, . . . to the exclusive jurisdiction of the court."), 11 U.S.C. § 203e & n (Supp. 1936) (expired March 1, 1949; repealed 1979). *See also* Act of April 21, 1948, 62 Stat. 198, ch. 225 & Pub. L. No. 95-598, §§ 401(a) & 402(a) (Nov. 6, 1978).

1658. *See, e.g.,* Bankruptcy Act §§ 189 & 343, 11 U.S.C. §§ 589 & 743 (1976) (repealed 1979).

Ass'n,[1659] the Court upheld the expenditure of proceeds from a mortgaged grape crop to pay for the harvesting of the crop and preserving the next year's crop, noting that this expense was necessary for preservation of the collateral and that the secured creditor benefited from the disbursements.[1660]

Under the Bankruptcy Code, the Court has not ruled directly on the power of a bankruptcy estate representative to use a secured party's collateral, but has clarified circumstances in which the bankruptcy trustee may use a secured party's collateral. In *United States v. Whiting Pools, Inc.,*[1661] the Court explained in broad dicta how Bankruptcy Code § 363 limits the secured party's rights to resist use of its collateral:[1662]

> At the secured creditor's insistence, the bankruptcy court must place such limits or conditions on the trustee's power to sell, use, or lease property as are necessary to protect the creditor. The creditor with a secured interest in property included in the estate must look to this provision for protection, rather than to the nonbankruptcy remedy of possession.

This clarification refines the Court's pronouncement in *Wright v. Vinton Branch of the Mountain Trust Bank,*[1663] that one of the five protected rights of secured creditors is to retain the lien on collateral until the indebtedness is paid.[1664] Indeed, as the Court foreshadowed in *Wright*, a statute might constitutionally modify some of the secured creditor's protected rights, but not all of them.[1665]

1659. 303 U.S. 350 (1938).

1660. *See id.* at 360-61.

1661. 462 U.S. 198 (1983).

1662. *See id.* at 204.

1663. 300 U.S. 440 (1937).

1664. *See id.* at 458.

1665. *See id.* at 457-58.

Abandonment

On its face, Bankruptcy Code § 554(a) gives the bankruptcy trustee an unrestricted right to abandon property of the estate that is burdensome to the estate or of inconsequential value and benefit to the estate.[1666] The same was true as a matter of case law under the Bankruptcy Act.[1667] Indeed, early on in *Brown v. O'Keefe*,[1668] the Court recognized the importance of a bankruptcy trustee's power to abandon burdensome assets.[1669] Abandonment results in property being returned to the debtor, but:[1670]

> that doctrine can have no application when the trustee is ignorant of the existence of the property and has had no opportunity to make an election. It cannot be that a bankrupt, by omitting to schedule and withholding from his trustee all knowledge of certain property, can, after his estate in bankruptcy has been finally closed up, immediately thereafter assert title to the property on the ground that the trustee had never taken any action in respect to it.

Moreover, despite the apparent unrestricted statutory power of the trustee to abandon, in *Midlantic National Bank v. New Jersey*

1666. Bankruptcy Code § 554(a), 11 U.S.C. § 554(a) (2000), provides as follows: "After notice and a hearing, the trustee may abandon any property of the estate that is burdensome to the estate or of inconsequential value and benefit to the estate."

1667. *See, e.g.*, First Nat'l Bank v. Lasater, 196 U.S. 115, 118-19 (1905) ("We have held that trustees in bankruptcy are not bound to accept property of an onerous or unprofitable character, and that they have a reasonable time in which to elect whether they will accept or not.") (dictum).

1668. 300 U.S. 598 (1937).

1669. *See id.* at 602 ("Whatever title or inchoate interest may have passed to the trustee was extinguished by relation as of the filing of the petition when the trustee informed the court that the shares were burdensome assets, and was directed by the court to abandon and disclaim them.").

1670. First Nat'l Bank v. Lasater, 196 U.S. 115, 119 (1905).

Department of Environmental Protection,[1671] the Court stated that "[t]he Bankruptcy Court does not have the power to authorize an abandonment [of toxic property] without formulating conditions that will adequately protect the public's health and safety."[1672] The Court went on to "hold that a trustee may not abandon property in contravention of a state statute or regulation that is reasonably designed to protect the public health or safety from identified hazards."[1673]

Sale of Property

Often the bankruptcy estate representative will want to sell property in which the bankruptcy estate asserts an interest, usually to raise cash or stem losses. Chapter 4 discusses the bankruptcy court's jurisdiction to authorize the sale of property to which the estate has title or possession. Bankruptcy law determines when the court may exercise its jurisdiction to order the sale of property.

Under the Bankruptcy Act, because statutory provisions governing sales of property were so basic,[1674] the courts identified terms and conditions under which the representative of the bankruptcy estate would be authorized to sell property. Thus, in *Van Huffel v. Harkelrode,*[1675] the Court upheld a bankruptcy court procedure enabling the trustee to sell property of the estate free and clear of encumbrances, with the rights of lien holders against the property to be transferred to

---

1671. 474 U.S. 494 (1986).

1672. *See id.* at 506-07.

1673. *See id.* at 507. *But see* Ohio v. Kovacs, 469 U.S. 274, 285 n.12 (1985) ("If the property were worth less than the cost of cleanup, the trustee would likely abandon it to its prior owner, who would have to comply with the state environmental law to the extent of his or its ability.").

1674. *See, e.g.,* Bankruptcy Act §§ 70f, 116(3) & 313(2), 11 U.S.C. § 110f, 516(3) & 713(2) (1976) (repealed 1979). *See also, e.g.,* Bankruptcy Rules 606, 10-607 & 11-54 (1976) (repealed 1979).

1675. 284 U.S. 225 (1931).

the proceeds of sale.[1676] In *Thompson v. Magnolia Petroleum Co.*,[1677] the Court extended this principle, holding that when other parties claimed ownership to property in possession of the debtor, the bankruptcy court could properly authorize the sale of the property with the proceeds to be impounded pending a determination of ownership in state court.[1678]

Financing

The Bankruptcy Act contained provisions authorizing the court to permit the receiver, trustee, or debtor in possession to obtain credit by issuing certificates of indebtedness.[1679] Moreover, Bankruptcy Code § 364 contains a broad authority for postpetition financing.[1680] During the last 111 years, however, the Court has not interpreted these provisions.

Executory Contracts

Executory contracts and unexpired leases present interesting challenges in bankruptcy cases because typically they involve both property interests and contractual obligations or claims.[1681] In 1916 the

---

1676. *See id.* at 227-28.

1677. 309 U.S. 478 (1940).

1678. *See id.* at 482-83.

1679. *See, e.g.,* Bankruptcy Act §§ 116(2) & 344, 11 U.S.C. §§ 516(2) & 744 (1976) (repealed 1979).

1680. *See* 11 U.S.C. § 364 (2000).

1681. *See supra* n.1296 and accompanying text and *infra* nn.1704-1708 and accompanying text, discussing whether and when an executory contract becomes property of the estate, and whether and when the non-debtor party to such a contract holds a claim. *See also* N.L.R.B. v. Bildisco & Bildisco, 465 U.S. 513, 530 (1984) (noting that "rejection of an executory contract which had not been assumed constitutes a breach of the contract which relates back to the date immediately preceding the filing of a petition in bankruptcy"); Cent. Trust Co. v. Chicago Auditorium Ass'n, 240 U.S. 581, 591-92 (1916) (holding that bankruptcy is an

Court held in *Central Trust Co. v. Chicago Auditorium Ass'n*,[1682] that bankruptcy is an anticipatory breach of contract which gives the non-debtor party the option to treat the contract as terminated and to assert a damage claim for anticipatory breach.[1683] In dictum, the Court also noted that although there was a stipulation in the contract precluding assignment of the contract without the consent of the non-debtor party, nevertheless the contract passed to the bankruptcy trustee by operation of law.[1684]

In *Connecticut Railway & Lighting Co. v. Palmer*,[1685] the Court noted that Congress placed leases on the same basis as executory contracts in railroad reorganization cases.[1686] Since then, bankruptcy statutory and case law has used the term "executory contracts" to include unexpired leases.[1687]

---

anticipatory breach of contract and allowing the non-debtor party the option to treat the contract as terminated and to assert a claim for anticipatory breach).

1682. 240 U.S. 581 (1916).

1683. *See id.* at 591-92. The Court noted that the measure of the damage claim was controlled by Roehm v. Horst, 178 U.S. 1, 20-21 (1900), a non-bankruptcy case in which the Court stated that the "plaintiff is entitled to compensation based . . . on the ascertainment of what he would have suffered by the continued breach of the other party down to the time of complete performance, less any abatement by reason of circumstances of which he ought reasonably to have availed himself."

1684. *See Cent. Trust Co.*, 240 U.S. at 590. On the facts of *Chicago Auditorium*, however, the trustee did not elect to assume the contract and so the matter was left as if the trustee did not elect to perform the debtor's obligations under the contract. *See id.*

1685. 305 U.S. 493 (1939).

1686. *See id.* at 502 ("Leases were placed upon the same basis as executory contracts.").

1687. *See, e.g.*, 11 U.S.C. §§ 365 & 1123(b)(2) (2000) (dealing with executory contracts and unexpired leases); Group of Institutional Investors v. Chicago, M., St. P. & Pac. R.R., 318 U.S. 523, 551-52 (1943).

Nevertheless, there are respects in which the Court has treated leases differently from executory contracts in bankruptcy cases. In *Group of Institutional Investors v. Chicago, Milwaukee, St. Paul & Pacific Railroad*,[1688] the Court upheld the provisions in a railroad reorganization plan that deferred the date of lease rejection and damage calculation, even though other damage claims were determined as of the date of the filing of the reorganization petition.[1689] The Court did so after setting forth the now familiar standard that "the question whether a lease should be rejected and, if not, on what terms it should be assumed is one of business judgment."[1690] This pronouncement came after the Court's recognition in *Philadelphia Co. v. Dipple*,[1691] that even though Bankruptcy Act § 77B contained no specific statutory authority for reorganization trustees to reject burdensome leases outside the context of a reorganization plan,[1692] the case law had filled that gap and gave them a reasonable time within which to exercise the rejection right.[1693] Pending the trustees' decision to seek assumption or rejection, the court could "order the trustees to pay a reasonable sum to be treated as payment for use and occupation in the event that the leases are disaffirmed or, on account of rent, in the event they are affirmed."[1694]

1688. 318 U.S. 523 (1943).

1689. *See id.* at 552.

1690. *See id.* at 550. In so holding, the Court left open whether only burdensome leases could be rejected. *Id.*

1691. 312 U.S. 168 (1941).

1692. Bankruptcy Act § 77B(b)(6), Act of June 7, 1934, ch. 424, § 77B(b)(6), 48 Stat. 912, 914, 11 U.S.C. § 207(b)(6) (1934) (superseded in 1938 by Chapter X, 52 Stat. 883, 11 U.S.C. §§ 501 et seq.) (permitting a plan of reorganization to "reject contracts of the debtor which are executory in whole or in part, including unexpired leases except contracts in the public authority[.]").

1693. *See Dipple*, 312 U.S. at 174.

1694. *See id.* (dictum).

In *National Labor Relations Board v. Bildisco & Bildisco*,[1695] the Court considered the application of Bankruptcy Code § 365 to rejection of a collective bargaining agreement in a chapter 11 reorganization case.[1696] The Court made many important holdings, including that a collective bargaining agreement was an executory contract.[1697] Another important *Bildisco* holding concerned the standard to reject a collective bargaining agreement. The N.L.R.B. contended that the standard for a debtor in possession to reject a collective bargaining agreement must be stricter than the business judgment standard.[1698] The Court agreed, but refused to adopt a strict test that would allow rejection only if the reorganization would fail without rejection.[1699] Instead, the Court opted for a middle ground, permitting rejection of a collective bargaining agreement under Bankruptcy Code § 365 "if the debtor [in possession] can show that the collective-bargaining agreement burdens the estate, and that after careful scrutiny, the equities balance in favor of rejecting the labor contract."[1700] In noting the special character of collective bargaining agreements, however, the Court permitted their rejection only if the debtor has: 1) made reasonable efforts to negotiate modifications; 2) the negotiations are not likely to produce a prompt and satisfactory solution; 3) the agreement burdens the estate; 4) the balance of the equities favors rejection; and 5) rejection will permit the successful rehabilitation of the debtor.[1701] These elements formed the basis for the modern test for modification or rejection of collective bargaining

---

1695. 465 U.S. 513 (1984).

1696. *See id.* at 516.

1697. *See id.* at 521-23.

1698. *See id.* at 523-24.

1699. *See id.* at 524-25.

1700. *See id.* at 526.

1701. *See id.* at 526-27.

agreements when Congress, in 1984, superseded *Bildisco* by enacting Bankruptcy Code § 1113.[1702]

The Court considered a second issue in *Bildisco:* whether the debtor in possession's rejection of the collective bargaining agreement constituted an unfair labor practice.[1703] The Court's analysis of this question resulted in several important holdings. First, the Court held that although the chapter 11 debtor in possession was not a "new entity," it is "empowered by virtue of the Bankruptcy Code to deal with its contracts and property in a manner it could not have employed absent the bankruptcy filing."[1704] As such, "the filing of the petition in bankruptcy means that the collective-bargaining agreement is no longer immediately enforceable, and may never be enforceable again."[1705] The *Bildisco* Court also reaffirmed the *Dipple* principles that rejection damages generally are computed as of the date of the filing of the bankruptcy petition,[1706] and that before assumption, the debtor in possession may elect to obtain the benefits of the contract by paying for the reasonable value of the services.[1707] Moreover, the Court noted that if the debtor in possession elects to assume a contract, it does so *cum onere*, with expenses and liabilities incurred treated as administrative expenses.[1708] Thus, even though Bildisco's standard for rejection of a collective bargaining agreement

---

1702. *See* Pub. L. No. 98-353, § 541(a), 98 Stat. 333, 390-91 (July 10, 1984).

1703. *See Bildisco*, 365 U.S. at 527.

1704. *See id.* at 528.

1705. *See id.* at 532.

1706. *See id.* at 530 (noting that "rejection of an executory contract which had not been assumed constitutes a breach of the contract which relates back to the date immediately preceding the filing of a petition in bankruptcy").

1707. *See id.* at 531.

1708. *See id.* at 531-32.

was legislatively superseded,[1709] its insights on executory contract law remain valuable as applied to executory contracts and unexpired leases generally.

AVOIDING POWERS: PREFERENCES, FRAUDULENT TRANSFERS (§§ 548 AND 544(B)), STRONG ARM CLAUSE, POSTPETITION TRANSFERS, SETOFF, OTHERS

Bankruptcy law gives the bankruptcy trustee certain avoiding powers to augment the bankruptcy estate and achieve an equitable distribution.[1710] For the most part, these powers are designed to undo transfers made in the period before bankruptcy,[1711] prevent similarly situated creditors from being treated differently, and prevent the debtor from diminishing assets that otherwise would become property of the estate.[1712] That is, the powers are designed to discourage a race of diligence among creditors, to prevent debtor favoritism among

---

1709. *See* Pub. L. No. 98-353, § 541(a), 98 Stat. 333, 390-91 (July 10, 1984).

1710. *See, e.g.,* Thomas v. Sugarman, 218 U.S. 129, 134 (1910) ("The legal title to the money had been in the bankrupt, and was transferred by the statute to the trustee, [Bankruptcy Act] § 70. . . . The law had put him in the bankrupt's shoes with additional powers.").

1711. The reach back period before bankruptcy differs depending on the avoiding power. For example, under Bankruptcy Code § 547, the trustee may avoid preferences made within 90 days before the date of the filing of the petition or one year, if the transferee is an insider. *See* 11 U.S.C. § 547(b)(4) (2000). Under Bankruptcy Code § 548, the trustee may avoid actual intent or constructive fraudulent transfers made within two years before bankruptcy. *See* 11 U.S.C. § 548(a)(1) (Supp. 2005). Under Bankruptcy Code § 544(b), the trustee may use the rights of an actual creditor holding an allowable unsecured claim to avoid transfers made under the applicable nonbankruptcy reach back period, which may be several years. *See* 11 U.S.C. § 544(b) (2000) &, *e.g.,* Uniform Fraudulent Transfer Act § 9(a)-(b), generally setting forth four year statute of limitations. *See also* n.1856 *infra.*

1712. *See generally* nn.1200-1202 *supra.*

creditors, and to prevent waste or gifting of property.[1713] The trustee or estate representative generally has two years[1714] to avoid the transfer and recover the property transferred or its value[1715] or preserve the transfer for the benefit of the bankruptcy estate.[1716] The trustee must

1713. *See, e.g.,* H.R. REP. NO. 595, 95th Cong., 1st Sess., 177-80 (1977). *But see* 11 U.S.C. § 548(a)(2) (2000) (insulating certain charitable contributions by individual debtors from fraudulent transfer attack).

1714. Bankruptcy Code § 546(a), 11 U.S.C. § 546(a) (2000), and Bankruptcy Act § 11e, 11 U.S.C. § 29e (1976) (repealed 1979), generally give the trustee two years from the entry of the order for relief (or adjudication) to file suit. In Herget v. Cent. Nat'l Bank & Trust Co., 324 U.S. 4 (1945), the Court held that the trustee could not take advantage of a longer state statute of limitations to file a preference suit beyond the two year period. *See id.* at 8-9.

1715. When the transferee no longer has the property transferred, the Court has affirmed orders awarding the trustee the value of the property transferred. *See, e.g.,* Eau Claire Nat'l Bank v. Jackman, 204 U.S. 522, 535-36 (1907) (the trustee may recover the value of a voidable preference where a demand for return of the property transferred would be futile). And, in the context of a fraudulent transfer, a defendant may not avoid liability for value of the property by buying back the property transferred. *See* Buffum v. Peter Barceloux Co., 289 U.S. 227, 236-37 (1933). Nor may the transferee be held in contempt if he no longer has the property and cannot turn it over to the trustee. *See* Maggio v. Zeitz (*In re* Luma Camera Serv., Inc.), 333 U.S. 56, 77 (1948). Furthermore, the grant of a preference is voidable, not void; so when the transferee is itself in an insolvency or bankruptcy case, the trustee must stand in line with other creditors of the transferee unless the trustee can prevail in imposing a trust on the property transferred. *See* Adams v. Champion, 294 U.S. 231, 236-38 (1935) (bankruptcy trustee not entitled to impose trust on property preferentially transferred to insolvent bank).

1716. Under Bankruptcy Code § 551, 11 U.S.C. § 551 (2000), most avoided transfers are automatically preserved for the benefit of the estate. Under Bankruptcy Act §§ 60b, 67a(3), 67c(2) & 70e, 11 U.S.C. §§ 96b, 107a(3), 107c(2) & 110e (1976) (repealed 1979), the court could order the avoided transfer preserved for the benefit of the estate. Moreover, before the Bankruptcy Act was amended to expressly authorize preservation of avoided transfers, the Court reached the same result by subrogating the trustee to the status of an avoided lien. *See* Moore v.

place recoveries of avoided transfers into the bankruptcy estate for ratable distribution to creditors in accordance with federal bankruptcy priorities.[1717] As noted previously, the entity from whom the avoided transfer is recoverable may be able to net the amount to be distributed on its claim against the amount required to be turned over to the trustee.[1718]

For the most part, these avoiding powers may not be asserted by the debtor,[1719] but only by the legal representative of the estate.[1720] Moreover, the Court has construed both the Bankruptcy Act and the Bankruptcy Code to apply these powers prospectively to permit avoidance of property rights established only after they were passed.[1721]

Bay, 284 U.S. 4, 5 (1931); Fallows v. Cont'l & Commercial Trust & Sav. Bank, 235 U.S. 300, 305 (1914).

1717. *See* Moore v. Bay, 284 U.S. 4, 5 (1931) ("[W]hat thus is recovered for the benefit of the estate is to be distributed in 'dividends of an equal percentum on all allowed claims, except such as have priority or are secured.'").

1718. *See* Page v. Rogers, 211 U.S. 575, 581 (1908) & *supra* nn.1430, 1440-1442 and accompanying text.

1719. *See* Connell v. Walker, 291 U.S. 1, 4 (1934) (only trustee, not debtor, had power to avoid attachment made within four months before bankruptcy while debtor was insolvent). *But see* Bankruptcy Code § 522(h)-(i), 11 U.S.C. § 522(h)-(i) (2000) (giving an individual debtor the power to exercise certain avoiding powers that the trustee has not exercised).

1720. Under Bankruptcy Code § 323, the bankruptcy trustee is the legal representative of the estate with the capacity to sue or be sued. *See* 11 U.S.C. § 323 (2000). In a chapter 11 reorganization case, the debtor in possession is authorized to exercise the avoiding powers. *See* 11 U.S.C. § 1107(a) (2000). In certain cases, the Bankruptcy Code also authorizes an examiner or an entity designated as a representative of the estate in a chapter 11 plan to exercise avoiding powers. *See* 11 U.S.C. §§ 1106(b) & 1123(b)(3)(B) (2000).

1721. *See* United States v. Sec. Indus. Bank, 459 U.S. 70, 79-80 (1982) (holding that the debtor's § 522(f)(2) power to avoid a lien to the extent it impaired an exemption did not apply retroactively to liens in effect before enactment of the 1978 Bankruptcy Code); Holt v. Henley, 232 U.S. 637,

Federal bankruptcy law avoiding power questions are almost always determined exclusively as a matter of federal bankruptcy law and policy.[1722] The bankruptcy trustee asserts these powers for the benefit of the bankruptcy estate and generally is not subject to defenses that might be asserted against the debtor. For example, in *Fairbanks Steam Shovel Co. v. Wills*,[1723] the Court permitted the trustee to avoid an unperfected chattel mortgage in a steam shovel notwithstanding any misrepresentations of the debtor that might have induced the secured party to record its security interest in the wrong county.[1724] Moreover, in *Cunningham v. Brown*,[1725] the Court held that parties who "invested" in a Ponzi scheme had to return monies distributed to them within the preference period, notwithstanding the debtor Ponzi's fraud.[1726] Although the Court has not squarely addressed whether the trustee of a solvent bankruptcy estate may assert avoiding powers, there is dictum in *Knapp v. Milwaukee Trust Co.*[1727] suggesting that the trustee's ability to sue others to recover

---

639-40 (1914) (prospectively applying the 1910 amendment of the Bankruptcy Act giving the trustee the status of a judicial lien creditor).

1722. Nonbankruptcy law might apply where federal law incorporates nonbankruptcy law as the rule of decision, such as in an action under Bankruptcy Code § 544(b). *See* 11 U.S.C. § 544(b) (2000). It also is possible for nonbankruptcy law to deprive the debtor of an interest in the property transferred such as through the imposition of a resulting or constructive trust. *See, e.g.,* Cunningham v. Brown, 265 U.S. 1, 11 (1924) (noting that property subject to a resulting or constructive trust would be excluded from property of the estate).

1723. 240 U.S. 642 (1916).

1724. *See id.* at 648 (holding that whatever equities arose out of any misrepresentation by the bankrupt could not have operated against the trustee).

1725. 265 U.S. 1 (1924).

1726. *See id.* at 13.

1727. 216 U.S. 545, 558-59 (1910) (leaving the question open but noting "[t]he suggestion . . . that the trustee in bankruptcy may possibly recover against directors and officers of the corporation . . . and against

assets sufficient to pay unsecured creditors in full does not preclude the trustee's avoidance of an unperfected mortgage.

Preferences

Under Bankruptcy Act § 60,[1728] the bankruptcy trustee could avoid certain transfers of property of the debtor (including the incurrence of consensual liens) made within four months before the bankruptcy petition while the debtor was insolvent.[1729] Under Bankruptcy Act § 67a,[1730] the bankruptcy trustee could avoid liens obtained by attachment, levy, or other legal or equitable process within four months before the filing of the bankruptcy petition while the debtor was insolvent.[1731] The 1978 Bankruptcy Code combined these two powers into § 547 dealing with avoidable preferences whether the transfer consisted of the debtor's disposition of an interest in property or incurrence of any kind of lien.[1732]

Under the Bankruptcy Act and the Bankruptcy Code, a preference has several essential elements. There must be a transfer of property of the debtor, to or for the benefit of a creditor, for or on account of an

---

stockholders . . . presents no reason why he may not resist an attempt to take all the available property in his hands to apply on a mortgage void as to creditors . . . .").

1728. 11 U.S.C. § 96 (1976) (repealed 1979). As noted *supra* in n.1602 Bankruptcy Act § 60d, 11 U.S.C. § 96d (1976) (repealed 1979) also gave the bankruptcy court power to review the reasonableness of debtors' attorneys fees paid by debtors before the filing of the petition in relation to the filing and to disgorge any excessive payments. *See In re* Wood, 210 U.S. 246, 257 (1908). The Bankruptcy Code removed this power from avoidable preferences in § 547, but placed it in Bankruptcy Code § 329, 11 U.S.C. § 329 (2000), where it remains a power of the bankruptcy court.

1729. *See* 11 U.S.C. § 96 (1976) (repealed 1979).

1730. *See* 11 U.S.C. § 107a (1976) (repealed 1979).

1731. *See, e.g.,* McHarg v. Staake, 202 U.S. 150 (1906) (*per curiam*); First Nat'l Bank v. Staake, 202 U.S. 141, 145-46 (1906).

1732. *See* 11 U.S.C. § 547 (2000).

antecedent debt of the debtor, made during the preference period, while the debtor was insolvent, that enables the transferee to receive more than the transferee would have received in a straight bankruptcy or chapter 7 liquidation case had the transfer not occurred.[1733] The Court has had occasion to clarify several of these elements.

The first element requires that the trustee prove the existence of a transfer. What constitutes a transfer and when it occurs is a matter of federal law.[1734] Although "transfer" is defined in both the Bankruptcy Act and the Bankruptcy Code, the Court has defined its contours. Early on, in *Pirie v. Chicago Title & Trust Co.*,[1735] the Court construed the term "property" to include a transfer of money.[1736] A few years later, however, in *New York County National Bank v. Massey*,[1737] the Court clarified that the deposit of money into the debtor's bank account is not a transfer,[1738] because to do so would cause the prefer-

---

1733. *See* Bankruptcy Act § 60a(1), 11 U.S.C. § 96a(1) (1976) (repealed 1979) & Bankruptcy Code § 547(b), 11 U.S.C. § 547(b) (2000). Bankruptcy Act § 60b also required the creditor to have reasonable cause to believe the debtor was insolvent. *See* 11 U.S.C. § 96b (1976) (repealed 1979); Coder v. Arts, 213 U.S. 223, 239-40 (1909) (refusing to avoid transfer because of absence of reasonable cause to believe debtor was insolvent). Because the "reasonable cause to believe" element does not apply in cases under the Bankruptcy Code, this book pays it little attention.

1734. *See* McKenzie v. Irving Trust Co., 323 U.S. 365, 369-70 (1945).

1735. Pirie v. Chicago Title & Trust Co., 182 U.S. 438 (1901).

1736. *See id.* at 443 ("[I]t would be anomalous in the extreme that in a statute which is concerned with the obligations of debtors and the prevention of preference to creditors, the readiest and most potent instrumentality to give a preference should have been omitted. Money is certainly property . . . .").

1737. 192 U.S. 138 (1904).

1738. *See id.* at 147 ("As we have seen, a deposit of money to one's credit in a bank does not operate to diminish the estate . . . . It is not a transfer of property . . . .").

ence section to conflict with Bankruptcy Act § 68[1739] preserving the bank's right of setoff.[1740] Under the Bankruptcy Act, the Court even went so far as to protect note payments made to a bank during the preference period when the bank would have had a right of setoff or bankers' lien had the money been deposited and the notes not paid.[1741] When a debtor moves bonds from one account to another, however, there will be a transfer if the accounts are held in different capacities; in *Clarke v. Rogers*,[1742] the Court affirmed the preference avoidance when the debtor transferred bonds from himself individually to himself as a trustee.[1743]

On at least two occasions, the Court has applied nonbankruptcy law to determine when a transfer is made by check. In *McKenzie v. Irving Trust Co.*,[1744] the Court applied nonbankruptcy law to hold that the debtor's transfer of a check under which the debtor was the payee occurred on delivery of the check, which the Court concluded occurred on the check's endorsement and mailing.[1745] As the Court

---

1739. 11 U.S.C. § 108 (1976) (repealed 1979).

1740. *See N.Y. County Nat'l Bank,* 192 U.S. at 147 (The "deposit of money to one's credit in a bank . . . does not . . . operate to enlarge the scope of the statute defining preferences so as to prevent set-off in cases coming within the terms of section 68a [of the Bankruptcy Act.]").

1741. *See* Studley v. Boylston Nat'l Bank, 229 U.S. 523, 527-29 (1913) (The result under the Bankruptcy Code should differ because payments are transfers and not treated as "equivalent to the voluntary exercise by the parties of the right of set-off.") *See id.* at 529.

1742. 228 U.S. 534 (1913).

1743. *See id.* at 548-49.

1744. 323 U.S. 365 (1945).

1745. *See id.* at 371-72 ("The Court of Appeals recognized that only such a 'parting with property' in the check, as would preclude the debtor from transferring any interest in the check to a creditor or bona fide purchaser, would perfect the transfer to respondent within the meaning of [Bankruptcy Act] § 60a. . . . It seems clear that at least from that time the transfer was perfected . . . [from] the time that the check was deposited in the mail . . ., delivery of the moneys to the assignee was complete.") *Id.* at 371

made clear in *Barnhill v. Johnson*,[1746] however, this is not the case regarding checks drawn by the debtor subject to the Uniform Commercial Code in which the transfer occurs only when the debtor's check is honored by the drawee bank.[1747] Thus, the delivery of a check drawn by the debtor is not a transfer at all; it gives the recipient no rights against the drawee bank if the bank refuses to honor the check.[1748] The debtor's claim against the drawee bank is transferred to the payee of the check only when the check is honored. Before the time of honor, a judicial lien creditor levying on the debtor's deposit account would prevail against the holder of the check.

By the same reasoning, the Court's holding in *McKenzie* must be wrong to the extent it conflates mailing of the third-party check with delivery. If the check is destroyed or lost in the mail before delivery, it is doubtful that any local law would hold the debtor's debt paid or that the debtor is precluded from seeking a replacement check from the third party who drew the original check to the debtor. On the other hand, debtor's endorsement of the check might have an impact on the result depending on whether the endorsement was special or in

---

& 372 n.3. The case does not specify whether the debtor's endorsement of the check was a general or restrictive endorsement. If the debtor endorsed the check in blank, then the Court's ruling is correct because the debtor has parted with all interests in the item at the time of general endorsement. But if the debtor made a restrictive endorsement on the check, it is not at all clear that the delivery of monies would occur under state law on the debtor's mailing of the check rather than at the time of endorsement by the restrictive endorsee after delivery of the check. *See* Negotiable Instruments Law, 37 McKinney's Consolidated Laws of New York §§ 64-67(3) (1943).

1746. 503 U.S. 393 (1992).

1747. *See id.* at 399-400. "[N]o transfer of any part of the debtor's claim against the bank occurred until the bank honored the check." *Id.* at 399.

1748. *See id.* at 398 n.6. Under UCC § 3-408, "[a] check or other draft does not of itself operate as an assignment of funds in the hands of the drawee available for its payment, and the drawee is not liable on the instrument until the drawee accepts it."

blank.[1749] The Court's result in *McKenzie* was probably correct if the debtor's special endorsement of the check made the transfer to the endorsee good against a bona fide purchaser irrespective of mailing or delivery; in 1940, as more fully discussed below, under the 1938 amendment to Bankruptcy Act § 60,[1750] the test for preference perfection inquired whether a bona fide purchaser from the debtor could acquire rights in the property transferred superior to the rights of the transferee. If the debtor endorsed the check in blank, however, a bona fide purchaser of the check would have rights superior to the bank and the Court's result in *McKenzie* would be erroneous.

Second, the transfer must be of property of the debtor.[1751] Thus, a transfer of services would not be preferential, because, at least in the nondischargeability context, as discussed below, the Court has recognized that services are not property.[1752] Also, the Court has held

---

1749. A blank endorsement does not affect the ability of a bona fide purchaser to acquire rights in the check superior to the bank; a special or restrictive endorsement to the bank, however, should preclude the existence of a bona fide purchaser with rights in the check superior to the bank. *See* UCC § 3-205.

1750. *See* The Chandler Act, Act of June 22, 1938, 75th Cong., 3d Sess., ch. 575, §1, 52 Stat. 840, 869-70, amending Bankruptcy Act § 60a, 11 U.S.C. § 96a (Supp. 1938), by adopting a bona fide purchaser perfection test to discourage secret liens.

1751. *See* Bankruptcy Act § 60a(1), 11 U.S.C. § 96a(1) (1976) (repealed 1979) & Bankruptcy Code § 547(b), 11 U.S.C. § 547(b) (2000) (referring to the transfer of an interest of the debtor in property). There is no requirement that the transfer be made by the debtor, as long as there is a transfer of the debtor's property or interest in property. *See, e.g.,* Rector v. Commercial Nat'l Bank, 200 U.S. 420, 423 (1906) (holding transferee liable for the debtor's property received from a clearing house holding checks on the debtor's behalf).

1752. *See* Gleason v. Thaw, 236 U.S. 558, 561-62 (1915) (holding that debt for obtaining services under false pretenses was dischargeable, because Bankruptcy Act § 17a(2) only made nondischargeable debts for obtaining property under false pretenses and services are not property: "Congress, we think, never intended that property . . . should include professional services." *Id.* at 561). *See also infra* nn.2254-2255 and accompanying text.

that the transfer to a customer of stocks held in pledge by an insolvent stockbroker is not preferential because the stocks are property of the customer, not the broker.[1753] Moreover, under the Bankruptcy Act, the Court held that the transfer of property possessed by the debtor under a conditional sale contract or bailment was not a transfer of property of the debtor because the debtor lacked title to the property.[1754] But when investors' property is commingled and not traceable, they will not be able to resist preference attack on the theory that the property transferred is theirs and not property of the debtor.[1755] Thus, in *Cunningham v. Brown*,[1756] as noted previously, the Court held that

---

1753. *See* Richardson v. Shaw, 209 U.S. 365, 380 (1908) ("We reach the conclusion, therefore, that although the broker may not be strictly a pledgee, as understood at common law, he is, essentially, a pledgee and not the owner of the stock, and turning it over upon demand to the customer does not create the relation of a preferred creditor within the meaning of the bankrupt[cy] law."). *Accord* Duel v. Hollins, 241 U.S. 523, 528 (1916); Sexton v. Kessler & Co., Ltd., 225 U.S. 90, 97-98 (1912) ("[T]he customer is held to have such an interest [an equitable lien in specifically identified stocks and bonds] that a delivery to him by an insolvent broker is not a preference."). *Id.* at 98.

1754. *See* Bailey v. Baker Ice Mach. Co., 239 U.S. 268, 274 (1915) (conditional sale contract); Ludvigh v. Am. Woolen Co., 231 U.S. 522, 528 (1913) (bailment). Under the Bankruptcy Code the result should differ because the debtor's possessory interest is an interest of the debtor in property that would have become property of the estate in the absence of the transfer. *See* 11 U.S.C. §§ 541(a)(1) & 547(b) (2000).

1755. *See* Cunningham v. Brown, 265 U.S. 1, 11 (1924) (The defrauded investors "could have followed the money wherever they could trace it and have asserted possession of it on the ground that there was a resulting trust in their favor, or they could have established a lien for what was due them in any particular fund of which he had made it a part. These things they could do without violating any statutory rule against preference in bankruptcy, because they then would have been endeavoring to get their own money, and not money in the estate of the bankrupt. But to succeed they must trace the money and therein they have failed.").

1756. 265 U.S. 1 (1924).

parties who "invested" in a Ponzi scheme had to return monies distributed to them within the preference period, notwithstanding the debtor Ponzi's fraud.[1757]

Third, the transfer of property of the debtor must be to or for the benefit of a creditor.[1758] The Bankruptcy Act[1759] and Bankruptcy Code[1760] define "creditor" for the most part to mean an entity that has a prepetition claim against the debtor.[1761] When the transfer is not to or for the benefit of a creditor, there is no preference. Thus, in *Richardson v. Shaw*,[1762] the Court held that an insolvent stockbroker's return of stock to a customer was not a preference because the customer was not a creditor of the broker.[1763] But in *Clarke v. Rogers*,[1764] the Court found a creditor relationship when the person serving as trustee of a trust is owed money from himself in his individual capacity.[1765]

Fourth, the transfer must be for or on account of an antecedent debt, i.e., a debt of the debtor that existed before the transfer was

---

1757. *See id.* at 13.

1758. *See* 11 U.S.C. § 547(b)(1) (2000). Early on, the Court noted that a transfer could be preferential if it was made for the benefit of a creditor rather than to the creditor directly. *See* Nat'l Bank of Newport v. Nat'l Herkimer County Bank, 225 U.S. 178, 184 (1912) (dictum).

1759. Bankruptcy Act § 1(11), 11 U.S.C. § 1(11) (1976) (repealed 1979), stated that "'Creditor' shall include anyone who owns a debt, demand, or claim provable in bankruptcy, and may include his duly authorized agent, attorney, or proxy."

1760. Bankruptcy Code § 101(10), 11 U.S.C. § 101(10), defines "creditor" in pertinent part to mean an "(A) entity that has a claim against the debtor that arose at the time of or before the order for relief concerning the debtor . . . ."

1761. The Bankruptcy Code includes in the definition of "creditor" a few postpetition claims against the estate that are deemed to arise prepetition. *See* 11 U.S.C. § 101(10)(B) (2000).

1762. 209 U.S. 365 (1908).

1763. *See id.* at 381.

1764. 228 U.S. 534 (1913).

1765. *See id.* at 548-49.

made[1766] (or deemed made[1767] as a matter of bankruptcy law). In
Western Tie & Timber Co. v. Brown,[1768] the Court held that funds
collected in trust by a collection agent were not preferential, because
the collection agent had no right to retain the money on account of its
claim against the debtor.[1769] Therefore, the transfer was not on account
of an antecedent debt, and the trustee's preference attack failed.[1770]

More commonly, when a transfer is made substantially contemporaneously with the creation of the debt, there will be no preference
because the transfer is not made on account of antecedent debt. Thus,
in *Dean v. Davis*,[1771] the Court held that when a debtor borrows money
on a secured basis and the lender uses the proceeds to buy notes of the
debtor held by an unsecured creditor, the mortgage securing the loan
is not avoidable as a preference because it does not secure an
antecedent debt.[1772]

In *National City Bank v. Hotchkiss*,[1773] the Court had previously
clarified the contours of "antecedent debt" in the context of a broker's
clearance day loan. Ordinarily, the broker's bank makes the clearance
loan in the morning to enable to the broker to clear trades and the

---

1766. *See* 11 U.S.C. § 547(b)(2) (2000).

1767. As discussed more fully below, under Bankruptcy Code § 547(e), 11
U.S.C. § 547(e) (2000), a transfer may be deemed to be made at a different
time than it actually occurs between the parties.

1768. 196 U.S. 502 (1905).

1769. *See id.* at 508-09.

1770. *See id.* at 509.

1771. 242 U.S. 438 (1917).

1772. *See id.* at 443 ("Preference implies paying or securing a preexisting
debt of the person preferred. The mortgage was given to secure [the
lender] for a substantially contemporaneous advance."). Of course "[m]ere
circuity of arrangement will not save a transfer which effects a preference
from being invalid . . . ." *Id.*

1773. 231 U.S. 50 (1913).

loan is repaid after clearance of trades at 3 p.m. on the same day.[1774] In *Hotchkiss*, however, after the bank made a clearance loan to the broker at 10 a.m., the market crashed before noon and the brokers were suspended from trading.[1775] Between 2 p.m. and 3 p.m., the bank demanded and received collateral for its clearance loan.[1776] At 4:10 p.m. creditors filed an involuntary bankruptcy petition against the brokers.[1777] The bankrupt brokers' trustee, Hotchkiss, brought suit against the bank to recover the collateral as a preference and was successful in both lower courts.[1778] The Court affirmed, holding in part that the bank's taking of collateral was not part of an instantaneous transaction, but was on account of an antecedent debt.[1779] This was not a case in which a bank intended to make a secured loan and waited a few hours to perfect its lien within a statutory grace period; rather it was a case in which the bank intended to make an unsecured loan and reconsidered a few hours later when the borrower's financial condition deteriorated.[1780]

1774. *See id.* at 55 ("The case arose upon what is known in New York as a clearance loan. Brokers need large sums to clear or pay for the stocks that they receive in the course of the day, and as the stocks must be paid for before they are received and can be pledged to raise the necessary funds, these sums are advanced by the banks. They are returned later on the same day by making deposits to the borrower's account and drawing a check to the order of the bank.").

1775. *See id.*

1776. *See id.* at 56.

1777. *See id.* at 55.

1778. *See id.*

1779. *See id.* at 57-58.

1780. *See id.* The *Hotchkiss* case underlies the requirement in the Bankruptcy Code's substantially contemporaneous exchange exception that the transfer must be *intended* to be contemporaneous in order to qualify for the preference defense. *See* 11 U.S.C. § 547(c)(1)(A) (2000) (emphasis added).

Fifth, the transfer must be made while the debtor was insolvent.[1781] Under both the Bankruptcy Act[1782] and the Bankruptcy Code,[1783] insolvency is determined by a so-called balance sheet test, roughly comparing the value of the debtor's assets at a fair valuation with the debtor's liabilities. The issue of the debtor's insolvency was raised infrequently under the Bankruptcy Act, because most of the preference litigation focused on whether the creditor had reasonable cause to believe the debtor was insolvent.[1784] The debtor's insolvency has been litigated even less so under the Bankruptcy Code due to the presumption of insolvency in § 547(f) during the 90 days before the date of the filing of the petition.[1785]

Sixth, the transfer must be made during the preference period.[1786] Under the Bankruptcy Act, the preference period was within four months before the date of the filing of the petition (or one year for the avoidance of insider liens). Under the Bankruptcy Code, the preference period is "on or within 90 days before the date of the filing of the petition"[1787] or, "between ninety days and one year before the date of the filing of the petition" if the creditor is an insider at the time of the transfer.[1788]

Although the preference period itself is well defined, whether a transfer is made during the preference period often is not straight forward. As noted previously, a transfer physically made during the preference period may relate back to an earlier time as a matter of law. If so, two consequences may result that affect the avoidability of

1781. *See* 11 U.S.C. § 547(b)(3) (2000).

1782. *See* 11 U.S.C. § 1(19) (1976) (repealed 1979).

1783. *See* 11 U.S.C. § 101(32) (2000).

1784. *See* H.R. REP. NO. 595, 95th Cong., 1st Sess. 178 (1977).

1785. *See id.* & 11 U.S.C. § 547(f) (2000).

1786. *See* 11 U.S.C. § 547(b)(4) (2000).

1787. *See* 11 U.S.C. § 547(b)(4)(A) (2000).

1788. *See* 11 U.S.C. § 547(b)(4)(B) (2000).

the transfer as a preference. First, the transfer may be deemed made concurrently with or before the creation of the debt and not on account of an antecedent debt. Alternatively, the transfer may be on account of an antecedent debt but deemed made outside of the preference period. In either event, the transfer would not be avoidable as a preference. The statute also has consequences based on the timing of the perfection of the transfer. Unless a transfer is perfected, it may be deemed to be made at a time later than the time it took effect between the parties, also resulting in two possible consequences. First, the transfer that was in fact contemporaneous with incurrence of the debt may now be deemed, as a matter of law, to be made on account of an antecedent debt. Second, a transfer in fact made outside of the preference period may be deemed made, as a matter of law, during the preference period. The Court's cases confront some of these possibilities.

In order to understand the cases, a review of the statutes is useful. Under Bankruptcy Code § 547(e)[1789] and Bankruptcy Act § 60a,[1790] a transfer is deemed made when: 1) it takes effect between the parties if timely perfected; 2) at the time of the perfection if not timely perfected; and 3) immediately before bankruptcy if not perfected at all. Under the Bankruptcy Code[1791] and the latter-day Bankruptcy Act,[1792] perfection occurred when the transfer was good against a

---

1789. 11 U.S.C. § 547(e) (2000).

1790. 11 U.S.C. § 96a (1976) (repealed 1979).

1791. *See* 11 U.S.C. § 547(e)(2) (2000).

1792. The modern perfection test applied under the Bankruptcy Act after the amendment of Bankruptcy Act § 60a in 1950 which adopted the judicial lien creditor perfection test for transfers of property other than real property. *See* Act of March 18, 1950, 81st Cong., 2d Sess., ch. 70, 64 Stat. 24-25, amending Bankruptcy Act § 60a(2), 11 U.S.C. § 96a(2) (1946) (repealed 1979). This amendment was in reaction to the 1938 Chandler Act amendment to Bankruptcy Act § 60 which deemed a transfer to be made when perfected against a bona fide purchaser, or if not so perfected, immediately before the date of the filing of the bankruptcy petition. *See* The Chandler Act, Act of June 22, 1938, 75th Cong., 3d Sess., ch. 575, §1,

judicial lien creditor on transfers of personal property and fixtures or against a bona fide purchaser on transfers of real property. From 1938 until 1950, however, under the Bankruptcy Act perfection occurred when the transfer was good against a bona fide purchaser, irrespective of the kind of property transferred.[1793] This caused problems for accounts receivables financiers and factors in cases such as *Corn Exchange National Bank & Trust Co. v. Klauder*,[1794] in which Pennsylvania law required the notification of account debtors in order to make the assignment of accounts receivable good against a bona fide purchaser.[1795]

In the early days of the Bankruptcy Act, however, the Court held that the Act did not require a transfer to be perfected against a judicial lien creditor or a bona fide purchaser; as long as perfection of the transfer under non-bankruptcy law related back to a time outside the preference period, there was no preference.[1796] Thus, in *Thompson*

---

52 Stat. 840, 869-70, amending Bankruptcy Act § 60a, 11 U.S.C. § 96a (Supp. 1938), to discourage secret liens by encouraging perfection.

1793. Congress adopted the bona fide purchaser test for perfection to discourage secret liens. *See* The Chandler Act, Act of June 22, 1938, 75th Cong., 3d Sess., ch. 575, §1, 52 Stat. 840, 869-70, amending Bankruptcy Act § 60a, 11 U.S.C. § 96a (Supp. 1938), to discourage secret liens by encouraging perfection. Before the 1938 amendments, creditors holding unrecorded liens could defeat the trustee if they took possession of their collateral during the preference period, as long as the perfection related back outside of the preference period under state law. *See, e.g.,* Thompson v. Fairbanks, 196 U.S. 516, 524-25 (1905), discussed more fully *infra* in nn.1797-1798 and accompanying text.

1794. 318 U.S. 434 (1943).

1795. *See id.* at 436-38. The Court avoided the assignments as preferential notwithstanding the harsh results and impact on the business of non-notification financing.

1796. *See* Carey v. Donohue, 240 U.S. 430, 432-34 (1916) (holding that where nonbankruptcy law does not require a deed to be recorded in order to be perfected, the transfer occurs when the deed is executed and delivered by the bankrupt, not when the deed is recorded).

v. Fairbanks,[1797] the Court held that there was no preference when a chattel mortgagee perfected a lien on after-acquired property by taking possession of collateral within four months before bankruptcy, because under nonbankruptcy law such perfection related back to a date outside the preference period, except as against an intervening attachment or execution creditor.[1798] The Court went further in *Humphrey v. Tatman*,[1799] holding that if taking possession of collateral by the mortgagee was valid against the bankruptcy trustee as a matter of state law, it also would be valid as a matter of bankruptcy law.[1800] Although the Court cited *Thompson v. Fairbanks*, it did not analyze whether the possession would relate back to the date of the mortgage. Instead, the Court stated "if the taking of possession [of the collateral] was good as against the trustee in bankruptcy so far as the Massachusetts law is concerned, it should be held good law here [under federal bankruptcy law]."[1801] This analysis appears not to go to the timing of the transfer, but whether it had a preferential effect. As discussed below, it is almost universally true that there is no preferential effect when a creditor with a valid lien[1802] takes possession of the collateral subject to the lien. Nevertheless, the Court's interpretation of the preference section protected "secret" liens that were not recorded until

---

1797. 196 U.S. 516 (1905).

1798. *See id.* at 524-25 (holding that the trustee did not enjoy the status of an attachment or execution creditor, and, thus, perfection related back outside of the preference period).

1799. 198 U.S. 91 (1905).

1800. *See id.* at 92, 94-95.

1801. *See id.* at 92.

1802. If the creditor's lien is avoided, the trustee may be able to prevail in preference actions to avoid transfers of property made to the creditor within the prepetition preference period. *See, e.g.,* Benedict v. Ratner, 268 U.S. 353, 364-65 (1925) (permitting trustee to avoid prepetition payments to receivables financier where lien on receivables was avoidable under nonbankruptcy law).

shortly before bankruptcy. In *Martin v. Commercial National Bank,*[1803] the debtor granted a chattel mortgage outside of the preference period and the mortgagee recorded the chattel mortgage on the day before bankruptcy.[1804] Because nonbankruptcy law did not require the mortgage to be recorded and made it junior only to liens of record before recordation, the transfer was made when the mortgage was granted and the trustee was unable to avoid the mortgage as a preference.[1805]

Seventh, the transfer must enable the creditor to receive more than the creditor would have received had the transfer not been made and the creditor received payment in a chapter 7 case of the debtor.[1806] In *Palmer Clay Products Co. v. Brown,*[1807] the Court held that although all other aspects of the preference test are determined when the transfer is made or deemed made, this aspect of the preference test is evaluated as of the date of the bankruptcy petition.[1808] That is, the amount received by the creditor during the preference period is measured against what the creditor would have received in a hypothetical chapter 7 case of the debtor filed on the date of the actual bankruptcy petition had the creditor filed a proof of claim and the

---

1803. 245 U.S. 513 (1918).

1804. *See id.* at 514.

1805. *See id.* at 519. Under Bankruptcy Code § 547(e) the result would differ, because the transfer would be deemed made when it was perfected against a judicial lien creditor. *See* 11 U.S.C. § 547(e) (2000).

1806. *See* 11 U.S.C. § 547(b)(5) (2000). Bankruptcy Act § 60a(1), 11 U.S.C. § 96a(1) (1976) (repealed 1979) contained a similar test making a transfer preferential, in pertinent part, when "the effect of which transfer will be to enable such creditor to obtain a greater percentage of his debt than some other creditor of the same class."

1807. 297 U.S. 227 (1936).

1808. *See id.* at 229. ("Whether a creditor has received a preference is to be determined, not by what the situation would have been if the debtor's assets had been liquidated and distributed among his creditors at the time the alleged preferential payment was made, but by the actual effect of the payment as determined when bankruptcy results.").

transfer not been made.[1809] If the amount the creditor receives as result of the transfer gives it a greater percentage recovery than other creditors in its class receive, then this element, the so-called "greater percentage test," is satisfied. The greater percentage test will always be satisfied when the transfer is to an unsecured or undersecured creditor when the debtor is insolvent.[1810] Ordinarily, however, the trustee will not be able to recover the debtor's transfers to a duly secured or oversecured creditor made within the preference period, because the greater percentage test will not be met. That is, the secured creditor would receive the equivalent distribution in the bankruptcy case even if the transfer never occurred, because the return of collateral would fully pay the debt. Of course if the trustee avoids the secured creditor's lien, as occurred in *Benedict v. Ratner*,[1811] the trustee may be able to recover amounts paid by the debtor prepetition in the same way the trustee could avoid transfers made to an unsecured creditor.[1812]

A series of Supreme Court cases adds an uncodified requirement that "[t]o constitute a preferential transfer within the meaning of the Bankruptcy Act there must be a parting with the bankrupt's property for the benefit of a creditor and a consequent diminution of the

---

1809. *See id.*

1810. When the debtor is insolvent, unsecured or undersecured creditors will receive less than payment in full on their claims in a bankruptcy case. The preferred creditor, however, received 100% on the portion paid. If this amount is instead disgorged to the trustee as though the transfer had not been made, the creditor will necessarily receive less in the bankruptcy on the claim it gets from disgorging the preference, because the estate will be augmented by the amount of the claim created and the amount distributed on the incremental claim will be less than 100% based on the debtor's insolvency.

1811. 268 U.S. 353 (1925).

1812. *See id.* at 364-65 (1925) (permitting trustee to avoid prepetition payments to receivables financier where lien on receivables was avoidable under nonbankruptcy law).

estate."[1813] In *Continental & Commercial Trust & Savings Bank v. Chicago Title & Trust Co.,*[1814] a third party took over the trades of an insolvent member of the Chicago board of trade and closed out several of the member's trades using its own securities.[1815] As a result, margin certificates that the insolvent member had pledged as collateral to other traders were released by the traders but set-off by the member's bank, which applied the proceeds of the certificates to indebtedness owed to it by the member.[1816] The member's bankruptcy trustee sued the bank to avoid the payment as a preference, but the Court held that there was no preference because there was no diminution of the member's bankruptcy estate.[1817] The Court reasoned that without the intervention of the third party, the margin certificates would have been available to the traders to cover damages for broken trades and of no value to the member's bankruptcy estate.[1818] Thus, even though the member's bank was benefited, there was no preference because there was no diminution of the estate.[1819]

The diminution of the estate requirement is a judicially-created short cut that undermines straight-forward application of the Bankruptcy statutes. The preference statute should rise or fall on its own plain language. If there is no transfer of property of the debtor, there is no preference. If the transfer is to a fully-secured creditor, the trustee will almost always be unable to satisfy the greater percentage test requirement. If, however, as might have been the case in *Conti-*

1813. *See, e.g.,* Cont'l & Commercial Trust & Sav. Bank v. Chicago Title & Trust Co., 229 U.S. 435, 443 (1913) (citing Nat'l Bank of Newport v. Nat'l Herkimer County Bank, 225 U.S. 178, 184 (1912) & N.Y. County Nat'l Bank v. Massey, 192 U.S. 138, 147 (1904)).

1814. 229 U.S. 435 (1913).

1815. *See id.* at 440.

1816. *See id.*

1817. *See id.* at 443-44.

1818. *See id.* at 443.

1819. *See id.* at 444.

nental & Commercial Trust, there is a transfer of certificates to an undersecured bank, then the insertion of a diminution of the estate requirement clouds the analysis and might produce the wrong result in other cases relying on its reasoning.[1820]

Both the Bankruptcy Act[1821] and the Bankruptcy Code[1822] give the transferee or creditor for whose benefit the transfer was made a series of defenses to resist preference attack or reduce the trustee's recovery. Shortly after enactment of the Bankruptcy Act, the Court had occasion in *Jaquith v. Alden*,[1823] to interpret Bankruptcy Act § 60c which gave a preferred creditor the right to setoff unsecured credit extended to the debtor in good faith during the preference period after receipt of preferential payments on a running account.[1824] Even though by its terms, § 60c provides a right of setoff only with respect to credit extended to the debtor after a creditor has been preferred, based on the augmentation of the estate occasioned by shipments to the debtor, the Court fashioned an equitable rule to permit the preferred creditor to net all of the transactions as though they were part of a single integrated transaction.[1825] Moreover, in *Kaufman v. Tredway*,[1826] the

---

1820. The Court's result in *Continental & Commercial Trust & Savings Bank* is correct based on the bank's right of set-off which is not subject to preference attack, or, alternatively, if the bank financed the third party who closed out the trades.

1821. *See, e.g.,* Bankruptcy Act §§ 11e & 60b-c, 11 U.S.C. §§ 29e & 96b-c (1976) (repealed 1979) (allowing statute of limitations defense to late-filed avoiding actions and substantive defenses to timely-filed actions).

1822. *See, e.g.,* 11 U.S.C. § 547(c) (2000) (enumerating preference defenses) and 11 U.S.C. § 546(a) (2000) (setting forth a statute of limitations).

1823. 189 U.S. 78 (1903).

1824. *See id.* at 80-82 (1903).

1825. *See id.* at 82-83. *Accord* Joseph Wild & Co. v. Provident Life & Trust Co., 214 U.S. 292, 296-97 (1909) (extending net result rule where estate benefits even though no shipments of goods after last payment); Yaple v. Dahl-Millikan Grocery Co., 193 U.S. 526, 527 (1904) (adopting net result rule).

1826. 195 U.S. 271 (1904).

Court extended the reasoning of *Jaquith* to permit setoff even when the subsequent credit was spent by the debtor prepetition and never became part of the bankruptcy estate.[1827] These principles became known as the net result rule. Following amendment of Bankruptcy Act §§ 57g and 60 in 1903,[1828] however, many lower courts refused to apply the running account defense or total net result rule, holding that it failed to survive the 1903 amendment of the Bankruptcy Act because innocent creditors would no longer be required to disgorge preferences under Bankruptcy Act § 57g.[1829]

1827. *See id.* at 274 ("It is the nonpayment and not the fact that the property remains still a part of the debtor's estate, which entitles to a setoff.").

1828. *See* Act of Feb. 5, 1903, ch. 487, §§ 12-13, 32 Stat. 799-800 (moving the four month preference period from § 60b, where it limited the trustee's ability to avoid preferences, to § 60a where it became an element of a preferential transfer, and limiting disgorgement of preferences under § 57g to circumstances where the creditor had reasonable cause to believe the debtor was insolvent at the time of the payment).

1829. *See, e.g.,* Cooper Petroleum Co. v. Hart, 379 F.2d 777, 781 (5th Cir. 1967) ("Indeed, several courts have persuasively indicated that where, as here, the creditor accepting payments on open account is found to have had reason to believe the debtor to be insolvent the rule is simply inapplicable, and *all* such payments, having been made in satisfaction of an antecedent debt, should be properly regarded as voidable preferences."); Campanella v. Liebowitz, 103 F.2d 252, 254 (3d Cir. 1939) ("The decision in Yaple v. Dahl-Millikan Grocery Co., supra, whatever its effect upon the Bankruptcy Act prior to the amendments of 1903, did not determine for all time that payments received on open accounts were, because of that fact alone, any the less voidable than payments on isolated transactions. As the law stands today, any payment, received within four months of bankruptcy by a creditor who has reasonable cause to believe that the debtor-payor is insolvent, is a voidable preference and may be recovered by the trustee. Section 60b, 11 U.S.C.A. § 96(b).") *See also* Bernstein v. Alpha Assocs., Inc. (*In re* Frigitemp Corp.), 753 F.2d 230, 232-34 (2d Cir. 1985) (dictum setting forth the history of the running account defense and indicating an inclination to refuse to follow it after the 1903 amendment because there is no reason to protect a creditor who has reasonable cause to believe the debtor is insolvent at the time of the preference).

Nevertheless, in 1978 Congress opted for a different approach by adopting a more restrictive subsequent advance rule in Bankruptcy Code § 547(c)(4),[1830] thereby superseding the net result rule in cases under the Bankruptcy Code.[1831] Instead of netting all transactions during the preference period, the subsequent advance rule provides a defense only for certain unsecured shipments or other extensions of unsecured credit made to or for the benefit of the debtor after preferential payments.

The 1978 Bankruptcy Code made another significant change, adopting an ordinary course of business defense[1832] in lieu of the requirement under Bankruptcy Act § 60b that the trustee prove the creditor had reasonable cause to believe the debtor was insolvent when the transfer was made.[1833] Under the Bankruptcy Act, the Court regarded the "reasonable cause to believe" test as a method of protecting transactions occurring in the ordinary course of business.[1834] Determination of the existence of "reasonable cause to believe" was an issue of fact on which the trustee had the burden of proof.[1835] Not surprisingly, the trustee failed to prevail in many preference actions due

---

1830. 11 U.S.C. § 547(c)(4) (2000).

1831. *See, e.g.,* McClendon v. Cal-Wood Door (*In re* Wadsworth Bldg. Components, Inc.), 711 F.2d 122, 124 (9th Cir. 1983); Waldschmidt v. Ranier (*In re* Fulgham Constr. Corp.), 706 F.2d 171, 173-74 (6th Cir.), *cert. denied*, 464 U.S. 935 (1983) (noting that judicially created net result rule did not survive enactment of the Bankruptcy Code).

1832. *See* 11 U.S.C. § 547(c)(2) (2000).

1833. *See* 11 U.S.C. § 96b (1976) (repealed 1979).

1834. *See, e.g.,* Pyle v. Texas Transp. & Terminal Co., 238 U.S. 90, 97-98 (1915) ("[T]heir transactions with the bank were in the usual course of business and without any intention on their part other than to conceal their true methods. . . . Considering the whole record we are unable to conclude that appellee banks had reasonable cause to believe that by transferring the genuine bills of lading to them a preference was intended or given.") (internal quotation marks omitted).

1835. *See id.* at 98 ("Whether such 'reasonable cause to believe' existed is a question of fact and the burden of proof is upon the trustee.").

to an inability to prove the creditor's belief and state of mind.[1836] To facilitate the recovery of preferences, Congress enacted the Bankruptcy Code's preference section without a reasonable cause to believe test.[1837] In order to avoid casting the preference net too broadly, however, Congress enacted an ordinary course of business preference defense.[1838] In *Union Bank v. Wolas*,[1839] the Court interpreted this defense literally to insulate from preference attack regularly scheduled payments to banks on long term debts, as well as payments on short term debts.[1840] Because Congress completely rewrote the preference section, the Court refused to limit the scope of the ordinary course of business defense under the Bankruptcy Code to apply only in the context of the "current expense" exception that was applicable to trade creditors under the Bankruptcy Act.[1841]

In order to protect purchase money financiers, the 1978 Bankruptcy Code contains an enabling loan exception in § 547(c)(3).[1842] The exception protects purchase money security interests perfected within the federal statutory period (currently 30 days) after the debtor receives possession of the purchased property.[1843] Without an enabling loan exception, the trustee would be able to avoid security interests

---

1836. *See* H.R. REP. No. 595, 95th Cong., 1st Sess., 178 (1977) ("[T]he requirement that the trustee prove the state of mind of his opponent is nearly insurmountable, and defeats many preference actions.").

1837. *See id.*

1838. *See* 11 U.S.C. § 547(c)(2) (2000); H.R. REP. No. 595, 95th Cong., 1st Sess., 373 (1977) ("The purpose of this exception is to leave undisturbed normal financial relations, because it does not detract from the general policy of the preference section to discourage unusual action by either the debtor or his creditors during the debtor's slide into bankruptcy.").

1839. 502 U.S. 151 (1991).

1840. *See id.* at 162.

1841. *See id.* at 160.

1842. *See* 11 U.S.C. § 547(c)(3) (2000).

1843. *See* 11 U.S.C. § 547(c)(3)(B) (Supp. 2005).

perfected when goods are delivered several weeks after the loan is made, because perfection can only occur once the debtor has rights in the purchased property collateral.[1844] In *Fidelity Financial Services, Inc. v. Fink*,[1845] the Court held that the federal statutory period within which to perfect a purchase money security interest (then 20 days) preempts any state statute that gave the creditor a longer period in which to perfect.[1846] Thus, "a creditor may invoke the enabling loan exception only by satisfying state law perfection requirements within the . . . period provided by the federal statute."[1847] Responding to *Fink*, in 2005 Congress amended Bankruptcy Code § 547(c)(3)(B) to increase the enabling loan perfection period from 20 days to 30 days after the debtor receives possession of the collateral, but it did not alter *Fink's* rule of federal preemption.[1848]

Fraudulent Transfers

Under both the Bankruptcy Act and the Bankruptcy Code, the trustee or estate representative is empowered to avoid fraudulent transfers. There are two general kinds of fraudulent transfers and two sources of law with which to avoid them.[1849] Under Bankruptcy Code § 548,[1850] which is the successor to Bankruptcy Act § 67d,[1851] the trustee has the ability to use federal fraudulent transfer law to avoid fraudu-

---

1844. *See* 11 U.S.C. § 547(e)(3) (2000).

1845. 522 U.S. 211 (1998).

1846. *See id.* at 212-13.

1847. *See id.* at 213.

1848. *See* 11 U.S.C. § 547(c)(3)(B) (Supp. 2005).

1849. Bankruptcy Code § 543 also provides for the turnover of property held by a custodian. *See* 11 U.S.C. § 543 (2000). To the extent this section applies to oust possession from a general assignee for the benefit of creditors, the Court has characterized it as akin to a constructive fraudulent transfer. *See* Randolph v. Scruggs, 190 U.S. 533, 536 (1903).

1850. 11 U.S.C. § 548 (2000).

1851. 11 U.S.C. § 107d (1976) (repealed 1979).

lent transfers made or deemed made within two years before bank-ruptcy.[1852] Moreover, under Bankruptcy Code § 544(b),[1853] which is the successor to Bankruptcy Act § 70e,[1854] the trustee can assert the rights of an actual creditor holding an allowable unsecured claim to avoid fraudulent transfers that could have been avoided by such creditor under applicable nonbankruptcy law,[1855] often several years before bankruptcy.[1856] Federal and state fraudulent transfer laws allow the trustee to avoid actual intent fraudulent transfers, i.e., when the debt-or had the actual intent to hinder, delay, or defraud creditors when the transfer was made or deemed made.[1857] These laws also allow the

1852. Bankruptcy Code § 548(a) was amended in 2005 to give the trustee a two year reach back period instead of the one year period previously in effect. *See* 11 U.S.C. § 548(a)(1) preamble (Supp. 2005); Pub. L. No. 109-8, § 1402(1), 119 Stat. 214 (2005).

1853. 11 U.S.C. § 544(b) (2000).

1854. 11 U.S.C. § 110e (1976) (repealed 1979).

1855. The existence of federal fraudulent transfer statutes in Bankruptcy Code § 548 and Bankruptcy Act § 67 does not preempt state fraudulent transfer laws. *See* Stellwagen v. Clum, 245 U.S. 605, 618 (1918).

1856. *See, e.g.,* Uniform Fraudulent Transfer Act § 9, 7A U.L.A. 194 (2006). *See also* Alabama Code 1975, § 8-9A-4(a) (2006) (Alabama state law extending the reach back period to ten years for real property and six years for personal property); 14 M. Rev. Stat. A. § 3757 (2006) (Maine state law extending the reach back period to six years or, if later, within one year after the transfer or obligation was or could reasonably have been discovered); Uniform Fraudulent Conveyance Act § 8, 7A U.L.A. 481 (2006). Even though, in 1981, the Uniform Commissioners on State Laws recommended that the UFTA supersede the UFCA, a few states, including New York, continue to retain the UFCA as their operative fraudulent transfer law. *See, e.g.,* Debtor and Creditor Law, 12 McKinney's Consol. Laws of N.Y. §§ 278-279 (2001); Le Café Crème, Ltd. v. Le Roux (*In re* Le Café Crème, Ltd.), 244 B.R. 221, 238 (Bankr. S.D.N.Y. 2000) (noting "the reach-back period under the [New York Debtor and Creditor Law U.F.C.A.] is six years . . . .").

1857. *See, e.g.,* Buffum v. Peter Barceloux Corp., 289 U.S. 227, 232-33 (1933) (holding that bankruptcy trustee could avoid a pledge made as part of an intentional scheme to defraud creditors).

trustee to avoid constructive fraudulent transfers, i.e., those made for less than a fair consideration or reasonable equivalent value that are made while the debtor is insolvent, leave the debtor with an unreasonably small capital, or with respect to which the debtor intends to incur debts beyond its ability to repay.

The Court has decided several cases interpreting fraudulent transfers under the bankruptcy laws. Under Bankruptcy Act § 67e, as originally enacted, the trustee could avoid a transfer made within four months before bankruptcy with actual intent to hinder, delay, or defraud the debtor's creditors except as to purchasers in good faith and for a fair consideration.[1858] Early on, in *Coder v. Arts*,[1859] the Court held that the debtor's mortgage of a large tract of land made in good faith within four months before bankruptcy was not avoidable as an actual intent fraudulent transfer.[1860] Not only did the trustee fail to prove the debtor's fraudulent intent, but the mortgagee had no reasonable cause to believe that the debtor was insolvent or that the mortgage was intended to give a preference.[1861] Although the Court held the mortgage was not avoidable, in dictum it noted that an actual intent fraudulent transfer may be set aside even if it was made on a valuable consideration.[1862] It also concluded that "the giving of the

---

1858. *See* Bankruptcy Act § 67e, Act of July 1, 1898, ch. 541, § 67e, 30 Stat. 544 (codified at 11 U.S.C. § 107e), and transferred to Bankruptcy Act § 67a(1)(b) by the Chandler Act, 52 Stat. 787 (1938), before its repeal in 1979.

1859. 213 U.S. 223 (1909).

1860. *See id.* at 245. (Congress had "not declared voidable merely preferential conveyances made in good faith and in which the grantee, as is found in this case, was ignorant of the insolvency of the grantor, and had no reason to believe that a preference was intended."). *Accord* Van Iderstine v. Nat'l Disc. Co., 227 U.S. 575, 582 (1913) ("It is therefore not unlawful to prefer nor fraudulent for one though insolvent to borrow in order to use the money in making a preference.").

1861. *See Coder*, 213 U.S. at 239.

1862. *See id.* at 242 (The law requires that "in order to invalidate a conveyance, that there shall be actual fraud; and it makes no difference

mortgage and its effect upon other creditors could . . . be considered as an item of evidence in determining the question of fraud."[1863]

This dictum proved to be prescient in *Dean v. Davis*,[1864] when the Court permitted the trustee to avoid as an actual intent fraudulent transfer a mortgage given shortly before bankruptcy.[1865] In *Dean v. Davis*, within four months before bankruptcy while the debtor was insolvent, the debtor borrowed money from his brother in law secured by a mortgage on substantially all of the debtor's property.[1866] The purpose of the loan was to pay outstanding notes bearing the debtor's forged endorsement.[1867] By the time the mortgage was recorded eight days after the loan was made, all of the new notes that the debtor owed to the mortgagee were past due.[1868] Not only did the debtor grant the mortgage with actual intent to hinder, delay, or defraud creditors, but the brother in law mortgagee knew the loan was being used to make a preference in contemplation of bankruptcy.[1869] The Court held that "where the advance is made to enable the debtor to make a preferential payment with bankruptcy in contemplation, the transaction presents an element upon which fraud may be predicated. The fact that the money advanced is actually used to pay a debt does not necessarily establish good faith."[1870] Thus, the lower courts were justified in finding the requisite fraudulent intent because the debtor "willingly sacrificed his property and his other creditors to avert a

---

that the conveyance was made upon a valuable consideration, if made for the purpose of hindering, delaying or defrauding creditors.").

1863. *See id.* at 244.

1864. 242 U.S. 438 (1917).

1865. *See id.* at 445.

1866. *See id.* at 442.

1867. *See id.*

1868. *See id.*

1869. *See id.* at 445.

1870. *See id.* at 444.

threatened criminal prosecution; and [the mortgagee] knowing the facts, cooperated in the bankrupt's fraudulent purpose, lack[ing] the saving good faith."[1871]

The Court has highlighted that actual intent to defraud is not required if the debtor has an actual intent to hinder or delay creditors. In *Shapiro v. Wilgus*,[1872] in order to avoid aggressive debt collection action by his creditors, the debtor transferred assets to a newly-formed solely owned corporation which also assumed his liabilities.[1873] The debtor next induced a friendly creditor to file a federal equity receivership complaint to which the debtor consented. The court promptly appointed a receiver and issued an injunction precluding attachment and execution in order to hold creditors at bay while the corporation reorganized.[1874] A hostile creditor proceeded to judgment against the debtor in state court and sought a lien on the debtor's personal property in federal court on the ground that the establishment of the corporation and equity receivership was avoidable as a single scheme that was an actual intent fraudulent transfer.[1875] The Court made clear that the judgment creditor could avoid a fraudulent transfer when the debtor had the actual intent to hinder or delay creditors even if there was no actual intent to defraud creditors.[1876] Writing for the Court, Justice Cardozo noted as follows:[1877]

> A conveyance is illegal if made with an intent to defraud the creditors of the grantor, but equally it is illegal if made with an intent to hinder and delay them. Many an embarrassed debtor holds the genuine belief that, if suits can be staved off for a season, he will weather a financial storm, and pay his

1871. *See id.* at 445.

1872. 287 U.S. 348 (1932).

1873. *See id.* at 352.

1874. *See id.* at 352-53.

1875. *See id.* at 353.

1876. *See id.* at 353-54.

1877. *See id.* at 354.

debts in full. The belief, even though well founded, does not clothe him with a privilege to build up obstructions that will hold his creditors at bay. This is true . . . under the Uniform Fraudulent Conveyance Act . . . . It is true under the Statute of Elizabeth . . . . Tested by either act, this conveyance may not stand.

The Court also held that the equity receivership was avoidable because it was part of a common scheme to hinder, delay, or defraud creditors.[1878] Of course the same result would occur if the attack were made in a bankruptcy case by a trustee who is empowered by bankruptcy law to avoid fraudulent transfers.[1879]

During the next year, the Court decided *Buffum v. Peter Barceloux Corp.*,[1880] in which Justice Cardozo, again writing for the Court, held that a stock pledge could be avoided as an actual intent fraudulent transfer because "[t]he pledge was a step in a general [fraudulent] plan which must be viewed as a whole with all its composite implications."[1881] Thus, the Court adopted the important principle that in evaluating a fraudulent transfer, a court will not consider each transfer in isolation but will view the "events consecutively as stages of an unfolding plot."[1882]

In *Benedict v. Ratner*,[1883] a receivables financier took an assignment of the debtor's accounts receivable but left the debtor with the

---

1878. *See id.* at 355. ("The conveyance to the corporation being voidable because fraudulent in law, the receivership must share its fate. It was part and parcel of a scheme whereby the form of a judicial remedy was to supply a protective cover for a fraudulent design.").

1879. *See, e.g.,* Sampsell v. Imperial Paper & Color Corp., 313 U.S. 215, 216-17 (1941) (Justice Douglas describes the bankruptcy trustee's avoidance of a fraudulent transfer in which an individual transferred assets to his family corporation to hinder and delay creditors).

1880. 289 U.S. 227 (1933).

1881. *See id.* at 232.

1882. *See id.* at 233.

1883. 268 U.S. 353 (1925).

unfettered discretion to collect the accounts and use the proceeds, thereby making the assignment void under New York law as a fraudulent conveyance.[1884] The Court held that state law "imputes fraud conclusively because of the reservation of dominion inconsistent with the effective disposition of title and creation of a lien."[1885] As such, the debtor's bankruptcy trustee could avoid the lien.[1886] The Court's conclusion in *Benedict v. Ratner* follows earlier cases in which the Court permitted the bankruptcy trustee to avoid pledges and chattel mortgages without a change of possession or meaningful restriction on use of proceeds that were void against creditors generally under state law.[1887]

Even if the bankruptcy trustee cannot prove that the debtor actually intended to hinder, delay, or defraud creditors, the trustee may be able to avoid the transfer as a constructive fraudulent transfer.

1884. *See id.* at 359-60. New York law currently allows an accounts receivable financier to have a perfected lien in the debtor's accounts even if the debtor retains discretion to collect the accounts and use proceeds. *See* McKinney's Uniform Commercial Code § 9-205, (New York 2001); Clarkson Co. v. Shaheen, 533 F. Supp. 905, 918 (S.D.N.Y. 1982) (when the security interest is perfected by filing, the secured party may allow the debtor to use, commingle, or dispose of the collateral without invalidating the security interest); *In re* Bennett Funding Group, 255 B.R. 616 (N.D.N.Y 2000) ("Although [floating liens] were initially prohibited under the Uniform Commercial Code, the drafters reluctantly recognized the validity of security interests created in general classes of after acquired property.").

1885. *See Benedict v. Ratner*, 268 U.S. at 363.

1886. *See id.* at 364-65.

1887. *See, e.g.,* Knapp v. Milwaukee Trust Co., 216 U.S. 545, 557-58 (1910) (avoiding chattel mortgage without change of possession under Wisconsin law); Sec. Warehousing Co. v. Hand, 206 U.S. 415, 425-27 (1907) (sham pledge where debtor kept possession of property void under Wisconsin law: "Such a scheme, under the facts and as carried out in this case, and with regard to Wisconsin law, was a fraud in fact, and neither the receipts nor the so-called pledge could be asserted against any of the creditors.").

Common to almost all[1888] of the tests for constructive fraud is the requirement that the transfer be made for less than a reasonably equivalent value or fair consideration. In *BFP v. Resolution Trust Corp.*,[1889] as discussed more fully in Chapters 1, 2, 3, and 6, the Court protected regularly-conducted, non-collusive real property foreclosure sales from constructive fraudulent transfer attack.[1890] The Court's holding is instructive in interpreting "reasonably equivalent value":[1891]

> [W]e decline to read the phrase "reasonably equivalent value" in [Bankruptcy Code] § 548(a)(2) to mean, in its application to mortgage foreclosure sales, either "fair market value" or "fair foreclosure price" (whether calculated as a percentage of fair market value or otherwise). We deem, as the law has always deemed, that a fair and proper price, or a "reasonably equivalent value," for foreclosed property, is the price in fact received at the foreclosure sale, so long as all the requirements of the State's foreclosure law have been complied with.

It remains to be seen how the Court will interpret "reasonably equivalent value" in other contexts.

Perhaps the Court's most important fraudulent transfer case is its shortest. *Moore v. Bay*[1892] is a unanimous opinion authored by Justice

---

1888. Some states have enacted statutes that make fraudulent and avoidable transfers of property not accompanied by a change of possession without regard to economic equivalence. *See, e.g.,* Cal. Civ. Code § 3440 (2007). In Moore v. Bay, 284 U.S. 4, 5 (1931), the Court allowed the bankruptcy trustee to assert the rights of an actual unsecured creditor under this statute to avoid a mortgage for failing to meet the requirements of Cal. Civ. Code § 3440.

1889. 511 U.S. 531 (1994).

1890. *See id.* at 542 ("When these procedures have been followed, however, it is 'black letter' law that mere inadequacy of the foreclosure sale price is no basis for setting the sale aside.").

1891. *See id.* at 545 (interpreting statutory language currently codified in 11 U.S.C. § 548(a)(1)(B) (2000)).

1892. 284 U.S. 4 (1931).

Holmes comprising two paragraphs of text in its entirety.[1893] In *Moore v. Bay*, the debtor executed a chattel mortgage without a change in possession of the collateral.[1894] Under applicable California law, the mortgage was void as against creditors who extended credit before the date the mortgage was recorded, but good against creditors who extended credit after that date.[1895] The question before the Court was whether the trustee could use Bankruptcy Act § 67a[1896] to assert the rights of an actual unsecured creditor to avoid the mortgage against future creditors. The most important aspect of the case is its holding that a transfer avoidable by some actual unsecured creditors is avoidable by or for the benefit of all of them.[1897] The Court reached its conclusion because the trustee's avoiding powers are enforced for the benefit of the estate and all general unsecured creditors share ratably in the estate.[1898] Moreover, the rule of *Moore v. Bay* endures under the Bankruptcy Code.[1899] Thus, if there is one unsecured creditor holding a small claim who could avoid a transfer under nonbankruptcy law, the

---

1893. *See id.* at 4-5.

1894. *See id.*

1895. *See id.*

1896. 11 U.S.C. § 107a (1928) (repealed 1979) (interpreted by the Court to mean that "claims which for want of record or for other reasons would not have been valid liens as against the claims of the creditors of the bankrupt shall not be liens against his estate."). *See Moore v. Bay*, 284 U.S. at 5. *See also* Bankruptcy Act § 70e, 11 U.S.C. § 110e (1928) (repealed 1979) ("The trustee may avoid any transfer by the bankrupt of his property which any creditor of such bankrupt might have avoided . . . .").

1897. *See Moore v. Bay*, 284 U.S. at 5 (answering in the affirmative the question "whether the mortgage is void also as against those who gave the bankrupt credit at a later date, after the mortgage was on record.").

1898. *See id.*

1899. The principles of Bankruptcy Act §§ 67a and 70e as interpreted by the Court in *Moore v. Bay* generally survive in Bankruptcy Code §§ 544(b) & 550(b), 11 U.S.C. §§ 544(b) & 550(b) (2000). *See* H.R. REP. NO. 595, 95th Cong., 1st Sess. 370 (1977).

trustee may assert the rights of that one creditor to avoid the entire transaction for the benefit of the estate.

The Strong Arm Clause

The trustee can use the strong arm clause of Bankruptcy Code § 544(a) (which is the successor to Bankruptcy Act § 70c[1900]) to defeat secret liens and conveyances. The strong arm clause gives the trustee the powers of a hypothetical judicial lien creditor or a creditor with an execution returned unsatisfied. Under the Bankruptcy Act, in *Bailey v. Baker Ice Machine Co.*,[1901] the Court held that the trustee's hypothetical creditor status was determined as of the date of the filing of the bankruptcy petition.[1902] Moreover, in *Lewis v. Manufacturers National Bank of Detroit*,[1903] following an amendment to Bankruptcy Act § 70c,[1904] the Court reaffirmed that the trustee's status as a hypothetical creditor is determined as of the time of the filing of the bankruptcy petition.[1905] The Bankruptcy Code specifically codifies this result.[1906]

The trustee's strong arm power can be used to defeat any kind of unperfected lien, whether a consensual security interest, a statutory lien,[1907] a judicial lien, or an equitable lien, depending on the rights of a

---

1900. 11 U.S.C. § 110c (1976) (repealed 1979).

1901. 239 U.S. 268 (1915).

1902. *See id.* at 275-76 (interpreting Bankruptcy Act § 47a, cl. 2, as amended in 1910, ch. 412, 36 Stat. 838, 840, the forerunner to Bankruptcy Act § 70c).

1903. 364 U.S. 603 (1961).

1904. *See* 11 U.S.C. § 110c (Supp. 1950) as amended by 64 Stat. 24, 26 (1950).

1905. *See Lewis*, 364 U.S. at 607 ("[T]he trustee acquires the status of a creditor as of the time when the petition in bankruptcy is filed.").

1906. *See* Bankruptcy Code § 544(a), 11 U.S.C. § 544(a) (2000).

1907. The trustee may assert the strong arm avoiding power of Bankruptcy Code § 544(a) independently of the trustee's power to avoid statutory liens under Bankruptcy Code § 545 (discussed below). *See* 11

judicial lien creditor under nonbankruptcy law. For example, consider the rights of a holder of an unrecorded federal tax lien. If the tax lien is unfiled at the time of the filing of the bankruptcy petition, the trustee's status as a judicial lien creditor will defeat it.[1908] Under state law, if a judicial lien creditor defeats the holder of an unperfected security interest in personal property, the trustee likewise can use Bankruptcy Code § 544(a) to defeat the security interest if it remains unperfected as of the date of the filing of the bankruptcy petition.[1909] But if state law makes an unrecorded security interest in personal property good except as against a bona fide purchaser, the trustee will lose.[1910] Likewise, if a secured creditor delays lien perfection, but perfects before the filing of the bankruptcy petition, the trustee will

---

U.S.C. §§ 544(b) & 545 (2000); United States v. Speers, 382 U.S. 266, 271-72 (1965) (so holding under Bankruptcy Act § 70c, 11 U.S.C. § 110c (1964) (repealed 1979), the predecessor to Bankruptcy Code § 544(b)).

1908. *See* United States v. Speers, 382 U.S. 266, 271-72 (1965).

1909. The same was true under Bankruptcy Act § 70c, 11 U.S.C. § 110c (1976) (repealed 1979). *See* Lewis v. Mfrs. Nat'l Bank of Detroit, 364 U.S. 603, 607 (1961) (holding that trustee's rights as a hypothetical judicial lien creditor operated at the date of the filing of the bankruptcy petition only). Before § 70c was inserted into the Bankruptcy Act in 1910, however, the Court held that the trustee had no lien status and simply stood in the bankrupt's shoes. *See, e.g.,* York Mfg. Co. v. Cassell, 201 U.S. 344, 352-53 (1906) (holding that the filing of the vendee's bankruptcy petition does not defeat the title of a conditional vendor with an unfiled contract under Ohio law, because "[u]nder the provisions of the bankrupt[cy] act the trustee in bankruptcy is vested with no better right or title to the bankrupt's property than belonged to the bankrupt at the time when the trustee's title accrued.").

1910. *See, e.g.,* Bryant v. Swofford Bros. Dry Goods Co., 214 U.S. 279, 290-91 (1909) (upholding unrecorded conditional sale contract as valid under Arkansas law); Hewit v. Berlin Mach. Works, 194 U.S. 296, 302-03 (1904) (holding under New York law that title retained as security under a conditional sale contract is good as against the bankruptcy trustee, who lacks the status of a purchaser). *Cf.* Zartman v. First Nat'l Bank of Waterloo, 216 U.S. 134, 138 (1910) (allowing postpetition reformation of a prepetition contract on the basis that the trustee does not have the status of a bona fide purchaser).

not prevail in defeating the transfer under the strong arm clause, because the trustee only acquires hypothetical judicial lien creditor status at the time of bankruptcy and is therefore subordinate and will lose to a previously perfected lien.[1911]

Postpetition Transfers

Bankruptcy Act § 70d[1912] and Bankruptcy Code § 549[1913] permit the trustee to avoid certain unauthorized postpetition transfers.[1914] Section 549(a)(2)(A) also permits the trustee to avoid transfers authorized under Bankruptcy Code § 542(c), i.e., transfers made when banks, without actual knowledge or actual notice of the bankruptcy, honor prepetition checks. The Bankruptcy Code permits the avoidance against immediate and subsequent transferees of the check, not against the drawee bank.[1915] Thus, current law codifies the Court's holding under Bankruptcy Act § 70d[1916] in *Bank of Marin v. England*,[1917] in which Justice Douglas, writing for the Court, invoked equitable principles to impose liability on the payee of the check but not on the drawee bank which cashed the check postpetition.[1918]

1911. *See* Lewis v. Mfrs. Nat'l Bank of Detroit, 364 U.S. 603, 607 (1961). The trustee may, however, be able to attack delayed perfection as a preference. *See id.* at 609.

1912. 11 U.S.C. § 110d (1976) (repealed 1979).

1913. 11 U.S.C. § 549 (2000).

1914. *See* 11 U.S.C. § 549(a)(2)(B) (2000). Bankruptcy Code § 549(b)-(c), 11 U.S.C. § 549(b)-(c) (2000), contains exceptions limiting the trustee's ability to avoid postpetition transfers. Bankruptcy Code § 549(d), 11 U.S.C. § 549(d) (2000), sets a statute of limitations within the trustee may sue to avoid a postpetition transfer, generally within two years after the date of the transfer.

1915. *See* 11 U.S.C. §§ 542(c), 549(a)(2)(A) & 550(b) (2000).

1916. 11 U.S.C. § 110d (1964) (repealed 1979).

1917. 385 U.S. 99 (1966).

1918. *See id.* at 103 ("[I]t would be inequitable to hold liable a drawee who pays checks of the bankrupt duly drawn but presented after bank-

The Bankruptcy Act also contained a provision permitting the trustee to seek disgorgement of postpetition compensation from debtor's officers who traded in the debtor's stock postpetition.[1919] In *Wolf v. Weinstein*,[1920] the Court interpreted the Bankruptcy Act broadly to require disgorgement of all postpetition compensation paid to officers of the debtor who traded in stock, not just compensation paid after the illicit trading.[1921] The Court found the debtor's senior officers to be fiduciaries, but commented that not all officers or managing officers would be considered fiduciaries.[1922] Even though the lower court had approved the officers' rate of compensation, this did not shield them from disgorgement liability under Bankruptcy Act § 249.[1923] Although the Bankruptcy Code did not codify Bankruptcy Act § 249, presumably the Court would apply the holding of *Wolf v. Weinstein* in a similar case under the Bankruptcy Code based on the inherent power of the bankruptcy court to regulate postpetition compensation.

Setoff

Both the Bankruptcy Act[1924] and the Bankruptcy Code[1925] have from their inception included provisions preserving the right of setoff.[1926] The federal bankruptcy laws do not create a federal right of

---

ruptcy, where no actual revocation of its authority has been made and it has no notice or knowledge of the bankruptcy.").

1919. *See* Bankruptcy Act Chapter X § 249, 11 U.S.C. § 649 (1976) (repealed 1979).

1920. 372 U.S. 633 (1963).

1921. *See id.* at 641.

1922. *See id.* at 651.

1923. *See id.* at 648.

1924. *See* Bankruptcy Act § 68, 11 U.S.C. § 108 (1976) (repealed 1979).

1925. *See* Bankruptcy Code § 553, 11 U.S.C. § 553 (2000).

1926. *See* Bankruptcy Act § 68a, 11 U.S.C. § 108a (1976) (repealed 1979) ("In all cases of mutual debts or mutual credits between the estate of a bankrupt and a creditor the account shall be stated and one debt shall be set off against the other, and the balance only shall be allowed or paid.");

setoff, but rather recognize rights of setoff that arise under nonbankruptcy law, usually federal or state law.[1927] The Court has described setoff in general terms as follows:[1928]

> What the old books called a right of stoppage – what business men call set-off, is a right given or recognized by the commercial law of each of the States and is protected by the Bankruptcy Act if the petition is filed before the parties themselves have given checks, charged notes, made book entries, or stated an account whereby the smaller obligation is applied on the larger.

The validity of a setoff in a bankruptcy case, however, is determined as a matter of federal bankruptcy law.[1929]

Notwithstanding the plain language of the statutes, the Court has construed the "right" of setoff as permissive rather than mandatory, based on the sound exercise of equitable discretion of the bankruptcy court.[1930] In the context of setoff in a railroad reorganization case under

---

Bankruptcy Code § 553(a) preamble, 11 U.S.C. § 553(a) preamble (2000) ("Except as otherwise provided in this section and in sections 362 and 363 of this title, this title [11] does not affect any right of a creditor to offset a mutual debt owing by such creditor to the debtor that arose before the commencement of the case under this title against a claim of such creditor against the debtor that arose before the commencement of the case . . . .").

1927. *See* Studley v. Boylston Nat'l Bank, 229 U.S. 523, 528 (1913) ("[Section 68a of the Bankruptcy Act] did not create the right of set-off but recognized its existence . . . .").

1928. *See id.*

1929. *See, e.g.,* McCollum v. Hamilton Nat'l Bank, 303 U.S. 245, 248 (1938) (holding that the validity of setoff does not depend on state law but on federal bankruptcy law).

1930. *See* Cumberland Glass Mfg. Co. v. DeWitt, 237 U.S. 447, 455 (1915) ("The provision is permissive rather than mandatory, and does not enlarge the doctrine of set-off, and cannot be invoked in cases where the general principles of set-off would not justify it. . . . The matter is placed within the control of the bankruptcy court, which exercises its discretion

Bankruptcy Act § 77,[1931] the Court in *Baker v. Gold Seal Liquors, Inc.*,[1932] refused to allow a creditor to offset freight charges owed to the estate against its claim against the estate.[1933] To do so would grant a priority to the creditor asserting the setoff and impede the prospects for railroad reorganization.[1934]

In order for a creditor to be able to setoff a debt it owes to the debtor against a claim it has against the debtor, there must be mutuality of obligations. That is, the right of setoff requires mutual debts and credits in the same capacity. Thus, in *Western Tie & Timber Co. v. Brown*,[1935] the Court held that when a creditor holds funds in trust that it owes to the debtor, it may not offset the trust funds against its claim against the debtor because mutuality is lacking.[1936] Moreover, in *McCollum v. Hamilton National Bank*,[1937] the Court held that a bank's non-contractual usury penalty owed to its customer was not mutual with the claim it held against the debtor-

---

in these cases upon the general principles of equity.") (internal citations omitted).

1931. 11 U.S.C. § 205 (1976) (repealed 1979).

1932. 417 U.S. 467 (1974).

1933. *See id.* at 474. The Court does not clarify whether the setoff provisions of Bankruptcy Act § 68 fail to apply in a railroad reorganization case under Bankruptcy Act § 77 or, alternatively, whether the reorganization court has discretion not to apply it. *See* Lowden v. Nw. Nat'l Bank & Trust Co., 298 U.S. 160, 163 (1936) (refusing to answer certified question about application of § 68 in a § 77 railroad reorganization case).

1934. *See Baker*, 417 U.S. at 473-74. The result in *Baker v. Gold Seal Liquors, Inc.* should differ in a railroad reorganization case under the Bankruptcy Code where the setoff provisions of § 553 would apply by their terms in a railroad reorganization case under subchapter IV of chapter 11. *See* 11 U.S.C. §§ 103(a) & 1161 (2000).

1935. 196 U.S. 502 (1905).

1936. *See id.* at 509-10.

1937. 303 U.S. 245 (1938).

customer because, under the Bankruptcy Act, the penalty liability was not a debt.[1938] Ordinarily, however, the debtor's deposit of money into a general bank account creates an ordinary debtor-creditor relationship mutual with debts owed to creditors, thereby enabling the bank to offset amounts in the deposit account against amounts that the debtor owes to the bank.[1939]

The right of set off is not unrestricted. Both the Bankruptcy Act[1940] and the Bankruptcy Code[1941] contain limitations when the right of set off

---

1938. *See id.* at 249 ("Liability for the penalty does not arise in contract but is laid *in invitum* as a disciplinary measure. Nor does the judgment determining the extent of guilt and declaring sentence change the liability for penalty to one for debt."). *But see* Pa. Dep't of Pub. Welfare v. Davenport, 495 U.S. 552, 562-63 (1990) (holding, in the context of nondischargeable debts, that criminal restitution obligations were "debts" giving rise to "claims" under the Bankruptcy Code).

1939. *See* N.Y. County Nat'l Bank v. Massey, 192 U.S. 138, 145 (1904) ("[A] deposit of money upon general account with a bank creates the relation of debtor and creditor. . . . It creates an ordinary debt, not a privilege or right of a fiduciary character.").

1940. Bankruptcy Act § 68b, 11 U.S.C. § 108b (1976) (repealed 1979), provides that "[a] set-off or counterclaim shall not be allowed in favor of any debtor of the bankrupt which (1) is not provable against the estate and allowable under . . . this Act; or (2) was purchased by or transferred to him after the filing of the petition or within four months before such filing, with a view to such use and with knowledge or notice that such bankrupt was insolvent or had committed an act of bankruptcy."

1941. Bankruptcy Code § 553(a)(1)-(3) & (b), 11 U.S.C. § 553(a)(1)-(3) & (b) (2000), precludes setoff when (1) the claim of the creditor is disallowed; (2) the creditor acquires the claim while the debtor is insolvent after the filing of the petition or within 90 days before the date of the filing; (3) the debt owed by the creditor to the debtor was incurred by the creditor while the debtor was insolvent and for the purpose of obtaining a right of setoff against the debtor later than 90 days before the filing of the petition; or (4) the creditor's prepetition setoff caused it to improve its position based on an insufficiency formula. The limitation contained in Bankruptcy Code § 553(b) is contrary to the policy under the Bankruptcy Act which allowed parties to setoff prepetition those amounts that would have been subject to offset postpetition. *Compare* 11 U.S.C. § 553(b)

is not permitted. As an alternative holding in *Western Tie & Timber Co. v. Brown*, the Court disallowed the setoff because the party owing money to the debtor acquired claims against the debtor shortly before bankruptcy, while the debtor was insolvent, with a view of using them to obtain a set-off.[1942] When the party is a bank and incurs an obligation to the debtor by virtue of the debtor's bank deposit, however, and the amounts deposited are subject to withdrawal, the bank's right of setoff is preserved.[1943] Surprisingly, however, in *Studley v. Boylston National Bank*,[1944] the Court equated the debtor's use of bank deposits used to pay a note with the bank's exercise of its right of setoff.[1945] Although this holding precluded the transferee from liability under the Bankruptcy Act,[1946] it could have the opposite effect under the Bankruptcy Code, under which treatment of the prepetition payment on the note as a setoff could subject the bank to disgorgement under the reduction-of-insufficiency test of Bankruptcy Code § 553(b).[1947] This result is unlikely, however, in light of the Court's recognition in *Citizens Bank of Maryland v. Strumpf*,[1948] that in a majority of jurisdictions "a setoff has

---

(2000) *with* Studley v. Boylston Nat'l Bank, 229 U.S. 523, 528-29 (1913) ("There is nothing in [Bankruptcy Act] § 68a which prevents the parties from voluntarily doing, before the petition is filed, what the law itself requires to be done after proceedings in bankruptcy are instituted.").

1942. *See* Western Tie & Timber Co. v. Brown, 196 U.S. 502, 510 (1905).

1943. *See* Cont'l & Commercial Trust & Sav. Bank v. Chicago Title & Trust Co., 229 U.S. 435, 446-47 (1913); N.Y. County Nat'l Bank v. Massey, 192 U.S. 138, 147-48 (1904) (holding that "a deposit of money upon an open account subject to check" is not a transfer and does not defeat the right of set off).

1944. 229 U.S. 523 (1913).

1945. *See id.* at 529. ("[W]hether the [deposited] checks for $5,000 were paid or notes for $5,000 were charged, was, in either event, a book entry equivalent to the voluntary exercise by the parties of the right of set-off.").

1946. Under the facts in *Studley*, the bank might have been liable for preference disgorgement in the absence of treatment of the note payment as a setoff. *See id.*

1947. *See* 11 U.S.C. § 553(b) (2000).

1948. 516 U.S. 16 (1995).

not occurred until three steps have been taken: (i) a decision to effectuate a setoff, (ii) some action accomplishing the setoff, and (iii) a recording of the setoff."[1949] The debtor's voluntary tender of third party checks to pay a note does not appear to meet these steps.

Avoiding Statutory Liens

Under Bankruptcy Code § 545,[1950] the policy to empower the trustee to avoid secret liens applies to statutory liens created under state or federal law. When the Bankruptcy Act of 1898 was enacted, there was no power to avoid statutory liens. Although the trustee could use Bankruptcy Act § 67f to avoid as a preference certain judicial liens[1951] or proceeds of an execution sale on such liens[1952]

1949. *See id.* at 19.

1950. 11 U.S.C. § 545 (2000).

1951. In Metcalf v. Barker, 187 U.S. 165, 174 (1902), the Court held that the trustee could not use Bankruptcy Act § 67f to avoid a judgment lien enforcing a perfected preexisting security interest: "In our opinion the conclusion to be drawn from this language is that it is the lien created by a levy, or a judgment, or an attachment, or otherwise, that is invalidated, and that where the lien is obtained more than four months prior to the filing of the petition, it is not only not to be deemed to be null and void on adjudication, but its validity is recognized. . . . A judgment or decree in enforcement of an otherwise valid preexisting lien is not the judgment denounced by the statute, which is plainly confined to judgments creating liens." But when the creditor's first property interest in the collateral arises by attachment within four months before bankruptcy while the debtor insolvent, the Court has upheld application of Bankruptcy Act § 67f to avoid the attachment lien. *See* Globe Bank & Trust Co. v. Martin, 236 U.S. 288, 304 (1915) ("Under the Bankruptcy Act, when the conveyance was set aside, the lien or attachment being within four months of the bankruptcy proceeding, the bankrupt being then insolvent, of which fact no question is made, and the Bankruptcy Court having ordered that the lien be preserved for the benefit of creditors, it became good under the provisions of the Bankruptcy Act for the benefit of all the creditors of the estate.").

1952. *See* Clarke v. Larremore, 188 U.S. 486, 488 (1903). In Taubel-Scott-Kitzmiller Co. v. Fox, 264 U.S. 426, 429 (1924), the Court clarified that Bankruptcy Act § 67f does not automatically void every lien or execution incurred within four months before bankruptcy while the debtor was insolvent,[1953] the Court held this power did not apply to statutory liens or liens of distress for rent.[1954] This result led Congress to add § 67c to the Bankruptcy Act, allowing the trustee to avoid certain statutory liens and all liens for rent or liens of distress for rent whether statutory or not.[1955]

When Congress enacted Bankruptcy Code § 545 in 1978,[1956] it continued to give the trustee the power to avoid certain statutory liens, statutory liens for rent, and liens of distress for rent whether or not statutory.[1957] As noted earlier, the status of the statutory lien is determined as of the date of the filing of the petition. If a creditor holds a valid statutory lien perfected by possession of the collateral, the creditor will not lose priority by voluntarily turning over the

---

sale. Rather, events occurring within four months of bankruptcy while the debtor is insolvent are voidable, not void. *See* Connell v. Walker, 291 U.S. 1, 3 (1934). Moreover, if the trustee loses the issue of lien avoidance and fails to appeal, his successor in interest will be disabled from challenging the title of a purchaser of the debtor's property at an execution sale within four months before bankruptcy. *See* Fischer v. Pauline Oil & Gas Co., 309 U.S. 294, 302-03 (1940).

1953. *See, e.g.,* Minnich v. Gardner, 292 U.S. 48, 52 (1934) (noting the general four-month rule, but denying trustee's efforts to avoid lien because state law revived the lien retroactively outside of preference period).

1954. *See* Henderson v. Mayer, 225 U.S. 631, 638-39 (1912) (holding that lien of distress for rent is not a judicial lien within the purview of Bankruptcy Act § 67f).

1955. *See* Bankruptcy Act § 67c(1)(C) as added by Pub. L. No. 89-495, 80 Stat. 269 (1966).

1956. 11 U.S.C. § 545 (2000).

1957. *See* 11 U.S.C. §§ 101(53) & 545(3)-(4) (2000) giving the trustee the right to avoid all statutory liens for rent and all liens of distress for rent respectively. Although Bankruptcy Code § 545 only allows the trustee to avoid "statutory liens," Bankruptcy Code § 101(53) defines the term "statutory lien" to encompass a lien of distress for rent whether or not statutory.

collateral to the trustee postpetition.[1958] If, however, the creditor's statutory lien is not perfected against a hypothetical bona fide purchaser, then, generally the bankruptcy trustee will be able to avoid the lien under Bankruptcy Code § 545(2).[1959]

PLANS OF REORGANIZATION, LIQUIDATION, AND REPAYMENT

Plans of Reorganization

Over the years, different chapters of the Bankruptcy Act[1960] and Bankruptcy Code[1961] have permitted debtors,[1962] and sometimes

---

1958. *See* Goggin v. Div. of Labor Law Enforcement of Cal., 336 U.S. 118, 130 (1949) (holding that the priority a of claimant's tax lien is determined at the time of the filing of the petition: "By his subsequent arrangement with the trustee for the sale of the bankrupt's property, the Collector did not lose the right to priority of payment accorded to the perfected tax liens, at the time of bankruptcy, as against the wage claims.").

1959. *See* 11 U.S.C. § 545(2) (2000).

1960. *See, e.g.,* Bankruptcy Act Chapters VIII (§ 77 railroad reorganizations), 11 U.S.C. § 205 (1976) (repealed 1979); IX (Adjustment of Debts of Political Subdivisions and Public Agencies and Instrumentalities, Bankruptcy Act §§ 81-98), 11 U.S.C. §§ 401-418 (1976) (repealed 1979) (replacing an earlier version of Chapter IX, 11 U.S.C. §§ 401-404 (50 Stat. 653 (1937)); X (Corporate Reorganizations, Bankruptcy Act §§ 101-276), 11 U.S.C. §§ 501-676 (1976) (repealed 1979); XI (Arrangements, Bankruptcy Act §§ 301-399), 11 U.S.C. §§ 701-799 (1976) (repealed 1979); XII (Real Property Arrangements By Persons Other Than Corporations, Bankruptcy Act §§ 401-526), 11 U.S.C. §§ 801-926 (1976) (repealed 1979); XIII (Wage Earners' Plans, Bankruptcy Act §§ 601-686), 11 U.S.C. §§ 1001-1086 (1976) (repealed 1979); & XV (Railroad Adjustments, Bankruptcy Act §§ 700-755), 11 U.S.C. §§ 1200-1255 (56 Stat. 787) (Supp. 1942) (terminated by its terms in § 1255 on Nov. 1, 1945).

1961. *See* Bankruptcy Code chapters 9 (Adjustment of Debts of a Municipality), 11 U.S.C. §§ 901-946 (2000); 11 (Reorganization), 11 U.S.C. §§ 1101-1174 (2000); 12 (Adjustment of Debts of a Family Farmer or Fisherman with Regular Annual Income), 11 U.S.C. §§ 1201-1231 (2000); & 13 (Adjustment of Debts of An Individual with Regular Income), 11 U.S.C. §§ 1301-1330 (2000).

1962. Each Chapter of the Bankruptcy Act and Bankruptcy Code permitted debtors to file plans. In some Chapters, only the debtor is permitted

trustees and other parties,[1963] to file plans of reorganization, liquidation,[1964] or repayment. The purposes of these plans vary. As a general proposition, a liquidation plan reduces the assets of the debtor's bankruptcy estate to money and distributes the net proceeds to creditors in accordance with their priorities.[1965] In this respect, "[a]ll of the consideration which is paid for a bankrupt's assets becomes part of the estate."[1966] A repayment plan for an individual debtor accomplishes a composition or extension of indebtedness whereby the debtor uses future income to repay creditors in whole or in part over the period of the plan.[1967] A plan of reorganization[1968] almost always separates the

---

to file a plan. *See, e.g.,* Bankruptcy Act Chapter XIII § 633(2), 11 U.S.C. § 1033(2) (1976) (repealed 1979) ("the debtor shall submit his plan"); Bankruptcy Code § 1321 (2000) ("The debtor shall file a plan.").

1963. *See, e.g.,* Bankruptcy Act Chapter X § 170(2), 11 U.S.C. § 570(2) (1976) (repealed 1979) (authorizing any creditor or indenture trustee to file a plan); Bankruptcy Code § 1121(c), 11 U.S.C. § 1121(c) (2000) (authorizing any party in interest, including a trustee and a creditor, to file a plan on expiration of the debtor's plan exclusivity period).

1964. Liquidating plans are specifically authorized in Bankruptcy Code § 1123(a)(5)(D), 11 U.S.C. § 1123(a)(5)(D) (2000).

1965. The same result may occur without a plan in chapter 7 or by order of the court if a plan has not been confirmed after five years in a railroad reorganization case. *See* 11 U.S.C. § 1174 (2000).

1966. *See* United States v. Knight, 336 U.S. 505, 508 (1949) (dictum). Moreover, "[n]o device or arrangement, however subtle, can subtract or divert any of it. It is the substance of the transaction, not its form, which controls." *Id.*

1967. *See, e.g.,* Bankruptcy Code §§ 1129(a)(15), 1225(b)(1)(B)-(C) & 1325(b)(1)(B), 11 U.S.C. §§ 1129(a)(15), 1225(b)(1)(B)-(C) & 1325(b)(1)(B) (Supp. 2005) (providing for repayment of debts out of an individual debtor's future income).

1968. In 1916 Paul Cravath described three kinds of reorganizations: "*First:* Reorganizations based on the foreclosure of mortgages or the enforcement of other rights of creditors and involving the organization of a new corporation to acquire the property which is the subject of the reorganization; *Second:* Readjustments of the debt or share capital of corporations because of insolvency or financial needs of some sort where

debtor's liabilities into classes of claims,[1969] adjusts the debtor's debts or recapitalizes the debtor's balance sheet[1970] and often restructures its business as well, either internally or by transfer of assets to a new entity.[1971]

---

the property is not transferred to a new corporation; *Third:* The recapitalization of corporations for some other purpose than to meet insolvency or correct defects of financial structure and which may be accomplished either with or without the transfer of the property to a new corporation." *See* Paul D. Cravath, "The Reorganization of Corporations; Bondholders' and Stockholders' Protective Committees; Reorganization Committees; and the Voluntary Recapitalization of Corporations," at 155-56 (A lecture delivered before the Association of the Bar of the City of New York, March 1 and 8, 1916) (located online at: http://books.google.com/books?id=KXE9AAAAIAAJ&pg=PA153&dq=paul+cravath+corporate+reorganization (last visited April 29, 2008).

1969. *See, e.g.,* Bankruptcy Code § 1122, 11 U.S.C. § 1122 (2000) (providing for a reorganization plan to place substantially similar claims and interests into separate classes). Typically postpetition priority administrative expenses are not classified at all and certainly are not similar to prepetition claims. *See* Bankruptcy Code §§ 503(b), 507(a) & 1123(a)(1), 11 U.S.C. §§ 503(b), 507(a) & 1123(a)(1) (2000). In Ecker v. W. Pac. R.R., 318 U.S. 448, 486 (1943), however, the Court made the extraordinary statement that all claims of the Reconstruction Finance Corp., including claims on postpetition trustees' certificates, could be considered as a single claim for purposes of allocating reorganization securities under a § 77 railroad reorganization.

1970. *See, e.g.,* Bankruptcy Code § 941, 11 U.S.C. § 941 (2000) (permitting a chapter 9 plan to adjust the debts of the debtor municipality or other political subdivision); Bankruptcy Code § 1123(a)(5)(E)-(H) & (J), 11 U.S.C. § 1123(a)(5)(E)-(H) & (J) (2000) (permitting a chapter 11 plan to satisfy or modify liens, indentures, or similar instruments; to cure or waive defaults, and to modify debts by extending debt maturity dates, interest rates, or other terms; and to issue new securities for cash or in exchange for other securities).

1971. *See, e.g.,* Bankruptcy Code § 1123(a)(5)(B)-(C), 11 U.S.C. § 1123(a)(5)(B)-(C) (2000) (permitting a chapter 11 plan to transfer all or part of the property of the estate to another entity; and merger or consolidation of the debtor with one or more persons).

Ordinarily after a plan is filed,[1972] the plan proponent solicits any necessary votes,[1973] and the court sets a hearing on confirmation of the plan. In determining whether sufficient holders of claims or interests have voted to accept the plan, the court may exclude the votes of certain creditors or equity holders whose interests conflict with others in the class[1974] or were not cast in good faith.[1975] In this respect, "[t]he court is not merely a ministerial register of the vote of the several classes of security holders."[1976]

Before a plan may be confirmed, both the Bankruptcy Act and the Bankruptcy Code offer parties in interest the opportunity to object to confirmation.[1977] An entity that purchases claims during the case may even object to confirmation on a basis that it would lack standing to

---

1972. The Bankruptcy Code permits prepetition solicitation of votes in certain so-called prepackaged or pre-negotiated chapter 11 cases. *See* 11 U.S.C. § 1126(b) (2000).

1973. *See, e.g.,* Bankruptcy Code § 1125-1126, 11 U.S.C. §§ 1125-1126 (2000).

1974. *See, e.g.,* Am. United Mut. Life Ins. Co. v. City of Avon Park, 311 U.S. 138, 146-48 (1940) (Chapter IX municipal reorganization case discussing the court's equitable power to limit or disqualify votes when there is "unfair dealing, a breach of fiduciary obligations, profiting from a trust, special benefits for the organizers, or the need for protection of investors against an inside few, or one class of investors from the encroachments of another.") *See id.* at 146.

1975. *See, e.g., id.* at 144-45 (discussing that full disclosure of a fiscal agent's interests was "[t]he very minimum requirement for fair dealing" and "[e]quity and good conscience obviously will not permit a finding that an acceptance of a plan by a person acting in a representative capacity is in 'good faith' where that person is obtaining an undisclosed benefit from the plan.").

1976. *See id.* at 145 citing Case v. Los Angeles Lumber Prods. Co., 308 U.S. 106, 114 (1939) (cited with approval to support the exclusion of plan acceptances).

1977. *See, e.g.,* Bankruptcy Code § 1128(b), 11 U.S.C. § 1128(b) (2000); Bankruptcy Act §§ 77(e), 179 & 337(3), 11 U.S.C. §§ 205(e), 579 & 737(3) (1976) (repealed 1979).

raise under non-bankruptcy law if the objections go to the fairness and equity of the plan.[1978]

Under Bankruptcy Act § 77 and Chapter X, the reorganization court could confirm a plan only if the plan was fair and equitable. In corporate reorganization cases and railroad reorganizations, the Court rendered many important decisions interpreting the words "fair and equitable" as words of art. Before discussing these cases, however, it is necessary to examine a few of the railroad equity receivership decisions from which they derived.

In 1869, the Court decided *Railroad Co. v. Howard*,[1979] affirming the challenge of unsecured guarantee judgment creditors to reach proceeds allocated to shareholders in the foreclosure sale of assets of an insolvent railroad.[1980] Bondholders and stockholders had agreed that shareholders of the insolvent railroad could participate in the foreclosure sale proceeds, even though the creditors were not paid in full.[1981] The Court held that "[e]quity regards the property of a corporation held in trust for the payment of the debts of the corporation . . . and the rule is well settled that stockholders are not entitled to any share . . . until all the debts of the corporation are paid."[1982] Once the secured mortgage bondholders accepted a percentage on their bonds in compromise of their claims, the remaining property or sale

---

1978. *See* Comstock v. Group of Institutional Investors, 335 U.S. 211, 227-28 (1948) (the court could entertain objections to a plan on their merits even if made by a person who might be barred from asserting a cause of action on his or her own behalf, if the subject matter of the objection is such that it goes beyond the objector's individual interests and affects the fairness and equity of the plan).

1979. 74 U.S. (7 Wall.) 392 (1869).

1980. *See id.* at 415.

1981. *See id.* at 408.

1982. *See id.* at 409-10.

proceeds belonged to the corporation and was subject to the senior claims of creditors before shareholders could participate.[1983]

Thirty years later, in 1899, the Court decided *Louisville Trust Co. v. Louisville New Albany & Chicago Railway*,[1984] clarifying that a foreclosing bondholder in an equity receivership could not preserve the rights of the railroad mortgagor and its stockholders while freezing out junior lien holders and unsecured creditors.[1985] The Court specifically left open "whether a court is justified in permitting a foreclosure and sale which leaves any interest in the mortgagor, to wit, the railroad company and its stockholders . . . ."[1986] *Louisville Trust Co.* set forth a seminal principle, however, that "any arrangement of the parties by which the subordinate rights and interests of the stockholders are attempted to be secured at the expense of the prior rights of either class of [secured or unsecured] creditors comes within judicial denunciation."[1987] Moreover, the Court roundly condemned efforts by foreclosing bondholders to circumvent this principle by "donating" part of their foreclosure proceeds to shareholders:[1988]

> It is no answer to these objections to say that a bondholder may foreclose in his own separate interest, and, after acquiring title to the mortgaged property, may give what interest he pleases to any one, whether stockholder or not, and so these several mortgagees foreclosing their mortgages, if proceeding in their own interest, if acquiring title for themselves alone, may donate what interest in the property acquired by foreclosure they desire. But human nature is something whose action

---

1983. *See id.* at 413-14.

1984. 174 U.S. 674 (1899).

1985. *See id.* at 683 ("[N]o such proceedings can be rightfully carried to consummation which recognize and preserve any interest in the stockholders without also recognizing and preserving the interests, not merely of the mortgagee, but of every creditor to the corporation.").

1986. *See id.*

1987. *See id.* at 684.

1988. *See id.* at 688.

can never be ignored in the courts, and parties who have acquired full and absolute title to property are not as a rule
donating any interest therein to strangers. It is one thing for a
bondholder who has acquired absolute title by foreclosure to
mortgaged property to thereafter give of his interest to others,
and an entirely different thing whether such bondholder, to
destroy the interest of all unsecured creditors, to secure a
waiver of all objections on the part of the stockholder and
consummate speedily the foreclosure, may proffer to him an
interest in the property after foreclosure. The former may be
beyond the power of the courts to inquire into or condemn.
The latter is something which on the face of it deserves the
condemnation of every court, and should never be aided by
any decree or order thereof. It involves an offer, a temptation,
to the mortgagor, the purchase price thereof to be paid, not by
the mortgagee, but in fact by the unsecured creditor.

The Court applied the rationale of the holding of *Louisville Trust
Co.* in the 1913 decision *Northern Pacific Railway Co. v. Boyd.*[1989]
Legal proceedings in *Boyd* began in 1893 when creditors filed a
creditors' bill against the Northern Pacific Railroad alleging its
insolvency and seeking the appointment of an equity receiver.[1990]
Shortly thereafter, certain mortgage bond trustees commenced suit to
foreclose on the railroad's mortgage bonds, and the cases were
consolidated.[1991] Shareholders of the railroad attempted to forestall
foreclosure and to file a reorganization plan that recognized the
superior claims of the bonds but still retained an interest in the
reorganized railroad for the old shareholders.[1992] The shareholders and
bondholders collaborated and issued a circular outlining a plan in
which assets of the railroad would be transferred to a new company
that would issue stock and notes for distribution to the old bondhold-

---

1989. 228 U.S. 482 (1913).

1990. *See id.* at 487.

1991. *See id.* at 488.

1992. *See id.*

ers and shareholders, but distribute nothing to the railroad's general unsecured creditors.[1993] General creditors of the railroad objected that the foreclosure sale under the plan "was the result of a conspiracy between the bondholders and shareholders to exclude general creditors" from ownership in the reorganized company.[1994] The general creditors contended that value could not be given to the shareholders unless first offered to and declined by the unsecured creditors.[1995] The trial court held that the Railroad was insolvent and that there was no value for unsecured creditors; at the same time, nothing precluded the former shareholders from getting an ownership interest in a new company that would purchase the assets.[1996] Boyd, a creditor of the old railroad, claimed the reorganization was invalid and sued the new railroad for payment of the old railroad's debts.[1997] The new railroad defended by saying that the plan was free from fraud and the property was transferred for a fair price.[1998] An amicus curiae contended that Boyd's remedy was against the former shareholders, not the new company.[1999]

In a 5-4 opinion, the Court agreed with Boyd and held that the transfer of assets to the new company was impermissible because, even in the absence of fraud, it reserved value to the old shareholders at the expense of unsecured creditors.[2000] "[I]f purposely or unintentionally a single creditor was not paid, or provided for in the reorganization, he could assert his superior rights against the

---

1993. *See id.*

1994. *See id.* at 490.

1995. *See id.*

1996. *See id.* at 490, 505. This holding was not res judicata because Boyd was not a party so that decree was not binding on him. *See id.* at 505.

1997. *See id.* at 492, 498, 501.

1998. *See id.* at 501.

1999. *See id.* at 492.

2000. *See id.* at 504.

subordinate interests of the old stockholders in the property transferred to the new company. They were in the position of insolvent
debtors who could not reserve an interest as against creditors."[2001] The
Court went on to note that:[2002]

> The invalidity of the sale flowed from the character of the re-
> organization agreement regardless of the value of the proper-
> ty, for in cases like this, the question must be decided
> according to a fixed principle, not leaving the rights of the
> creditors to depend upon the balancing of evidence as to
> whether, on the day of sale the property was insufficient to
> pay prior encumbrances.

The *Boyd* Court's holding was based on the following rationale:[2003]

> If the value of the road justified the issuance of stock in ex-
> change for old shares, the creditors were entitled to the benefit
> of that value, whether it was present or prospective, for divi-
> dends or only for purposes of control. In either event it was a
> right of property out of which the creditors were entitled to be
> paid before the stockholders could retain it for any purpose
> whatever.

The Court also made the following observation:[2004]

> This conclusion does not, as claimed, require the impossible
> and make it necessary to pay an unsecured creditor in cash as
> a condition of stockholders retaining an interest in the reorga-
> nized company. His interest can be preserved by the issuance,
> on equitable terms, of income bonds or preferred stock. If he
> declines a fair offer he is left to protect himself as any other
> creditor of a judgment debtor, and, having refused to come in-
> to a just reorganization, could not thereafter be heard in a
> court of equity to attack it. If, however, no such tender was
> made and kept good he retains the right to subject the interest

---

2001. *See id.*

2002. *See id.* at 507.

2003. *See id.* at 508.

2004. *See id.*

of the old stockholders in the property to the payment of his debt. If their interest is valueless, he gets nothing. If it be valuable, he merely subjects that which the law had originally and continuously made liable for the payment of corporate liabilities.

Three years after the *Boyd* case was decided, Paul Cravath, leader of the New York reorganization bar, described the impact of the case as "materially reduc[ing] the opportunities for stockholders to participate in reorganizations controlled by mortgage bondholders, for manifestly, the simplest way . . . to avoid the embarrassments of the *Boyd* case is completely to exclude the stockholders and thereby gain freedom to exclude the unsecured debt."[2005] Cravath stated that:[2006]

> [I]n most large reorganizations . . . it is still the preference of most bondholders' committees to afford [the stockholders] participation, partly to avoid the dissatisfaction, litigation and delay which might result from their exclusion, and partly to secure new capital by appealing to the desire of the stockholders to retain their interest in the property and their consequent willingness to furnish new capital on more favorable terms than could be obtained from strangers.

In 1926, the Court decided another railroad equity receivership case, *Kansas City Terminal Railway v. Central Union Trust Co.*[2007] *Kansas City Terminal* provided more definition to the contours of the absolute priority rule:[2008]

2005. Paul D. Cravath, "The Reorganization of Corporations; Bondholders' and Stockholders' Protective Committees; Reorganization Committees; and the Voluntary Recapitalization of Corporations," at 195 (A lecture delivered before the Association of the Bar of the City of New York, March 1 and 8, 1916) (located online at: http://books.google.com/ books?id=KXE9AAAAIAAJ&pg=PA153&dq=paul+cravath+corporate+ reorganization (last visited April 29, 2008).

2006. *See id.*

2007. 271 U.S. 445 (1926).

2008. *See id.* at 454-55.

[W]hen necessary, [creditors] may be protected through other arrangements [than the issuance of income bonds or preferred stock] which distinctly recognize their equitable right to be preferred to stockholders against the full value of all property belonging to the debtor corporation, and afford each of them fair opportunity, measured by the existing circumstances, to avail himself of this right.

The Court went on to note that "[i]f creditors decline a fair offer based upon the principles above stated, they are left to protect themselves. After such refusal, they cannot attack the reorganization in a court of equity."[2009]

The Court applied these principles to evaluate the fairness of the reorganization plan in *Kansas City Terminal*, which provided for the distribution of various combinations of mortgage lien bonds, secured income bonds, preferred stock, and common stock to outstanding classes of secured bonds, unsecured creditors, and stockholders.[2010] Certain objecting creditors contended that in order to be fair, the plan had to preserve the relative priority of creditors over shareholders with respect to the form of the consideration distributed; i.e., it was impermissible for the plan to give the same grade of securities to both creditors and shareholders.[2011] The Court squarely rejected this contention, holding that "it does not follow that in every reorganization the securities offered to general creditors must be superior in rank or grade to any which stockholders may obtain."[2012] "[C]ircumstances may justify an offer of different amounts of the same grade of securities to both creditors and stockholders."[2013] At the same time, the Court recognized the importance of protecting creditors' rights: "The primary right of unsecured creditors to the assets of an insolvent

---

2009. *See id.* at 455.

2010. *See id.* at 450-51.

2011. *See id.* at 452.

2012. *See id.* at 455.

2013. *See id.* at 456.

corporation . . . must be adequately protected; and to each [unsecured creditor] there must be given such opportunity as the circumstances permit to secure the full enjoyment of this preference."[2014] Finally, *Kansas City Terminal* is noteworthy because it lays the groundwork for the new value corollary to the absolute priority rule: "Generally, additional funds will be essential to the success of the [reorganization], and it may be impossible to obtain them unless stockholders are permitted to contribute and retain an interest sufficiently valuable to move them [to inject fresh capital]."[2015]

The Court's 1939 decisions in *Taylor v. Standard Gas & Electric Co.*[2016] and *Case v. Los Angeles Lumber Products Co.*,[2017] extended the principles of the fair and equitable test formed in the Court's railroad equity receivership cases to the reorganization of non-railroad businesses.[2018] In *Taylor*, debtor Deep Rock Oil Corporation was engaged in the business of producing, refining and selling gasoline, oil, and other petroleum products,[2019] and it filed a petition for reorganization under Bankruptcy Act § 77B.[2020] Standard Gas and Electric

---

2014. *See id.* at 455-56.

2015. *See id.* at 455.

2016. 306 U.S. 307 (1939).

2017. 308 U.S. 106 (1939).

2018. The Court did not distinguish railroad reorganizations from the reorganization of ordinary commercial corporations where the public interest is not at stake.

2019. *See Taylor*, 306 U.S. at 309.

2020. Bankruptcy Act § 77B, Act of June 7, 1934, ch. 424, § 77B, 48 Stat. 912-22, 11 U.S.C. § 207 (1934) (superseded in 1938 by Chapter X, 52 Stat. 883, 11 U.S.C. §§ 501 et seq.). According to the Court, "[l]ack of knowledge and control by the court of the conditions attending formulation of reorganization plans, the inadequate protection of widely scattered security holders, the frequent adoption of plans which favored management at the expense of other interests, and which afforded the corporation only temporary respite from financial collapse, so often characteristic of reorganizations in equity receiverships, led to the

Company owned practically all of the common stock of Deep Rock and also was a creditor.[2021] Because Standard Gas had operated Deep Rock as its instrumentality to the detriment of Deep Rock's preferred stockholders, the Court held that the district court abused its discretion in approving the compromise of Standard Gas's claim against Deep Rock in a reorganization plan that gave common stock to both the preferred and common stockholders;[2022] the preferred stockholders were entitled to rights superior to those of the common stockholders, and it was unfair and inequitable for the plan to treat Standard's rights as a common stockholder on a parity with the preferred stockholders.[2023]

In *Los Angeles Lumber Products*, the debtor was a holding company for a shipbuilding and drydock corporation under § 77B of the Bankruptcy Act.[2024] Justice Douglas, who had worked diligently to persuade the Court to grant certiorari in *Los Angeles Lumber Products*,[2025] authored the opinion of the Court and framed the

---

enactment of 77B." *See* S.E.C. v. U.S. Realty & Imp. Co., 310 U.S. 434, 448 (1940) (footnote omitted).

2021. *See Taylor*, 306 U.S. at 309.

2022. *See id.* at 315.

2023. *See id.* at 323 ("Equity requires the award to preferred stockholders of a superior position in the reorganized company.").

2024. Bankruptcy Act § 77B, Act of June 7, 1934, ch. 424, § 77B, 48 Stat. 912-22, 11 U.S.C. § 207 (1934) (superseded in 1938 by Chapter X, 52 Stat. 883, 11 U.S.C. § 501 et seq.).

2025. *See* May 10, 1939, Memorandum of Justice Douglas to Justice Reed (stating that "[t]his plan, in my opinion, is a clear fraud in law") and May 15, 1939, Addendum to Memorandum of 5-10-39 (arguing that certiorari should be granted based on the split in the Circuits and "since the matter is so enormously important to prior lienholders as well as to stockhold-ers . . . ."). In his private papers (23-124), Justice Reed writes a Memo on Case v. Los Angeles Lumber Prods. Co. as follows: "Mr, [sic] Justice Douglas this morning convinced me that his position on this is correct and that my trouble of yesterday evening was born of misconception." He then sets forth at length his reasons for being convinced. On May 22,

question "of the conditions under which stockholders may participate in a plan under § 77B of the Bankruptcy Act where the debtor corporation is insolvent both in the equity and in the bankruptcy sense."[2026] In 1924, the holding company issued mortgage bonds secured by a lien on stock in the debtor's subsidiaries.[2027] The debtor defaulted in the payment of bond interest in 1929; negotiations ensued, and, in 1930, the parties agreed to an out of court voluntary reorganization in which 97% of the bondholders agreed to reduce interest under a plan that eliminated the old shares of stock in the holding company and issued new shares to bondholders in payment of outstanding interest and to old shareholders in exchange for $400,000 in new money that was used as working capital by the shipbuilding subsidiary.[2028] In 1937, the holding company prepared a plan of reorganization that was accepted by over 80% of the bondholders and 90% of the stockholders.[2029] The plan provided for the formation of a new corporation that would acquire the assets of the shipbuilding subsidiary in exchange for newly issuing preferred stock to the bondholders and common stock to the old share holders (without any new cash infusion).[2030]

In 1938, the holding company filed a petition for reorganization under Bankruptcy Act § 77B to consummate the plan.[2031] Over 90% of

---

1939, the Court voted 5-4 to grant certiorari in *Los Angeles Lumber Products*. *See* 307 U.S. 619 (1939) and private papers of Justice Douglas (23-124) October Term 1939 noting that Justices Douglas, Frankfurter, Reed, Black, and Roberts voted to grant certiorari whereas Justices Stone, Butler, McReynolds, and Hughes voted to deny the petition.

2026. *See Los Angeles Lumber Prods.*, 308 U.S. at 108-09 (citation omitted). Justice Douglas's internal private memorandum on the case characterized it as involving a "plan of the most outrageous sort."

2027. *See id.* at 109.

2028. *See id.* at 109-10.

2029. *See id.* at 110.

2030. *See id.* at 111.

2031. *See id.* at 110.

the bondholders and stockholders voted to accept the plan.[2032] Bondholders, who never consented to the 1930 reorganization, dissented from the 1937 plan on the basis that it was not fair and equitable.[2033] The Court agreed, noting that Bankruptcy Act § 77B(f)'s words requiring that the plan be "fair and equitable" were "words of art" which "had acquired a fixed meaning through judicial interpretations in the field of equity receivership reorganizations" including the "fixed principle" of the *Boyd* case.[2034] Justice Douglas described this as a "rule of full or absolute priority" and it has since become to be known as the absolute priority rule.[2035] Relying on the principle expressed in *Kansas City Terminal* that "to the extent of their debts creditors are entitled to priority over stockholders against all the property of an insolvent corporation," the Court held that it was error to confirm a plan diverting value to shareholders when bondholders are not receiving full value.[2036]

Even though the *Los Angeles Lumber Products* Court struck down confirmation of the plan, it reaffirmed the observation of *Kansas City Terminal* that "stockholders may participate in a plan of reorganization of an insolvent debtor," especially when seeking new money from the stockholders is "essential to the success of the undertaking."[2037] "Where that necessity exists and the old stockholders make a fresh contribution and receive in return a participation reasonably

---

2032. *See id.* at 111-12.

2033. *See id.* at 112.

2034. *See id.* at 115-16.

2035. *See id.* at 117.

2036. *See id.* at 120.

2037. *See id.* at 121. In Marine Harbor Props., Inc. v. Mfrs. Trust Co., 317 U.S. 78, 85 (1942), the Court noted in dictum that the fair and equitable rule and the new value principle applied under Chapter X as well as under § 77B.

equivalent to their contribution, no objection can be made."[2038] The Court concluded:[2039]

> In view of these considerations we believe that to accord "the creditor his full right of priority against the corporate assets" where the debtor is insolvent, the stockholder's participation must be based on a contribution in money or money's worth, reasonably equivalent in view of all the circumstances to the participation of the stockholder.

> The alleged consideration furnished by the stockholders in this case falls far short of meeting those requirements.

Having established the elements of the new value principle, the Court then applied it to the facts to reach its holding that the principle was not satisfied in this case.[2040] Specifically, the Court found that "financial standing and influence in the community" and a "continuity of management" did not constitute money or money's worth constituting a legal justification for the issuance of new stock to the old shareholders.[2041]

The Court followed its *Los Angeles Lumber Products* decision with several more decisions interpreting the absolute priority rule under Chapter X corporate reorganizations or § 77 railroad reorganizations.[2042] These decisions refined the absolute priority rule and set forth

---

2038. *See Los Angeles Lumber Prods.*, 308 U.S. at 121.

2039. *See id.* at 122.

2040. On at least two occasions, the Court has characterized as "dicta" or "dictum" this application of facts to the new value principle. *See* Bank of Am. Nat'l Trust & Sav. Ass'n v. 203 N. LaSalle St. P'ship, 526 U.S. 434, 445-46 (1999); Norwest Bank Worthington v. Ahlers, 485 U.S. 197, 203 (1988).

2041. *See Los Angeles Lumber Prods.*, 308 U.S. at 122-23 ("[T]hey cannot possibly be translated into money's worth reasonably equivalent to the participation accorded the old stockholders. They have no place in the asset column of the balance sheet of the new company. They reflect merely vague hopes or possibilities.").

2042. From 1933 until 1979, railroad reorganization cases were decided under § 77 of the Bankruptcy Act. *See* Act of March 3, 1933, 47 Stat.

many important clarifications.[2043] In *Consolidated Rock Products Co. v. DuBois*,[2044] the Court held that although "[f]ull compensatory provision must be made for the entire bundle of rights which the creditors surrender[,]"[2045] including priority rights,[2046] creditors have no right to be paid out of specific properties to satisfy their claims.[2047] Specifically, the Court stated as follows:[2048]

> If the creditors are adequately compensated for the loss of their prior claims, it is not material out of what assets they are paid. So long as they receive full compensatory treatment and so long as each group shares in the securities of the whole enterprise on an equitable basis, the requirements of "fair and equitable" are satisfied.

Thus, it is commensurate with the absolute priority rule for a reorganization plan to give preferred and common stock in the reorganized debtor to classes of senior secured creditors even though these securities are of lower stature than notes given to unsecured creditors.[2049] Moreover, a reorganization plan may eliminate creditors' liens on specific items of collateral in favor of new securities secured

---

1467, 1474, ch. 204, 72d Cong., 2d Sess.; 11 U.S.C. § 205 (1976) (repealed 1979).

2043. *See* Kenneth N. Klee, *Cram Down II*, 64 AM. BANKR. L.J. 229 (1990).

2044. 312 U.S. 510 (1941).

2045. *See id.* at 528.

2046. *See id.* at 528-29 ("[T]hose prior rights are not recognized, in cases where stockholders are participating in the plan, if creditors are given only a face amount of inferior securities equal to the face amount of their claims. They must receive, in addition, compensation for the senior rights which they are to surrender.").

2047. *See id.* at 530.

2048. *See id.*

2049. *See Ecker v. W. Pac. R.R.*, 318 U.S. 448, 484 (1943).

by liens on all assets of the reorganized entity.[2050] Furthermore, "[i]n the case of first and second liens on the same property, senior lienors, of course, would be entitled to receive, in case the junior lienors participated in the plan, not only 'a face amount of inferior securities equal to the face amount of their claims' but, in addition, 'compensation for the senior rights' which they surrendered."[2051]

The Court also has stated that when creditors' claims are not satisfied fully, the absolute priority rule forbade the distribution of reorganization securities under the plan to classes of creditors or equity interests that were out of the money based on the reorganization value of the debtor enterprise,[2052] even with respect to the issuance of warrants to stockholders whose equity was valueless (at least without their infusion of new value in money or money's worth).[2053]

2050. *See Consol. Rock Prods.*, 312 U.S. at 530-31 ("Certainly where unified operations of separate properties are deemed advisable and essential, . . . the elimination of divisional mortgages may be necessary as well as wise."). *Accord* Group of Institutional Investors v. Chicago, M., St. P. & Pac. R.R., 318 U.S. 523, 558 (1943) (applying the same principle in the context of a railroad reorganization under Bankruptcy Act § 77: "So far as the law is concerned, there is no obstacle to the substitution of system mortgages for divisional ones.").

2051. *See Group of Institutional Investors*, 318 U.S. at 562-63 (citation omitted).

2052. *See id.* at 541-42 (1943) ("The finding of the Commission, affirmed by the District Court under § 77(e) that the stock had "no value" is supported by evidence. The issue involved in such a determination is whether there is a reasonable probability that the earning power of the road will be sufficient to pay prior claims of interest and principal and leave some surplus for the service of the stock. If it is established that there is no reasonable probability of such earning power, then the inclusion of the stock would violate the full priority rule . . . .").

2053. *See* Consol. Rock Prods. Co. v. DuBois, 312 U.S. 510, 529 n.27 (1941) (noting in dictum "as respects the warrants issued to the old common stockholders that they admittedly have no equity in the enterprise. Accordingly, it should have been shown that there was a necessity of seeking new money from them and that the participation accorded them was not more than reasonably equivalent to their contribution."). *But see* Ecker v. W. Pac. R.R., 318 U.S. 448, 476 (1943)

"That is to say, senior claims first receive securities of a worth sufficient to cover their face and interest before junior claims [or interests] receive anything."[2054]

Although the Court has written many opinions about the application of the absolute priority rule to the debtor's capital structure, only one opinion discusses application of the rule to corporate governance issues. In *St. Joe Paper Co. v. Atlantic Coast Line Railroad Co.*,[2055] the Court held that a reorganization plan under § 77 could not be confirmed as fair and equitable if it included a forced merger of the debtor with another railroad.[2056] Bankruptcy Code § 1123(a)(5)(C)[2057] overturns this result in chapter 11 cases so that a plan providing for a forced merger will be consistent with the requirements for confirmation.[2058]

Both the Bankruptcy Act[2059] and the Bankruptcy Code[2060] have provisions that preclude plans from being unfairly discriminatory in

---

("After all of the reasonable value had been exhausted by senior securities, warrants might have been authorized for otherwise unsatisfied claims. Such warrants would represent merely the possibility of recoupment, just as the equity of redemption in judicial sales. But there is no constitutional or statutory requirement that such immediately valueless paper should be issued.") (dictum).

2054. *See Ecker*, 318 U.S. at 483.

2055. 347 U.S. 298 (1954).

2056. *See id.* at 306.

2057. 11 U.S.C. § 1123(a)(5)(C) (2000).

2058. *See* H.R. REP. NO. 595, 95th Cong., 1st Sess. 407 (1977).

2059. *See* Bankruptcy Act § 77B(f)(1), 11 U.S.C. § 207(f)(1) (1936) (superseded in 1938 by Chapter X, 52 Stat. 883, 11 U.S.C. § 501 et seq.) (corporate reorganization) ("the judge shall confirm the plan if satisfied that . . . [i]t . . . does not discriminate unfairly in favor of any class of creditors or stockholders . . . ."); Bankruptcy Act § 77(e)(1), 11 U.S.C. § 205(e)(1) (1976) (repealed 1979) (railroad reorganization) ("the judge shall approve the plan if satisfied that . . . [i]t . . . does not discriminate unfairly in favor of any class of creditors or stockholders . . . .") & Bankruptcy Act § 94(b)(1), 11 U.S.C. § 314(b)(1) (1976) (repealed 1979) (municipal reorganization) ("The court shall confirm the plan if . . . the plan . . . does not discriminate unfairly in favor of any creditor or class of creditors . . . .").

2060. *See* Bankruptcy Code § 1129(b)(1), 11 U.S.C. § 1129(b)(1) (2000) (reorganization) (permitting court to confirm a cramdown plan "if the plan

treatment of classes of claims or ownership interests. The statutory prohibition against unfair discrimination stems from the principle that creditors with equal or similar legal rights are entitled to be treated similarly.[2061] The Court has interpreted the prohibition against unfair discrimination to apply in evaluating fairness of the plan in reorganizations in which there is no appropriate allocation of asset values among creditors of affiliated debtors in a joint plan.[2062]

Moreover, in order to confirm a reorganization plan, the reorganization court must find that the plan is feasible. "A basic requirement of any reorganization is the determination of a capitalization which makes it possible not only to respect the priorities of the various classes of claimants but also to give the new company a reasonable prospect for survival."[2063] The Court has recognized that the interdependence of the feasibility requirement and the fair and equitable test may dictate a deleveraged capital structure in which debt is converted to equity or senior debt is subordinated:[2064]

> The absolute priority rule does not mean that bondholders cannot be given inferior grades of securities, or even securities of the same grade as are received by junior interests. Require-

---

does not discriminate unfairly . . . with respect to each class of claims or interests that is impaired under, and has not accepted, the plan."); Bankruptcy Code § 1222(b)(1), 11 U.S.C. § 1222(b)(1) (2000) (debt adjustments of family farmer or fisherman) ("[T]he plan may . . . not discriminate unfairly against any class . . . ."); Bankruptcy Code § 1322(b)(1), 11 U.S.C. § 1322(b)(1) (2000) (debt adjustments of individuals) ("[T]he plan may . . . not discriminate unfairly against any class . . . .").

2061. *See, e.g.,* H.R. REP. NO. 595, 95th Cong., 1st Sess. 416 (1977) (applying unfair discrimination to test treatment given "to equal classes").

2062. *See* Consol. Rock Prods. Co. v. DuBois, 312 U.S. 510, 524-25 (1941) (requiring the court to determine allegations of unfair discrimination based on "some appropriate formula for at least an approximate ascertainment" of respective asset values despite the difficulties of commingling).

2063. *See* Group of Institutional Investors v. Chicago, M., St. P. & Pac. R. Co., 318 U.S. 523, 540 (1943) (citation omitted).

2064. *See Consol. Rock Prods. Co. v. DuBois,* 312 U.S. at 528 (footnote omitted).

ments of feasibility of reorganization plans frequently necessitate it in the interests of simpler and more conservative capital structures.

Nevertheless, as noted previously, the Court has stated that if creditors and stockholders share the same class of securities in the reorganized debtor, the absolute priority rule requires the creditors to be given compensation in excess of the face amount of their claims to compensate for the loss of their seniority rights under the plan.[2065] "But whether in case of a solvent company the creditors should be made whole for the change in or loss of their seniority by an increased participation in assets, in earnings or in control, or in any combination thereof, will be dependent on the facts and requirements of each case."[2066] For example, in *Reconstruction Finance Corp. v. Denver & Rio Grande Western Railroad Co.,*[2067] the Court approved a plan that gave senior claimants common stock in the reorganized debtor because "one thing that gave the senior creditors compensation for the admission of junior claimants to participation in securities before the seniors obtained full cash payment was their chance to share in the unlimited dividends that might be earned and paid on the common stock to have a part in the 'lush years.'"[2068] Thus, the underlying principle to be served is that the absolute priority rule "protects the rights of senior creditors against dilution either by junior creditors or

---

2065. *See id.* at 528-29; *Kansas City Terminal*, 271 U.S. at 454. It remains to be seen whether the Bankruptcy Code's reference to the fair and equitable rule in § 1129(b)(1) incorporates this judicial rule of over-compensation for loss of seniority rights or whether the Bankruptcy Code's statutory reference to satisfying up to the allowed amount of a claim in § 1129(b)(2)(B)(i) leads to a different result. *Compare* 11 U.S.C. § 1129(b)(1) (2000) *with* 11 U.S.C. § 1129(b)(2)(B)(i) (2000).

2066. *See Consol. Rock Prods. Co. v. DuBois*, 312 U.S. at 529 (dictum) (footnote omitted).

2067. 328 U.S. 495 (1946).

2068. *See id.* at 518.

by equity interests."[2069] Nevertheless, neither senior creditors, nor any other creditors, are "entitled to more than full payment" and are under a duty to account to junior claims and interests "for any surplus remaining after they have been made whole."[2070]

Both the financial fairness test and the feasibility requirement are driven by valuation of the enterprise which in turn is driven by how much the reorganized enterprise can earn.[2071] In this respect, the Court has acknowledged that "Mankind's foresight is limited. The uncertainties of future estimates are recognized."[2072] "The basic question in a valuation for reorganization purposes is how much the enterprise in all probability can earn."[2073] In this respect, in *Protective Committee v. Anderson (In re TMT Trailer Ferry, Inc.)*,[2074] the Court held that it is error for a reorganization court to base a valuation on past earnings without considering whether past earnings are "a reliable criterion of

---

2069. *See* Marine Harbor Props. v. Mfrs. Trust Co., 317 U.S. 78, 87 (1942) (citing *Los Angeles Lumber Prods.* and *Consol. Rock Prods. Co. v. DuBois*).

2070. *See Reconstruction Fin. Corp. v. Denver & R.G.W.R. Co.*, 328 U.S. at 530-31.

2071. *See, e.g., Group of Institutional Investors*, 318 U.S. at 540 ("[I]n connection with a reorganization of an industrial company, . . . the 'criterion of earning capacity is the essential one . . . if the allocation . . . is to be fair and equitable.' . . . That is equally applicable to a railroad reorganization." (citing Consol. Rock Prods. Co. v. DuBois, 312 U.S. 510, 526 (1941)); Consol. Rock Prods. Co. v. DuBois, 312 U.S. 510, 525 (1941) ("Findings as to the earning capacity of an enterprise are essential to a determination of the feasibility as well as the fairness of a plan of reorganization."). *See also* Ecker v. W. Pac. R.R., 318 U.S. 448, 482 (1943) ("The requirements for valuation are the same in a § 77B proceeding as in a railroad reorganization.").

2072. *See Reconstruction Fin. Corp. v. Denver & R.G.W.R. Co.*, 328 U.S. at 522 n.29.

2073. *See Group of Institutional Investors*, 318 U.S. at 540.

2074. 390 U.S. 414 (1968).

future performance."[2075] "If it is shown that the record of past earnings is not a reliable criterion of future performance, the court must form an estimate of future performance by inquiring into all foreseeable factors which may affect future prospects. In forming this estimate, 'mathematical certitude' is neither expected nor required."[2076] As noted by the Court in *Consolidated Rock Products Co. v. DuBois:*[2077]

> [T]hat estimate must be based on an informed judgment which embraces all facts relevant to future earning capacity and hence to present worth, including, of course, the nature and condition of the properties, the past earnings record, and all circumstances which indicate whether or not that record is a reliable criterion of future performance. A sum of values based on physical factors and assigned to separate units of the property without regard to the earning capacity of the whole enterprise is plainly inadequate.

Under the absolute priority rule, the enterprise valuation is applied to distribute reorganization securities or assets to classes of allowed prepetition claims in strict order of priority, thereby resulting in the elimination of valueless claims and equity interests from participation in the reorganization.[2078] Valuation of the enterprise differs from valuation of a secured creditor's collateral. The collateral package

---

2075. *See id.* at 452 (1968) (citation omitted).

2076. *See id.*

2077. 312 U.S. 520, 526 (1941).

2078. *See* Reconstruction Fin. Corp. v. Denver & R.G.W.R. Co., 328 U.S. 495, 509 (1946) ("We see no more constitutional impediment to the elimination of [valueless] claims against railroad debtors . . . than we do to their elimination by an accepted bid in a depression market."); *Id.* at 516 ("The aggregate [enterprise valuation] was too small to allow anything to former stockholders. Thus, they were eliminated from the reorganization." (footnote omitted)); *Group of Institutional Investors* at 537-38 (eliminating valueless common and preferred stock from participation under the plan); *Ecker v. Western Pac. R.R.*, 318 U.S. at 475-76 ("[W]e hold that the elimination of the claims of stockholders and creditors which are valueless from participation in the reorganization is in accordance with valid provisions of [Bankruptcy Act] § 77(e).").

might comprise less than all of the assets of the bankruptcy estate, and the method of valuation might differ depending on the debtor's proposed use of the collateral.[2079] Moreover, there might be items that contribute to the value of the enterprise in which the secured creditor cannot take a valid security interest, such as future labor.

Under Chapter XI of the Bankruptcy Act,[2080] for most of its existence, the feasibility test applied, but the only financial fairness standard that applied was the so-called best interest of creditors test.[2081] This financial fairness standard also applied in Chapter X and § 77 railroad reorganization cases. The best interest of creditors test protected dissenting members of an accepting class of claims by requiring the Chapter XI plan of arrangement to give dissenting creditors at least as much under the plan as they would receive in a straight bankruptcy liquidation of the debtor. The valuation testimony to meet this test often was far less cumbersome than the going concern valuation necessary to prove that the plan complied with the fair and equitable test.[2082]

2079. *See* Assocs. Commercial Corp. v. Rash, 520 U.S. 953, 955-56 (1997) (chapter 13 case adopting replacement value when debtor seeks to retain and use collateral under chapter 13 plan).

2080. Bankruptcy Act §§ 301-399, 11 U.S.C. §§ 701-799 (1976) (repealed 1979). The National Association of Credit Men and other trade creditor groups urged Congress to adopt Chapter XI to provide a less expensive and more speedy alternative to Chapter X for the arrangement of unsecured debts. *See* S.E.C. v. U.S. Realty & Imp. Co., 310 U.S. 434, 450, 450 n.8 (1940).

2081. *See* Bankruptcy Act § 366(2), 11 U.S.C. § 766(2) (1976) (repealed 1979), allowing the bankruptcy court to confirm a Chapter XI plan of arrangement if, inter alia, "it is for the best interests of the creditors and is feasible."

2082. *See* n.2071 *supra* and accompanying text and Consol. Rock Prods. Co. v. DuBois, 312 U.S. 510, 525-26 (1941) (requiring capitalization of future earnings to generate an enterprise valuation to evaluate the fairness of a plan of reorganization under Bankruptcy Act § 77B, 11 U.S.C. § 207 (1934) (superseded in 1938 by Chapter X, 52 Stat. 883, 11 U.S.C. § 501 et seq.)).

Because the fair and equitable test did not apply in Chapter XI after 1952[2083] and in most cases the Chapter XI debtor served as a debtor in possession[2084] with the exclusive right to file a plan of arrangement,[2085] debtors commonly preferred filing for rehabilitation under Chapter XI than Chapter X. The Securities and Exchange Commission, which had oversight of the reorganization of public companies,[2086] closely monitored whether cases belonged under Chapter XI rather than Chapter X. The SEC could seek leave to intervene to petition the bankruptcy court to convert a Chapter XI case to Chapter X, and often used this leverage to achieve plan modifications or force dismissal of Chapter XI cases to protect the public interest.

2083. Before the 1952 amendment to Chapter XI, Bankruptcy Act § 366(3), 11 U.S.C. § 766(3) (1940), provided that the bankruptcy court could confirm the Chapter XI plan of arrangement only if, inter alia, "it is fair and equitable and feasible." Pub. L. No. 75-696, ch. 575, § 366(3), 52 Stat. 840, 912 (1938). The 1952 amendment, however, deleted the fair and equitable test and moved the feasibility test into paragraph (2) of Bankruptcy Act § 366. *See* Pub. L. No. 456, 82d Cong., 2d Sess, ch. 579, 66 Stat. 420, 433 (1952). The 1952 amendment specifically removed the fair and equitable test from Bankruptcy Act Chapters XI, XII, and XIII because its presence impaired or made valueless the relief provided by those Chapters. *See* S. REP. NO. 1995, 82d Cong., 2d Sess. 11 (1952).

2084. *See* Bankruptcy Act § 342, 11 U.S.C. § 742 (1976) (repealed 1979) (permitting the debtor to remain in possession where no trustee or receiver is appointed).

2085. Under Bankruptcy Act §§ 306(1), 323 & 357, 11 U.S.C. §§ 706(1), 723 & 757 (1976) (repealed 1979), only the debtor could propose a Chapter XI plan of arrangement and creditors were left with the option of voting for or against the plan.

2086. Chapter X provided for the S.E.C. to file an advisory report with the reorganization court on the plan of reorganization. Bankruptcy Act § 172, 11 U.S.C. § 572 (1976) (repealed 1979). Moreover, the S.E.C. could file a notice of appearance in the reorganization, and on court approval, became a party in interest in the Chapter X reorganization case. *See* Bankruptcy Act § 208, 11 U.S.C. § 608 (1976) (repealed 1979).

In *SEC v. United States Realty & Improvement Co.*,[2087] even before deletion of the fair and equitable test from Chapter XI, the Court held that the SEC could intervene in Chapter XI cases to move to dismiss the case on the basis that it interferes with the exercise of the SEC's duties and violates public policy.[2088] The Court also endorsed the SEC's position that modification of unsecured debt in a large public company case had to be done under Chapter X,[2089] if at all, and that the bankruptcy court, as a court of equity, should dismiss the pending Chapter XI case to protect the public interest.[2090] The Court's holding was based "on considerations growing out of the public policy of the Act found both in its legislative history and in an analysis of its terms, and of the authority of the court clothed with equity powers and sitting in bankruptcy to give effect to that policy through its power to withhold relief under Chapter XI when relief is available under Chapter X, which is adequate and more consonant with that policy."[2091]

The Bankruptcy Code consolidated the various business reorganization chapters of the Bankruptcy Act[2092] into chapter 11.[2093] Chapter 11 combines and modifies the financial fairness tests of the Bankruptcy Act. All plans must comply with the best interest of creditors test[2094] to assure that dissenting members of an accepting impaired

---

2087. 310 U.S. 434 (1940).

2088. *See id.* at 458-60 (allowing permissive intervention).

2089. *See id.* at 444-45 ("The Commission argues that Chapter X of the Bankruptcy Act prescribes the exclusive procedure for reorganization of a large corporation having its securities outstanding in the hands of the public such as respondent, and that consequently the district court was without jurisdiction to entertain respondent's petition under Chapter XI . . . .").

2090. *See id.* at 455-57.

2091. *See id.* at 448.

2092. *See* Bankruptcy Act § 77 & Chapters X, XI & XII, 11 U.S.C. §§ 205, 501-676, 701-799 & 801-926 (1976) (repealed 1979).

2093. *See* 11 U.S.C. §§ 1101-1174 (2000).

2094. *See* Bankruptcy Code § 1129(a)(7), 11 U.S.C. § 1129(a)(7) (2000).

class[2095] of claims or interests receive at least as much on account of such claims and interests as they would have received in a hypothetical liquidation of the debtor on the effective date of the plan. In addition, if at least one impaired class of claims or interests does not vote to accept the plan,[2096] the court may confirm the plan only if it does not discriminate unfairly and is fair and equitable with respect to the dissenting class.[2097]

The Court has provided limited guidance on the application and interpretation of the fair and equitable test under the Bankruptcy Code. In *Norwest Bank Worthington v. Ahlers*,[2098] undersecured creditors filed motions for relief from the automatic stay based on allegations that the debtor had no equity in the collateral and it was not necessary for an effective reorganization.[2099] In considering whether the debtors could propose an effective reorganization plan, the Court held that individual debtors could not retain a proprietorship interest when creditors refused to accept the plan and the reorganization plan did not satisfy creditors' claims in full.[2100] The Court noted that "the Code provides that a 'fair and equitable' reorganization plan is one which complies with the absolute priority rule . . . and . . . that it is up to the creditors – and not the courts – to accept or reject a reorganization plan which fails to provide them adequate protection or fails to honor the absolute priority rule."[2101] In reaching its decision, the Court rejected the debtors' contention that the retention of a

---

2095. Bankruptcy Code § 1124 sets forth the circumstances under which a class of claims or interests is not impaired. *See* 11 U.S.C. § 1124 (2000).

2096. Plan acceptance is governed by Bankruptcy Code § 1126, 11 U.S.C. § 1126 (2000).

2097. *See* 11 U.S.C. § 1129(b) (2000).

2098. 485 U.S. 197 (1988).

2099. *See id.* at 200 & 201 n.1 & 11 U.S.C. § 362(d)(2) (1988).

2100. *See id.* at 208-09.

2101. *See id.* at 207 (citations omitted).

"worthless" proprietorship interest did not violate the absolute priority rule, because "there may still be some value in the control of the enterprise . . . ."[2102] The Court also rejected the debtors' contention that their contribution of future "labor, experience, and expertise" constituted new value in money or money's worth in satisfaction of the new value exception to the absolute priority rule.[2103] In so holding, the Court refused to rule on the Solicitor General's suggestion, as amicus curiae, that "codification of the absolute priority rule has eliminated any 'exception' to that rule . . . ."[2104] "Rather, we simply conclude that even if an 'infusion–of—"money–or–money's–worth"' exception to the absolute priority rule has survived the enactment of the Bankruptcy Code, this exception does not encompass [the debtors'] promise to contribute their 'labor, experience, and expertise' to the reorganized enterprise."[2105] In 2005, Congress amended the Bankruptcy Code to overrule this result to permit individual chapter 11 debtors to retain under the plan property specified in Bankruptcy Code § 1115, even if impaired classes of claims vote to reject the plan.[2106]

In *Bank of America National Trust & Savings Ass'n v. 203 North LaSalle Street Partnership*,[2107] the Court considered a single asset real estate partnership's efforts to confirm a new value plan over the dissent of the undersecured nonrecourse mortgagee.[2108] The partner-

2102. *See id.* at 208.

2103. *See id.* at 203-04.

2104. *See id.* at 203 & n.3 ("[O]ur decision today should not be taken as any comment on the continuing vitality of the Los Angeles Lumber exception.").

2105. *See id.* at 203 n.3. *See also id.* at 205 (rejecting any expansion of exceptions to the absolute priority as they existed in 1978).

2106. *See* Bankruptcy Code § 1129(b)(2)(B)(ii) (Supp. 2005) (permitting an individual debtor to retain under the plan property specified in Bankruptcy Code § 1115).

2107. 526 U.S. 434 (1999).

2108. *See id.* at 437-39.

ship filed a reorganization plan during the plan exclusivity period[2109] under which former partners had the sole right to invest over $6 million in new value over five years in exchange for complete ownership of the reorganized debtor.[2110] The plan provided that the bank's secured claim would be paid in full over seven to ten years on a present value basis and its separately classified[2111] unsecured nonrecourse deficiency claim[2112] would receive consideration worth about 16% of the allowed amount of the deficiency claim.[2113] By comparison, the plan provided for outside trade creditors holding general unsecured claims to be paid in full, without interest, on the effective date of the plan.[2114] The impaired classes comprised of the bank's claims voted against the plan, but the impaired class of outside general unsecured claims voted to accept the plan.[2115] The bankruptcy court confirmed the cram down[2116] plan over the dissent of the bank,

2109. *See id.* at 438-39. Under Bankruptcy Code § 1121(b), unless a trustee is appointed, the debtor has a period during which it retains the exclusive right to file a reorganization plan. *See* 11 U.S.C. § 1121(b) (2000).

2110. *See 203 N. LaSalle*, 526 U.S. at 440.

2111. In accordance with Seventh Circuit law, the plan separately classified the bank's nonrecourse deficiency claim from unsecured claims of the other creditors. The Court did not review the propriety of this classification because the issue was not before the Court. *See id.* at 439 & n.7.

2112. *See* Bankruptcy Code § 1111(b)(1)(A), 11 U.S.C. § 1111(b)(1)(A) (2000), providing in certain circumstances for the allowance in chapter 11 cases of a deficiency claim on a nonrecourse loan, notwithstanding the absence of recourse against the debtor for such deficiency under non-bankruptcy law.

2113. *See 203 N. LaSalle*, 526 U.S. at 440.

2114. *See id.*

2115. *See id.* at 440-41.

2116. The Court explained the term "cram down" in the *New Haven Inclusion Cases* by reference to the court's ability to confirm a plan over the dissent of a class. *See* New Haven Inclusion Cases, 399 U.S. 392, 433 n.60 (1970).

holding that the infusion of new capital was not on account of the former partners' ownership interests and was authorized under the new value corollary to the absolute priority rule as stated by the Court in *Los Angeles Lumber Products*.[2117]

Once again, as it had done in *Ahlers*[2118] and *Bonner Mall*,[2119] the Court in *203 N. LaSalle* refused to decide whether the new value corollary survived enactment of the 1978 Bankruptcy Code.[2120] Instead, the Court held that the debtor's prebankruptcy equity holders may not, "over the objection of a senior class of impaired creditors, contribute new capital and receive ownership interests in the reorganized entity, when that opportunity is given exclusively to the old equity holders under a plan adopted without consideration of alternatives."[2121] The Court grounded its holding on its interpretation of Bankruptcy Code § 1129(b)(2)(B)(ii)[2122] which, when a plan fails to fully satisfy an impaired class of claims, precludes junior classes from receiving or retaining under the plan any property "on account of" their junior claims or interests.[2123] Rather than interpreting "on account of" to mean "in exchange for," the Court interpreted it to mean "because of," thereby recognizing "that a causal relationship between holding the prior claim or interest and receiving or retaining property is what activates the absolute priority rule."[2124] Applying this

---

2117. *See id.* at 442-43.

2118. *See* Norwest Bank Worthington v. Ahlers, 485 U.S. 197, 203 n.3 (1988).

2119. *See* U.S. Bancorp Mortgage Co. v. Bonner Mall P'ship, 513 U.S. 18, 20 n.1 (1994) (expressing no view on the existence of the new value exception under the Bankruptcy Code).

2120. *See 203 N. LaSalle*, 526 U.S. at 443 ("We do not decide whether the statute includes a new value corollary or exception . . . .").

2121. *See id.* at 437.

2122. 11 U.S.C. § 1129(b)(2)(B)(ii) (2000).

2123. *See 203 N. LaSalle*, 526 U.S. at 449-51.

2124. *See id.* at 451.

interpretation, the Court concluded that the plan did not provide for the bank's deficiency claim in full and gave former partners the exclusive right to buy equity in the reorganized debtor "on account of" their former partnership interests:[2125]

> Hence it is that the exclusiveness of the opportunity, with its protection against the market's scrutiny of the purchase price by means of competing bids or even competing plan proposals, renders the partners' right a property interest extended "on account of" the old equity position and therefore subject to an unpaid senior creditor class's objection.

Writing in dissent, Justice Stevens concluded otherwise, noting "that a holder of a junior claim or interest does not receive property 'on account of' such a claim when its participation in the plan is based on adequate new value."[2126] Nevertheless, the Court majority held that even if the new value corollary survived enactment of the Bankruptcy Code, the plan did not meet the requirements of the corollary because it did not subject valuation of the reorganized debtor's equity to a market test.[2127] The Court expressly refused to decide whether a market test would be satisfied by termination of plan exclusivity, affording others the opportunity to file a competing plan, or whether a market sale or auction would be required.[2128]

2125. *See id.* at 456 (giving old equity the exclusive right to invest in equity of the reorganized debtor is "to do old equity a favor" which is an opportunity and benefit "because of old equity's prior interest within the meaning of [§ 1129] (b)(2)(B)(ii).").

2126. *See id.* at 464 (Stevens, J., dissenting).

2127. *See id.* at 457-58. ("Under a plan granting an exclusive right, making no provision for competing bids or competing plans, any determination that the price was top dollar would necessarily be made by a judge in bankruptcy court, whereas the best way to determine value is exposure to a market.") *Id.* at 457.

2128. *See id.* at 458 ("Whether a market test would require an opportunity to offer competing plans or would be satisfied by a right to bid for the same interest sought by old equity, is a question we do not decide here. It is enough to say, assuming a new value corollary, that plans providing

Except with respect to issues of res judicata and collateral estoppel discussed in Chapter 4,[2129] the Court has written very little about the effect of confirmation of a composition or reorganization plan. Under the Bankruptcy Act, the Court held that a composition was in the nature of a contractual voluntary settlement and would not release endorsers of a note from a composition which functioned only to discharge the maker of the note.[2130] Although a confirmed plan of reorganization binds parties with respect to preconfirmation claims, the Court has held that it does not bind parties with respect to claims that arise post-confirmation.[2131] Moreover, in extraordinary circumstances, a Justice may stay consummation of the plan to permit the reorganization court to consider alteration or modification of the plan, proposal of a new plan, or dismissal of the case.[2132]

---

junior interest holders with exclusive opportunities free from competition and without benefit of market valuation fall within the prohibition of § 1129(b)(2)(B)(ii).").

2129. *See generally supra* Ch. 4, nn.1159-1197 and accompanying text. The Court has given preclusive effect to orders confirming a plan of reorganization in Prudence Realization Corp. v. Ferris, 323 U.S. 650, 654-55 (1945); Chicot County Drainage Dist. v. Baxter State Bank, 308 U.S. 371, 375-76 (1940); and Stoll v. Gottlieb, 305 U.S. 165, 171-72 (1938). *See also* New Haven Inclusion Cases, 399 U.S. 392, 481 (1970) (giving preclusive effect to asset sale order).

2130. *See* Myers v. Int'l Trust Co., 273 U.S. 380, 383-85 (1927) (composition of a partnership under Bankruptcy Act § 12 discharged the partnership as the maker of a note, but not the individual partners who endorsed the note).

2131. *See* Holywell Corp. v. Smith, 503 U.S. 47, 58 (1992) (allowing the Internal Revenue Service to seek payment of postconfirmation taxes from the trustee of a liquidating trust established under the confirmed plan, because "[e]ven if §1141(a) binds creditors of the corporation and individual debtors with respect to claims that arose before confirmation, we do not see how it can bind the United States or any other creditor with respect to postconfirmation claims.").

2132. *See In re* Equitable Office Bldg. Corp., 72 S. Ct. 1086, 1089-90 (1946) (Justice Reed granting stay of consummation of Chapter X reorganization plan).

Individual Debt Repayment Plans

The Court has rendered several decisions regarding individual repayment plans under Chapter XIII of the Bankruptcy Act and Chapter 13 of the Bankruptcy Code. Although these decisions are important in their own right, it is unclear the extent to which they influence the Court's interpretation of similar issues in business reorganization cases.[2133]

In an individual debtor repayment plan, the debtor pays a portion of future earnings to a disbursing agent to repay creditors in whole or in part over a repayment period, usually three to five years. If the debtor successfully completes payments under the plan, the debtor receives a discharge. Even if the debtor fails to complete payments under the plan, in certain circumstances, the court may grant the debtor a hardship discharge. Under the Bankruptcy Act, a debtor eligible for discharge in a straight bankruptcy case might nevertheless choose to file a Chapter XIII repayment plan in order to pay creditors in full over time and avoid the stigma of having been adjudicated a bankrupt.[2134] Alternatively, even a debtor who is time-barred from receiving a straight bankruptcy discharge might be eligible to confirm a Chapter XIII repayment plan and receive a Chapter XIII discharge.[2135] From 1978 until 2005, this policy remained in effect under the Bankruptcy Code in which a chapter 7 discharge did not serve as

---

2133. *See, e.g.,* Till v. SCS Credit Corp., 541 U.S. 465, 476 n.14 (2004) (noting despite similar statutory language that the difference in efficient markets in chapter 11 and chapter 13 cases might cause the Court to choose a different methodology in each chapter to select a cram down rate).

2134. *See, e.g.,* Perry v. Commerce Loan Co., 383 U.S. 392, 397 (1966).

2135. *See id.* at 399 ("In view of these considerations and the purposes of Chapter XIII as outlined above, we do not believe that the Congress intended to apply the six-year bar of [Bankruptcy Act] § 14(c)(5) to the confirmation of wage-earner extension plans.").

a basis to bar a discharge in a later case filed under chapter 13.[2136] Supporting this statutory theme, the Court held in *Johnson v. Home State Bank*[2137] that the Bankruptcy Code contained no statutory prohibition precluding a chapter 7 debtor from filing for relief under chapter 13 to deal with debts that survived the chapter 7 discharge.[2138] In 2005, however, Congress partially overturned this policy when it enacted Bankruptcy Code § 1328(f), providing a four year bar to discharge in a chapter 13 case for a previous chapter 7, 11, or 12 discharge and a two year bar for a previous chapter 13 discharge.[2139]

From the debtor's perspective, a key benefit of Chapter XIII or chapter 13 is the ability to retain possession and use of property while restructuring secured and unsecured debt obligations.[2140] The debtor's ability to restructure debts, however, is subject to constraints. The repayment plan must give unsecured creditors at least as much as they would receive in a chapter 7 liquidation case.[2141] Often this is not a practical barrier because the debtor has no non-exempt assets available for distribution to unsecured creditors in a chapter 7 case.

2136. *Compare* 11 U.S.C. § 727(a)(8)-(9) (2000) (providing that a discharge under any chapter within the previous six years bars a discharge under chapter 7) *with* 11 U.S.C. § 1328 (2000) (containing no bar).

2137. 501 U.S. 78 (1991).

2138. *See id.* at 87.

2139. 11 U.S.C. § 1328(f) (Supp. 2005) (as amended by 119 Stat. 87 (2005)).

2140. As noted *supra* in the text accompanying nn.1637-1640, however, a bank with a right of setoff may impose an administrative freeze on the chapter 13 debtor's bank account, pending the outcome of a motion for relief from the automatic stay. *See* Citizens Bank of Md. v. Strumpf, 516 U.S. 16, 21 (1995).

2141. *See* 11 U.S.C. § 1325(a)(4) (2000) (The court shall confirm a plan if "the value, as of the effective date of the plan, of property to be distributed under the plan on account of each allowed unsecured claim is not less than the amount that would be paid on such claim if the estate of the debtor were liquidated under chapter 7 . . . on such date.").

With respect to secured claims, however, the constraints are more formidable.[2142] In order to protect the home mortgage industry, in 1978 Congress enacted a special protection in Bankruptcy Code § 1322(b)(2)[2143] precluding the chapter 13 plan from modifying the rights of holders of secured claims whose debts are secured only by security interests in real property that is the debtor's principal residence. In *Nobelman v. American Savings Bank*,[2144] the Court considered how this protection applied when the amount of mortgage debt exceeded the value of the residence.[2145] Under Bankruptcy Code § 506(a),[2146] when a claim is secured by a first lien on collateral worth less than the amount of the debt, the holder of the claim has an allowed secured claim equal to the value of the collateral and an unsecured deficiency claim for the balance. The Court considered whether the statutory protection applied only to the allowed secured claim or the entire debt.[2147] As a matter of statutory construction and purpose, the Court held that this prohibition extended to the entire claim secured by the residence, even if under Bankruptcy Code § 506(a) the allowed secured claim was less than the debt, because the value of the residence was less than the amount owing on the mortgage.[2148] The Court reasoned that the statute precluded modification of the rights of holders of secured claims, and satisfaction of only part of the amount owing on the mortgage would alter the mortgagee's contractual rights.[2149]

2142. *See, e.g.,* 11 U.S.C. §§ 1322(b)(2) & 1325(a)(5) (2000).

2143. 11 U.S.C. § 1322(b)(2) (2000).

2144. 508 U.S. 324 (1993).

2145. *See id.* at 326.

2146. 11 U.S.C. § 506(a) (2000).

2147. *See Nobelman*, 508 U.S. at 326-27.

2148. *See id.* at 332.

2149. *See id.*

For most other kinds of secured claims,[2150] however, even if the secured creditor votes to reject the plan,[2151] the chapter 13 plan may return the collateral to the creditor,[2152] or, if the debtor wants to keep the collateral, strip the debt down to the collateral value and repay that value over time, with interest, in deferred payments.[2153] This broad statutory formula caused a split in statutory interpretation in the lower courts, ultimately leading the Court to consider the appropriate valuation of the collateral and the interest rate that a holder of an allowed secured claim is entitled to receive under a chapter 13 plan. In *Rake v. Wade*,[2154] the Court held that whether or not home mortgage documents provided for postpetition interest on arrearages, Bankruptcy Code §§ 506(b) and 1325(a)(5)[2155] require the payment of postpetition interest on all oversecured claims.[2156] To overrule this decision legislatively, in 1994 Congress amended the Bankruptcy Code to require the amount to cure a default under a plan to "be determined in accordance with the underlying agreement and applicable non-

---

2150. In 2005, Congress amended chapter 13 to preclude the strip down of certain purchase money motor vehicle loans. *See* 11 U.S.C. § 1325 hanging paragraph (Supp. 2005), Pub. L. No. 109-8, § 309, 119 Stat. 83 (2005).

2151. If the creditor holding an allowed claim votes to accept the chapter 13 plan, then that consent serves to replace the financial standards applicable to secured creditors who do not vote to accept the plan. *See* 11 U.S.C. § 1325(a)(5)(A) (2000).

2152. *See* 11 U.S.C. § 1325(a)(5)(C) (2000).

2153. *See* 11 U.S.C. § 1325(a)(5)(B) (2000) (permitting confirmation of the chapter 13 plan if the secured creditor retains the lien on the collateral and receives property (usually deferred cash payments) with a present value equal to the value of the allowed secured claim). Congress amended the statute in 2005 to provide less leeway in altering allowed secured claims. *See id.* (Supp. 2005).

2154. 508 U.S. 464 (1993).

2155. 11 U.S.C. §§ 506(b) & 1325(a)(5) (2000).

2156. *See Rake v. Wade*, 508 U.S. at 471.

bankruptcy law."[2157] Although the 1994 amendments appear to overrule *Rake v. Wade* legislatively in chapter 12 and chapter 13 cases, it is unclear whether the amendment to chapter 11 accomplishes its objective.[2158]

In *Associates Commercial Corp. v. Rash*,[2159] the Court addressed valuation of collateral under a chapter 13 plan in which the debtor wanted to retain a truck worth less than the debt outstanding.[2160] The Court rejected "a ruleless approach allowing use of different valuation standards based on facts and circumstances of individual cases."[2161] Instead, the Court determined that when the debtor's plan proposes to retain and use collateral, Bankruptcy Code § 506(a)[2162] directs application of a replacement-value standard rather than a foreclosure-value standard or something in between.[2163] The Court's use of the term "replacement value" was equivalent to the Ninth Circuit's meaning of fair market value, i.e., "the price a willing buyer in the debtor's trade, business, or situation would pay a willing seller to

---

2157. *See* The Bankruptcy Reform Act of 1994, Pub. L. 103-394, 103d Cong., 2d Sess. § 305, 108 Stat. 4106, 4134 (Oct. 22, 1994), amending chapters 11, 12, and 13, 11 U.S.C. §§ 1123(d), 1222(d) & 1322(e) (2000).

2158. The chapter 11 amendment to Bankruptcy Code § 1123(d), 11 U.S.C. § 1123(d) (2000) may not accomplish its objective, because the amendment applies notwithstanding only Bankruptcy Code §§ 506(b), 1129(a)(7) & 1129(b), 11 U.S.C. §§ 506(b), 1129(a)(7) & 1129(b) (2000). Bankruptcy Code § 1123(d) does not override Bankruptcy Code § 1124(2), 11 U.S.C. § 1124(2) (2000), which apparently allows a chapter 11 plan to reinstate and cure a default without payment of default interest on arrearages.

2159. 520 U.S. 953 (1997).

2160. *See id.* at 956-57.

2161. *See id.* at 964 n.5.

2162. 11 U.S.C. § 506(a) (2000).

2163. *See Rash*, 520 U.S. at 955-56.

obtain property of like age and condition."[2164] Notwithstanding its rejection of a ruleless approach, the Court left[2165]

> to bankruptcy courts, as triers of fact, identification of the best way of ascertaining replacement value on the basis of the evidence presented. Whether replacement value is the equivalent of retail value, wholesale value, or some other value will depend on the type of debtor and the nature of the property.

Nevertheless, the Court was clear that replacement value should not include certain items of retail value "such as warranties, inventory storage, and reconditioning."[2166]

In 2005, Congress overturned this decision, in part, when it amended Bankruptcy Code § 506(a)(2)[2167] to value consumer collateral in chapter 7 or 13 cases at replacement value of the collateral as of the date of the filing of the bankruptcy petition "without deduction of costs for sale or marketing."[2168] Congress specified that when courts determine the replacement value of property acquired for personal, family, or household purposes, "replacement value shall mean the price a retail merchant would charge for property of that kind considering the age and condition of the property at the time value is determined."[2169] Unlike the Court's holding in *Rash*, however, nothing in the amended Bankruptcy Code limits the use of replacement cost to situations when the debtor retains the collateral.[2170]

2164. *See id.* at 959 n.2.

2165. *See id.* at 965 n.6.

2166. *See id.*

2167. 11 U.S.C. § 506(a)(2) (Supp. 2005).

2168. *See id.* as added by Pub. L. No. 109-8, § 327, 119 Stat. 100 (April 20, 2005).

2169. *See id.*

2170. Apparently, based on the plain language of the statute, if the debtor returns the collateral to the secured creditor under Bankruptcy Code § 1325(a)(5)(C), the replacement value standard of Bankruptcy Code § 506(a)(2) would apply. *See* 11 U.S.C. §§ 506(a)(2) & 1325(a)(5)(C) (Supp. 2005).

The Court's valuation holding in *Rash* had an impact on its determination of an appropriate postconfirmation interest rate in *Till v. SCS Credit Corp.*,[2171] another chapter 13 case in which the debtor sought to retain an over-encumbered truck.[2172] In *Till*, a sharply divided Court[2173] rejected the Seventh Circuit's holding that the contract rate of interest was presumptively proper as the postconfirmation rate of interest on an allowed secured claim under a chapter 13 plan.[2174] Justice Stevens announced the judgment of the Court and authored a plurality opinion in which Justices Souter, Ginsberg, and Breyer joined.[2175] Rejecting the coerced loan, presumptive contract rate, and cost of funds approaches, these Justices adopted a formula approach whereby the bankruptcy court starts with the prime rate and adjusts upward for risk[2176] to select the postconfirmation "cramdown" rate of interest on an allowed secured claim under a chapter 13 plan.[2177] Justice Scalia authored a dissent, in which Chief Justice Rehnquist and Justices O'Connor and Kennedy joined,[2178]

2171. 541 U.S. 465 (2004).

2172. *See id.* at 469-70.

2173. Four justices delivered the opinion of the Court, in which Justice Thomas concurred, and four justices dissented resulting in a 4-1-4 decision. *See id.* at 468, 485, 491.

2174. *See id.* at 477 (plurality opinion rejecting the coerced loan, presumptive contract rate, and cost of funds approaches); 487 (concurring opinion holding that "the plan need only propose an interest rate that will compensate a creditor for the fact that if he had received the property immediately rather than at a future date, he could have immediately made use of the property. In most, if not all, cases, where the plan proposes simply a stream of cash payments, the appropriate risk-free rate should suffice.").

2175. *See id.* at 468.

2176. The Court noted that risk adjustment usually varies between 1% and 3%, but explicitly did "not decide the proper scale for the risk adjustment." *See id.* at 480.

2177. *See id.* at 477-79.

2178. *See id.* at 491, Scalia, J., dissenting.

adopting the contract rate as the presumptive chapter 13 cramdown rate for allowed secured claims.[2179] Although these eight Justices agreed that the chapter 13 secured claim cramdown rate would have a risk adjustment,[2180] the judgment of the Court depended on Justice Thomas's concurrence in which he found that "the statute that Congress enacted does not require a debtor-specific risk adjustment . . . ."[2181] Instead, based on the plain language of the statute, the risk-free rate adequately compensates the secured creditor for receiving a stream of future payments based on the time value of money.[2182] Justice Thomas buttressed his position by noting that under *Rash*, "secured creditors are already compensated in part for the risk of nonpayment through the valuation of the secured claim" because *Rash* "utilized a secured-creditor-friendly replacement-value standard rather than the lower foreclosure-value standard for valuing secured claims when a debtor has exercised Chapter 13's cram down option."[2183]

DISCHARGE AND NONDISCHARGEABLE DEBTS

Often the main incentive for a debtor to file for bankruptcy relief is to obtain a discharge of debts. In a chapter 11 reorganization case, debts incurred before confirmation are subject to discharge under the plan.[2184] Generally the discharge applies to benefit the debtor and not

---

2179. *See id.* at 492, Scalia, J., dissenting. In doing so, Justice Scalia assumed, inter alia, that the "subprime lending markets are competitive and therefore largely efficient." *Id.*

2180. *See id.* at 508, Scalia, J., dissenting. ("Eight Justices are in agreement that the rate of interest set forth in the debtor's approved plan must include a premium for risk.").

2181. *See id.* at 486, Thomas, J., concurring.

2182. *See id.* at 486-87, Thomas, J., concurring.

2183. *See id.* at 489, Thomas, J., concurring.

2184. *See* Bankruptcy Code § 1141(d)(1)(A), 11 U.S.C. § 1141(d)(1)(A) (2000). The Bankruptcy Act also contained broad discharge provisions in compositions, arrangements, and plans of reorganization. *See* Bank-to benefit codebtors, guarantors, indorsers, or other third parties.[2185] The indemnity claim of a surety against the principal is, however, subject to discharge in the principal's bankruptcy, even if the surety has not paid on the bond by the time of the filing of the bankruptcy petition.[2186] In a chapter 7 liquidation case the discharge makes debts incurred before the order for relief unenforceable as a personal liability against the individual debtor.[2187] Debts arising after the order

---

ruptcy Act §§ 228, 371, 476 & 660-661, 11 U.S.C. §§ 628, 771, 876 & 1060-1061 (1976) (repealed 1979) (providing for discharge in Chapters X, XI, XII & XIII cases). In Chapter XIII and § 77B cases, however, the discharge ran from completion of payments under the plan and entry of the final decree rather than from entry of the confirmation order. *See, e.g.,* Meyer v. Kenmore Granville Hotel Co., 297 U.S. 160, 166 (1936) (§ 77B case in which the Court stated that "[d]ischarge is effected not by confirmation of the plan but by the final decree."). *See also* Nassau Smelting & Ref. Works v. Brightwood Bronze Foundry Co., 265 U.S. 269, 271 (1924) (noting that when a composition under Bankruptcy Act § 12 is "confirmed the bankrupt is discharged from all debts 'other than those agreed to be paid by the terms of the composition and those not affected by a discharge.'").

2185. *See* Myers v. Int'l Trust Co., 273 U.S. 380, 383-85 (1927) (composition of a partnership under Bankruptcy Act § 12 discharged the partnership as the maker of a note, but not the individual partners who endorsed the note). *But see* Bankruptcy Code § 524(g)(4)(A)(ii), 11 U.S.C. § 524(g)(4)(A)(ii) (2000), providing for an injunction in asbestos mass tort cases to protect third parties from liability in certain circumstances.

2186. *See* Williams v. U.S. Fid. & Guar. Co., 236 U.S. 549, 556-57 (1915) ("It would be contrary to the basal spirit of the Bankrupt Law to permit a surety, by simply postponing compliance with his own promise in respect of a liability until after bankruptcy, to preserve a right of recovery over against his principal notwithstanding the discharge . . . ."). *See id.* at 557.

2187. *See* Brown v. O'Keefe, 300 U.S. 598, 603 (1937) (considering the "question whether the effect of the discharge in bankruptcy was to extinguish the personal liability" of the debtor on a debt attached to the ownership of shares in an insolvent bank). *See also* Bankruptcy Code § 727(b), 11 U.S.C. § 727(b) (2000). The order relief occurs on the date of the filing of a voluntary bankruptcy petition and on adjudication in an involuntary bankruptcy case. *See* Bankruptcy Code §§ 301, 303(h) (2000).

for relief and before the discharge are not discharged in a straight bankruptcy or chapter 7 case.[2188] Nor are a creditor's lien rights discharged under chapter 7.[2189]

The Court has underscored the importance of the discharge to the individual debtor's fresh start. In *Williams v. United States Fidelity & Guaranty Co.*,[2190] the Court noted that "[i]t is the purpose of the Bankrupt[cy] Act to convert the assets of the bankrupt into cash for distribution among creditors and then to relieve the honest debtor from the weight of oppressive indebtedness and permit him to start afresh free from the obligations and responsibilities consequent upon business misfortunes."[2191] The Court expanded this policy in *Local Loan Co. v. Hunt*,[2192] when it held that "the clear and unmistakable policy of the bankruptcy act" precluded post-discharge enforcement by a prebankruptcy lender of an assignment of the bankrupt's future wages.[2193] In so holding, the Court made a powerful statement that would serve as the backbone of American consumer bankruptcy law for the next 70 years:[2194]

2188. *See* Zavelo v. Reeves, 227 U.S. 625, 632 (1913) (holding that a promise to pay a prepetition provable debt made postpetition and before discharge is nondischargeable, because the postpetition promise is not itself a provable debt). Under current law, such a postpetition promise would be treated as a reaffirmation agreement, the validity of which is governed by Bankruptcy Code § 524(c)-(d), 11 U.S.C. § 524(c)-(d) (2000).

2189. *See* Johnson v. Home State Bank, 501 U.S. 78, 80 (1991) ("[T]he Bankruptcy Court discharged petitioner from personal liability on his promissory notes to the Bank. Notwithstanding the discharge, the Bank's right to proceed against petitioner *in rem* survived the Chapter 7 liquidation.").

2190. 236 U.S. 549 (1915).

2191. *See id.* at 554-55.

2192. 292 U.S. 234 (1934).

2193. *See id.* at 244.

2194. *See id.* at 245. This policy was undercut somewhat by the 2005 amendments to the Bankruptcy Code which denied a chapter 7 discharge and fresh start to some debtors. *See* 11 U.S.C. § 707(b) (Supp. 2005).

When a person assigns future wages, he, in effect, pledges his future earning power. The power of the individual to earn a living for himself and those dependent upon him is in the nature of a personal liberty quite as much as, if not more than, it is a property right. To preserve its free exercise is of the utmost importance, not only because it is a fundamental private necessity, but because it is a matter of great public concern. From the viewpoint of the wage earner there is little difference between not earning at all and earning wholly for a creditor. Pauperism may be the necessary result of either. The amount of the indebtedness, or the proportion of wages assigned, may here be small, but the principle, once established, will equally apply where both are very great. The new opportunity in life and the clear field for future effort, which it is the purpose of the bankruptcy act to afford the emancipated debtor, would be of little value to the wage earner if he were obliged to face the necessity of devoting the whole or a considerable portion of his earnings for an indefinite time in the future to the payment of indebtedness incurred prior to his bankruptcy.

Although the debtor's discharge is the centerpiece of the fresh start afforded by bankruptcy, this privilege is limited by a moral constraint. The bankruptcy laws of the United States do not, for the most part,[2195]

2195. As originally enacted, Bankruptcy Code chapter 13, 11 U.S.C. §§ 1301 et seq. (2000) granted debtors who complete payments under a chapter 13 individual debt repayment plan a so-called "super discharge" that included discharge of debts involving moral turpitude such as fraud, crime, and willful and malicious injury. *See* 11 U.S.C. § 1328(a) (Supp. 1980). As discussed more fully below, in Pa. Dep't of Pub. Welfare v. Davenport, 495 U.S. 552, 555 (1990), the Court held criminal restitution debts dischargeable under chapter 13, and Congress responded by amending the Bankruptcy Code to change the result. *See infra* n.2321. In 1994 Congress narrowed the scope of the super discharge to exclude from discharge in chapter 13 cases debts for drunk driving. *See* Pub. L. No. 103-394, 103d Cong., 2d Sess., § 501(d)(38), 108 Stat. 4106, 4147 (Oct. 22, 1994). The 2005 amendments made the super discharge far less "super" for debtors by excluding even more categories of debts of moral turpitude. *See* Bankruptcy Code § 1328(a) (Supp. 2005) (as amended by Pub. L. No. 109-8, 109th Cong., 1st Sess., §§ 106(c), 213(11), 312(2),

confer a discharge on a dishonest debtor.[2196] Moreover, even when the Bankruptcy Code permits the discharge of a civil debt arising from an act for which the debtor may have criminal liability, the Court has emphasized that discharge of the debt does not relieve the debtor from criminal prosecution.[2197] The discharge does, however, operate to relieve the debtor from personal liability on the debt and from any specific performance that is connected to the debt.[2198]

There are two fundamental ways in which debts may survive a debtor's bankruptcy. The first is if the debtor is denied a discharge, usually based on the commission of a bad act. The second is if a creditor succeeds in proving that a particular debt is nondischargeable.[2199]

The Court has addressed each, with the bulk of the cases involving nondischargeable debts rather than objections to discharge. If a creditor succeeds in an objection to discharge, then all creditors are

314(b), 330(d) & 707, 109 Stat. 23, 38, 53, 87, 88, 102, 126 (April 20, 2005)). *See also* n.2308 *infra*.

2196. *See, e.g.,* Williams v. U.S. Fid. & Guar. Co., 236 U.S. 549, 554-55 (1915) ("It is the purpose of the Bankrupt Act to convert the assets of the bankrupt into cash for distribution among creditors and then to relieve the honest debtor from the weight of oppressive indebtedness and permit him to start afresh free from the obligations and responsibilities consequent upon business misfortunes.").

2197. *See* Ohio v. Kovacs, 469 U.S. 274, 284 (1985) ("[W]e do not suggest that [the debtor's] discharge will shield him from prosecution for having violated the environmental laws of Ohio or for criminal contempt for not performing his obligations under the injunction [to clean up the property] prior to bankruptcy.").

2198. *See id.* at 285 ("[W]e here address . . . only the affirmative duty to clean up the site and the duty to pay money to that end.").

2199. Under the Bankruptcy Act, the discharge released the debtor from personal liability on provable debts. Because the concept of provability does not apply under the Bankruptcy Code, this book seldom discusses the topic. *See* Brown v. O'Keefe, 300 U.S. 598, 603-06 (1937) where the Court charitably interpreted provability of a contingent debt in order to give an honest debtor the benefit of a fresh start.

free to pursue the debtor and the debtor's property. If a creditor succeeds in making a particular debt nondischargeable and the debtor receives a discharge, then only creditors holding nondischargeable debts and post-bankruptcy creditors may make such a pursuit. This economic incentive might explain why creditors bring far more non-dischargeability complaints that objections to discharge.

The Court has recognized that a debtor has no constitutional right to receive a discharge, and, therefore, a bankruptcy court could deny a discharge to an indigent debtor who did not pay the fee required to file the bankruptcy petition.[2200] On the other hand, as discussed extensively in Chapter 3, the Court has used the Supremacy Clause to protect the debtor's discharge from being undermined by state regulatory statutes designed to frustrate the fresh start.[2201]

Over 100 years ago, in *Hanover National Bank v. Moyses*,[2202] the Court granted Congress broad latitude in fashioning procedures governing the discharge, including giving notice of the bankruptcy to creditors by mail and publication: "Congress may prescribe any regulations concerning discharge in bankruptcy that are not so grossly unreasonable as to be incompatible with fundamental law, and we cannot find anything in [the Bankruptcy] [A]ct on that subject which would justify us in overthrowing its action."[2203] Moreover, "the court

---

2200. *See* United States v. Kras, 409 U.S. 434, 446 (1973).

2201. *See supra* Ch. 3, nn.845-855 & 875-895 and accompanying text. Notably, in Perez v. Campbell, 402 U.S. 637 (1971), the Court overturned an Arizona statute that would have suspended the debtors' driver's licenses for failure to pay a discharged tort debt. In so holding, the Court overturned earlier inconsistent nondischargeability opinions in Reitz v. Mealey, 314 U.S. 33 (1941) and Kesler v. Dep't of Pub. Safety, 369 U.S. 153 (1962). *See Perez*, 402 U.S. at 651-52. ("Thus, we conclude that *Kesler* and *Reitz* have no authoritative effect to the extent they are inconsistent with the controlling principle that any state legislation which frustrates the full effectiveness of federal law is rendered invalid by the Supremacy Clause.").

2202. 186 U.S. 181 (1902).

2203. *See id.* at 192.

has jurisdiction to decree discharge, if sufficient opportunity to show cause to the contrary is afforded, on notice given in the same way. . . . Service of process or personal notice is not essential to the binding force of the [discharge] decree."[2204] More recently, the Court has recognized that Congress has the power to designate diverse categories of nondischargeable debts:[2205]

> The statutory provisions governing nondischargeability reflect a congressional decision to exclude from the general policy of discharge certain categories of debts – such as child support, alimony, and certain unpaid educational loans and taxes, as well as liabilities for fraud. Congress evidently concluded that the creditors' interest in recovering full payment of debts in these categories outweighed the debtors' interest in a complete fresh start.

Both the Bankruptcy Act[2206] and the Bankruptcy Code[2207] permit creditors to object to discharge in straight bankruptcy or chapter 7 liquidation cases, usually[2208] on the basis of the debtor's bad acts. For example, in *Levy v. Industrial Finance Corp.*,[2209] the Court affirmed the denial of a discharge under Bankruptcy Act § 14b(3)[2210] to a debtor who fraudulently obtained money for a wholly owned corporation.[2211] The Court rejected on policy grounds the debtor's argument that denial of discharge should be limited to a debtor who fraudulently

---

2204. *See id.*

2205. Grogan v. Garner, 498 U.S. 279, 287 (1991).

2206. Bankruptcy Act § 14, 11 U.S.C. § 32 (1976) (repealed 1979).

2207. Bankruptcy Code § 727, 11 U.S.C. § 727 (2000).

2208. The Bankruptcy Code contains some bases for denial of discharge not based on bad acts. *See, e.g.,* 11 U.S.C. § 727(a)(1) (2000) (denying partnership and corporate debtors discharges in chapter 7 cases based on their status).

2209. 276 U.S. 281 (1928).

2210. 11 U.S.C. § 32b(3) (1922) (amended by Act of May 27, 1926, ch. 406, § 6, 44 Stat. 662, 663) (repealed 1979).

2211. *See id.* at 282-84.

obtains money directly for himself: "It would seem that so far as policy goes there is no more reason for granting a discharge to a man who has fraudulently obtained a loan to a corporation which is owned by him . . . than for granting one to a man who has got money directly for himself."[2212] Similarly, in *Morimura, Arai & Co. v. Taback*,[2213] the Court held that discharge should be denied to individual partner business debtors who knowingly or recklessly made materially false written statements for the purpose of obtaining credit for the business which credit was actually extended on the basis of the false statements.[2214] Likewise, in *Fidelity & Deposit Co. v. Arenz*,[2215] the Court reversed the grant of discharge to a debtor who obtained a surety bond by means of materially false written statements.[2216] Interpreting amended Bankruptcy Act § 14b(3),[2217] the Court held that the discharge should have been denied, because the debtor obtained a surety bond (which was a form of "property") on credit by making a materially false statement.[2218] Moreover, for purposes of denying the debtor's discharge, the debtor may give the materially false statement long before the creditor extends credit as long as the creditor relies on it in extending credit.[2219]

2212. *See id.* at 283. The Court noted that the 1926 amendment to Bankruptcy Act § 14b(3) which limited denial of discharge to "a materially false statement . . . respecting his financial condition" was not before the Court in this case. *See id.* at 283-84.

2213. 279 U.S. 24 (1929).

2214. *See id.* at 33-34 (citing Bankruptcy Act § 14b(3)).

2215. 290 U.S. 66 (1933).

2216. *See id.* at 70.

2217. 11 U.S.C. § 32b(3) (as amended by Act of May 27, 1926, ch. 406, § 6, 44 Stat. 662, 663) (repealed 1979).

2218. *See Fid. & Deposit Co. v. Arenz*, 290 U.S. at 68 ("'Property' is a word of very broad meaning, and when used without qualification . . . it reasonably may be construed to include obligations, rights and other intangibles as well as physical things.").

2219. *See* Gerdes v. Lustgarten, 266 U.S. 321, 326 (1924) ("[T]he lapse of time is only material in determining whether credit was extended within

In order to prevent bankruptcy recidivism and to keep bankruptcy as a remedy of last resort, both the Bankruptcy Act[2220] and the Bankruptcy Code[2221] contain a statutory bar to discharge if the debtor in a straight bankruptcy or chapter 7 liquidation case has been discharged in another bankruptcy case within a period of time before the filing of the current bankruptcy petition.

The Bankruptcy Act and Bankruptcy Code delineate several categories of nondischargeable debts. A creditor litigating the issue in bankruptcy court must prove the nondischargeability of a debt by a preponderance of the evidence.[2222] Moreover, under the Bankruptcy Code, once a debt is found to be nondischargeable, any damage award arising from the debt is nondischargeable, including an award of attorneys' fees and treble damages.[2223] Furthermore, postpetition interest relating to the nondischargeable debt is likewise nondischargeable.[2224]

Both the Bankruptcy Act[2225] and the Bankruptcy Code[2226] make many kinds of tax debts nondischargeable. Taxes are involuntary

---

the period intended, while the statement was still binding on the bankrupt, and whether the creditor in fact extended the credit upon the faith of the statement.").

2220. *See* Bankruptcy Act § 14c(5), 11 U.S.C. § 32c(5) (1976) (repealed 1979) (providing six year bar).

2221. *See* Bankruptcy Code § 727(a)(8)-(9), 11 U.S.C. § 727(a)(8)-(9) (Supp. 2005) (providing eight year and six year bars, respectively).

2222. *See* Grogan v. Garner, 489 U.S. 279, 291 (1991).

2223. *See* Cohen v. de la Cruz, 523 U.S. 213, 223 (1998) (holding that if debt is incurred by fraud and is nondischargeable under Bankruptcy Code § 523(a)(2), so are attorneys' fees and treble damages associated with the debt).

2224. *See* Bruning v. United States, 376 U.S. 358, 362-63 (1964) (holding debtor liable for postpetition interest on nondischargeable tax debt).

2225. Bankruptcy Act § 17a(1), 11 U.S.C. § 35a(1) (1976) (repealed 1979).

2226. Bankruptcy Code §§ 523(a)(1) & 1141(d)(6)(B), 11 U.S.C. §§ 523(a)(1) & 1141(d)(6)(B) (Supp. 2005).

claims that are the life-blood of government, and it would create a moral hazard to permit the discharge of tax claims that the government has not had a reasonable opportunity to collect. Some kinds of tax obligations are nondischargeable without time limit. In *United States v. Sotelo*,[2227] by a vote of 5-4, the Court held nondischargeable under Bankruptcy Act § 17a(1)(e)[2228] so-called trust fund withholding taxes that an individual responsible debtor is required to collect or withhold.[2229] The Court found that even though the employer corporation that paid wages was required to collect and withhold employee taxes, the Bankruptcy Act's nondischargeability language would extend to a responsible officer of the corporation who was liable to pay a penalty to the government when the corporation failed to pay the withholding tax.[2230] The Court reached such a conclusion notwithstanding the Bankruptcy Act's strong fresh start policy: "[W]hile it is true that a finding of nondischargeability prevents a bankrupt from getting an entirely 'fresh start,' this observation provides little assistance in construing a section expressly designed to make some debts nondischargeable."[2231]

Bankruptcy Code §§ 507(a)(8)(C) and 523(a)(1)(A)[2232] provide a statutory basis to continue *Sotelo's* holding under the Bankruptcy Code. Moreover, as more fully discussed below, in *Young v. United States*,[2233] the Court unanimously extended *Sotelo's* policy of broad interpretation of tax exceptions to discharge. Under Bankruptcy Code § 523(a)(1)(A),[2234] priority tax claims are nondischargeable in cases in

---

2227. 436 U.S. 268 (1978).

2228. 11 U.S.C. § 35a(1)(e) (1976) (repealed 1979).

2229. *See Sotelo*, 436 U.S. at 282.

2230. *See id.* at 274.

2231. *See id.* at 279-80.

2232. 11 U.S.C. §§ 507(a)(8)(C) & 523(a)(1)(A) (2000).

2233. 535 U.S. 43 (2002). *See* n.2237 *infra* and accompanying text.

2234. 11 U.S.C. § 523(a)(1)(A) (2000).

which the debtor is an individual.[2235] In particular, Bankruptcy Code
§ 507(a)(8)(A)(i)[2236] confers priority status to taxes for income and gross
receipts taxes for which the return was due within three years before
the date of the bankruptcy petition. In *Young*, however, the Court
invoked the doctrine of equitable tolling to stop the running of time
during the debtor's previous bankruptcy case, thereby extending the
three year reachback in the debtor's subsequent bankruptcy case.[2237]
As a result, the Court's broad interpretation of the tax exception to
discharge rendered nondischargeable debts for taxes that would have
been discharged under the plain language of the statute.

The Court also has adopted a broad interpretation of the exception
to discharge for alimony, maintenance, and support.[2238] Indeed, as
noted more fully previously,[2239] before Congress adopted an express
statutory exception to discharge in 1903, the Court interpreted the
statute charitably on three occasions to accomplish that result.[2240]
Chapter 2 contains a more detailed discussion of the history and
substance of the exception to discharge for alimony, maintenance, and
support.[2241]

2235. *See* 11 U.S.C. § 507(a)(8) (2000) according priority to certain tax
claims.

2236. 11 U.S.C. § 507(a)(8)(A)(i) (2000).

2237. *See Young*, 535 U.S. at 54.

2238. *See* Bankruptcy Act § 17a(7), 11 U.S.C. § 35a(7) (1976) (repealed
1979); Bankruptcy Code § 523(a)(5) & (15), 11 U.S.C. § 523(a)(5) & (15)
(2000).

2239. *See supra* Ch. 2, nn.319-337 and accompanying text.

2240. *See id.* at nn.322-335 and accompanying text, citing and discussing
Wetmore v. Markoe, 196 U.S. 68 (1904); Dunbar v. Dunbar, 190 U.S. 340
(1903); and Audubon v. Shufeldt, 181 U.S. 575 (1901).

2241. *See supra* Ch. 2, nn.320-337 and accompanying text and nn.363-366
and accompanying text, discussing the Bankruptcy Act's exception to
discharge for debts from seduction and criminal conversation.

In order to protect the debtor's fresh start, typically the Court has narrowly interpreted non-tax[2242] and non-alimony exceptions to discharge.[2243] Under the Bankruptcy Act of 1867, the Court held that statutory references to nondischargeability of a "debt created by the fraud . . . of the bankrupt" required "positive fraud, or fraud in fact, involving moral turpitude or intentional wrong . . . and not implied fraud, or fraud in law, which may exist without the imputation of bad faith or immorality."[2244] The Court justified its rationale as follows:[2245]

> Such a construction of the statute is consonant with equity, and consistent with the object and intention of Congress in enacting a general law by which the honest citizen may be re- lieved from the burden of hopeless insolvency. A different construction would be inconsistent with the liberal spirit which pervades the entire bankrupt system.

Thus, the Court held that a debtor's participation in constructive fraudulent transfer did not give rise to a nondischargeable debt.[2246] By contrast, in *Forsyth v. Vehmeyer*,[2247] when the debtor made an intentional misrepresentation of fact, "knowingly, falsely, and fraudu- lently for the purpose of obtaining money from another," the debt was

---

2242. Justice Rehnquist, writing for the four dissenters in *Sotelo*, would have maintained the policy of narrow interpretation of exceptions to discharge even for tax debts: "I would hesitate to depart from our longstanding tradition of reading the Bankruptcy Act with an eye to its fundamental purpose – the rehabilitation of bankrupts. This has always led the Court, at least until today, to construe narrowly any exceptions to the general discharge provisions." *Sotelo* at 285-86 (citations omitted).

2243. *See, e.g.,* Gleason v. Thaw, 236 U.S. 558, 562 (1915) ("In view of the well-known purposes of the Bankrupt[cy] Law exceptions to the operation of a discharge thereunder should be confined to those plainly expressed . . . .").

2244. *See, e.g.,* Neal v. Clark, 95 U.S. 704, 706, 709 (1877).

2245. *See id.* at 709.

2246. *See id.* at 706, 709.

2247. 177 U.S. 177 (1900).

nondischargeable because it was created "by means of a fraud involving moral turpitude and intentional wrong."[2248] Moreover, because the debtor had suffered a state court judgment in which the jury made a finding of fraud, "the question of fraud was not open for a second litigation" in the nondischargeability trial.[2249]

The Court reached a similar result under the Bankruptcy Act of 1898, which initially limited nondischargeability to judgments for fraud.[2250] In *Bullis v. O'Beirne*,[2251] the Court held a judgment for actual fraud nondischargeable,[2252] citing its decision and rationale under the Bankruptcy Act of 1867 in *Forsyth v. Vehmeyer*.[2253]

The Court continued to interpret the scope of nondischargeable debts narrowly under the Bankruptcy Act of 1898. In *Gleason v. Thaw*,[2254] the Court held that a debtor's fraudulent inducement of an attorney to provide services did not come within the category of non-dischargeable debts because the services were not "property" obtained by false pretenses.[2255]

When the nature of the underlying debt is a debt for money obtained by fraud, the creditor will be able to timely obtain an order of the bankruptcy court holding the debt nondischargeable.[2256]

2248. *See id.* at 182 (construing the Bankruptcy Act of 1867).

2249. *See id.* at 180.

2250. *See* Bankruptcy Act § 17a(2), 11 U.S.C. § 35a(2) (Supp. 1900), 30 Stat. 544, 550, before its amendment on February 5, 1903.

2251. 195 U.S. 606 (1904).

2252. *See id.* at 618-19.

2253. *See id.* at 620 (noting that "the real question is, was the relief granted in the judgment, based upon actual as distinguished from constructive fraud of the bankrupt.").

2254. 236 U.S. 558 (1915).

2255. *See id.* at 561-62.

2256. *See* Brown v. Felsen, 442 U.S. 127, 138 (1979) (all debts that "arise out of" fraud are nondischargeable). *Cf.* Friend v. Talcott, 228 U.S. 27, 40-41 (1913) (holding that an order confirming a composition plan

Likewise, if the creditor has reduced the fraudulent debt to judgment prepetition, the character of the debt does not merge into the judgment; thus, the bankruptcy court may look behind the judgment to determine that the underlying fraudulent debt is nondischargeable.[2257] Moreover, if the fraudulent debt has been resolved in a prepetition settlement stipulation and consent decree, claim preclusion does not prevent the bankruptcy court from looking behind the decree and stipulation and holding the debt nondischargeable.[2258] Similarly, if the debt has been reduced to a promissory note as part of a prepetition settlement in which the tort for fraud is released contractually, the bankruptcy court nevertheless can look behind the note and hold the debt nondischargeable.[2259]

Since 1960, the bankruptcy laws have conditioned nondischargeability of a debt based on a materially false statement in writing for the purpose of obtaining credit on the creditor's reasonable reliance on the false financial statement.[2260] The bankruptcy laws do not, however,

---

granting the debtor a general discharge does not preclude a creditor from suing to exempt a particular debt from discharge on the basis that the debtor obtained the creditor's goods by deceit).

2257. *See* Grogan v. Garner, 498 U.S. 279, 290 (1991) (assuming that the Bankruptcy Code seeks to "permit exception from discharge of all fraud claims creditors have successfully reduced to judgment.").

2258. *See* Brown v. Felsen, 442 U.S. 127, 138-39 (1979) ("In sum, we reject respondent's contention that res judicata applies here and we hold that the bankruptcy court is not confined to a review of the judgment and record in the prior state-court proceedings when considering the dischargeability of respondent's debt. Adopting the rule respondent urges would take [Bankruptcy Act] § 17 issues out of bankruptcy courts well suited to adjudicate them, and force those issues onto state courts concerned with other matters, all for the sake of a repose the bankrupt has long since abandoned. This we decline to do.") (footnote omitted).

2259. *See* Archer v. Warner, 538 U.S. 314, 320-21 (2003).

2260. *See* Bankruptcy Act § 17a(2), 11 U.S.C. § 35a(2) (Supp. 1960) (as amended by Act of July 12, 1960, Pub. L. No. 86-621, 74 Stat. 409); Bankruptcy Code § 523(a)(2)(B), 11 U.S.C. § 523(a)(2)(B) (2000).

specify the level of reliance required when the debtor commits fraud other than through a written false financial statement.[2261] In *Field v. Mans*,[2262] the Court considered "what, if any level of justification a creditor needs to show above mere reliance in fact in order to exempt the debt from discharge under [Bankruptcy Code] § 523(a)(2)(A)."[2263] The Court held that the appropriate reliance requirement for Bankruptcy Code § 523(a)(2)(A) was not "reasonable reliance," as would be required for a written false financial statement under Bankruptcy Code § 523(a)(2)(B),[2264] but the lesser requirement of "justifiable reliance."[2265] The Court reasoned that the term "fraud" in § 523(a)(2)(A) was a term of art including common law actions for debts based on "false pretenses, a false representation, or actual fraud."[2266] As such, the Court purported to adopt the common-law understanding of the term as it was used in 1978 when the language was added to Bankruptcy Code § 523.[2267] The Court held that since suits at common law in 1978 required a showing of both actual and justifiable reliance to establish fraudulent misrepresentation,[2268] that was the appropriate standard for Bankruptcy Code § 523(a)(2)(A).[2269] A creditor will be found to justifiably rely "where the facts should be apparent to one of his knowledge and intelligence from a cursory glance, or he has discov-

---

2261. *See* Bankruptcy Code § 523(a)(2)(A), 11 U.S.C. § 523(a)(2)(A) (2000).

2262. 516 U.S. 59 (1995).

2263. *See id.* at 66.

2264. *See* Bankruptcy Code § 523(a)(2)(B), 11 U.S.C. § 523(a)(2)(B) (2000).

2265. *See Field v. Mans*, 516 U.S. at 74-75, 77.

2266. *See id.* at 69; 71 n.9 ("We construe the terms in § 523(a)(2)(A) to incorporate the general common law of torts.").

2267. *See id.* at 70.

2268. *See id.*

2269. *See id.* at 74-75.

ered something which should serve as a warning that he is being deceived, that he is required to make an investigation of his own."[2270]

Both the Bankruptcy Act[2271] and the Bankruptcy Code[2272] require that a debtor[2273] timely schedule debts with the name of the creditor; otherwise the debt will be nondischargeable unless the creditor had notice or actual knowledge of the bankruptcy. Moreover, when the debtor does not schedule the name of the creditor, the Court has held that the debtor bears the burden of proving that the creditor had notice or actual knowledge of the bankruptcy case.[2274] Early on, in *Birkett v. Columbia Bank*,[2275] the Court determined when actual knowledge would render the debt dischargeable:[2276]

> Actual knowledge of the proceedings contemplated by the section is a knowledge in time to avail a creditor of the benefits of the law – in time to give him an equal opportunity with other creditors – not a knowledge that may come so late as to deprive him of participation in the administration of the affairs of the estate or to deprive him of dividends . . . .

2270. *See id.* at 71 (citing W. Prosser, Law of Torts § 108, p. 718 (4th ed. 1971).

2271. Bankruptcy Act § 17a(3), 11 U.S.C. § 35a(3) (1976) (repealed 1979).

2272. Bankruptcy Code § 523(a)(3), 11 U.S.C. § 523(a)(3) (2000) (applying to debts of individual debtors).

2273. The nondischargeability provisions of the Bankruptcy Act applied to all kinds of debtors in straight bankruptcy cases. Under the Bankruptcy Code, however, the nondischargeability provisions generally apply only to individual debtors. *See* 11 U.S.C. § 523(a) (2000) preamble. In chapter 7 liquidation cases, corporate and partnership debtors are ineligible to receive a discharge. *See* 11 U.S.C. § 727(a)(1) (2000).

2274. *See* Hill v. Smith, 260 U.S. 592, 595 (1923) ("We agree with the Court below that justice and the purpose of the section justify the technical rule that if the debtor would avoid the effect of his omission of a creditor's name from his schedules he must prove the facts upon which he relies.").

2275. 195 U.S. 345 (1904).

2276. *See id.* at 350.

Moreover, in *Miller v. Guasti*,[2277] the Court affirmed the nondischarge-ability of a debt because the debtor knew, but scheduled as "unknown," the residence and post office address of the creditor, and the creditor did not have notice or knowledge of the bankruptcy in time to file a proof of claim.[2278]

For the most part, however, the Court has been lenient in determining what the debtor must do to discharge scheduled debts. In *Kreitlein v. Ferger*,[2279] the Court held that a debtor's schedule listing the creditor's initials and last name along with the creditor's city of residence was *prima facie* sufficient to comply with the statute and avoid nondischargeability.[2280] Evidently the Court's holding was based on its observation that "letters directed to persons by their initials are constantly, properly and promptly delivered in the greatest cities of the country even when the street number is not given."[2281] As such, "it becomes evident that to lay down the general rule that the schedule must give the name of the creditor and the city and street number of the residence of those living in the largest cities would, in a multitude of cases, destroy the beneficent effect of the Bankruptcy Act."[2282] Nev-ertheless, *Kreitlein* might not remain good law today, because, over the years, as times have changed, the notice requirements of Bank-ruptcy Code § 342(c)[2283] are much more stringent than the standard 100 years ago, even though the scheduling and nondischargeability standards look much the same.[2284]

2277. 226 U.S. 170 (1912) (mem.).

2278. *See id.* at 171.

2279. 238 U.S. 21 (1915).

2280. *See id.* at 33-34.

2281. *See id.* at 33.

2282. *See id.* at 34.

2283. 11 U.S.C. § 342(c) (2000).

2284. *See* Bankruptcy Code §§ 521(1) & 523(a)(3), 11 U.S.C. §§ 521(1) & 523(a)(3) (2000) (dealing with the debtor's duty to schedule and the non-dischargeability of unscheduled debts respectively).

Beginning with the Bankruptcy Act of 1841,[2285] debts for defalcation in a fiduciary capacity have been included in the categories of nondischargeable debts.[2286] In *Chapman v. Forsyth*,[2287] the Court held that the Bankruptcy Act of 1841's reference to fraud or misappropriation while acting in a fiduciary capacity "speaks of technical trusts, and not those which the law implies from the contract."[2288] Thus, "a factor, who owes his principal money received on the sale of his goods, is not a fiduciary debtor within the meaning of the act."[2289] "Within the meaning of the exception in the bankruptcy act, a debt is not created by a person while acting in a 'fiduciary character,' merely because it is created under circumstances in which trust or confidence is reposed in the debtor, in the popular sense of those terms."[2290]

The Court extended its reasoning in *Chapman v. Forsyth* to discharge under the Bankruptcy Act of 1867 the obligations of a bankrupt who appropriated "to his own use collateral securities deposited with him as security for the payment of money or the performance of a duty . . . ."[2291] The Court concluded that "there is not so much - - of the character of a trustee, in one who holds collateral securities for a debt . . . . The creditor who holds a collateral, holds it for his own

---

2285. *See* Act of Aug. 19, 1841, ch. 9, 5 Stat. 440 (repealed by Act of Mar. 3, 1843, ch. 82, 5 Stat. 614).

2286. *See* Act of Aug. 19, 1841, ch. 9, 5 Stat. 440 § 4 (repealed by Act of Mar. 3, 1843, ch. 82, 5 Stat. 614); Act of Mar. 2, 1867, ch. 176, 14 Stat 517 § 33 (repealed by Act of June 7, 1878, ch. 160, 20 Stat. 99); Act of July 1, 1898, ch. 541, 30 Stat. 544 § 17d (repealed 1979); and Act of Nov. 6, 1978, Pub. L. No. 95-598, 92 Stat. 2549, 2591 (enacting 11 U.S.C. § 523(a)(4)).

2287. 43 U.S. (2 How.) 202 (1844).

2288. *See id.* at 208 (interpreting the Bankruptcy Act of 1841).

2289. *See id.*

2290. *See* Upshur v. Briscoe, 138 U.S. 365, 375 (1891) (interpreting the Bankruptcy Act of 1867).

2291. *See* Hennequin v. Clews, 111 U.S. 676, 678, 684 (1884).

benefit under contract. He is in no sense a trustee."[2292] This is particularly so when a debtor, without fraud or actual fraudulent intent, commingles another person's money that he agreed to collect and hold as an accommodation party without compensation.[2293]

Section 17a(4) of the Bankruptcy Act of 1898 refers not only to debts from defalcations in a fiduciary capacity, but also to fraud, embezzlement, and misappropriation while acting in any fiduciary capacity.[2294] In *Crawford v. Burke*,[2295] the Court held that this language imposed a fiduciary capacity limitation on debts for fraud,[2296] embezzlement, and misappropriation, as well as defalcation.[2297] Stated differently, whereas embezzlement or misappropriation might have been nondischargeable under the Bankruptcy Act of 1867 whether or not the bankrupt was a fiduciary, under the Bankruptcy Act of 1898 these debts are nondischargeable only if the bankrupt is acting in a fiduciary capacity.[2298] Thus, in *Crawford v. Burke*, the Court upheld

---

2292. *See id.* at 682.

2293. *See* Noble v. Hammond, 129 U.S. 65, 67-68, 70 (1889) (interpreting Bankruptcy Act of 1867).

2294. *See* Bankruptcy Act § 17a(4), 11 U.S.C. § 35a(4) (1976) (repealed 1979) ("A discharge in bankruptcy shall release a bankrupt from all of his provable debts . . . except such as . . . (4) were created by his fraud, embezzlement, misappropriation or defalcation while acting . . . in any fiduciary capacity . . . .").

2295. 195 U.S. 176 (1904).

2296. The limitation on debts for fraud is no longer very meaningful in light of the nondischargeability provisions in Bankruptcy Code § 523(a)(2), 11 U.S.C. § 523(a)(2) (2000) discussed previously. Thus, cases such as Tindle v. Birkett, 205 U.S. 183 (1907), in which the debtor made false and fraudulent misrepresentations to induce creditors to ship goods to the debtor, should be decided differently today.

2297. *See id.* at 189-90.

2298. As noted previously, Bankruptcy Act § 17a(2), 11 U.S.C. § 35a(2) (1976), provides an alternative basis to make nondischargeable debts incurred by fraud whether or not the debtor is acting in a fiduciary capacity. *See* nn.2250, 2260 *supra*.

the discharge of an investor against stockbrokers who sold stocks of the investor and converted the proceeds to their own use, because the frauds were not committed by the stockbrokers while acting in a fiduciary capacity.[2299]

The Court once again adhered to its reasoning in *Chapman v. Forsyth* when it interpreted the scope of Bankruptcy Act § 17a(4)[2300] in *Davis v. Aetna Acceptance Co.*[2301] In *Davis*, the debtor automobile dealer sold an automobile in the ordinary course of business but without permission of the holder of the trust receipt on the car.[2302] The automobile financier claimed that because it held a trust receipt, the debt for conversion was nondischargeable under Bankruptcy Code § 17a(4) as a debt from fraud or misappropriation while acting in a fiduciary capacity.[2303] The Court, relying on over 100 years of legal history, held that the debt was dischargeable because the debtor was not a trustee before the creation of the obligation.[2304] Moreover, the parties' efforts to label the obligation as arising from a trust did not make it so in substance.[2305]

2299. *See Crawford v. Burke*, 195 U.S. at 194.

2300. 11 U.S.C. § 35a(4) (Supp. 1920).

2301. 293 U.S. 328, 333-34 (1934) (finding no trust relationship where automobile dealer sold automobile without permission of holder of trust receipt).

2302. *See id.* at 330.

2303. *See id.* at 333.

2304. *See id.* at 333-34.

2305. *See id.* at 334 ("The resulting obligation is not turned into one arising from a trust because the parties to one of the documents have chosen to speak of it as a trust.").

Under both the Bankruptcy Act[2306] and the Bankruptcy Code,[2307] the law generally[2308] makes debts for "willful and malicious injury" nondischargeable in an individual debtor's bankruptcy case. Early on, in *Tinker v. Colwell*,[2309] the Court decided that this language excludes intentional torts from the scope of the discharge without any specific holding of "particular malice" or "personal malevolence" toward the creditor.[2310] Thus, in *McIntyre v. Kavanaugh*,[2311] the Court found nondischargeable a debt for intentional conversion of another person's property.[2312] On the other hand, "a willful and malicious injury does

2306. Bankruptcy Act § 17a(8), 11 U.S.C. § 35a(8) (1976) (repealed 1979), excludes from discharge debts "for willful and malicious injuries to the person or property of another . . . ."

2307. Bankruptcy Code § 523(a)(6), 11 U.S.C. § 523(a)(6) (2000), excludes from an individual debtor's discharge debts "for willful and malicious injury by the debtor to another entity or to the property of another entity."

2308. Under the Bankruptcy Code, the so-called "super discharge" provisions of chapter 13 originally discharged debts for willful and malicious injury in chapter 13 cases. *See* 11 U.S.C. § 1328 (as enacted 1978), 92 Stat. 2650 (Nov. 6, 1978). The 2005 amendments restored nondischargeability in chapter 13 "for restitution, or damages, awarded in a civil action against the debtor as a result of willful and malicious injury by the debtor that caused personal injury to an individual or the death of an individual." *See* 11 U.S.C. § 1328(a)(4) (as amended by Pub. L. No. 109-8, § 314(b), 119 Stat. 88 (2005)). Nevertheless, debts for intentional torts to property remain dischargeable in chapter 13 as, apparently, do debts for intentional torts to a person that have not been reduced to judgment.

2309. 193 U.S. 473 (1904). *See supra* Ch. 2, nn.363-366 and accompanying text.

2310. *See id.* at 485, 490 (holding nondischargeable the debtor's "criminal conversation" debt to another man for seducing his wife, when "the act [of seduction] itself necessarily implies that degree of malice which is sufficient to bring the case within the exception stated in the statute.").

2311. 242 U.S. 138 (1916).

2312. *See id.* at 141 (nondischargeable debt from deprivation of property through deliberate disposition of it without semblance of authority).

not follow as of course from every act of conversion;" debts caused by the debtor's negligence, gross negligence, or recklessness are dischargeable.[2313] In *Kawaauhau v. Geiger*,[2314] the Court reaffirmed this principle and expanded it beyond debts for conversion, holding that "debts arising from recklessly or negligently inflicted injuries do not fall within the compass of [nondischargeability under Bankruptcy Code] § 523(a)(6)."[2315] Moreover, in defining the contours of nondischargeable "intentional torts," the *Geiger* Court clarified that "[i]ntentional torts generally require that the actor intend 'the consequences of an act,' not simply 'the act itself.'"[2316] Thus, it is not enough to make a debt nondischargeable that the debtor intended to perform the act that resulted in injury; rather, in order to render the debt nondischargeable under Bankruptcy Code § 523(a)(6), the debtor must have intended the act to cause injury.

The Court also has addressed the nondischargeability of penalties. Under Bankruptcy Code § 523(a)(7), a debt is nondischargeable if it is "a fine, penalty, or forfeiture payable to and for the benefit of a governmental unit, and is not in compensation for actual pecuniary loss."[2317] In *Kelly v. Robinson*,[2318] the Court strained to interpret this language to hold, in the context of a chapter 7 liquidation case, that restitution obligations owed by the debtor to individuals and imposed

---

2313. *See* Davis v. Aetna Acceptance Co., 293 U.S. 328, 332 (1934) (holding dischargeable a debt for conversion arising from an automobile dealer's sale of an automobile without consent of the dealership financier).

2314. 523 U.S. 57 (1998).

2315. *See id.* at 64.

2316. *See id.* at 61-62.

2317. *See* 11 U.S.C. § 523(a)(7) (2000).

2318. 479 U.S. 36 (1986).

as a condition of criminal probation are nondischargeable.[2319] In *Pennsylvania Department of Public Welfare v. Davenport*,[2320] however, the Court held that restitution orders are debts that are dischargeable under chapter 13.[2321]

As noted previously, receipt of a discharge in a bankruptcy case may bar the debtor from receiving a discharge in a subsequent bankruptcy case filed within a specified time after receipt of the discharge.[2322] Likewise, if a debtor is denied a discharge in a bankruptcy case or the discharge is pending and contested, the court, in a subsequent bankruptcy, will not discharge the debts subject to the first proceeding.[2323] Moreover, discharge or nondischargeability of a debt in a previous bankruptcy case may affect the nondischargeability

---

2319. *See id.* at 50. Although the Court's policy result is understandable to protect state criminal proceedings from federal interference, its statutory construction is questionable because a restitution obligation owed to a private individual is in no sense payable to and for the benefit of a governmental unit. *See id.* at 55 ("I find unconvincing the majority's conclusion that the criminal restitution order at issue here is not 'compensation for actual pecuniary loss.' While restitution imposed as a condition of probation under the Connecticut statute is in part a penal sanction, it is also intended to compensate victims for their injuries.") (footnote omitted) (Justice Marshall dissenting).

2320. 495 U.S. 552 (1990).

2321. *See id.* at 555. In response to the Court's decision in *Davenport*, Congress amended Bankruptcy Code § 1328(a)(3) to make criminal restitution obligations and, later, criminal fines nondischargeable in chapter 13 cases. *See* The Crime Control Act of 1990, Pub. L. No. 101-647, 104 Stat. 4792 (1990) excepting criminal restitution obligations from discharge under Chapter 13; Criminal Victims Protection Act of 1990, Pub. L. No. 101-581 §§ 2(b), 3, 104 Stat. 2865 (1990) enacting a portion of the Crime Control Act of 1990. *See also* Bankruptcy Reform Act of 1994, Pub. L. No. 103-394, 108 Stat. 4106, 4132 (1994) excepting criminal fines from discharge (amending 11 U.S.C. § 1328(a)(3) (Supp. 1992)).

2322. *See generally supra* nn.2135-2139, discussing the history of bar periods in cases filed under Chapter XIII or chapter 13.

2323. *See* Freshman v. Atkins, 269 U.S. 121, 122-23 (1925).

of a debt in a subsequent bankruptcy case.[2324] If a creditor succeeds in having a debt declared nondischargeable in the earlier case, with certain exceptions,[2325] it will likewise be nondischargeable in the later case if the creditor pleads res judicata, but will be discharged if the creditor fails to plead the previous adjudication.[2326]

Some exceptions pertain to the nondischargeability of debts incurred within a specified time, such as a chapter 7 discharge of an individual debtor which does not extend to priority income or gross receipts tax claims for which a return is last due within three years before bankruptcy.[2327] In *Young v. United States*,[2328] two chapter 13 debtors dismissed their joint chapter 13 case, having filed a joint petition under chapter 7 one day before dismissal.[2329] So much time had elapsed during the chapter 13 case, that certain income tax claims were well beyond the three-year reachback period of Bankruptcy Code § 507(a)(8)(A)(i),[2330] unless the running of the three-year period was equitably tolled during the chapter 13 case. In order to close this

---

2324. *See* Bankruptcy Act § 17b, 11 U.S.C. § 35b (1976) (repealed 1979); Bankruptcy Code § 523(b), 11 U.S.C. § 523(b) (2000).

2325. Under Bankruptcy Code § 523(b), 11 U.S.C. § 523(b) (2000), debts excepted from discharge under Bankruptcy Code § 523(a)(1), (3), or (8), 11 U.S.C. § 523(a)(1), (3), or (8) (2000), or Bankruptcy Act § 17a(1), (3), or (5), 11 U.S.C. § 35a(1), (3), or (5) (1976) (repealed 1979), in a prior case may be reevaluated in a subsequent case and discharged unless nondischargeable on the merits in the subsequent case.

2326. In Bluthenthal v. Jones, 208 U.S. 64, 66 (1908), the Court held that the debt will be discharged in the subsequent case if the creditor "intentionally remained away from the court and allowed the discharge to be granted without objection."

2327. *See* 11 U.S.C. §§ 507(a)(8)(A)(i), 523(a)(1)(A) (2000).

2328. 535 U.S. 43 (2002).

2329. *See id.* at 45.

2330. 11 U.S.C. § 507(a)(8)(A)(i) (2000).

legal loophole,[2331] the Court held that the tax debt was nondischargeable because the three-year reachback period was a period of limitation that was equitably tolled during the debtors' chapter 13 case.[2332]

BANKRUPTCY LITIGATION

As discussed in specific contexts previously, many aspects of the bankruptcy case involve litigation in adversary proceedings or contested matters. As discussed more fully in Chapters 1, 3, and 4, although the Court has clarified whether a party is entitled to or has waived a jury trial in certain instances, the Court has avoided deciding whether the bankruptcy court may conduct a jury trial.[2333] Chapter 4 also discusses in detail whether a bankruptcy court has jurisdiction to conduct various kinds of litigation.[2334] This chapter discusses specific contexts and issues that arise in bankruptcy litigation.

Once the debtor files a petition, a party in interest may file a motion to dismiss on the basis of the debtor's ineligibility or lack of good faith. Bankruptcy Act § 146 required a debtor to sustain the burden of showing that the petition was filed in good faith. In this regard, the statute deemed a bad faith filing if, inter alia, "a prior proceeding is pending in any court and it appears that the interests of creditors and stockholders would be best subserved in such prior proceeding."[2335] Interpreting this law, the Court held that the Chapter

---

2331. *See Young*, 535 U.S. at 46 ("The terms of the lookback period appear to create a loophole: Since the Code does not prohibit back-to-back Chapter 13 and Chapter 7 filings (as long as the debtor did not receive a discharge under Chapter 13, *see* §§ 727(a)(8)-(9)), a debtor can render a tax debt dischargeable by first filing a Chapter 13 petition, then voluntarily dismissing the petition when the lookback period for the debt has lapsed, and finally refiling under Chapter 7.").

2332. *See id.* at 47, 54.

2333. *See supra* Ch. 1, nn.16-23, 25; Ch. 3, nn.723-740; and Ch. 4, nn.1069-1072.

2334. *See supra* Ch. 4, nn.1011-1087 and accompanying text.

2335. *See* Chapter X § 146(4), 11 U.S.C. § 546(4) (1976) (repealed 1979).

X petitioner "must demonstrate that at least in some substantial particular the prior proceedings withhold or deny creditors or stockholders benefits, advantages, or protection which Ch. X affords."[2336] When the debtor is insolvent, a previous state court case is pending, and the stockholders show no inclination to contribute new value, the court will dismiss the Chapter X petition as a bad faith filing in order to avoid "giving the equity owners a nuisance value wholly unjustified by the reorganization standards which are incorporated into Ch. X."[2337]

It is common for creditors to file proofs of claims to participate in bankruptcy distributions and also common for the bankruptcy trustee to file objections to claims. The Court has had occasion to deal with the burden of proof in one specialized aspect of claims litigation. Ordinarily, a party asserting a claim against a bankruptcy estate bears the burden of proof.[2338] In *Raleigh v. Illinois Department of Revenue*,[2339] the Court held "that in the absence of modification expressed in the Bankruptcy Code the burden of proof on a tax claim in bankruptcy remains where the substantive tax law puts it."[2340] The Court reached its conclusion in part because the burden of proof was a "'substantive' aspect" of the claim.[2341]

A substantial volume of bankruptcy court litigation involves nondischargeability complaints. The Court has granted bankruptcy courts discretion to extend the time within which discharge or nondischarge-

2336. *See* Marine Harbor Props., Inc. v. Mfrs. Trust Co., 317 U.S. 78, 84 (1942).

2337. *See id.* at 86.

2338. *See* Fed. R. Bankr. P. 3001(f) ("A proof of claim . . . shall constitute prima facie evidence of the validity and amount of the claim.").

2339. 530 U.S. 15 (2000).

2340. *See id.* at 26.

2341. *See id.* at 20-21.

ability complaints may be filed.[2342] Moreover, in *Kontrick v. Ryan*,[2343] the Court held that the debtor may waive a timeliness objection; specifically, if a creditor fails to timely file such a complaint, the debtor must raise the timeliness objection before the court reaches the merits of the objection to discharge.[2344] Furthermore, if the bankruptcy court reaches the merits of a nondischargeability complaint, it also may adjudicate counterclaims filed by the debtor in response to the complaint.[2345]

The Court also has addressed the burden of proof in nondischargeability litigation. As noted previously, in *Grogan v. Garner*[2346] the Court held that a creditor seeking to prove the nondischargeability of a debt need only do so by a preponderance of the evidence rather than clear and convincing evidence.[2347] The Court was well aware of the practical consequences of its holding:[2348]

> In sum, if nondischargeability must be proved only by a preponderance of the evidence, all creditors who have secured fraud judgments, the elements of which are the same as those of the fraud discharge exception, will be exempt from dis-

---

2342. *See* Lerner v. First Wis. Nat'l Bank, 294 U.S. 116, 119 (1935) ("Under Order XXXVII, and permissive provisions of the Bankruptcy Act, we think the courts may exercise discretion sufficient for the successful conduct of proceedings in varying circumstances. Thus, while an objecting creditor must file specifications showing the grounds of his opposition on the day when creditors are required to show cause, that day may be fixed or postponed by the court in view of the existing situation."). *Accord* Fed. R. Bankr. P. 4004(b), 4007(c)-(d) & 9006(b)(3).

2343. 540 U.S. 443 (2004).

2344. *See id.* at 460 ("No reasonable construction of complaint-processing rules, in sum, would allow a litigant situated as Kontrick is to defeat a claim, as filed too late, after the party has litigated and lost the case on the merits.").

2345. *See* Marshall v. Marshall, 547 U.S. 293, 314 (2006).

2346. 498 U.S. 279 (1991).

2347. *See id.* at 291.

2348. *See id.* at 285.

charge under collateral estoppel principles. If, however, non-dischargeability must be proved by clear and convincing evidence, creditors who secured fraud judgments based only on the preponderance standard would not be assured of qualifying for the fraud discharge exception.

In reaching its conclusion, the Court reasoned as follows: "Because the preponderance-of-the-evidence standard results in a roughly equal allocation of the risk of error between litigants, we presume that this standard is applicable in civil actions between private litigants unless 'particularly important individual interests or rights are at stake.'"[2349] The Court's rationale is so broad that the preponderance of the evidence standard probably applies to all or almost all matters litigated in a bankruptcy case, with the exception of certain nonbankruptcy causes of action.[2350]

Settlements in bankruptcy cases and proceedings may arise during a bankruptcy case or proceeding or under a plan. Under the Bankruptcy Act, the Court recognized that "compromises, settlements, and concessions are a normal part of the reorganization process."[2351] At least under a plan when the fair and equitable rule applies, the Court has held that "[t]he requirements . . . that plans of reorganization be both 'fair and equitable,' apply to compromises just as to other

---

2349. *See id.* at 286 (citations omitted).

2350. The *Grogan* Court was careful to note that nonbankruptcy law, usually state law, governs "the standard of proof that a creditor must satisfy in order to establish a valid claim against a bankrupt estate . . . ." *See id.* at 283 & n.9.

2351. *See* Protective Comm. v. Anderson, 390 U.S. 414, 424 (1968) ("Compromises are 'a normal part of the process of reorganization'") (citation omitted); Group of Institutional Investors v. Chicago, M., St. P. & Pac. R.R., 318 U.S. 523, 565 (1943) (citation omitted); Case v. Los Angeles Lumber Prods. Co., 308 U.S. 106, 130 (1939) ("There frequently will be situations involving conflicting claims to specific assets which may, in the discretion of the court, be more wisely settled by compromise rather than by litigation.").

aspects of reorganization."[2352] Threats to the jurisdiction of the bankruptcy court or to exercise "hold up" value does not support a compromise or settlement.[2353] Moreover, "[w]hatever might be the strategic nuisance value of such parties outside of [bankruptcy] is irrelevant to the duties of the court in confirming or disapproving a plan . . . ."[2354]

Instead, the court has promulgated the so-called *TMT Trailer Ferry* test, requiring "the bankruptcy judge [to] apprise[] himself of all facts necessary for an intelligent and objective opinion of the probabilities of ultimate success should the claim be litigated."[2355] Moreover, "the judge should form an educated estimate of the complexity, expense, and likely duration of such litigation, the possible difficulties of collecting on any judgment which might be obtained, and all other factors relevant to a full and fair assessment of the wisdom of the proposed compromise."[2356] In essence, the court must perform a cost/benefit analysis, comparing "the terms of the compromise with the likely rewards of litigation."[2357]

Most settlements are reviewable on appeal under an abuse of discretion standard, if the appeals are not dismissed as moot[2358] based

---

2352. *See* Protective Comm. v. Anderson, 390 U.S. 414, 424 (1968) (citations omitted).

2353. *See* Los Angeles Lumber Prods., 308 U.S. at 130-31 ("[A]ny strategic position occupied by the stockholders prior to these proceedings vanished once the court invoked its jurisdiction. Threats by the stockholders of the kind here in question are merely threats to the jurisdiction of the court . . . . Consequently, these claims of the stockholders are . . . entitled to no more dignity than any claim based upon sheer nuisance value.").

2354. *See id.* at 129.

2355. *See* Protective Comm. v. Anderson, 390 U.S. 414, 424 (1968).

2356. *See id.*

2357. *See id.* at 425.

2358. *See, e.g.,* U.S. Bancorp Mortgage Co. v. Bonner Mall P'ship, 513 U.S. 18, 21 (1994) ("'If a judgment has become moot [while awaiting review], this Court may not consider its merits, but may make such disposition of the whole case as justice may require.'") (citation omitted).

on consummation of an unstayed settlement pending appeal. More-over, the Court has provided the following guidance when an appellate court reviews a settlement order: "It is essential, however, that a reviewing court have some basis for distinguishing between well-reasoned conclusions arrived at after a comprehensive considera-tion of all relevant factors, and mere boiler-plate approval phrased in appropriate language but unsupported by evaluation of the facts or analysis of the law."[2359] As noted previously, in *Taylor v. Standard Gas & Electric Co.*,[2360] the Court held that the district court abused its discretion in approving the compromise of the claim asserted by a creditor who had operated the debtor as its own instrumentality.[2361] The Court also has clarified that a settlement order is binding on a successor in interest, holding that a bankruptcy court-approved agreement between a receiver, as predecessor in interest to the bank-ruptcy trustee, and a third party is binding on the trustee even if it is detrimental to the estate.[2362]

Sometimes, parties will settle litigation while an appeal is pending and provide for vacatur of the lower court judgment in the settlement agreement. In *U.S. Bancorp Mortgage Co. v. Bonner Mall Partner-ship*,[2363] the Court made clear that if an appeal is mooted based on a voluntary action of the parties, such as entering into a settlement, the

---

Cf. Foley v. Blair, 414 U.S. 212, 215-16 (1973) (remanding matter so Court of Appeals could consider whether confirmation of consensual arrangement mooted appeal).

2359. *See id.* at 434.

2360. 306 U.S. 307 (1939).

2361. *See id.* at 308, 314-15. ("[I]t was an abuse of discretion to approve the compromise . . . .") *Id.* at 314.

2362. *See* Bryant v. Swofford Bros. Dry Goods Co., 214 U.S. 279, 291-92 (1909) (holding that bankruptcy trustee was bound by court–approved agreement between receiver and third party).

2363. 513 U.S. 18 (1994).

Court generally will not permit vacatur of the lower court judgment.[2364] As a matter of public policy, because judicial precedents are in the public domain, equitable considerations and the public interest usually will not be served by permitting private parties to bargain to vacate judicial precedent.[2365]

BANKRUPTCY CRIMES

Whenever people control other people's money, there is a temptation to use that money wrongly for one's own benefit. Often this temptation starts with an innocent intention to "borrow" the money; ultimately it may result in embezzlement, larceny, criminal conversion, or some other crime. From the beginning, federal criminal laws have functioned to deter and punish debtors, trustees, and other fiduciaries from these wrongful acts.[2366] The modern federal criminal code contains several provisions specifying different kinds of bankruptcy crimes[2367] which the Court has seldom interpreted in the bank-

---

2364. *See id.* at 29 (holding "that mootness by reason of settlement does not justify vacatur of a judgment" except in "exceptional circumstances").

2365. *See id.* at 26-29. ("This is not to say that vacatur can never be granted when mootness is produced in that fashion. As we have described, the determination is an equitable one, and exceptional circumstances may conceivably counsel in favor of such a course."). *See id.* at 29.

2366. *See, e.g., see* United States v. Knight, 336 U.S. 505 (1949) (reversing acquittal of defendant attorneys who aided and abetted the bankruptcy trustee in appropriating property of the bankruptcy estate in violation of the statute preceding modern 18 U.S.C. § 152 (2000)).

2367. *See* 18 U.S.C. §§ 151-158 (bankruptcy crimes); 1519 (obstruction of justice); 2516 (authorization for interception of wire, oral, or electronic communications); 3057 (bankruptcy investigations); 3284 (limitations re: concealment of bankrupt's assets); 3613 (civil remedies re: satisfaction of unpaid fine); & 6001 (definitions) (2000).

ruptcy context.[2368] The Court, however, has rendered decisions involving crimes during the early regime of the Bankruptcy Act.

Before 1979, Bankruptcy Act § 7a(9)[2369] and other federal statutes[2370] precluded the use of testimony given by the bankrupt at the first meeting of creditors from being offered in evidence in a criminal prosecution against him. The Court rendered several decisions limiting the scope of these provisions.[2371] A few of these may contain important principles applicable in current cases. For example, in *Burrell v. Montana*,[2372] the Court held that the statutory limitation on the introduction of evidence in a criminal trial did not prevent its use

---

2368. *See* United States v. Knight, 336 U.S. 505, 507-08 n.1 (1949) (reversing acquittal of defendant attorneys who aided and abetted the bankruptcy trustee in appropriating property of the bankruptcy estate in violation of the statute preceding modern 18 U.S.C. § 152 (2000)).

2369. Bankruptcy Act § 7a(9), 11 U.S.C. § 25a(9) (1898) (amended in 1938 and recodified into § 7a(10) & repealed 1979) ("The bankrupt shall . . . (9) [w]hen present at the first meeting of his creditors, and at such other times as the court shall order, submit to an examination concerning . . . all matters which may affect the administration and settlement of his [bankruptcy] estate; but no testimony given by him shall be offered in evidence against him in any criminal proceeding."). As amended in 1938, Bankruptcy Act § 7a(10) permitted the use of testimony given by the bankrupt in any hearing on objections to discharge. *See* Bankruptcy Act § 7a(10), 11 U.S.C. § 25a(10) (Supp. 1938) (repealed 1979), Act of June 22, 1938, 52 Stat. 847.

2370. *See, e.g.,* Rev. Stat. § 860 (1875) (repealed 36 Stat. 352 (1910)) ("No pleading of a party, nor any discovery or evidence obtained from a party or witness by means of a judicial proceeding . . . shall be given in evidence, or in any manner used against him or his property or estate . . . in any criminal proceeding . . . .") and Act of Feb. 11, 1893, ch. 83, 27 Stat. 443 ("[N]o person shall be prosecuted or subjected to any penalty or forfeiture for or on account of any transaction, matter or thing, concerning which he may testify . . . before said Commission . . . .").

2371. *See, e.g.,* Cameron v. United States, 231 U.S. 710 (1914); Ensign v. Pennsylvania, 227 U.S. 592 (1913); Glickstein v. United States, 222 U.S. 139 (1911); Burrell v. Montana, 194 U.S. 572 (1904).

2372. 194 U.S. 572 (1904).

in leading to the bankrupt's prosecution.[2373] The Court also held that the bankrupt could waive statutory immunity if not timely claimed.[2374] Moreover, in *Glickstein v. United States*,[2375] the Court held that the statutory immunity excluding the use of testimony given at the first meeting of creditors only applied to truthful testimony; the prosecution could use false testimony against the bankrupt in a perjury trial.[2376]

The bankruptcy process for an individual debtor embraces a fundamental bargain: the debtor accounts for and turns over property to the bankruptcy estate for sale and distribution to creditors in exchange for which the honest debtor gets a fresh start. In accounting for property and turning over records, the debtor runs a risk that the books produced contain incriminating information that may be used in a criminal prosecution. Nevertheless, as discussed in Chapter 3, the Court has held that notwithstanding the Fourth and Fifth Amendments, the debtor has an absolute duty to turn over books and records to the bankruptcy estate and information in those books may be used against the debtor in a criminal prosecution.[2377] Thus, although the debtor may invoke the Fifth Amendment privilege to avoid testifying or producing evidence at trial,[2378] the debtor may not invoke the

---

2373. *See id.* at 578 (Section 7(9) of the Bankruptcy Act "does not say that [the bankrupt] shall be exempt from prosecution, but only, in case of prosecution, his testimony cannot be used against him.").

2374. *See id.* at 577, 579.

2375. 222 U.S. 139 (1911).

2376. *See id.* at 143 ("[I]t is impossible in reason to conceive that Congress commanded the giving of testimony, and at the same time intended that false testimony might be given with impunity . . . .").

2377. *See supra* Ch. 3 nn.644-649 and accompanying text, citing, inter alia, *Ex parte* Fuller , 262 U.S. 91 (1923); Johnson v. United States, 228 U.S. 457 (1913); *In re* Harris, 221 U.S. 274 (1911).

2378. *See, e.g.,* McCarthy v. Arndstein, 266 U.S. 34, 39-40 (1924), 262 U.S. 355, 359-60 (1923) (holding that the debtor was entitled to invoke his Fifth Amendment privilege in refusing to answer questions in a civil bankruptcy case when to do so might tend to incriminate him). *But see* 11 U.S.C. § 727(a)(6)(B) (2000) (providing for denial of discharge when debtor refuses to testify after grant of immunity).

privilege to prevent the bankruptcy estate from producing books and records in its possession at trial.[2379]

When a debtor conceals money or property from the bankruptcy trustee, the debtor is subject to indictment for a federal bankruptcy crime.[2380] Moreover, the Court has held that conspiracy to commit a bankruptcy crime is a separate offense from the underlying bankruptcy crime and is not an offense that arises under the Bankruptcy Act for purposes of the statute of limitations.[2381] Furthermore, if the debtor induces another to make a false oath in the bankruptcy court, the debtor may be prosecuted for subornation of perjury.[2382] But the Court has held that the debtor cannot be convicted of perjury when the only evidence is the unsupported testimony of the perjurer.[2383] Moreover, "[i]n substance subornation is the same as perjury."[2384] Therefore, the Court has held that the uncorroborated testimony of one witness that he was suborned to make a false oath in a bankruptcy case is not enough to establish falsity in a prosecution for subornation of perjury.[2385]

2379. *See Ex parte* Fuller, 262 U.S. 91, 93-94 (1923) ("his privilege in respect to what was his and in his custody ceases on a transfer of the control and possession [of the books and records] which takes place by legal proceedings . . . ."); Johnson v. United States, 228 U.S. 457, 458 (1913). *Cf.* Ensign v. Pennsylvania, 227 U.S. 592, 599-601 (1913) (permitting bankruptcy schedules to be used in prosecution against bankrupts, because statutory exclusion of testimony only applies to oral testimony).

2380. *See Johnson*, 228 U.S. at 458.

2381. *See* United States v. Rabinowich, 238 U.S. 78, 85-87, 89 (1915).

2382. *See* Hammer v. United States, 271 U.S. 620, 624-26 (1926).

2383. *See id.* at 626 ("The general rule in prosecutions for perjury is that the uncorroborated oath of one witness is not enough to establish the falsity of the testimony of the accused set forth in the indictment as perjury.").

2384. *See id.* at 628.

2385. *See id.* at 629.

CHAPTER 6

LANDMARK CASES AND OLD FAVORITES

INTRODUCTION

This chapter discusses a few of the most significant bankruptcy cases over the past 111 years in which the Court sharply changed the course of bankruptcy law. The chapter continues with a discussion of favorite cases regardless of their impact on bankruptcy law or doctrine and concludes with speculation about how bankruptcy law might have developed had the Court decided none of these cases.

LANDMARK CASES

The Supreme Court cases of the past 111 years range in importance from relatively insignificant to very consequential. This chapter discusses some of the most important cases of the past century that have had the greatest impact on the practice of bankruptcy law.

CASES RULING ON THE CONSTITUTIONALITY OF BANKRUPTCY LAWS

Some of the Court's most significant cases declared all or part of the bankruptcy law unconstitutional or upheld its constitutionality.[2386] During the 1930's, a conservative Supreme Court twice struck down bankruptcy laws as unconstitutional. Twice Congress amended and reenacted the laws. And twice the Court, probably responding to the

---

2386. Although this chapter discusses several of the Court's more important decisions, Ch. 3 *supra* contains a more thorough discussion of bankruptcy law and the Constitution. *See* pp. 122-165.

pressure of President Franklin Roosevelt's court packing plan,[2387] reversed course and upheld the constitutionality of the legislation.

In 1935, the Court considered the constitutionality of bankruptcy laws designed to retard the progress of farm foreclosures. The Court's holding in *Louisville Joint Stock Land Bank v. Radford*,[2388] unanimously struck down the first Frazier-Lemke Act[2389] for unconstitutionally taking a mortgagee's property rights without just compensation.[2390] As such, *Radford* identified certain protected constitutional rights of secured creditors. Specifically, the *Radford* Court held that the Frazier-Lemke Act unconstitutionally deprived the mortgagee of the following specific state property rights:[2391]

1. The right to retain the lien until the indebtedness thereby secured is paid.

2. The right to realize upon the security by a judicial public sale.

3. The right to determine when such sale shall be held, subject only to the discretion of the court.

4. The right to protect its interest in the property by bidding at such sale whenever held, and thus to assure having the mortgaged property devoted primarily to the satisfaction of the debt, either through receipt of the proceeds of a fair competitive sale or by taking the property itself.

5. The right to control meanwhile the property during the period of default, subject only to the discretion of the court, and to have the rents and profits collected by a receiver for the satisfaction of the debt.

2387. *See, e.g.,* Barry Cushman, *Rethinking the New Deal Court*, 80 VA. L. REV. 201 (1994); Laura Kalman, *Law, Politics, and the New Deal(s)*, 108 YALE L.J. 2165 (1999).

2388. 295 U.S. 555 (1935).

2389. Pub. L. No. 73-486, 48 Stat. 1289 (1934).

2390. *See Radford*, 295 U.S. at 588-90.

2391. *See id.* at 594-95.

The taking of these rights occurred because the Act deprived the mortgagee of possession for five years while the debtor was permitted to retain possession by paying a fair annual rent or purchasing the property at its appraised value with deferred payments bearing annual interest at 1% and paid under an amortization that has 85% of the principal paid after six years.[2392] The Court did not opine whether the Constitution required protection of each of these five property rights.

As more fully discussed in Chapter 3, almost immediately after the Court declared the first Frazier-Lemke Act unconstitutional, to protect farmers from losing their farms in foreclosures Congress enacted the second Frazier-Lemke Act,[2393] which the Court upheld as constitutional in *Wright v. Vinton Branch of the Mountain Trust Bank.*[2394] Significantly, *Vinton Branch* sustained constitutionality based on the second Frazier-Lemke Act's preservation of only three of the five property rights identified in *Radford.*[2395] The three preserved rights are the right to retain the lien until the secured indebtedness is paid; the right to realize on the security by a judicial public sale; and the right to bid in the secured debt at a foreclosure sale.[2396] These three rights continue to serve as a base line protection for secured creditors in bankruptcy cases.[2397] Whether these rights survive as constitutional guarantees or only as statutory protections is open to doubt.[2398] In *Wright v. Union Central Life Insurance Co.,*[2399] the Supreme Court

---

2392. *See id.* at 591-92, 601-02 & n.21.

2393. Act of Aug. 28, 1935, Pub. L. No. 74-384, 49 Stat. 941 (1935).

2394. 300 U.S. 440, 458-61 (1937) ("*Vinton Branch*").

2395. *See id.* at 458.

2396. *See id.* at 458-59, noting that the last of these rights was not provided for in the Frazier-Lemke Act but in the legislative history.

2397. *See supra* Ch. 3, nn.671-677 and accompanying text.

2398. *See supra* Ch. 3, nn.678-684 and accompanying text.

2399. 311 U.S. 273 (1940).

clarified and defined the basic constitutional rights of secured creditors in the context of a sale of farm property: "Safeguards were provided to protect the rights of secured creditors, throughout the proceedings, to the extent of the value of the property. There is no constitutional claim of the creditor to more than that."[2400]

In a parallel but narrower context, in 1936 the Court overturned the nation's first municipal bankruptcy law[2401] as unconstitutional before upholding the constitutionality of its successor statute.[2402] In *Ashton v. Cameron County Water Improvement District*,[2403] the Court held that Congress lacked the power to require creditors to accept a composition plan offered by a public corporation.[2404] The Court reasoned that since Congress cannot exercise its taxing power to tax municipal bonds without infringing state sovereignty, it likewise cannot exercise its bankruptcy power to infringe municipal bonds because the bankruptcy power cannot have any higher "rank or importance in our scheme of government" than the taxing power.[2405] Moreover, because the Contracts Clause[2406] forbids the states from impairing the obligations of their municipal bonds, the States cannot consent to federal legislation under the bankruptcy clause that accomplishes an end run around this restriction.[2407] Furthermore, for Congress to do so directly without the consent of the states would

---

2400. *See id.* at 278-79. (citations omitted).

2401. Act of May 24, 1934, Pub. L. No. 73-251, 73d Cong., 2d Sess., ch. 345, §§ 78-80, 48 Stat. 798.

2402. Act of Aug. 16, 1937, Pub. L. No. 75-302, 75th Cong., 1st Sess., ch. 657, 50 Stat. 653.

2403. 298 U.S. 513 (1936).

2404. *See id.* at 530-31.

2405. *See id.* at 530.

2406. U.S. CONST. art. I, § 10.

2407. *See Ashton*, 298 U.S. at 531.

impermissibly violate state sovereignty.[2408] Thus, the Court struck down Chapter IX of the Bankruptcy Act[2409] as unconstitutional.[2410]

Two years later in *United States v. Bekins*,[2411] however, the Court examined the constitutionality of Chapter X of the Bankruptcy Act,[2412] a municipal debt adjustment statute passed by Congress after the Court's decision in *Ashton* struck down Chapter IX. The Court held that Congress could constitutionally provide a composition chapter applicable to arms of the state without violating state sovereignty reserved under the Tenth Amendment, because the state retains both ultimate approval of the composition plan under state law and the ability to limit access of its instrumentalities to bankruptcy relief.[2413] The Court distinguished its decision in *Ashton* by noting that Chapter X was carefully crafted to avoid federal interference with the power of the state or its subdivisions to manage their own affairs.[2414]

The Court also has declared more modern bankruptcy laws unconstitutional. In 1982, the Court decided *Railway Labor Executives' Ass'n v. Gibbons*[2415] and, on Uniformity Clause grounds, struck down bankruptcy legislation drafted so specifically on its face that it would apply in practice to the reorganization of only one large

---

2408. *See id.*

2409. Act of May 24, 1934, Pub. L. No. 73-251, 73d Cong., 2d Sess., ch. 345, §§ 78-80, 48 Stat. 798.

2410. *See Ashton*, 298 U.S. at 532.

2411. 304 U.S. 27 (1938).

2412. Act of Aug. 16, 1937, Pub. L. No. 75-302, 75th Cong., 1st Sess., ch. 657, 50 Stat. 653.

2413. *See Bekins*, 304 U.S. at 54.

2414. *See id.* at 49-51. ("The statute is carefully drawn so as not to impinge on the sovereignty of the State. The State retains control of its fiscal affairs."). *See id.* at 51.

2415. 455 U.S. 457 (1982).

railroad debtor.[2416] Later in 1982, within a few years after the enactment of the 1978 Bankruptcy Code, in *Northern Pipeline Construction Co. v. Marathon Pipe Line Co.*[2417] the Court[2418] declared the Bankruptcy Code's pervasive grant of jurisdiction to non-Article III judges to be unconstitutional.[2419] Although the controversy arose in an adversary proceeding in which the debtor in possession, as plaintiff, asserted a state law breach of contract and warranty cause of action,[2420] the Court held the jurisdictional infirmity to be non-severable and struck the constitutionality of the entire bankruptcy court system.[2421] Two years later, Congress enacted the "Bankruptcy Amendments and Federal Judgeship Act of 1984" proposing a new bankruptcy court system.[2422] The Court has not yet ruled on the constitutionality of the current jurisdictional scheme.[2423]

The Court also has used the Supremacy Clause of the Constitution to overturn state statutes that conflict with the bankruptcy laws.

2416. *See id.* at 469-73. ("A law can hardly be said to be uniform throughout the country if it applies only to one debtor and can be enforced only by the one bankruptcy court having jurisdiction over that debtor.") *Id.* at 470.

2417. 458 U.S. 50 (1982).

2418. The *Northern Pipeline* decision must be analyzed with great care because the judgment of the Court was accompanied by a four justice plurality opinion authored by Justice Brennan, a two justice opinion authored by Justice Rehnquist concurring in the judgment, and a three justice dissent authored by Justice White. Chief Justice Burger joined in Justice White's dissent and wrote his own dissenting opinion. *See id.*

2419. *See id.* at 87.

2420. *See id.* at 56, 89.

2421. *See id.* at 87-88, 91-92.

2422. *See* Bankruptcy Amendments and Federal Judgeship Act of 1984, Pub. L. No. 353, 98th Cong., 2d Sess., 98 Stat. 333, § 101 (1984) (enacting 28 U.S.C. §§ 157 & 1334 (1988)).

2423. The scope of Bankruptcy Court jurisdiction, including the responses to *Northern Pipeline*, is discussed more fully in Ch. 4 *supra*, pp. 200-220.

Thus, in *Perez v. Campbell*,[2424] the Court used the Supremacy Clause to invalidate an Arizona motor vehicle safety responsibility statute[2425] as inconsistent with the dischargeability provisions of the Bankruptcy Act.[2426] Adolfo Perez and his wife confessed judgment in a suit arising from personal injuries and property damage he caused while operating his uninsured motor vehicle. Shortly after the confession of judgment, Mr. and Mrs. Perez each filed voluntary bankruptcy petitions and received a discharge of the judgment. Because the Perez's did not pay the judgment, the Superintendent of the Arizona Motor Vehicle Division suspended their drivers' licenses as required by the Arizona statute, notwithstanding discharge of the judgment.[2427] The Court engaged in "a two-step process of first ascertaining the construction of the two statutes and then determining the constitutional question whether they are in conflict."[2428] After ascertaining that the Arizona statute was designed to protect judgment creditors from "financially irresponsible persons" and the Bankruptcy Act was designed to give the financially-troubled debtor a fresh start, the Court determined that the Arizona statute unconstitutionally interfered with and frustrated the discharge provisions of the Bankruptcy Act because it stood "as an obstacle to the accomplishment and execution of the full purposes and objectives of Congress."[2429] Congress later codified and expanded the anti-discrimination principle of *Perez* in Bankruptcy Code § 525(a).[2430]

2424. 402 U.S. 637 (1971).

2425. *See id.* at 651-52.

2426. *See id.* at 638. (The Arizona statute was based on the Uniform Motor Vehicle Safety Responsibility Act).

2427. *See id.* at 641-42.

2428. *See id.* at 644.

2429. *See id.* at 644-49 (citation omitted).

2430. *See* 11 U.S.C. § 525(a) (2000).

Perhaps the most important Court opinion on bankruptcy law and the Constitution upheld the constitutionality of bankruptcy reorganization provisions. In *Continental Illinois National Bank & Trust Co. of Chicago v. Chicago, Rock Island & Pacific Railway Co.*,[2431] the Court rejected the argument that congressional power to enact bankruptcy laws is confined to liquidation cases, noting that, taken as a group, the bankruptcy laws passed by Congress before enactment of § 77, "far-reaching though they be, have not gone beyond the limit of congressional power; but rather have constituted extensions into a field whose boundaries may not yet be fully revealed."[2432] The Court confirmed Congress' power to provide for railroad reorganizations by noting that § 77 "does no more than follow the line of historical and progressive development projected by previous acts."[2433] This important holding affirmed the power of Congress to enact corporate reorganization statutes, including chapter 11 of the Bankruptcy Code.

DECISIONS SUPPORTING EXPANSIVE BANKRUPTCY POWERS

As discussed more fully in Chapter 5, other important Court cases upheld creative or expansive applications of bankruptcy law or jurisdiction. For example, in *Moore v. Bay*,[2434] the Court held unanimously that a transfer avoidable by some actual unsecured creditors is avoidable by or for the benefit of all of them.[2435] In a few cases, this decision greatly benefits administrative and unsecured creditors by increasing the magnitude of the trustee's recovery. On the other hand, the rule of *Moore v. Bay* subjects transactions to uncertainty, not just

---

2431. 294 U.S. 648 (1935).

2432. *See id.* at 671.

2433. *See id.* at 672.

2434. 284 U.S. 4 (1931).

2435. *See id.* at 5 (answering in the affirmative the question "whether the mortgage is void also as against those who gave the bankrupt credit at a later date, after the mortgage was on record").

to the extent an actual creditor may avoid the transfer under non-bankruptcy law but often in its entirety.

Moreover, in *Van Huffel v. Harkelrode*,[2436] in the absence of an explicit statutory reference, the Court upheld a bankruptcy court procedure under which the trustee sold property of the estate free and clear of encumbrances, with the rights of lien holders against the property to be transferred to the proceeds of sale.[2437] This holding solidified the power of the bankruptcy court to exercise full *in rem* jurisdiction over property of the estate. Also, the decision gave the estate representative freedom to choose when to sell property of the estate without having to accommodate the timing considerations of secured creditors or others with interests in the property.

Furthermore, in *United States v. Whiting Pools, Inc.*,[2438] the Court established that under the Bankruptcy Code, as was the case under Chapter X of the Bankruptcy Act, the estate representative had the power to compel turnover of property seized by a secured creditor but not yet sold at a foreclosure sale.[2439] This power gives the debtor in possession or bankruptcy trustee the ability to gain possession of assets which may enhance prospects of reorganization or amounts received in liquidation.

As set forth in Chapter 4, several Court decisions have established broad equity powers in the bankruptcy courts, although a few have circumscribed those powers. In *Pepper v. Litton*,[2440] the Court not only established the bankruptcy court's power of equitable subordination

---

2436. 284 U.S. 225 (1931).

2437. *See id.* at 227-28.

2438. 462 U.S. 198 (1983).

2439. *See id.* at 208 (holding that "the bankruptcy court could order the turnover of collateral in the hands of a secured creditor") (citations omitted).

2440. 308 U.S. 295 (1939).

and equitable disallowance,[2441] but also held that a bankruptcy court, as a court of equity, may look through form to substance when determining the true nature of a transaction as it relates to the rights of parties against a bankrupt's estate.[2442] Moreover, two noteworthy Court decisions invoke equitable principles to circumscribe the allowance of postpetition interest or interest on interest. In *Sexton v. Dreyfus*,[2443] the Court held that based on equitable principles, the accumulation of interest on undersecured and unsecured claims is suspended as of the date of the bankruptcy petition.[2444] Later, in *Vanston Bondholders Protective Committee v. Green*,[2445] the Court held that "an allowance of interest on interest under the circumstances shown by this case would not be in accord with the equitable principles governing bankruptcy distributions."[2446]

Although cases more recent than *Vanston* tended to cut back on the bankruptcy courts' equitable powers,[2447] most recently in *Marrama v. Citizens Bank of Massachusetts*,[2448] the Court held, despite

---

2441. *See id.* at 305-06 (holding that the bankruptcy court may equitably disallow claims under Bankruptcy Act § 57k when allowance of the claims would not be fair and equitable to other creditors).

2442. *See id.* at 305 (The bankruptcy court's equitable powers "have been invoked to the end that fraud will not prevail, that substance will not give way to form, that technical considerations will not prevent substantial justice from being done.").

2443. 219 U.S. 339 (1911).

2444. *See id.* at 344-45.

2445. 329 U.S. 156 (1947).

2446. *See id.* at 163.

2447. *See, e.g.,* Norwest Bank Worthington v. Ahlers, 485 U.S. 197, 206 (1988) ("[W]hatever equitable powers remain in the bankruptcy courts must and can only be exercised within the confines of the Bankruptcy Code.").

2448. 546 U.S. 365, 127 S. Ct. 1105 (2007).

apparently clear language of the statute to the contrary,[2449] that Bankruptcy Code § 105(a) gave the bankruptcy court power to deny a debtor's right, under Bankruptcy Code § 706(a), to convert a chapter 7 case to a chapter 13 case.[2450] The Court also intimated that such a power was inherent and not dependent on congressional enactment of Bankruptcy Code §105(a): "[E]ven if § 105(a) had not been enacted, the inherent power of any court to sanction 'abusive litigation practices,' . . . might well provide an adequate justification for a prompt, rather than a delayed, ruling on an unmeritorious attempt to qualify as a debtor under Chapter 13."[2451]

The Court has rendered important decisions dealing with the intersection of bankruptcy law and labor law.[2452] Of these, perhaps the most significant is *National Labor Relations Board v. Bildisco & Bildisco*[2453] in which the Court confronted the status of collective bargaining agreements in bankruptcy. In *Bildisco*, the Court held that a collective bargaining agreement was an executory contract[2454] that could be rejected under Bankruptcy Code § 365 "if the debtor [in possession] can show that the collective-bargaining agreement burdens the estate, and that after careful scrutiny, the equities balance in favor of rejecting the labor contract."[2455] Even though Congress

---

2449. *See id.*, 127 S. Ct. at 1112 (Alito, J., dissenting) ("The Bankruptcy Code unambiguously provides that a debtor who has filed a bankruptcy petition under Chapter 7 has a broad right to convert the case to another chapter.").

2450. *See id.*

2451. *See id.*

2452. For a more complete discussion of this topic, *see supra* Ch. 2 nn.374-398 and accompanying text.

2453. 465 U.S. 513 (1984).

2454. *See id.* at 521-23.

2455. *See id.* at 526.

overturned *Bildisco's* rejection standard in 1984,[2456] the Court's reasoning in *Bildisco* formed the basis for the modern test for modification or rejection of collective bargaining agreements under Bankruptcy Code § 1113.[2457]

CASES WITH SIGNIFICANT ECONOMIC IMPLICATIONS

A few of the Court's bankruptcy decisions, including some of those discussed previously,[2458] declared or clarified the law with an economic impact on the market. For example in *BFP v. Resolution Trust Corp.*,[2459] the Court refused to permit the trustee to use the constructive fraudulent conveyance avoiding powers of Bankruptcy Code § 548 to unwind a real property foreclosure sale.[2460] A majority of the Court steadfastly protected state real property foreclosure systems, rejecting that Congress could have intended to upset over 400 years of mortgage foreclosure law by allowing bankruptcy judges to determine whether the value received at the sale constituted a reasonably equivalent value.[2461] Had the Court decided *BFP* the other way, the bankruptcy trustee's ability to attack real property foreclosures would have had a dramatic impact on distressed real estate values and title insurance policy premiums or exclusions.[2462]

2456. *See* Pub. L. No. 98-353, § 541(a), 98 Stat. 333, 390-91 (July 10, 1984).

2457. For a more comprehensive discussion of *Bildisco*, *see supra* Ch. 5, nn.1695-1709 and accompanying text.

2458. *E.g., Bildisco, Sexton*, and *Vanston*.

2459. 511 U.S. 531 (1994). For a more complete discussion of *BFP*, *see supra* Ch. 1, nn.128-142 and accompanying text.

2460. *See id.* at 536.

2461. *See id.* at 542-43.

2462. *See* Ronald J. Mann, "The Supreme Court, The Solicitor General and Bankruptcy: *BFP v. Resolution Trust Corporation*," BANKRUPTCY LAW STORIES 77, 80 (Robert K. Rasmussen, ed., Foundation Press 2007) ("Invalidating such a sale would interfere with the ability of the secured-credit system to redeploy collateral to a solvent owner in an expeditious

Dewsnup v. Timm[2463] is another case in which the Court protected the market by precluding the bankruptcy laws from interfering with liens securing real estate loans. As discussed in Chapter 5, in *Dewsnup* the Court considered whether a chapter 7 individual debtor could use Bankruptcy Code § 506(d)[2464] to strip an undersecured real property lien down to the judicially-determined value of the collateral.[2465] Bankruptcy Code § 506(a)[2466] bifurcates an undersecured recourse claim into an allowed claim equal to the value of the collateral and an unsecured claim for the deficiency. Despite the plain language of Bankruptcy Code § 506(a) and (d), the Court forbade a chapter 7 individual debtor from using Bankruptcy Code § 506(d) to strip liens securing claims of undersecured creditors.[2467] In doing so, the Court found the statutory language to be ambiguous.[2468] Instead of reading § 506 (a) and (d) together, the Court instead embraced the secured creditor's position that subsection (d) could be construed without regard to subsection (a):[2469]

---

manner."); *See also id.* at 83 n.26 (noting that such a rule "troubled insurers and likely affected the market for distressed real estate").

2463. 502 U.S. 410 (1992).

2464. 11 U.S.C. § 506(d) (Supp. 1992) ("(d) To the extent that a lien secures a claim against the debtor that is not an allowed secured claim, such lien is void . . . .") (exceptions omitted)).

2465. *See Dewsnup*, 502 U.S. at 411.

2466. 11 U.S.C. § 506(a) (Supp. 1992) ("(a) An allowed claim of a creditor secured by a lien on property in which the estate has an interest . . . is a secured claim to the extent of the value of [the collateral], and is an unsecured claim to the extent that the value of [the collateral] is less than the amount of such allowed claim. . . .").

2467. *See id.* at 417.

2468. *See id.*

2469. *See id.* at 415. As noted *supra* in Ch. 1, nn.137-142 and accompanying text, Justice Scalia authored a scathing dissent attacking the Court's statutory interpretation. *See* Dewsnup v. Timm, 502 U.S. 410, 420-36 (1992) (Scalia, J., dissenting).

[T]he words "allowed secured claim" in § 506(d) need not be read as an indivisible term of art defined by reference to § 506(a), which by its terms is not a definitional provision. Rather, the words should be read term-by-term to refer to any claim that is, first, allowed, and, second, secured. Because there is no question that the claim at issue here has been "allowed" pursuant to § 502 of the Code and is secured by a lien with recourse to the underlying collateral, it does not come within the scope of § 506(d), which voids only liens corresponding to claims that have *not* been allowed and secured.

On the other hand, some of the Court's opinions have restricted the collateral that creditors may encumber to secure their loans. In *Local Loan Co. v. Hunt*,[2470] the Court precluded creditors from tying up a bankrupt's future earnings when it held that "the clear and unmistakable policy of the bankruptcy act" precluded post-discharge enforcement by a prebankruptcy lender of an assignment of the bankrupt's future wages.[2471] In so holding, the Court made a powerful statement that would serve as the backbone of American consumer bankruptcy law for the next 70 years:[2472]

When a person assigns future wages, he, in effect, pledges his future earning power. The power of the individual to earn a living for himself and those dependent upon him is in the nature of a personal liberty quite as much as, if not more than, it is a property right. To preserve its free exercise is of the utmost importance, not only because it is a fundamental private necessity, but because it is a matter of great public concern. . . . The new opportunity in life and the clear field for future effort, which it is the purpose of the bankruptcy act to afford the emancipated debtor, would be of little value to the wage earner if he were obliged to face the necessity of devot-

---

2470. 292 U.S. 234 (1934).

2471. *See id.* at 244.

2472. *See id.* at 245. This policy was undercut somewhat by the 2005 amendments to the Bankruptcy Code which denied a chapter 7 discharge and fresh start to some debtors. *See* 11 U.S.C. § 707(b) (Supp. 2005).

ing the whole or a considerable portion of his earnings for an indefinite time in the future to the payment of indebtedness incurred prior to his bankruptcy.

Thus, the Court took future wages off the table as an effective source of collateral and, at least theoretically, altered the economics of consumer credit.

In *Union Bank v. Wolas*,[2473] the Court strengthened the position of financial unsecured creditors to retain preferential payments made in the ordinary course of business. Instead of interpreting the ordinary-course-of-business defense to apply to protect only regular payments to trade creditors, the Court interpreted the defense literally to insulate from preference attack regularly scheduled payments to banks on long term debts, as well as payments on short term debts.[2474] Thus, the Court prevented the bankruptcy laws from disrupting settled commercial financial transactions.

As noted at length in Chapter 5, *Northern Pacific Railway Co. v. Boyd*[2475] and its progeny have had a dramatic impact on corporation reorganizations with the establishment of the absolute priority rule.[2476] At stake is whether, and under what conditions, junior interests may receive or retain value under a reorganization plan when senior creditors are not paid or given property that satisfies their interests in full. Moreover, it is still unsettled whether, under a cram down plan, the owners of a corporate or partnership business may receive or retain an ownership interest in the reorganized enterprise for a contribution of fresh capital in money or money's worth. The answer appears to turn on whether the new value principle of *Case v. Los Angeles Lumber Products Co.*[2477] survived enactment of the Bank-

---

2473. 502 U.S. 151 (1991).

2474. *See id.* at 162.

2475. 228 U.S. 482 (1913).

2476. *See supra* Ch. 5, nn.1979-2128 and accompanying text.

2477. 308 U.S. 106 (1939).

ruptcy Code, and, if so, the conditions under which the new value principle may be satisfied.[2478] The uncertainty surrounding these issues affects the bargaining dynamic in business reorganization cases and the economics of both consensual and cram down plans.

OLD FAVORITES

The sands of time tend to obscure all but the most prominent cases. Nevertheless, the Court regards its old precedents just as binding as its recent decisions.[2479] There is much to learn from reexamining older cases that may be significant in modern practice.

Not surprisingly, in the early decades after the enactment of the Bankruptcy Act of 1898, the Court decided many issues of first impression that still have vitality under the Bankruptcy Code. A favorite is *Page v. Rogers*.[2480] Under Bankruptcy Act § 57g,[2481] as well as under § 502(d) of the Bankruptcy Code, if a creditor owes or might owe property to the estate under one of the avoiding powers, the creditor's claim is disallowed until the property is delivered to the estate. Based on the plain language of the statute, one might think that a creditor would have to pay over the full amount of the avoided transfer and then assert a claim against the estate. In 1909, however, the Supreme Court decided otherwise. Resolving an issue that had not been briefed or argued, the Court held that the creditor might be able

---

2478. *See supra* Ch. 5, nn.2037-2039 & 2098-2128 and accompanying text.

2479. *See, e.g.,* United States v. Sec. Indus. Bank, 459 U.S. 70, 80-81 (1982) (citing Holt v. Henley, 232 U.S. 637, 639 (1914) (prospectively applying the 1910 amendment of the Bankruptcy Act giving the trustee the status of a judicial lien creditor) and other old precedents dealing with the prospective nature of bankruptcy statutes).

2480. 211 U.S. 575, 581 (1909).

2481. Bankruptcy Act § 57g provided that "[t]he claims of creditors who have received or acquired preferences, liens, conveyances, transfers, assignments or encumbrances, void or voidable under this Act, shall not be allowed unless such creditors shall surrender such preferences, liens, conveyances, transfers, assignments, or encumbrances."

to net any "dividend" on its claim against sums to be turned over to the estate.[2482] One can only speculate how many trustees or avoiding powers defendants are unaware that this old precedent supports such a netting.

Another favorite early case is *Ivanhoe Building & Loan Ass'n v. Orr*, decided in 1935.[2483] As a matter of policy, one could argue either way whether a creditor holding third party collateral should be required to net that collateral or any recovery on that collateral to reduce it's allowed claim against the debtor's bankruptcy estate. The issue is not whether the creditor should be entitled to more than a single recovery, but whether the face amount of the allowed claim is diminished by the proceeds or value of third party collateral.

Ivanhoe stands for the proposition that a creditor holding a claim secured only by third party collateral is an unsecured creditor of the debtor and is entitled to an unsecured claim against the estate for the full amount of the debt until a recovery in full is had from all sources.[2484] Ivanhoe, a creditor of the debtor Sash and Door Company, filed a claim in the bankruptcy case seeking to recover an amount due on a bond executed to Ivanhoe on a mortgage assumed by the debtor.[2485] Before bankruptcy, the debtor had conveyed the mortgaged property to a third party.[2486] After the debtor defaulted, Ivanhoe commenced a foreclosure against the mortgaged property and

---

2482. *See* Page v. Rogers, 211 U.S. at 581 ("[I]t is entirely practicable to avoid the circuitous proceeding of compelling the defendant to pay into the bankruptcy court the full amount of the preference which he has received, and then to resort to the same court to obtain part of it back by way of dividend. The defendant may be permitted, if he shall be so advised, to prove his claim against the estate of the bankrupt, and the bankrupt court then may settle the amount of the dividend coming to him, and the final decree may direct him to pay over the full amount of this preference, with interest, less the amount of his dividend.").

2483. 295 U.S. 243 (1935).

2484. *See id.* at 245-46.

2485. *See id.* at 244.

2486. *See id.*

purchased the property by a credit bid of $100 at the foreclosure sale.[2487] After the sale, Ivanhoe asserted a claim against the debtor's bankruptcy estate for the principal amount due on the mortgage debt less the amount credit bid at the foreclosure sale.[2488] The bankruptcy referee limited Ivanhoe's allowed claim to the difference between the claim presented and the stipulated value of the property acquired at the foreclosure sale, less the amount of the credit bid.[2489] Both lower courts affirmed.[2490]

The Supreme Court reversed. The question presented to the Court was "whether a creditor of a bankrupt, who has recovered a portion of the debt owed him by foreclosure of a mortgage on property not owned by the bankrupt, may prove for the full amount of the debt, or only for the balance required to make him whole."[2491] The Court held that Ivanhoe did not fall within the definition of "Secured creditor" as defined in Bankruptcy Act § 1(23).[2492] Therefore, under Bankruptcy Act § 57e,[2493] Ivanhoe's unsecured proof of claim for the principal of the bond with interest was allowable.[2494] The Court, however, limited Ivanhoe to a single satisfaction so that Ivanhoe was not able to collect and retain dividends which, with the sum realized from the foreclosure, would more than satisfy the principal amount of the bond plus interest.[2495] Because Ivanhoe was not a secured creditor of the debtor, Ivanhoe was entitled to recover the full amount of the debt, less the purchase price at the sale, and the Court accordingly reversed the

---

2487. *See id.* at 244-45.

2488. *See id.* at 245.

2489. *See id.*

2490. *See id.*

2491. *See id.* at 244.

2492. *See id.* at 245-46 & 11 U.S.C. § 1(23) (1934) (repealed 1979 as § 1(28)).

2493. *See* 11 U.S.C. § 93e (1934) (repealed 1979).

2494. *See Ivanhoe*, 295 U.S. at 245-46.

2495. *See id.* at 246.

lower court's judgment.[2496] The Supreme Court expressly affirmed its holding in *Ivanhoe* a decade later in *Reconstruction Finance Corp. v. Denver & Rio Grande Western Railroad Co.*,[2497] noting that "[t]he rule is settled in bankruptcy proceedings that a creditor secured by the property of others need not deduct the value of that collateral or its proceeds in proving his debt."[2498]

The *Ivanhoe* decision remains good law under the Bankruptcy Code.[2499] As such, parties structuring transactions have an economic incentive to place collateral in special purpose vehicles or with third parties. Structuring a transaction in this manner gives the creditor the opportunity both to optimize recourse to the collateral and to increase the amount of any pro rata distribution on unsecured claims against the original debtor.

Another old favorite is *Gleason v. Thaw*[2500] in which the Court determined that the professional services of an attorney were not property for purposes of determining whether a debt for services procured by fraud was nondischargeable.[2501] The Court noted that property "denotes something subject to ownership, transfer or

---

2496. *See id.* at 246-47.

2497. 328 U.S. 495 (1946).

2498. *See id.* at 529 (citation omitted).

2499. *See, e.g.*, Nat'l Energy & Gas Transmission, Inc. v. Liberty Elec. Power, LLC (*In re* Nat'l Energy & Gas Transmission, Inc.), 492 F.3d 297, 301 (4th Cir. 2007); *In re* Emergency Beacon Corp., 48 B.R. 341, 352 (S.D.N.Y. 1985) ("[I]t is settled law that a creditor, secured by property of a third party, may assert the full amount of its claim against the debtor's estate without deduction for the security."); *In re* Sacred Heart Hosp., 182 B.R. 413, 417 (Bankr. E.D. Pa. 1995) (explicitly interpreting *Ivanhoe* as allowing a creditor to "prove its entire claim in the bankrupt's case notwithstanding the existence of third party collateral or guarantees of payment so long as the claimant does not seek to recover more than one full payment of its claim from whatever source."); *In re* F.W.D.C., Inc., 158 B.R. 523, 528 (Bankr. S.D. Fla. 1993).

2500. 236 U.S. 558 (1915).

2501. *See id.* at 561.

exclusive possession or enjoyment, which may be brought within the dominion and control of a court through some recognized process."[2502] Although the Court limited its statutory construction to the nondischargeability statute, similar reasoning could be used to hold that a transfer of services is not a transfer of property in other contexts. For example, under the reasoning of *Gleason*, the fraudulent transfer avoiding powers would not apply when the debtor provided services for free or less than a reasonably equivalent value. Nor would the preference avoiding power apply when the debtor provides services during the preference period in payment of an antecedent debt.

Dean v. Davis[2503] is another old case that lurks in the nightmares of many secured creditor lawyers. In *Dean v. Davis*, discussed in Chapter 5, the Court permitted the trustee to avoid, as an actual intent fraudulent transfer, a mortgage given contemporaneously to secure a loan borrowed from the debtor's brother in law shortly before bankruptcy.[2504] The purpose of the loan was to pay outstanding notes bearing the debtor's forged endorsement.[2505] Not only did the debtor grant the mortgage with actual intent to hinder, delay, or defraud creditors, but the brother in law mortgagee knew the loan was being used to make a preference with bankruptcy in contemplation.[2506] The Court held that "where the advance is made to enable the debtor to make a preferential payment with bankruptcy in contemplation, the transaction presents an element upon which fraud may be predicated. The fact that the money advanced is actually used to pay a debt does not necessarily establish good faith."[2507] Thus, the lower courts were justified in finding the requisite fraudulent intent because the debtor

---

2502. *See id.*

2503. 242 U.S. 438 (1917).

2504. *See id.* at 442, 445.

2505. *See id.*

2506. *See id.* at 445.

2507. *See id.* at 444.

"willingly sacrificed his property and his other creditors to avert a threatened criminal prosecution; and [the mortgagee] knowing the facts, cooperated in the bankrupt's fraudulent purpose, lack[ing] the saving good faith."[2508] The principles of *Dean v. Davis* remain viable and could well apply to certain modern securitization or leveraged buyout transactions when lenders facilitate bad-faith transfers shortly before bankruptcy.[2509]

CONCLUSION

In reflecting on the Supreme Court's bankruptcy jurisprudence over the past 111 years, it is fair to ask whether these cases make much of a difference outside the context of the particular case in which they are decided. Certainly, a significant number of unpopular decisions induced Congress to amend the bankruptcy laws to overturn the decisions.[2510] Most notably, the Court's decision in *Bildisco*, permitting the rejection of a collective bargaining agreement in bankruptcy,[2511] provided the political impetus for Congress to enact legislation mending an unconstitutional bankruptcy court system.[2512]

Nevertheless, most of the Court's bankruptcy decisions have had little impact outside of the context in which they were decided other

---

2508. *See id.* at 445.

2509. *See* Kenneth C. Kettering, *Securitization and its Discontent: The Dynamics of Financial Product Development*, 29 CARDOZO L. REV. 1553, 1601-08 (March 2008) (citing *Shapiro v. Wilgus* and its progeny for the proposition that securitization transactions may be avoidable as transfers that actually intend to hinder or delay creditors even in the absence of intent to defraud).

2510. *See, e.g.,* Daniel J. Bussel, *Textualism's Failures: A Study of Overruled Bankruptcy Decisions*, 53 VANDERBILT L. REV. 887-946 (2000).

2511. *See supra* nn.2453-2457 and accompanying text.

2512. *See* Pub. L. No. 98-353, §§ 101-211, 98 Stat. 333, 333-51 (July 10, 1984) (enacting a new bankruptcy court system) & *supra* Ch. 4, nn.1057-1061 and accompanying text.

than to resolve Circuit court splits. Resolving these splits is one of the Court's core functions and serves to minimize forum shopping and provide more uniform rules of decision across the country. Admittedly, resolution of a conflict brings certainty and predictability to the law and to the financial markets. But unless there is a large policy question at stake or a great impact on the financial markets, often the fact that the Court has resolved the conflict in some fashion is more important that the rule of substantive law that the Court adopts in the resolution.

Indeed, many lower courts and lawyers are pragmatists. Although they are bound by the Court's decision, courts and lawyers show resilience and creativity in adapting to Court decisions that threaten efficient operation of the bankruptcy system. One need look no farther than the response to the Court's *Northern Pipeline* decision declaring the entire bankruptcy court jurisdictional scheme unconstitutional.[2513] Rather than leaving bankruptcy cases to be adjudicated by state courts as courts of last resort, the Administrative Office of the United States Courts promulgated an Emergency Rule permitting the bankruptcy judges to continue to exercise jurisdiction in bankruptcy cases.[2514] Moreover, as noted in Chapter 5,[2515] lawyers responded to the Court's interpretation of the absolute priority rule in *Boyd*[2516] by designing equity receivership practices to circumvent the rule by giving value to shareholders while squeezing out junior creditors.[2517]

2513. *See* N. Pipeline Constr. Co. v. Marathon Pipe Line Co., 458 U.S. 50 (1982), discussed more fully *supra* in Chs. 3 & 4, pp. 154, 201, 213-214.

2514. *See* H.R. REP. NO. 807, 97th Cong., 2d Sess. at 30 (1982) and *supra* Ch. 4, nn.1055-1056 and accompanying text.

2515. *See supra* Ch. 5, nn.2005-2006 and accompanying text.

2516. N. Pac. Ry. v. Boyd, 228 U.S. 482 (1913).

2517. *See* Paul D. Cravath, "The Reorganization of Corporations; Bondholders' and Stockholders' Protective Committees; Reorganization Committees; and the Voluntary Recapitalization of Corporations," at 198 (A lecture delivered before the Association of the Bar of the City of New

The resilience of lower courts and lawyers to adapt to Court decisions gives the Supreme Court a margin for error in most of its decisions. Apparently, many of the Justices lose little sleep over bankruptcy decisions compared with cases involving fundamental constitutional rights and liberties. Indeed, the Court usually grants certiorari in bankruptcy cases only to resolve a conflict of laws or a Circuit split. Nevertheless, even though the Justices are generalists with little previous understanding of the nuances of bankruptcy law, for the most part they decide bankruptcy cases correctly by making sound policy choices or adhering to strict statutory interpretation as serves their purpose. When the Court shapes the bankruptcy law in a direction with which Congress disagrees, in many instances the legislative response is swift and decisive. Once Congress amends the law, most of the time the Court follows congressional intent and refines the law. Thus, upon reflection, in evaluating the Court's role in the development of bankruptcy law and policy, instead of being "Supremely Wrong," as some colleagues suggested as a title for this book, it might more properly be argued that the Court is, on the whole, "Supremely Right."

York, March 1 and 8, 1916) (located online at: http://books.google.com/books?id=KXE9AAAAIAAJ&pg=PA153&dq=paul+cravath+corporate+reorganization (last visited June 24, 2008) (praising a recent decision that "affords some hope that mortgage bondholders could carry through a Plan of Reorganization which admitted the stock and excluded the floating debt provided it could be shown that the value of the property did not exceed the mortgage lien . . . .").

Index

A

B

BANKRUPTCY CRIMES (See CRIMES)

BANKRUPTCY JUDGES

BANKRUPTCY POWER

F

J